Is the International Legal Order Unraveling?

Is the International Legal Order Unraveling?

Edited by

DAVID L. SLOSS

OXFORD
UNIVERSITY PRESS

OXFORD
UNIVERSITY PRESS

Oxford University Press is a department of the University of Oxford. It furthers the University's objective of excellence in research, scholarship, and education by publishing worldwide. Oxford is a registered trade mark of Oxford University Press in the UK and certain other countries.

Published in the United States of America by Oxford University Press
198 Madison Avenue, New York, NY 10016, United States of America.

CIP data is on file at the Library of Congress

ISBN 978–0–19–765280 0

DOI: 10.1093/oso/9780197652800.001.0001

1 3 5 7 9 8 6 4 2

Printed by Integrated Books International, United States of America

Contents

List of Tables and Figures vii
Acknowledgments ix
Author Biographies xi
List of Abbreviations xix

Introduction: Preserving a Rules-based International Order 1
David L. Sloss

PART ONE SYSTEMIC ISSUES

1. The Rise and Decline of a Liberal International Order 37
Richard H. Steinberg

2. The West and the Unraveling of the Economic World Order: Thoughts from a Global South Perspective 62
James T. Gathii and Sergio Puig

3. The Future of Liberal Democracy in the International Legal Order 82
Tom Ginsburg

4. Revolution or Collapse?: Climate Change and the International Legal Order 106
Maxine Burkett

PART TWO INTERNATIONAL PEACE AND SECURITY

5. War and Words: The International Use of Force in the UN Charter Era 143
Lauren Sukin and Allen S. Weiner

6. The *Jus in Bello* under Strain: Diluted But Not Disintegrating 184
Laura A. Dickinson

7. Autonomous Weapons 216
Chris Jenks

8. Cyber Conflict and the Thresholds of War 251
Ido Kilovaty

PART THREE INTERNATIONAL ECONOMIC LAW AND INSTITUTIONS

9. The Experimental Evolution of Trade Law 285
Kathleen Claussen

10. Strength in Obscurity: The Resilience of International Investment Law 307
Jeremy Rabkin

11. Anti-Bribery Law 338
Paul B. Stephan

PART FOUR HUMAN RIGHTS AND RELATED ISSUES

12. Authoritarianism, International Human Rights, and Legal Change 363
Wayne Sandholtz

13. The International Criminal Law of the Future 397
Leila N. Sadat

14. Migration and International Legal Disorder 425
Jaya Ramji-Nogales

Index 453

List of Tables and Figures

Tables

I.1. Evolution of a Rules-Based International Order 7
I.2. Summary of Major Threats 21
3.1. Number of Democracies Since 2006 86
3.2. Countries by Category, 2020 86
5.1. Justifications in Article 51 Communications and Sample Dictionary Terms 164
5.2. Frequency of Justifications 165
5.A1. Automated Coding Accuracy 183
12.1. States Parties to Human Rights Treaties, 2021 370
12.2. Autocracies in the Human Rights Council, 2020 373
12.3. Authoritarian Strategies, V-Dem Indicators 379
12.4. Average Number Out of Six Indicators Showing an Authoritarian Shift, 2009–19 381
12.A1. Change in Indicators of Core Authoritarian Strategies, 2009–19 393
12.A2. Change in Indicators of Core Authoritarian Strategies, 2009–19 395

Figures

1.1. GATT/ WTO Members' Shares of Aggregate GDP of GATT/ WTO Members (1948–2019) 43
1.2. IMF Quota Distribution 44
1.3. IMF Quotas vs. Net Capital Inflows (US$ in Billions—60 Countries) 45
1.4. Liberal International Order: Three Periods 53
5.1. Frequency of Militarized Interstate Disputes Involving Use of Force 156
5.2. MIDs and Article 51 Communication Frequencies 158
5.3. Communications with Mentions of Counterattacks 166
5.4. Communications with Mentions of Collective Self-Defense 167

5.5. Communications with Mentions of Ceasefire Violations 168

5.6. Communications with Mentions of Anticipatory Self-Defense 170

5.7. Communications with Mentions of Nonstate Actors 172

5.8. Communications with Mentions of Humanitarianism 174

5.9. Communications with Mentions of Reprisals 176

5.10. Correlations between Legal and Extralegal Justifications 178

12.1. Global Human Rights Treaties, Total Ratifications 370

Acknowledgments

As an author and editor, it is a distinct pleasure to thank the many people who contributed to the production of this volume. First and foremost, I want to thank the contributing authors: Maxine Burkett, Kathleen Claussen, Laura A. Dickinson, James T. Gathii, Tom Ginsburg, Chris Jenks, Ido Kilovaty, Sergio Puig, Jeremy Rabkin, Jaya Ramji-Nogales, Leila N. Sadat, Wayne Sandholtz, Richard H. Steinberg, Paul B. Stephan, Lauren Sukin, and Allen S. Weiner. The contributing authors represent a broad range of ideological and scholarly perspectives; the book as a whole benefited greatly from that diversity. Moreover, I learned a great deal from each of the authors individually over the course of this project. Every contributing author made a significant intellectual contribution to the book. It has been a pleasure and a privilege to work with all of them.

This book grows out of the work of a study group convened by the American Branch of the International Law Association (ABILA). ABILA approved the formation of the study group in December 2018, with the title "Threats to a Rules-Based International Order and Possible Responses." I want to thank the ABILA leadership, without whose support and encouragement this project would not have happened. In particular, I thank David Stewart, the outgoing ABILA president when I first proposed the study group; Leila Sadat, the current ABILA president who approved the formation of the study group; and Peter Yu, the ABILA director of studies.

A few scholars who did not write chapters for the book nevertheless made important contributions to the project. Susan Pascocello participated actively in the study group, but ultimately decided not to contribute a chapter for this edited volume. Oona Hathaway and Kristen Eichensehr each attended one study group meeting; they both made important intellectual contributions to the project. I had several conversations with Greg Shaffer about the work of the study group, and I benefited greatly from his insights.

I thank Lisa Kloppenberg, the former dean of Santa Clara Law, and Anna Han, who served as interim dean for much of the time I worked on this book. They both provided generous support for my scholarship. I also want to thank Tseming Yang, the director of the Center for Global Law and Policy at

Santa Clara, for helping to fund a crucial study group meeting at Santa Clara in February 2020. Katherine Blake, Jonathan Greene, Michael Romero, and Rory Hayes all provided valuable research assistance for the project.

I also want to thank my editors at Oxford University Press. Merel Alstein has supported this project since I first discussed it with her, even before I had developed a formal book proposal. David Lipp, Iona Jacob, Fiona Blee, and Rebecca Lewis have helped shepherd the book through various stages of the production process.

Finally, I want to thank my wife, Heidi Sloss, and my children, Dakin and Kamala Sloss. Their presence in my life provides an ongoing source of joy and inspiration that helps sustain all of my scholarly work.

Author Biographies

Maxine Burkett is a Professor of Law at the William S. Richardson School of Law, University of Hawaii (on leave). An international expert in the law and policy of climate change, with a specific focus on climate justice, climate-induced migration, and climate and conflict, she is currently serving in the Biden administration as a Senior Adviser to the Special Presidential Envoy for Climate. She is a member of the International Law Association's Committee on International Law and Sea Level Rise and a former member of the Center for Progressive Reform and the Lancet Commission on Reparations and Redistributive Justice, and the American Law Institute. Professor Burkett received her BA from Williams College, which awarded her the Bicentennial Medal for Distinguished Achievement in 2016. She also attended Exeter College, Oxford University. She received her JD from Berkeley Law, University of California, and served as a law clerk for the Honorable Susan Illston of the US District Court, Northern District of California.

Kathleen Claussen is Associate Professor at the University of Miami School of Law and Non-Resident Senior Fellow at the Georgetown Institute of International Economic Law. She is the author of more than thirty articles and essays concerning trade, investment, and international dispute settlement, among other related research areas. Among other leadership roles, she serves on the Executive Council and Executive Committee of the American Society of International Law and as co-Editor-in-Chief of the *Journal of International Economic Law*. Prior to joining the academy, Professor Claussen was Associate General Counsel at the Office of the US Trade Representative. Earlier in her career, she was Legal Counsel at the Permanent Court of Arbitration in The Hague, covering disputes between countries and investment law arbitrations. She is a graduate of the Yale Law School; Queen's University Belfast, where she was a Mitchell Scholar; and Indiana University where she was a Wells Scholar.

Laura A. Dickinson is the Oswald Symister Colclough Research Professor and Professor of Law at George Washington University. Her work focuses on national security, human rights, the law of armed conflict, and foreign affairs privatization. She has authored numerous articles and book chapters, including scholarship that has appeared in the *American Journal of International Law*, the *Yale Journal of International Law*, the *NYU Journal of International Law and Politics*, the *William & Mary Law Review*, the *Emory Law Journal*, and the *Southern California Law Review*. Her prize-winning book, *Outsourcing War and Peace*, outlines a framework of accountability and oversight to protect core public values threatened in the current era of growing military and security privatization. Professor Dickinson has served as Special Counsel to the General Counsel of the US Department of Defense and as a senior policy adviser in the Bureau of Democracy, Human Rights, and Labor at the US Department of State. She served as the 2020–21 Lieber Scholar at the Lieber Institute for Law and Land Warfare at the US Military Academy at West Point.

James T. Gathii is a Professor of Law and the Wing-Tat Lee Chair in International Law at Loyola University Chicago School of Law. He is a graduate of the University of Nairobi, Kenya, and Harvard Law School. He sits on the board of editors of the *American Journal of International Law*, the *Journal of African Law*, and the *Journal of International Trade Law and Policy*, and on the Advisory Board of the International Journal of Constitutional Law. He is a founding editor of http://www.afronomicslaw.org/ and the *African Journal of International Economic Law*. He was the Grotius Lecturer at the 2020 Annual Meeting of the American Society of International Law. Professor Gathii has sat as an arbitrator in international commercial arbitrations hosted by the Permanent Court of Arbitration. He sits on the China International Economic and Trade Arbitration Commission. His books include: *African Regional Trade Agreements as Legal Regimes* (Cambridge University Press, 2011, Paperback 2013); *War, Commerce and International Law* (Oxford University Press, 2010); *The Contested Empowerment of Kenya's Judiciary, 2010–2015: A Historical Institutional Analysis* (Sheria Publishing House, 2016); and an edited volume, *The Performance of Africa's International Courts: Using Litigation for Political, Legal and Social Change* (Oxford University Press, 2020).

Tom Ginsburg is the Leo Spitz Professor of International Law at the University of Chicago, where he also holds an appointment in the Political Science Department. He is also a Research Professor at the American Bar Foundation.

He holds BA, JD, and PhD degrees from the University of California at Berkeley, and currently co-directs the Comparative Constitutions Project, an NSF-funded data set cataloging the world's constitutions since 1789, that runs the award-winning Constitute website. His latest book is *How to Save a Constitutional Democracy* (2018, with Aziz Huq), winner of the Best Book Prize from the International Society for Constitutional Law. His other books include *Judicial Reputation: A Comparative Theory* (2015) (with Nuno Garoupa), *The Endurance of National Constitutions* (2009) (with Zachary Elkins and James Melton), and *Judicial Review in New Democracies* (2003), the latter two both winning best book awards from the American Political Science Association. He is a member of the American Academy of Arts and Sciences. Before entering law teaching, he served as a legal adviser at the Iran-US Claims Tribunal in the Netherlands. He currently serves a senior adviser on Constitution Building to International IDEA.

Chris Jenks is a Professor of Law at the SMU Dedman School of Law in Dallas, Texas, and a professorial fellow in the Program on the Regulation of Emerging Military Technology in Australia. Professor Jenks's research focuses on the efficacy of the law of armed conflict as applied to autonomous weapons. He is the co-author of a law of armed conflict textbook and has published articles and book chapters on autonomous weapons. In 2020, he testified on autonomous weapons at a US Congress Helsinki Commission Hearing. Between 2017 and 2018, while on leave from SMU and serving as the Special Counsel to the General Counsel for the Department of Defense, Professor Jenks twice served on the US delegation to the UN Group of Governmental Experts meetings on Lethal Autonomous Weapons in Geneva, Switzerland. He previously presented on autonomous weapons at a similar UN meeting. In 2015, he was awarded a Fulbright Senior Scholars Grant to research autonomous weapons as part of a multidisciplinary research group based in Melbourne, Australia.

Ido Kilovaty is the Frederic Dorwart and Zedalis Family Fund Associate Professor of Law at the University of Tulsa College of Law. Before joining the faculty at the College of Law, Ido spent two years as a Research Scholar in Law at Yale Law School. At Yale, Ido was a Cyber Fellow at the Center for Global Legal Challenges and a Resident Fellow at the Information Society Project, where he remains an affiliated fellow. Ido specializes in the intersection of technology, law, and society, with a focus on cybersecurity—both domestic and international. His specific areas of research include cybersecurity law, computer crime law, and domestic and global technology regulation. His research has appeared in the *UC Irvine Law Review*, *Ohio State Law Journal*, *Tennessee Law Review*, *Harvard National Security Journal*, *Berkeley Technology Law Journal*, and more. Professor Kilovaty's op-eds and essays have appeared in *Harvard Law Review Blog*, *Lawfare*, *Just Security*, *WIRED*, and *TechCrunch*.

Sergio Puig is a Professor of Law at the James E. Rogers College of Law, University of Arizona. His previous academic track includes positions as lecturer and teaching fellow at the Stanford University School of Law and Duke University School of Law. He is the author of multiple articles and essays on international economic law, international dispute settlement, and international law more generally—all available on SSRN. He is also the author of *At the Margins of Globalization: Indigenous Peoples and International Economic Law* (Cambridge University Press, 2021). Before entering academia, Professor Puig practiced international law and arbitration in leading firms in Washington, D.C., and Mexico and worked at ICSID and the World Bank. He has been appointed as arbitrator and has testified as expert before international tribunals. Professor Puig holds a law degree from Instituto Tecnológico Autónomo de México—ITAM (México), and two degrees (Master and Doctor of the Science of Law, respectively) from Stanford Law School.

Jeremy Rabkin is Professor of Law at Scalia Law School of George Mason University, where he teaches (among other subjects) international law. Before coming to Mason in 2007, he taught for over two decades at the Department of Government of Cornell University. He holds a PhD in political science from Harvard University. Many of his academic publications have analyzed changing perspectives on national sovereignty over the past three centuries. His books include *Law Without Nations? Why Constitutional Government Requires Sovereign States* (2007) and *Striking Power: How Cyber, Robots and Space Weapons Change the Rules of War* (with John Yoo) (2017). In addition to academic journals, his writings have appeared in *The Washington Post*, the *Wall Street Journal*, and other periodicals. He was appointed to the Board of Directors of the US Institute of Peace by President George W. Bush and confirmed by the US Senate. He also serves on the International Law Practice

Group of the Federalist Society. He has lectured on international law topics in Australia, China, Belgium, the Netherlands, Poland, and Israel.

Jaya Ramji-Nogales is Associate Dean for Academic Affairs and the I. Herman Stern Research Professor at Temple University's Beasley School of Law. She is the co-author, with Georgetown Law Professors Andrew I. Schoenholtz and Philip G. Schrag, of *The End of Asylum* (2021), which assesses asylum law and policy under the Trump administration; *Refugee Roulette: Disparities in Asylum Adjudication and Proposals for Reform* (2011), an empirical study of adjudication at all four levels of the US asylum system; and *Lives in the Balance: Asylum Adjudication by the Department of Homeland Security* (2014), a quantitative and qualitative study of asylum adjudication before the Department of Homeland Security's Asylum Offices. Her work also seeks to generate conversations around the concept of global migration law, including a symposium in the *American Journal of International Law Unbound*. Her recent publications uncover the role of international law in constructing migration emergencies and critique human rights law as insufficiently attentive to the interests of undocumented migrants. Professor Ramji-Nogales has also authored articles on the situation of forced migrants under international criminal law and international humanitarian law, as well as on regional migration law in Southeast Asia.

Leila N. Sadat is the James Carr Professor of International Criminal Law and longtime Director of the Whitney R. Harris World Law Institute at Washington University. Leila Sadat served as Special Adviser on Crimes Against Humanity to ICC Prosecutor Fatou Bensouda (2012–21) and as a member of the US Commission on International Religious Freedom (2001–03). Sadat is an internationally recognized authority in the fields of public international law, international criminal law, human rights, and foreign affairs, and has published more than 150 books and articles in leading journals, academic presses, and media outlets throughout the world. She was the first woman selected to hold the Alexis de Tocqueville Distinguished Fulbright Chair in Paris, France (2011) and received an Honorary Doctorate from Northwestern University as well as the Arthur Holly Compton Faculty Achievement Award from Washington University in 2017. Sadat directs the *Crimes Against Humanity Initiative*, a groundbreaking project launched in 2008 to write the world's first global treaty on crimes against humanity. Sadat is the President of the International Law Association (American Branch), a Counselor to the American Society of International Law, and a member of the US Council on Foreign Relations and the American Law Institute.

Wayne Sandholtz holds the John A. McCone Chair in International Relations and is Professor of International Relations and Law at the University of Southern California. He has been a visiting fellow at the Graduate Institute for International and Development Studies (Geneva) and the Research Group "International Law—Rise or Decline?" (Berlin). Professor Sandholtz has written on international human rights law, international human rights courts, human rights and constitutionalism, international law in domestic courts, and wartime cultural plunder (*Prohibiting Plunder: How Norms Change*, Oxford, 2007). He is co-editor (with Christopher Whytock) of the *Research Handbook on the Politics of International Law* (Edward Elgar, 2017) and of *International Norms and Cycles of Change* (Oxford, 2009, with Kendall Stiles). Current projects focus on international norm resilience, the international rule of law, the Inter-American Court of Human Rights, and a comparative analysis of the regional human rights courts.

David L. Sloss is the John A. and Elizabeth H. Sutro Professor of Law at Santa Clara University. He is the author of *The Death of Treaty Supremacy: An Invisible Constitutional Change* (Oxford University Press, 2016) and *Tyrants on Twitter: Protecting Democracies from Information Warfare* (Stanford University Press, 2022). He is the co-editor of *International Law in the U.S. Supreme Court: Continuity and Change* (Cambridge University Press, 2011) and sole editor of *The Role of Domestic Courts in Treaty Enforcement: A Comparative Study* (Cambridge University Press, 2009). He has also published several dozen book chapters and law review articles. His book on the death of treaty supremacy and his edited volume on international law in the US Supreme Court both won prestigious book awards from the American Society of International Law. Professor Sloss is a member of the American Law Institute and a Counselor to the American Society of International Law. His scholarship is informed by extensive government experience. Before entering academia, he spent nine years in the federal government, where he worked on US-Soviet arms control negotiations and nuclear proliferation issues.

Richard H. Steinberg is the Jonathan D. Varat Professor of Law, and Professor of Political Science, at the University of California, Los Angeles. He has written over sixty articles and published eight books in the fields of international law and international relations. He is a Member of the Council on Foreign Relations, a Member of United States Trade Representative's Trade and Environment Policy Advisory Committee, Chair of the International Trade Law Committee of the International Law Association (American Branch), and Editor-in-Chief of the award-winning http://iccforum.com/. Dr. Steinberg has served as Counselor to the American Society of International Law, on the Board of Editors of the *American Journal of International Law*, and on the Editorial Board of *International Organization*. He has taught law courses on six continents, including at Stanford Law School, the University of California Berkeley (Boalt Hall) School of Law, Sciences Po (Institut d'Etudes Politiques) in France, and the University of São Paulo in Brazil. Professor Steinberg holds a BA degree from Yale, and JD and PhD degrees from Stanford.

Paul B. Stephan is the John C. Jeffries, Jr., Distinguished Professor and the David H. Ibbeken 1971 Research Professor at the University of Virginia School of Law, where he has taught since 1979. Stephan has taken leave from Virginia to serve as an adviser to the US Treasury Department for tax reform in Central and Eastern Europe and Eurasia in 1993–98, as the Counselor on International Law to the Legal Adviser of the US State Department in 2006–07, and Special Counsel to the General Counsel of the US Defense Department in 2020–21. He has also taught at Duke Law School and Columbia Law School in the United States, and abroad at the Moscow State Institute for International Relations, the University of Vienna, Westfälische Wilhelms-Universität Münster, University of Lausanne, Sciences Po, Paris I, Paris II, Melbourne University, Sydney University, Interdisciplinary Research Center Herzliya, Peking University School of Transnational Law, and the University of Tartu Pärnu College. He was coordinating reporter for the American Law Institute's Restatement (Fourth) of the Foreign Relations Law of the United States. He has published many monographs, book chapters, and articles and maintains a consulting practice on issues of international and foreign relations law.

Lauren Sukin is a postdoctoral fellow at the Center for International Security and Cooperation in the Freeman Spogli Institute at Stanford University.

She will soon join the Department of International Relations at the London School of Economics and Political Science as an Assistant Professor. Sukin's scholarship focuses on issues of international security, primarily on the role of nuclear weapons in international politics. Her other research interests include the laws of armed conflict, crisis politics, cybersecurity, and public opinion on the use of force. She takes a multimethod approach to research, and her scholarship involves the use of survey experiments, machine learning for text analysis, causal analysis, case studies, and myriad other techniques. Sukin received her PhD in Political Science from Stanford University, specializing in international relations. She also holds an MA in Political Science from Stanford University as well as ABs in Political Science and Literary Arts from Brown University.

Allen S. Weiner is Senior Lecturer in Law and Director of the Program in International and Comparative Law at Stanford Law School. He is also the Director of the Stanford Center on International Conflict and Negotiation. Weiner's scholarship and teaching focus on international and national security law, the law of war, international conflict resolution, and international criminal law (including transitional justice). His scholarship is deeply informed by experience; before joining the Stanford faculty, he practiced international law in the US Department of State for more than a decade, serving first as an Attorney Adviser in the Office of the Legal Adviser and later as Legal Counselor to the US Embassy in The Hague. Weiner received his JD degree from Stanford Law School and his AB from Harvard University.

List of Abbreviations

ABILA	American Branch of the International Law Association
BIT	bilateral investment treaty
BRI	Belt and Road Initiative
CAT	Convention Against Torture
CCW	Convention on Certain Conventional Weapons
CEDAW	Convention on the Elimination of All Forms of Discrimination Against Women
CERD	Convention on the Elimination of All Forms of Racial Discrimination
CPTPP	Comprehensive and Progressive Agreement for Trans-Pacific Partnership
CRC	Convention on the Rights of the Child
CSO	civil society organization
DDoS	distributed denial-of-service attack
ECJ	European Court of Justice
ECOWAS	Economic Community of West African States
EEC	European Economic Community
FAA	Federal Aviation Administration
FCPA	Foreign Corrupt Practices Act
FDI	foreign direct investment
FTA	free trade agreement
GATT	General Agreement on Tariffs and Trade
GGE	Group of Government Experts
IAC	international armed conflict
IACtHR	Inter-American Court of Human Rights
IBRD	International Bank for Reconstruction and Development
ICC	International Criminal Court
ICCPR	International Covenant on Civil and Political Rights
ICESCR	International Covenant on Economic, Social, and Cultural Rights
ICJ	International Court of Justice
ICRC	International Committee of the Red Cross
ICSID	International Centre for Settlement of Investment Disputes
ICSID Convention	Convention on the Settlement of Investment Disputes Between States and Nationals of Other States
ICT	information and communications technology

ICTR	International Criminal Tribunal for Rwanda
ICTY	International Criminal Tribunal for the former Yugoslavia
IEL	international environmental law
IHL	international humanitarian law
IHRL	international human rights law
ILO	international legal order
IMF	International Monetary Fund
IMO	International Maritime Organization
IPPC	Intergovernmental Panel on Climate Change
iPRAW	International Panel on the Regulation of Autonomous Weapons
ISDS	investor-state dispute settlement
ITLOS	International Tribunal for the Law of the Sea
LAWS	lethal autonomous weapons systems
MAI	Multilateral Agreement on Investment
MID	militarized interstate dispute
MTCR	Missile Technology Control Regime
NAFTA	North American Free Trade Agreement
NIAC	non-international armed conflict
NSG	Nuclear Suppliers Group
OAS	Organization of American States
OAU	Organization of African Unity
ODA	official development assistance
OECD	Organisation for Economic Co-operation and Development
RSCI	Resilient Supply Chain Initiative
SEC	Securities and Exchange Commission
TWAIL	Third World Approaches to International Law
TPP	Trans-Pacific Partnership
TTIP	Transatlantic Trade and Investment Partnership
UN GGE	UN Group of Governmental Experts
UNCITRAL	UN Commission on International Trade Law
UNCLOS	UN Convention on the Law of the Sea
UNCTAD	UN Conference on Trade and Development
USMCA	United States–Mexico–Canada Agreement
WMD	weapons of mass destruction
WTO	World Trade Organization
WTO AB	World Trade Organization Appellate Body

Introduction

Preserving a Rules-based International Order

David L. Sloss

This book grows out of the work of a study group convened by the American Branch of the International Law Association (ABILA). ABILA approved the formation of the study group in December 2018, with the title, "Threats to a Rules-Based International Order and Possible Responses." Key assumptions that prompted formation of the study group were: (1) that we have reached a watershed moment in the evolution of the international system in which the rules-based international order confronts multiple threats that have the potential to undermine or seriously erode that order; and (2) that the United States should try to preserve a rules-based international order, if possible.

Although several members of the ABILA study group prefer the phrase "liberal international order," I believe that the phrase "rules-based international order" provides a better frame for the project. The phrase "liberal international order" is problematic because the meaning of the term "liberal" is contested and because the term "liberal" fails to capture key features of the current international legal order. One of the central goals of the international legal order—arguably the central goal—is to preserve peace and minimize the human suffering caused by armed conflict. That goal is neither liberal nor illiberal. Indeed, it is debatable whether liberal states have a better track record than illiberal states when it comes to compliance with international legal rules governing the use of force. Regardless, those rules are at the heart of the project to maintain a rules-based international order.

For at least some "liberals," a normative commitment to free movement of people is a central pillar of liberal internationalist ideology. Even so, as Jaya Ramji-Nogales explains in her contribution to this volume,[1] the post–World War II international order has never codified that commitment in law.

[1] *See* Jaya Ramji-Nogales, *Migration and International Legal Disorder* (Chapter 14 in this volume).

David L. Sloss, *Introduction* In: *Is the International Legal Order Unraveling?*. Edited by: David L. Sloss, Oxford University Press. © Oxford University Press 2022. DOI: 10.1093/oso/9780197652800.003.0001

Thus, the current international legal order is illiberal insofar as it reinforces the sovereign power of states to close their borders to transnational migrants.

The two features of the current international legal order that are most closely associated with liberal values are international human rights law and international economic law. In both areas, current international rules expose a rift between competing versions of liberalism, which I call "humanitarian liberalism" and "free market liberalism." The Universal Declaration of Human Rights is based on the principle that economic/social rights and civil/political rights are indivisible; it therefore manifests a commitment to humanitarian liberalism. However, the United States, which has been the dominant power in the international system since World War II, has traditionally privileged civil and political rights over economic and social rights. The US view of the hierarchical relationship between the two sets of rights is consistent with free market liberalism, but not humanitarian liberalism.

James Gathii and Sergio Puig argue persuasively that domination of the Global South by the Global North is a key feature of the post–World War II international economic order.[2] The persistence of North-South inequality can be partially explained by the fact that international economic institutions have been guided largely by free market liberalism, not humanitarian liberalism. Moreover, as Richard Steinberg shows, after the end of the Cold War the United States deployed its hegemonic power in pursuit of what he calls economic "hyper-liberalism," which is an extreme form of free market liberalism.[3] Those hyper-liberal policies provoked substantial pushback, which is arguably contributing to the unraveling of the international legal order.

The preceding comments explain why the phrase "liberal international order" may be problematic for some analytic purposes. In contrast, although no terminology is perfect, the phrase "rules-based international order" provides a more helpful frame for this project. Here, I contrast the idea of a rules-based order with a "sovereignty-based international order." The distinction between a rules-based order and a sovereignty-based order is not black and white. Even in an international order that is primarily sovereignty-based, there are international legal rules that govern the behavior of states. Therefore, the distinction is best understood as a continuum with many shades of grey. Moreover, the distinction between rules-based

[2] *See* James T. Gathii & Sergio Puig, *The West and the Unraveling of the Economic World Order: Thoughts from a Global South Perspective* (Chapter 2 in this volume).

[3] *See* Richard H. Steinberg, *The Rise and Decline of a Liberal International Order* (Chapter 1 in this volume).

and sovereignty-based can be applied to the international system as a whole, or to specific subfields within international law.

Bearing in mind these caveats, a rules-based order differs from a sovereignty-based order along three dimensions: the nature of international obligations, the degree to which states delegate authority to international institutions, and the degree to which rules are actually enforced.[4] In a sovereignty-based order, most international legal rules operate horizontally: states owe obligations to other states, not to private actors. Rules governing the initiation of use of force, the *jus ad bellum*, are horizontal rules.[5] In contrast, a rules-based international order includes numerous rules that operate vertically: they create obligations that states owe to private parties.[6] The rules embodied in international human rights law and international investment law are primarily vertical rules. In the decades after World War II, the international system became more rules-based as states added more vertical legal rules, creating a thicker set of obligations that states owe to private parties.

Second, in a sovereignty-based order, states either do not create international institutions or they delegate very limited authority to those institutions. In contrast, in a rules-based order, states delegate more robust authority to international institutions. Thus, after World War II, states gradually strengthened the rules-based international order by delegating authority to institutions like the UN Security Council (1945), the European Court of Human Rights (1959), the World Trade Organization (1995), and the International Criminal Court (2002).

Third, in a sovereignty-based order, enforcement of international rules is weak or nonexistent. In contrast, in a rules-based order, enforcement of

[4] My concept of rules-based versus sovereignty-based orders has some commonalities with the concept of "legalization" explained by Professor Abbott and his co-authors in their seminal article in *International Organizations*. *See* Kenneth W. Abbott et al., *The Concept of Legalization*, 54 INT'L ORG. 401 (2000). They define the term "legalization" as "a particular form of institutionalization characterized by three components: obligation, precision, and delegation." *Id.* at 401. Their concept of obligation focuses on the question whether a rule is legally binding, *id.* at 408–12, whereas mine focuses on the distinction between horizontal and vertical obligations. Their concept of delegation includes delegation of authority to actors other than international institutions, *id.* at 415–18, whereas I focus on delegation of authority to international institutions. They explicitly exclude questions about the effectiveness of enforcement from their concept of legalization. *See id.* at 402. In contrast, I claim that effective enforcement is a key distinguishing feature of a rules-based order.

[5] *See* Lauren Sukin & Allen S. Weiner, *War and Words: The International Use of Force in the UN Charter Era* (Chapter 5 in this volume).

[6] *See* David L. Sloss & Michael P. Van Alstine, *International Law in Domestic Courts*, *in* RESEARCH HANDBOOK ON THE POLITICS OF INTERNATIONAL LAW 79, 83–85 (Wayne Sandholtz & Christopher A. Whytock eds., 2017) (discussing horizontal and vertical obligations).

international legal rules is more effective. It bears emphasis that many vertical rules of international law are enforced, albeit imperfectly, without delegating authority to international institutions. For example, enforcement of international investment law relies primarily on investor-state arbitration;[7] enforcement of the *jus in bello* relies heavily on national military systems;[8] and states have created a fairly robust mechanism for enforcing anti-bribery rules by tacitly delegating enforcement authority to the United States and a handful of other powerful states.[9] More broadly, the term "enforcement," as used in this introduction, includes both domestic and international enforcement mechanisms, and both judicial and nonjudicial enforcement mechanisms.

Ultimately, in evaluating the degree to which a particular area of international law is rules-based or sovereignty-based, one must consider all three dimensions: the nature of vertical versus horizontal obligations; the degree to which states have delegated authority to international institutions; and the effectiveness of various enforcement mechanisms. Some areas of international law are "rules-based" in the sense that they create vertical obligations for states, and there are reasonably effective mechanisms for enforcing those rules, even though they do not delegate significant authority to international institutions. To reiterate, the distinction between rules-based and sovereignty-based orders is not black and white: it is a continuum with many shades of grey.

Although states have made significant gains in strengthening the rules-based international order over the past several decades, there has been significant backsliding toward a more sovereignty-based order since the turn of the century, especially in the areas of international human rights law[10] and international trade law.[11] In his contribution to this volume, Tom Ginsburg considers the possibility that the rising power of China might steer the international order in a direction that is both more sovereignty-based and more illiberal.[12] As he explains, such changes are arguably already underway.

[7] *See* Jeremy Rabkin, *Strength in Obscurity: The Resilience of International Investment Law* (Chapter 10 in this volume).

[8] *See* Laura A. Dickinson, *The* Jus in Bello *under Strain: Diluted But Not Disintegrating* (Chapter 6 in this volume).

[9] *See* Paul B. Stephan, *Anti-Bribery Law* (Chapter 11 in this volume).

[10] *See* Wayne Sandholtz, *Authoritarianism, International Human Rights, and Legal Change* (Chapter 12 in this volume).

[11] *See* Kathleen Claussen, *The Experimental Evolution of Trade Law* (Chapter 9 in this volume).

[12] *See* Tom Ginsburg, *The Future of Liberal Democracy in the International Legal Order* (Chapter 3 in this volume).

Even so, I remain hopeful that key features of the rules-based international order will endure. The several chapters in this book generally support the conclusion that the rules-based international order confronts significant challenges, but it is not unraveling—at least, not yet. Climate change is the biggest wild card in trying to predict the future. Maxine Burkett argues persuasively that climate change represents the single greatest threat to the future of a rules-based international order.[13] If the world's major powers—especially the United States and China—cooperate with each other to combat climate change, then other threats to the rules-based order should be manageable. If the world's major powers fail to address the climate crisis by 2040 or 2050, the other threats addressed in this volume may come to be seen as trivial in comparison.

The remainder of this introduction is divided into three sections. Section I presents a brief history of the rules-based international order. It shows that—between 1945 and the first decade of the twenty-first century—the international system evolved from a primarily sovereignty-based order to a much more rules-based order. However, since about 2008 or 2010, we have witnessed significant backsliding toward a more sovereignty-based order, especially in the areas of international trade and international human rights law. Section II then briefly surveys the major, current threats to the rules-based international order. Finally, section III outlines a potential strategy to mitigate those threats in the interest of preserving a rules-based international order that is consistent with liberal, humanitarian values.

I. A Brief History of the Rules-based International Order

In Chapter 1, Richard Steinberg divides the history of the post–World War II international order into three periods: 1945–90, 1991–2008, and 2009–present.[14] As he admits, any line-drawing exercise that divides history into discrete periods is somewhat arbitrary. Even so, Steinberg's proposed division into discrete periods is analytically useful,[15] because these three periods correspond roughly to the Cold War; a post–Cold War period when the

[13] *See* Maxine Burkett, *Revolution or Collapse?: Climate Change and the International Legal Order* (Chapter 4 in this volume).

[14] Steinberg, Chapter 1.

[15] One potential criticism of this periodization is that the 9/11 attacks—which had a substantial impact on the evolution of the international legal order—fall right in the middle of the second period.

United States was the world's sole superpower; and a recent period characterized by declining US power and rising Chinese power. For the purpose of this introduction, I add a fourth period: the period before World War II, when the international order was largely sovereignty-based, not rules-based. It bears emphasis that the sovereignty-based order that existed before World War II reinforced the sovereign power of mostly European states; it excluded large portions of the globe occupied by dependent colonies that lacked sovereign powers.[16]

This book consists of fourteen chapters (plus this introduction), eight of which address specific substantive areas of international law. Those eight chapters deal with: *jus ad bellum*,[17] *jus in bello*,[18] international trade law,[19] international investment law,[20] anti-bribery law,[21] human rights law,[22] international criminal law,[23] and international migration law.[24] (The *jus ad bellum* involves rules for the initiation of armed conflict. The *jus in bello* involves rules for conducting armed conflict after it has been initiated.) This section analyzes the evolution of a rules-based international order in those eight substantive areas, dividing the history into four periods. Table I.1 summarizes the historical analysis. To reiterate, though, the distinction between rules-based and sovereignty-based orders is a continuum with many shades of grey. In Table I.1, the labels "rules-based" and "sovereignty-based" reflect a qualitative judgment about the location on that continuum of particular legal regimes during particular historical eras.

A. The International Legal Order before World War II

Before World War II, international law established a rules-based order in only one of the eight substantive areas referenced above: the *jus in bello*, also known as "international humanitarian law" (IHL). IHL rules were first codified in the 1864 Geneva Convention, and later strengthened and expanded in agreements reached at the 1899 Hague Peace Conference, the 1907 Hague

16 *See* Gathii & Puig, Chapter 2.
17 Sukin & Weiner, Chapter 5.
18 Dickinson, Chapter 6.
19 Claussen, Chapter 9.
20 Rabkin, Chapter 10.
21 Stephan, Chapter 11.
22 Sandholtz, Chapter 12.
23 Leila N. Sadat, *The International Criminal Law of the Future* (Chapter 13 in this volume).
24 Ramji-Nogales, Chapter 14.

Table I.1 Evolution of a Rules-Based International Order

	Before WW II	1945–1990	1990–2008	2009–present
Jus in bello	Rules-based	Rules-based	Rules-based	Stable
Jus ad bellum	Sovereignty-based	Rules-based	Rules-based	Backsliding??
Int'l Trade Law	Sovereignty-based	Rules-based	Rules-based	Backsliding
Int'l Human Rights	Sovereignty-based	Rules-based	Rules-based	Backsliding
Int'l Criminal Law	Sovereignty-based	Sovereignty-based	Rules-based	Stable
Investment Law	Sovereignty-based	Sovereignty-based	Rules-based	Stable
Bribery	Sovereignty-based	Sovereignty-based	Rules-based	Stable
Migration	Sovereignty-based	Sovereignty-based	Sovereignty-based	Sovereignty-based

Peace Conference, and the 1929 Geneva Conference.[25] None of the IHL treaties concluded during this period created international institutions with significant enforcement powers; enforcement relied primarily on national militaries. Regardless, there were internationally agreed rules creating vertical obligations that states owed to individuals. Numerous states incorporated those obligations into national military law and enforced the rules against their own citizens.

Before World War II, the international order was generally sovereignty-based, not rules-based, in the other seven areas of substantive law covered in this volume. There were no internationally agreed rules governing bribery or migration. With respect to migration, states had the sovereign right to exclude any persons they chose to exclude, subject to modest restrictions in some bilateral treaties. Bribery was an accepted part of the transnational business environment. Bilateral treaties addressed topics related to international trade and investment law, but there were few globally or even regionally accepted norms governing international trade and investment, despite efforts by capital-exporting states to persuade capital-importing states to

[25] *See* International Committee of the Red Cross, *Treaties, States Parties and Commentaries*, https://ihl-databases.icrc.org/applic/ihl/ihl.nsf/vwTreatiesHistoricalByDate.xsp (last visited Jan. 2, 2021).

accept a legal rule requiring compensation for expropriation.[26] States began to lay a foundation for development of international criminal law by concluding bilateral extradition treaties and by prohibiting both piracy and the slave trade, but there were few international rules obligating states to punish individuals for criminal conduct.[27] The International Labor Organization, created in 1919, began to sow the seeds for modern international human rights law, but international law imposed few restrictions on the power of sovereign states to abuse the human rights of their own citizens.

Some scholars have argued that the Kellogg-Briand Pact of 1928[28] created a rules-based order related to *jus ad bellum* before World War II.[29] Even if one accepts that view, which is disputed, it is undisputed that international law before 1928 imposed few meaningful constraints on the power of sovereign states to initiate armed conflicts whenever they determined that they had good cause to do so. Thus, with respect to *jus ad bellum*, the international order was primarily sovereignty-based, not rules-based, until at least 1928, and arguably until adoption of the UN Charter in 1945.

B. The Cold War Era: 1945 to 1990

In the period after World War II, the international order moved much further along the spectrum from a sovereignty-based order toward a rules-based order. By the end of the Cold War, internationally agreed legal rules had established a rules-based order in four of the eight substantive areas covered in this volume: *jus ad bellum*, *jus in bello*, trade, and human rights. However, anti-bribery law, investment law, migration law, and international criminal law remained primarily sovereignty-based as of 1990.

Article 2(4) of the UN Charter codified a general prohibition on the use of force with only two exceptions: force is permitted in self-defense or with Security Council authorization. The Charter also delegated substantial authority to a new international institution, the UN Security Council,

[26] During this period, numerous decisions by international arbitral tribunals ordered states to compensate foreign investors for expropriation of property, but states in the Global South challenged the asserted rules on expropriation. Moreover, in many cases, their agreement to submit claims to arbitration was coerced by an express or implied threat of military force. *See* Rabkin, Chapter 10.

[27] *See* Sadat, Chapter 13.

[28] Kellogg-Briand Pact, 46 Stat. 2343, TIAS No. 796 (1928) (providing that parties "renounce" war as a solution for any "disputes or conflicts of whatever nature or whatever origin they may be").

[29] *See* Oona A. Hathaway & Scott J. Shapiro, The Internationalists: How a Radical Plan to Outlaw War Remade the World (2017).

and vested the Council with significant enforcement powers. In particular, Chapter VII of the Charter authorizes the Council to "determine the existence of any threat to the peace, breach of the peace, or act of aggression" and to "take such action by air, sea, or land forces as may be necessary to maintain or restore international peace and security."[30] Although the Charter granted the Security Council robust enforcement powers, the Council rarely exercised those powers before 1990. Critics argue that the Article 2(4) prohibition on use of force is not "real law" because powerful states violate that prohibition at will.[31] However, in Chapter 5, Lauren Sukin and Allen Weiner present persuasive empirical evidence showing that the incidence of armed conflict has not increased significantly since 1945 and that states have generally felt the need to justify the use of force within the legal framework established by the Charter.[32]

During the Cold War, states strengthened the *jus in bello* by codifying detailed legal rules in six separate treaties: the four Geneva Conventions of 1949 and the two Additional Protocols of 1977.[33] As of 1990, approximately 160 states were parties to the 1949 Geneva Conventions, 96 states were parties to the first Additional Protocol, and 86 states were parties to the second Additional Protocol.[34] The International Committee of the Red Cross (ICRC) has an oversight role, but states have not created an international institution with significant enforcement powers. Hence, enforcement continues to rely primarily on national militaries.

In October 1947, twenty-three states concluded the General Agreement on Tariffs and Trade (GATT), thereby creating the world's first, broad-based multilateral trading system founded on the liberal principle of free movement of goods.[35] During seven rounds of negotiations between 1949 and 1973, GATT members agreed to a series of progressively more stringent restrictions on tariff and nontariff barriers to trade. By 1990, approximately one hundred states had joined the GATT system. Thus, GATT laid the foundation for a rules-based order for international trade. However, that order was not global in scope: China and Soviet bloc nations were excluded.

[30] U.N. Charter, arts. 39, 42.

[31] *See, e.g.*, Michael J. Glennon, *The Fog of Law: Self-Defense, Inherence, and Incoherence in Article 51 of the United Nations Charter*, 25 HARV. J.L. & PUB. POL'Y 539 (2002).

[32] Sukin & Weiner, Chapter 5.

[33] *See* Dickinson, Chapter 6.

[34] International Committee of the Red Cross, *State Parties to the Following International Humanitarian Law and Other Related Treaties as of 15-Dec-2020*, https://ihl-databases.icrc.org/applic/ihl/ihl.nsf/vwTreatiesHistoricalByDate.xsp.

[35] General Agreement on Tariffs and Trade, Oct. 30, 1947, 55 U.N.T.S. 187.

Moreover, GATT did not create a robust institutional framework for oversight and enforcement. Disputes between states were submitted to panels for resolution, but decisions by GATT panels were binding only if approved by consensus of the contracting parties, and the losing party could block that consensus.

The UN General Assembly established the foundation for modern international human rights law when it adopted the Universal Declaration of Human Rights in 1948. Although the Declaration is nonbinding, states have acknowledged that many of its provisions are now customary international law. By 1990, states had also adopted several multilateral human rights treaties, including the International Covenant on Civil and Political Rights (ICCPR), the International Covenant on Economic, Social, and Cultural Rights (ICESCR), the Convention on the Elimination of All Forms of Racial Discrimination (CERD), the Convention on the Elimination of All Forms of Discrimination Against Women (CEDAW), the Convention Against Torture (CAT), and the Convention on the Rights of the Child (CRC). The institutional framework for international human rights law included the UN Commission on Human Rights and several human rights treaty bodies. In Europe and Latin America, states supplemented these global treaties and institutions by adopting regional treaties and creating regional human rights courts with significant enforcement authority. The network of global and regional treaties and institutions created a rules-based order in the field of human rights. However, as Wayne Sandholtz notes, the basic institutional design relies primarily on domestic courts and other domestic institutions to enforce governmental compliance with human rights treaty obligations.[36] During the Cold War, the quality of domestic enforcement was generally quite good in liberal democracies, but quite poor in authoritarian states.

As of 1990, the international order in the areas of bribery, investment law, migration, and criminal law remained largely sovereignty-based. The United States enacted the Foreign Corrupt Practices Act (FCPA) in 1977 to criminalize transnational bribery.[37] However, as of 1990, very few other states had followed the US lead and there were no international agreements proscribing the practice. States began to conclude bilateral investment treaties (BITs) as early as 1959. By 1988, states had concluded a total of 309 BITs,[38]

[36] *See* Sandholtz, Chapter 12.

[37] Foreign Corrupt Practices Act of 1977, Pub. L. No. 95-213, Tit. I, Dec. 19, 1977, 91 Stat. 1495, *codified as amended at* 15 U.S.C. §§ 78dd-1, 78dd-2, 78dd-3.

[38] Jeswald W. Salacuse & Nicholas P. Sullivan, *Do BITs Really Work?: An Evaluation of Bilateral Investment Treaties and Their Grand Bargain*, 46 HARV. INT'L. L.J. 67, 75 (2005).

which codified significant international law protections for foreign investors. However, as recently as the 1980s, many states continued to assert their sovereign right to expropriate property owned by foreign investors. A UN study conducted in the 1970s "identified 875 distinct acts of governmental taking of foreign property in sixty-two countries" between 1960 and 1974.[39]

States adopted the UN Convention Relating to the Status of Refugees in 1951; it codified a rule prohibiting states from expelling refugees to countries where they have reasonable grounds to fear persecution.[40] The 1967 Protocol on the Status of Refugees broadened the scope of protection for refugees.[41] But despite these important international law protections for refugees, the field of migration law remains primarily sovereignty-based, not rules-based, because international law does not obligate any state to admit refugees, and because the definition of "refugee" is so narrow that it excludes millions of migrants who desperately need protection.[42]

As of 1990, states had planted the seeds of a rules-based order in the field of international criminal law, but the international order at that time was still primarily sovereignty-based. After World War II, the International Military Tribunal at Nuremberg and the International Military Tribunal for the Far East (in Tokyo) prosecuted German and Japanese defendants, respectively, for crimes against peace and war crimes. However, after the 1940s, there were no additional prosecutions before international criminal tribunals until the 1990s. The Genocide Convention, adopted in 1948, codified an international obligation to prevent and punish genocide. Similarly, the 1949 Geneva Conventions obligated states to punish individuals who commit "grave breaches." However, there are no recorded cases of genocide prosecutions during the Cold War period, and war crimes were generally treated as domestic matters requiring internal discipline by national militaries.[43]

C. The Post–Cold War Era: 1991 to 2008

Between 1991 and 2008, the fields of investment law, anti-bribery law, and international criminal law transitioned from sovereignty-based orders to

[39] *Id.*
[40] Convention Relating to the Status of Refugees, July 28, 1951, 189 U.N.T.S. 137.
[41] Protocol Relating to the Status of Refugees, Jan. 31, 1967, 606 U.N.T.S. 267.
[42] *See* Ramji-Nogales, Chapter 14.
[43] For more on the history of international criminal law during this period, *see* Sadat, Chapter 13.

rules-based orders. During the same period, states and international organizations strengthened enforcement of the rules-based orders related to *jus ad bellum*, *jus in bello*, trade, and human rights. As of 2008, migration law was the only area of law covered in this survey that remained primarily sovereignty-based.

Members of the Organisation for Economic Co-operation and Development (OECD) adopted the OECD Bribery Convention in 1997.[44] The treaty entered into force in 1999; forty-four states are parties to the Convention. (The United Nations adopted the UN Convention Against Corruption in 2003;[45] it now has 187 parties.) The OECD Convention focuses on the relatively narrow problem of bribery, not the broader problem of corruption. The treaty targets individuals who pay bribes, not the government officials who receive them. The Convention does not create any new international institutions to combat bribery. Instead, it facilitates prosecution of individuals who commit transnational bribery offenses by removing traditional sovereignty-based barriers to extraterritorial regulation.[46] In the words of Paul Stephan, the Convention created "a remarkably robust regulatory regime with almost all of the action occurring at the national level."[47] The OECD Convention has been fairly successful because the United States and a small number of other countries actively prosecute crimes covered by the Convention, while other countries quietly acquiesce when their nationals are prosecuted.

As of 1990, states had concluded about four hundred BITs. "By 2005, there were more than 2,000 BITs, a five-fold increase in the 15 years after 1990."[48] The proliferation of BITs manifested widespread acceptance of an international legal rule prohibiting sovereign states from expropriating private property owned by foreign investors. Capital-exporting states had favored that rule for more than a century, but the rule failed to gain broad acceptance during the Cold War. In addition to banning expropriation, BITs include several other substantive protections for foreign investors. Most BITs also empower private investors to sue host states in arbitration proceedings,

[44] OECD Convention on Combating Bribery of Foreign Public Officials in International Business Transactions, Dec. 17, 1997, S. Treaty Doc. No. 105-43, 2802 U.N.T.S. 225 (entered into force Feb. 15, 1999) [hereinafter OECD Convention].

[45] United Nations Convention Against Corruption, Oct. 31, 2003, S. Treaty Doc. No. 109-6, 2349 U.N.T.S. 41 (entered into force Dec. 14, 2005).

[46] *See* Stephan, Chapter 11.

[47] *Id.* at (p. 339)

[48] Rabkin, Chapter 10, at (p. 313)

a process known as investor-state dispute settlement (ISDS). ISDS existed on paper before 1990, but the number of ISDS proceedings exploded over the next two decades. The International Centre for Settlement of Investment Disputes (ICSID) reported only seven ISDS cases registered between 1990 and 1994. In contrast, ICSID reported a total of 113 ISDS cases registered between 2000 and 2004.[49] By relying on ISDS as the primary enforcement mechanism for investor protection rules, states created a robust rules-based order in the field of international investment law without delegating substantial enforcement authority to any international institution.[50]

During the post–Cold War era, the Security Council created the International Criminal Tribunal for the former Yugoslavia (ICTY) in 1993 and the International Criminal Tribunal for Rwanda (ICTR) in 1994. Both tribunals prosecuted individuals for genocide, war crimes, and crimes against humanity.[51] Over the next ten to fifteen years, the international community established several other hybrid tribunals, including the Extraordinary Chambers in the Courts of Cambodia, the Supreme Iraqi Criminal Tribunal, the Special Court of Sierra Leone, and the Special Tribunal for Lebanon. Most importantly, states adopted the Rome Statute for the International Criminal Court (ICC), which entered into force in 2002.[52] By 2008, almost 120 states were parties to the Rome Statute. Creation of the ICC was a landmark achievement that established a rules-based order in the field of international criminal law. However, the effectiveness of that order is hampered by the fact that neither the United States nor China nor Russia has ratified the Rome Statute. Their nonparticipation is driven at least partly by sovereignty-based objections to the ICC.

For proponents of a rules-based international order, creation of the World Trade Organization (WTO) was clearly one of the signature accomplishments of the post–Cold War era. States adopted the Agreement Establishing the World Trade Organization in 1994;[53] the WTO came into existence on January 1, 1995. The GATT had previously established a rules-based order for international trade, but the WTO strengthened and broadened that order. In contrast to GATT, the WTO agreement created a permanent international institution staffed by international civil servants. The Dispute Settlement

[49] *See* ICSID, *Cases Database*, at https://icsid.worldbank.org/cases/case-database.

[50] ICSID serves an important coordination function, but ICSID itself does not have significant enforcement powers.

[51] *See* Sadat, Chapter 14.

[52] Rome Statute of the International Criminal Court, July 17, 1998, 2187 U.N.T.S. 3.

[53] Agreement Establishing the World Trade Organization, Apr. 15, 1994, 1867 U.N.T.S. 3.

Understanding, an integral part of the WTO agreements, strengthened the international enforcement mechanism for resolving trade disputes, in part by creating a permanent appellate body to hear appeals from panel decisions.[54] The admission of China into the WTO in 2001 represented a significant expansion of the international trading system to include countries that were once deemed off limits. Whereas only about one hundred states were parties to the GATT agreements in 1990, the WTO had more than 150 member states as of 2008. Today, trade among WTO member states—all of which is governed by WTO rules—accounts for more than 95 percent of total world trade.[55]

The UN response to Iraq's 1990 invasion of Kuwait marked a significant turning point in the Security Council's role in enforcing the Charter's *jus ad bellum* regime. One day after the invasion, the Council adopted Resolution 660, declaring "a breach of international peace and security" and demanding Iraq's immediate and unconditional withdrawal from Kuwait.[56] A few months later, in Resolution 678, the Council authorized "Member States co-operating with the Government of Kuwait . . . to use all necessary means to . . . re store international peace and security in the area."[57] Over the next thirteen years, the Council invoked its authority under Chapter VII of the Charter to authorize enforcement actions in Somalia (1992), the former Yugoslavia (1991–93), Rwanda (1994), Haiti (1994), Albania (1997), the Central African Republic (1997), East Timor (1999), Kosovo (1999), Afghanistan (2001), Liberia (2003), the Democratic Republic of Congo (2003), and Cote d'Ivoire (2003).[58] During this period, states and commentators expressed guarded optimism that the Security Council was finally fulfilling its primary mission under the UN Charter: to maintain international peace and security. That optimism faded after 2003, for reasons discussed in the next section.

The core *jus in bello* norms remained largely unchanged in the post–Cold War period, but creation of the ICC and other international criminal tribunals strengthened international enforcement of those norms. The ICTY and ICTR prosecuted hundreds of people for war crimes during this period. Decisions by those tribunals helped refine and clarify *jus in bello* norms,

54 *See* Claussen, Chapter 9.

55 *See* World Trade Organization, *Accession in Perspective*, https://www.wto.org/english/thewto_e/acc_e/cbt_course_e/c1s1p1_e.htm.

56 S.C. Res. 660 (Aug. 2, 1990).

57 S.C. Res. 678 (Nov. 29, 1990).

58 *See* Christine Gray, International Law and the Use of Force 289–300, 341–59 (4th ed. 2018).

especially with respect to non-international armed conflicts. Still, the principle of complementarity codified in the Rome Statute reflects the expectation that national governments retain primary responsibility for prosecuting individuals who commit war crimes. After adoption of the Rome Statute, many states parties enacted new domestic legislation to clarify and enhance their authority to prosecute individuals who commit war crimes and other international crimes. The evidence is inconclusive, but some studies suggest that states began using their domestic legal systems to prosecute international crimes more aggressively during this period.[59]

The core human rights norms remained largely unchanged during this period, but there was modest institutional innovation at the international level. For example, the Organization of African Unity (OAU) created the African Court on Human and Peoples' Rights in 1998. The UN Commission on Human Rights created several new working groups and special rapporteurs during this period, and the Human Rights Council replaced the Commission in 2006. However, the global spread of democracy was arguably the most significant development related to human rights enforcement in the post–Cold War era. The number of democracies in the world increased from 57 countries in 1990 to 96 countries in 2008. During the same period, the number of liberal democracies increased from 28 to 43 countries.[60] Given that domestic courts and executive agencies are the institutions with primary responsibility for enforcing states' international human rights obligations, the spread of democracy generally, and liberal democracy in particular, strengthened enforcement of human rights norms, although the world's autocracies continued to violate those norms on a regular basis.

D. The End of US Hegemony: 2009 to Present

In the past decade or so, blogs and scholarly journals have been filled with essays about the decline of the rules-based international order. However, if

[59] *See* Geoff Dancy & Florencia Montal, *Unintended Positive Complementarity: Why International Criminal Court Investigations May Increase Domestic Human Rights Prosecutions*, 111 Am. J. Int'l L. 689 (2017); Geoff Dancy & Kathryn Sikkink, *Ratification and Human Rights Prosecutions: Towards a Transnational Theory of Treaty Compliance*, 44 Int'l L. & Politics 751 (2012).

[60] These figures are based on the v2x_regime variable in the Varieties of Democracy database. That variable divides countries into four groups: liberal democracies, electoral democracies, electoral autocracies, and closed autocracies. The database and codebook are available at https://www.v-dem.net/vdemds.html.

one focuses on the eight areas of law covered in this survey, the rules-based order appears to be in fairly good health. Robust enforcement continues in the areas of anti-bribery law and international investment law, albeit without any significant involvement from international institutions. (Indeed, the decision not to delegate substantial authority to international institutions may be one factor contributing to the success of those regimes.) The norms constituting the *jus in bello* regime remain essentially unchanged. Despite various factors that place strain on the *jus in bello*,[61] domestic enforcement by national militaries continues, supplemented occasionally by international prosecutions. Similarly, international criminal law continues on the same basic trajectory established in the aftermath of the Cold War. The ICC may not be thriving, but neither is it unraveling. International migration law remains primarily sovereignty-based, but that has been true for the entire post–World War II period.[62] Thus, in five of the eight areas under review, there has not been any significant backsliding from a rules-based order toward a sovereignty-based order.

In contrast, there has been some backsliding toward a sovereignty-based order in the fields of trade, human rights, and *jus ad bellum*. Despite major changes in the global economy, states have not concluded any significant new trade agreements on a global basis since the founding of the WTO in 1995. As of this writing, negotiation of a Transatlantic Trade and Investment Partnership (TTIP) has not yielded a final agreement, despite substantial efforts. The United States and eleven other countries finalized the text of a Trans-Pacific Partnership Agreement in 2016, but President Donald Trump repudiated the agreement shortly after taking office.[63] President Trump also launched a major trade war with China, not to mention minor trade wars with key US allies. Additionally, he effectively halted all appeals to the WTO Appellate Body by blocking all judicial appointments to that body.[64] President Joe Biden may reverse some of the Trump administration actions that damaged the international trade regime, but opposition to free trade within the Democratic Party constrains his options. Thus, most experts agree

[61] *See* Dickinson, Chapter 6.

[62] The growth of anti-migrant animus since about 2015 may pose a significant threat to the rules-based international order, as discussed in the next section.

[63] After the United States withdrew, the other TPP countries concluded an agreement without the United States, calling it the Comprehensive and Progressive Agreement for Trans-Pacific Partnership (CPTPP).

[64] *See* Claussen, Chapter 9.

that the rules-based order in the field of trade law has grown weaker since 2016, and the future of the "trade rule of law" remains in doubt.[65]

The core human rights norms remain essentially the same in 2021 as they were in 2008. Similarly, the international institutions related to human rights law remain largely unchanged. However, the total number of democracies in the world decreased from a peak of ninety-eight countries in 2010 to a trough of eighty-seven countries in 2019. Similarly, the number of liberal democracies declined from a peak of forty-five countries in 2009 to a low point of thirty-seven countries in 2019.[66] As Wayne Sandholtz demonstrates, the global decline of democracy between 2008 and 2020 adversely affected human rights enforcement at the domestic level.[67] Moreover, to reiterate, the basic institutional design of the international human rights regime relies primarily on domestic legal systems to enforce international human rights norms.

Backsliding in trade law can be traced to the global financial crisis in 2008–09, and progress on human rights arguably peaked in about 2009–10 (as measured by the number of democracies or liberal democracies in the world). In contrast, backsliding in the use of force regime began earlier. As noted in the previous section, the Security Council achieved a remarkable degree of consensus on use of force after the end of the Cold War. However, the invasion of Iraq in 2003 under the banner "Operation Iraqi Freedom" marked an important turning point in the Security Council's approach to use of force. The United States tried unsuccessfully to persuade other Council members to authorize use of force in Iraq. When that effort failed, the United States and its allies proceeded without express Security Council authorization, claiming that Operation Iraqi Freedom was implicitly authorized by prior Council resolutions. According to one leading scholar, the disingenuous claim of implied authorization had a significant impact on "subsequent Security Council decision-making. . . . When the Security Council wished to express its concern that North Korea and Iran were in violation of their non-proliferation obligations, the language it used . . . was designed deliberately to exclude any possible invocation of implied Security Council authorization."[68] More broadly, the perceived illegitimacy and failure of Operation

[65] *See id.*
[66] These figures are based on the v2x_regime variable in the Varieties of Democracy database. *See supra* note 59.
[67] *See* Sandholtz, Chapter 12.
[68] Gray, *supra* note 58, at 383.

Iraqi Freedom probably led to a much more cautious approach within the Security Council, and a greater willingness on the part of both China and Russia to wield their vetoes to block Chapter VII enforcement actions.[69] Thus, the era of robust Security Council enforcement actions under Chapter VII was very short-lived: from about 1990 to 2003. Even so, Lauren Sukin and Allen Weiner argue persuasively that "[t]he reports of the demise of the U.N. Charter's legal regime governing the use of force are greatly exaggerated."[70]

II. Threats to the Rules-based Order

In thinking about threats to the rules-based international order, it is helpful to begin by considering the broader goals of a rules-based order. This book assumes that those goals generally fit into three baskets: peace (Part II of the book), prosperity (Part III), and human rights (Part IV). Certain threats to the rules-based order relate primarily to one or two of those baskets. Other threats relate to all three.

Two chapters in this book address *new weapons technologies* that could potentially undermine the effectiveness of international rules designed to preserve peace and minimize the destructiveness of armed conflict. Chris Jenks contends that the development of autonomous weapons threatens to erode the effectiveness of the core prohibition on use of force in Article 2(4), but that such weapons are unlikely to have an adverse impact on the key humanitarian principles of the *jus in bello*.[71] Ido Kilovaty has a less sanguine view about the potential impact of cyber weapons. He argues that—in light of the development of new cyber technologies—we need to recalibrate the key thresholds that distinguish prohibited "uses of force" from less violent acts and that distinguish "armed conflict" from situations where IHL does not apply, in order to accomplish the main goals of the *jus ad bellum* and *jus in bello*.[72]

[69] Between 1990 and 2003, China and Russia exercised their veto powers a total of four times in fourteen years. Between 2004 and 2020, they exercised their veto powers a total of twenty-five times in seventeen years. *See* Security Council—Veto List, at https://research.un.org/en/docs/sc/quick. Some vetoes were unrelated to Chapter VII enforcement actions. Nevertheless, the frequency of vetoes gives some indication of the degree of consensus, or lack thereof, among the five permanent members.

[70] Sukin & Weiner, Chapter 5, at (p. 181)

[71] Chris Jenks, *Autonomous Weapons* (Chapter 7 in this volume). For an insightful analysis of current threats to the *jus in bello* regime, *see* Dickinson, Chapter 6.

[72] Ido Kilovaty, *Cyber Conflict and the Thresholds of War* (Chapter 8 in this volume).

Richard Steinberg's contribution to this volume highlights the *dispersion of power* in the international system.[73] Many factors contribute to the dispersion of power. The number of sovereign states in the world has increased from about fifty states that signed the UN Charter in 1945 to almost two hundred states today. Numerous nonstate actors—including large private corporations, terrorist groups, and transnational criminal enterprises—wield much greater power today than they did in 1950. For most of the period since World War II, the United States served as the "glue" that preserved order in the international system, but the presidency of Donald Trump put the world on notice that the United States may no longer be willing or able to exert its power to preserve the rules-based international order. In short, the international order is fraying because the multiplicity of state and nonstate actors is nudging the system toward chaos, and it is uncertain whether the United States (or any combination of states) has the will or capacity to preserve order in a highly decentralized system.

The dispersion of power could potentially weaken all three "baskets" of the rules-based order—peace, prosperity, and human rights—because international legal rules in all three areas are difficult to enforce without a dominant hegemon that is willing and able to exert its power to maintain a rules-based order. Of course, when the United States was the world's dominant power, it did not always wield that power for benign purposes. However, from 1945 until the 2010s, the United States exercised its power to enforce rules that served its perceived interests, and in doing so generally helped to promote and strengthen the rules-based order.

Two chapters address threats to the rules-based order associated with the *rise of China* as a major world power. Richard Steinberg contends that the rise of China is one of the key causal factors contributing to the decline of the liberal international order.[74] Similarly, Tom Ginsburg warns that the rise of China could push the international system away from a rules-based order in the direction of a more sovereignty-based order.[75] In my view, the growth of Chinese power will likely have a major impact on two areas of substantive law covered in this volume: international human rights and international trade law. Indeed, we have already seen shifts toward a more sovereignty-based order in those areas, and we could see further movement

[73] *See* Steinberg, Chapter 1.
[74] *See id.*
[75] *See* Ginsburg, Chapter 3.

in that direction. Rising Chinese power also contributes to paralysis in the UN Security Council, which adversely affects the *jus ad bellum*. However, as of this writing, there is little evidence that rising Chinese power is undermining the effectiveness of the rules-based order related to the *jus in bello*, international investment law, anti-bribery law, or international criminal law. Moreover, Chinese power has no apparent adverse impact on international migration law, which, as previously noted, has remained primarily sovereignty-based for the past seventy-five years.

Several chapters address threats to the rules-based order related to the ongoing phenomenon of *democratic decline*. As noted previously, both the number of liberal democracies and the total number of democratic countries has been declining since about 2009 or 2010. Jaya Ramji-Nogales notes that the rise of anti-migrant animus is a key factor contributing to democratic decline in many democratic (or formerly democratic) states.[76] In some cases, anti-migrant animus is a thinly disguised form of racial animus. James Gathii and Sergio Puig highlight the fact that economic inequality is also a key factor contributing to democratic decline.[77] Economic inequality perpetuates racial inequality because global wealth is concentrated in countries with a majority white population, whereas global poverty is concentrated in countries populated mostly by non-white people.

Wayne Sandholtz argues persuasively that ongoing democratic decline threatens the integrity of the international human rights regime.[78] Tom Ginsburg warns that continued democratic decline could nudge the entire international legal order toward a system of "authoritarian international law."[79] Although a system of authoritarian international law would be more sovereignty-based, and less rules-based, than the current system, it would still be more rules-based than the international legal order before World War II. Table I.2 summarizes the major threats to a rules-based international order.

The major threats I have discussed so far—new technologies, dispersion of power, the rise of China, democratic decline, inequality, and anti-migrant animus—may well weaken the rules-based international order, but they are unlikely to revolutionize that order, or drive us back to the type of sovereignty-based order that existed before 1945. The same cannot be said

[76] *See* Ramji-Nogales, Chapter 14.
[77] *See* Gathii & Puig, Chapter 2.
[78] *See* Sandholtz, Chapter 12.
[79] *See* Ginsburg, Chapter 3.

Table I.2 Summary of Major Threats

Underlying Causes	Key Threats	Potential Consequences
	Autonomous Weapons; Cyber Weapons	Could weaken or undermine both *jus in bello* and *jus ad bellum*
	Rise of China	Tends to weaken int'l human rights. Will likely contribute to fragmentation of int'l trade law.
Anti-migrant sentiment. Increased inequality within rich countries. Continued North-South inequality.	Democratic Decline	Tends to weaken or undermine int'l human rights.
Increasing # of states. Increased influence of nonstate actors. Decline of US power and leadership.	Dispersion of Power	Makes it more challenging to maintain and enforce a wide range of rules affecting peace, prosperity, and human rights.
	Climate Change	Could potentially threaten the entire rules-based international order.

with respect to climate change. As Maxine Burkett warns us, "[g]iven the current state of the climate, the international legal order (ILO) must evolve simply to avoid collapse."[80] Climate change threatens to disrupt every aspect of the international legal order. Therefore, if we want to preserve a rules-based international order and avoid a descent into the type of sovereignty-based order that existed before World War II, the world's major carbon emitters—especially the United States and China—will need to cooperate to combat climate change.

III. Responding to Those Threats

Until this point, this introduction has been largely descriptive. Section III turns from description to prescription. I assume that there is a need for global cooperation to address global threats, like pandemics and climate

[80] Burkett, Chapter 4, at (p. 106)

change. I also assume that the United States and China will be powerful adversaries for the next several decades and that China will use its power to nudge the system in the direction of a more sovereignty-based international order. Hence, the question arises: How can the United States and other liberal democracies best respond to the threats summarized in section II, preserve a rules-based order that is consistent with liberal, humanitarian values,[81] and balance the reality of strategic competition with the need to cooperate with China in areas of common interests? In addressing this question, I speak only for myself and not for the other contributing authors to this volume.

A. Dispersion of Power

The dispersion of power in the international system is a simple fact that must be accepted in the twenty-first century. Between 2000 and 2018, China's share of global GDP increased from about 3 percent to about 14 percent. During that same period, the US share of global GDP decreased from about 26 percent to about 21 percent.[82] Moreover, as noted previously, the number of UN member states has increased dramatically since 1945.

In the post–Cold War era, the United States attempted to create a rules-based order that was both liberal and global. It pursued that agenda by expanding membership in the WTO to encompass almost all nations, by leveraging US economic power to promote the so-called Washington Consensus and by engaging in military adventurism based on a misguided attempt to use US military power to spread democracy and human rights around the globe.[83] In the current geopolitical environment, it is no longer possible (if it ever was) to spread humanitarian liberalism on a global basis in the areas of international trade and human rights. The United Nations and the WTO will continue to serve important functions, but those organizations have so many member states with so many diverse interests that they are not likely to be effective instruments for promoting a humanitarian liberal agenda. Moreover, China exerts significant influence in both the WTO

[81] For present purposes, the phrase "liberal, humanitarian values" encompasses a normative commitment to free trade and free markets, as well as a normative commitment to the values embodied in the Universal Declaration of Human Rights, including a commitment to racial equality and to the principle that economic and social rights are inseparable from civil and political rights.

[82] TheGlobalEconomy.com, *Percent of World GDP: Country Rankings*, https://www.theglobaleconomy.com/rankings/gdp_share/.

[83] *See* Steinberg, Chapter 1.

and the United Nations, and it will use that influence to resist such an agenda. Therefore, the dispersion of power in the international system means that future efforts to advance the goals of humanitarian liberalism in the international order are more likely to succeed if they focus on regional and plurilateral arrangements, not global institutions.

As Anne-Marie Slaughter has argued persuasively, a range of nonstate actors play an increasingly important role in the modern world.[84] In the first quarter of 2021, Amazon produced total sales of about $108 billion[85]—substantially more than the annual gross domestic product of Nepal, a country of thirty million people.[86] In 2019, the Bill and Melinda Gates Foundation distributed more than $5 billion in total direct grantee support.[87] In contrast, Japan, which is the third wealthiest country in the world, spent about $16 billion on official development assistance in 2020.[88]

Some nonstate actors are making an important contribution to the task of preserving a rules-based order. Microsoft's advocacy for a "Digital Geneva Convention" is one excellent example.[89] However, other nonstate actors—including terrorist organizations and transnational criminal enterprises—pose a significant threat to the rules-based order. To preserve and potentially strengthen a rules-based international order in the future, the United States will need to collaborate with private companies and charitable foundations whose goals align with liberal, humanitarian values. At the same time, we need to devise ways to combat terrorism and transnational crime without condoning lawless behavior by governments that is inconsistent with those values. More broadly, in thinking about strategies to preserve a rules-based international order, scholars and practitioners must acknowledge that sovereign states are no longer the only important actors in the international system. Accordingly, we need to reconceive international law in a way that recognizes the important influence of a range of nonstate actors.

[84] *See* Anne-Marie Slaughter, A New World Order (2004).

[85] Tugba Sabanoglu, *Amazon: Quarterly Net Revenue 2007–2021* (Apr. 30, 2021), https://www.statista.com/statistics/273963/quarterly-revenue-of-amazoncom/

[86] Nepal's GDP in 2017 was about $79 billion. CIA, The World Factbook: Nepal, https://www.cia.gov/the-world-factbook/countries/nepal/ (last visited July 1, 2021).

[87] Bill and Melinda Gates Foundation, *2019 Annual Report*, https://www.gatesfoundation.org/about/financials/annual-reports/annual-report-2019.

[88] *See* OECD.Stat, *Total Flows by Donor*, https://stats.oecd.org/Index.aspx?DataSetCode=TABLE1# (last visited July 1, 2021).

[89] *See* Microsoft, *A Digital Geneva Convention to Protect Cyberspace*, https://www.microsoft.com/en-us/cybersecurity/content-hub/a-digital-geneva-convention-to-protect-cyberspace (last visited July 1, 2021).

B. New Weapons Technologies

During the Cold War, the United States and the Soviet Union cooperated to promote their common interest in combating the proliferation of nuclear weapons and other weapons of mass destruction (WMD), despite the generally adversarial nature of the US-Soviet relationship. Similarly, in the twenty-first century, the United States must collaborate with China and Russia to counter the threat posed by new weapons technologies—including autonomous weapons and cyber weapons—without allowing the ideological competition in areas like human rights to stymie needed cooperation in areas of common interests. The Cold War precedent provides grounds for guarded optimism that the United States and China will find ways to cooperate to promote their shared interests, while simultaneously competing as adversaries in other areas.

Consider, first, existing arms control regimes. The Nuclear Non-Proliferation Treaty[90] and the Chemical Weapons Convention[91] have achieved notable success in limiting the proliferation of nuclear and chemical weapons. Similarly, existing export control regimes like the Missile Technology Control Regime (MTCR)[92] have helped control the spread of ballistic missile technology and other weapons technologies. As of this writing, the evidence suggests that the rules-based order related to ballistic missiles and weapons of mass destruction is not unraveling. It is fair to assume that the United States, China, and Russia will continue to cooperate to maintain these existing regimes.

In contrast, new technologies like cyber weapons and autonomous weapons pose greater challenges. States created a Group of Government Experts (GGE) on lethal autonomous weapons in 2016–17, but the GGE has made little progress to date in negotiating agreed limitations on such weapons.[93] Progress in negotiating agreed rules governing the use of cyber weapons has been equally slow. In thinking about strategies to preserve a

[90] Treaty on the Non-Proliferation of Nuclear Weapons, July 1, 1968, 729 U.N.T.S. 161 (entered into force Mar. 5, 1970) [hereinafter NPT].

[91] Convention on the Prohibition of the Development, Production, Stockpiling and Use of Chemical Weapons and on Their Destruction, Jan. 13, 1993, 1974 U.N.T.S. 317 (entered into force Apr. 29, 1997) [hereinafter CWC].

[92] *See* Missile Technology Control Regime, *MTCR Guidelines and Equipment, Software and Technology Annex*, https://mtcr.info/mtcr-guidelines/ [hereinafter MTCR guidelines].

[93] *See* United Nations Office for Disarmament Affairs, *Background on LAWS in the CCW*, https://www.un.org/disarmament/the-convention-on-certain-conventional-weapons/background-on-laws-in-the-ccw/ (last visited July 1, 2021).

rules-based order in this area, it is helpful to distinguish between arms control and export controls. An arms control treaty would limit the capabilities of powerful states like the United States, China, and Russia. At present, none of the major world powers appears to have any significant interest in concluding a treaty that would limit its own military capabilities with respect to either cyber or autonomous weapons.

However, the world's major powers do have a shared interest in restricting the proliferation of cyber and autonomous weapons. These are areas where the world is divided between "haves" and "have nots." The "haves" share a common interest in preventing the spread of sophisticated weapons technology both to smaller states and to nonstate actors. Hence, one could imagine the development of a new, multilateral export control regime, similar to the Nuclear Suppliers Group (NSG) dual-use guidelines[94] or the MTCR. Of course, the technical challenges to designing an effective export control regime are daunting. As Chris Jenks notes in his chapter for this volume, "what distinguishes an autonomous weapon is essentially lines of computer code."[95] The same point applies equally to cyber weapons. Since computer code can be transmitted almost instantaneously across national borders, traditional approaches to multilateral export control agreements—which tend to focus primarily on hardware[96] not software—would have to be modified to address both cyber and autonomous weapons.

Even so, two factors suggest that the challenge of designing an effective export control regime for cyber and autonomous weapons is not insurmountable. First, the United States, Russia, and China all have a strong interest in restricting the spread of cyber and autonomous weapons to small states and nonstate actors to preserve their military advantage—not in relation to each other but in relation to less powerful actors. One should be hesitant to bet against the ability of powerful states to devise rules that advance their shared interests.

Second, technical knowledge is arguably the most important input in creating effective cyber weapons and/or autonomous weapons. The United

[94] *See* Nuclear Suppliers Group, *Guidelines for transfers of nuclear-related dual-use equipment, materials, software, and related technology*, INFCIRC/254, Part 2, https://www.nuclearsuppliersgroup.org/en/guidelines [hereinafter NSG dual-use guidelines]. During my government service, I had a major hand in drafting an early version of the NSG dual-use guidelines.

[95] Jenks, Chapter 7, at (p. 249)

[96] Existing export control regimes do regulate software exports. *See, e.g.*, MTCR guidelines, *supra* note 92, NSG dual-use guidelines, *supra* note 94. However, existing regimes focus primarily on hardware, treating regulation of software as an adjunct. A different approach will probably be necessary to develop effective controls for cyber and autonomous weapons.

States and other major powers have extensive experience regulating the diffusion of technical knowledge related to nuclear weapons, cryptography, and other sensitive technologies. Of course, no regime can completely halt the diffusion of knowledge. However, a set of controls designed to slow the diffusion of knowledge could help ensure that any weapons developed by small states or nonstate actors would be largely ineffective against the relatively sophisticated defenses that the United States and other major powers are capable of deploying to defend themselves against cyber and autonomous weapons.

In sum, there are grounds to believe that the threat posed by cyber and autonomous weapons can be mitigated to some extent by a type of great power condominium that divides the world between "haves" and "have nots." A multilateral export control regime along these lines could potentially make an important contribution to the project of preserving a rules-based order related to the *jus in bello* and *jus ad bellum*.

C. Climate Change

Climate change, to reiterate, is the single greatest current threat to the rules-based international order. As Daniel Bodansky says, it is "the mother of all global commons problems. Solving it will require collective action by the entire international community to reduce and eventually phase out net greenhouse gas emissions."[97] A report prepared by scholars at Princeton University shows that the United States must overcome extraordinarily complex technical and political challenges to reach "net zero" carbon emissions by 2050.[98] For the international community to achieve net zero emissions by 2050 on a worldwide basis is an even more daunting challenge. It is beyond the scope of this introduction to offer a detailed prescription for combatting climate change, but two general points bear emphasis.

[97] Daniel Bodansky, *Climate Change: Reversing the Past and Advancing the Future*, 115 AJIL Unbound 80, 80 (2021).

[98] *See* Eric Larson et al., Net-Zero America: Potential Pathways, Infrastructure, and Impacts (2020), https://netzeroamerica.princeton.edu/the-report. The phrase "net zero emissions" means that the amount of carbon introduced into the atmosphere by various carbon emitting technologies must be no more than the amount of carbon removed from the atmosphere by various techniques for carbon capture.

First, according to Susan Biniaz, a former State Department lawyer who worked on several international environmental agreements, "[n]on-State entities have become more significant as climate actors, not just in the United States . . . but all over the world."[99] Key nonstate entities include: international organizations, such as the International Maritime Organization (IMO);[100] subnational governments, such as the government of California;[101] private companies that are making substantial investments in climate-friendly technology;[102] and a wide range of nongovernmental organizations that continue to pressure governments to take more aggressive measures to combat climate change. Thus, climate change illustrates the broader point that a successful response to some of the most challenging threats to the rules-based international order (including global pandemics[103]) requires coordination among a broad range of state and nonstate actors.

Second, a successful approach to combating climate change clearly requires cooperation between the United States and China, the world's two largest carbon emitters (and the world's two largest economies). However, to remain faithful to its core values, the United States must confront China when China engages in behavior that is simply unacceptable, such as the forcible extinguishment of democracy in Hong Kong and the persecution of almost one million Uighurs and other Muslims detained in facilities that resemble concentration camps.[104] Thus, to quote Dan Bodansky again, the United States "must balance leadership with humility," and it must "balance the use of cooperative and confrontational tools."[105] It will be an ongoing challenge for US diplomats and political leaders to strike the right balance. Proponents of a rules-based international order must hope that they get it right. Our future depends on it.

[99] Susan Biniaz, *"Multilateralism," The Climate Challenge and the (Greater Metropolitan) Paris Agreement*, Wilson Center (Sept. 30, 2020).

[100] *See* Tae-Hwan Joung et al., *The IMO Initial Strategy for Reducing Greenhouse Gas (GHG) Emissions, and Its Follow-up Actions Towards 2050*, 4 J. Int'l Maritime Safety, Envt'l Aff. & Shipping 1 (2020).

[101] *See* David L. Sloss, *California's Climate Diplomacy and Dormant Preemption*, 56 Washburn L.J. 507 (2017).

[102] *See, e.g.*, Carly Anderson, *Carbon Capture: Part 1, An Introduction and a Look Ahead*, Mar. 11, 2020, https://medium.com/prime-movers-lab/carbon-capture-part-i-147c0d64ca29.

[103] *See* Lawrence O. Gostin et al., *How the Biden Administration Can Reinvigorate Global Health Security, Institutions, and Governance*, 115 AJIL Unbound 74 (2021).

[104] *See* Austin Ramzy & Chris Buckley, *Absolutely No Mercy: Leaked Files Expose How China Organized Mass Detentions of Muslims*, N.Y. Times, Nov. 16, 2019.

[105] Bodansky, *supra* note 97, at 80–81.

D. The Rise of China and a New Cold War

The United States must prepare itself for long-term geopolitical competition with China. Many people fear the onset of a new Cold War. However, in my view, there are good reasons to welcome a Cold War with China. During the last Cold War, the United States made significant domestic reforms related to racial equality—including both landmark US Supreme Court decisions and landmark civil rights legislation—driven in part by the geopolitical goal of persuading foreigners that the US system was better than the Soviet system.[106] Similarly, in the current geopolitical environment, the United States should pursue a foreign policy designed to persuade countries in the Global South that the US system is better than the Chinese system. To make that case persuasively, the United States will need to adopt progressive domestic reforms to promote racial equality and to promote economic security and economic opportunity for those at the bottom of the economic ladder. Although proposals for such domestic reforms will undoubtedly encounter political resistance, the rhetoric of "a new Cold War with China" could be a useful rallying cry (as it was in the 1950s and 1960s) to help overcome political polarization at home and build bipartisan support for progressive domestic reforms.

For the United States to win the battle for hearts and minds in the Global South, we will need to compete more effectively with China in the information warfare domain. As I have argued elsewhere, we have a potential strategic advantage in this area because much of the competition in information warfare is occurring on the "battlefield" of US social media platforms (Facebook, Twitter, YouTube, etc.), and the US government has the power to regulate those platforms.[107] The US is currently squandering that potential strategic advantage by failing to regulate social media, and by granting Chinese and Russian agents unrestricted access to US social media platforms. Moreover, Chinese and Russian cyber troops are exploiting US social media platforms to spread propaganda and disinformation to a global audience. Therefore, to win the information warfare competition, the United States should ban Chinese and Russian agents from US social media platforms.[108]

[106] *See* Mary L. Dudziak, Cold War Civil Rights: Race and the Image of American Democracy (2000).

[107] *See* David L. Sloss, Tyrants on Twitter: Protecting Democracies from Information Warfare (2022).

[108] *See id.*

Assuming that the United States is entering into a Cold War with China, we will not win that war militarily. Indeed, avoiding military confrontation with China should be a central goal of US foreign policy in the coming decades. However, as the saying goes, "if you want peace, prepare for war." Thus, the United States must maintain strong military forces to help ensure that the Cold War with China does not become a hot war. The potential for military conflict in and around Taiwan presents the greatest danger in this respect.[109] Deterring China from attempting a forcible takeover of Taiwan will be a major challenge for the next decade or more. Failure to maintain an effective deterrent would have serious negative ramifications for the future of a rules-based international order.

Managing economic relations with China will require a delicate balance of cooperation and competition. In the twentieth century Cold War, the United States and its NATO allies operated economies that were almost completely independent from the economies of the Soviet Union and other Warsaw Pact countries. The economic reality today is quite different because Chinese and Western economies are highly interdependent. China has demonstrated its willingness to exploit that interdependence by using economic coercion to achieve its political goals. For example, in fall 2020, China "ordered traders to stop purchasing at least seven categories of Australian commodities," to retaliate against Australia after "Prime Minister Scott Morrison's government . . . called for an independent probe into the origins of the coronavirus."[110]

During the euphoria of the post–Cold War era, "globalisation led people to believe that companies could build supply chains wherever there was a labour or other cost advantage. The result would be lower prices, higher profits and greater prosperity internationally."[111] More recently, though, "great-power competition between the US and China piled on, making it obviously not in either country's national interest to have deeply entangled systems of research and production for their defence items and high technology."[112] Thus, Australia, India, and Japan recently introduced a "Resilient Supply Chain Initiative" (RSCI) to allay concerns about "security risks associated with

[109] *See* Oriana Skylar Mastro, *The Taiwan Temptation: Why Beijing Might Resort to Force*, Foreign Aff., July–Aug. 2021.

[110] *China to Halt Key Australian Imports in Sweeping Retaliation*, Bloomberg News, Nov. 2, 2020.

[111] Michael Shoebridge, *Coronavirus and the Death of Xi's China Dream*, Australian Strategic Policy Institute, Feb. 28, 2020, https://www.aspistrategist.org.au/coronavirus-and-the-death-of-xis-china-dream/.

[112] *Id.*

production networks significantly embedded in, or connected to, China. By disengaging strategic supply chains—semiconductors, automobiles, pharmaceuticals, and telecommunications—from China, and repositioning them substantially in countries without security threats, proponents of the RSCI hope to decouple from China in a broader strategic sense."[113]

It is neither realistic nor desirable to try to end economic interdependence with China completely. However, in the context of the new Cold War, compelling geopolitical considerations support a partial decoupling to reduce supply chain vulnerability in areas of strategic significance. At the same, it remains true that liberal international trading rules promote economic prosperity for everyone. For reasons explained by Kathleen Claussen in her contribution to this volume, the WTO is unlikely to be a viable forum for negotiating new agreements to broaden or deepen trade liberalization.[114] Therefore, the United States should attempt to broaden and deepen free trade with other democracies by joining the Comprehensive and Progressive Agreement for Trans-Pacific Partnership (CPTPP) and by reviving negotiations for the TTIP. Liberal trading rules under these mega-regional trade agreements would help generate the wealth that the United States and its allies need to compete effectively with China, while simultaneously allowing states parties to reduce their vulnerability to Chinese economic coercion. Finally, the United States should adopt appropriate domestic policies to ensure that the economic benefits of free trade agreements accrue to a broad segment of the population, not just to the privileged elite.[115]

E. Democratic Decline and a New Marshall Plan

As explained previously, the ongoing trend of democratic decline is weakening the international human rights regime and nudging the broader system in the direction of a more sovereignty-based international order. The United States has a strong national interest in reversing democratic decline because a world with more democracies and fewer autocracies will generally be more hospitable to US interests and values.

[113] Amitendu Palit, *The Resilient Supply Chain Initiative: Reshaping Economics Through Geopolitics*, THE DIPLOMAT, Sept. 10, 2020.
[114] *See* Claussen, Chapter 9.
[115] *See* Judith Goldstein, *A New Era for Trade?*, 115 AJIL UNBOUND 52 (2021).

After World War II, the United States helped rebuild the domestic economies in Japan and Western Europe by devoting substantial resources to the Marshall Plan. The goals of the Marshall Plan were not merely economic; US assistance also helped establish stable democracies in both Japan and Germany, despite the prior history of autocratic governments in both countries. As of 2021, the United States does not have the wealth (or the generous spirit) to fund a new Marshall Plan for the entire world. However, we can combat the trend of democratic decline by: (1) partnering with other G7 countries, wealthy philanthropic foundations, and large private companies; and (2) targeting as recipients a select group of low- and middle-income countries that have reasonably good democratic credentials.

In selecting a group of beneficiary countries for the new Marshall Plan, donors should consider both economic need and democratic bona fides because a central goal of the new Marshall Plan should be to reverse the trend of democratic decline. I developed an illustrative list of potential beneficiaries by combining data from two sources. To measure economic need, I used the World Bank list of economies to classify national economies into four groups: "high income," "low income," "lower middle income," and "upper middle income."[116] To measure democratic credentials, I used the V-Dem "liberal democracy" index. According to the V-Dem codebook, "the liberal principle of democracy emphasizes the importance of protecting individual and minority rights against the tyranny of the state and the tyranny of the majority. The liberal model takes a 'negative' view of political power insofar as it judges the quality of democracy by the limits placed on government."[117] Countries with strong protection for individual rights score closer to one on the liberal democracy index, whereas countries with autocratic governments score closer to zero.

Since countries that are lower on the income scale tend to score lower on the liberal democracy index, I adopted a "sliding scale" approach to select an illustrative list of beneficiary countries for the new Marshall Plan. The resultant list includes: low-income countries with a score of .35 or better on the libdem index (The Gambia, Liberia, Malawi, and Sierra Leone); lower middle income countries with a score of .45 or better (Benin, Bhutan, Cape Verde,

[116] Umar Serajuddin & Nada Hamadeh, *New World Bank Country Classifications by Income Level: 2020–2021* (July 1, 2020), https://blogs.worldbank.org/opendata/new-world-bank-country-classifications-income-level-2020-2021.

[117] V-Dem Institute, V-Dem Codebook 43 (v10 Mar. 2020), https://www.v-dem.net/en/data/data-version-10/.

Ghana, Lesotho, Mongolia, Nepal, Sao Tome and Principe, Senegal, Solomon Islands, Sri Lanka, Timor-Leste, Tunisia, and Vanuatu); and upper middle income countries with a score of .55 or better (Argentina, Armenia, Botswana, Costa Rica, Jamaica, Namibia, Peru, South Africa, and Suriname). Notably, the list of beneficiaries is shaped less by the economic factors that tend to guide traditional development assistance and more by political calculations about which countries have the greatest potential to become stable democracies. If the G7 and other partners decide to pursue a new Marshall Plan, the donors will invariably develop their own criteria for selecting beneficiary countries. Regardless, my illustrative list is instructive because the group of beneficiary countries is geographically diverse (an important goal), and the total of twenty-seven beneficiary countries is neither too small nor too large for the program to be effective.

The United States cannot and should not try to implement the new Marshall Plan by itself; the United States will need to partner with other G7 countries,[118] large private corporations, and large charitable foundations to develop a coordinated strategy. One key element of that strategy should be an agreement among G7 countries to increase the number of employment-related visas for migrants from the agreed list of beneficiary countries.[119] In recent years, the total level of remittances sent by migrant workers in rich countries to family members in their home countries has been far greater than the total level of official development assistance (ODA) sent from wealthy countries to poorer countries. For example, "remittances reached a record high of $548 billion in 2019 . . . outstripping international aid three times over."[120] Moreover, "worker remittances have a democratizing effect" because they "are often the only source of foreign income that circumvents the government. Beyond the reach of the state, those funds facilitate protest and undermine authoritarian tactics, tipping the balance of power toward citizens who mobilize for democratic change."[121]

[118] For these purposes, the G7 could be expanded to include other members of the OECD Development Assistance Committee (DAC) that have a proven record of providing generous development assistance. However, the full DAC, which includes thirty countries, is probably too large a group to permit efficient policy coordination. *See* OECD, Development Assistance Committee, https://www.oecd.org/dac/development-assistance-committee/ (last visited July 6, 2021).

[119] *See* Tom Ginsburg, Democracies and International Law (2021) (developing this idea in more detail).

[120] Abel Escriba-Folch, Covadonga Meseguer, & Joseph Wright, *Global Migration Drives Global Democracy: How Workers Abroad Weaken Dictators Back Home*, Foreign Aff., June 2, 2021.

[121] *Id.*

Private investment in the information and communications technology (ICT) sector in beneficiary countries should also be a critical element of the new Marshall Plan. In the past decade, Chinese companies have been actively involved in exporting ICT equipment and technology to the Global South.[122] Chinese exports in the ICT sector have contributed to the rise of "digital authoritarianism"—a set of laws, policies, and technical practices that empower governments to exploit digital technologies for surveillance, censorship, and online content manipulation.[123] Empirical analysis shows "that those authoritarian regimes that rely more heavily on digital repression are among the most durable."[124] In short, the exploitation of information and communications technologies by states that practice digital authoritarianism strengthens autocratic control. To counter this trend, the United States should partner with Western ICT companies to promote investments in Marshall Plan beneficiary countries that support an open information environment that is largely free from government control.

The new Marshall Plan should also include traditional forms of development assistance that promote economic growth in developing countries. As James Gathii and Sergio Puig note in their contribution to this volume, persistent North-South inequality is a major source of dissatisfaction with the current rules-based international order.[125] The new Marshall Plan should aim to reduce the income gap between poor countries and wealthy countries by providing targeted development assistance to selected beneficiary countries. The twenty-seven countries in my illustrative list have a combined population of about 320 million people,[126] roughly the equivalent of the current US population. If the United States partners with other G7 countries and major philanthropic foundations, we can help lift millions of people out of poverty without breaking the bank at home. Moreover, if development assistance is combined with rule-of-law programs, we can help beneficiary countries build stable democracies, while simultaneously promoting economic security for millions of people.

122 *See generally* Danielle Cave et al., *Mapping China's Technology Giants*, Australian Strategic Policy Institute (Apr. 2019).
123 *See* Andrea Kendall-Taylor, Erica Frantz, & Joseph Wright, *The Digital Dictators: How Technology Strengthens Autocracy*, Foreign Aff., Mar.–Apr. 2020.
124 *Id.* at 112.
125 Gathii & Puig, Chapter 2.
126 *See* https://www.worldometers.info/world-population/population-by-country/.

Finally, it bears emphasis that the effort to resist democratic decline must begin at home.[127] The quality of democratic governance in the United States has deteriorated significantly in recent years. According to Freedom House, "the United States' aggregate *Freedom in the World* score has declined by 11 points," from 94 to 83, between 2010 and 2020.[128] Reversal of that trend is essential not only to support a global effort to resist democratic decline but also to prevail in the broader ideological competition with China. To get its domestic house in order, the United States will need to adopt progressive domestic reforms to promote racial equality and to promote both economic security and economic opportunity for those at the bottom of the economic ladder. We must also take steps to combat the electronic amplification of lies and misinformation, which is a major factor contributing to democratic decline in the United States.[129]

The program outlined here is undoubtedly ambitious; some will say that it is unrealistic. However, in the polarized political environment in the United States today, partisans on both sides agree that rising Chinese power poses a significant threat to American values and interests. Astute political leaders may be able to exploit widespread fear of China to mobilize support for a progressive political agenda designed to revitalize democracy at home and abroad.[130] If that effort fails, the international system will drift further in the direction of a sovereignty-based international order, because continued erosion of liberal democracy within domestic legal systems will inevitably undermine protection for human rights, which is a central element of the modern, rules-based international order.

[127] *See, e.g.*, Stacey Abrams, *American Leadership Begins at Home: The Global Imperative to Rebuild Governance and Restore Democracy*, Foreign Aff., May 1, 2020.

[128] Freedom House, Freedom in the World 2021: Democracy Under Siege 10 (2021).

[129] *See* David L. Sloss, *Stop Electronic Amplification of Lies*, 66 St. Louis Univ. L.J. 129 (2021).

[130] *See* Michael Beckley, *Enemies of My Enemy: How Fear of China Is Forging a New World Order*, Foreign Aff., Mar.–Apr. 2022.

PART ONE
SYSTEMIC ISSUES

1

The Rise and Decline of a Liberal International Order

*Richard H. Steinberg**

I. Introduction

The liberal international order established by Western powers in the postwar era is in decline due to an international dispersion of power and political blowback from distributive consequences of the freer movement of goods, services, and people that was a product of that order. The postwar structure has shifted from bipolarity, to a unipolar moment at the end of the Cold War, to multipolarity today. In today's multipolar world, a liberal international order is increasingly difficult to maintain. While it will not be possible to halt the decline of that order, the United States could adopt policies that would decelerate the decline and reconstitute a largely liberal plurilateral order over much of the world.

The postwar "liberal international order" has been primarily rules-based, led by the United States and Europe, organized around the principles of open markets, multilateralism, liberal democracy, and human rights, and defended by a web of military alliances and security guarantees—but it has not been static in form, breadth, or depth.

During Cold War bipolarity, the US-shaped order was Western embedded liberalism: limited to the West; liberalism embedded in the context of a social contract that demanded deviation from pure laissez-faire rules in order to protect national political-economic structures and those hurt most by liberalization; and tolerant of engagement with authoritarian states. NATO stood ready to defend the West in the heart of Europe, its forces facing off

* The author thanks Kathleen Claussen, James Gathi, Sergio Puig, Leila Sadat, Wayne Sandholtz, David Sloss, and Alan Weiner for helpful comments on earlier drafts, Robert O'Brien for research assistance, and Ben Nyblade for assistance with data visualization.

Richard H. Steinberg, *The Rise and Decline of a Liberal International Order* In: *Is the International Legal Order Unraveling?*. Edited by: David L. Sloss, Oxford University Press. © Oxford University Press 2022.
DOI: 10.1093/oso/9780197652800.003.0002

against the Warsaw Pact in the East, while the US military guaranteed the security of our most important economic partners in East Asia—Japan, South Korea, Taiwan, Australia, and New Zealand—through various agreements and guarantees.

After the Cold War, until roughly 2009 (the Great Recession), through cooperative transatlantic governance, the international order transformed to global hyperliberalism. It became global in that international economic regimes expanded to include most of the former Soviet and COMECON states, China, and just about everyone else. It became hyperliberal in that international rules more deeply adhered to laissez-faire capitalism and were less embedded in an egalitarian social contract; international relations were subject to deeper judicialization (e.g., more courts and tribunals); and the United States and many allies embraced regime change to spread democracy and human rights. US alliances in Asia held fast, while NATO enlarged eastward and its mission creeped from a nearly exclusive focus on security against the Soviet threat to protecting human rights in Bosnia and Kosovo, facilitating regime change, participating in the war on terror in Afghanistan, and combating human trafficking.

Since 2009, that liberal international order has been receding—and at an accelerating rate during the Trump years. In the economic realm, the World Trade Organization (WTO) is incapable of legislating new rules, old rules have been flouted, and its judicial system has been rendered dysfunctional—while bilateral and regional trade arrangements have expanded. Substantial protectionism has reemerged for the first time since the interwar period. The International Monetary Fund (IMF) has continued to diminish in importance as a global lender of last resort: IMF quotas are now a small fraction of global capital flows. Capital controls have reemerged. Lines of fracture have become apparent in the European Union, with Brexit emblematic. Politically, we are in a democratic recession[1]—or depression: nativism and elements of authoritarianism have emerged as forces in the United States, the United Kingdom, Hungary, Poland, Germany, and Brazil, among others. Russia went from a fledgling democracy to autocracy under Putin, with revisionist ambitions in southwest Asia, the Middle East, Eastern Europe, and the Baltics. China has become an autocratic surveillance state, more deeply committed to its version of a "socialist market economy," and it aggressively asserts illegal, revisionist territorial claims. US security alliances have held

[1] Larry Diamond, *Facing Up to the Democratic Recession*, 26 J. DEMOCRACY 141 (2015).

together, but are subtly changing, with some continuing signs of strain and undercapacity in NATO.

Consistent with hegemonic stability theory,[2] a dispersion of power in the international system has driven the recent decline of the liberal international order. In the 2000s, international structure shifted from a moment of perceived unipolarity toward multipolarity. Structural change across the postwar era has taken place slowly. Relative US power has diminished as China and other countries' military and economic power have grown, and as the United States has suffered waves of blowback against its international activities[3] and tolerated free-riding on its security guarantees in Asia, the Middle East, and Europe. Those guarantees were established seventy years ago, when the United States was far more powerful; today, the United States is overstretched. While no state could credibly challenge the US military in the immediate post–Cold War period, China's military has now achieved at least parity with the United States in the Western Pacific,[4] and Russia poses an ongoing military threat to US interests and allies all along the Russian border,[5] and in the Middle East.

Relative US economic power has also declined. To some extent, it was natural that US economic dominance declined as Europe rebuilt after the Second World War, and many poorer countries began to catch up with the advanced industrialized countries.[6] However, consistent with classical[7] and neoclassical[8] liberal trade theory (but not with the "new" economic theory[9]), postwar US trade policy did not demand absolute reciprocity (i.e., that other countries open their markets to the same extent as the United States

[2] Robert Gilpin, War and Change in World Politics (1981); Stephen D. Krasner, *State Power and the Structure of International Trade*, 28 World Pol. 317 (1976); Charles P. Kindleberger, The World in Depression 1929–1939 (1973).

[3] Chalmers Johnson, Blowback: The Costs and Consequences of American Empire (2004).

[4] Eric Heginbotham et al., RAND Corp., The U.S.-China Military Scorecard: Forces, Geography, and the Evolving Balance of Power, 1996–2017 (2015); Ryan Pickrell, *The US Has Been Getting 'Its Ass Handed to It' in War Games Simulating Fights Against Russia and China*, Bus. Insider (Mar. 8, 2019), https://www.businessinsider.com/the-us-apparently-gets-its-ass-handed-to-it-in-war-games-2019-3. *See also* Comm'n on Nat'l Def. Strategy, U.S. Inst. Peace, Providing for the Common Defense: The Assessment and Recommendations of the National Defense Strategy Commission (2018).

[5] David A. Shlapak & Michael W. Johnson, RAND Corp., Reinforcing Deterrence on NATO's Eastern Flank: Wargaming the Defense of the Baltics (2016).

[6] Convergence of Productivity: Cross-National Studies and Historical Evidence (William J. Baumol et al. eds., 1994).

[7] David Riccardo, On the Principles of Political Economy and Taxation (1817).

[8] Eli F. Heckscher & Bertil Ohlin, Heckscher-Ohlin Trade Theory (1991).

[9] Elhanan Helpman & Paul Krugman, Market Structure and Foreign Trade: Increasing Returns, Imperfect Competition, and the International Economy (1987).

opened its market), and access to large US and European markets accelerated the BRICs' growth rates, China's in particular. Meanwhile, China has pursued domestic economic subsidization on a scale unparalleled in the postwar period,[10] and a policy of export-led growth, maintaining a relatively closed market, performance requirements for investors, and for many years an undervalued Yuan, which have buttressed a constant trade surplus with the United States. Thus, since the late 1940s, the relative position of the US economy has fallen precipitously. The US share of GATT/WTO GDP has fallen from around 75 percent in 1948 to approximately 25 percent today.[11] The IMF quota share of the United States has fallen from 42 percent in 1947 to 17 percent today.[12]

These shifts have transformed governance of these important multilateral economic regimes from hegemonic control by the United States in the early postwar period, to hegemonic duopoly or triopoly (the United States, the European Union, and Japan) in the middle years,[13] to increasingly diffuse multipolarity today. Multipolar governance among countries with often divergent views and interests now makes it far more difficult for these multilateral regimes to function effectively.

Simultaneously, in recent decades, global hyperliberalism, which was a product of US and EU policies beginning after the collapse of the Soviet Union, sowed the seeds of its own destruction. *Economic* hyperliberalism (freer movement of goods, services, labor, and capital) contributed to economic growth globally, but also worsened inequality within countries. In the Global North, unskilled and semiskilled workers lost jobs; in the South, small-scale agriculture, telecommunications, banking, insurance, and other sectors were overwhelmed by US and European firms.[14] Free trade and laissez-faire mantras and interpretations narrowed the scope of exceptions to WTO trade liberalizing rules, diminishing the extent to which trade remedy laws (i.e., safeguards measures, countervailing duties, and antidumping duties) could be used to address social dislocations resulting from trade, and

[10] Mark Wu, *The "China, Inc." Challenge to Global Trade Governance*, 57 HARV. INT'L L.J. 261 (2016).

[11] GDP 1948 from *International Financial Statistics (IFS)*, IMF, https://data.imf.org/?sk=4c514d48-b6ba-49ed-8ab9-52b0c1a0179b (last updated Mar. 29, 2021); GDP 2018 from *World Development Indicators*, WORLD BANK, https://datacatalog.worldbank.org/dataset/world-development-indicators (last updated Mar. 19, 2021).

[12] *See infra* Figure 1.2.

[13] Richard H. Steinberg, *In the Shadow of Law or Power? Consensus-Based Bargaining and Outcomes in the GATT/WTO*, 56 INT'L ORG. 339 (2002).

[14] *Id.*

tightening the conditions under which WTO Members may use trade measures to protect the environment.[15] And instead of increased trade adjustment assistance and redistributive policies to offset the adverse distributive consequences of liberalization, US federal tax policy became more regressive over the past fifty years.[16]

Political hyperliberalism, in the form of exporting democracy through regime change, was disastrous: interventions in Afghanistan, Iraq, and Libya destabilized the Middle East. For the most part, the Arab Spring, which was at least tacitly supported by civil society in the West, failed miserably. Deeply discounting the lessons of political modernization theory,[17] Americans and Europeans widely supported pro-democracy protesters and regime change over strongmen almost everywhere, regardless of whether there were democratically favorable social, economic, and institutional conditions, which led not to democracy but to massive bloodshed and a doubling down on authoritarianism, autocracy, or anarchy. Millions of political and economic refugees have spilled over borders. In the United States and Europe, many of those who have suffered economically from hyperliberalism were further threatened by refugees; they now find hope in political and economic nationalism and nativism—and they vote that way.

With diminished US power to drive forward a liberal international order, and domestic political backlash against the global liberal order, the world has begun to shift—away from globalism, liberalism, and associated elements of a rules-based order.

II. Conceptualizing and Operationalizing a "Liberal International Order": Three Dimensions

The concept of a liberal international order has three dimensions, each of which is on a continuum.

[15] Richard H. Steinberg, *The Impending Dejudicialization of the WTO Dispute Settlement System?*, 112 ASIL Proc. 316 (2019).

[16] Thomas Piketty & Emmanuel Saez, *How Progressive Is the U.S. Federal Tax System? A Historical and International Perspective*, 21 J. Econ. Persp. 3 (2007).

[17] Democracy in Developing Countries: Latin America (Larry Diamond et al. eds., 1989); Samuel P. Huntington, Political Order in Changing Societies (1968); Seymour Martin Lipset, *Some Social Requisites of Democracy: Economic Development and Political Legitimacy*, 53 Am. Pol. Sci. Rev. 69 (1959).

First, how *liberal* are international relations? The ideal-type of classical liberalism, rooted in Enlightenment thought, favors liberty, consent of the governed, and equality before the law. Many philosophers, theorists, and economists have tied liberalism to laissez-faire capitalism. Politically, liberalism favors democracy, and civil and political rights. Liberal international economic policy favors the free movement of goods, services, labor, and capital.

Second, how *international* are these liberal policies? This is a spatial question: To what extent are these liberal policies established and maintained globally, plurilaterally, regionally, or by only a handful of states?

Third, to what extent are these policies maintained via an international *legal order*? Liberal policies may be adopted and maintained voluntarily by states, driven by Manchesterism or a similar ideology, or other domestic political forces that favor free trade. Liberal economic policies might be imposed and maintained through a direct exercise of coercive power and imperial governance, as within the British Empire. Or one can imagine establishing a liberal order, or any order, through a Pareto-improving contract between states. Whether established voluntarily, coercively, or transactionally, elements of a liberal order could be maintained, or at least administered, by way of international law, and administrative, judicial, or quasi-judicial processes.

III. Power Shifts and the Postwar Orders

The rise and decline of a postwar liberal international order is explained largely by the changing structure of power in international relations. "Power" is defined here as the ability to get states to do what they would not otherwise do. The two most important levers of power are economic and military. Dominant military power enables effective defense or conquest, but military power requires economic power, which is also necessary to hold foreign territory or govern it (directly or indirectly). Hard power, military or economic, is exercised primarily through coercion, coercive diplomacy,[18] deterrence,[19] or contracting. The resulting policies generate outcomes with a distribution of benefits across states that reflect the underlying power structure.[20] Some

[18] ALEXANDER L. GEORGE, FORCEFUL PERSUASION: COERCIVE DIPLOMACY AS AN ALTERNATIVE TO WAR (1992); KENNETH A. SCHULTZ, DEMOCRACY AND COERCIVE DIPLOMACY (2009).

[19] ALEXANDER L. GEORGE & RICHARD SMOKE, DETERRENCE IN AMERICAN FOREIGN POLICY: THEORY AND PRACTICE (1974).

[20] STEPHEN D. KRASNER, SOVEREIGNTY: ORGANIZED HYPOCRISY (1999).

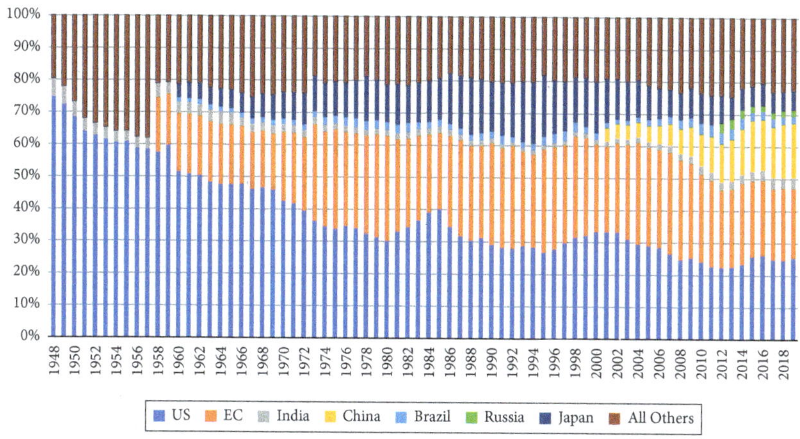

Figure 1.1 GATT/WTO Members' Shares of Aggregate GDP of GATT/WTO Members (1948–2019)

* GDP from 1948 to 1959: *International Financial Statistics*, IMF, https://data.imf.org/?sk=4c514d48-b6ba-49ed-8ab9-52b0c1a0179b (last accessed June 2021).

* GDP from 1960 to 2019: *World Development Indicators*, World Bank, https://datacatalog.worldbank.org/dataset/world-development-indicators (last accessed June 2021).

* Subtle changes in the form of available exchange-rate data pre-1960 versus post-1959 result in a discontinuity of GDP shares between 1959 and 1960. GDP or exchange rate data are unavailable for some small economies in certain years, but the aggregate missing data is estimated to be less than 1 percent of the combined GDP of GATT/WTO members and so does not meaningfully affect the trends represented in the chart.

think that "soft power," shaping the preferences of others through appeal and attraction, may also influence behavior.[21]

A. Change in Economic Power

Bargaining power in trade has typically depended on promises by a country with a large market to open it further—or a threat to close it. Hence, state power to affect rules in the GATT/WTO, the world's most important trade regime, may be approximated by relative market size. Figure 1.1 shows leading states' GDP as a proportion of GATT/WTO GDP from 1948 to 2019.

Over that time period, the US share of GATT/WTO GDP declined steadily from approximately 75 percent to around 25 percent. In the years immediately after the Second World War, the United States was the West's dominant

[21] Joseph Nye, Soft Power: The Means to Success in World Politics (2004).

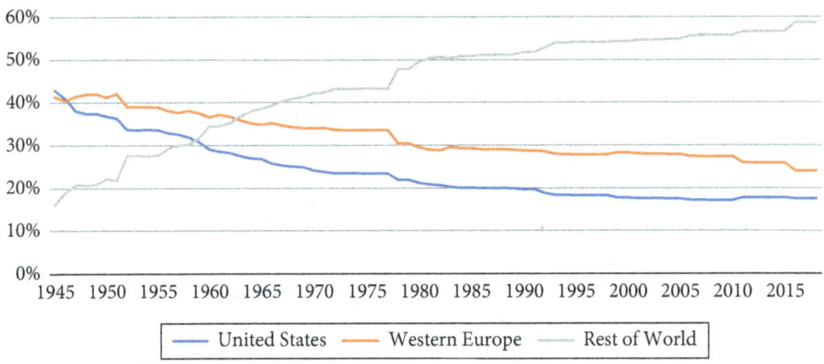

Figure 1.2 IMF Quota Distribution*

*International Financial Statistics, IMF, https://data.imf.org/?sk=4c514d48-b6ba-49ed-8ab9-52b0c1a0179b (last accessed Nov. 2019).

economic power, and it established most substantive GATT undertakings.[22] In the middle postwar years, roughly 1970–95, the United States shared GATT governance with the European Union;[23] the two territories combined accounted for around 60 percent of GATT GDP. Since 1995, however, the transatlantic share has fallen, while the shares of Brazil, Russia, India, and especially China (the BRICs) have risen, suggesting an increasingly multipolar distribution of power.

Figure 1.2 shows the US share of the IMF quota from inception through 2015. An individual member's quota, denominated in Special Drawing Rights, which is the IMF's unit of account, broadly reflects that member's relative position in the world economy. Here too it is clear that the United States was once the world's dominant financial power, but that position has been in decline for decades. While the US dollar retains its position as the world's reserve currency and the United States remains one of the world's biggest financial powers, it is not as powerful as it once was. Moreover, as shown by Figure 1.3, the IMF's financial market power is dwarfed by the size of global capital flows, and so it is far less capable than it once was of serving as the world's lender of last resort with capacity to avert sovereign debt crises or a systemic crisis.

[22] Steinberg, *supra* note 13.
[23] *Id.*

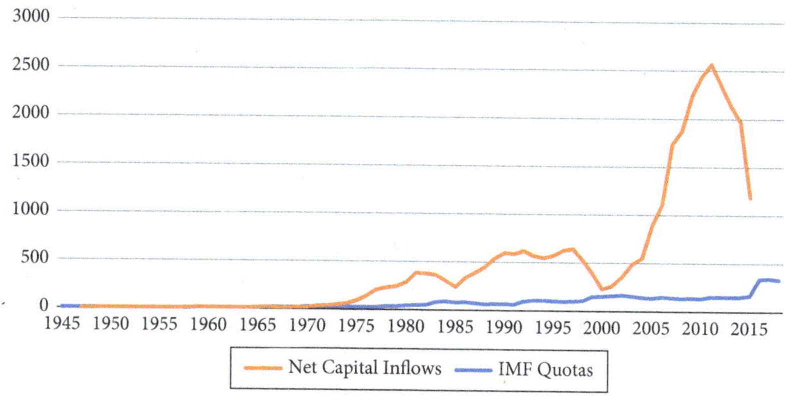

Figure 1.3 IMF Quotas vs. Net Capital Inflows (US$ in Billions—60 Countries)*

* IMF Quotas from *International Financial Statistics*, IMF, https://data.imf.org/?sk=4c514d48-b6ba-49ed-8ab9-52b0c1a0179b (last accessed Nov. 2019).

* Estimated net capital inflows from Carmen M. Reinhart et al., *Capital Flow Cycles: A Long, Global View* (Portfolio Construction Forum, First Conference Draft, Oct. 31, 2017), https://portfolioconstructionforum.edu.au/obj/articles_perspectives/Portfolio-Construction-Forum_CR_Capital-Flow-Cycles-A-Long-Global-View.pdf.

B. Change in Military Power

Relative military power may be assessed in a few ways. Quantitatively, military power may be roughly approximated by such factors as military spending; counting hardware, taking into account the quality and technological sophistication of that hardware; and number of personnel, taking into account training and quality. Military power may also be assessed by considering conflict scenarios. Retrospectively, which country or countries prevailed in conflicts in different theaters? Prospectively, through simulations or other analysis, which country would likely prevail in a posited contemporary or future conflict? A fine-grained metric could consider the extent of prevalence in a particular region or context. By some definitions, an imperial power is able to prevail and effectively hold and govern territory within a defined geographic region, often subsuming conquered territory into its own borders, whereas a hegemonic power prevails or can be expected to prevail in a particular geographic region, and sets the rules of the system within the territory it dominates, but is unable or unwilling to hold and directly govern conquered territory.[24]

[24] Michael W. Doyle, Empires (1986).

During the Cold War, the United States and the Soviet Union were the two great military powers, each with military capacity far greater than any other state, and roughly at parity with each other. At no time in the 1945–90 period did either of these two states risk conquest of its own territory. Each had a navy, air force, and nuclear arsenal far larger than any third country, and each enjoyed geographic spheres of influence or dominance, some of which demanded projecting power to far reaches of the globe. The nuclear arsenals and delivery systems of the United States and the Soviet Union enabled them to offer security guarantees to, and deter aggression against, third countries located anywhere on the planet. Of course, each faced asymmetric challenges and was unwilling to use its entire arsenal in particular conflicts—in Vietnam for the United States and in Afghanistan for the Soviet Union, for example. The Soviet Union was imperial in that Moscow held and governed territory directly throughout the USSR and in much of Eastern Europe. The United States maintained a substantial empire in the early postwar period, occupying and governing Japan, part of Germany, and a handful of other territories. Thereafter, the United States continued (and still continues) to govern or administer some islands and archipelagos in the Pacific and Caribbean, but governance of other territories beyond its borders has been at best indirect, by means of international law and economic and diplomatic pressure. Despite their great power rivalry, during the Cold War years, the United States and the Soviet Union were able to conclude several agreements with each other that made each better off: arms control agreements, in particular, as well as solutions to territorial disputes among proxies in the Middle East, Asia, and elsewhere.

In the immediate aftermath of the Cold War, the US military was uncontested as the most powerful in the world, attributable largely to its nuclear arsenal, broad web of foreign military bases, a large and seemingly invulnerable navy built around aircraft carrier task forces, its relative technological sophistication—and the sudden and unexpected collapse from within of the Soviet Union. From 1990 until roughly 2010, it seemed that the United States was invincible on the battlefield anywhere in the world, except in and along the borders of China and Russia: the first Gulf War was a rout, as were the initial US military conquests in Afghanistan and Iraq. While these were coalition wars, US technology, hardware, and strategy drove the outcomes.

Since the late 2000s, however, China and Russia have both increased their military strength, increasingly able to project force over longer distances, with Russia re-establishing itself as a regional hegemon and China bent on emerging as one, as well. Under Putin, Russia began enacting major military reforms in 2008, starting with flattening its command and control structure, initiating and regularizing inter-service exercises across military districts, integrating its combat branches, and enhancing its non-nuclear strategic deterrence. Russia has since added space and missile defense forces, and a substantial cruise missile capability. It now possesses formidable cyber, information, and electronic warfare capabilities. It is also upgrading its fighter jets, modernizing its strategic weapons arsenal, and deploying a hypersonic glide vehicle, which could threaten US missile defenses. While Russia's navy lacks the broad capabilities that would warrant its status as an "ocean-going" navy, limiting its capacity to project force across the high seas, its heavily mechanized ground forces include approximately 400,000 persons with 2,100 battle tanks, backed by a tactical nuclear weapons capability that is likely superior to that of the United States and its allies.[25] Meanwhile, since the end of the Cold War, NATO's ground forces have substantially declined in readiness, and NATO has shifted focus away from high-intensity conventional combat.[26]

With renewed will and enhanced capacity, by the early 2000s, Russia had reasserted itself over many of its former Soviet "republics" in southwest Asia. In the 2010s, as the US military began withdrawing from the Middle East, Russia filled the vacuum, re-emerging as a rival to the United States there. It is now the dominant external actor in Iran, Syria, and Lebanon. And its 2022 war of aggression against Ukraine increased the threat to NATO's eastern flank.

Similarly, China, once a minor power, except along its immediate border, has radically improved its military capacity, establishing itself as a regional power. Moreover, China is on a trajectory to be able to project force effectively beyond the region. The 1996 Taiwan Strait Crisis, which triggered the biggest US display of military force in Asia since the Vietnam War, and demonstrated China's inability to stop US forces from coming to Taiwan's assistance, catalyzed modernization of the People's Liberation Army (PLA), with its military budget growing at an average of 11 percent per year between 1996 and 2015, focused on improving and expanding its air, naval, and ballistic

[25] Off. Sec'y Def., Nuclear Posture Review 9 (2018).

[26] Scott Boston et al., RAND Corp., Assessing the Conventional Force Imbalance in Europe: Implications for Countering Russian Local Superiority (2018).

missile capabilities, and building counter-space and cyber capacity.[27] China's 2015 defense white paper marked a change in the PLA's targeted geographic scope, announcing that "the armed forces will actively participate in both regional and international security cooperation and effectively secure China's overseas interests,"[28] a strategic shift echoed in subsequent official Chinese documents. The Chinese military has now asserted its interests, at least on paper, not only in Tibet and Turkestan but also the East China Sea and South China Sea, as well as in the "first island chain" of Japan, Taiwan, the Philippines, and Indonesia.[29] Moreover, official Chinese documents establish a goal of strike capability into the "second island chain," demarcated by the Aleutian Islands, Mariana Islands, Guam, Palau, and Northern Papua New Guinea.[30]

With China's persistent large investments in the PLA since the late 1990s, military analyses uniformly conclude that US military power is no longer unchallenged and unrivaled in the Western Pacific.[31] In case of conflict with the United States, China's network of anti-access area denial will push any US fleet, including aircraft carrier task forces, to operate further from the immediate area of conflict,[32] and China's military now has the capability to disrupt the operation of US airbases throughout much of the Western Pacific, including Japan and Guam.[33] China's military capabilities have shifted from a being at a "major disadvantage" in cases of conflict with the United States over Taiwan or the Spratly Islands, to at least parity.[34]

[27] Heginbotham, *supra* note 4.

[28] State Council Info. Off., People's Republic China, China's Military Strategy (2015).

[29] Anthony Cordesman, *China's New 2019 Defense White Paper: An Open Strategic Challenge to the United States, but One Which Does Not Have to Lead to Conflict* 1 (Ctr. For Strategic & Int'l Stud., Working Draft, 2019), https://csis-prod.s3.amazonaws.com/s3fs-public/publication/190724_China_2019_Defense.pdf.

[30] *Hearing on U.S. Indo-Pacific Command Posture Before the S. Armed Servs. Comm.*, 116th Cong. 5 (2019) (statement of Philip S. Davidson, Commander, U.S. Indo-Pacific Command).

[31] *Id. See also* RAND Corp. Project Air Force, Forecasting China's Military Spending Through 2025 (2005).

[32] Robert Clifford, *The U.S. Navy and China's Anti-Access Bubble*, Real Clear Def. (Dec. 19, 2019), https://www.realcleardefense.com/articles/2019/12/19/the_us_navy_and_chinas_anti-access_bubble_114938.html. *See China's Anti-Access Area Denial*, Missile Def. Advoc. Alliance (Aug. 24, 2018), https://missiledefenseadvocacy.org/missile-threat-and-proliferation/todays-missile-threat/china/china-anti-access-area-denial/.

[33] Heginbotham, *supra* note 4, at 337.

[34] *Id.* at 282.

C. Change in Soft Power

Many scholars and political leaders have come to embrace "soft power" as a means of getting others to do what they would not otherwise do. The extent to which and contexts in which culture, political values, and diplomacy might affect international outcomes are contested. Culture, diplomacy, and political values could be independent sources of power to the extent that the *vision* they constitute legitimates foreign policy; appeals to other societies; is applied consistently and without contradiction; delivers what is promised; and competing visions fail. Conversely, culture, political values, or diplomacy could undermine the effectiveness of economic or military power when they fail to deliver what is promised by the vision; they are applied inconsistently, with internal or external contradictions; when soft power policies require spending too much hard power currency; or a competing power with different political-economic values and structure is more successful. Perhaps only very powerful states—the greatest powers—can afford to spend blood and treasure trying to advance a particular social structure in the world.

American culture has been a constant source of US soft power throughout the postwar period, but the influence of American political values has varied. For most of the postwar era, US economic and military power has been complemented by a claim of moral force through liberalism. The United States at least purported to lead by example and by maintaining a foreign policy that has championed democracy, civil and political rights, economic development through capitalism, freer trade and capital movements, and rule of law. The credibility of that moral claim, however, has varied.

To a large extent, the global structure of soft power mirrors the structure of hard power. In a bipolar system, two great powers are likely to offer competing visions of social structure. In a unipolar system, there can be only one vision. In a multipolar system, there will likely be two or more visions, though very few countries can afford to use their economic or military power to coerce or pay other states to follow their vision of the best social structure.

During the Cold War, the United States embraced and supported liberalism, including civil and political rights where it could, while the Soviet Union offered its communist vision and claimed to favor economic, social, and cultural rights. The United States claimed to be supporting democracy in some conflicts, such as the Vietnam War and Central American civil conflicts, while the Soviets spoke of liberation from capitalism in its engagements. Neither great power, however, was free to champion its vision credibly in all conflicts: for example, Thiệu's Vietnam was hardly a democracy, and communism was not a driving force behind Soviet intervention in Afghanistan. Nor could the United States afford to offer military and diplomatic support to democracies alone—so it supported autocrats in places like Argentina, Chile, Taiwan, and South Korea. Engaged in great power competition with the USSR, the United States needed to focus on the balance of power and protecting allies, whether or not they were democracies, while voicing support for democracy and making the world safe for democracy.[35]

In the period following the collapse of the Soviet Union, US soft power in the form of credible advocacy of liberalism reached its apex. Without a hard power competitor, and with liberalism's apparent triumph over communism, then depicted as a failed ideology, the world could look to the United States as *the* model for appropriate and effective policy. The "Washington Consensus," a normative claim and policy prescription that the various dimensions of a liberal order are good and all go together, and support for regime change to democratize the world, drove US foreign policy. Democratization and human rights were a rallying cry for interventions in the Middle East, North Africa, and the Balkans. A surge forward in freer trade and the elimination of capital controls were touted as the best way forward to replace socialism, import substitution industrialization policies, and other non-market-oriented development paths. Rule of law, even at the international level, was favored by the United States in many areas. With the apparent triumph of the US order and with no great power or alternative ideology to challenge it, it appeared to some as the end of history.[36]

The end of history was short-lived. The US response to 9/11 included policies such as waterboarding and other forms of torture that undercut US moral authority. The abject failure of US efforts at regime change demonstrated that not all countries could democratize and that military efforts to free them from autocracy could lead to anarchy instead. The 2008–09 Great Recession and its aftermath dealt a fatal blow to important elements of the Washington Consensus, revealing that the US brand of hyperliberalism had deep vulnerabilities. In contrast, the Chinese "socialist market economy with Chinese

[35] Stephen D. Krasner, Defending the National Interest (1978).
[36] Francis Fukuyama, The End of History and the Last Man (1992).

characteristics," and even the German social democratic system with its macro-economic stabilizers, experienced only an economic slowdown, not a recession. China enjoyed double-digit annual growth rates through most of the 2000s; after the Great Recession the Chinese system seemed to gain credibility as a model for development and governance. Chinese foreign policy increasingly embraced that role, engaging in diplomatic, cultural, and economic outreach throughout Asia and Africa, in particular, complementing its Belt and Road Initiative, billed as an effort to stimulate development. By 2016, many viewed US foreign policy as contradicted by its failures and inconsistent application across countries and peoples. Meanwhile, China's vision, and a European vision that focused on social democracy with greater equality and exceptions to laissez-faire capitalism to foster social welfare, were garnering attraction. US soft power was diminishing.

Then arrived Donald Trump. Trump's "America First" approach deprived US foreign policy of moral force: a nation that staked its foreign policy solely on pursuit of its own interests cared not about the interests of any other country. And during those same years, Trump, supported by roughly half the US electorate, behaved autocratically, inviting foreign adversaries to interfere in US elections, demanding imprisonment of his political competitors, deeming the free press the enemy of the people, and—at the end of his term—falsely claiming that American elections are rigged and that votes in states he lost should be disregarded. Internationally, Donald Trump embraced dictators and autocrats in China, Brazil, Saudi Arabia, and North Korea as friends—the Egyptian president was his "favorite dictator"—while launching personal attacks on many democratic leaders, including Trudeau, Macron, and Merkel. It is hard to see how a country led by such a president could stand for liberal political values that would inspire the world. As US soft power diminished under Trump, France and Germany stepped up their roles as beacons of liberal democracy.

Although the Biden administration promises a return to the status quo ante in American foreign policy and political culture, the extent to which a declining power can afford the luxury of using military and economic resources to advance or sustain liberalism in other countries is uncertain,[37] as is the extent to which the deeply divided American electorate can return to the shared norms and practices of a functional, stable democracy.

[37] Stephen D. Krasner, How to Make Love to a Despot: An Alternative Foreign Policy for the Twenty-First Century (2020).

IV. Periodization

Periodization of complex social change must be understood as an exercise in approximation, and can be wrongly interpreted as suggesting sudden historical breaks (rather than social evolution) or implying that the multiple dimensions being analyzed change at the same rate. Nonetheless, properly employed and understood, periodization is a heuristically powerful tool that offers clarity and parsimony.

The analysis in the previous section of economic and military factors, as well as soft power considerations, suggests three periods of the postwar international power structure: bipolarity (1945–90); a unipolar moment (1991–2008); and multipolarity (2009–present). Figure 1.4 summarizes the periodization.

A. 1945–90: Bipolarity and the Rise of the Western Order

From roughly 1945 to 1990, the interstate order was not purely liberal, not truly international, and not deeply legalized.

Most important regimes were structured on a *bipolar* basis, not globally: the West defended itself through NATO and organized its economic relations through the GATT, IMF, and World Bank, while the East defended itself through the Warsaw Pact and organized its economic relations through COMECON. Western regimes were driven by the United States. Most of the text of the GATT 1947 was drafted in Washington, with changes to accommodate the request of Great Britain (the world's second largest economy at the time) to grant preferences for its former colonies, and was effectively presented as a *fait accompli* to other countries if they wanted access to the world's largest market.[38] Similarly, the IMF and International Bank for Reconstruction and Development (IBRD) Articles of Agreement were each derived from plans initially drafted by a US Treasury official, with changes suggested by British officials, and were concluded in Bretton Woods, New Hampshire.[39] And the North Atlantic Treaty that established NATO was also drafted by US diplomats and finalized in Washington, D.C., with relatively

[38] Steinberg, *supra* note 13.
[39] The Bretton Woods Transcripts (Kurt Schuler & Andrew Rosenberg eds., 2013).

	LIBERAL	INTERNATIONAL	ORDER
~1945–1990 **BIPOLAR**	**Economic:** Embedded Liberalism	Western	International Organizations
	Political: Democracy & Authoritarianism		Legalization Begins
~1991–2008 **UNIPOLAR**	**Economic:** Hyperliberalism	Global	International Organizations
	Political: The Third Wave		Legalization Broadens & Judicialization Broadens and Deepens
~2009–Present **MULTIPOLAR**	**Economic:** Liberalism Curtailed	Fractured & Overlapping	International Organizations
	Political: Democratic Recession		Delegalization/Dejudicialization

Figure 1.4 Liberal International Order: Three Periods

few changes[40]—and, of course, NATO routinely designates an American to be Supreme Allied Commander.[41]

Moreover, the West was not purely liberal economically: its economic regimes were characterized by embedded liberalism[42]—a version of liberalism tempered by social safety nets and with exceptions such as capital controls; broad trade remedy laws; express protection of agriculture and textiles; and regulations to protect the environment, health, intellectual property, and public morals. Nor was the West purely liberal politically: while the West championed democracy and civil and political rights, it tolerated or backed authoritarian allies in Latin America, Asia, and Africa.

The Western order was maintained partly through nascent legalization: the codification of customary law, and a plethora of treaties

[40] Richard D. McKinzie, *Oral History Interview with Theodore Achilles*, Harry S. Truman Library, https://www.trumanlibrary.gov/library/oral-histories/achilles (last visited Apr. 4, 2021).

[41] North Atlantic Treaty, Apr. 4, 1949, 63 Stat. 2241, 34 U.N.T.S. 243; *1949–1952: Creating A Command Structure for NATO*, Supreme Headquarters Allied Powers Eur., https://shape.nato.int/page14612223.aspx (last visited Apr. 4, 2021).

[42] John Gerard Ruggie, *International Regimes, Transactions, and Change: Embedded Liberalism in the Postwar Economic Order*, 36 Int'l Org. 379 (1982).

establishing the UN, GATT, IMF, World Bank, and other organizations, each of which developed operational procedures and norms. But rules and procedures for adjudication and legislation, which H.L.A. Hart refers to as "secondary" rules,[43] were largely absent from those organizations. The international and Western legal systems were "primitive" in both Hart's and Brierly's schemas.[44]

B. 1991–2008: The Unipolar Moment and the End of History

The end of the Cold War ushered in a new era, in which the United States acted as a global hegemon and interstate relations came closest to approaching a liberal international order.

With the dissolution of bipolarity, Western regimes expanded spatially. In economic affairs, the GATT internationalized, expanding from a club of 100 members in 1990, to 160 GATT/WTO members by 2008, adding the world's two largest non-Western powers, China and Russia.

Liberalism deepened, broadened, and morphed into hyperliberalism, partly unembedding from the postwar social contract. During this period: the IMF conditioned bailouts on ending capital controls;[45] the United States concluded fifteen free trade agreements and more than three dozen bilateral investment treaties; the European Union enlarged from 15 to 27 Member States, deepened, and concluded free trade agreements (or variants) with nearly 100 countries; the GATS liberalized trade in services; the WTO Agreement on Agriculture reduced subsidies and other protection; the Technical Barriers to Trade and Sanitary and Phytosanitary agreements constrained regulation; and WTO Appellate Body decisions substantially reduced the effective scope of trade remedy laws.

At the same time, immigration (and internal migration) increased sharply in Europe, as did legal immigration into the United States. Annual legal immigration into the United States averaged 1.1 million in the 1990s and rose to an annual average of 1.4 million in the 2000s. In the 2000–10 decade, the United States experienced the largest number of immigrants in its history,

[43] H.L.A. Hart, The Concept of Law (1961).

[44] J.L. Brierly, The Law of Nations: An Introduction to the International Law of Peace (1928).

[45] Stanley Fischer, *The IMF and the Asian Crisis—Address by Stanley Fischer*, IMF (Mar. 20, 1998), https://www.imf.org/en/News/Articles/2015/09/28/04/53/sp032098.

triple the number of the 1980s and quadruple that of the 1970s. By 2010, immigrants who had arrived legally made up 12.9 percent of the US population, up from 4.7 percent in 1970.[46]

This freer movement of goods, services, and people put downward pressure on wages and employment of unskilled and semi-skilled workers in the United States, wealthier European states, and many other advanced industrialized countries. In the United States, these distributive consequences were not accompanied by substantial trade adjustment assistance, and the structure of the federal income taxation system became more regressive, exacerbating wealth inequality.

The Washington Consensus dominated policy globally: capitalism, democracy, development, and rule of law—"all good things go together." Central planning in the former COMECON countries disappeared, and in China the proportion of GDP produced by state owned enterprises fell from 65 percent to 35 percent. Meanwhile, the Third Wave of democratization,[47] which enveloped Latin America in the 1980s, now spread through most of Central and Eastern Europe—even Russia, so it seemed. International legalization deepened.[48] Not only did the United Nations and Western international organizations persist, but international criminal law legalized; human rights law became more expansive in Europe and Latin America; EU legal competence expanded substantially; and some areas of law judicialized through establishment of new tribunals such as the International Criminal Tribunal for the former Yugoslavia (ICTY), International Criminal Tribunal for Rwanda (ICTR), International Criminal Court (ICC), and the WTO Appellate Body.[49]

Finally, US military cooperation with other countries also expanded through a broad range of international agreements to strengthen the US-centered liberal international order—and in some cases to expand it geographically. In Europe, NATO enlarged, effectively adding East Germany through reunification, then adding Poland, Hungary, and the Czech Republic in 1999, seven more Central and Eastern European countries in 2004, and

[46] *Number of Immigrants and Their Share of the Total U.S. Population, 1850–2019*, Migration Pol'y Inst., https://www.migrationpolicy.org/programs/data-hub/charts/immigrant-population-over-time (last visited Dec. 7, 2020).

[47] Samuel P. Huntington, The Third Wave: Democratization in the Late Twentieth Century (1991).

[48] Kenneth W. Abbott et al., *The Concept of Legalization*, 54 Int'l Org. 401 (2000).

[49] Karen J. Alter et al., *Theorizing the Judicialization of International Relations*, 63 Int'l Stud. Q. 449 (2019).

Albania and Croatia in early 2009. In the Western Pacific, the United States demonstrated its commitment to defend Taiwan by sending two aircraft carrier task forces to international waters off Taiwan during the 1996 Taiwan Strait Crisis, and then concluded agreements to increase arms sales to the island. US military cooperation with Japan also expanded: in the early 2000s, Japan began moving away from its purely defensive postwar policy, agreeing to provide logistical support to US military operations in Afghanistan, and aiding reconstruction efforts in Iraq. In 2001, the United States greatly expanded the scale of its military exercises with South Korea, reaching agreement to inaugurate the annual Foal Eagle exercises. In the Middle East, the United States established a coalition of 60 countries to participate in Operation Enduring Freedom in Afghanistan after the Al Qaeda attack of September 11, 2001; and a coalition of 40 countries in 2003 to participate in Multi-National Force Iraq.

C. 2009–Present: Multipolarity and the Decline of the Western International Liberal Order

Domestic and international blowback from the hyperliberalism that preceded the Great Recession and a dispersion of global power that makes governance of multilateral regimes increasingly difficult have combined to weaken the liberal international order and political support for it. The 2008–09 global financial crisis, attributed by many to the underregulation of banking and China's deft and important role in addressing the crisis contributed to diminished confidence in the American Way.

Spatially, important multilateral regimes have fractured or stagnated. Multilateral trade liberalization stopped—and then reversed during the Trump years—and the focus of regime development has become regional or subregional. Lines of fracture appear in the European Union, which is working through Brexit and other powerful centripetal forces. The WTO has been deadlocked between North and South, and China versus the West, on the negotiation of any important new rules. Meanwhile, bilateral or plurilateral trade agreements and economic regimes have become focal points for further liberalization, many of them on a regional basis with a powerful state at the center. These include: China's Belt and Road Initiative and its Regional Comprehensive Economic Partnership; the US hub-and-spokes structure of free trade agreements with almost twenty countries; Russia's

Commonwealth of Independent States and free trade zone; MERCOSUR and other South-South arrangements.

Hyperliberalism is retreating. In the United States and Europe, those hurt economically by the hyperliberalism of the 1990s and 2000s have rebelled. In the last several years many have supported right wing, anti-globalization, populist politicians, many of whom challenge the foundations of liberal democracy and a liberal global economy. Democracy is in a recession or worse.[50] Since 2009, civil and political rights have been on the decline across the globe, a shift analyzed in depth by Wayne Sandholtz in this volume.[51] Elements of authoritarianism emerged in Brazil, Hungary, Poland, India, the United States, and elsewhere. Putin hardened his control in Russia. China, which some thought would be in the midst of a democratic transition by now, has moved in the opposite direction, becoming a totalitarian surveillance state.

Economic liberalism is also in decline. In trade, after seventy years of continuous annual tariff reductions, the trans-Atlantic and trans-Pacific trade wars that began in 2017 increased US tariffs from 2.6 percent to more than 16 percent on about 13 percent of imports, covering about 10,000 products, including steel, aluminum, and technology.[52] US trade partners retaliated by raising their tariffs from around 7 percent to more than 20 percent on just over 8 percent of US exports.[53] The United States withdrew from the Trans-Pacific Partnership and effectively abandoned a comprehensive Transatlantic Trade and Investment Partnership (TTIP), in favor of a shift from the North American Free Trade Agreement (NAFTA) to the United States–Mexico–Canada Agreement (USMCA) (that is likely to yield only slight welfare improvements for the United States, at best), and—as of 2021—small, partial deals with India, Japan, and Kenya. Privatization in China has stalled. Government subsidies are provided to more than 20 percent of its economy, including steel, aluminum, energy, chemicals, solar panels, batteries and electric vehicles, and other sectors, leading to overcapacity and subsidized exports in many of those industries, putting additional pressure on unskilled

[50] Diamond, *supra* note 1.

[51] Wayne Sandholtz, *Authoritarianism, International Human Rights, and Legal Change* (Chapter 12 in this volume). *See also* the last decade of Freedom House annual reports, *Publication Archives*, FREEDOM HOUSE, https://freedomhouse.org/reports/publication-archives (last visited Apr. 5, 2021) (showing that the number of free countries has dropped from 90 in 2013 to 82 in 2021); FREEDOM HOUSE, FREEDOM IN THE WORLD 2020: A LEADERLESS STRUGGLE FOR DEMOCRACY (2020).

[52] Pablo D. Fajgelbaum et al., *The Return to Protectionism*, 135 Q.J. ECON. 1 (2020).

[53] *Id.*

and semi-skilled US workers. Many countries have reinstated capital controls.

Meanwhile, there are few examples since 2009 of continuing international legalization, and there are significant signs of decline. The WTO dispute settlement system has dejudicialized and is barely functional.[54] The ICC has lost two members, the Philippines and Burundi, with other countries threatening withdrawal, and a majority of African Union states[55] and the United States[56] have engaged intermittently in diplomatic war on it. China is ignoring the UN Convention on the Law of the Sea (UNCLOS) tribunal decision[57] on the South China Sea.

Finally, security alliances are shifting in response to the rise of China and the resurgence of Russia, both of which have expanded cooperation with foreign governments. Since 2009, China has acquired foreign military installations in Cambodia, Sri Lanka, Pakistan, Burma, the Maldives, and Djibouti. Beginning in 2015, Russia deployed forces into Syria and has since concluded several military cooperation agreements with the Assad government and with Iran, as well as understandings with Hezbollah in Lebanon. Notably, just prior to Russia's invasion of Ukraine, China and Russia declared a "no limits" partnership. Some US alliance relationships have frayed, while US cooperation with some other countries—most notably the other Quad countries of Japan, India, and Australia—has increased to counter the new security threats from Russia and China. Turkey's commitment to NATO seems diminished, with its purchase of S-400 anti-aircraft missile systems from Russia, renewed disputes with Greece in the Aegean, and repeated threats to expel US forces from Incirlik Air Base. President Trump repeatedly equivocated on the US commitment to NATO and in June 2020 ordered the withdrawal of 10,000 US troops from Germany. While President Biden has recommitted the United States to NATO, some key European leaders have voiced deep concern about whether the United States will be consistently reliable in the defense space given US internal divisions. Accordingly, some European leaders have announced policies that would reduce that reliance. On the other hand, since 2015, in response to a perceived Russian threat in the Baltics, Estonia, Lithuania, and Latvia have all signed bilateral defense cooperation agreements with the United States, and Poland has

[54] Steinberg, *supra* note 15.
[55] African Union, Assembly Dec. 621, Assembly/AU/Dec.621(XXVIII) (Jan. 31, 2017).
[56] Exec. Order No. 13,928, 85 Fed. Reg. 36139 (June 11, 2020).
[57] The South China Sea Arbitration (Phil. v. China), 33 R.I.A.A. 153 (Perm. Ct. Arb. 2016).

been encouraging increased US troop presence in that country. In reaction to Russia's attack on Ukraine, NATO allies expanded the scale and scope of weapons deliveries to Ukraine, Finland and Sweden asked to join the alliance, and several NATO countries promised to increase defense spending.

In Asia, there has been a similar mix of fluctuating or inconsistent US cooperation with allies, though there are now clear, fledgling efforts to build relationships to deter China. In 2017, the United States and South Korea scaled back their annual Foal Eagle exercises, which were then discontinued indefinitely in 2019. In the 2017–22 period, Philippines President Rodrigo Duterte repeatedly declared his willingness to downgrade military ties with the United States in exchange for increased Chinese investment. At the same time, partly in reaction to China's military build-up and illegal maritime claims, US military and diplomatic cooperation has improved, to varying degrees, with Australia, India, Indonesia, Japan, Singapore, Taiwan, Thailand, and Vietnam.

While China is clearly a rising, revisionist power, leading some to suggest a new era of bipolarity featuring the United States and China, for the moment power seems more dispersed than would be suggested by bipolarity. China wields growing economic power, currently second only to the United States, and its long-term geopolitical ambitions are global, but its current capacity to project military power is confined to East Asia and the Western Pacific. Russia flexes its muscles along its borders and into the Middle East, but it too is unable to project power much further than those surrounding territories. Japan and the European Union's larger constituent states both have substantial economic power and strong defense capabilities, but are unable to project force effectively beyond their borders. For the Europeans, China is far away, so engaging deeply in Sino-American competition seems unlikely. We are in a multipolar world.

V. Conclusion

The hyperliberal, global, judicialized legal order will not be fully reconstituted, even in the post-Trump era. With increasingly dispersed global economic and military power, no one state has the power to supply a set of regimes to constitute a particular rules-based political-economic order on a global scale. While a liberal, democratic revival, along the lines suggested by Tom Ginsburg in this volume is possible,[58] it will not be on a global scale.

[58] Tom Ginsburg, *The Future of Liberal Democracy in the International Legal Order* (Chapter 3 in this volume).

New economic regimes, which have been taking shape for the last two decades, have been bilateral, regional, and overlapping, with spheres of influence mirroring the multipolar structure. While no prominent US politician currently supports mega-deals or substantially deeper liberalization, political support for mega-deals or further liberalization *among like-minded countries* can be imagined, if complemented by a heavy investment in trade adjustment assistance, broader trade remedy laws, redistributive policies, or other means of protecting socioeconomic structure. China's socialist market economy, with its massive subsidization, state enterprises, and other illiberal elements, would likely be excluded from any mega-deal that includes the United States.

At the global level, the multilateral economic order will become shallower and narrower. The WTO will continue to erode due to its inability to create new rules to address new problems, and the collapse of its dispute settlement system, which, if revived, would be less judicialized than the 1995–2019 system. IMF reserves will become even smaller relative to capital flows, and while IMF action may be supplemented by central bank coordination, that coordination will be increasingly difficult as the number of countries required to effectuate successful bailouts increases and their national interests diverge. While regional regimes might be rules-based, global delegalization seems more likely than deepening global legalization.

There are, however, many shared interests among competing great powers that could form the bases of new arrangements among them. Even as international relations become increasingly regional, less classically liberal, and less legalized globally, the fundamentals of public international law will remain intact. Most obviously, treaty-making and the principle of *pacta sunt servanda* will survive, as it remains in everyone's interest to maintain the global rules that allow Pareto-improving contracts between states. While the contemporary international power structure is too diffuse for any state to supply a truly liberal, global, rules-based order, there will remain, as always, a demand for agreements that make all states better off. A new generation of arms control agreements among the great powers is possible, as is an evolving set of global commitments to address climate change.

Some go much further and imagine a *modus vivendi* between the United States and China,[59] or more broadly still, a concert of powerful states—including China, the European Union, India, Japan, Russia, and the United

[59] *Id.*

States—that would manage conflict and facilitate limited cooperation.[60] But neither a *modus vivendi* nor an inclusive concert of great powers seems likely as long as China or Russia continues to display, use, or threaten to use force to assert revisionist territorial claims and engages in other fundamental challenges to the contemporary rules-based international order.

[60] Richard N. Haas & Charles A. Kupchan, *The New Concert of Powers*, FOREIGN AFF., Mar. 23, 2021.

2

The West and the Unraveling of the Economic World Order

Thoughts from a Global South Perspective

James T. Gathii and Sergio Puig

I. Introduction

Between 1950 and 1970, newly decolonized states condemned the then-emerging world economic order as inequitable and illegitimate because it lacked input legitimacy and reproduced entrenched colonial era patterns of economic and racist subjugation, as well as their attendant ideas and practices. Many states sought to reform it through initiatives like the New International Economic Order, resisted by Western states and its scholars, and dismissed as nothing more than destabilizing economic nationalism. In the first quarter of the twenty-first century, the global economic world order is again under attack. This time the attack is not coming from the countries of the Global South, as was the case in the 1950–70 period. Instead, the United States and certain European countries now claim that rules of the global economic order—such as those relating to trade and investment—that are not working for them should be repudiated.

This chapter argues that a more inclusive and therefore legitimate way of addressing the disenchantment with the global economic order from the Global North is to address squarely the inequities built into that economic order. We contend that the global economic order requires unprecedented reforms to make it more equitable and democratic. For that reason, we depart from David Sloss's introduction to this book to the extent it is predicated on preserving "a rules-based international order that is consistent with liberal, democratic values, and to prevent the transformation of the international

James T. Gathii and Sergio Puig, *The West and the Unraveling of the Economic World Order* In: *Is the International Legal Order Unraveling?*. Edited by: David L. Sloss, Oxford University Press. © Oxford University Press 2022.
DOI: 10.1093/oso/9780197652800.003.0003

order into a system of authoritarian international law."[1] Without a deeper engagement with the legacies of colonial dispossession and postcolonial exploitation that lie at the heart of the current global economic order, preserving this system will not resolve one of the most problematic aspects of the post–World War II international order.

We make our argument in two sections. Section II explores the parallels between earlier calls to transform colonial legacies and the current discontent with the effects of the international economic order. Section III explores the problems with preserving the "liberal" economic order, and presents an alternative roadmap to establish a less unfair and racialized economic order.

II. The Post–Second World War Order and Normalization of Injustice

In this section, we uncover the colonial and racialized origins of the post–World War II international economic order. We also discuss how former colonial powers thwarted the efforts of the then newly decolonized countries to reform it.

A. The Liberal World Order Preserved and Continued Colonial Era Inequities

Writing against the backdrop of the global protests against systemic racism in April 2021, Gideon Rachman, the chief foreign affairs commentator of the *Financial Times*, argued that "[t]he fact that four of the 'perm five' are predominantly white countries arguably represents an international form of 'white privilege,' inherited from the age of empires. It looks unsustainable when roughly 5.8 billion of a global population of about 7.6 billion live in Asia and Africa."[2] Rachman's argument that the decision to grant higher status to the five permanent members of the UN Security Council is an inheritance from the age of empire applies equally to the global economic system: the International Monetary Fund (IMF) is led by Europe, the World Bank is led

[1] David L. Sloss, *Introduction: Preserving a Rules-based International Order* (Introduction to this volume).

[2] Gideon Rachman, *Race Is also a Geopolitical Matter*, Fin. Times, Apr. 6, 2021, at 15.

by the United States, and the World Trade Organization (WTO) is a compromise where Japan is also invited to the big table.

Rachman's analysis of the racialized and unequal global system is unfortunately not represented in mainstream international economic law scholarship. Rather, mainstream international economic law scholarship overwhelmingly represents rules of international law as neutral, universal, fair, and raceless. By contrast, scholars from the Global South have focused on how rules of international economic law arose in the crucible of racialized colonial extractivism, and how the interpretation and application of those rules continues to justify the subordinate economic position of countries of the Global South.[3] *The Guardian* has recently documented these inequalities in a study showing that foreign multinationals dominate mineral, fish, and timber industries in the South Pacific; that China is the leading destination for these exports; that the hundreds of millions of dollars' worth of exports are underreported in the profits of those multinationals; and that this massive resource extraction often leaves a trail of "environmental devastation, poisoning rivers and forests, and degrading food security."[4] African countries have in the recent past foregrounded the fact that illicit financial flows from Africa far outweigh foreign aid and investment from the Global North.[5]

These adverse outcomes and asymmetrical financial flows are possible in no small measure because the current structure of international economic legal rules produces economic gains that disproportionately favor the interests of the Global North at the expense of the Global South—very often along racist and other immoral lines. These highly uneven outcomes are a direct inheritance from and continuation of the rules that justified the extraction of resources from colonized territories to the metropole. The current rules of many international institutions are vestiges of and the direct result of prior eras that benefited Europe, the United States, and other predominately white countries (e.g., Australia) at the expense of the non-white world. Especially in Latin America, leading (often white) elites of these non-white nations have now circled the wagons and captured the value produced and

[3] *See, e.g.*, Cedric J. Robinson, Black Marxism: The Making of the Black Radical Tradition (3rd ed. 2020); Histories of Racial Capitalism (Destin Jenkins & Justin Leroy eds., 2020).

[4] *Pacific Plunder*, The Guardian, May 31, 2021.

[5] United Nations Economic Commission for Africa, Illicit Financial Flows: Report of the High-Level Panel on Illicit Financial Flows from Africa (2015), https://repository.uneca.org/handle/10855/22695. *See also* James Thuo Gathii, *Recharacterizing Corruption to Encompass Illicit Financial Flows*, 113 AJIL Unbound 336 (2019).

protected by such rules in the postcolonial period in what Kwame Nkurumah called neocolonialism.[6] As Nkurumah argued, the goal of struggles against neocolonialism was to ensure that capital investments from the Global North would not impoverish the newly independent countries, rather than excluding those capital imports altogether.

The continuation of uneven rules from the colonial period to date can be illustrated with several examples. Perhaps the international investment regime—a system that empowers corporations to sue states before ad hoc arbitral tribunals to enforce rights that are guaranteed in very broadly crafted treaty and customary international law rules—is the most commonly referred to example.[7] In the early twentieth century, Latin American states strenuously opposed gunboat diplomacy for the enforcement of the rights of Western creditors.[8] They advocated for doctrines like the Drago Doctrine, which would make war and the right of diplomatic protection illegal for enforcement of civil obligations. It is key to note here that rules of international economic law—such as the minimum standard of treatment, and various property and contract rules—were tools in the formulation of doctrines for acquisition, such as discovery, occupation, conquest, and cession. These doctrines were used to justify European acquisition of title to territory previously occupied by non-European peoples.[9] In places like Australia, the British justified title to the territory on the basis that it was uninhabited, *terra nullius*, and therefore belonged to no one.[10] This view that Indigenous people did not have title to their own territory, even though they had occupied it for thousands of years, formed part of the racist justification for colonial rule.[11] Non-European peoples were measured against an idealized European standard of "civilized nations" that included presumptions such as property ownership as a hallmark of civilization, and lack of it as a justification for conquest. In short, "imperial international law was constructed on the basis of white racial superiority—as rational stewards of the territories

[6] Kwame Nkurumah, Neo-Colonialism: The Last Stage of Imperialism (1965).

[7] For a great recent analysis from this point of view, *see* John Linarelli, Margot E. Salomon & M. Sornarajah, The Misery of International Law: Confrontations with Injustice in the Global Economy (2018).

[8] *See* Jeremy Rabkin, *Strength in Obscurity: The Resilience of International Investment Law* (Chapter 10 in this volume).

[9] Antony Anghie, Imperialism, Sovereignty and the Making of International Law 82 (2005).

[10] *Id.* at 83.

[11] *Id.* at 84.

of non-Europeans—and on the basis of racist myths of Indigenous savagery, primitivism and pathology."[12]

From the 1950s to the 1970s, newly decolonized African and Asian countries argued that commercial concessions, such as those relating to minerals, procured under colonial rule should be repudiated so that these countries could begin with a clean slate.[13] They argued that these colonial-era economic advantages were the result of unfair dispossession and embedded in treaties. Therefore, they should be repudiated so that newly formed states could begin their political independence with economic independence, free from contractual obligations in resource extraction concessions and from the dominance exercised by multinational commercial interests created under colonial rule. In the context of succession of treaties, this doctrine is referred to as the Nyerere Doctrine, which rejects the idea "of automatic succession to the treaty obligations of the predecessor state, particularly as regards those treaties which inhibit the sovereign status of the newly independent."[14] By contrast, the former colonial powers argued that the quest of these newly independent states to have control over their natural resources had to respect the rights held by investors, which had been acquired under colonial rule.[15]

In a 1967 speech to the Group of 77, then Senegalese Foreign Minister Doudou Thiam argued that Africa demanded a new international legal order that required the dissolution of colonial international law.[16] In that speech, Thiam argued that "Africa demands a new international order" to replace colonial international law ("pacte du conquete" or "pact of conquest").[17] That new international law would have a right to development for the nations in the Third World. He concluded: "nous devons proclaimer . . . pour les nations

[12] James Thuo Gathii, *Writing Race and Identity in a Global Context: What CRT and TWAIL Can Learn from Each Other*, 67 UCLA L. Rev. 1613 (2020).

[13] *See, e.g.*, O. Selolwane, *Colonization by Concession: Capitalist Expansion in the Bechuanaland Protectorate (1885–1950)*, 2 Botswana J. African Stud. 74 (1980). For the case of Zambia, *see* Peter Slinn, *Commercial Concessions and Politics during the Colonial Period: The Role of the British South Africa Company in Northern Rhodesia 1890–1964*, 70 African Aff. 365 (1971).

[14] N.S. Rembe, *The Vienna Convention on State Succession in Respect of Treaties: An African Perspective on Its Applicability and Limitations*, 17 Comp. & Int'l L.J. Southern Africa 131 (1984).

[15] Anghie, *supra* note 9, at 212.

[16] The following account is taken from James Thuo Gathii, *Africa and the Radical Origins of the Right to Development*, 1 Third World Approaches to Int'l L. Rev. 28 (2020).

[17] *See* Doudou Thiam, *L'Afrique Demande un Droit International d'un Nouveau*, 1 Verfassung und Recht in Übersee 52 (1968) (reprinting speech delivered at the meeting of the Group of 77 in Algiers in October 1967). *See also* Philip Alston, *The Right to Development at the International Level*, *in* The Right to Development at the International Level 100 (Rene-Jean Dupuy ed., 1990) (noting that Ecuador had drafted a version of the Declaration of Rights and Duties of States in the 1940s that included a reference to states having a right to peaceful and secure development).

du Tiers-Monde le droit au developpement."[18] Under this vision, a right to development existed and belonged to the nations of the Third World, the then former colonies. He conceptualized it as a collective right to correct the wrongs wrought by unfair colonial rules, its resulting dispossessions and lasting inequities.

The role of international law then, through this demand for a right to development, included a rejection of the old international law that Mohammed Bedjaoui argued undergirded colonial subjugation. The old international law had a slant in favor of the privileged, reflecting the role of power in social, political, and economic relations. According to Bedjaoui, "[t]he new legal order must make provision within itself for the development of all nations in the world and must provide for international economic cooperation raised to the dignity of a legal institution acknowledged to be fundamental."[19] This "radical" vision of a right to development, which was a clarion call of the New International Economic Order and the Charter of the Rights and Duties of States, was ridiculed by officials and scholars in Europe and the United States. First, representatives of those powers argued that these demands constituted an unjustifiable effort to extend the concept of sovereignty to economic relations.[20] On this account, economic relations were best left to market forces, free from government intervention. Second, scholars engaging with these demands argued that academic voices like those of Bedjaoui, who supported this vision, were shrill, inept, or polemical at best, and had no basis in legal text.[21]

For Global South countries and its scholars, therefore, colonialism and its legacies are a central feature not only of postcolonial Africa and Asia but also of the modern international economic order. Mohammed Bedjaoui again sharply linked the centuries of domination and exploitation with "the right to development."[22] Then and now this means "the right to an equitable share

[18] Thiam, *supra* note 17 ("we must proclaim . . . for Third World nations the right to development.").

[19] Mohammed Bedjaoui, Towards a New International Economic Order 114 (1977).

[20] *See, e.g.*, Norbert Horn, *Normative Considerations of a New International Economic Order*, 16 J. World Trade L. 338, 343 (1982). For an alternative view, *see* B.S. Chimni, *The Principle of Permanent Sovereignty Over Natural Resources: Toward a Radical Interpretation*, 38 Indian J. Int'l L. 208, 214 (1998) (arguing in favor of examining material as opposed to statist interpretations of international law).

[21] *See, e.g.*, Marc Williams, *Book Review*, 2 Third World Q. 782 (1980) (reviewing four different books).

[22] Bedjaoui, *supra* note 19, at 22. Bedjaoui elaborates further, noting that "the most important and comprehensive [aspect of the right to development] is the right of each people freely to choose its economic and social system without outside interference or constraint of any kind, and to determine, with equal freedom, its own model of development." *Id.* at 35.

in the economic and social well-being of the world. It reflects an essential demand of our time since four fifths of the world population no longer accept that the remaining fifth should continue to build its wealth on their poverty."[23] From this perspective, Bedjaoui went on to argue that the right to development flows from the right of self-determination. In fact, the right to development was an inherent and built-in right forming an inseparable part of the right to self-determination.

The link between self-determination and development is not surprising since, prior to his appointment to the International Court of Justice (ICJ), Bedjaoui advocated for Algerian self-determination in his earlier writings.[24] The right to development then, according to Bedjaoui, was "much more of a right of the State or of the people, than a right of the individual:" a collective right. Bedjaoui's account of international law here is that it had "made use of a series of justifications and excuses to create legitimacy for the subjugation and pillaging of the Third World, which was pronounced uncivilized."[25] Today, Article 38 of the Statute of the ICJ, considered the most authoritative enumeration of international law sources, maintains the term "civilized nations" despite its problematic origin. In a welcome development, the International Law Commission's 2019 discussion on General Principles of Law alluded to the fact that General Principles "had underpinned the depredations of ruthless colonialism and the domination, by a handful of states in a small geographical area, of the states and peoples of the rest of the world."[26] A "nearly unanimous" view seems to be emerging that the racist notion of civilized nations associated with sources of international law in the Statute of the ICJ should be abandoned in favor a framing that recognizes the sovereign equality of all states.[27]

[23] *Id.* at 49. Bedjaoui further argued that classic international law "recognized and enforced a 'right of domination' for the benefit of the 'civilized nations.' This was a colonial and imperial right, institutionalized at the Berlin Conference on the Congo." *Id.* at 49.

[24] *See generally* Umut Özsu, *Determining New Selves*, *in* The Battle for International Law: South-North Perspectives on the Decolonization Era (Jochen von Bernstorff & Philipp Dann eds., 2019).

[25] Mohammed Bedjaoui, *The Right to Development*, *in* Mohammed Bedjaoui, International Law: Achievements and Prospects (1991).

[26] International Law Commission, Seventy-First Session, Provisional Summary Record of the 3491st Meeting, A/CN.4/SR.3491, at 6 (Oct. 2, 2019).

[27] *Id.* at 16 ("The nearly unanimous view was that the expression was an outdated relic of the past that should be replaced with words that reflected the sovereign equality of States.").

B. The Reforms to Overcome Colonial Legacies Have Been Thwarted

The political leaders who supported a right to development from the mid-twentieth century, particularly in the debates surrounding the New International Economic Order and the Charter for the Economic Rights and Duties of States, centered their focus on the legacy of colonial-capitalist modernity and its violent processes of domination and exploitation. Newly independent countries from Asia, America, and Africa in the post–World War II period demanded a transformation toward a fairer and more equitable world. Critics of the right to development approach, such as Jack Donnelly, argued that conceptualizing development as a right was a fallacy, since there was no right to be developed.[28]

Since then and in other critical moments, leaders of the developed nations have failed to adjust to similar demands for change, contributing to what William Barber calls the "five interlocking injustices" of our times: systemic racism, poverty, ecological devastation, the war economy, and religious nationalism.[29] At a global level, each of these structural injustices can be paired with other similar instances of ignoring the lasting legacies of colonialism. In the Bretton Woods Institutions, for example, the economic dominance of the former colonial powers is entrenched in their governance structures. Thus, in both the World Bank and the IMF, the system of weighted voting—according to which each country gets one vote for each share of the Bank's or IMF's capital stock held by the member—ensures the dominance of former colonial powers. Thus, as of March 1, 2021, the United States controlled 15.9 percent of the total voting power at the Bank, while Chad, one of the poorest countries in the world and a former French colony, controls just 0.07 percent of the total voting power.[30] At the IMF, even after governance reforms eventually approved by the US Congress in 2016, the United States controls a majority of quotas that gives it a de facto veto.[31] And as a recent report noted,

[28] Jack Donnelly, *In Search of the Unicorn: The Jurisprudence and Politics of the Right to Development*, 15 Cal. Western Int'l L.J. 473 (1985).

[29] NPR, *Co-Chairs of the Poor People's Campaign on the Impact of Their Virtual Demonstration*, June 21, 2020 ("there are five of them—systemic racism, systemic poverty, ecological devastation, the war economy and the false moral narrative of religious nationalism. And they all represent five interlocking injustices that are undermining the hopes and the dreams of this society.").

[30] World Bank Group, *IBRD Subscriptions and Voting Power of Member Countries*, https://finances.worldbank.org/Shareholder-Equity/IBRD-Subscriptions-and-Voting-Power-of-Member-Coun/rcx4-r7xj/data (last visited June 10, 2021).

[31] Notably, 22 U.S.C. § 286c provides in part: "Unless Congress by law authorizes such action, neither the President nor any person or agency shall on behalf of the United States (a) request or

"European countries 'present at the creation' remain overrepresented on the Executive Board."[32] In fact, Western powers together hold nearly 58 percent of the voting shares of the IMF, giving them the formal power to delay or defeat any changes that would water down their very consequential control of the IMF, such as increasing China's shares in the IMF as its economy quickly becomes one of the largest in the world.[33]

Thus, the overwhelming majority of the former colonized countries do not have an effective voice or vote in the IMF or World Bank, notwithstanding the very consequential effect these institutions have on the economies of the Global South. Since 2000, the share of the world's economy held by emerging and developing markets has increased from 40 percent to 60 percent, while the share of those of the Global North has fallen.[34] This institutional rigidity has led to experimentation with alternatives to the Bretton Woods Institutions, as illustrated by the Asian Infrastructure Investment Bank.[35] As explained by Shaffer and Gao, at the WTO, "through China's investment in legal capacity, it was able to become a legal rival to the United States and Europe, who now suggest that the rules favor China."[36]

Other examples of the United States thwarting or vetoing multilateral reforms include: the abandonment of the Kyoto Protocol, which delayed multilateral climate change action to benefit oil conglomerates in industrialized countries with high cumulative CO_2 emissions; the failure to take seriously the Doha Round of Development at the WTO, leading to the increase in unsustainable pressures to our planet; the pretense of multilateralism in building a "coalition of the willing" for the invasion of Iraq and subsequent wars; and the stigmatization of communities of color (Muslims and immigrants in particular), especially after the Great Recession, to distract

consent to any change in the quota of the United States under article III, section 2(a), of the Articles of Agreement of the Fund."

[32] José de Gregorio et al., IMF Reform: The Unfinished Agenda 1 (2018), https://cepr.org/sites/default/files/events/Geneva20.pdf.

[33] *Id.* at 67. *See also* J. Vestergaard & R.H. Wade, *Protecting Power: How Western States Retain Their Dominant Voice in the World Bank's Governance*, *in* Rising Powers and Multilateral Institutions (Dries Lesage & Thijs Van de Graaf eds., 2015).

[34] Rakesh Mohan, IMF Quota Reforms and Global Economic Governance: What Does the Future Hold? (2020), https://csep.org/working-paper/imf-quota-reforms-and-global-economic-governance-what-does-the-future-hold/#_ftn3.

[35] Dong Kyu Kim, Jaein Lee, & Byungwon Woo, *Institutional Rigidity of the Bretton Woods Institutions, Domestic Politics of the U.S. and the Establishment of the Asian Infrastructure Investment Bank*, 19 Korean J. Int'l Stud. 105 (2021).

[36] Gregory Shaffer & Henry Gao, *China's Rise: How It Took on the U.S. at the WTO*, 2018 Univ. Ill. L. Rev. 115, 118–19 (2018).

from its own failures of governance. Therefore, we need a more ambitious plan—one that follows the spirit of a right to development and that is committed to challenging and displacing the colonial-era legacies of international economic law.

III. Preserving the Economic World Order?

In this section, we argue that the current wave of discontent in the Global North has a similar root. Amidst problems of economic inequality rooted in fallacious ideas and practices of capitalism that reproduce colonial institutions, communities across the world perceive an ongoing abandonment of a moral vision for a world order. The lack of attention to these problems has had devastating consequences in Latin America, the Middle East, and Africa. Therefore, preserving this economic order is not a viable option.

A. The Problem with Liberalism

In the introduction to this volume, David Sloss argues in favor of preserving a rules-based international order. We agree with this, but depart from his argument that a future rules-based system should be a liberal one. As José Álvarez argued in response to Anne-Marie Slaughter's advocacy of a post–Cold War liberal order, the type of liberalism that she advocated was one consistent with the neoliberal order of the Washington Consensus—one underpinned by free markets and free and fair elections.[37] This claim that liberalism ought to underpin the global order also dovetails very well with the post–Cold War arguments that liberal democracies behave better than illiberal regimes. The decline of democracy in the early part of the twenty-first century in the United States and other liberal democracies in Europe and elsewhere undermines the argument that liberal democracies should set the example for other regimes. This claim also assumes that Western liberalism, however it is defined, should be the basis for organizing global order—as if there are no other imperfect alternatives to liberalism. Making such an assumption

[37] Jose Alvarez, *Do Liberal States Behave Better? A Critique of Slaughter's Liberal Theory*, 12 EUR. J. INT'L L. 190 (2001).

belies the fact that human rights norms often have been mobilized to support neoliberal economic restructuring by the Bretton Woods Institutions in the Global South, a factor that suggests severe limits to embracing them as an unproblematic global benchmark.[38]

Further, characterizing China as an antithesis to the kind of liberalism that David Sloss argues should underpin a new rules-based international order underestimates the ways in which liberal democracies behave illiberally in global governance. For example, the virulent Islamophobia and xenophobia that has in the recent past characterized US immigration policy, resulting in shutting its borders to individuals from Muslim majority countries and non-white peoples generally, is also shared by populist European governments. In the United States, this racialization of immigration has become a central pillar of the "counterterrorism and the national security state" that emerged after September 11, 2001, and has been consolidated since then.[39] This racialization has been an important driver of US foreign policy, with its UN-sanctioned intervention in Libya in 2011, its now decades old targeted killing campaign using drone strikes, as well as its unilateral uses of force, such as the assassination of Qasem Soleimani in early 2020. As Asli Bali and Aziz Rana recently argued, the US global war on terror "brought into focus an international order in which American exceptionalism was no longer tied to a commitment to rule-based presumptions."[40] While open disregard for international law rules became routine during the Donald Trump era, his administration was not exceptional in this respect; prior administrations over the last quarter century have contributed to this descent into international legal lawlessness.[41]

For us, though, it is not just that making the case for liberalism to underpin a rules-based global order is based on ethnocentric assumptions that assume the universality of Western values, but rather like José Álvarez, we are

[38] *See* Antony Anghie, *Inequality, Human Rights, and the New International Economic Order*, 10 Humanity 429 (2019).

[39] Asli Bâli & Aziz Rana, *Constitutionalism and the American Imperial Imagination*, 85 Chi. L. Rev. 257, 261 (2018). For further analysis, especially with regard to the racialized and gendered nature of the wars in Syria and Iraq led by the United States, *see generally* Ntina Tzouvala, Capitalism as Civilization: A History of International Law (2020).

[40] Bali & Rana, *supra* note 39, at 282.

[41] *See, e.g.*, Henry J. Richardson III, *U.S. Hegemony, Race, and Oil in Deciding United Nations Security Council Resolution 1441 on Iraq*, 17 Temple Int'l & Comp. L.J. 27 (2003); Henry J. Richardson III, *The Gulf and African-American Interests Under International Law*, 87 Am. J. Int'l L. 42 (1993); Ruth Gordon, *Racing U.S. Foreign Policy*, 17 Nat'l Black L.J. 1 (2003); Ruth Gordon, *Critical Race Theory and International Law: Convergence and Divergence*, 45 Villanova L. Rev. 827 (2000).

especially skeptical that liberal democracies behave better than nonliberal states with regard to compliance with treaties,[42] respect for socioeconomic rights, protection of minorities, or, as we have alluded to earlier, with regard to using force consistent with the United Nations (UN) Charter framework.[43] In our view, José Álvarez is correct in his criticism that the liberal/nonliberal distinction has not characterized the United States' foreign policy goals, and that the United States has traditionally entered into numerous treaty relationships with countries characterized as nonliberal and even undemocratic. Even though Álvarez was writing at the end of the Cold War, the rise of populism and retreat from democratic tenets in the Global North has not changed in this first part of the twenty-first century. To quote José Álvarez:

> If Slaughter is claiming not that liberal states tend to act in accord with liberal tenets all or most of the time but merely that they are more apt to do so than non-liberal states as a whole, she gives us little to undertake comparative assessment except conjecture and anecdotal evidence.[44]

Like José Álvarez, we fail to find convincing, systematic evidence that justifies why the behavior of a few powerful states that claim an attachment to liberalism ought to form the benchmark against which a rules-based system of global governance should be based. The world is after all very heterogeneous. Other ways of arriving at a baseline for global governance that involve more democratic input would be more legitimate and have more staying power than the presumption that liberalism is the de facto benchmark for global governance.[45] Yet this benchmark, as Makau Mutua reminds us, "is not concerned about the asymmetries of power among citizens, or the ability of entrenched interests to maintain social control over politics,"[46] some of the most important issues that go to the root of political, social, and economic disenfranchisement.

The liberal international order that Sloss contemplates is consistent with the United States' economic interests, not just because, as we saw earlier, the United States dominates the Bretton Woods Institutions. This is also because the liberal international order comes with inbuilt limitations that protect

[42] Alvarez, *supra* note 37, at 210.
[43] *Id.* at 194.
[44] *Id.* at 205.
[45] For more on this view in the context of human rights law, *see* Makau Mutua, *Human Rights in Africa: The Limited Promise of Liberalism*, 51 African Stud. Rev. 17 (2008).
[46] *Id.* at 21.

certain economic prerogatives from public deliberation and therefore democratic choice. Sloss argues that a rules-based international order is necessary "because continued erosion of liberal democracy within domestic legal systems will inevitably undermine protection for human rights, which is a central element of the modern, rules-based international order."[47] Sloss proposes a Marshall Fund to combat the trend of democratic decline by targeting "low and middle-income countries that have reasonably good democratic credentials." Although all the details of the Marshall Fund are underspecified, it seems that it would target countries that already have good market governance credentials. Those low- and middle-income countries that Sloss has in mind for his Marshall Fund are countries operating under the aegis of the neoliberal economic regimes of the World Bank and IMF. These two international financial institutions are first and foremost committed to privatizing or re-regulating economies in ways beneficial to private capital and that are immiserating for many ordinary people.[48] Most importantly, neoliberal economic arrangements at the national level in non-Western countries are adopted by governments or imposed by conditionalities of the Bretton Woods Institutions without much public discussion, deliberation, and debate.[49] Therefore, we are especially critical of Sloss's rules-based international order because it is limited to protection of civil and political rights that more likely than not fails to take into account the economic and social policies that are constitutive of the entire spectrum of the rights of citizens.[50]

So, while we acknowledge that there has been progress since the end of the Second World War, it is also true that many of the elements of the global economic system—including massive inequalities between countries and growing inequality within countries—are the rule rather than the exception. As Thomas Picketty powerfully demonstrated in his 2014 book, *Capital in the Twenty-First Century*, returns on capital and existing wealth, held overwhelming by the wealthiest, had far exceeded the rate of growth of the economy as a whole. The result, he showed convincingly, was a rate

[47] *See* Sloss, Introduction to this volume.

[48] For more on this, *see* Michael A. Wilkinson, *Authoritarian Liberalism as Authoritarian Constitutionalism*, *in* AUTHORITARIAN CONSTITUTIONALISM: COMPARATIVE ANALYSIS AND CRITIQUE 317 (Helena Alviar Garcia & Günter Frankenberg eds., 2019) [hereinafter AUTHORITARIAN CONSTITUTIONALISM].

[49] For the case of Latin America, *see* Helena Alviar Garcia, *Neo-Liberalism as a Form of Authoritarian Constitutionalism*, *in* AUTHORITARIAN CONSTITUTIONALISM, *supra* note 48, at 41.

[50] For the African case, *see* James Thuo Gathii, *Representations of Africa in Good Governance Discourse: Policing and Containing Dissidence to Neo-Liberalism*, 18 THIRD WORLD L. STUD. 65 (1998–1999).

of inequality that compared to the period before the Gilded Age. In his next book, *Capital and Ideology*, Picketty traces the populist backlash and anti-immigrant sentiments to growing inequality in the United States and Europe. He argues in favor of high taxes on the rich to fund affordable health care and other public goods, like childcare and education, with a view to providing more economic security and opportunity for citizens.[51]

Picketty's findings ring true in the richest country today, with nearly a fifth of the population concentrated among minority populations living in poverty, or struggling to make ends meet. As the COVID-19 pandemic illustrated, those at the lowest end of the economic ladder—often racial minorities—were the ones most adversely and disproportionately affected by the pandemic.[52] That has been the case at the global level as well. Robbie Shilliam's *Race and the Undeserving Poor* traces the institutionalization of oppressive political structures over many decades in Britain to create an undeserving poor working class that was not Indigenous and not white. Through this analysis, Shilliam shows how the "moral worth" and "political agency of the poor" brought the colony and metropole together.[53] Consistent with Shilliam's analysis of a racialized underclass produced by oppressive political structures, in the Global South, the most vulnerable segments of the global population negatively impacted by the COVID-19 pandemic are the most marginalized by the postcolonial state, especially Indigenous populations and individuals excluded from the market economy or living on its very edges. Therefore, an uncritical examination of change in the international legal order may sadly lead to another mistaken inference: that the liberal oriented states of the Global North perform much better than those elsewhere, and should therefore be the baseline for reforms toward a new rules-based international order.

A major problem with that kind of argument, to reiterate, is that the liberal international order has been built on prioritizing the economic interest of Western nations, and in particular its wealthiest citizens. The Bretton Woods Institutions (World Bank, IMF, General Agreement on Tariffs and Trade

[51] For a great analysis of the reluctance of the left and the right to ensure more economic opportunity and security for all in the United States, *see* James T. Patterson, America's Struggle Against Poverty: 1900–1994 (2000).

[52] Catherine Powell, *Color of COVID and Gender of COVID: Essential Workers, Not Disposable People*, 33 Yale J.L. & Feminism 1 (2021), https://papers.ssrn.com/sol3/papers.cfm?abstract_id=3713395.

[53] Robbie Shilliam, Race and the Undeserving Poor 31 (2018).

(GATT), WTO) are all controlled by the United States, Europe, Canada, and Japan. The policies of these institutions reflect their priorities rather than those countries and populations that these countries formerly colonized. In particular, these institutions have played a key role in consolidating a global capitalist economy that safeguards the interests that produce profits for the Global North. However, with China's economic rise and its growing success on the technological frontier, the United States is largely abandoning liberal goals. The undermining of the WTO by effectively closing the doors of the Appellate Body is an example at hand. This removes any checks on the United States in its trade wars with China and other countries. By single-handedly contributing to the Appellate Body's demise, the United States has signaled its determination to undermine multilateral institutions that do not play by its rules, even if these rules are unjust. The unraveling of the rules-based post–World War II order at the current moment is not surprising for countries of the Global South. Countries in the Global South were always critical of this rules-based international order because they experience its dark underbelly. Many of the major criticisms against institutions of international economic law were not only completely justified but remain as valid today as they were particularly in the 1970s. Most importantly, we believe that in this first part of the twenty-first century, institutions and rules of the international economic order must play a key role in building solutions to the interlocking crises we face, while rejecting the colonial legacies embedded in existing rules.

B. Transforming Rather than Preserving

We believe that the international economic order has the capacity to (and must) adapt and should become an important part of the solution to major global challenges—from inequality between and within countries to climate justice. For that to happen, international economic law needs to recognize that the structural inequality of the magnitude that we continue to experience cannot and should not be treated as normal, but rather as unjust and unsustainable. This has been the attitude by policy makers in many countries and it needs to change. Both the nature and the scale of the problem are unique and demand transformative action—not preserving a system that works well for the interests of a handful of countries who benefited from racist colonialism.

Of course, international law cannot redress all wrongs, and we don't expect a legal transformation without a deeper social transformation. But with the demands of our times, scholars should push for an international law concerned with systemic injustice and racism. Hence, calls for preserving the international system fail to see the issue from "A Global South Perspective" and the importance and moral value of a more radical transformation addressing its complex origins. Preserving international law without a critical evaluation of its effects would not serve to mitigate the abuses of state sovereignty; advocates of preservation too readily dismiss the potential that international law has to transform ideas about justice and catalyze collective action around it. Preserving the system means that international law will continue to serve as an adjunct of global business instead of the more capacious project embedded in a development perspective.

We have explained why we depart from Sloss's uncritical embrace of a rules-based international order, whose goal is not to transform but rather to preserve it. Without a deeper engagement with how this rules-based order formalizes problematic legacies of the colonial and postcolonial past, this proposal will not resolve the current discontent, missing a critical opportunity for reform. Instead, we provide some suggestions to broaden the lens, acknowledging the complex character of such changes. Our proposal lies in three broad axes.

Legitimacy and Equality: International economic law can start by enhancing input as well as external legitimacy by adopting participation rules that are more suited to the challenges faced by many communities in many places. International economic organizations must include representatives of all nations on a fair basis; this will require changes to the voting and shareholding structure of decision-making bodies. A system that allocates decision-making power on the basis of material wealth, as is currently true, will perpetuate the effects of colonial racist institutions. The best example of this alluded to earlier in this chapter is the weighted voting system of the IMF and the World Bank. Here, the wealthiest nations of the post–World War II period continue to dominate, and in fact have a veto on the economic policy choices that these institutions impose on the rest of the world. For example, in 2023 there is an opportunity for voice and vote reform in the IMF after the United States blocked the latest efforts in 2020.[54]

[54] Rakesh Mohan, IMF Quota Reforms and Global Economic Governance: What Does the Future Hold? (Oct. 2020), https://csep.org/working-paper/imf-quota-reforms-and-global-economic-governance-what-does-the-future-hold/#_ftn3.

Such governance reforms to address these inequities that exclude the voice and vote of most of the world are necessary, not only to address the legitimacy deficit of these institutions but also to reform economic policymaking. Future policies should be more consistent with the interests of a broader swath of the global population, particularly those in the Global South. In short, the underrepresentation of countries of the Global South in multilateral institutions that have global lawmaking power—including the UN Security Council—is long overdue. In addition, such reforms must include efforts to hold corporate actors accountable under international law, in effect reversing the virtual disappearance of these powerful actors from the gaze of international legal accountability.[55] Just as the Bandung Conference of 1955 initiated a discussion of the fairness of the international system, we believe that we "must wrench open the possibility of an alternative, fairer, and more just world order,"[56] and not ever give up on it.

Democracy and Self-determination: As we understand it, democracy should extend beyond paying attention to civil and political rights. It should extend to giving citizens and countries the right to determine their own economic policies, free from the constraints imposed by international institutions or inflexible treaties. As we have argued earlier, neoliberal economic policies limit policy innovation and weaken social protections, such as spending on basic needs, while rewarding returns to the owners of capital. For many scholars, this is a "form of governing in opposition to democracy."[57] To the extent the adoption of the austerity programs of neoliberal economics that reduce social spending circumvent parliamentary authority and debate through powerful Executive branch managerialism, those programs are antidemocratic in practice. This kind of "democratic deficit," as it has been referred to in Europe,[58] is a familiar story in the Global South. Overcoming these constraints in part involves subjecting the economic policies that states

[55] For an account of the disappearance of corporate actors from the gaze of accountability in international law, *see* DOREEN LUSTIG, VEILED POWER: INTERNATIONAL LAW AND THE PRIVATE CORPORATION, 1886–1981 (2020).

[56] Luis Eslava, Michael Fakhri, & Vasuki Nesiah, *The Spirit of Bandung*, *in* BANDUNG, GLOBAL HISTORY, AND INTERNATIONAL LAW: CRITICAL PASTS AND PENDING FUTURE (Luis Eslava, Michael Fakhri, & Vasuki Nesiah eds., 2017) [hereinafter BANDUNG AND INTERNATIONAL LAW].

[57] Wilkinson, *supra* note 48.

[58] Simon Hix & Andreas Follesdal, *Why There Is a Democratic Deficit in the EU: A Response to Majone and Moravcsik*, 44 J. COMMON MARKET STUD. 533 (2006).

pursue to democratic legitimation, beyond free and fair elections and the enjoyment of civil and political rights.[59]

One way to ensure democratic control of economic decisions at the local level is to focus on the political legitimacy of policymaking. According to Trubek et al., for this to happen "legal regimes must ensure accountability, transparency, and participation in development policies, which requires norms for disclosure, frameworks for participation, methods to hold policymakers accountable for results, and ways to avoid industry capture of government at the same time public-private dialogue is fostered."[60] In some contexts this can be achieved by mechanisms of prior consultation—similar to the consultations with Indigenous communities.[61] In others, strong rules against corruption could deter some practices that lead to capture. Finally, risk- and benefit-sharing agreements can encourage research and innovation and expand industry capacity and exports of local communities. For this to happen, international conditions like investment treaties, lending safeguards and conditionalities, and international trade law must enable sufficient flexibility for policy experimentation and encourage political legitimacy. With the fast pace of change and social acceleration, policies should be altered as domestic and international conditions change. Rigid frameworks that result in violations of international law rules for the adoption of legitimate policies and regulation—a likely possibility under some bilateral investment treaties—should be avoided. Overall, decision makers should embrace the ways in which different societies determine their own priorities, while critically and creatively engaging with the way local communities manage economic activity.

Fair and Differential Treatment: We suggest strengthening rules of international law to address the failure of current rules of international economic law to meet the needs of the least well-off countries. At the WTO, for example, developing countries (particularly since the Doha Round) have made the case that "all special and differential treatment provisions shall be reviewed with a view to strengthening them and making them more precise, effective

[59] For an articulation of this argument, *see* James T. Gathii, *Neoliberalism, Colonialism, and International Governance: Decentering the International Law of Government Legitimacy*, 98 Mich. L. Rev. 1996 (2019).

[60] For examples of such initiatives, *see* Sergio Puig, At the Margins of Globalization: Indigenous Peoples and International Economic Law 104–25 (2021).

[61] David M. Trubek, Diogo R. Coutinho, & Mario G. Schapiro, *New State Activism in Brazil and the Challenge for Law*, *in* Law and the New Developmental State: The Brazilian Experience in Latin American Context (David M. Trubek et al. eds., 2013).

and operational."[62] In the context of international environmental law, developing countries have made the case for common and differentiated responsibilities, acknowledging that while they have responsibility for remedying environmental harms, they are not equally responsible for causing them and therefore the weight attributed to their share of remediation should be proportionately smaller.[63] Other initiatives to nudge international economic law toward a more inclusive future, sensitive to the needs of developing countries, include the Convention on Access to Genetic Resources and the Fair and Equitable Sharing of Benefits Arising from their Utilization to the Convention on Biological Diversity (Nagoya Protocol) that creates access and benefit sharing standards so that developing countries can earn a return on their rich biodiversity. Ensuring that the traditional knowledge and genetic resources of Indigenous communities and groups, especially in the Global South, are not subject to biopiracy but rather are underpinned by equitable frameworks, has been a primary agenda item of developing countries.[64]

This inclusive future also includes the 2018 Declaration on the Rights of Peasants and Other People Working in Rural Areas.[65] This Declaration, more than other human rights instruments, seeks to ensure that peasants and people working in rural areas have the right to control their land, a critical means of production for them. With ownership, these groups would have control over their own livelihoods, given the centrality of land for their survival. They would also be better able to resist acquisition of their lands by well-heeled domestic or local investors. For this reason, this Declaration buttresses the economic self-determination over land for people who might otherwise be displaced because they may not have ancestral or other links to it.[66] Another important proposal to level the global playing field in a way that takes into account developing country interests is the current proposal in the WTO, proposed by Brazil and India, to suspend patent protection and

[62] World Trade Organization, Ministerial Declaration of 14 November 2001, WTO Doc. WT/MIN(01)/DEC/1, ¶ 44, 41 ILM 746 (2002).

[63] For more on this point, *see* Carmen G. Gonzalez, *The Sacrifice Zones of Carbon Capitalism: Race, Expendability, and Loss and Damage*, *in* RESEARCH HANDBOOK ON CLIMATE CHANGE LAW AND LOSS AND DAMAGE (Meinhard Doelle & Sara Seck eds., forthcoming 2022), https://ssrn.com/abstract=3838069.

[64] Sergio Puig, *International Indigenous Economic Law*, 52 U.C. DAVIS. L. REV. 1243, 1272–74 (2019).

[65] *See generally* Lorenzo Cotula, *The Right to Land in* THE UNITED NATIONS' DECLARATION ON PEASANTS' RIGHTS (M. Alabrese et al. eds., forthcoming 2022), https://ssrn.com/abstract=3867153.

[66] *Id.*

increase investment in production capacity to ensure access to COVID-19 vaccines for a majority of the world's population.

Overall, international economic law must contribute to restructuring the imbalance of power that translates into marginalization of many people in different parts of the world. We conclude by noting that the Bandung Declaration of 1955 sought to achieve "a world where there is respect for human rights, equality, racial equality and justice."[67] We believe that this clarion call is still relevant in this first quarter of the twenty first century.[68]

IV. Conclusion

The disenchantment with the current international economic order is real, and it is not new; the problems lie deep. We need an inclusive and legitimate way to eliminate the inequities built within the global economic order. Resolving these structural issues will require unprecedented reforms that make international economic law more equitable and democratic and address its racist origins. For that reason, we depart from the proposal of preserving rather than transforming the post–Second World War rules-based international order. We propose instead a deeper engagement with the legacies of colonial dispossession and postcolonial exploitation that lie at the heart of the current global economic order. That deeper engagement can provide a foundation for a more profound and progressive transformation of international economic law.

[67] Final Communiqué of the Asian-African conference of Bandung (Apr. 24, 1955), https://www.cvce.eu/en/obj/final_communique_of_the_asian_african_conference_of_bandung_24_april_1955-en-676237bd-72f7-471f-949a-88b6ae513585.html.

[68] For an extensive exploration of this theme, *see* BANDUNG AND INTERNATIONAL LAW, *supra* note 56.

3
The Future of Liberal Democracy in the International Legal Order

Tom Ginsburg

I. Introduction

Liberal democracy is a feature of national political order that can be promoted, defended, or undermined by international legal institutions. It is not a feature of international legal order itself, nor can it be, given the inherent pluralism about ways of organizing government that is constitutive of the international legal system. But neither is it the case that any particular liberal democracy is an island; liberalism is itself a transnational ideology, and both the expansion and recession of democracy around the world have been the result of interdependent decisions made by states and other transnational actors.

Of particular importance has been the role of hegemons in the system, promoting particular kinds of governance, notably the United States in the post–World War II period. The liberal international order whose death has become a matter of conventional wisdom was largely a product of US empire. For this reason, the single biggest factor affecting the future of liberal democracy going forward will be the role of hegemons and large powers. For the near term, those are the United States, the People's Republic of China (PRC), Russia, and the European Union, with India obviously a relevant player as well. As these powers interact, they will create conditions that will advance or retard liberal democracy.

We already see some trends under way that seem likely to continue, and they are not pretty. Liberal democracies have had their confidence challenged in recent years, and bureaucrats in Brussels and Geneva are favored targets. Liberal democracies are perceived to have delegated too much power upward, rendering them unable to deliver policies that people want. This has led some to turn away from the liberal brand. Certainly, the United States

Tom Ginsburg, *The Future of Liberal Democracy in the International Legal Order* In: *Is the International Legal Order Unraveling?*. Edited by: David L. Sloss, Oxford University Press.
DOI: 10.1093/oso/9780197652800.003.0004

under President Donald Trump gave up its role as chief promoter of democracy, ceding that role to the European Union and the United Nations. Whether Joe Biden is able to reverse that course, or is instead, as Philip Cunliffe described him, a kind of "Brezhnev-like figure" for the liberal order, remains to be seen.[1] But authoritarian regimes have become skillful mimics of democratic forms at the national level, contributing to what some have called a democratic recession.

This chapter asks the question: What will the international law of democratic governance look like in 2050? The question reflects the fact that notwithstanding pluralism, there is much normative architecture supporting liberal democratic norms on the international plane. This architecture is not matched by equally expansive enforcement, but weak mechanisms do exist. This chapter speculates on alternative scenarios and what they might mean for the persistence of liberal democracy as a going concern, through the lens of international law.

II. Definition and Trends

A. The Architecture of Democracy

Preliminaries first. Aziz Huq and I define constitutional liberal democracy as having three essential elements: free and fair elections; core rights related to those elections, such as rights to speech, association, and voting as well as a free press; and the bureaucratic rule of law, by which we mean independent courts and agencies that act according to law, especially when dealing with matters related to democratic governance.[2] This is a relatively thin definition, which helps in applying it across widely different cultural contexts.

The definition highlights that international law *has* made contributions to supplying norms, institutions, and ideas that can reinforce national actors in their democratic practice. The Universal Declaration of Human Rights guarantees citizens the right to participate in public affairs, and to vote in genuine and periodic elections using a secret ballot.[3] The International Covenant

[1] PHILIP CUNLIFFE, THE NEW TWENTY YEARS' CRISIS: A CRITIQUE OF INTERNATIONAL RELATIONS, 1999–2019 (2020).

[2] TOM GINSBURG & AZIZ Z. HUQ, HOW TO SAVE A CONSTITUTIONAL DEMOCRACY (2018).

[3] Universal Declarations of Human Rights, art. 3, G.A. Res. 217 (III) A, U.N. Doc. A/RES/217(III) (Dec. 10, 1948).

on Civil and Political Rights (ICCPR) reinforces these norms in a legally binding treaty.[4] The United Nations, while recognizing the plurality of legitimate regime types, has also supported democratic practice in a variety of ways, including election monitoring and normative articulation. In a 2017 report, the Secretary-General of the United Nations noted that his organization had provided electoral assistance to roughly one-third of its member states.[5] And in the 1990s, the organization made democracy central to its mission. In 1996, UN Secretary-General Boutros Boutros-Ghali submitted *An Agenda for Democratization* to the General Assembly, seeking to clarify state practice, and emphasizing an independent judiciary, governmental accountability, the rule of law, and popular participation. Several other UN documents follow similar conceptions.[6]

Beyond these global documents, regional activity in Africa, Latin America, and Europe has supported the spread and maintenance of democracy.[7] The Organization of American States and the African Union have each issued "democracy charters" entrenching democracy as a regional norm, as has the

[4] International Covenant on Civil and Political Rights, art. 5, Dec. 19, 1966, 999 U.N.T.S. 171.

[5] United Nations, General Assembly, *Strengthening the Role of the United Nations in Enhancing the Effectiveness of the Principle of Periodic and Genuine Elections and the Promotion of Democratization: Report of the Secretary-General*, U.N. Doc. A/72/260 (Aug. 1, 2017).

[6] In 1999, the UN Commission on Human Rights adopted a resolution entitled *A Right to Democracy*, E/CN.4/RES/1999/57, stating that democracy includes "the rights to freedom of opinion and expression, of thought, conscience and religion, and of peaceful association and assembly; the right to freedom to seek, receive and impart information and ideas through any media; the rule of law, including legal protection of citizens' rights, interests and personal security, and fairness in the administration of justice and independence of the judiciary; the right of universal and equal suffrage, as well as free voting procedures and periodic and free elections; the right of political participation, including equal opportunity for all citizens to become candidates; transparent and accountable government institutions; the right of citizens to choose their governmental system through constitutional or other democratic means; and the right to equal access to public service in one's own country." A later document added elements of pluralism. U.N. Human Rights Council Res. 19/36, Human rights, democracy and the rule of law, 19th. Sess., U.N. Doc. A/HRC/Res/19/36, at para. 1 (2012) ("democracy includes respect for all human rights and fundamental freedoms, *inter alia*, freedom of association and of peaceful assembly, freedom of expression and opinion, freedom of thought, conscience, religion or belief, the right to be recognized everywhere as a person before the law and the right to take part in the conduct of public affairs, directly or through freely chosen representatives, to vote in a pluralistic system of political parties and organizations and to be elected at genuine, periodic, free and fair elections by universal and equal suffrage and by secret ballot guaranteeing the free expression of the will of the people, as well as respect for the rule of law, the separation of powers, the independence of the judiciary, transparency and accountability in public administration and decision-making and free, independent and pluralistic media.").

[7] Regional organizations with clauses related to democracy include the Council of Europe (CoE), the European Union (EU), the Andean Community, the Common Market of the South (Mercosur), the Central American Integration System (SICA), the Organization of American States (OAS), the Union of South American Nations (UNASUR), the African Union (AU), the Common Market for Eastern and Southern Africa (COMESA), the East African Community (EAC), and the Economic Community of West African States (ECOWAS).

Economic Community of West African States (ECOWAS).[8] The European Convention of Human Rights also has an architecture in this regard, as does the European Union. As international institutions devote more attention to promoting democracy, they reinforce the normative consensus around it. Evidence for the normative consensus is that even regional organizations that are composed mainly of nondemocracies, such as the Association of Southeast Asian Nations, assert that they adhere to principles of democracy.[9]

This normative consensus has been accompanied with institutional structure as well, even if the latter has not been as expansive as the former. The United Nations has promoted elections and constitutional reform, as well as providing technical advice. Human rights organizations and private foundations have also played a role. And regional courts, human rights commissions, and trade blocs have all encouraged countries to maintain and deepen democracy. They have done so through reports that expose practices falling short of democratic ideals; judgments sanctioning violations; threats of expulsion or outcasting; and occasionally through direct intervention or the threat thereof. To be sure, the record is mixed. However, international institutions can help resist democratic backsliding, in part by providing resources to democrats trying to advance their cause on the national level.

B. Trends

This normative consensus, however, has not prevented democratic erosion and backsliding in practice. Indeed, democratic erosion is one of the great trends of our time. Consider some statistics. According to the influential Freedom House Survey, the number of democracies peaked around 2006, and has declined since then. Other democracy indices show a similar decline in the number of liberal or full democracies (see Table 3.1). The quality of democracy has also declined: each year since 2006, more countries have suffered declines in their levels of democracy than have improved.

[8] Organization of American States, The Inter-American Democratic Charter, Sept. 11, 2001, O.A.S.T.S.; African Union (AU), Charter on Democracy, Elections and Governance (ACDEG), Jan. 30, 2007; Protocol of the Economic Community of West African States (ECOWAS) on Democracy and Good Governance, Dec. 10, 1999; Olabisi D. Akinkugbe, *Towards an Analysis of the Mega-Politics Jurisprudence of the ECOWAS Community Court of Justice*, *in* The Performance of Africa's International Courts: Using Litigation for Political, Legal, and Social Change (James Thuo Gathii ed., 2020).

[9] Preamble, *in* The ASEAN Charter (ASEAN ed., 2008).

Table 3.1 Number of Democracies since 2006

	2006	2010	2014	2019
Freedom House # Free countries	90	87	89	83
V-Dem # Liberal Democracies	41	45	43	37
Economist Intelligence Unit Full Democracies	28	26	24	22

Table 3.2 Countries by Category, 2020

	# Countries	% Countries	% World Population
Full Democracies	23	13.8	8.4
Flawed Democracies	52	31.1	41.0
Hybrid Regimes	35	21.0	15.0
Authoritarians	57	34.1	35.6

Source: Economist Intelligence Unit.

These declines have affected even established democracies: between 2014 and 2019, for example, the Economist Intelligence Unit downgraded South Korea, Japan, and the United States from "Full Democracies" to "Flawed Democracies." The decline has led us to a point where, for the first time in three decades, less than half of the countries in the world are considered to be even flawed democracies (Table 3.2). Furthermore, more than half of the world's population lives in nondemocracies, whether true authoritarians, or "Hybrid" regimes that exhibit some democratic forms, such as elections, but do not have genuine competition for political power.

Many of these flawed democracies and hybrid regimes reflect the fact that backsliding does not involve a sudden collapse of democracy, but instead a gradual process of erosion.[10] This involves a series of steps that attack component parts of a democratic order, one at a time, so as to facilitate a takeover of the political system. Indeed, some of the leaders who have consolidated power in their own political systems enjoy a good deal of popularity. Narendra Modi, for example, has extraordinary charisma

[10] Nancy Bermeo, *On Democratic Backsliding*, 27 J. Dem. 5 (2016); Ginsburg & Huq, *supra* note 2.

and has consolidated his Bharatiya Janata Party's control over national institutions, while eroding some of India's liberal traditions. India was recently downgraded from "Free" to "Partly Free" in the Freedom House categorization, and characterized as an electoral autocracy in the V-Dem assessment. Viktor Orbán, though less popular, valorizes "illiberal democracy" and has consolidated personal control over the Hungarian political system, assuming the ability to rule by decree without regard to law during the COVID-19 emergency.[11]

These trends toward illiberalism are beginning to affect international law in several ways, notwithstanding the stability of the de jure normative framework codified in the UN Charter and international covenants. First, authoritarians are forming their own international organizations to cooperate across borders. Authoritarian cooperation has, of course, long been a feature of international law, going back to the Congress of Vienna, through the Axis bloc, the Warsaw Pact, and the COMINTERN. But as I have argued elsewhere, we are seeing a new level of sophistication in authoritarian use of international organizations, in which new norms to promote order and stability are being articulated.[12] Authoritarian international organizations are expanding in number, type, and ambition, enhancing their ability to dilute democratic norms. Some, like the Shanghai Cooperation Organization, sponsor election monitors and provide technical "assistance," which dilutes the efforts by European institutions to ensure electoral integrity. By 2050, we may see authoritarian-dominated international organizations that sponsor their own "democracy charters" paying lip service to democracy promotion, but functioning primarily to dilute the operation of the real deal. Election interference may become so subtle that it is hard to detect, in turn undermining public confidence in voting machinery.

Second, proto authoritarians are eroding the pro-democratic quality of governance in established international institutions. Central here are battles over the rule of law in the European Union. In late 2020, the self-described "illiberal democracies" of Hungary and Poland delayed the adoption of the European Union budget and were able to dilute (though not eliminate) provisions reinforcing the commitment to the rule of law among member

[11] Each of these countries has experienced a decline over time in its democratic status. According to V-Dem, India was an electoral democracy consistently until the 2020 downgrade. Hungary was a liberal democracy through 2005, then was an electoral democracy in 2010; it was downgraded to an electoral autocracy in 2018.

[12] Tom Ginsburg, *Authoritarian International Law?*, 114 Am. J. Int'l L. 221 (2020).

states. Both governments had engaged in systematic programs of taking over the courts in their countries, purging them of liberals, and promoting like-minded jurists who would advance the political agendas of the governing parties. At the international level, these countries have proven immune to discipline from the European Union or the Council of Europe. That a rich industrialized region could fall prey to democratic backsliding suggests that no country is immune, and also illustrates the weakness of the international mechanisms to enforce democratic norms in the face of strong and sustained political movements.

C. Causes

The causes of this trend of democratic erosion are contested. Some blame the global financial crisis of 2008–09. Technological change may also play a role, especially because it has eroded the media as an authoritative gatekeeper of information. Disruption has allowed anti-democrats to flood the information environment with disinformation.[13]

The neoliberal economic order is a favorite target of critics. By hollowing out industrial workforces in the rich world, it resulted in both job insecurity and increased movement of people, leading to backlash in the rich democracies of the world.[14] The famous "Elephant graph" produced by Branko Milanovic purported to show that the era of globalization benefited a large majority of the global population, but hurt the members of the working classes in rich democracies. The argument was that these groups then rebelled against globalization. However, the data underlying this account is highly sensitive to which countries are included in the analysis, and Milanovic's thesis has not generated consensus.[15] Perhaps we need to look elsewhere for a viable theory of democracy's decline.

My view is that the key factors lie in the realm of culture and identity, rather than economy. Migration is critical here.[16] With the increased ability

[13] David L. Sloss, Tyrants on Twitter: Protecting Democracies from Information Warfare (2022).

[14] *See* Richard H. Steinberg, *The Rise and Decline of a Liberal International Order* (Chapter 1 in this volume).

[15] Caroline Freund, *Deconstructing Branko Milanovic's "Elephant Chart": Does It Show What Everyone Thinks?*, PIIE (Nov. 30, 2016), https://www.piie.com/blogs/realtime-economic-issues-watch/deconstructing-branko-milanovics-elephant-chart-does-it-show.

[16] Jaya Ramji-Nogales, *Migration and International Legal Disorder* (Chapter 14 in this volume).

to move, massive numbers of poorer citizens contributed to the displacement of lower-class wage earners in the rich world; the "Polish plumber" of the European Union was the "illegal immigrant" of California. Even though data seem to suggest that these immigrants raised the average wages of the natives, the sense of losing control provided rich soil for demagogues. Fear of cultural change, in other words, was a key dimension contributing to pressures on established democracies.[17]

Another factor in democratic decline has been the trajectory of certain authoritarian states, particularly Russia and China, that have accumulated material and symbolic power in recent years. Russia and China have become perhaps the most vocal defenders of the sovereigntist view of international order, and have attacked its liberal basis. They had very strong responses to the US policy of regime change in the Middle East, and to the dismemberment of sovereign states as exemplified in the 1999 invasion of Kosovo. They thus perceived, accurately, a threat in the US-led world order. Their responses were measured, but the overall increased leverage that they enjoyed no doubt contributed to pressure on the liberal democratic model.

III. Three Scenarios

In this section, I speculate on three different scenarios and explain how they matter for international law and institutions. One is authoritarian dominance; the second is democratic revival; and the third is a duopoly, in which the United States and China come to a modus vivendi.

The single biggest change that will occur between now and 2050 is the dominance that China will exert over much of Eurasia, Africa, and the Pacific. Because China is extremely unlikely to liberalize or democratize, this means that an authoritarian power will play a central role in the world economy as well as regional—and perhaps global—security. China's strategy to date has been to try to dilute and repurpose the language of liberal democracy, while embedding its own concepts in the United Nations and other fora. The rise of Xi Jinping since 2013 has been accompanied by a new language of international relations, including "win-win" (共赢- "gong ying") foreign policy, "mutually beneficial cooperation," and "a Community

[17] Milada Anna Vachudova, *Ethnopopulism and Democratic Backsliding in Central Europe*, 36(3) E. Eur. Pol. 318 (2020).

of Shared Future for Mankind."[18] China is promoting these concepts at the United Nations, sponsoring resolutions and initiatives to provide legal imprimatur for its policies.[19]

The future of liberal democracy in the international legal order will depend very much on whether these trends continue, and how existing democratic powers react to them. The United States will play an outsized role in this regard, but lacks the weight to dictate responses unilaterally and so will need to work with other democratic powers. In this section, I outline three scenarios. The law, as always, follows power imperfectly, and so the enforcement of the existing norms will depend very much on the relationship between the United States and China as the world's two largest economies, and the world's most powerful democracy and autocracy, respectively.

Before launching into the three scenarios, it is worth identifying a fourth outcome that will surely not occur: a return to a Westphalian golden age. Westphalian sovereignty is an ideal type that international lawyers often use to locate principles like noninterference and sovereign equality, principles embodied in the UN Charter. Professor Gerry Simpson describes this system as embodying "Charter Liberalism": just as in a liberal society, each individual is free to engage in any behavior that does not harm others, so in international society, each state is free to organize its internal affairs in whatever way it likes, so long as it does not abuse its citizens too much, or cause harm to another state.[20] And while powerful states have often contravened the principle of noninterference, it remains a touchstone of the international legal order. Practically, this means that countries are free to pick their regimes, whether an Islamic Republic, Communist dictatorship, or absolute monarchy. Nevertheless, the ideal of absolute autonomy is, and always has been, a fiction. Even the Treaty of Westphalia itself allowed for some international rules governing internal affairs of states.[21] And various forms of coercion to get states to adopt favored policies remain a feature of international life, exercised by the United States, Russia, the European Union, and China. There is no return to an imagined past. Instead, the future of the international legal order will be determined by how these powerful states, with their different visions for international law, interact in the coming decades.

[18] Congyan Cai, The Rise of China and International Law 324–26 (2019).
[19] Gady Epstein, *In the UN, China Uses Threats and Cajolery to Promote Its Worldview*, The Economist, Dec. 7, 2019.
[20] Gerry Simpson, *Two Liberalisms*, 12 Eur. J. Int'l L. 537 (2001).
[21] Stephen Krasner, Sovereignty: Organized Hypocrisy (1999).

The utility of these kinds of scenario-building exercises, which have been engaged in by national defense agencies, large oil companies, and other actors, is to sharpen the alternatives to help inform strategic thinking. The scenarios are in some sense themselves ideal-types, and reality is invariably messier. Nevertheless, the three have starkly different predictions for the future of liberal democracy.

A. Authoritarian Dominance

Since the dawn of the reform and opening era under Deng Xiaoping, China has transformed from a bit player in global affairs to a major power in every field. The extraordinary shift has been driven by massive economic growth, and some political evolution, that has made the PRC more powerful and secure than at any time in its modern history. China's rise raises the question of whether liberal democracy will remain viable outside a core set of rich industrial democracies, such as South Korea, Japan, and Western Europe.

China's relationship with international law during the period of the PRC has been consistently pragmatic, which is quite remarkable given the deployment of that law as an instrument of Western colonialism in Chinese history. International law facilitated the dismemberment of Chinese territory during the Opium Wars and after the Sino-Japanese War of 1895. It justified "Unequal Treaties," which reversed China's traditional hierarchical view of international order by positing white Europeans as the source of civilization. In the post-revolutionary era, the PRC was kept out of the United Nations until 1971.[22] Despite all this, China has engaged with international law since the 1950s, for example, by helping to convene the Bandung Conference in 1955.[23] In the reform and opening era, it has joined many international regimes and signed many treaties, including the World Trade Organization (WTO) and bilateral investment treaties (BITs) that structure international economic law. It has become a major player at the United Nations and other international institutions. And in the face of American rejection of this architecture during the Trump administration, China has emerged as a leading defender of multilateralism.

[22] Phil C. Chan, *China's Approaches to International Law since the Opium War*, 27 Leiden J. Int'l L. 859 (2014).

[23] Bandung, Global History and International Law: Critical Pasts and Pending Futures (Luis Eslava, Michael Fakhri, & Vashuki Nesiah eds., 2017).

China's approach is not fully evolved, but like domestic reform, more experimental and incremental, in keeping with Deng Xiaoping's famous aphorism "cross the river by feeling the stones." There is a mix of compliance and resistance to international norms, depending on the issue at stake.

China has, however, taken a consistent approach. It has been extraordinarily aggressive in pursuing its self-defined core interests. Detlev Vagts coined the term "hegemonic international law" to characterize the attitude of the United States in the early twenty-first century, in the midst of the Global War on Terror.[24] China has similarly sought to avoid obligations that impinge on its flexibility in areas of vital strategic importance, such as the South China Sea. In the face of the Philippines' victory in the arbitration over maritime delimitation there,[25] in which China refused to participate, economic coercion was swift and effective. China's aggressive tactics induced a complete change of course in the Philippines under the government of strongman Rodrigo Duterte. Any hint of recognition of Taiwan brings furious retaliation, and China has stepped up pressure on the island, even sabre rattling before the 2020 re-election of Tsai Ing-Wen. Its diplomats presented a list of fourteen demands to Australian Prime Minister Scott Morrison in late 2020, in response to perceived slights committed by that country. It initiated a border clash with India in the high Himalayas, and has ended tolerance of political liberalism in Hong Kong.

The implications for the international legal order are significant. China has declared that reunification with Taiwan is a non-negotiable core goal. If it attempts to achieve reunification by using force, it would likely succeed. The fact that both countries agree that Taiwan is a part of China means that this may not itself be considered a violation of international law, although other states reacted to the Anti-Secession Law of 2005 as if it were an international matter. The United States has retained a studied ambiguity on these questions, which presents a possibility of future conflict.

The "feelings of the Chinese people" has emerged as a rhetorical trump card. China acts like a thin-skinned bully on certain issues, and a confident superpower on others. This behavior may be self-defeating, and there is a school of thought that says China is acting too aggressively too early. Just as the concentration of power in the person of Mao Zedong led to massive errors during the Cultural Revolution, so the Xi Jinping era is seeing a single

[24] Detlev Vagts, *Hegemonic International Law*, 95 Am. J. Int'l L. 843 (2001).
[25] The South China Sea Arbitration (Phil. v. China), 33 R.I.A.A. 153 (Perm. Ct. Arb. 2016).

individual dominate the system, driving major shifts in behavior. If its aggressive approach, combined with international suspicion related to the novel coronavirus, leads to backlash, China may not end up dominating the twenty-first century. There are also internal sources of brittleness that may present challenges.[26]

However, there are forces at work that will be hard to avoid. China's economy continues to grow at a rapid clip. Its system of techno-authoritarianism means that there is strict control of internal criticism. It is likely to prove a resilient authoritarian.[27] Furthermore, every Western strategy has failed to change China. The idea that the WTO would lead to internal liberalization has obviously not played out.[28] Embedding China in the rules-based international order has led to its takeover of some of that architecture. It has used the nominally private character of its firms to capture markets, even as Western firms are kept out of the Chinese market. It has engaged in systematic programs of state-sponsored industrial espionage. Its investment in military capacity continues at a rapid clip. If engagement failed to domesticate China, neither does confrontation, as practiced by the Trump administration, appear to have paid off.

While China may be unlikely to become a true global hegemon, in the sense of being the dominant power in a unipolar world, that scenario is still a distinct possibility. Should it come to pass, China will act as hegemons do. It will be the single most powerful player in the global standards game, displacing Europe; the so-called Brussels effect may become the Beijing effect.[29] China will also work with other dictatorships to advance a specifically authoritarian international law.

In the first place, this law will be defensive, as we have already seen for example in the 2016 Russia-China Declaration on the Promotion of International Law.[30] While committing to the peaceful settlement of international disputes, the Declaration reaffirms the importance of consent and good faith, a position that "applies equally to all types and stages of dispute

[26] *See* Minxin Pei, *China's Coming Upheaval*, FOREIGN AFF., May–June 2020.

[27] *See* Andrea Kendall-Taylor, Erica Frantz, & Joseph Wright, *The Digital Dictators: How Technology Strengthens Autocracy*, FOREIGN AFF., Mar.–Apr. 2020.

[28] *But see* a nuanced account by Yeling Tan, *Disaggregating "China, Inc": The Hierarchical Politics of WTO Entry*, 53 COMP. POL. STUD. 13 (2020).

[29] ANU BRADFORD, THE BRUSSELS EFFECT: HOW THE EUROPEAN UNION RULES THE WORLD (2020).

[30] Kenneth Anderson, *Text of Russia-China Joint Declaration on Promotion and Principles of International Law*, LAWFARE (July 7, 2016), https://www.lawfareblog.com/text-russia-china-joint-declaration-promotion-and-principles-international-law.

settlement."[31] One might read this as requiring specific consent to each instance of interstate dispute resolution. The Declaration specifically mentions the United Nations Convention on the Law of the Sea (UNCLOS) and the requirement of consistent application of its provisions, "in such a manner that does not impair rights and legitimate interests of States Parties"[32]—a thinly veiled reference to the South China Sea Arbitration. The Declaration also condemns terrorism, unilateral sanctions, and coercive measures outside the context of the Security Council process, while reaffirming state immunity. Though sounding in classical Westphalian sovereignty, the Russia-China Declaration is in fact more sophisticated; it reflects a good deal of learning and experimentation by authoritarian leaders, enabling them to extend their own rule and reinforce each other.[33] A changing balance of power in favor of authoritarians will give these countries greater weight in the formation of international law generally, as well as the ability to deploy specific strategies within the field.

China's more active role would seem to belie its rhetorical emphasis on Westphalian norms of state sovereignty and nonintervention.[34] Yet China has been consistent on one point. China's brand does not include promoting a specific model of domestic governance, and I doubt that this will change in the future. Chinese authoritarianism is decidedly not ideological in terms of its external footprint.[35] This is not the Soviet Union, exporting global communism; nor even Saudi Arabia, whose subsidy of Wahhabism has colored the character of Islam in many parts of the world. China's particular international profile takes Bandung seriously to some extent. China is perfectly willing to let national leaders be chosen through democratic or nondemocratic means. It simply asks those leaders not to cross certain red lines. Obviously, there are exceptions, such as Taiwan, which is considered to be a fundamental part of the national territory. But, to give just one example, China has tolerated multiparty democracy in Mongolia, over which it gave up claims in January 1946, for three decades. The massive Belt and Road Initiative (BRI) incorporates all kinds

[31] *Id.*, para 5.
[32] *Id.*, para 9.
[33] Kendall-Taylor et al., *supra* note 27.
[34] Yin He, *China's Changing Policy on UN Peacekeeping Operations*, Inst. for Security & Dev. Pol'y (July 2007), http://isdp.eu/content/uploads/publications/2007_he_chinas-changing-policy.pdf.
[35] Jessica Chen Weiss, *An Ideological Contest in U.S.-China Relations? Assessing China's Defense of Autocracy*, 28 J. Contemp. China 679 (2019).

of regimes into the warm embrace of a Beijing-centered economic system. This might suggest that democracy in some form has a fighting chance in a China-centered world.

However, the importance of getting along with China may determine who gets elected in democracies. And China's need for certainty in its relations along the Belt and Road may push it to intervene on behalf of particular favored partners who can deliver. China has demonstrated its interest in picking winners in domestic politics in certain cases. For example, it openly backed the Rajapaksa regime in Sri Lanka, as it veered in a strongly authoritarian direction. Similarly, China openly backed the corrupt President Abdulla Yameen in the Maldives, though voters still threw him out of power in 2018. And China's ability to export the technology of repression, particularly in the digital realm, will make it an attractive partner to leaders with authoritarian aspirations.[36]

Thus, even without active promotion of authoritarian governance, there will be hydraulic pressures that will diminish the space of liberal democracy. Criticism of Papa Xi will be de facto forbidden in vast swaths of the earth, even as the ICCPR and national constitutions provide for freedom of speech. Other terms will be given new, thinner meanings. The rule of law will remain a powerful ideal, but its meaning will be transformed: it will mean that the rulers will act through laws, as in the "rule of law with Chinese characteristics."

At the same time, a China-dominated world may very likely be more peaceful than one led by the United States. The country has not fought a war, other than on its borders with Korea and Vietnam, since World War II. It is not going to use armed forces to export autocracy in the same way that the liberal United States has done for democracy, though it surely wants to make the world safe for dictatorship. (This distinguishes China from Russia, whose invasion of Ukraine began well after this chapter was completed.) Thus, we might predict that Chinese hegemony will reinforce the prohibition on the use of military force. Pro-democratic interventions, even those done by regional powers like ECOWAS, will be disfavored, except in the rare cases in which China for some reason favors it, or is not sufficiently interested to push back. Interstate war may still occur among small countries, but Beijing can play a mediating role. So far, its attempts to do so, for example between Sudan and South Sudan, have not been particularly effective. But it may learn.

[36] Kendall-Taylor et al., *supra* note 27; Sloss, *supra* note 13.

International legal discourse will have completely internalized Chinese-promoted virtues and values: principles of amity, sincerity, dialogue, mutual benefit from "win-win" governance, and inclusiveness furthering a "community of shared destiny." The father of these terms, Xi Jinping, will celebrate his ninety-seventh birthday in 2050, just a few months after the PRC's centenary. Xi will be comfortably retired, but still highly influential in resolving disputes among his chosen successors, now in the "seventh generation" of leadership since the founding of the PRC.

Authoritarian international law tends to involve very thin commitments. Wary of unexpected costs, authoritarians are less likely to entrust matters to binding third-party dispute resolution. Their forms of cooperation tend to be informal, thin, and flexible. Only in international economic law—the WTO and the network of BITs—have we observed systematic willingness to submit to third-party dispute resolution, and even here the approach has not been as open as some other countries, having retrenched since 2007.[37]

The model of the BRI lays the groundwork for what authoritarian international law with Chinese characteristics might look like in years to come. The BRI features loose forms of economic cooperation, taking the form of framework agreements that allow for mutual adjustment over time. The BRI also has a hub-and-spokes quality, with each participant interacting bilaterally with Beijing, rather than through a multilateral forum in which smaller nations can cooperate with each other.[38] This approach allows China to maximize leverage vis-à-vis each participating country while minimizing the possibility that others will band together to make demands. Flexibility, a blurring of the public-private divide, and minimal use of third-party dispute resolution at a state-to-state level are key features of this model.

China has in recent years become a skilled player at the United Nations. The United Nations will remain at the center of international legal order, and in some areas, such as the use of force, its norms may be strengthened. China has been a major player, seeking to head off criticism of its internal practices and to promote its interests. A China-dominated United Nations will be less of a force for human rights and democracy. In economic law, China will be quite willing to play by regional and multilateral rules that it has largely shaped, unless there is some reason to do otherwise. Whether the WTO is revived after the assault by the Trump administration, there is no doubt that

[37] Yuwen Li & Cheng Bian, *China's Stance on Investor-State Dispute Settlement: Evolution, Challenges, and Reform Options*, 67 NETH. INT'L L. REV. 503 (2020).

[38] Heng Wang, *China's Approach to the Belt and Road Initiative*, 22 J. INT'L ECON. L. 29 (2019).

a formally open trade regime is in China's interest. At the same time, bilateralism rather than multilateralism tends to be its preferred approach for economic commitments, an approach that allows it to bring its full weight to bear vis-à-vis any particular partner.

Cyber law is one of the great areas in play at present. China has taken an approach to the internet that emphasizes national sovereignty and security, rather than the "free and open internet" pushed by democracies.[39] China's prodigious technical capacities will be brought to bear here, establishing standards that can then be used to ensure its complete internal control, and possibly external control, of what gets seen where. Look for cyber-erasure of Taiwan, meaning the elimination of references to the jurisdiction, and possibly extraterritorial criminalization of "splittists," who sit in its government or call for independence. Even if Taiwan manages to remain independent for the next thirty years, it will have ever narrower scope for action.

Human rights, of course, will remain a centerpiece of global rhetoric, but will be less rigorously enforced than ever. Here, China will be joined by a wide array of illiberal regimes, which have targeted LGBT individuals and religious minorities, in emphasizing national cultures rather than a homogeneous globalized one. Less well appreciated is China's pivot away from an internal policy that tolerated and indeed formally celebrated cultural pluralism. The erasure of internal cultural minorities, currently on display in Xinjiang, Inner Mongolia, and Tibet, will proceed apace. This may have implications for foreign causes that sound in self-determination. The Western Sahara, Kurdistan, Palestine, and other causes will find less support as the forces of order dominate the forces of freedom. Instead, the recently articulated norms of the Shanghai Cooperation Organization against "extremism" and "separatism" will be globalized.

But none of this will mean the complete erasure of democratic discourse on the international plane. Liberal discourses of freedom and self-governance will continue to be popular among national publics. The world's prior hegemon, the United States, may selectively promote these discourses and could provide a counterweight for those fearing the yoke of repression, but its toolkit will be very limited. Democrats may retain the moral high ground, but the institutionalization of democratic norms will diminish on the international level.

[39] Jack Goldsmith & Andrew Keane Woods, *Internet Speech Will Never Go Back to Normal*, The Atlantic, Apr. 25, 2020.

In short, a China-dominated world will not be good for liberal democracy on the international plane. The rich normative architecture of democracy charters and human rights instruments will lay mostly dormant, further eroding protection for human rights and democratic norms.

To be sure, there are many potential roadblocks in the way of this scenario becoming a reality. There are many obstacles to Chinese hegemony, not least its aggressive behavior that, as of 2020, has soured many other nations on its approach. Hegemons, China is learning, are feared and not loved, and there is something of a backlash against China at this writing. And of course, American military power continues to be overwhelming. But even if China's global hegemony is not realistic, "authoritarian dominance" is certainly a realistic scenario. In this scenario, liberal democracy will gradually recede to a small group of core states, and authoritarianism will gradually expand in terms of the number of governments, their resilience, and their use of international law to cooperate with each other and to shape international norms.

B. Democratic Revival

The United States has just barely survived its experiment with authoritarian populism in the person of Donald Trump. Although the 1990s, when the liberal order seemed to be the only game in town, will never return, our recent "near miss" may trigger efforts to shore up America's political and economic vulnerabilities. This could lead to a renewal of liberal democracy at home and a return to a vigorous set of alliances abroad. One might even contemplate a revival of the idea of a "community of democracies," which as it stands is a relatively unimportant international organization,[40] but could be a more deeply integrated set of alliances, linked by trade and common values. Perhaps the democracies will work with each other to achieve a partial decoupling from a prickly Chinese regime that has shown itself willing to use maximal leverage in response to fairly minor perceived slights. This implies a trade system that is less focused on the WTO and more focused on serving strategic interests. Groupings like the "Five Eyes" (which brings together Australia, Canada, New Zealand, the United Kingdom, and the

[40] Formed as an intergovernmental organization in 2000, and with thirty-one current members, the group is based on the idea that democracies should self-consciously engage in collective action to defend common interests. *See* COMMUNITY OF DEMOCRACIES, https://community-democracies.org/.

United States) could expand from a focus on security and intelligence to encompass common liberal traditions and approaches.

If liberalism is to survive and thrive, the existence of current international laws and institutions that favor democracy may play an important role in preventing decline. The UN human rights machinery has lost credibility in some quarters because of its obsessive focus on Israel, while ignoring severe repression by dictatorships. But regional machinery has been more effective at both developing norms and enforcing them. Already we have seen a series of pro-democratic regional interventions. For example, the Organization of American States (OAS) played a role in resolving the Honduran crisis of 2009, when President Manuel Zelaya was removed from office and spirited out of the country. The OAS has had less success with Venezuela. But the other Bolivarian regimes of Ecuador and Bolivia have remained in the democratic camp. Similarly in Africa, the African Union and ECOWAS have conducted a series of regional interventions that have staved off would-be authoritarians. The African Union has gone further than other international organizations by specifically targeting unconstitutional changes in government, a category which includes not only coups and mercenary takeovers but also manipulation of term limits by incumbent leaders.[41] Since most democracies these days die through incumbent takeover rather than military coup, this is a particularly important norm.

The return of a liberal order will not mean that every project of the 1990s is plausible. The International Criminal Court (ICC) has suffered attacks on its capacity by the United States as well as African countries. The willingness of the ICC to indict national political leaders around the issue of electoral violence has produced backlash. But international criminal law is not an essential liberal democratic project.

At the same time, human rights will do much better in a liberal world. The machinery of the United Nations will remain ineffectual, but national level pressures from Europe and the Western powers will have a strong deterrent effect on the worst abuses in some smaller countries. Regional human rights bodies will revive and thrive. Their jurisprudence on rights of speech and association, which are at the core of the liberal project, will become definitive and will lead to national level compliance even by some hybrid regimes.

[41] Lome Declaration of July 2000 on the Framework for an OAU Response to Unconstitutional Changes of Government, AHG/Decl.5 (XXXVI), July 12, 2000.

In this scenario, the European Union will eventually grapple with the presence of nondemocratic Hungary in its midst. The Brexit experience will demonstrate that having a country leave the Union is feasible, and the Europeans will threaten to disband the entire Union and re-form it without Hungary, instituting large tariffs on Hungarian goods entering the new European Union. The resulting economic pressures may eventually unseat Viktor Orban. The European Union will allow Poland to remain in the European Union after Polish voters reject the current illiberal government and a new liberal government is voted in.

The endurance of liberal democracy, giving substance to the rich normative architecture of democracy, does not mean that every country will become a democracy. The resurgence of liberal power will survive because it won't overreach. Liberalism in the 1990s came crashing down on the shore of the Iraq war, as well as its support for a global neoliberal regime that benefited wealthy elites on the promise of redistribution that never occurred. A revival of liberal democracy will, paradoxically, require recognizing that authoritarian powers have legitimate spheres of influence that should be respected. Chinese power in Asia is sure to rise. But it has already shown that it can coexist with vital liberal countries such as South Korea and Japan. (Taiwan is, of course, a special problem.) Similarly, NATO will have to come to terms with Russia, an inherently authoritarian power. Russia's immediate neighborhood will be in its control, but there may be opportunities for liberal advances in particular countries so long as they do not threaten Russia militarily. As I write, a liberal government has taken over in Armenia, but is remaining in the Russian military sphere. These kinds of opportunities will require restraint on the part of large Western powers.

Yet this scenario will also require aggressive policing when a country appears to be backsliding too severely. Refraining from unilateral "regime change" interventions is the first order of business for a chastened United States, but multilateral interventions may still be worth pursuing in some parts of the world to prevent coups and other sudden democratic collapses. In terms of the other more serious threat, the risk of slow erosion, international cooperation may be less effective. Deploying nonmilitary resources, including economic access and soft power, can go a long way in the absence of the use of force. But at the end of the day, the direction that democracies take will be determined by their citizens, and in our era of nationalism, liberalism is under threat in many countries.

International economic law will have adjusted to recognize a growing role for the state in national economies, in democracies as well as dictatorships. Rules for state-owned enterprises and publicly subsidized markets will require sophisticated negotiations, but the collective market power of liberal democracies can be coordinated to keep rules from being abused by statist economies.

Liberalism's survival will require a robust engagement in the realms of cyber governance, artificial intelligence, and other technological developments.[42] The precise shape of this engagement is not yet clear, but liberal states will need to agree on a common set of principles and approaches, instantiated in technical standards, to ensure that technology does not erode democracy. It may involve a modus vivendi with large authoritarian powers. It probably involves engaging in a serious revisiting of the current free-market approach to companies like Facebook and Google, which have tremendous power to control political messaging. More vigorous antitrust enforcement is now in the works, although the tools of antitrust were not devised with platform economies in mind. Some solution to the political dominance of these small number of firms will be essential.[43] In turn, this will require transnational regulatory harmonization, and possibly even formal agreements, so that the platforms do not simply relocate to low-regulation jurisdictions.

If this scenario is to become a reality, it will require American leadership and cooperation from the couple dozen mature democracies around the world. Together they can help liberal democracy overcome its current malaise to develop enhanced capacity to coordinate regulatory approaches, while allowing relatively unrestricted flows of goods and services among democracies. The challenge of mass migration will have to be addressed as well.

C. Duopoly

If the first two scenarios rely on the dominance of China and the United States, respectively, the third is based on the cooperation of the two. The

[42] Jared Cohen & Richard Fontaine, *Uniting the Techno-Democracies: How to Build Digital Cooperation*, Foreign Aff., Nov.–Dec. 2020.

[43] Francis Fukuyama, Barak Richman, & Ashish Goel, *How to Save Democracy from Technology*, Foreign Aff., Jan.–Feb. 2021.

international legal order is founded on sovereign equality, but some sovereigns are more equal than others. Many of the greatest problems facing mankind will require common action that can only be achieved if large powers coordinate their policies in areas of vital interests. The duopoly idea is that the United States and China come to a modus vivendi to accommodate each other's core interests.

In the security sphere, this will require accommodation of Chinese interests in the Western Pacific. This means a creative resolution of the Taiwan problem in a complex federation that allows permanent autonomy for the "renegade province," avoiding the mistakes of the now failed Hong Kong experiment. The autonomy would be externally guaranteed, and the deployment of Chinese military forces on the island would be strictly limited. Other Western Pacific powers would have to reduce their cooperation with the US military, perhaps being limited to strictly defensive postures.

International economic law will remain relatively open and markets will be competitive. China and the United States will continue to engage in interdependent economic relations, and WTO rules will remain a floor for global trade relations. At the same time, the WTO exception for free trade areas will allow for special spheres of economic influence by both major powers. The recently enacted Regional Comprehensive Economic Partnership, which brings in states from Australia to Japan, provides a framework, and may provide a multilateral counterpart to China's so-far bilateral approach.

In this scenario, the very weak current rules of international environmental law are reinvigorated by US-China cooperation on the existential issue of climate change. A framework treaty is negotiated in the 2020s that effectively confronts problems of carbon leakage and uses the market power of the G2 to ensure compliance by smaller states. Technological innovations in carbon sequestration allow the world to begin to remove carbon from the atmosphere, although the untold suffering of rising seas and weather-related disasters continues unabated. Still, close coordination of the two countries' scientific communities is facilitated by blockchain-based schemes that reduce levels of industrial espionage and ensure that dual-use technologies are restricted to their nonmilitary usages. Furthermore, the two countries develop a common approach to the Law of the Sea that facilitates exploration of the deep seabed, while saving the world's fisheries from the collapse that was threatened earlier in the century. Finally, there is great potential for cooperation on global public health issues, something which the COVID-19 virus has made highly salient. The cooperation of the two largest powers helps tackle global problems.

In this scenario, liberal democracy stands a fighting chance. China is no friend of liberal democracy, but neither is it an implacable enemy, when practiced outside its own borders. The United States will surely have to accommodate China's preferences in its sphere of influence, and there may be tensions that arise for the democracies of the Western Pacific. But we could see a flourishing of liberal democracy in regions like Latin America and Africa. This outcome will depend on a particular approach from the United States and Europe, namely, not to be overly aggressive in pushing for regime change, but rather to let countries' internal dynamics play out. In this sense the outcome is not unlike that described earlier under the "democratic revival scenario," except that the relative sizes of the democratic and nondemocratic spheres are more balanced. The United States and China will need to have some rules of engagement in this regard, but given China's generally non-ideological stance, this should be feasible.

IV. Prospects

To summarize, I see three possibilities for global order going forward, each with its own implications for liberal democracy. The three can be arrayed in terms of the relative space for liberal democracy as a going concern around the world. In the event of liberal resurgence, liberal norms and international cooperation will thrive, not just in the core but in a growing number of states. This, as noted, cannot take place at the barrel of a gun. But liberal democracies remain attractive places and contribute an outsized share to global culture. Their brand may be currently diminished, but democracies are capable of reinvention.

In the duopoly scenario, the United States and China will cooperate to solve global problems and agree to disagree about the others' systems of governance. This will require recognition of a Chinese sphere of influence in much of Central Asia and the Western Pacific.[44] Countries within this sphere will move in an illiberal direction, in ways that are already being

[44] Graham Allison, Destined for War: Can America and China Escape Thucydides's Trap? (2017).

demonstrated in the Philippines and India. Global democracy promotion will not disappear, but for practical purposes it will be limited to the regions of Latin America and Africa and led largely by local institutions like the OAS and ECOWAS.

The scenario of authoritarian dominance will have profound implications for international law as a whole. Authoritarians, and especially China, do not emphasize thick forms of legally binding cooperation but instead utilize thinner forms of cooperation that are less intrusive, at least outside the economic sphere. They have no interest in enforcing human rights abroad, and fear the open discourse associated with liberal democracy. As it stands, they are developing tools to undermine democracies, though so far these have only been deployed around the margins. In this scenario, the number and quality of democracies will continue to diminish, and freedom will remain a dim hope for many of the world's citizens.

There are certain commonalities across the scenarios. There will continue to be some space for liberal democracy on the international legal plane in all of them: no one is going to retract the ICCPR, as it is too ineffectual to be worth dismantling. International norms related to democratic participation, human rights, and the rule of law will remain on paper, even if their practice is affected by global political developments. And in none of these scenarios does the United Nations become a significant actor, even as it is the authoritative keeper of many of the norms. Instead, the action of enforcement will turn on lower-level actors, at either the national, regional, or plurilateral level.

Of course, these three scenarios do not exhaust the possibilities. But they do capture alternatives that are sufficiently different to allow us to consider normative implications going forward. I take it as an assumption that the authoritarian scenario is worth avoiding, even though I do not have space to work out a complete normative evaluation of the other two. But it is worth noting that, whether duopoly or liberal resurgence turns out to better describe the world in 2050, the strategy for today's democratic leaders is similar. They should invest in the existing normative architecture and provide support for it by explicitly prioritizing liberal democracy in their international relations, including trade and investment. Unilateral use of force should be avoided, because much of the authoritarian backlash that has emerged in this century is a direct reaction to US efforts to engineer regime change by military means. But regional entities that have intervened militarily to support democracy, such as ECOWAS, should be supported and reaffirmed, both materially and symbolically.

Liberal democracy is not the end of history, as developments in the last two decades have well shown. As my colleague Dan Slater put it in conversation, "democracy is a grind," requiring constant hard work in difficult conditions. It is not pretty, and there are missteps and severe challenges. Being a citizen of a democracy can be depressing, as leaders continually come up short. But it is the least bad alternative at present among the forms of government on offer.

4

Revolution or Collapse?

Climate Change and the International Legal Order

Maxine Burkett

I. Introduction

Given the current state of the climate, the international legal order (ILO) must evolve simply to avoid collapse. All elements of the ILO either impact or are impacted by the changing climate. The climate crisis is not a discrete issue or one causal factor to manage. It is the *context* within which law, economy, and culture will develop while attempting to avoid the worst outcomes. This chapter analyzes the geophysical phenomenon of climate change as a key frame for the discourse on the twenty-first-century international legal order. I hope to galvanize action that is commensurate with the true options before us: revolution or collapse.

With each release of the Intergovernmental Panel on Climate Change's (IPPC) comprehensive assessments, preeminent physical and social scientists state with great clarity the scale and urgency of the crisis. Because they are consensus documents based on peer-reviewed articles, the IPCC Assessment Reports are inherently conservative and always time-delayed in their accounts. In other words, the documents do not reflect outlier projections, however sound, nor those published at or close to the time of Report release. As a result, even the troubling conclusions of the 2018 Special Report[1] are likely to be understated. Nonetheless, the documents recount remarkable findings, detailing the significant projected disruption to current socioeconomic systems and the lives and livelihoods of all human and non-human beings.

[1] Int'l Panel on Clim. Change [IPCC], *Global Warming of 1.5°C. An IPCC Special Report on the impacts of global warming of 1.5°C above pre-industrial levels and related global greenhouse gas emission pathways, in the context of strengthening the global response to the threat of climate change, sustainable development, and efforts to eradicate poverty* (2018), https://www.ipcc.ch/sr15/.

Maxine Burkett, *Revolution or Collapse?* In: *Is the International Legal Order Unraveling?*. Edited by: David L. Sloss, Oxford University Press. DOI: 10.1093/oso/9780197652800.003.0005

Pronouncements of climate change producing a "new normal"—whether it is melting in the Arctic region, continent-consuming wildfires in Australia, or erosive flooding in densely populated delta communities worldwide—are jarring and, at the same time, incomplete. In fact, climate change is not a static phenomenon producing a definitive and steady state of extremes, however new and unfamiliar. It is a process of continuous change as average global temperatures rise over time. Further, the *rate* of change is also increasing over time. In sum, we can expect more significant disorder, more swiftly.

Because of its causes and effects, and the deeply lopsided nature of them, "climate change" is a geopolitical term as well as a geophysical one.[2] One's contribution and vulnerability to climate change is a consequence of historical and systemic inequality. It reflects a series of decisions and differential inputs by states and multinational actors across geographic and temporal scales. To date, however, international environmental law (IEL) has been the primary legal domain to address climate change. Those engaged in other areas of law have not seen their relevance to it. Legal scholars and practitioners actively disregard the significance of climate change and ecological integrity,[3] despite the global consequences. The effect of this positioning is that environmental law, constructed with the limited capacity to save the trees, is now freighted with saving each and every forest, as well as the peoples and political economies that depend upon them.[4] Carmen Gonzalez diagnoses IEL as a "field in crisis" because it confronts problems like carbon pollution and ecosystem degradation that are intricately embedded in the existing economic order, an order which IEL cannot meaningfully touch.[5]

In its effort to understand the current direction of the international order, the underlying premise of this volume is that the prior contexts,

[2] For deeper exploration of the expanded significance of the term, *see* Maxine Burkett, *Justice and Climate Migration*, *in* CLIMATE REFUGEES: BEYOND THE LEGAL IMPASSE? (Simon Behrman & Avidan Kent eds., 2018).

[3] *See, e.g.*, Luca Enriques et al., *The Basic Governance Structure: Minority Shareholders and Non-Shareholder Constituencies*, *in* THE ANATOMY OF CORPORATE LAW: A COMPARATIVE AND FUNCTIONAL APPROACH 93 (Reinier Kraakman et al. eds., 3d ed. 2017) (stating that the proper channel to address corporate impacts on environmental degradation is environmental law, not corporate law, and that "the use of legal rules and standards . . . to promote interests extraneous to the corporate form is, almost by definition, not corporate law"). *But see* Sarah E. Light, *The Law of the Corporation as Environmental Law*, 71 STAN. L. REV. 137 (2019).

[4] For further exploration of this quite useful analogy, *see* Klaus Bosselmann, *Losing the Forest for the Trees: Environmental Reductionism in the Law*, 2 SUSTAINABILITY 2424 (2010).

[5] Carmen Gonzalez, *Global Justice in the Anthropocene*, *in* ENVIRONMENTAL LAW AND GOVERNANCE FOR THE ANTHROPOCENE 223, 229 (Louis J. Kotze ed., 2017).

frameworks, and institutional actors will shape the path forward—either by committing anew to the rule of law or regressing toward lawlessness. This chapter examines how the climate system—disrupted by those very contexts/frameworks/institutional actors—will serve as the backdrop and a driver of a perpetually more unpredictable world. To determine whether revolution or gradual evolution will prevail, the difference between prognosis and prescription matters. The climate crisis is dire and is rapidly hurtling us toward unprecedented disruption. Collapse is completely plausible. International legal order based on the rule of law is not guaranteed. And, as I will argue, given international law's complicity in producing the current state of affairs, a change is necessary. Any intervention or prescription to arrest unmanageable disruption must aim for a fundamental while rapid shift in the international legal order.

This chapter will discuss the core assumptions in international law and related modalities in ILO that have gotten us to this precipice. It will explore the key levers of the ILO that elide the environment, generally, and the climate system, specifically, and then make an argument for a more sophisticated understanding of what a "new and everchanging *abnormal*" means for any sound attempt at prognosticating about or planning for order in the twenty-first century. Consistent with the book's framing, "revolution" appears inevitable, as a descriptive and normative matter. As a descriptive matter, unless we act quickly, climate change will lead to revolutionary changes in the world. Section II defends this claim. As a normative matter, we need to make revolutionary changes in international law and ILO to avert catastrophe. I defend this claim in section III. Section III, generally, addresses the assumptions about the natural world embedded in the current law and law's role in producing climate disruption and entrenched inequities, inequities that increase the climate vulnerability of billions of people. Section III closes with a consideration of the ways in which these centuries-old North-South dynamics are redolent in international law, in code and in practice, and how that dynamic impacts our (in)ability to address effectively the disparate impacts of climate change. Section IV follows with a closer look at the specific impacts of climate change on North-South inequality, the nagging and worsening crises of international borders and migration, and the prospect of increased national and regional conflict. These constitute just a handful of the climate-induced disruptions that will test ILO's resilience and, more consequential, its ability to evolve to respond to the radical disruption that climate change will cause to both geophysical and legal systems.

II. Understanding Climate Change as Context

A. The Climate Forecast

The climate system, on which we rely, is set to experience an average global temperature increase of at least 3° Celsius around mid-century. Without major emissions reduction, the increase in annual average global temperatures could reach 5° Celsius above preindustrial times by 2081.[6] For context, an increase of just 1.1° Celsius above normal, our current status, has produced summer 2020's simultaneous dry lightning storms, firenadoes,[7] red-orange skies and smoke-filled air crippling the American West, the massive and repetitive hurricanes hitting the gulf coast, as well as 100° Fahrenheit heat waves in Siberia buckling oil pipelines and producing arctic wildfires, massive sinkholes, and methane explosions—among innumerable other global disasters.

The projections published in national and international assessment documents detailing this change are not hyperbolic. As consensus documents, the IPCC reports and related US National Climate Assessments are conservative and time-delayed in their accounts of the state of the climate. Studies have found that international policy makers are relying on outdated projections that underestimate the depth and intensity of change and the cuts in emissions necessary to stave off greater devastation.[8]

The socioeconomic consequences are just as dire. Climate change will "decimate" the global economy at even the lower average temperature increases predicted. At just 2° Celsius, the world would suffer losses totaling 13 percent of global GDP and $69 trillion of damages.[9] According to the UN Special Rapporteur on extreme poverty and human rights, there are life-or-death consequences for everyone, and especially the global poor: "Even

[6] D.R. Easterling et al., *Our Globally Changing Climate, in* I CLIMATE SCIENCE SPECIAL REPORT: FOURTH NATIONAL CLIMATE ASSESSMENT 35, 42 (D.J. Wuebbles et al. eds., 2017).

[7] Alicia Victoria Lozano, *Rare "Firenado" Spotted in California as Heat Wave Scorches State*, NBC NEWS, Aug. 15, 2020.

[8] *See generally* Patrick T. Brown & Ken Caldeira, *Greater Future Global Warming Inferred From Earth's Recent Energy Budget*, NATURE, Dec. 07, 2017, at 45; Georgina Gustin, *The Most Accurate Climate Models Predict Greater Warming, Study Shows*, INSIDE CLIMATE NEWS (Dec. 6, 2017), https://insideclimatenews.org/news/06122017/climate-change-warming-forecast-worst-case-best-models-ipcc-study. According to a 2017 study, there is a 93% chance that the planet will warm more than 4° Celsius—previous studies suggested that it was 62 percent. Four degrees of warming would eradicate coral reefs, create prolonged heat waves, and drown small islands, if they have not already been abandoned by the lack of freshwater and arable land.

[9] IPCC Special Report, *supra* note 1, at 264, 453.

under the best-case scenario, hundreds of millions will face food insecurity, forced migration, disease and death. Climate change threatens the future of human rights and risks undoing the last 50 years of progress in development, global health and poverty reduction."[10]

The lived experience of that change, and how it varies across human populations, reflects broader geopolitical disharmonies. The impacts to human health, for example, are worrisome and telling. One documented health threat, extreme humid heat, has more than doubled in frequency since 1979 in some coastal subtropical locations. Despite our bodies being well adapted for heat, extreme heat remains one of the most dangerous natural hazards to human physiology, with tens of thousands of fatalities occurring in the deadliest events so far this century.[11] Under the business as usual scenario, in as few as fifty-five years temperatures in parts of South Asia and the Middle East will regularly exceed the upper limit of the human body.[12] In fact, countries and communities closer to the equator or located in tropical or subtropical climates are projected to experience a large increase in future heat wave–related excess mortality, absent significant adaptations.[13] There is also evidence of grievous public health emergencies just short of death, as heat waves induce the onset of cardiovascular diseases, respiratory disease, and diabetes, among other things. European countries and the United States will have smaller percent increases in heat wave–related excess mortality and morbidity in the near term, whereas countries like Colombia, the Philippines, and Brazil are among those at the frontlines.[14]

Similarly, a recent study garnering popular attention found that the "human climate niche" is under unparalleled threat. The niche, according to researchers, describes the narrow part of the "climatic envelope" available on the globe in which human populations have consistently resided. Given current emissions, the geographical position of this niche will move so dramatically over the coming fifty years that more than 3.5 billion people may live outside the climate conditions that have been amenable to human survival for the past six thousand years. Without either a level of climate mitigation

[10] Special Rapporteur on Extreme Poverty and Human Rights, *Rep. on Climate Change and Poverty*, U.N. Doc. A/HRC/41/39 (July 17, 2019) [hereinafter *Special Rapporteur Report*].

[11] Colin Raymond, Tom Matthews, & Radley M. Horton, *The Emergence of Heat and Humidity Too Severe For Human Tolerance*, Science Advances, May 6, 2020, at 6; Yuming Guo et al., *Quantifying Excess Deaths Related to Heatwaves under Climate Change Scenarios: A Multicountry Time Series Modelling Study*, PLOS Medicine, July 31, 2018.

[12] Raymond, Matthews, & Horton, *supra* note 11.

[13] Guo et al., *supra* note 11.

[14] *Id.*

not evident in any present agreement, or contentious and increasingly dangerous migration, average annual temperatures presently found in the Sahara will envelop up to a third of humanity. In sheer magnitude and systemic strain, human migration is one of the most impactful indicators of the complexity of climate change.[15] Extant migration governance is already poor and impacting the ILO. The acute strain of just one climate impact threatens to buckle key constituent systems of that order.[16]

Of course, climate crises do not act independently. They are overlapping and simultaneous, compounding individual effects. As witnessed in the days following Hurricane Laura in Louisiana, the storm was followed by crushing and deadly heat as well as a conveyor belt of subsequent storms. Without aggressive emissions reduction, researchers estimate that by 2100 major climate hazards such as heat waves, fires, floods, and precipitation events will frequently strike the world's population concurrently. Some tropical coastal areas, including the most exposed regions of coastal Southeast Asia, East and West Africa, and the Atlantic coast of South and Central America, will face up to six simultaneous disasters under a business-as-usual emissions scenario.[17] Future projections are disconcerting and are unable to account for "climate surprises," as the worst effects may occur in a nonlinear or abrupt fashion.[18] Researchers cannot predict with accuracy the onset of "tipping points," or thresholds, at which tiny changes can push a system into a completely new state. They do, however, know what is at stake, such as the disappearance of the Amazon rainforest, coral reef die-off, shifting of the West African and Indian monsoons, or all of the above, among others.[19] These tipping points usher in shifts in the state and viability of global ecosystems.

These descriptions of global trends can obscure the community and household level toll of climate change, which is dystopian in the retelling. A vivid description of the 2014 flooding in the United Kingdom effectively conveys the climate surprises that hit even the wealthiest of countries: "Not everyone

[15] *See* Maxine Burkett, *Behind the Veil: Climate Migration, Regime Shift, and a New Theory of Justice*, 53 Harv. C.R.-C.L. L. Rev. 445 (2018).

[16] *See infra* section IV.B.

[17] Camilo Mora et al., *Broad Threat to Humanity from Cumulative Climate Hazards Intensified by Greenhouse Gas Emissions*, Nature Climate Change, Nov. 19, 2018, at 1062.

[18] Int'l Panel on Clim. Change [IPCC], *AR5 Synthesis Report: Climate Change 2014. Contribution of Working Groups I, II and III to the Fifth Assessment Report of the Intergovernmental Panel on Climate Change*, (2014), https://www.ipcc.ch/report/ar5/syr/.

[19] Robert McSweeney, *Explainer: Nine "Tipping Points" That Could Be Triggered by Climate Change*, CarbonBrief (Feb. 10, 2020), https://www.carbonbrief.org/explainer-nine-tipping-points-that-could-be-triggered-by-climate-change?utm_campaign=RevueCBWeeklyBriefing&utm_medium=email&utm_source=Revue%20newsletter%20.

watching the news coverage of the . . . flooding . . . will be aware, for example, of the fields full of dead badgers and raw sewage or of rats invading homes to escape newly submerged sewers—or of the complex ecosystem implications for crops, planned production patterns, economic futures."[20] The upheaval to the legal and regulatory infrastructure mirrors the level of comprehensive disruption on the ground. The international legal community, however, has not fully appreciated the system-wide exposure and vulnerability of the field.

B. Implications for ILO: Revolution or Collapse

Avoiding worst-case scenarios, which by all accounts are catastrophic, requires far steeper greenhouse gas emissions reductions than previously calculated. At present, therefore, collapse of multiple systems is a plausible outcome. The nature and scope of the upheaval could range from the collapse of multiple domestic economies to the collapse of international relations due to domination of stronger countries over the weak to the complete collapse of international institutions and perhaps civilizations. At this moment of unabated carbon emissions, the degree of breakdown is uncertain and difficult to forecast. Given the existential nature of the threat, any adequate response will likely require a "radical," "fundamental," or "seismic" "transformation."[21] Of course, the scope of the geophysical crisis is, perhaps, fundamentally at odds with the traditional rule of law, which is meant to serve as a "bulwark against hasty change."[22] Arguably, the rule of law is inherently opposed to revolution and provides steady friction to slow evolution.[23] According to London School of Economics (LSE) Law Professor Stephen Humphreys, the law is the vehicle that ensures that "*past* decisions, *past* claims, *past* reasoning, *past* justification have effect into the future."[24] But, he rightly asks: "How far into the future?" Indeed, the obsolescence of firm border agreements, like those

[20] Anna Grear & Conor Gearty, Editorial, *Choosing a Future: The Social and Legal Aspects of Climate Change*, 5 J. HUM. RTS. & ENV'T 1, 1–7 (2014).
[21] *See id.*; *Special Rapporteur Report*, *supra* note 10; Stephen Humphreys, *Climate Justice: The Claim of the Past*, 5 J. HUM. RTS. & ENV'T 134 (2014); Robin Kundis Craig, *"Stationarity Is Dead"—Long Live Transformation: Five Principles for Climate Change Adaptation Law*, 34 HARV. ENV'T L. REV. 9 (2010) (exhorting the law to declare, "long live transformation!").
[22] Humphreys, *supra* note 21, at 146.
[23] *Id.*
[24] *Id.* (emphasis added).

between Italy and Switzerland, for example,[25] demonstrate the indifference of the climate crisis—and the ushering in of unprecedented legal concepts, like a fluid border. Italy's northern border moves with the natural, morphological boundaries of the shared glacier's frontiers. The glacier is melting and borders are shifting. Past agreement leads to novel, contemporary disputes and indeterminate futures.

Bridging current agreements with future exigencies need not lead inevitably to lawlessness or abandonment of the rule of law. As Humphreys explains, however, "we cannot expect the necessary 'evolution' of law simply to take place because it is 'right' or 'reasonable.'"[26] The global economy is saturated with fossil fuels and other carbon intensive processes. The story of how we got to this moment is complex. Suffice it to say, however, that the way forward may be fundamentally disruptive to the ILO as currently constructed.

III. From Root to Branch: Environment, Global Divides, and the Complicity of International Law

In our efforts to slow or arrest climate change, global leaders have generally favored low-hanging fruit. Few have explored the root of the problem, which is a fundamental misapprehension of the environment. Opening with an exploration of critical research on the law's assumptions about the natural world, this section explores the dominant worldviews and approaches that have ignored, subsumed, or compartmentalized the natural environment in contemporary legal and social orders. It will also explore the way in which colonialism disseminated and accelerated the impacts of this worldview and effectuated the political economy that has destabilized the global environment. Finally, this section considers the ways in which centuries-old North-South dynamics pervade the international order—in law and in practice—and how that dynamic impacts our ability to address adequately the extreme and inequitable impacts of climate change.

[25] Elza Bouhassira, *As the Climate Shifts a Border Moves*, GlacierHub (Apr. 30, 2020), https://glacierhub.org/2020/04/30/as-the-climate-shifts-a-border-moves/.

[26] Humphreys, *supra* note 21, at 147.

A. The Stationarity Myth and Global Instability

The predominate approaches to the environment[27] and its health or degradation belie a fundamental misapprehension of it and the way in which its integrity is paramount to our existence and overall well-being. In her critique of US domestic environmental and natural resources law, Robin Craig notes that the fields are based on assumptions of ecological stationarity, which is the notion that natural systems "fluctuate within an unchanging envelope of variability."[28] This notion has never accurately depicted the dynamism of the natural world, and it remains an antiquated and dangerous operating assumption in an increasingly climate-disrupted world. Further, according to Craig, an assumption that pervades Anglo-American laws is that anthropogenic change is "non-transformative and hence reversible."[29] Climate change, however, is proving just the opposite: we have drastically transformed and degraded our natural environment and irreversibility[30] inheres in that transformation.

The horizon for lawmaking is also inconsistent with the longer arc and complex character of the environment. According to Klaus Bosselmann, short-term-oriented decision-making is hostile to these complexities and often conflates the environment with natural resources, a potentially fatal flaw as it turns out.[31] Natarajan and Khoday also note that conceptions of development and economy in international law are equally reductionist, transforming nature into "limitless commodification processes."[32] This approach furthers a disciplinary commitment to infinite economic growth and technocratic, market-based solutions,[33] which are severely limited in their

[27] Like Natarajan and Khoday, I also use nature and environment interchangeably, adopting their rationale for collapsing the terms as well as their critique of terms like "environmental law." Usha Natarajan & Kishan Khoday, *Locating Nature: Making and Unmaking International Law*, 27 Leiden J. Int'l L. 573, 575 n.6 (2014) ("We adopt the ordinary usage of these terms in the mainstream discipline to reference our physical surroundings in a general sense. The term 'environmental law' to some extent assumes that the environment can be identified, and that problems in the environment 'out there' can be addressed by applying law to human activity. This article argues the impossibility of such an endeavour as law is itself situated within the broader constitutive context of how humans collectively self-organize their relationship with their physical surroundings.").

[28] Craig, *supra* note 21, at 6.

[29] *Id.* at 22.

[30] Susan Solomon, *Irreversible Climate Change Due to Carbon Dioxide Emissions*, PNAS, Feb. 10, 2009, at 1704.

[31] Klaus Bosselmann, *A Vulnerable Environment: Contextualizing Law with Sustainability*, 2 J. Hum. Rts. & Env't 45, 49 (2011).

[32] Natarajan & Khoday, *supra* note 27, at 576.

[33] *Id.*

ability to curb dynamic and comprehensive ecological calamities like climate change.[34]

Accordingly, in addition to a limiting conception of natural systems within a static envelope, the environment is reduced to its economic utility. It is at once fixed and purely instrumental in value. A more appropriate response to its actual dynamism is to construct regulatory goals and legal mechanisms, according to Craig, that center on the concept of change itself.[35] Uniquely relevant to the present discussion, to also deliver equitable approaches amidst such change presents a particular challenge for international law as, according to Humphreys, "the law—human rights law, trade law—is not ready made to deliver climate justice";[36] that is, equitable responses based on distributional and corrective justice, among other climate justice principles.

B. Pruning the "Environment": Compartmentalization and Fragmentation in Practice and Worldview

The fundamental misapprehension of nature is related to prevailing Western understandings of the human relationship to the natural world. Many scholars have explored the deep roots of these understandings, as well as its departure from non-Western worldviews and even worldviews within the West that did not prevail.[37] Exploring the foundations of the law and its approach to the natural environment is critical to understanding both international law's complicity in the current climate crisis, the embedded limitations it has to respond to the crisis, and the unequivocal need for revolution in order to maintain order through the rule of law while avoiding collapse.

International law emerged from a particular soil. Bosselmann points to "European cosmology" as a root cause and explanatory factor in the emergence of "economic rationality."[38] Using the acronym DAMAGE,[39]

[34] *Id.* at 592.

[35] Craig, *supra* note 21, at 21. *See also* Bosselmann, *supra* note 31, at 47–48.

[36] Humphreys, *supra* note 21, at 141.

[37] Bosselmann, *supra* note 4, at 2436 (noting that there is "a wealth of sustainability wisdom in the history of all cultures and European culture is no exception"). Looking prior to European Enlightenment is also revealing. According to Natarajan and Khoday, "Before [the European Enlightenment], societal change was assumed to be cyclical, with advances in knowledge, economy, and culture followed by stabilization and eventual decline. Examples include the Aristotelian perception of rising and falling civilizations, or the Augustinian notion of humanity's journey from creation to revelation." Natarajan & Khoday, *supra* note 27, at 588.

[38] Bosselmann, *supra* note 4, at 2430.

[39] *See also* Bosselmann, *supra* note 31, at 47.

Bosselmann notes that this cosmology is rooted in: dualism, anthropocentrism, materialism, atomism, greed, and economism. While all are relevant, at least three are uniquely relevant to the present state of international law and its historic roots. Dualism emphasizes separateness rather than complementarity and is manifest in Western concepts of assumed dichotomies: human versus nature, individual versus community, and—perhaps most consequentially as it relates to delayed climate action—economy versus environment. Materialism has roots in the Enlightenment and is linked with Descartes' mind-matter dichotomy, which tends to view matter as dead, inert, and without inherent value.[40] A disenchantment with nature is a dangerous consequence and, as Bosselmann explains, "leads to the belief that humans can control and rearrange the material world purely as a matter of utility, with no moral or ethical constraints, duties or obligations."[41] Finally, the atomistic or "reductionist"[42] worldview has yielded ill-fitting concepts, such as stationarity, in that it seeks to atomize complex objects, assuming intricate systems are no more than the interaction of its disaggregated parts.

This parsing has also influenced the metastructure of the law, including international law, and, by the way, is a significant departure from the conception of the natural world and legal orders in other worldviews. Anna Grear cogently demonstrates how reductionism manifests in the law: "[It] is expressed . . . in a complexly disembodied juridical notion of the human subject and a related juridical objectification of the 'natural world'. Thus, in law, as in science, the modern 'rational human subject' forms the epistemic 'centre' surrounded by its 'environment', understood as mere 'matter' 'out there.' "[43] This narrow frame causes international law to buckle when confronted with the dynamic pace and content of myriad ecological crises.

Perhaps the greatest threat to a dynamic approach to law is the compartmentalization of the environment and the fragmentation of it in our "environmental management" regimes, on which there is rich scholarly critique. Consider that environmental law has a uniquely sweeping mandate. Its subject is each person. Its object is the commons; and, the space and time it covers

[40] *See also* Anna Grear, *Towards "Climate Justice"? A Critical Reflection on Legal Subjectivity and Climate Injustice: Warning Signals, Patterned Hierarchies, Directions for Future Law and Policy*, 5 J. Hum. Rts. & Env't 103, 111 (2014) (describing Descartes' carving of an ontological rift between *res cogitans* (the mind) and *res extensa* (everything else—including the human body)).

[41] Bosselmann, *supra* note 4, at 2430.

[42] *Id.* (defining "environmental reductionism" as the compartmentalized, fragmented, and anthropocentric idea of the environment).

[43] Grear, *supra* note 40, at 111.

is the entire globe—yesterday, today, and the near- and long-term future. Nonetheless, the management domain at the domestic level is compartmentalized in comparatively weak agencies like the Environmental Protection Agency and similarly situated Ministries of the Environment. At the international level, international environmental law, discussed in more detail later, is similarly constrained in reach. By contrast, agencies managing trade, and other core political institutions related to finance, economic growth, or social welfare, set sweeping public policy,[44] and international trade law is noted for its ability to ensure compliance and accountability consistent with the prevailing political economy.

There is, however, no governing rule or principle running through the law that prohibits a thorough compromise of ecosystems' fundamental integrity.[45] This absence is noteworthy and peculiar given that functioning ecosystems are necessary to sustain life. In international negotiations on trade in natural resources (read: the environment), for example, "environmental provisions" are a nagging afterthought, if considered at all.[46] Tellingly, key elements of the trade regime, namely the WTO, and the climate regime developed contemporaneously, and during a critical window for the global community to combat climate change aggressively in the 1990s and 2000s. The weight and enforceability of those commitments are deeply divergent. States have created, for example, specialized international tribunals to enforce obligations under international trade and investment regimes, but they have not created specialized international tribunals to enforce climate related obligations.[47]

[44] *See* Bosselmann, *supra* note 4, at 2432; Bosselmann, *supra* note 31, at 48.

[45] *See e.g.*, Humphreys, *supra* note 21, at 144 (noting that the trade regime is a cornerstone of the international system; the climate regime is not; and, at the same time, within the WTO itself—including its Dispute Settlement Body—there is little sense that climate change requires any rethinking of WTO rules). Humphreys presumes that the WTO was not intended as a "suicide pact" and wonders "to what extent might we look forward to the evolution of international law (human rights law, trade law, environmental law)?" *Id.*

[46] Here I depart significantly from Bosselmann's construction of the solution. He states, "Fundamentally, only two solutions are available: either protection of the commons must set a benchmark against which all rights and duties are to be measured or environmental protection will be considered as merely relative to competing concerns such as economic prosperity and social equity." Bosselmann, *supra* note 4, at 2428. I strenuously disagree with the notion that social equity is a competing concern. Indeed, as discussed in depth later, such inequity and injustice is intimately intertwined with the causes and consequences of environmental degradation, namely, the othering and objectification inherent in Cartesian dualism.

[47] On this discrepancy between the "conclusion of a dizzying number of international trade and investment treaties" and the singular and ineffectual climate-related agreement, *see Special Rapporteur Report*, *supra* note 10.

Governance of conduct vis-à-vis the natural environment is also hampered by its fragmentation. It is fragmented in that, for the most part, decision makers manage specific aspects of the environment independently rather than as an integrated whole. And a commitment to constructing "legal taxonomies"[48] and "bounded domains" has stymied progress in remedying systemic challenges like climate change as well as notably and relatedly race, indigeneity, and gender. In many respects, this makes sense in the environmental context. To be specific and enforceable, laws need to carve out sensible domains, even if roughly demarcated. Indeed, that is perhaps why conventions like the Law of the Sea Convention and organs like the International Maritime Organization that are delimiting boundaries and setting standards are more effective instantiations of international environmental governance.[49] What is missing however, is a system-wide approach throughout international law that "holds the environment as the foundation of life and the integrity of the ecological systems as non-negotiable."[50] That is why the individual successes of environmental laws, such as regional air quality improvements, have not "trickled up and out" to cover the scale and scope of emerging, interrelated crises such as precipitous loss of biodiversity and climate change. Indeed, environmental governance is no match for larger economic objectives at the core of the global legal architecture.[51]

Without essentializing or suggesting that there were not Western notions of interdependence—there were[52]—Indigenous legal systems and philosophies throughout the Global South tend to regard human beings as part of their ecosystems, with ethical and legal rules flowing from that conception.[53] That proximity to nature, in ontology and practice, was not only viewed as distinct from the "civilizing" forces of Enlightenment but justified colonization in as a means of enlightenment and progress. Relationships with nature, in fact, were one of the earliest and most consequential points at which inequality and environmental and climate degradation collided. As Natarajan

[48] Grear, *supra* note 40, at 105 (noting that law's "taxonomical and linear tendencies, if anything, tend to exacerbate law's inadequate systemic grasp of the challenges").

[49] Bosselmann, for example, concedes that the reductionist concept of environmental protection has not been entirely without success. Bosselmann, *supra* note 31, at 51. The global environment is, nonetheless, in rapid decline.

[50] Bosselmann, *supra* note 4, at 2432.

[51] *See, e.g.*, Grear, *supra* note 40, at 106.

[52] Bosselmann, *supra* note 4, at 2437 ("living from the yield, not from the substance").

[53] *See* Gonzalez, *supra* note 5, at 232 (describing the worldview and rules that have facilitated "each group's adaptation to its distinct ecological niche and to protect the ecological systems upon which human and non-human life depend.").

explains, scholars and philosophers of the Enlightenment viewed societies in the Global South as being "trapped in a state of nature,"[54] a designation that justified the subjugation of "savages" and "barbarians," and similarly justified "imperial projects of transformation."[55]

The consequences of this worldview and its global spread through colonialism and neocolonialism have been devastating, facilitating the overconsumption of global resources and rendering much of the Global South ill-equipped to adapt to the consequences of that overconsumption.[56] The Western idea of the "modern state," for example, brought sometimes arbitrary nation-state boundaries to the Global South, with significant consequences for the specter of uncoordinated migration as well as the proliferation of exclusionary policy.[57] It has also brought to the Global South "the assertion of state control over nature as the basis for modernity and progress."[58] It persisted through to the postcolonial period, as Natarajan explains, at which time postcolonial states were "imbued with a civilizing mission" in which the nation-state was tied to a specific understanding of development, one that equated "development progress with the degree of state control over nature."[59] At the roots of the contemporary international legal order, therefore, are the intertwined missions to "civilize" and "modernize" through increasingly sophisticated modes of exploitation of both land and peoples.[60]

C. Order as Hierarchy: Shared Origins of Climate Change and the Global North-South Divide

Commingled with environmental degradation is racial subjugation. The two are inextricably intertwined. Indeed, the climate crisis might not have been possible without conceptions of peoples and places that a few could sacrifice

[54] Usha Natarajan, *TWAIL and the Environment: The State of Nature, the Nature of the State, and the Arab Spring*, 14 Or. Rev. Int'l L. 177 (2012).

[55] *Id.*

[56] *See infra* section IV.A. Statistics regarding the amount of "natural resources" needed to maintain a Western lifestyle evince the North's overconsumption of global resources. For example, despite being only about 20% of global population, the North consumes about 80% of the planet's resources. *See, e.g.*, Gonzalez, *supra* note 5, at 221–22; Mathis Wackernagel et al., *The Ecological Footprint of Cities and Regions: Comparing Resource Availability with Resource Demand*, 18 Env't & Urbanization 103, 105–08 (2006).

[57] Natarajan, *supra* note 54, at 192.

[58] *Id.*

[59] *Id.*

[60] *See, e.g.*, Grear, *supra* note 40, at 112.

for "wealth" and "progress." The relationship is at least five centuries old, at which point European contact appears immediately transformational at the scale of the global climate. Data show that the mini Ice Age of the 1600s may have been the byproduct of the prior century's massive genocide of Americas' Indigenous peoples, estimated at over fifty million dead.[61] Native farming collapsed and forests rebounded to the extent that newly forested areas captured enough carbon to spur measurably cooler global temperatures, as forests sequestered significant amounts of carbon dioxide. This section introduces the ongoing and disproportionately negative effects of global climate change on the Global South and impaired abilities to adapt.[62] It also explores the ways in which colonial and postcolonial legal orders made the climate crisis possible.

Related to the discussion in the prior section, the domination of the environment has produced adverse results for centuries, with the current climate crisis serving as a dangerous denouement. From the beginning, international law has held a similar view of nature, treating it as a "resource for wealth generation" and a singular formulation of "development."[63] As the disciplinary scaffolding of the international legal order, international law has universalized and normalized that understanding.[64] Further, norms fundamental to international law, such as sovereignty,[65] economy, and development are modeled on the political economy of the North, which itself is ill-suited to "perceiving or observing ecological limits,"[66] much less correcting for them in a rapid, wholistic, and inclusive manner.

At the same time, international law has also been deeply complicit in the subjugation of peoples, from the doctrine of *terra nullius* driving colonialism through to trusteeship and structural adjustment in the postcolonial era. Gonzalez argues that international law paints a very vivid picture, as it depicts "Southern peoples as so primitive, savage, uncivilized, backward, and underdeveloped that their lives, livelihoods, and cultures are unworthy of protection."[67] Nomadic societies operated distinctly from societies with

[61] *See* Alexander Koch et al., *Earth System Impacts of the European Arrival and Great Dying in the Americas after 1492*, Quatenary Science Reviews, Mar. 1, 2019, at 13; *see also* Gonzalez, *supra* note 5.
[62] Section IV.A. explores climate change's impact on the Global North-South divide in greater depth.
[63] *See, e.g.*, Natarajan & Khoday, *supra* note 27.
[64] *Id.*
[65] *See* Natarajan, *supra* note 54, at 193.
[66] Natarajan & Khoday, *supra* note 27.
[67] Gonzalez, *supra* note 5.

strong conceptions of "sovereignty," in that they did not exert the requisite degree of control over nature and did not maximize "nature's productive capacity through consistent agriculture and farming."[68] *Terra nullius* is perhaps the clearest example of early norms that justified the colonial project in the territory of nomadic cultures.[69]

1. Colonialism and the Domination of People and Place

Colonialism was the period of aggressive and globally exported "progress." Colonizers commodified and exploited nature,[70] simultaneous with the exploitation of certain humans, almost exclusively in the Global South. Scholars of TWAIL (Third World Approaches to International Law) understand colonialism as "a cultural project of control. Colonized societies were classified and labeled. New distinctions and oppositions came into being between colonizers and colonized, modern and primitive, and West and East,"[71] mirroring the dualism discussed earlier. As Gonzalez explains, colonialism reduced subsistence economies into "economic satellites of Europe," wreaking havoc on the in situ people and environments.[72] The South exported massive amounts of raw goods and imported the manufactured end products.[73] The knock-on effect was, among other things, a shift to export production that not only diverted prime agricultural lands but created poverty and inequality by "concentrating landholding in the hands of local elites, converting farmers into landless peasants, promoting the use of [the labor of the enslaved], and degrading the natural resource base necessary for food production."[74] Of course, colonizers routinely met resistance with brutal repression,[75] and this kind of repression to maintain control was tolerated if not sanctioned by the ILO.

2. Postcolonialism and Shadows of Hierarchy

This understanding of civilization and the classifying of non-European societies relative to "the civilized" persisted in the waning days of colonialism. The League of Nation's Mandate Systems, in which "European states would

[68] Natarajan & Khoday, *supra* note 27, at 586–87.
[69] *Id.*
[70] *See* Gonzalez, *supra* note 5.
[71] Natarajan, *supra* note 54.
[72] Carmen Gonzalez, *Environmental Justice and International Environmental Law*, *in* ROUTLEDGE HANDBOOK OF INTERNATIONAL ENVIRONMENTAL LAW (S. Alam et al. eds., 2013).
[73] *See generally* JASON HICKEL, THE DIVIDE (2017); Gonzalez, *supra* note 72, at 80.
[74] Gonzalez, *supra* note 72, at 80.
[75] *Id.*

assist non-European territories to evolve towards sovereignty,"[76] is evidence of persisting notions of civilization into the postcolonial period. As before, control and productive use of the natural environment were also, in some respects, key to sovereignty during the postcolonial period. As Natarajan and Khoday explain, "In their quest to gain equal footing under international law, non-European states had to considerably transform their domestic spheres to enable the increasingly efficient exploitation of nature through instituting appropriate European systems of land tenure, private property, contracts, torts, and so on."[77] Notions of European racial and cultural superiority were also imprinted and later exploited by postcolonial elites, who have justified exploiting indigenous peoples and places,[78] among others, within their sovereign boundaries.

Modern investment law exemplifies the strength and durability of these precepts in the fabric of international law. It adopts the colonial era "instrumentalist view of the environment" and facilitates the North's overuse of ecosystem services.[79] This occurs without a parallel obligation to protect healthy ecosystems and local communities. Indeed, such gestures are not only frowned upon in favor of "stable legal and business" environments; they are forbidden. Gonzalez explains that instruments like bilateral and regional investment agreements have sought to provide "foreign investors with unfettered access to natural resources by restricting the ability of host states to adopt health and safety, environmental, labour and human rights standards."[80] These arrangements may even stymie a country's ability to adapt to climate change in the Global South as a result of requirements to compensate investors when measures to respond to drought-induced water shortages, for example, "depress the value of foreign investment."[81] Indeed, the progeny of the Washington Consensus was an international economic regime that uncritically and unabashedly facilitated the Global North's overconsumption and offshored much of the waste byproduct and environmental degradation to the Global South.[82] Of course, climate change has now enhanced the scale and scope of that degradation, which now has an

[76] Natarajan & Khoday, *supra* note 27, at 587.

[77] *Id.*

[78] *See, e.g.*, Gonzalez, *supra* note 72, at 81; *see also* Renato Antunes dos Santos, Denise Osorio Severo, & Maria da Graça Luderitz Hoefel, *Bolsonaro's Hostility Has Driven Brazil's Indigenous Peoples to the Brink*, Nature, Aug. 27, 2020, at 524.

[79] Gonzalez, *supra* note 5, at 224.

[80] *Id.*

[81] *Id.*

[82] Gonzalez, *supra* note 72, at 82–83.

irrefutably global reach of the kind that even the North cannot outsource. Nonetheless, these underlying legal structures remain.

IV. Case Studies

Changes in climate affect all aspects of contemporary life. This section provides three case studies to illustrate the breadth of disruption that threatens the existing order. It explores the role of the Global North-South divide in producing and accelerating global change, as well as the profound impact climate extremes will continue to have on the welfare gaps between them. Regarding refugee and migration law, the emergence of displacement, migration, and relocation scenarios induced by climate change is one example of how climate amplifies old pressures (border tensions and xenophobia) and introduces novel scenarios (statelessness and atoll island states). Finally, it considers the emerging, though at times contradictory, evidence of climate change's impact on regional conflict and the destabilizing nature of a world that is just 2° Celsius warmer. In sum, the case studies introduce a small handful of the phenomena that touch innumerable areas of international law, affect all countries without exception, and threaten to upend the livelihoods of hundreds of millions, possibly billions, of people.

A. North-South Inequality

The nature of the contemporary North-South divide is rooted in the colonial encounter and demonstrates the long-standing relationship between environmental change and disparate vulnerabilities to that change. The "underdevelopment" of the Global South was initiated and accelerated through mass enslavement, dispossession of Indigenous peoples, and colonial and postcolonial domination through neoliberal economic reforms.[83] This was then normalized and extended through space and time by the ILO. Raqul Islam explains: "This historic legacy of economic disparity continues unabated under current international economic law, which requires the South

[83] *See generally* Carmen Gonzalez, *Racial Capitalism, Climate Justice, and Climate Displacement*, 11 OÑATI SOCIO-LEGAL SERIES 108 (2020) (citing the works of political theorist Cedric Robinson and sociologist Aníbal Quijano).

to compete with the North that has accumulated wealth through a method no longer available."[84] It is no longer available because international law no longer sanctions formal slavery, of course, and the climate system cannot bear the expansion of Western-style development. From an Indigenous perspective, and with respect to settler colonialism, Kyle Powys White notes the way in which colonial campaigns both "dramatically changed ecosystems—such as through deforestation, overharvesting, and pollution—*and* obstructed indigenous peoples' capacities to adapt to the changes, through removal and containment on reservations."[85] Qualitative and quantitative studies and empirical data demonstrate that similar campaigns repeat throughout the Global South—from the Pacific to the Caribbean to the southwest Indian Ocean.[86]

1. *Evidence*

There have been multiple pronouncements of varied threads of injustice that inhere in the climate crisis. In 2007, UK economist Nicholas Stern described it as an "externality" entailing costs not paid for by the chief emitters and borne by those least responsible.[87] More pointedly, the UN Special Rapporteur on Extreme Poverty and Human Rights describes the divide between the affluent who can protect themselves and everyone else as "climate apartheid."[88] Consistent with these assessments, scientists have long postulated that higher temperatures will have the greatest impact on the world's most vulnerable and poorest people. Recent research suggests that this has already happened over the last several decades. In a 2019 study, Diffenbaugh and Burke found that between 1961 and 2000, climate change "dampened" per capita incomes in the world's poorest countries between 17 percent and 30 percent.[89] In wealthier, cooler countries the effect has had a less negative—or in some cases even beneficial—effect on per capita gross domestic product. For poor countries, researchers found a greater

[84] M. Rafiqul Islam, *History of the North-South Divide in International Law: Colonial Discourses, Sovereignty, and Self-Determination*, *in* International Environmental Law and the Global South 23–49 (Shawkat Alam et al. eds., 2015).

[85] Kyle Powys Whyte, *Our Ancestors' Dystopia Now: Indigenous Conservation and the Anthropocene*, *in* Routledge Companion to the Environmental Humanities 206, 209 (Ursula K. Heise, Jon Christensen, & Michelle Niemann eds., 2016).

[86] *See* Leon Sealey-Huggins, *"1.5°C to Stay Alive": Climate Change, Imperialism and Justice for the Caribbean*, 38 Third World Q. 2444 (2017).

[87] Nicholas Stern, The Economics of Climate Change: The Stern Review 25 (2011).

[88] *Special Rapporteur Report*, *supra* note 10.

[89] Somini Sengupta, *Global Wealth Gap Would Be Smaller Today Without Climate Change, Study Finds*, N.Y. Times, Apr. 22, 2019.

than 90 percent likelihood that per capita GDP is lower today than if global warming had not occurred. In short, countries like Norway are among the winners, while those like India and Nigeria have lost, and will continue to do so as the planet warms further.[90]

Growing evidence supports the notion that poorer countries are more negatively affected for two independent, though often overlapping, reasons: they lack the resources to protect against the impacts and they tend to sit in warmer regions of the globe, where additional warming is detrimental to both productivity and health.[91] Diffenbaugh and Burke describe this increasing gap as "warming-induced penalties" in poor countries and "warming-induced benefits" in some rich countries, a dynamic that has a long time horizon. Overall, they explain, the "pattern of impacts is robust, but the cumulative magnitude is larger over the longer period."[92] In other words, according to Diffenbaugh and Burke, the full impact of warming since the Industrial Revolution has been even greater than impacts calculated over the last fifty years.[93] The study's findings add to previous research on the topic, which found a strong negative correlation between baseline income and baseline temperature, demonstrating that global warming may drive more extreme global inequality as hotter, poorer countries face the biggest reduction in growth.[94]

In addition to greater exposure to climate impacts, colonial legacies have depressed capacities to adapt at various scales. The Caribbean experience is a helpful illustration. The geographical factors that render the region more vulnerable to extreme heat, drought, and storms, for example, are exacerbated by the imprints of "empire."[95] Douglass and Cooper detail specific ways in which colonial legacies exacerbate present climate exposures through study of archaeological and palaeoecological research.[96] The precolonial record both unveils the deleterious effect of colonialism and also suggests strategies and mechanisms to inform resilience building for climate adaptation

[90] *See id.*

[91] Noah S. Diffenbaugh & Marshall Burke, *Global Warming Has Increased Global Economic Inequality*, PROC. NAT'L ACAD. SCI., May 14, 2019, at 9808.

[92] *Id.*

[93] *Id.*

[94] Marshall Burke, Solomon M. Hsiang, & Edward Miguel, *Global Non-Linear Effect of Temperature on Economic Production*, NATURE, Oct. 21, 2015, at 235.

[95] *Id.*

[96] Kristina Douglass & Jago Cooper, *Archaeology, Environmental Justice, and Climate Change on Islands of the Caribbean and Southwestern Indian Ocean*, PROC. NAT'L ACAD. SCI., Apr. 14, 2020, at 8254.

moving forward. The landscapes and material records of the Caribbean islands reveal the loss of thousands of years of traditional ecological knowledge resulting from the genocide of millions of Indigenous peoples.[97] Island ecologies were further transformed with the seventeenth- and eighteenth-century translocation of European and African lifeways, with further modification during nineteenth- and twentieth-century industrialization. With the "adoption of European settlement patterns" and household architectures and building materials, for example, new towns were built in river valleys and estuaries increasing the relative vulnerability of "post-Columbian communities to hurricane-related flooding and wind shear."[98] A fixed built environment evidenced by the ubiquity of reinforced concrete is a sharp departure from the Indigenous technology of a thousand years prior, which included resilient architecture that also facilitated swift post-hurricane reconstruction using locally available materials.[99]

Archaeological samples also demonstrate that water scarcity is often a key tipping point in forcing island abandonment. Douglass and Cooper explain: "The 16th century translocation of monoculture agriculture later exacerbated by island-dependent cash crop economies has reduced water retention, increased soil erosion, and exposed people to greater vulnerability to droughts. At the same time, increasingly urbanized communities with high water consumption have depleted freshwater supplies and require engineered water management systems."[100] Douglass and Cooper make similar observations in the southwest Indian Ocean, noting that "European colonialism and the postcolonial 20th and 21st centuries have seen the advent of massive extractive industries (fisheries, logging, and mining) and efforts to 'modernize' indigenous communities, all of which have exacted a heavy toll on local livelihoods and environments."[101] Further, "[I]ndigenous farmers and herders were pushed onto marginal lands where soils were quickly depleted, a process that led to increasing economic inequality; energy insecurity; and more rapid deforestation, erosion, and sedimentation of waterways and fragile coastal habitats."[102] All of these preexisting conditions compound climate vulnerability.

[97] *Id.*
[98] *Id.* at 8256.
[99] *Id.*
[100] *Id.*
[101] *Id.* at 8257.
[102] *Id.* at 8259.

The Pacific has had a similar experience. As Skillington explains: "Prior to colonization, many of the traditional communities of the Pacific, for instance, lived in protected, high land areas chiefly as a defense against sudden storms or flooding. Colonial authorities, however, encouraged the amalgamation and establishment of coastal villages in areas more vulnerable to tropical cyclone events and increased exposure to storm."[103] The throughline from Western contact to contemporary exposure is consistent and pervasive.

Colonial legacies introduce other systemic obstacles to adaptation. They are, among other things: (1) chronic indebtedness, leaving states more dependent on external financial aid and curbing their ability to fund development and action; (2) economic dependence on tourism, fishing, and agriculture, sectors which are particularly sensitive to climate change; and (3) power imbalances in diplomatic negotiations, leading to climate change discussions prioritizing the needs of the developed North over those of the Global South.[104] In a review of diplomatic correspondence released in 2010, Sealey-Huggins found that economic coercion, "bullying tactics" and use of intelligence resources were key levers in limiting the rigor of key climate targets.[105] The long-standing refrain of the Caribbean states and other members of the Alliance of Small Island States negotiating bloc was "1.5° to Stay Alive." This has been consistently foreclosed over the first decades of the UN Framework Convention on Climate Change (UNFCCC), becoming almost entirely aspirational in the Paris Agreement.[106] The Pacific island countries have had similarly dispiriting experiences in other fora. Since the early 2000s, there have been perennial efforts to bring related concerns to the International Court of Justice, which, if successful, would have limited but symbolic value. One such effort by the Republic of Palau was quickly dropped purportedly because of warnings of requital from the United States (with which Palau has close ties under the Compact of Free Association).[107]

[103] Tracey Skillington, *Reconfiguring the Contours of Statehood and the Rights of Peoples of Disappearing States in the Age of Global Climate Change*, Soc. Sci., Aug. 31, 2016, at 46.

[104] *Id.*

[105] Sealey-Huggins, *supra* note 86.

[106] Paris Agreement to the United Nations Framework Convention on Climate Change, art. 2, Dec. 12, 2015, T.I.A.S. No. 16-1104.

[107] Margaretha Wewerinke-Singh & Diana Hinge Salili, *Between Negotiations and Litigation: Vanuatu's Perspective on Loss and Damage from Climate Change*, Climate Pol'y, June 10, 2019, at 681. *See also* Maxine Burkett, *A Justice Paradox: On Climate Change, Small Island Developing States, and the Quest for Effective Legal Remedy*, 35 U. Haw. L. Rev. 633 (2013).

2. Projections

Consistent with Diffenbaugh and Burke's assessment of the past fixing present inequalities, a 2016 study by Carleton and Hsiang found that, with all other factors remaining constant, locations that are subject to hotter temperatures with more extreme precipitation patterns and more major environmental shocks, such as tropical cyclones or drought, will likely lead to higher health costs, lower productivity, higher economic costs, increased population movement, and higher rates of violence.[108] Other projections on the climate-inequality nexus include a paper by Taconet et al. in 2020, which argues that climate change affects international inequality in two ways: (1) low-income countries are more vulnerable to the effects of rising temperatures from greenhouse gas emissions; and (2) the expense of climate mitigation could hinder the "economic catch-up" of poor countries.[109] The study stresses the need for climate mitigation policies to regulate the rise of future inequalities between states.[110] This research also builds on previous work, such as Burke et al.'s 2015 study, which predicts that the average income in the poorest countries will decrease 75 percent by 2100 compared to a world without warming.[111]

B. Borders and Migration

There is general agreement that there is a link between the environment and human mobility, that today there is more than one driver of almost all migration events, and that environmentally induced migration is growing.[112] Research has identified links between international migration and weather outcomes, with temperature having a considerably stronger impact than disasters on permanent emigration to other areas.[113] Like the climate-conflict nexus discussed later, however, the relationship between climate change and

[108] Tamma A. Carleton & Solomon M. Hsiang, *Social and Economic Impacts of Climate*, SCIENCE, Sept. 9, 2016, at 9837.

[109] Nicolas Taconet, Aurélie Méjean, & Céline Guivarch, *Influence of Climate Change Impacts and Mitigation Costs on Inequality between Countries*, CLIMATIC CHANGE, Feb. 26, 2020, at 15.

[110] *Id.*

[111] Diffenbaugh & Burke, *supra* note 91.

[112] Lezlie C. Erway Morinière & Mohammed Hamza, *Environment and Mobility: A View from Four Discourses*, AMBIO, Aug. 12, 2012, at 795.

[113] Pratikshya Bohra-Mishra et al., *Climate Variability and Migration in the Philippines*, POPULATION & ENV'T, Oct. 8, 2016, at 286; V. Mueller, C. Gray, & K. Kosec, *Heat Stress Increases Long-Term Human Migration in Rural Pakistan*, NATURE CLIMATE CHANGE, Jan. 26, 2014, at 182.

migration is highly context-dependent and deeply influenced by cultural, economic, political, and social factors.[114]

1. Evidence

In recent decades, the role of climate change in driving human migration has emerged as a prominent research focus.[115] Some studies argue that extreme climate events are *not* significant drivers of migration. However, others have found that the impact of climate change on human mobility depends on its interaction with other socioeconomic and political drivers, particularly those related to livelihood.[116]

Quantifying environmental migration is challenging given the multiple drivers of such movement, related methodological challenges, and the lack of data-collection standards. Although comprehensive data sets on environmental migration or planned relocation do not yet exist at the global level, a number of initiatives have begun to collect information across several countries.[117] For example, a twenty-one-year longitudinal survey conducted by Mueller et al. in rural Pakistan measured the relationship between weather and long-term migration. That study found that while flooding (a climate shock commonly associated with large relief efforts) has "modest to insignificant impacts on migration," heat stress "consistently increases the long-term migration of men, driven by a negative effect on farm and non-farm income."[118] Similarly, Bohra-Mishra, Oppenheimer, and Hsiang demonstrated that temperature has a much stronger effect on permanent emigration to other areas than disasters.[119] Another study by Feng, Krueger, and Oppenheimer revealed that migrants from Mexico to the United States respond to weather shocks in the origin states in Mexico. Other research found that asylum applications to the European Union strongly and significantly respond to weather shocks in the host country. The more that temperatures

[114] Robert A. McLeman, Climate and Human Migration: Past Experiences, Future Challenges (2014).

[115] David J. Kaczan & Jennifer Orgill-Meyer, *The Impact of Climate Change on Migration: A Synthesis of Recent Empirical Insights*, Climatic Change, Nov. 7, 2019, at 281.

[116] Colette Mortreux & Jon Barnett, *Climate Change, Migration and Adaptation in Funafuti, Tuvalu*, 19(1) Global Envtl. Change 105 (Feb. 2009).

[117] François Gemenne, *Why the Numbers Don't Add Up: A Review of Estimates and Predictions of People Displaced by Environmental Changes*, 21 Global Envtl. Change, Supp. 1, at 541 (Dec. 2011).

[118] Mueller, Gray, & Kosec, *supra* note 113.

[119] Bohra-Mishra et al., *supra* note 113.

in a country's key agricultural regions rose above 20° Celsius in the growing season, the more people left their homes for another country.[120]

The type of event—sudden or slow onset—appears to affect the direction and length of displacement. Migrations and displacements that result from extreme, sudden events vary greatly by socioeconomic groups and create multiple patterns of temporary and permanent migration relative to the affected area.[121] Researchers have described this as the "migration churn," underscoring that any current measure or projection of future migration will "inevitably lack precision and contain numerous caveats."[122] Slower onset events, like droughts and prolonged extreme heat events, undermine household incomes and food security. This does not typically generate immediate, large-scale displacement or migration.[123] In these instances, there is time for interventions that can increase adaptive capacity and the ability to stay in place, including water conservation measures and/or insurance or government assistance. Persistent in situ heat and/or drought, however, may trigger an increase in rural out-migration.[124] Furthermore, research has shown that climate change will contribute to a "planetary redistribution of economic activity, which will result in a redistribution of international trade flows," underlining the profound impact of climate change on global economic patterns and associated local livelihoods.[125] All of this, of course, depends on international policy's ability to influence the rate of continued greenhouse gas emissions and local-level adaptive capacity.[126]

Sound strategies and coordinated policy approaches are critical to implement; their absence may have greater influence on migration than slow or sudden onset disasters in the near term. Novel legal questions abound, with very few clear answers as to appropriate next steps. Among the many

[120] Anouch Missirian & Wolfram Schlenker, *Asylum Applications Respond to Temperature Fluctuations*, Science, Dec. 22, 2017, at 1610; S. Feng, A.B. Krueger, & M. Oppenheimer, *Linkages Among Climate Change, Crop Yields and Mexico-US Cross-Border Migration*, Proc. Nat'l Acad. Sci., Aug. 10, 2010, at 14257.

[121] Robert McLeman, *International Migration and Climate Adaptation in an Era of Hardening Borders*, Nature Climate Change, Nov. 26, 2019, at 911.

[122] *Id.*

[123] *Id.*

[124] *Id.* (noting that "International migration outcomes in the wake of droughts are multidirectional, with out-migration from low-income countries tending to decline temporarily, while out-migration from middle-income countries temporarily increases).

[125] Wolfram Schlenker & Maximilian Auffhammer, *The Cost of a Warming Climate*, Nature News & Views Forum (May 23, 2018), https://www.nature.com/articles/d41586-018-05198-7.

[126] *See, e.g.*, D.J. Wrathall et al., *Meeting the Looming Policy Challenge of Sea-level Change and Human Migration*, Nature Climate Change, Nov. 26, 2019, at 898 (noting the contingencies when considering predictions related to sea-level change).

challenges for international law, there are several that are potentially destabilizing for the field. The possibility of substantial territorial loss and deterritorialization as a result of rising sea levels, particularly among small atoll states, like Kiribati and the Marshall Islands, has been the subject of scholarly inquiry and has now been taken up by both the International Law Association and the International Law Commission. This one possibility implicates fundamental aspects of international law, including: elements of statehood, human rights, refugee law, and broader issues of international peace and security.[127] Notably, the islands' complete uninhabitability may occur before they lose physical territory, as extreme heat and drought stressing freshwater resources are immediate, near-term threats. These triggers raise similarly thorny legal questions, as island abandonment has implications for the nation-state as well as displaced individuals and communities seeking protection.

The movement of people is helped or hindered by the levels of resistance in domestic policy and international collaboration regarding migration. McLeman notes that—despite the fact that the Global Compact for Migration imposes no legal obligations—important destination or transit countries like the United States, Australia, and several European states have not endorsed the compact.[128] Those countries have cited concerns regarding erosion of national sovereignty and limitations on their ability to implement strict immigration and border policies to justify their decisions. In some instances, racialized xenophobia is thinly veiled, if veiled at all.[129]

2. *Projections*

As for the future, and as new risks arise, migration forecasting becomes more difficult to do with reasonable certainty. The uncertainty is self-evident in the broad range of estimates of the number of migrants who will be internally displaced and moving across borders—numbers that vacillate between the hundreds of millions to greater than a billion. Moreover, as one commentator has noted, "models can't say much about the cultural strain that might result from a climate influx; there is no data on anger or prejudice."[130] McLeman

[127] Davor Vidas, David Freestone, & Jane McAdam, *International Law and Sea Level Rise: The New ILA Committee*, 21 ILSA J. Int'l & Comp. L. 397 (2015).

[128] McLeman, *supra* note 121.

[129] *See* Gonzalez, *supra* note 83 (citing Andrew Telford, *A Threat to Climate-Secure European Futures? Exploring Racial Logics and Climate-Induced Migration in US and EU Climate Security Discourses*, 96 Geoforum 268 (2018)).

[130] Abrahm Lustgarten, *Where Will Everyone Go?*, ProPublica (July 23, 2020), https://features.propublica.org/climate-migration/model-how-climate-refugees-move-across-continents/.

notes that "the morphology of migration networks changes in terms of the destinations, duration of movement, participation rates and demographic characteristics of migrants."[131] He cites three potential outcomes that could result:

> (1) Larger flows of people along established migration routes, because the destinations become safer or more attractive, sending areas become less safe or less viable, and migration network effects continue to facilitate movement. (2) Unchanged or even decreased flows of people along established migration routes, either because the destinations become less attractive or less viable relative to the sending area, or because migrant networks are not able to facilitate greater levels of migration. (3) New flows of migrants between sending and destination areas that have not historically been connected, leading to the creation of new migration networks.[132]

Social and policy decisions will necessarily influence movement.

The current state of international refugee, migration, and labor laws—among others, including human rights[133] and humanitarian law—provide little useful direction for cross-border migration. Based on current policy, there are only a handful of options for those who travel across borders. Formal movement includes relocating to a neighboring country that allows unrestricted entry and applying to a formal international migration program such as skilled worker visa programs in higher income countries.[134] Informal or extralegal pathways include clandestine travel across borders and, according to McLeman, travel to another country and, once arriving "misrepresent[ing] oneself to authorities as a political refugee."[135] These suboptimal and dangerous options are what produce current day migration "crises" and, notably, this is happening today absent the full force of climate change. In this regard, critiques of migration law are important to consider. In a recent and trenchant assessment of international migration law, Professor Jaya Ramji-Nogales suggests that this field of law is itself a chief

[131] McLeman, *supra* note 121.

[132] *Id.*

[133] *But see* U.N. Hum. Rts. Comm., Views adopted by the Committee under article 5(4) of the Optional Protocol, concerning communication No. 2728/2016, U.N. Doc. CCPR/C/127/D/2728/2016 (Sept. 23, 2020).

[134] McLeman, *supra* note 121. *See, e.g.*, Ama Francis, *Free Movement Agreements & Climate-Induced Migration: A Caribbean Case Study*, Colum. L. Pub. Res. (https://ssrn.com/abstract=3464594).

[135] McLeman, *supra* note 121.

contributor—if not the progenitor—of many contemporary migration and refugee crises.[136] Taking international refugee law as one example, Ramji-Nogales notes that it benefits only a select group of migrants who fit into its narrow definition. It also encourages risk-taking activity to enjoy its promised protections, often resulting in exacerbated emergencies. This complexity becomes more knotted as climate-induced migration is more frequently framed as a "looming security crisis" and emerges as a common rationale for "strengthening" or weaponizing borders in the Global North as well as common destination countries in the South.[137]

C. Conflict

Climate change is already transforming the way we think about security. Although researchers have long been divided about the relationship between climate and conflict, studies are increasingly revealing how the effects of global warming on the world's physical landscape have led to geopolitical changes that destabilize already vulnerable regions. Indeed, as the global community draws ever nearer to irreversible climate "tipping points," reaching an understanding about the relationship between climate-related stressors and conflict becomes increasingly urgent.

From a historical standpoint, researchers have attributed armed conflict to political and/or ideological tensions that, in turn, provide grounds for violence.[138] It is important, however, to keep in mind that when looking at the historical record, its "salience . . . is unclear."[139] The hallmark of climate change is a sharp departure from the past. Although research on climate and conflict has not yet fully matured to the point of establishing well-accepted general findings, several studies discern a link between disasters and conflict onset. Using new methods, Ide et al. have found that climate-related disasters increase the risk of armed conflict.[140] The relationship is not linear. Under

[136] Jaya Ramji-Nogales, *Migration Emergencies*, 68 Hastings L.J. 609 (2017). *See also* Jaya Ramji-Nogales, *Migration and International Legal Disorder* (Chapter 14 in this volume).

[137] *See generally* Ingrid Boas et al., *Climate Migration Myths*, Nature Climate Change, Nov. 26, 2019, at 901. On weaponized borders, *see* Todd Miller, Storming the Wall (2017).

[138] Frances Stewart, *Root Causes of Violent Conflict in Developing Countries Commentary: Conflict—From Causes to Prevention?*, BMJ, Feb. 9, 2002, at 342.

[139] Richard Matthew, *Integrating Climate Change into Peacebuilding*, Climatic Change, Sept. 13, 2013, at 83.

[140] Tobias Ide et al., *Multi-Method Evidence for When and How Climate-related Disasters Contribute to Armed Conflict Risk*, Global Env't Change, Apr. 2, 2020, at 102063.

certain circumstances, however, climate-related change can influence factors that lead to or exacerbate conflict, especially in areas already lacking in strong political leadership, social equality, and/or access to natural resources.[141] As one study posits, the link between the onset of climate-related disasters and the occurrence of various forms of violent conflict is "often dependent on the presence of scope conditions like ethnic heterogeneity, political expulsion, or autocratic governance."[142] This relationship is therefore complicated, country-specific, and highly context-dependent.

1. Evidence

The effects of climate change (such as extreme weather events, sea-level rise, and increasing resource scarcity) are commonly assumed to lead to loss of livelihood, economic decline, and increased insecurity, either directly or through forced migration.[143] In short, fragile situations emerge when states are less able to absorb shocks and handle stresses peacefully. Researchers warn that one must avoid deterministic and reductionist narratives and instead take into account the entirety of factors that account for conflict-prone scenarios.

Nevertheless, there are a few triggers that are useful to consider when assessing climate-conflict relationships. Extreme climate events, such as hurricanes or droughts, have been linked to conflict either through economic loss or through weakening of government authority, but empirical studies on this remain inconclusive.[144] There is sufficient evidence to support the idea, however, that extreme weather events and disasters will exacerbate fragility challenges and can increase people's vulnerability and grievances, especially in conflict-affected countries. Nina von Uexkull demonstrates that areas experiencing sustained droughts have a higher risk of conflict because the exposure of such events "undermines alternative coping mechanisms of individuals."[145] Using data on civil conflict events in Sub-Saharan Africa from 1989 to 2009, she finds that areas dependent upon rain-fed agriculture are more likely to see civil conflict following drought because individuals in

[141] Joshua S. Goldstein, *Climate Change as a Global Security Issue*, 1 J. GLOB. SEC. STUD., 95 (2016).

[142] Ide et al., *supra* note 140.

[143] Ole Magnus Theisen et al., *Is Climate Change a Driver of Armed Conflict?*, CLIMATIC CHANGE, Jan. 3 2013, at 613.

[144] JUDITH M. BRETTHAUER, CLIMATE CHANGE AND RESOURCE CONFLICT: THE ROLE OF SCARCITY (1st ed. 2015).

[145] Nina Von Uexkull, *Sustained Drought, Vulnerability and Civil Conflict in Sub-Saharan Africa*, 43 POL. GEOGRAPHY, Nov. 2014, at 16.

these regions are more likely to partake in rebellion in order to redress economic grievances or to obtain food and income. Uexkull's findings align with existing research that finds that climate shocks affect the likelihood of conflict through individual economic outcomes, which change the individual opportunity costs of participation in violent activities.[146] Theisen et al. propose that climate change results in less rainfall and hotter temperature that jointly causes droughts; they find higher risks of poverty and violence where there is limited access to the natural resources that sustain livelihoods. They point out that various climate change impacts (such as food scarcity) lead or contribute to various kinds of violence. By examining a number of studies that focus on individual-level behavior and drawing on "relative deprivation or opportunity cost arguments," Theisen et al. show that scarcity is associated with more armed violence or crime: "[I]f we were to make an inference from unorganized events with low levels of violence to organized armed conflict, we would expect worsening climatic conditions to coincide with more armed conflict."[147]

In 2016, Schleussner et al. similarly hypothesized that climate-related disasters increase the risk of armed conflict in ethnically fractionalized countries. The study found no evidence of a direct causal relationship between environmental disasters and armed conflicts. It maintained, however, that disasters might act as a threat multiplier in several of the world's most conflict-prone regions.[148] It also warns that country-specific risks may prevail over the next decades if no adequate progress in ethnic inclusiveness regarding power sharing is achieved, highlighting that some of the most fractionalized countries are African and Central Asian nations. According to the paper, these areas are "hot spots" of increased armed-conflict risk because of their socioeconomic position and climate vulnerability.[149]

Other key triggers of instability that might yield conflict-sensitive scenarios are the volatility of food prices and food security, generally. Climate change is likely to reduce food production in many regions, increasing prices and market fluctuations, and raising the risk of protests, rioting, and civil

[146] Jonas Vestby, *Climate Variability and Individual Motivations for Participating in Political Violence*, 56 Global Env't Change, May 2019, at 114.

[147] *Id.*

[148] Lukas Rüttinger et al., A New Climate for Peace—Taking Action on Climate and Fragility Risks (2015).

[149] Håvard Hegre et al., *Forecasting Civil Conflict along the Shared Socioeconomic Pathways*, 11(5) Env't Res. Letters, Apr. 25, 2016, at 054002.

conflict.[150] In one study, Wischnath and Buhaug concentrated their analysis on conflict severity and food production across India and found that harvest loss is strongly associated with increased levels of political violence in the subsequent year, providing evidence that, at least for India, food scarcity is linked to an increase in armed conflict.[151]

Local resource competition, scarcity, and disasters are additional identified pathways to conflict. Research suggests that the availability of "small arms, persistent social and political inequities, and a struggle for resources," will continue to drive organized deadly assaults against civilian populations.[152] Increased competition over natural resources will also see higher demand for them in areas with growing populations and rapid economic development, creating a likely environment for tension and local conflict. These local struggles can (and are likely to) trigger problems at the national and international levels.[153]

Climate-related resource scarcity may not only increase conflict risk and exacerbate preexisting climate-conflict connections but also reveals "missing" institutions for which governance mechanisms do not yet exist to address emergent climate change risks, such as substantial increases in migration.[154] Mach et al. note that such resource pressures can "stimulate cooperation to ensure the fair distribution of resources, or decrease conflict risk if more time is spent on procuring food or because conditions are unfavourable for sustaining an armed group."[155] For conflicts to date, experts calculate with a 67 percent probability that improving the status and stability of known drivers such as illiberal democracy or intergroup inequality could reduce climate-related conflict risk.[156]

2. *Projections: Research and Methodology*

Despite the noise of current research on the climate-conflict nexus, it seems that there is a discernible signal of increased conflict as the impacts of climate worsen. The signal, as well as the causal factors, may become clearer as the research methodologies themselves evolve to capture the ubiquity of

[150] Katharine J. Mach et al., *Climate as a Risk Factor for Armed Conflict*, NATURE, June 12, 2019, at 193.

[151] *Id.*; Gerdis Wischnath et al., "*Rice or Riots: On Food Production and Conflict Severity across India*, 43 POL. GEOGRAPHY, Nov. 2014, at 6.

[152] *Id.*

[153] Vestby, *supra* note 146.

[154] Mach et al., *supra* note 150.

[155] *Id.*

[156] *Id.*

climate impacts. For example, Mach et al.'s 2019 study found that climate change is only a modest contributor to armed conflict since World War II,[157] citing factors such as "low socioeconomic development, low state capacity, and intergroup inequality emerging as vastly more consequential."[158] One member of the team of leading climate experts, Cullen Hendrix, asserted in hindsight that they may be "massively underestimating" the impacts of climate on armed conflict because standard methodologies fail to explore and incorporate the pathways through which climate change affects key factors not deemed as strictly environmental.[159] Taking their review of Kenya as an example, Hendrix explains that the researchers "have focused more attention on comparing Kenya in times of drought to Kenya in times of heavy rains than asking whether the vast differences in socioeconomic development and state capacity across the world are in part attributable to climatic conditions."[160] He says: "Low socioeconomic development and low state capacity are two factors most associated by climate-conflict scholars with armed conflict, surpassing by a large margin factors like climate change and physical geography. But what if socioeconomic development and state capacity are themselves products—at least in part—of climatic conditions?"[161] Here, the compartmentalization of the environment is evident in social science research. The effect on the ability to forecast future vulnerabilities is not only salient, it is potentially dangerous.

Failing to see these linkages in the first place belies a broad blind spot in the research itself, which mirrors blind spots that are pervasive across numerous disciplines, international law included. Citing the "large and relatively influential literature" that links climate to economic development and state capacity, Hendrix finds consistent conclusions. As noted earlier, "countries with less temperate climates are systematically poorer and governed by less capable states than those countries with more temperate climates."[162] It is possible, Hendrix concludes, that the conflict experts are "missing large indirect effects of climate operating through low socioeconomic development and state capacity."[163] Therefore, when looking to future projections, it is wise

[157] *Id.*
[158] Cullen Hendrix, *Are We Radically Underestimating the Effects of Climate on Armed Conflict?*, New Security Beat (Mar. 3, 2020), https://www.newsecuritybeat.org/2020/03/radically-underestimating-effects-climate-armed-conflict/.
[159] *Id.*
[160] *Id.*
[161] *Id.*
[162] *Id.*
[163] *Id.*

to consider the destabilizing effect of climate change on factors that are just one step removed and erroneously categorized as independent variables vis-à-vis a changing climate. In light of this, the future of climate-fueled conflict, without concerted intervention, is likely trending toward disorder, if not collapse.

V. Conclusion

The global community is now at the precipice of a great shift requiring a revolution in how we organize ourselves and our relationship to the environment. Coined by ecologists, though completely relevant to the present discussion, a "regime shift" or "critical transition" is a large, abrupt, and persistent change in the structure and function of a system occurring when a critical threshold is crossed.[164] It is a change that affects the system's very identity;[165] yet most shifts, strikingly, are a "complete surprise" to the people living in or managing the system.[166] Notable for ILO in the climate context, once a shift has occurred, return to the previous regime is appreciably more difficult.[167] It is a mistake to assume that cascading regime shifts in the physical system will not trigger and inflame similar shifts in our human systems that will prompt, without aggressive action, international legal disorder.

It is critically important, therefore, to frame the analysis of ILO in the context of climate change. As we lament the indicators of a weakened rule of law, it is necessary to consider what a strong "rule of law" enforces vis-à-vis the environment, the environment's criticality to our well-being as well as its rapid and dystopian decline. In other words, if the law and the concomitant legal order is weak or, as Grear would contend, suffering from a "structural pathology," then doubling down on that iteration of the law is dangerous. Recognizing the law's reductionist nature and the nature of climate change's comprehensive disruption is a first and crucial step to sound, enduring, and equitable responses. Grear advises: "This sense of epistemic limitation in turn readily implies the need for epistemic humility—for an open acknowledgment in both theoretical and practical terms of the vulnerability of

[164] Juan Carlos Rocha, R. Biggs, & G. Peterson, *Regime Shifts: What Are They and Why Do They Matter?*, REGIME SHIFTS DATABASE (2014), www.regimeshifts.org.
[165] *Id.*
[166] *Id.* at 3.
[167] *Id.* at 4.

perspective arising from the limitations (both real and symbolic) of the body itself as a field of perception."[168] The remedy, therefore, lies in a review of "our epistemic practices,"[169] favoring an openness and inclusivity in the development of international law and, by extension, the order (re)constructed within a climate on the verge of collapse.

In the meantime, given that avoiding collapse will require radical action on the timescale of years, rather than the generation(s) likely needed for a true epistemic shift, there are glimmers of a shift in practice—at least on the part of the United States. The new Biden administration has signaled a clear-eyed understanding of the urgency of the crisis and has also outlined priorities and specific intentions regarding even the more contentious elements of climate disruption, such as climate-induced migration.[170] Further, key voices within the administration have affirmed the fundamental relevance of climate change to international agreements and institutions beyond the Paris Agreement and IEL generally—as well as all elements of foreign policy.[171] The importance of this perceptual shift is difficult to overstate. The byproduct of that shift signals, at a minimum, a possible evolution in the ILO that, depending on the speed with which it develops, may well be revolutionary.

[168] Grear, *supra* note 40, at 131.

[169] *Id.*

[170] *See* Exec. Order No. 14008, 86 Fed. Reg. 7619 (Jan. 27, 2021); Exec. Order No. 14013, 86 Fed. Reg. 8839 (Feb. 4, 2021).

[171] *See* Sue Biniaz, *Multilaterialism, the Climate Challenge, and the (Greater Metropolitan) Paris Agreement*, *in* 21st Century Diplomacy: Foreign Policy is Climate Policy (Carius et al. eds., Sept. 2020), https://www.wilsoncenter.org/publication/21st-century-diplomacy-foreign-policy-climate-policy-full-report.

PART TWO

INTERNATIONAL PEACE AND SECURITY

5

War and Words

The International Use of Force in the UN Charter Era

Lauren Sukin and Allen S. Weiner

I. Introduction

The evolution of the international strategic environment since World War II and the emergence of new security threats present challenges to the legal regime governing the use of force adopted in the UN Charter in 1945. These developments raise the question of whether the Charter's use of force regime—a central pillar of the post–World War II international legal order—remains relevant and effective in regulating or constraining the behavior of states.

In this chapter, we answer this question in part by looking at the actual behavior of states, in particular by examining the incidence of the transnational use of force from 1945 until today. We find that the level of transnational use of force has not significantly increased, despite the emergence of new security threats unanticipated at the Charter's adoption. Although there could be many explanations for this pattern other than the constraining power of international law, the data, at a minimum, undermines the claim that the Charter's use of force regime is collapsing due to changes in the international security environment. The evidence suggests the legal regime governing the use of force has served, and continues to serve, as a meaningful constraint on state behavior.

To gain deeper insight into the law's role in contributing to the relative stability in the overall level of transnational violence, we investigate *how* states engage with the Charter's use of force regime by examining their justifications for military action. Are states increasingly using force without seeking to justify their behavior within the UN Charter's legal framework? Have states pushed for adaptations to that framework to address new security challenges? Or do states facing a changing security environment increasingly

Lauren Sukin and Allen S. Weiner, *War and Words* In: *Is the International Legal Order Unraveling?*. Edited by: David L. Sloss, Oxford University Press. © Oxford University Press 2022. DOI: 10.1093/oso/9780197652800.003.0006

justify their actions on political, strategic, or moral bases rather than legal grounds, implicitly acknowledging that their actions are not reconcilable with the black letter law of the Charter?

Our examination of the justifications that states offer for their uses of force reveals that states remain committed to the existing UN Charter's legal framework. The proportion of transnational instances of the use of force for which states provide formal justifications to the Security Council has remained relatively static from 1945 through today. The changing patterns of justificatory discourse also reveal limited reliance by states on several legally contested bases for using force we examine, suggesting an absence of state claims for the adaptation of the black letter law to accommodate these contested justifications. The one notable exception reflects evolving recognition that the right of states to exercise self-defense against nonstate actors located in other states prevails over the right of the territorial integrity of the state where force is used. We also find increasing reliance by states on extralegal justifications, but these extralegal justifications frequently *complement* contested legal arguments. That is, states are more likely to use extralegal language along with contested legal justifications to bolster support for their use of force. The use of extralegal justifications in this way suggests that even when states use force in circumstances that are difficult to reconcile with the black letter law of the Charter, they do not directly challenge the applicability of the Charter's use of force regime. They instead combine legal arguments with moral, political, and strategic ones in order to persuade Security Council members to support, or at a minimum not to oppose, their actions.

II. The Law Governing the Use of Force: Clear Cases and Controversies

A. The Black Letter Law of the UN Charter

During most of the post–Westphalian era, the legal regime governing the use of force was not highly restrictive; the right to go to war was a sovereign right, unrestricted by treaty or customary international law.[1] In response to

[1] Ian Brownlie, International Law and the Use of Force by States 16, 49–50 (1963). *See also* Christian Henderson, The Use of Force and International Law 11 (2018).

the horrors of World War II, states created the United Nations and adopted the UN Charter, which severely limited the right of states to resort to force. Article 2(4) of the UN Charter categorically prohibits "the threat or use of force against the territorial integrity or political independence of any state."

The general prohibition on the use of armed force is subject to two exceptions. First, states may use force in self-defense. Article 51 of the Charter preserves the "inherent right of individual . . . self-defense if an armed attack occurs." This is a unilateral right; each state can invoke it without any review by or approval of any other state or institution. In addition to this right of individual self-defense, the Charter also recognizes the right of "collective self-defense," that is, the right of states that have not themselves been attacked to use force to assist other states that have.

The second exception to the prohibition on the use of force permits armed activity authorized by the Security Council pursuant to the Charter's collective security mechanism. The Charter vests the Security Council with "primary responsibility for the maintenance of international peace and security."[2] In cases of "threats to the peace, breaches of the peace, and acts of aggression,"[3] the Council has broad powers to impose coercive measures against states (and others), including the power to authorize the use of force.[4]

B. Challenges to the Charter Regime: Obsolescence or Adaptation?

Almost immediately after adoption of the UN Charter, developments in the international security realm—including the escalation of the Cold War, the shift by the United States and the USSR to the use of proxy forces, and the emergence of new weapons technologies—began to place great pressure on the Charter's use of force regime. More recent security challenges include the imperatives states face to: (1) counter international terrorism carried out by nonstate actors; (2) halt the spread of weapons of mass destruction (WMD); and (3) stop mass atrocities occurring within other states. The transformation of a world with two main blocs of security rivals into a multipolar world has further altered the international security environment. But

[2] U.N. Charter, art. 24.
[3] *Id.*, ch. VII (chapeau).
[4] *Id.*, art. 42.

the international legal regime governing use of force has not undergone any formal transformation to respond to these dramatic changes in the international security realm.

Some commentators argue that the changing international security environment has led to "a persistent effort" to weaken the restriction on the use of force.[5] Others suggest that the "postwar consensus on the illegality of war is under greater assault today than it has been in seven decades."[6] Some commentators go even further; they conclude that the Charter's use of force regime is simply obsolete and no longer affects the behavior of states. Michael Glennon, for instance, argues that "[t]he *de jure* system consists of illusory rules that would govern the use of force among states in . . . a world that does not exist."[7] Glennon continues:

> No rules will work that do not reflect underlying geopolitical realities. The use-of-force regime set out in the U.N. Charter failed because the Charter sought to impose rules that are out-of-sync with the way states actually behave. A new use-of-force regime that does work will have to rest far more firmly upon actual patterns of practice that reveal, with solid empirical evidence, what regulation of force is possible and what is not. . . . There is no use in telling ghost stories, Holmes said, to people who do not believe in ghosts.[8]

Other commentators believe the Charter's use of force regime, instead of collapsing in the face of a changing security environment, has demonstrated the ability to adapt and evolve. Thomas Franck argues that the Charter is susceptible to changing interpretations based on state practice: "[T]he Charter [is] subjected to continuous interpretation and adaptation through the member states' individual and collective practice: their actions, voting, and rhetoric."[9] Christian Henderson similarly sees the Charter's use of force regime as a "living instrument" that "evolves and develops" over time.[10]

[5] Mary Ellen O'Connell, The Art of Law in the International Community 72 (2019).

[6] Oona A. Hathaway & Scott Shapiro, The Internationalists 417–18 (2017).

[7] Michael J. Glennon, *The Fog of Law: Self-Defense, Inherence, and Incoherence in Article 51 of the United Nations Charter*, 25 Harv. J.L. & Pub. Pol'y 539, 540 (2002).

[8] *Id.* at 557.

[9] Thomas M. Franck, Recourse to Force: State Action Against Threats and Armed Attacks 6–7 (2002).

[10] Henderson, *supra* note 1, at 121.

Michael Reisman describes the process of adaptation as one grounded in contested state claims urging evolution of the law:

> Claims to change inherited security arrangements . . . ignite a process of counterclaims, responses, replies, and rejoinders until stable expectations of right behavior emerge. . . . [This generates] the ceaseless dialectic of international law: Whether by diplomatic communication or state behavior, one state claims from others acquiescence in a new practice. Insofar as that new practice is accepted in whole or in part, the practice becomes part of the law.[11]

But states might not make claims calling for the evolution of the legal understanding of the Charter in *all* cases in which they use force in ways that are not clearly consistent with the black letter law of the Charter. A state might recognize that a legal regime in which all states claimed the right to use force in like circumstances would be inferior to the existing Charter regime. In such cases, states might seek to justify their actions on an exceptional basis, hoping the international community will essentially excuse what, in effect, constitutes a formal breach of the Charter. States may in such cases invoke other legal principles, even though they do not formally authorize the use of force, or they may rely on other considerations—moral claims, political considerations, or strategic arguments—in support of legally questionable uses of force. Franck argues that the international community can be receptive to such approaches, noting that "those with responsibility for interpreting and implementing the law employ a concept of mitigation to bridge the gap between the law and a common sense of moral justice."[12]

C. The Article 51 Reporting Requirement and Security Council Debates

The Security Council is a particularly important forum in which states advance justifications for their recourse to armed force. Article 51 of the Charter—in addition to prescribing states' substantive self-defense rights—also provides a procedural mandate requiring states to report all instances

[11] W. Michael Reisman, *Assessing Claims to Revise the Laws of War*, 97 AM. J. INT'L L. 82, 82 (2003).
[12] FRANCK, *supra* note 9, at 184.

in which they use force in self-defense.[13] It provides that "[m]easures taken by Members in the exercise of this right of self-defense shall be immediately reported to the Security Council." Since the Charter prohibits all uses of force by states other than those taken in self-defense or authorized by the Council, any unilateral use of force that a state does not report to the Council under Article 51 as an exercise of self-defense would presumably violate international law. This provides a strong incentive for states to report their uses of force to the Security Council and to characterize them as conforming with Article 51. States may seek to convey that their use of force accords with prevailing legal rules, both for normative reasons and also on prudential grounds, as states benefit from a reputation for complying with international law.[14] Since the Security Council is not a judicial body, states may also advance strategic, political, and moral justifications for using force. In general, states are likely to believe they can secure greater international support for their armed actions through the justifications they provide to the Security Council. And the responses of Security Council members to these justifications, through "their actions, voting, and rhetoric," contribute to the ongoing "interpretation and adaptation" of the Charter's use of force legal regime.[15]

D. Accepted Grounds for the Unilateral Use of Force

We next identify widely accepted legal justifications for the use of force and indicate how states might be expected to invoke or refer to those justifications in their Article 51 communications.[16]

[13] For earlier work on the Article 51 reporting requirement, see James A. Green, *The Article 51 Reporting Requirement for Self-Defense Actions*, 55 Va. J. Int'l L. 563 (2015); D.W. Greig, *Self-Defence and the Security Council: What Does Article 51 Require?*, 40 Int'l & Compar. L.Q. 366 (1991).

[14] Andrew T. Guzman, How International Law Works: A Rational Choice Theory 34–41 (2018); Bernd Lahno, Trust and Strategic Rationality (1995).

[15] Franck, *supra* note 9, at 7.

[16] Our focus is on the *unilateral* use of force by states, i.e., actions taken by states based on their own legal authority (whether alone or in conjunction with other states acting on the basis of their own legal authority). Another accepted legal justification for the use of force is collective security action authorized by the Security Council pursuant to its Chapter VII powers. *See* Allen S. Weiner, *The Use of Force and Contemporary Security Threats: Old Medicine for New Ills?*, 59 Stan. L. Rev. 415, 423–25 (2006). Particularly since the end of the Cold War, the Security Council has authorized a "wide range of member state [forcible] operations" on this basis, Christine Gray, International Law and the Use of Force 382 (4th ed. 2018), although the number of such cases remains a slight fraction of unilateral uses of force. We do not examine collective security cases here because authorizations to use force by the Security Council under the terms of the UN Charter do not involve the same purported challenges to the Charter's legal regime for regulating force as do actions states take on their

1. *Response to an "Armed Attack"*

The paradigmatic basis for a unilateral use of force is in response to an armed attack, either as a matter of individual self-defense by the victim state, or in collective self-defense by those invited to assist the victim state. The precise degree of violence necessary to trigger the right of self-defense is contested. The International Court of Justice (ICJ) indicated in the *Nicaragua* case that not all measures that "involve a use of force" are sufficiently "grave" to qualify as "armed attack[s]" within the meaning of Article 51; whether an episode of violence amounts to an armed attack must be evaluated in light of its "scale and effects."[17] The United States has periodically rejected this differentiation between armed attacks and less grave uses of force, asserting that states have the right to respond in self-defense to "any illegal use of force."[18]

We expect states would often explicitly identify attacks or uses of force against them or their allies in their Article 51 communications, emphasizing their right to mount an individual counterattack or assist an ally in collective self-defense.[19]

2. *Violations of Ceasefire Agreements*

Once a state of armed conflict erupts, international law does not require the states involved to provide a new justification for "each armed operation or to make a *de novo* self-defense determination with respect to each military action against" the adversary.[20] States may continue to wage war against each other until the armed conflict is over. If the parties to an armed conflict reach an agreement providing for a temporary cessation of hostilities, such as an armistice, truce, interim territorial demarcation agreement, or any other ceasefire agreement, they may take the view that the

own. Moreover, unlike unilateral uses of force, which states are required to report to the Council under Article 51 of the Charter, we would not expect states to submit notifications to the Security Council regarding uses of force the Council has itself authorized.

[17] Military and Paramilitary Activities (Nicar. v. U.S.), Judgment, 1986, I.C.J. 14, 101, 103, 110 (June 27).

[18] Harold Koh, *International Law in Cyberspace*, 54 Harv. Int'l L.J. 1, 7 (2012).

[19] Questions have arisen about whether hostile cyber operations constitute either a "use of force" prohibited by Article 2(4) or an "armed attack" triggering the right of self-defense under Article 51. *See* Ido Kilovaty, *Cyber Conflict and the Thresholds of War* (Chapter 8 in this volume). Our data shows there have not yet been any instances in which states in their Article 51 communications claim to be victims of hostile cyber operations or defend their uses of force as lawful responses to such operations.

[20] Allen S. Weiner, Book Review, 113 Am. J. Int'l L. 859, 859 (2019) (reviewing Christian Henderson, The Use of Force and International Law (2018)).

state of armed conflict is merely suspended rather than concluded.[21] In such cases, a state may claim that the breach of a ceasefire agreement by the other side results in the resumption of a state of armed conflict and justifies its renewed use of force. Article 40 of the 1907 Hague Regulations reflects an early codification of this view; it provides that "[a]ny serious violation of [an] armistice by one of the parties gives the other party the right of denouncing it, and even, in cases of urgency, of recommencing hostilities immediately."[22]

States that are parties to ceasefire agreements might accordingly justify uses of force as responses to the other side's violations of such agreements, without necessarily invoking their right of self-defense in response to an armed attack.

E. Contested Claims for Legal Adaptation

The changing international security landscape has generated a series of recurring use-of-force scenarios distinct from the classic armed attack/self-defense model. The legal justifications for using force in these scenarios range from being somewhat to extremely difficult to reconcile with the black letter law of the Charter. The following sections describe prominent contested forms of the use of force for which states or commentators have advanced legal justifications that call for adaptation of the traditional understanding of the black letter law of the Charter and how states might invoke them in their Article 51 communications.

[21] By some accounts, terms like "truce" or "ceasefire" signify merely "an interlude in the fighting," whereas the term "armistice" could be an agreement on "peace preliminaries" prior to the conclusion of a peace agreement or even, in contemporary usage, an agreement to terminate a war. Yoram Dinstein, *The Initiation, Suspension, and Termination of War*, *in* International Law Across the Spectrum of Conflict: Essays in Honour of Professor LC. Green on the Occasion of His Eightieth Birthday 131, 140–41 (Michael N. Schmitt ed., 2000). We use the term "ceasefire" here to refer to any cessation of hostilities agreement that suspends fighting temporarily but that does not, as a legal matter, terminate an armed conflict. "A termination of hostilities means that the war is over—the parties are no longer belligerents, and any subsequent hostilities between them would indicate the outbreak of a new war." *Id.* at 150. The traditional conception of an "armistice" as a ceasefire agreement is captured in the 1907 Hague Regulations on the Law of War on Land: "An armistice suspends military operations by mutual agreement between the belligerent parties." Hague Convention (IV) Respecting the Laws and Customs of War on Land, Annex (Regulations), art. 36, October 18, 1907, 36 Stat. 2295, 1 Bevans 643.

[22] *Id.*, art. 40.

1. *Anticipatory Self-defense*

Because Article 51 recognizes the right of self-defense "if an armed attack occurs," the Charter was widely understood when it was adopted as eliminating the preexisting customary international law right of states to use force in anticipation of an imminent attack. Through the adaptive interpretive process described earlier, however, widespread (although not uniform) support has emerged for a contemporary interpretation of the Charter that permits states to use force to prevent an imminent attack,[23] in what is known as "anticipatory self-defense." However, uses of force meant to confront nascent or growing threats that are not yet imminent (or "preventive self-defense") are still widely seen as impermissible. Citing the vast potential harm associated with WMD attacks, the George W. Bush administration challenged the notion that states must wait until an armed attack is imminent before they act,[24] but this view was met with widespread criticism among legal commentators.[25] To the extent this basis for using force is accepted as permissible, anticipatory self-defense can also occur against conventional threats.

In light of the contingent support for the right of states to respond to imminent threats, states that use force in cases where they have not actually sustained an armed attack by an adversary might justify their actions by invoking the purported right of anticipatory self-defense.

2. *Use of Force Abroad vs. Nonstate Actors*

Another legally controversial scenario involves a state's use of force against a nonstate group located on the territory of another state, where the use of force occurs without the territorial state's consent.[26] As a threshold matter, there is general agreement that the right of self-defense is available to respond to armed attacks by nonstate groups, not just those by states. Exercising the right of self-defense against nonstate actors abroad, however, violates the territorial integrity of the state where force is used.[27]

[23] U.N. High-level Panel on Threats, Challenges and Change, A More Secure World, U.N. Doc. A/59/565, at 63 (2004). *See also* W. Michael Reisman & Andrea Armstrong, *The Past and Future of the Claim of Preemptive Self-Defense*, 100 AM. J. INT'L L. 525, 526 (2006). *But see* GRAY, *supra* note 16, at 175 (arguing that the majority of states reject anticipatory self-defense).

[24] THE WHITE HOUSE, THE NATIONAL SECURITY STRATEGY OF THE UNITED STATES OF AMERICA 15 (2002), https://2009-2017.state.gov/documents/organization/63562.pdf.

[25] *See, e.g.*, HENDERSON, *supra* note 1, at 287; YORAM DINSTEIN, WAR, AGGRESSION, AND SELF-DEFENCE 234 (6th ed. 2017).

[26] If a state invites outside states to use force against nonstate armed groups on its territory, that consent eliminates any legal concerns about violations of its territorial integrity.

[27] Weiner, *supra* note 16, at 431.

This tension persists even though states are under an international legal obligation not to harbor nonstate groups that use force against other states. Some commentators endorse the "unwilling or unable" test championed by the United States as a means of resolving this tension.[28] This test provides that a state that has suffered an armed attack at the hands of a nonstate group may use force against it on the territory of another state, without that state's consent, if that state is unwilling or unable to suppress the threat the nonstate group poses to the victim state.[29] Others, in contrast, continue to see the nonconsensual use of force against nonstate groups on another state's territory as an impermissible use of force against that state.[30]

3. *Reprisals*

Prior to adoption of the Charter, states were permitted to use force by way of reprisal, that is, in "retaliation for acts contrary to international law on the part of the offending State, which have remained unredressed after a demand for amends."[31] By prohibiting force except in self-defense in response to an armed attack, the Charter is widely seen as categorically prohibiting forcible reprisals as a form of self-help.[32] Nevertheless, state behavior appears more nuanced, and in some cases international "tolerance has been manifest in U.N. passivity when faced with actual recourse to force" in self-help.[33] Although such use of force is prohibited by the text of the Charter, in practice it may in exceptional cases "be justified by the evident legitimacy of the cause in which self-help is deployed."[34]

Under these circumstances, states that use force in cases that do not involve a response to an armed attack by another state might justify their actions based on that state's prior unlawful actions.

4. *Humanitarianism and "Humanitarian Intervention"*

An additional contested basis for the use of force is humanitarian intervention, that is, the use of force against a state to halt atrocities its government is perpetrating against its own population. Since the state against which force is

[28] Ashley S. Deeks, *"Unwilling or Unable": Toward a Normative Framework for Extraterritorial Self-Defense*, 52 VA. J. INT'L L. 483, 486 (2012).

[29] *Id.* at 487.

[30] *See, e.g.*, O'CONNELL, *supra* note 5, at 185; GRAY, *supra* note 16, at 243.

[31] Sir Humphrey Waldock, *The Regulation of the Use of Force by Individual States in International Law*, 81 RECUEIL DES COURS 455, 460 (1952) (quoting the *Naulilaa* Case, Portuguese-German Mixed Arbitral Tribunal (1928)).

[32] ELISABETH ZOLLER, PEACETIME UNILATERAL REMEDIES: AN ANALYSIS OF COUNTERMEASURES 38–39 (1984).

[33] FRANCK, *supra* note 9, at 132.

[34] *Id.*

used in such circumstances has not committed an armed attack against other states, humanitarian intervention cannot be reconciled with the right of self-defense expressed in the Charter. Nevertheless, there are cases in which states have used force against others largely for humanitarian purposes—including India's 1971 intervention in East Pakistan, Tanzania's 1978–79 intervention in Uganda, and Vietnam's 1978–79 intervention in Cambodia—although the states involved did not expressly claim a legal right of humanitarian intervention in those cases. While some commentators have asserted that there are circumstances in which humanitarian intervention is permissible,[35] only a few states have expressly asserted that humanitarian intervention is an acceptable legal basis for using force. The United Kingdom has stated that states are "permitted under international law, on an exceptional basis, to take measures in order to alleviate overwhelming humanitarian suffering."[36] Before the ICJ, Belgium defended NATO's 1999 bombing campaign aimed at halting abuses perpetrated by the Federal Republic of Yugoslavia against Kosovar Albanians as an "armed humanitarian intervention justified by international law."[37] The Constitutive Act of the African Union also seems to endorse the right of humanitarian intervention, recognizing the Union's right to authorize intervention "in respect of grave circumstances, namely: war crimes, genocide and crimes against humanity."[38] However, the African Union has never invoked this principle as a basis for a nonconsensual intervention in an African state.

Alternatively, states might emphasize the humanitarian *goal* of protecting another country's nationals in order to buttress the legitimacy of their use of force, without formally invoking humanitarian intervention as the *legal* basis for using force.[39] The language of humanitarianism can, in this way, provide states with moral or political justifications that complement what might otherwise be recognized as legally dubious uses of force.

Our results show that no states have relied on a legal right of humanitarian intervention in their Article 51 communications to the Security Council.

[35] *See, e.g.*, FERNANDO R. TESÓN, HUMANITARIAN INTERVENTION: AN INQUIRY INTO LAW AND MORALITY (3rd ed. 2005); NICHOLAS J. WHEELER, SAVING STRANGERS: HUMANITARIAN INTERVENTION IN INTERNATIONAL SOCIETY (2000).

[36] U.K. PRIME MINISTER'S OFFICE, SYRIA ACTION—UK GOVERNMENT LEGAL POSITION (2018).

[37] Legality of the Use of Force (Serbia & Montenegro v. Belg.), Verbatim Record, 1999 I.C.J. CR 99/15 (May 10).

[38] Org. of African Unity, Constitutive Act of the African Union, art. 4(f), 2158 U.N.T.S. 3 (July 11, 2000).

[39] The US justification for the 1999 bombing campaign against the Federal Republic of Yugoslavia is a prominent example. The State Department spokesman cited "humanitarian dangers," among other factors, in asserting that there were "legitimate" grounds to use of force; he conspicuously did not assert that the use of force would be "lawful." James P. Rubin, Briefer, U.S. Dep't of State, Daily Press Briefing (Mar. 23, 1999), https://1997-2001.state.gov/briefings/9903/990323db.html.

States do, however, frequently cite humanitarian factors as extralegal considerations to complement legal justifications.

F. Extralegal Arguments

As noted earlier, states may have reasons to rely not only on legal arguments in their Article 51 communications but also on strategic, political, or moral claims. For example, a state might invoke a notion of self-defense going beyond the meaning of Article 51 by arguing that its use of force was necessary not only to respond to an armed attack but also to protect its economy. Or a state may emphasize the gravity of the crisis that required it to act. Other justifications might involve a more strategic focus, emphasizing the potential regional spillover risks associated with a conflict. States might also focus on the desirable policy benefits of their uses of force, arguing, for instance, that they are protecting human rights or promoting good governance. Alternatively, states may seek to gain international support by calling out objectionable aspects of an adversary's conduct or character or by highlighting their own moral stature.

III. Patterns in the Use of Force

Several commentators point to the level of armed conflict in the international system as evidence of the failure of the UN Charter's legal regime to constrain the use of force. Michael Glennon, who argues that the Charter regime "has all but collapsed," notes that between 1945 and 1999, two-thirds of UN member states, or 126 states, fought a total of 291 interstate conflicts.[40] Relying on the Correlates of War database and other empirical studies, John Yoo argues that "the rate of interstate wars either roughly remained the same or increased during the period of the UN Charter and the League of Nations."[41] Glennon and Yoo emphasize the more recent security threats of terrorism[42] and the risk of WMD attacks[43] as phenomena that highlight the

[40] Glennon, *supra* note 7, at 540.

[41] John C. Yoo, *Force Rules: UN Reform and Intervention*, 6 CHI. J. INT'L L. 641, 645 (2006). Yoo acknowledges that if the incidence of interstate war is adjusted for the significant increase in the number of states in the international system after 1945, the frequency of interstate war has dropped in the post-Charter period. *Id.*

[42] Glennon, *supra* note 7, at 541–49.

[43] Yoo, *supra* note 41, at 650.

incompatibility of the Charter's use of force regime with "underlying geopolitical realities,"[44] suggesting that the Charter is becoming increasingly irrelevant to the conduct of states. Tom Farer sees US unilateralism after September 11 as part of a pattern threatening to "break" the "basic force-regulating provisions of the UN Charter."[45] Anthony Arend, after canvassing a series of post-1945 uses of force, suggests that in light of "this historical record of violations, it seems very difficult to conclude that the charter framework is truly controlling of state practice."[46] His pithier conclusion is that "[f]or all practical purposes, the UN Charter framework is dead."[47]

The view that the Charter's use of force regime is increasingly misaligned with the international system's emerging security challenges would suggest a corresponding increase in the overall level of transnational armed conflict. In fact, the use of force has been relatively static since the advent of the United Nations, with only a slight increase in violence over time. Figure 5.1 shows the yearly frequency of militarized interstate disputes (MIDs) that amount to uses of force.[48] The MIDs data set tracks militarized activities of all states in the international system.[49] Because instances of violence included in the MIDs data set do not have to meet the one-thousand-fatality threshold for a war, this data is more inclusive than the Correlates of War data cited by John Yoo. It therefore provides a more comprehensive view of the level of violence in the international system, particularly by tracking low-level uses of forces more reliably. From the MIDs data set, we included instances involving at least two states in which at least one of the following events is present: blockades; occupations of territory; seizures of territory; attacks; clashes; declarations of war; uses of chemical, biological, and/or radiological weapons; beginning interstate wars; or joining interstate wars. Each of these events potentially involves a "use of force" within the meaning

[44] Glennon, *supra* note 7, at 557.

[45] Tom J. Farer, *Beyond the Charter Frame: Unilateralism or Condominium?*, 96 AM. J. INT'L L. 359, 364 (2002).

[46] Anthony Clark Arend, *International Law and the Preemptive use of Military Force*, 26 WASH. Q. 89, 100 (2003).

[47] *Id.* at 101.

[48] The trend in the pattern of MIDs is visualized using a loess smoothing function, a nonparametric, locally weighted smoothing function designed to create a smooth line through scatterplot data in order to visualize trends. It creates a line of best fit without assuming a particular underlying distribution. Essentially, the line in the figure shows the average number of MIDs occurring at any given time, weighted by the density of MIDs occurring around that time period. This smoothing method helps minimize the bias resulting from outliers. It can be useful for interpreting trends during time periods where data is sparse. A 95% confidence interval surrounds the trend line.

[49] We use dispute-level MIDs data (MIDA 4.3) from Glenn Palmer et al., *The MID4 Data Set, 2002–2010*, 32 CONFLICT MGMT. & PEACE SCI. 222–42 (2015).

of Article 2(4). While lower-level MIDs exist—including instances in which states make threats against their adversaries—these almost certainly do not constitute uses of force and are therefore omitted from our analysis. Because we are more inclusive about defining the use of force, we identify many more instances than Yoo or Glennon; between 1945 and 2008, we record 1,138 MIDs potentially involving the use of force.

In Figure 5.1, we also consider trends in two subsets of MIDs involving the use of force: those in which the use of force is *reciprocal*—where both sides in the dispute use force—as well as instances in which at least one fatality occurs. These subsets may provide better proxies for episodes that amount to armed uses of force for the purpose of Article 2(4). In both cases, there is no significant increase in violence over time. Between 1945 and 2008, we record 800 reciprocated uses of force and 313 fatal uses of force.

The relatively static pattern evident in the occurrence of MIDs contradicts the claim that changing security circumstances have led to an increase in the frequency of interstate violence and the corresponding demise of the Charter's use of force regime. However, this pattern does not, on its own, demonstrate that the *legal framework* governing use of force has constrained interstate conflict. At a minimum, though, our results undermine the suggestion that the legal regime governing the use of force is "dead," having collapsed in the face of increasing bellicosity in the international system. In

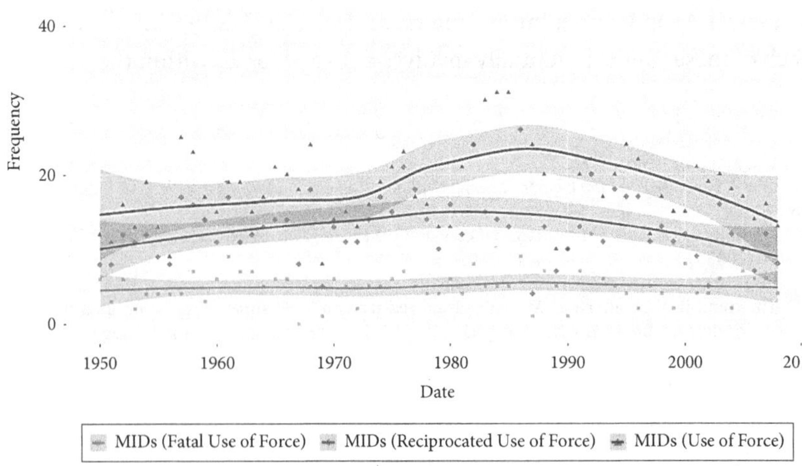

Figure 5.1 Frequency of Militarized Interstate Disputes Involving Use of Force

the remainder of this chapter, we explore states' claims about *when* and *why* they use force and identify implications for the continuing viability of the Charter's use of force regime.

IV. Justifications for the Use of Force

A. Article 51 Communications to Justify the Use of Force

In this section, we describe how states' justifications for the use of force have evolved since 1945 in view of the changing security environment, and we illuminate the implications of these changing patterns for the continued efficacy of the Charter's use of force regime.

For this analysis, we collected a data set of UN member states' Article 51 justifications for the use of force between 1945 and 2018. We build on the work of Dustin Lewis, Naz Modirzadeh, and Gabriella Blum to compile a systematic data set of communications to the Security Council about instances of the use of force that were, purportedly, in self-defense.[50] Lewis, Modirzadeh, and Blum produced a data set that identified all communications they judge to be "communications to the United Nations Security Council of measures taken by U.N. Member States in purported exercise of the right of self-defense."[51] Their methodology involved searching the UN Official Documents System (ODS) for documents including the terms "self-defense," "self-defence," or "Article 51." The authors then identified and removed several "false positives," where the concept of self-defense was mentioned in the context of its perceived *absence*. In essence, the data set catalogues written communications to the UN from member states about acts of self-defense. It is our understanding that this is the only data set that purports to provide a comprehensive set of such communications.[52] Building on this,

[50] Dustin A. Lewis, Naz K. Modirzadeh, & Gabriella Blum, Quantum of Silence: Inaction and Jus Ad Bellum (2019), https://papers.ssrn.com/sol3/papers.cfm?abstract_id=3420959.

[51] *Id.*, Annex. The Charter prescribes no particular form or mechanism for submitting reports under Article 51.

[52] Green reports having compiled an original data set of Article 51 communications, but it covers only reports submitted between 1998 and 2013. *See* Green, *supra* note 13, at 566. Green identifies the existence of two hundred Article 51 reports submitted by states between 1998 and 2013, *id.* at 575, while our data set includes only 163 reports during this time period. After removing "repeated reporting" by Iraq, Green reports ninety-seven Article 51 communications during the 1998–2013 period. *Id.* at 583. Because Green's article does not explicitly identify the data collection methods used, it is not possible to assess the basis for the differences between the two data sets.

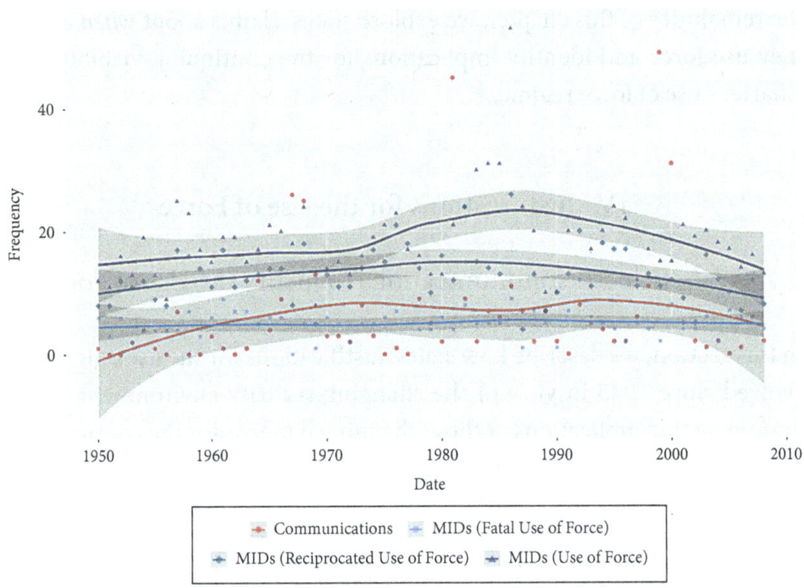

Figure 5.2 MIDs and Article 51 Communication Frequencies

we collected the full text of each communication,[53] dropping from the data set repeated communications and verbal communications (those evidenced in meeting notes from UN Security Council sessions). In total, we collected 416 written communications between 119 unique directed dyads[54] between May 7, 1951, and November 15, 2018.[55]

Like the frequency of conflict, the use of Article 51 communications has been relatively constant over time since adoption of the Charter. While not all uses of force are justified via an Article 51 communication, states submit them with relative frequency, especially for more intense uses of force. Figure 5.2 shows the yearly frequency of Article 51 communications—in red—as well as the yearly frequency of interstate uses of force—in dark blue. Between 1945 and 2008, there were an average of eighteen MIDs potentially involving the use of force per year and an average of six Article 51 communications

[53] We identified each document in the ODS archives and then used one of three transcription methods: webscraping, OCR, or manual transcription.

[54] For example, Israeli communications about Syria are distinct from Syrian communications about Israel.

[55] The Lewis, Modirzadeh, and Blum data set contains 433 observations.

per year.[56] Crucially, this 1:3 ratio remains largely unchanged over time. This indicates that states are *not* justifying their uses of force less frequently—which presumably would be true if a changing international security environment meant that states, in their "actual patterns of practice,"[57] were increasingly using force in circumstances deviating from the Charter's traditional self-defense model, as the commentators noted earlier suggest. While there are prominent cases in which states did not seek to justify their uses of force in the Security Council—such as Israel's preventive strikes on Syrian nuclear assets in 2007, Russia's 2014 intervention into Ukraine, and the US-led 1999 bombing campaign against the Federal Republic of Yugoslavia—in many other instances, states used the legal mechanisms associated with Article 51 to explain their militarized actions.[58] Contrary to what we would expect to see if the use of force regime had become obsolete, states invoke the Article 51 reporting mechanism as frequently today as they did during the Charter's early days.

Moreover, the 1:3 reporting ratio of Article 51 communications to *all* MIDs potentially involving the use of force likely significantly understates the rate of reporting. The MID database includes low intensity acts of violence that states might not see as warranting a forcible response in self-defense. For example, one MID describes an event where the United States condemned

[56] Our findings differ in this respect from those of James Green, who argues that Article 51 "reporting frequency" during the 1998–2013 period is "significantly higher than it was during the Cold War." Green, *supra* note 13, at 575. Green himself acknowledges, however, that assessments of Article 51 reporting rates prior to 1998 "have not been based on a systematic study of state reporting," *id.* at 575, and Green provides no quantitative data on Article 51 reporting prior to 1998. Moreover, in comparing reported instances of self-defense to the total number of self-defense cases, Green relies on the Uppsala Conflict Data Program *Dyadic Dataset Version 1-2014* (1946–2013), *id.* at 577, rather than the subsets of the MIDs data we rely on. The Uppsala data identifies instances of "state-based armed conflict," defined as "a contested incompatibility that concerns government and/or territory where the use of armed force between two parties, of which at least one is the government of a state, results in at least 25 battle-related deaths in a year." Lotta Themnér, *UCDP Dyadic Dataset Codebook Version 1-2014* § 2.1 (2014), https://ucdp.uu.se/downloads/replication_data/2014_c_666956-l_1-k_ucdp-dyadic-dataset_codebook-2014.pdf. Many instances of the use of force do not involve twenty-five or more deaths; the use of Uppsala's data as a proxy for the use of force, in our opinion, thus undercounts. We believe that our MIDs data subsets present more accurate representations of the true underlying incidence of the "use of force" in international relations within the meaning of Article 2(4) of the Charter. In addition, because we include a broader set of the uses of force than previous analyses, and because states may be less likely to submit Article 51 documentation for less intensive uses of force, our approach biases against our hypothesis that the legal use-of-force regime has maintained its relevance.

[57] Glennon, *supra* note 7, at 557.

[58] O'Connell cites the failure by the United States to provide legal justifications for its 2017 and 2018 attacks against Syria to argue that "decades of ever thinner arguments justifying the use of force may have reached the vanishing point." O'Connell, *supra* note 5, at 155 n.17. Notwithstanding these and other prominent cases in which states do not report their actions to the Security Council, the data on the broader pattern of state justifications for the use of force belies O'Connell's argument.

Cuba for shooting down two private aircraft belonging to a US-based anti-Castro group while they were flying over international waters. The MIDs data codes this event as an "attack," but it did not provoke the United States to use force in self-defense. The data may thus reflect *underresponding* by states more than underreporting.

To assess the rate of reporting more precisely, we also compare the frequency of Article 51 communications to the frequency of reciprocal MIDs and to the frequency of fatal MIDs. If states do not act on or report about minor forcible incidents, but only submit communications when uses of force meet a threshold of significance that implicates international peace and security, then comparing the rate of communications to MIDs in which an exchange of force or at least one fatality occurs may provide better proxies for understanding how often the Article 51 reporting requirement is invoked. For both these of comparisons, the reporting rate is higher and largely consistent, suggesting again that there has not been a decline in the rate of justifications. There are half as many communications as *reciprocal* MIDs, although it is possible for both sides in a reciprocal MID to use low levels of force not rising to the level of an "armed attack," and that accordingly do not trigger the right of self-defense under Article 51. For example, in a 1995 MID, Costa Rican civil guards crossed into Nicaragua while pursuing illegal immigrants; the guards were seized by Nicaraguan forces. Costa Rica then seized two Nicaraguan policemen who crossed the Costa Rican border to drink water. The two sides later exchanged their prisoners. The fact that neither state submitted an Article 51 report in connection with this MID should not be construed as evidence of disregard of the Charter's use of force regime. The rate of reporting is much higher in the context of more violent interactions. On average, there are almost twice as many Article 51 communications per year as *fatal* MIDs.[59] This rate may reflect the fact that states on both sides of a MID might submit a communication when a fatal MID occurs. The rate of reporting in comparison to fatal conflicts offers richer insight into how the Charter is functioning. As Monica Hakimi writes:

[59] Katherine Irajpanah and Kenneth Schultz find that forty of one hundred thirty-five (thirty percent) "war participants" produced Article 51 reports. They define wars using the Correlates of War database, which has a threshold of one thousand battle deaths. Irajpanah and Schultz use a different data set of Article 51 reporting which combines the Lewis, Modirzadeh, and Blum data set with additional documents identified through Irajpanah and Schultz's search of "letters or other official documents" in the UN Dag Hammarskjöld Library's DAG Repository that mention the phrases "Article 51," "self-defense," or "defend itself." Katherine Irajpanah & Kenneth A. Schultz, *Off the Menu: Revisiting the Disappearance of War Declarations after 1945*, 30 Security Stud. 485, 499 n.66, 500 (2021).

> It is not clear to what extent the violations that have occurred betray an overall lack of constraint. . . . [P]erhaps the Charter has effectively constrained conduct that hits at the core of Article 2(4)—large-scale invasions or annexations of foreign territory—but has been less effective on lower level or indirect uses of force. . . . Not all violations are the same.[60]

Even when considering fatal MIDs, however, some underreporting persists. Some states participate in fatal MIDs but do not use the Article 51 reporting mechanism at all. For example, Afghanistan, Congo, Albania, and North Korea are all nonreporting states that participated in at least four fatal MIDs. Other states do submit Article 51 communications at times, but chronically underreport, such as Turkey, Russia, Yugoslavia, Uganda, Croatia, and Sudan.[61] At the same time, there are also many states with rates of reporting largely commensurate with the number of fatal MIDs in which they are involved, including the United States, Pakistan, India, Thailand, China, Syria, Ethiopia, and Poland.

The non-increase in the use of force, the steady use of the Charter regime over time, and the high rate of reporting relative to fatal uses of force all evidence the regime's continued importance and suggest that the regime's alignment with the international security environment has not changed significantly since adoption of the Charter. States' continued use of Article 51 communications implies that they gain concrete utility from exercising this option.

B. Identifying States' Justifications for the Use of Force

Using primarily dictionary-based computational text-analysis methods, we analyzed the content of states' Article 51 communications.[62] That is, we manually compiled dictionaries of words associated with certain justifications for

[60] Monica Hakimi, *What Might (Finally) Kill the* Jus ad Bellum?, 74 CURRENT LEGAL PROBS. 101, 107 (2021).

[61] In a draft version of their study of war declarations, *supra* note 59, Irajpanah and Schultz find that a country's military capabilities are inversely related to the likelihood of submitting an Article 51 report, and that permanent members of the Security Council (except the United States) and states with a connection to them are less likely to submit Article 51 reports. Katherine Irajpanah & Kenneth Schultz, *Off the Menu: Revisiting the Disappearance of War Declarations After 1945*, at 28–29 (2020 draft manuscript) (on file with author).

[62] We removed symbols, special characters, numbers, punctuation, and capitalization from the speeches, consistent with previous work. *See* Justin Grimmer & Brandon M. Stewart, *Text as Data: The Promise and Pitfalls of Automatic Content Analysis Methods for Political Texts*, 21 POL. ANALYSIS 267 (2013). We also removed "stop words," i.e., words that generally lack content, such

the use of force and then tracked the use of those justifications over time. Dictionary-based methods can be used to classify any type of text into any type of group, and they are one of the most exhaustive and efficient computer-assisted methods of text-analysis.[63] We developed dictionaries for the accepted[64] and contested[65] legal claims that states employ to justify their uses of force. In addition, we identified several extralegal justifications and developed dictionaries of terms associated with those topics.[66] We determined

as "the" or "and," and we employed a "Porter Stemmer," which improves the information-retrieval performance of text-analysis algorithms. The stemmer shortens words to their stems—changing, for example, "defending" and "defender" to "defend"—allowing us to more accurately determine the content of communications without as much concern for elements like whether US or British spellings are employed, what tense is used, or whether some types of spelling mistakes have occurred. See Wahiba Karaa Ben Abdessalem, *A New Stemmer to Improve Information Retrieval*, 5 INT'L J. NETWORK SEC. & ITS APPLICATIONS 143 (2013).

[63] *See* Lei Guo et al., *Big Social Data Analytics in Journalism and Mass Communication: Comparing Dictionary-Based Text Analysis and Unsupervised Topic Modeling*, 93 JOURNALISM & MASS COMM'N Q. 332 (2016); DANIEL RIFFE ET AL., ANALYZING MEDIA MESSAGES: USING QUANTITATIVE CONTENT ANALYSIS IN RESEARCH (2019).

[64] Each dictionary has a threshold, or a number of times that words in the dictionary must appear. Thresholds are determined by the authors, taking into account dictionary size, frequency, crossover, and the justification's scope. For the accepted legal justifications, the thresholds are set to three for counterattacks and to one for collective self-defense and ceasefire violation.

[65] The contested legal justifications are anticipatory self-defense, cyber, nonstate actors, humanitarianism, and reprisals. Cyber has a threshold of one. Nonstate actors and humanitarianism have thresholds of five. However, while this approach helps us identify *when* states mention humanitarianism, to determine *how* they employ humanitarianism requires further investigation. Therefore, we qualitatively examined each of the cases above the threshold to evaluate who the alleged victims of humanitarian abuses were and how the state using force claimed to be responding to them. As elaborated later, we assess whether a state is invoking a legal right of humanitarian intervention or instead citing humanitarian concerns as a complementary extralegal justification. For anticipatory self-defense, the authors read all communications that met a threshold of one, then determined if an actual anticipatory self-defense legal justification was included in the communication. For reprisals, the authors evaluated all communications that met a threshold of one and that did *not* discuss violations of ceasefire agreements. This second condition is necessary because language discussing breach of ceasefire agreements—unlike forcible responses to violations of other legal obligation—is indicative of an accepted justification for the use of force. The authors then evaluated whether these communications included a true reprisal claim.

[66] The extralegal justifications use the following thresholds:

Justification	Threshold
Character of Actors	10
Governance	5
Gravity	5
Normative Values	5
Regional Stability	5
Transparency	5
Economy	3
Premeditation	3

the content of all dictionaries by reading all 416 communications in our data set, identifying distinguishing and high-content words associated with the various justifications for the use of force. The resulting process created dictionaries of words associated with each justification. Table 5.1 displays these justifications and a sample of the dictionary terms associated with each justification.[67] Using these dictionaries, we can identify how often any communication mentions words associated with each justification. This methodology allows us to categorize documents accurately[68] by justification and to track the use of the various justifications over time.

Using these dictionaries, we coded each communication for whether or not it mentions any of the justifications under study. Table 5.2 presents the frequency with which each of these justifications was mentioned in the full set of communications. The uniformly accepted legal justification—self-defense in the form of a counterattack—is present in nearly all communications, consistent with the traditional interpretation of self-defense in the use of force regime. Other accepted justifications, such as uses of force in collective self-defense or in response to violations of ceasefire agreements, are less common (8.17 percent and 35.58 percent, respectively). This is presumably because they describe rare events to begin with. The contested claims are made less frequently, although their frequency varies. On the low end are cyber operations (appearing in no communications), discussions of anticipatory self-defense (2.16 percent), and reprisals (9.38 percent). References to nonstate actors (22.36 percent) are more common. Almost 40 percent of communications mention humanitarian concerns. As explained later, however, the vast majority of invocations of humanitarian considerations involve states' claims about abuses being perpetrated against their own nationals in the context of uses of force rooted in accepted justifications, like countering an enemy's armed attack or responding to a violation of a ceasefire agreement. The use of extralegal justifications occurs in 80 percent of communications.

[67] The full dictionaries can be found in the online Appendix A.1, available at laurensukin.com. Dictionary terms are all lowercase and the Porter Stemmer is applied to them before analysis takes place. Full terms are provided in Table 5.1, however, for clarity.

[68] *See infra* Appendix.

Table 5.1 Justifications in Article 51 Communications and Sample Dictionary Terms

	Sample Dictionary Terms				
Justification	1	2	3	4	5
Accepted Legal Claims					
Counterattack	Defense	Protect	Reciprocal	Repercussion	Reversed
Collective Self-defense	Collective self defense	Collective self defence	Collective self-defense	Collective self-defence	Collective selfdefense
Ceasefire Agreement Violation	Armistice	Cease	Demilitarized	Moratorium	Truce
Contested Legal Claims					
Anticipatory Self-defense	Inevitable	Preemption	Premeditation	Pretext	Preventative
Cyber Operations	Cyber	Cyberwarfare	Cyberwar	Hacker	Internet
Humanitarianism	Abuse	Brutality	Crimes	Extermination	Genocide
Nonstate Actors	Extremism	Insurgency	Irregular	Terrorism	Separatist
Reprisals	Broken	Compliance	Enshrined	Illegal	Unlawful
Extralegal Justifications					
Character of Actors	Bad	Colonizer	Expansionist	Hegemonic	Hero
Economy	Disruption	Economic	Factory	Farm	Trade
Governance	Constitution	Democratic	Dictator	Elections	Junta
Gravity	Critical	Daily	Endanger	Heavy	Incessant
Normative Values	Equitable	Ethical	Freedom	Inhumane	Justice
Premeditation	Calculated	Deliberate	Premeditated	Preplanned	Willful
Regional Stability	Destabilization	Escalation	International	Region	Spillover
*Transparency***	Evidence	Eyewitness	Factual	Information	Propaganda

* "Character of actors" refers to both negative and positive descriptors of actors, including of both the state that submitted the Article 51 communication and its adversary. "Economy" refers to discussions of primarily domestic economic conditions, often in relation to the impact of conflict on these factors. "Governance" refers to discussions of the governing systems and styles of one or more of the states involved in a conflict. "Gravity" refers to language indicating the seriousness of a threat or situation covered by an Article 51 communication. "Normative values" refers to statements about systems of ethics and other normative attitudes that states hold. "Premeditation" refers to language used to describe ways in which an adversary's harmful actions were preplanned. "Regional stability" refers to ways in which violence might affect regional political dynamics. "Transparency" refers to evidentiary issues and openness, generally as they relate to determining the facts of a situation. *See supra*, section II.F, for more details on the extralegal justifications.

** Transparency is a critical mechanism in treaty enforcement. *See* Abram Chayes & Antonia Handler Chayes, *Compliance Without Enforcement: State Behavior under Regulatory Treaties*, 7 NEGOT. J. 311 (1991); Kal Raustiala & Anne-Marie Slaughter, *International Law, International Relations and Compliance*, *in* HANDBOOK OF INTERNATIONAL RELATIONS 538 (Walter Carlsnaes et al. eds., 2002).

Table 5.2 Frequency of Justifications

Justification Type	Justification	Percent Communications
Accepted Claims	Counterattack	96.15
	Ceasefire Agreement Violation	35.58
	Collective Self-defense	8.17
Contested Claims	Humanitarianism/Humanitarian Intervention	39.90
	Nonstate Actors	22.36
	Reprisals	9.38
	Anticipatory Self-defense	2.16
	Cyber Operations	0.00
Extralegal Justifications	Premeditation	42.79
	Character of Actors	41.11
	Governance	26.44
	Gravity	26.20
	Regional Stability	18.99
	Economy	14.90
	Normative Values	14.90
	Transparency	9.38

C. Patterns in Accepted Justifications: Counterattacks, Collective Self-defense, and Violations of Ceasefire Agreements

Arguably, the best test of our hypothesis that the functioning of the use of force regime has not undergone significant change since the Charter's adoption is whether states continue to rely heavily on the accepted legal justifications for their uses of force. Our results indicate this is the case. Nearly all communications in our data set involve claims that states are engaging in counterattacks in response to adversary attacks.

In Figures 5.3–5.9, each point on the graph indicates a communication. All communications are coded as either using a justification and are given a value of "1," or as not using a justification ("0"). For any given date, the points on the graph show all communications submitted to the Security Council. Within any given time period, the figures display the density of communications mentioning a justification compared to the density of failing to mention it. This reveals trends in the use of justifications over time. Loess smoothers and 95 percent confidence intervals are also used to visualize trends in the data.

Figure 5.3 shows that mentions of counterattacks are extremely common. Since this is the most accepted legal basis for the use of force, it is unsurprising that this justification is so consistently advanced, if states indeed care about their reputations for legality. That is, if states used Article 51 communications only as a way to transmit messages about their interests, without regard to considerations of legality, they would have little reason to rely so heavily on the accepted legal justification. Instead, we see that states routinely justify their uses of force in terms of accepted legal standards. This suggests that states are generally neither disregarding the formal legal regime governing the use of force nor advocating for changes to it. Figure 5.3 therefore implies that, as in 1945, states recognize that legal standards departing from the limited and clearly demarcated grounds for using force recognized in the Charter would result in greater instability and insecurity in the international system. In other words, our data reflects that states continue to favor

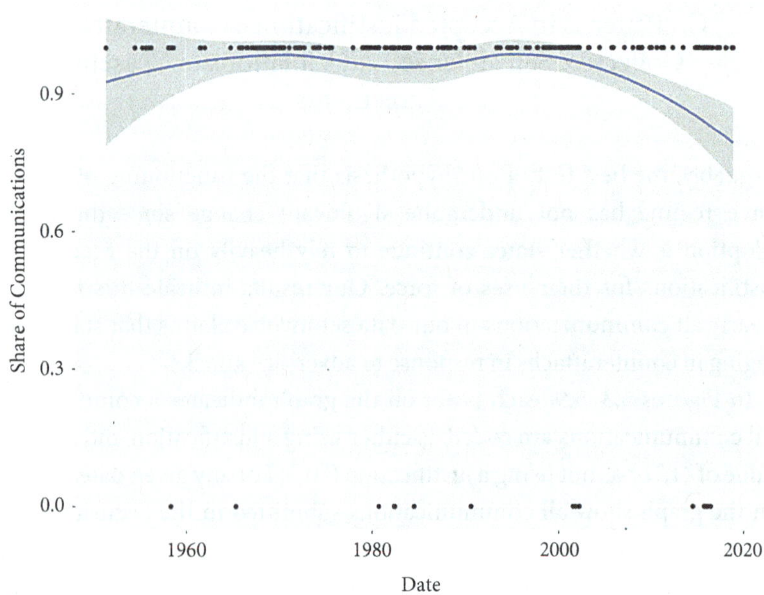

Figure 5.3 Communications with Mentions of Counterattacks

a formal legal framework that favors "peace rather than preserving justice and redressing injustice."[69]

The frequency of reliance on this traditional self-defense interpretation has been declining slightly since 2000, with only 90 percent of communications since 2000 including this justification. The decline, however, does not indicate that states are moving away from traditional justifications for the use of force. Instead, the decline is explained by an increase in the occurrence of collective self-defense, which is also uncontroversial under black letter law. Since 2000, 27 percent of communications have involved collective self-defense, compared to just 4 percent of communications in prior years. This is largely due to the collective self-defense of Iraq undertaken by a number of states against ISIS in Iraq and Syria. Ninety-five percent of post-2000 communications mention either counterattacks or collective self-defense, and that rate does not differ significantly from before the turn of the century. Patterns in the frequency of the collective self-defense justification are visualized in Figure 5.4.

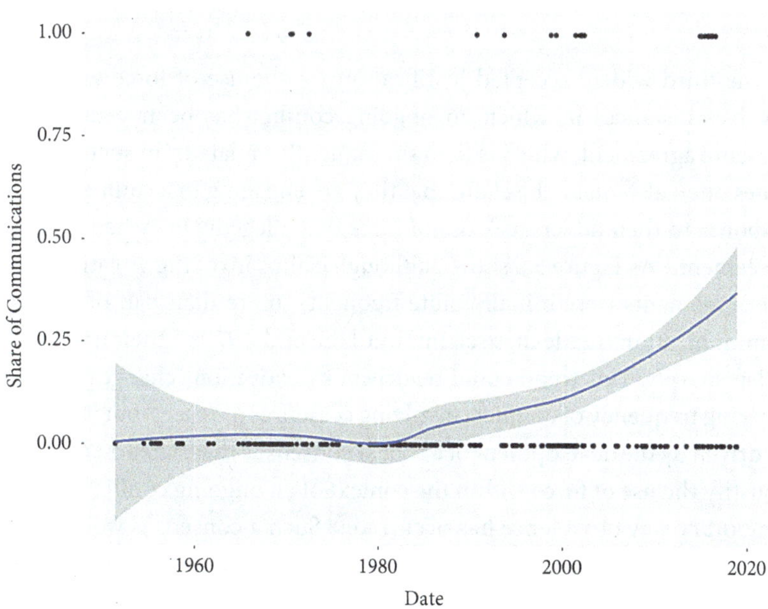

Figure 5.4 Communications with Mentions of Collective Self-Defense

[69] Franck, *supra* note 9, at 16.

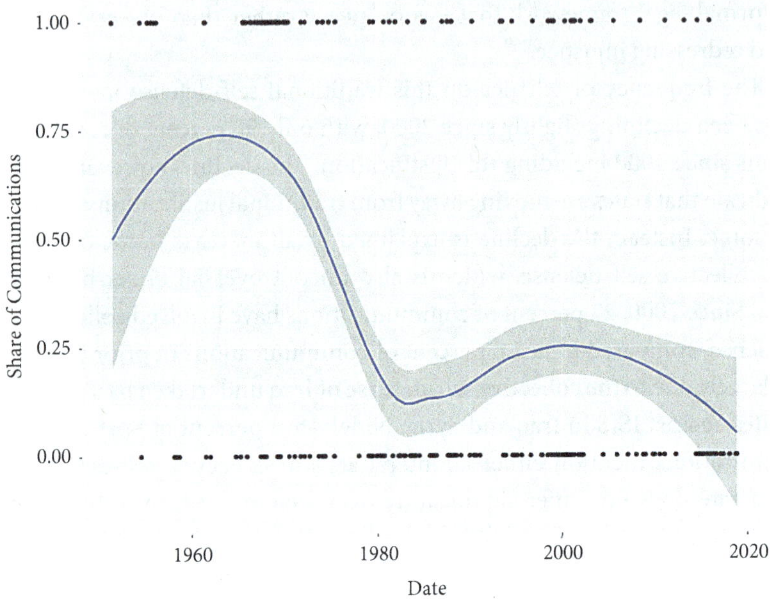

Figure 5.5 Communications with Mentions of Ceasefire Violations

The third widely accepted justification for the use of force we examine involves instances in which an ongoing conflict has been paused with a ceasefire agreement, which is then subsequently violated. (In such instances, states often also make the claim that they are engaging in a counterattack, in response to their adversary's use of force that allegedly breached a ceasefire agreement.) As Figure 5.5 shows, although claims invoking violations ceasefire agreements were initially quite frequent—more than half of Article 51 communications made these claims until the mid-1970s—their use has since fallen sharply. This trend could be driven by exogenous changes in the underlying frequency of conflicts involving ceasefires or truces, but it could also be driven by the development of a robust consensus that states do not need to rejustify the use of force within the context of an ongoing conflict—even if a temporary stay of violence has occurred.[70] Such a consensus would obviate the need for states to submit Article 51 communications when ceasefires are

[70] As Michael Schmitt notes, "Conventional military campaigns seldom occur as either a single blow or an extended period of uninterrupted combat. On the contrary, pauses are the norm, not the exception, in conflict." Michael N. Schmitt, *Preemptive Strategies in International Law*, 24 MICH. J. INT'L L. 513, 535 (2003).

violated. In this way, the decline in the use of ceasefire violation justifications for uses of force may illustrate what happens when justifications become commonly accepted; these norms influence state behavior in myriad ways, delineating when force is and is not acceptable.

D. Patterns in Contested Claims: Anticipatory Self-defense, Nonstate Actors, Reprisals, and Humanitarian Intervention

In contrast to the aforementioned justifications, which enjoy general acceptance within the international community, there are several contested claims that states sometimes invoke in an effort to justify their uses of force. One such claim is that a state was acting in anticipatory self-defense, preempting an imminent use of force by an adversary. Notwithstanding the notable degree of support for such a doctrine in the legal literature and diplomatic discourse, there are few Article 51 communications in which states have claimed the right to use force on the basis of anticipatory self-defense. This suggests that it is *not* generally accepted as a legitimate reason for the use of force. Changing the trigger for the lawfulness of the unilateral use of force from a clear and objective bright-line rule (the existence of an "armed attack") to a more flexible and subjectively ascertained standard (the "threat of attack") would "greatly increase the opportunity for states to find legal pretexts for attacking their adversaries" and would be a "highly subjective and difficult-to-falsify standard that . . . can easily be invoked by states seeking to use force to engage in aggression or to pursue other national interests."[71] States' continuing "fear of misuse"[72] of the doctrine of anticipatory self-defense may thus explain why states have largely avoided explicitly invoking that justification for the use of force during the Charter period.

Nevertheless, the notion of using force in the face of threats is not entirely absent from states' justifications for the use of force. For example, in a communication from October 2, 1985, South Africa defended its military operations against nonstate armed groups in Botswana by claiming that it had "exercised its inherent and natural right of self-defence in order to curtail further imminent acts of violence" against it. In other cases, even though a

[71] Weiner, *supra* note 16, at 495.

[72] Michael D. Ramsey, *Reinventing the Security Council: The U.N. as a Lockean System*, 79 Notre Dame L. Rev. 1529, 1556 (2004).

state cites a use of force by the adversary that might trigger a right of self-defense, it seems clear that the use of force described in the Article 51 communication is, in fact, aimed at threatened actions that have not yet occurred. For example, in a communication from January 15, 2008, Chad initially refers to "acts of aggression and destabilization committed by the Sudan" in invoking its right of self-defense. Chad further contends, though, that Sudan "is determined and secretly plotting to use every possible means to install a compliant regime" in Chad. Under the circumstances, Chad asserts, it "cannot continue to wait indefinitely, and is only exercising its legitimate right to defend itself." In this case, and in a small number of others, the use of force is directed against a perceived threat, rather than (or in addition to) a specific attack a state has already sustained. Anticipatory self-defense also sometimes emerges in a collective self-defense context, where states suggest they are deploying forces to another state to prevent (further) uses of force against that state; an anticipatory logic is present in these cases, even though no anticipatory use of force has occurred.

Figure 5.6 illustrates the frequency with which the anticipatory self-defense justification is employed in Article 51 communications. The figure

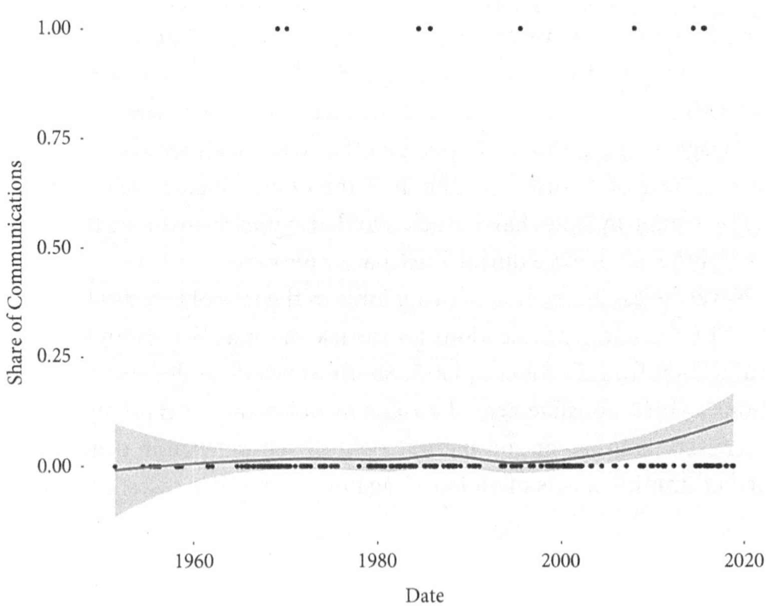

Figure 5.6 Communications with Mentions of Anticipatory Self-Defense

shows the invocation of the logic of anticipatory self-defense is very rare. In fact, there are only nine cases of its use in our data set, many of which are not clear-cut. Nevertheless, in rare cases, states do appear to take anticipatory action, either because of pressing strategic reasons or, perhaps, because they believe they can confidently demonstrate their adversary's attack was indeed imminent.

Scholars have often discussed anticipatory self-defense in the context of advanced weaponry—such as planes, missiles, drones, WMD, and rockets—that may lower states' response times and thus incentivize preemptive first strikes.[73] However, mentions of anticipatory self-defense do not occur in any Article 51 communications that contain mentions of WMD. Despite changes in the international security environment that might provide states with incentives to use force preemptively, states have not invoked anticipatory self-defense at significantly increasing rates since the Charter's adoption.

Other contested justifications have emerged since 1945 as responses to the changing security environment. For example, as Figure 5.7 shows, states have increasingly referenced the right to respond to attacks by nonstate actors, even when the nonstate actor is located in a third state that does not consent to the use of force on its territory. Such justifications have increased dramatically since the early 1980s.

This pattern may be driven by particular recurring conflicts that feature in the Article 51 data. For example, Israel's justifications for its various interventions into Lebanon include discussions of the right to retaliate against Hezbollah, a nonstate actor. The frequency of those communications may skew the data to overvalue justifications that Israel invokes. To address this, we reweight the data such that the set of all communications between each directed dyad are weighted equally.[74] For example, the fifteen communications from Israel about Lebanon are given equal weight in their effect on the loess trend as has the single communication between Mauritania and Algeria. When utilizing this approach, the trend remains the same; justifications for the use of force relying on the right to respond to nonstate actors have increased dramatically since the early 1980s.

This increase in the invocation of a right to use force abroad against nonstate actors is a response to the changing international security environment,

[73] Antony Anghie & Charles Hill, *The Bush Administration Preemption Doctrine and the United Nations*, 98 ASIL Proc. 326 (2004); Matthew C. Waxman, *The Use of Force Against States that Might Have Weapons of Mass Destruction*, 31 Mich. J. Int'l L. 11 (2009).

[74] *See* online Appendix A.2, at laurensukin.com.

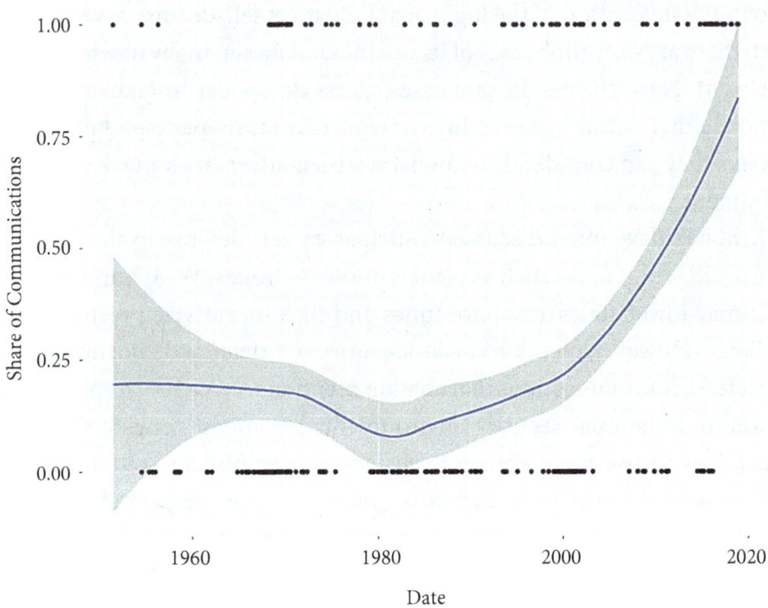

Figure 5.7 Communications with Mentions of Nonstate Actors

in which conflict involving nonstate actors has become more frequent. Transnational nonstate armed conflicts and Article 51 justifications involving nonstate actors are highly and significantly correlated.[75] The positive correlation suggests that increasingly frequent claims of a legal right to attack another state's territory in response to the use of force by nonstate actors are a product of a security environment in which traditional, interstate conflict is no longer the predominant mode of warfare. In this new environment, states are embracing an adaptive interpretation of the Charter to address nonstate armed groups located in the territory of another state.

Although the transnational use of force against nonstate actors has become more prominent in states' Article 51 communications, those communications do not exhibit widespread support for the "unwilling or unable" doctrine advanced by the United States.[76] Notwithstanding the significant increase in transnational uses of force involving nonstate actors, states have

[75] *See* online Appendix A.3, at laurensukin.com.
[76] *See supra* notes 28–30 and accompanying text.

expressly invoked the "unwilling or unable" doctrine in only three Article 51 communications. Instead, states facing nonstate actors typically invoke their right of self-defense in response to attacks they have sustained, offering little additional legal elaboration regarding the basis for acting on the territory of another state. The combination of the increasing invocation of the right to use force against nonstate actors along with the absence of an embrace of the "unwilling or unable" doctrine suggests that no consensus has emerged about the legal conditions under which states may use force against nonstate actors located abroad, and that the international community's "ceaseless dialectic"[77] on this subject is ongoing. But while the boundaries delimiting *when* states may legally retaliate against nonstate actors on the territory of other states are unclear, there does appear to be a consensus that states *do* have a right to respond in other countries to uses of force by nonstate actors.

Just as the threat emanating from nonstate actors has become more acute since 1945, challenges around responses to atrocities committed by governments against their own populations have also placed growing pressure on the Charter's use of force regime. As noted earlier, some scholars have suggested there are circumstances in which the use of force to halt severe humanitarian abuses abroad is legally permissible, even though the state using force has not sustained an armed attack. However, explicit invocations by states of a right of humanitarian intervention—like the United Kingdom's formal embrace of the doctrine and Belgium's 1999 argument before the ICJ—are empirically quite rare. Indeed, the Article 51 communications reinforce the position that states are *not* advocating for an adaptive interpretation of the law that would endorse a right of unilateral armed humanitarian intervention. We find no cases in which states have explicitly claimed the legal right to use force against another state based on that state's mistreatment of its own population. This may be because states recognize potentially negative consequences of embracing humanitarian intervention as an accepted formal legal justification for the use of force; doing so could significantly expand the circumstances in which states use force against one another, potentially exacerbating international instability. It might also increase states' sense of vulnerability to the risk of foreign intervention in their own internal affairs. Thus, even states that engage in humanitarian interventions in particular circumstances, or that might defend intervention on humanitarian

[77] Reisman, *supra* note 11, at 82.

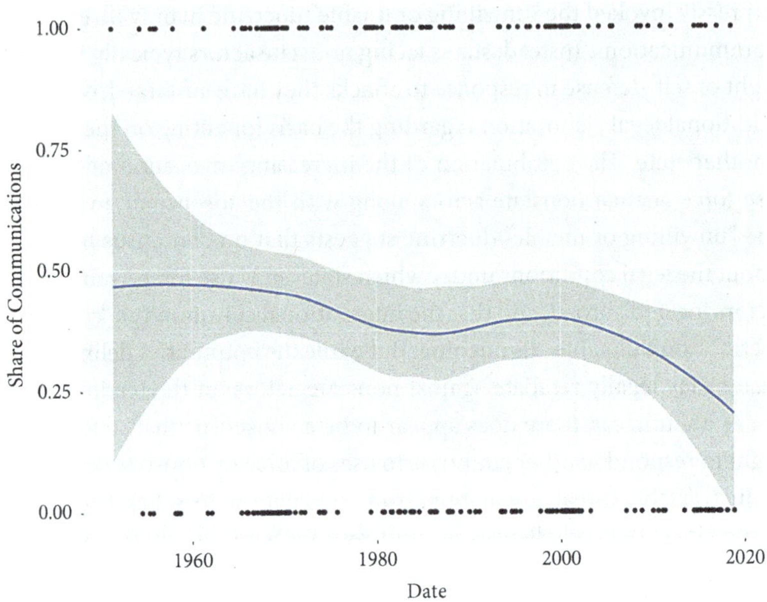

Figure 5.8 Communications with Mentions of Humanitarianism

grounds in other fora, may be reticent to invoke this argument as a formal legal principle in the Security Council.

Even so, states routinely use language about humanitarian issues to justify uses of force; in fact, this justification has featured prominently since the beginning of the Charter era. As Figure 5.8 shows, just under half of Article 51 communications mentioned humanitarian issues throughout the 1950s. But states are not invoking humanitarian concerns in support of a legal doctrine that would permit them to use force to save citizens of other countries. To the contrary, in 85 percent of the 141 cases that contain humanitarian considerations, states cite the humanitarian harm sustained by *their own population* in the context of an armed attack (either by a state or nonstate actor) or a breach of a ceasefire agreement. A small number of cases (4 percent) involve claims about mistreatment of the notifying state's own citizens living in the adversary country and, as such, can be considered part of a "defense of nationals" or "protection of citizens abroad" legal justification for using force.[78] In both of these scenarios, states focus on the humanitarian protection of their own

[78] DINSTEIN, *supra* note 25, at 219–21, 275–79.

citizens. In another notable proportion of cases (12 percent), states refer to the humanitarian interests of the citizens of the adversary state by emphasizing the precautions they are taking in their armed operations to minimize harm to enemy civilians. In only a small number of cases (9 percent) do states cite the adversary state's mistreatment of its own civilians (or third country civilians) as part of a broader moral and political justification for their use of force. In all such cases, however, these concerns are complementary to reliance on accepted legal justifications for using force, like responding to the adversary's armed attack or its violation of a ceasefire agreement.[79] As such, there are no "pure" cases of humanitarian intervention. Principles about international human rights or humanitarianism accordingly are referenced, essentially, as extralegal considerations. They provide moral and political support for, or are intended to mitigate international criticism of, uses of force, including some that could be difficult to reconcile with the black letter law. More on extralegal justifications follows.

The final contested justification for using force involves legal reprisals. States invoking legal reprisals use general language associated with violations of legal obligations—such as "breach," "duty," "enshrined," "illegal," "liable," and so forth—but are *not* using these terms in relation to specific alleged violations of ceasefire agreements. For example, an Article 51 communication dated June 8, 2004, from the Israeli government described the firing of explosive devices and infiltration attempts by nonstate armed groups operating from Lebanese territory. In justifying its use of force against the nonstate actors on Lebanon's territory, Israel stated that the attacks against it "were enabled by the complicity of the Government of Lebanon, and with the

[79] For example, in December 1971, India used force against Pakistan, including East Pakistan (now Bangladesh), which was engaged in a war of independence against Pakistan. In its Article 51 communication justifying its use of force, India highlighted the suffering of the people of East Pakistan, but particularly emphasized the massive influx of refugees into India fleeing oppression in East Pakistan:

> [I]f one State deliberately drives millions of its citizens across the territory of another State and casts upon the receiving State unconscionable burdens, what remedies are open to the receiving State which has become a victim of domestic policies of a Member State of the United Nations? . . . For nine long months India staggered under this load and exercised the utmost self-restraint.

Permanent Rep. of India to the U.N., Letter dated 12 December 1971 from the Permanent Rep. of India addressed to the Secretary-General, U.N. Doc. S/10445 (Dec. 12, 1971).

Although safeguarding a state against the burdens imposed by refugees fleeing disorder in a neighboring state is not an accepted basis for the use of force, India nevertheless reportedly planned to attack East Pakistan on December 4, 1971. Pakistan, however, struck first and launched attacks against Indian territory on December 3. *See* Gary J. Bass, *The Indian Way of Humanitarian Intervention*, 40 YALE J. INT'L L. 227, 235 (2015). India accordingly also invoked its right of self-defense in response to the Pakistani attacks in its Article 51 communication. Letter from the Permanent Rep. of India to the U.N., *supra*.

support of the Syrian and Iranian regimes that have long sponsored, trained and financed these terrorist groups." Israel continued that Lebanon's "grave violation" of its obligation to "prevent crossborder attacks from its territory" was the "direct cause of instability in the area and of the necessity for Israel to take measures in self-defense." Israel's reproach of Lebanon's violations of international law cited obligations imposed on Lebanon in several Security Council resolutions to ensure the restoration of effective Lebanese government authority in southern Lebanon (UN Security Council Resolutions 425, 426, 1310, 1337) and to prevent persons who "commit terrorist acts from using [a state's territory] for those purposes against other States" (Security Council Resolution 1373). Yet violations of these legal obligations by themselves would not necessarily provide Israel with a legal basis for using force against Lebanon. Nevertheless, the communication depicts Lebanon as a persistent violator of its international legal obligations. Israel, in this way, seeks the international community's tolerance of its use of force in self-help, even if it does not expressly invoke a legal right of reprisal.

Despite this example, the use of this type of self-help or reprisal justification is infrequent, as Figure 5.9 shows. Reliance on the language of reprisal,

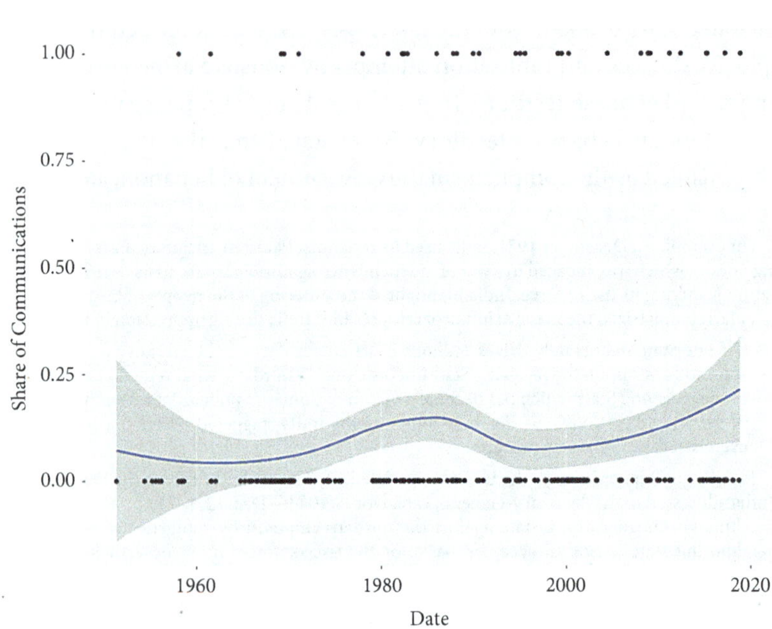

Figure 5.9 Communications with Mentions of Reprisals

that is, claims highlighting the adversary's breach of legal obligations *other* than the Charter's prohibition on the use of force, has never come close to approximating the frequency with which states rely on the accepted understanding of the right to use force in response to an adversary's attack in their Article 51 communications. When states do allege that their adversary has breached legal duties (outside of the context of ceasefire agreements), this usually occurs in tandem with a claim that the state using force has sustained an attack triggering the right of self-defense. There are only nine Article 51 communications in which a state emphasizes the adversary's breach of legal obligations (other than ceasefire agreements) without also claiming that the adversary had used force against it. Moreover, in none of these cases do states explicitly claim a right of reprisal under international law. Our results therefore do not suggest that states are pressing for an adaptive interpretation of the Charter to restore a right of reprisal. The data suggests that states do, however, highlight other states' breaches of their legal obligations as part of the justificatory discourse to bolster support for their uses of force. In short, the data suggests that states, in some cases, seek to avail themselves of the "tolerance" Tom Franck suggests may be afforded to states that use force in self-help.[80]

E. Extralegal Justifications: Complementary Support for the "Contested Claims"

Discussion of the contested claims highlights the limited ways in which the use of force regime has adjusted to the changing international security environment. In the case of uses of force in response to the growing phenomenon of transnational armed conflicts against nonstate actors, states embrace and increasingly rely on an interpretation that changes the traditional understanding of the use of force regime. States using force on the basis of other legally contested rationales, in contrast, increasingly rely on extralegal rationales as complements to their legal assertions. By doing so, states effectively seek to persuade others to overlook the legally problematic aspects of their use of force by highlighting moral and political reasons why

[80] FRANCK, *supra* note 9, at 132.

their action was not especially egregious in that *particular* case, even if it might be legally debatable.

To evaluate whether and to what extent states pad their legal arguments with extralegal justifications for the use of force—that is, normative, strategic, or other reasons why their use of force should be accepted by the international community—we assess the correlations between the use of different justifications for the use of force. Figure 5.10 presents Pearson's correlations between every pair of justifications. Red backgrounds indicate negative correlations, while blue backgrounds represent positive correlations, with darker blue backgrounds indicating more positive correlations than lighter blue backgrounds. The figure reveals that accepted legal justifications are rarely used in conjunction with extralegal "padding," while contested legal justifications often co-occur with extralegal claims.

	Counterattack	Ceasefire Violations	Economy	Premeditation	Transparency	Governance	Normative Values	Humanitarianism	Gravity	Regional Stability	Character of Actors	Collective Self-Defense	Nonstate Actors	Anticipatory Self-Defense	Reprisals
Counterattack		0.12	0.08	0	0.06	0.06	0.08	0.16	0.12	0.1	0.14	-0.21	-0.04	-0.14	0.02
Ceasefire Violations	0.12		0.04	0.09	0.14	0	0.04	0.14	0.19	-0.09	0.02	-0.13	0.07	-0.04	-0.24
Economy	0.08	0.04		0.12	0.28	0.18	0.28	0.27	0.24	0.07	0.03	-0.03	0.02	-0.06	0.03
Premeditation	0	0.09	0.12		0.21	0.31	0.28	0.23	0.29	-0.25	0.15	0.01	0.07	0.14	0.16
Transparency	0.06	0.14	0.28	0.21		0.29	0.44	0.29	0.31	-0.03	0.2	-0.04	0.1	0.01	0.07
Governance	0.06	0	0.18	0.31	0.29		0.51	0.3	0.32	-0.1	0.43	0.02	0.18	-0.01	0.24
Normative Values	0.08	0.04	0.28	0.28	0.44	0.51		0.4	0.36	-0.01	0.36	0	0.15	-0.02	0.26
Humanitarianism	0.16	0.14	0.27	0.23	0.29	0.3	0.4		0.33	-0.01	0.25	-0.08	0.18	-0.02	0.07
Gravity	0.12	0.19	0.24	0.29	0.31	0.32	0.36	0.33		-0.09	0.21	0	0.19	-0.01	0.15
Regional Stability	0.1	-0.09	0.07	-0.25	-0.03	-0.1	-0.01	-0.01	-0.09		0.47	-0.1	-0.17	-0.07	-0.11
Character of Actors	0.14	0.02	0.03	0.15	0.2	0.43	0.36	0.25	0.21	0.47		-0.11	-0.04	-0.06	0.17
Collective Self-Defense	-0.21	-0.13	-0.03	0.01	-0.04	0.02	0	-0.08	0	-0.1	-0.11		0.2	0.08	-0.1
Nonstate Actors	-0.04	0.07	0.02	0.07	0.1	0.18	0.15	0.18	0.19	-0.17	-0.04	0.2		0.04	0.06
Anticipatory Self-Defense	-0.14	-0.04	-0.06	0.14	0.01	-0.01	-0.02	-0.02	-0.01	-0.07	-0.06	0.08	0.04		0.07
Reprisals	0.02	-0.24	0.03	0.16	0.07	0.24	0.26	0.07	0.15	-0.11	0.17	-0.1	0.06	0.07	

Figure 5.10 Correlations between Legal and Extralegal Justifications

Consider the three widely accepted legal justifications for the use of force: counterattacks, collective self-defense, and responses to violations of ceasefire agreements. None are highly correlated with extralegal justifications; counterattacks are correlated, only to a small extent, with discussions of the character of actors, which occur quite frequently throughout the data (in over 40 percent of communications), and with humanitarianism, which also occurs frequently (in approximately 40 percent of communications) and which mainly involves accounts of harm to the civilians of the state that has sustained an attack. Similarly, the justification regarding breaches of ceasefire agreements is slightly correlated with language about transparency, humanitarianism, and gravity—again, arguments that appear very frequently throughout the data set. Collective self-defense is somewhat correlated with discussions of nonstate actors, largely because of a series of conflicts in the Middle East in which US action has gained significant support from a large network of allies.

The counterattack justification is negatively correlated with the invocation of collective self-defense. Given that *collective* self-defense is exercised by states that have not themselves sustained an attack, whereas states invoking *individual* self-defense must identify an armed attack triggering their right of self-defense, the negative correlation between these categories is unsurprising. The counterattack justification is also negatively correlated with anticipatory self-defense. Anticipatory self-defense ordinarily cannot occur in conjunction with a traditional, counterattack exercise of self-defense.

Collective self-defense justifications are also negatively correlated with justifications about ceasefire agreements. When parties to an ongoing armed conflict have reached an agreement to stop waging war against one another, it is unsurprising that communications regarding violations of the agreement that induce a state to *reignite* the formerly stagnant conflict implicate the interests of only the parties to that conflict and agreement. On the other hand, collective self-defense communications emphasize the motives of states *entering* what is typically a new conflict. Collective self-defense is positively correlated with only one extralegal theme—nonstate actors. This is the result of collective self-defense being invoked in several Middle Eastern conflicts that feature nonstate actors. That no other extralegal themes co-occur with the collective self-defense justification is notable.

Finally, invocation of the right to respond to violations of ceasefire agreements is negatively correlated with justifications based on legal reprisals, which are defined as *excluding* any cases involving ceasefire agreements. The ceasefire violation justification correlates positively with three extralegal claims—in which states appeal to the gravity of a particular threat or crisis, discuss issues of transparency, or appeal to humanitarian values. Once states have reached a temporary cessation of their conflict, it is understandable that they feel the need to demonstrate that their decision to resume armed conflict is due to a serious violation of the agreement by the adversary, not merely a technical or minor breach; this explains why discussions of gravity and humanitarianism likely intersect with this justification. Transparency is often involved in debates over which party violated a ceasefire agreement first.

With the exception of anticipatory self-defense, which is extremely rare in the data, the contested legal claims—unlike the accepted claims—are all positively correlated with multiple extralegal justifications for the use of force. For example, states emphasizing humanitarian considerations are likely to mention economic reasons for their actions, to discuss democracy promotion and principles of good governance, to espouse the normative value of their intervention, and to highlight their own transparency and their adversaries' lack thereof, as well as their own good character in contrast to their adversary's bad character. The nonstate actor justification for the use of force is similarly correlated with a number of extralegal themes: normative concerns, regional politics, transparency, good governance, and the gravity of crises. Finally, the legal reprisal justification is also associated with discussions of extralegal topics, namely, the character of actors, good governance, normative values, gravity of crises, and premeditation. That contested justifications are often bolstered by extralegal justifications is telling; it suggests that states may be aware that their legal justifications are suspect and that they therefore attempt to drum up support—or, at a minimum, tolerance—for their actions on other grounds.

We also find that Article 51 communications are getting longer over time.[81] The average communication length for the first twenty years of the United Nation was 5,265 characters, with an average of seven justifications per document. For the past twenty years, the average communication length has been 6,645 characters, with an average of nine justifications per document. Longer communications allow states to provide more details and more justifications.

[81] *See* online Appendix A.4, at laurensukin.com.

This can add legitimacy to uses of force grounded in nonconsensus legal doctrines. As such, extralegal justifications do not *replace* legal arguments, but instead *complement* them. They help states make the argument that a use of force should be accepted—or at least that its legally debatable character should be overlooked. If states are concerned that anticipatory self-defense, for example, may not be a credible justification for the use of force in the eyes of some Security Council members, they may be able to tip support in their favor by citing additional justifications regarding compelling normative or strategic concerns. States may also seek to build consensus about the legitimacy of certain contested legal claims.

Notably, states are *not* using extralegal doctrines to complement their legal arguments when relying on more "accepted" claims, such as the rights to individual and collective self-defense. In these cases, extralegal "padding" is not necessary to generate consensus support for the use of force.

V. Conclusions

The reports of the demise of the UN Charter's legal regime governing the use of force are greatly exaggerated. Notwithstanding significant changes in the international security environment since 1945, the overall level of transnational violence since the adoption of the Charter has remained relatively constant. In other words, the additional security threats that have arisen in the post–World War II era have not resulted in additional exercises of the use of force between states.

State behavior, moreover, seems to reflect a normative commitment to the preservation of the Charter's use of force regime. Procedurally, states have relied on the Article 51 reporting mechanism at essentially consistent rates over the past seventy-five years. This reflects a desire by states to justify their actions as consistent with the black letter law of the Charter and implicitly to signal their support for the Charter regime. Even as new security threats emerge that present challenges that differ from the classic state attack/counterattack model embodied in the Charter, states continue seeking to justify their actions as falling within the scope of that model.

The patterns of state efforts to justify their uses of force in the Security Council reflect their continuing support for a legal regime in which the unilateral use of force by states is generally prohibited, except in cases of armed attacks. States consistently and overwhelmingly justify their uses of force as responses to armed attacks by other states. States have not relied heavily on contested justifications for using force, such as anticipatory self-defense, which is infrequently cited, or an explicit legal right of humanitarian intervention, which no state has formally invoked in an Article 51 communication.

The one notable exception reflecting change from the traditional regime concerns the use of force against nonstate actors located on the territory of other states. Although there is disagreement among scholars about whether attacking nonstate actors abroad violates the territorial integrity of the state where the nonstate actors are located, we observe a steady increase in state invocation of the need to confront nonstate actors abroad as a justification for the use of force. Growing reliance on this rationale may imply that states believe this justification for using force has won acceptance in the international community. State behavior reflects the judgment that there has been an adaptive interpretation of the understanding of the balance in the Charter between the self-defense rights of states that have been attacked by nonstate groups and the territorial integrity rights of the states where those groups are located. That balance has now tipped in favor of the state that sustains the initial armed attack. Despite this change, the proposed doctrinal test advanced primarily by the United States to delineate *when* it is permissible to use force against nonstate actors abroad—the unwilling or unable test—has not been widely embraced by the international community. It accordingly appears that no consensus has been reached with respect to the precise conditions governing when states may use force against nonstate actors abroad. Importantly, this shift represents an evolution in how states are interpreting the right of self-defense—not the emergence of a fundamentally new legal basis for the right to use force.

To the extent that states do invoke contested grounds for using force, they tend to buttress their justifications with extralegal arguments, such as references to the need to protect their civilians from harm, the bad character of their adversary, or contributions made by the use of force to good governance. This suggests that when states rely on controversial legal justifications for using force, they often also rely heavily on moral and political justifications applicable to their *particular* use of force, in effect to secure international support for the notion that their use of force was appropriate or legitimate, even though it may not have strictly conformed with the black letter law of the Charter.

Appendix

Assessing Automated Coding Accuracy via Comparison with Human Coders

As a robustness check for coding done using automated text-analysis, a research assistant and both co-authors of this chapter examined a random sample of Article 51 communications to determine the justifications that each communication used. Table 5.A1 displays the percent of one hundred randomly selected documents determined to mention each justification by our automated text analysis process and by the discretion of the authors and research assistant. We consider our automated categorization to be accurate if it is within ten percentage points of the results from the human coder. The only inaccurate category is the character of actor category; because this justification is expansive and often uses very general terms, we cannot effectively capture all relevant language in a single dictionary. However, underinclusivity biases against our hypothesis that states frequently use extralegal claims as complements to legal justifications to garner support for their uses of force.

Table 5.A1 Automated Coding Accuracy

Category	Automated Coding	Hand-Coding	Assessment
Anticipatory Self-defense		5	Hand-Coding Only
Ceasefire Violation	34	29	Accurate
Character of Actors	41	56	Underinclusive
Collective Self-defense	0	6	Accurate
Counterattack	95	93	Accurate
Cyber Operations	0	0	Accurate
Economy	12	8	Accurate
Governance	25	16	Accurate
Gravity	30	35	Accurate
Humanitarianism	45	57	Accurate
Nonstate Actors	18	26	Accurate
Normative Values	22	12	Accurate
Premeditation	42	48	Accurate
Regional Stability	20	11	Accurate
Reprisals		39	Hand-Coding Only
Transparency	11	20	Accurate

6

The *Jus in Bello* under Strain

Diluted But Not Disintegrating

Laura A. Dickinson

I. Introduction

The *jus in bello* is perhaps the most stable branch of public international law. Forged out of the tragedy of modern warfare in the nineteenth and twentieth centuries, this body of law seeks to balance the reality of military necessity with humanitarian values. Its core tenets are some of the most widely accepted principles of public international law, and they have been enshrined in the four Geneva Conventions of 1949[1] and two Additional Protocols,[2] as well as customary international law. In addition, well-established international institutions—most notably the International Committee of the Red Cross (ICRC), but also the United Nations and international courts and tribunals—have played a key role in implementing and interpreting this body of law.

Yet multiple contemporary forces have placed even this sturdy body of law under considerable strain. These forces include: (1) the rise of nonstate armed groups, in particular the proliferation of transnational terrorist organizations; (2) the increased use of military and security contractors; (3) the emergence of new military technologies; and (4) rapid urbanization, such

[1] Geneva Convention for the Amelioration of the Condition of the Wounded and Sick in Armed Forces in the Field (First Geneva Convention), Aug. 12, 1949, 6 U.S.T. 3114, 75 U.N.T.S. 31; Geneva Convention for the Amelioration of the Condition of Wounded, Sick and Shipwrecked Members of Armed Forces at Sea (Second Geneva Convention), Aug. 12, 1949, 75 U.N.T.S. 8; Geneva Convention Relative to the Treatment of Prisoners of War, Aug. 12, 1949, 75 U.N.T.S. 135 [hereinafter POW Convention]; Geneva Convention Relative to the Protection of Civilian Persons in Time of War, Aug. 12, 1949, 75 U.N.T.S. 287 [hereinafter Civilian Persons Convention].

[2] Protocol Additional to the Geneva Conventions of 12 August 1949, and relating to the Protection of Victims of International Armed Conflicts, 8 June 1977, 1125 U.N.T.S. 3 [hereinafter AP I]; Protocol Additional to the Geneva Conventions of 12 August 1949, and relating to the Protection of Victims of Non-International Armed Conflicts, June 8, 1977, 1125 U.N.T.S. 609 [hereinafter AP II].

Laura A. Dickinson, *The* Jus in Bello *under Strain* In: *Is the International Legal Order Unraveling?*. Edited by: David L. Sloss, Oxford University Press. © Laura Dickinson 2022. DOI: 10.1093/oso/9780197652800.003.0007

as the proliferation of megacities. The fact that the *jus in bello* has already weathered some of these challenges indicates that it may well survive the others. Fundamentally, most states remain committed to the core values that undergird this body of law. It therefore appears less likely that the *jus in bello* will unravel than that gaps and fissures will emerge as states seek to translate the underlying values and norms to meet new challenges. Moreover, these gaps and fissures may expand, enabling states and others to adopt competing, often self-serving, interpretations. In short, the risk is one of long-term dilution rather than rapid disintegration.

II. Nonstate Armed Groups

The *jus in bello* has actually coped surprisingly well with the rise of nonstate armed groups, including transnational terrorist organizations, suggesting that this body of international law remains relatively resilient. This resilience is a bit surprising. As efforts to combat terrorism accelerated following the 9/11 attacks on the United States, many questioned whether the then existing *jus in bello* was up to the task—or even relevant—to non-international armed conflicts (NIACs) that crossed state boundaries. For a time, countries such as Israel[3] and the United States (during the early part of President George W. Bush's administration)[4] contended that existing *jus in bello* rules did not apply to transnational NIACs at all, and that members of certain terrorist groups fell outside *jus in bello* protections. However, other countries, international organizations, nongovernmental organizations (NGOs), and even members of the US and Israeli governments pushed back against this view. Ultimately, most states have accepted that the *jus in bello* governs contemporary trans-border NIACs, including some extraterritorial counterterrorism operations, and that there are no legal "black holes."[5]

These lengthy counterterrorism NIACs, therefore, have not ultimately threatened the fabric of the *jus in bello* itself. Indeed, the scope of the *jus in bello* has arguably expanded, as many states have embraced a broad approach to the circumstances in which armed conflict is occurring, both geographically and temporally. In this respect, the *jus in bello* has actually encroached

[3] *See* HCJ 769/02 Public Committee Against Torture in Israel v. The Government of Israel (2) IsrSC 459 (2006) (Isr.).
[4] *See infra* text accompanying notes 9–13.
[5] *See* Public Committee Against Torture, *supra* note 3.

on other bodies of law, such as international human rights law (IHRL). The bigger challenge for the durability of the *jus in bello* in the face of nonstate armed groups and global terrorism has been the propensity of states to exploit gaps and uncertainties in the law. This is because the *jus in bello* offers more specificity and guidance in international armed conflicts (IACs) than it does for NIACs. The vagueness of the *jus in bello*'s NIAC rules has created confusion for all actors in armed conflicts, and it has provided a large opening for states to adopt competing and sometimes self-serving interpretations.

This section first recounts the existential threat to the *jus in bello* in the early twenty-first century and the surprising resilience of the basic framework. Then I sketch the new gaps and fissures in that framework, when applied to NIACs and nonstate armed groups. Illustrative examples include how the *jus in bello* applies to targeting decisions and detention operations. Finally, I point to the possibility that as the *jus in bello* expands to address NIACs and nonstate armed groups, it could displace other legal regimes, such as IHRL, thus leading to a less robust overall international legal framework.

A. The Post–9/11 *Jus in Bello* "Black Hole"

States developed the *jus in bello* when war consisted primarily of contests between and among large, hierarchical, organized militaries.[6] The foundational treaties defining a significant portion of this body of law, the Geneva Conventions, contain only one provision, Common Article 3, devoted to conflicts involving nonstate actors.[7] Granted, subsequent treaties such as Additional Protocol II (AP II) to the Geneva Conventions addressed wars with nonstate groups, such as guerilla movements or insurgents.[8] But AP II did not really contemplate the prospect of *transnational* conflicts with nonstate actors crossing the boundaries of multiple states. In the aftermath of the terrorist attacks on the United States on September 11, 2001, therefore, the conditions were ripe for governments to exploit the possibility that the *jus in bello* simply did not govern this type of transnational armed conflict and that military operations undertaken in this context existed in a kind of law-free zone.[9]

[6] *See* Laura A. Dickinson, Outsourcing War and Peace: Preserving Public Values in a World of Privatized Foreign Affairs 40–68 (2011).

[7] *See, e.g.*, Civilian Persons Convention, *supra* note 1, art. 3.

[8] *See, e.g.*, AP II, *supra* note 2.

[9] *See* Public Committee Against Torture, *supra* note 3.

The United States pushed this argument most strongly in the context of military detention. Following the 9/11 terrorist attacks, the United States, supported by many allies, entered into an armed conflict with Al Qaeda, the Taliban, and associated forces in Afghanistan. During that conflict (which soon spread beyond the borders of Afghanistan) and the US-led armed conflict in Iraq in 2003 to oust Saddam Hussein, the US military took custody over thousands of detainees. Some of them were detained in theater by the United States. Others were handed over to allies. Hundreds were brought to the US Naval base at Guantánamo Bay, Cuba.[10]

The US government made sweeping legal arguments that these detentions fell outside the domain of international law entirely. Due to the transnational nature of the conflict and the fact that terrorists did not fit into any category of "lawful" combatants defined by this body of law, the government argued that the *jus in bello* did not impose any binding restrictions on the United States when it detained such individuals.[11] Some scholars echoed this view, arguing that the existing *jus in bello* simply did not regulate this new type of conflict.[12] In addition, US government officials argued that IHRL also did not apply, in part because that body of law did not obligate the United States outside its territorial borders.[13]

The US government's view that the detainees stood largely outside *any* international legal regime prompted vociferous criticism from the international community and civil society organizations.[14] US allies, international organizations, and NGOs rejected US claims that neither the *jus in bello* nor IHRL governed US extraterritorial military detention. Many contended that not only should the *jus in bello* apply, but that the detainees were entitled to the more robust IHRL rights and protections. They decried the notion that these individuals could fall into a legal "black hole.[15] The ICRC, for example,

[10] For an overview, *see* Inter-Am. Comm'n H.R. [IACHR], *Toward the Closure of Guantanamo*, IACHR Doc. OAS/Ser.L./V/II, Doc. 20/15 (June 3, 2015) [hereinafter 2015 IACHR Report].

[11] Brief for Respondents at 48–50, Hamdan v. Rumsfeld, 548 U.S. 557 (2006) (No. 05-184).

[12] For a discussion of this debate, *see, e.g.*, Rosa Brooks, *War Everywhere: Rights, National Security Law, and the Law of Armed Conflict in the Age of Terror*, 153 U. PA. L. REV. 675 (2004); Marco Sassoli, *Use and Abuse of the Laws of War in the War on Terrorism*, 22 LAW & INEQUALITY 195 (2004).

[13] *See* Robert M. Chesney, *Leaving Guantanamo: The Law of International Detainee Transfers*, 40 RICH. L. REV. 657, 673 (2006).

[14] *See, e.g., Guantanamo: Implications for U.S. Human Rights Leadership: Hearing Before the U.S. Comm'n on Sec. and Cooperation in Eur.*, 110th Cong. 26–30 (2007) [hereinafter 2007 Guantanamo Hearing] (statements of Tom Malinowski, Advocacy Dir., Human Rights Watch, and Gabor Rona, Legal Dir., Human Rights First); Letter from Anthony D. Romero, Exec. Dir., ACLU, to Robert M. Gates, Sec'y of Def. (Mar. 23, 2007), https://perma.cc/H9ET-7NNF.

[15] *See* 2007 Guantanamo Hearing, *supra* note 14 (Leahy Statement).

maintained that the *jus in bello* governed and that detainees in long-term military detention were entitled to be charged and prosecuted in a regular court within a certain period of time, rather than being held "indefinitely."[16]

In the face of these criticisms, the US government ultimately accepted the view that the *jus in bello* governs US detention of terrorists and other military operations in transnational NIACs. The Obama administration explicitly accepted that the *jus in bello* applies in such conflicts, including military detention operations.[17] The US Supreme Court's decision in *Hamdan v. Rumsfeld*[18] was also a significant turning point. There, the Court considered the legality of military commission trials for detainees held at Guantánamo Naval Base. In the context of defending the commissions, the US executive branch articulated its position that the *jus in bello* did not apply at all to transnational armed conflicts with nonstate groups. The Court soundly rejected that view, reasoning that Common Article 3 of the Geneva Conventions was not limited to conflicts internal to one state but also governed transnational NIACs.

By embracing the *jus in bello* in the face of this new challenge, the US government helped avert what may have been the biggest test of the *jus in bello* regime. Indeed, the Trump administration, despite its hostility to international law, never retreated from this position.[19] And other states, such as Israel, which had made similar arguments in the context of counterterrorism operations, also ultimately accepted the broad scope of the *jus in bello* to address transnational NIACs.[20]

B. Applying the *Jus in Bello* to Nonstate Actors

Even though the *jus in bello* bounced back from what initially appeared to be an existential threat from the growing role of nonstate armed groups, the

[16] *See* Inter-Am. Comm'n H.R. [IACHR], Res. 2/11, *Regarding the Situation of the Detainees at Guantanamo Bay, United States*, IACHR Doc. MC 259-02 (July 22, 2011) [hereinafter 2011 IACHR Resolution] (describing ICRC position).

[17] *See, e.g.*, Office of the White House, Report on the Legal and Policy Frameworks Guiding the United States' Use of Military Force and Related National Security Operations (2016) [hereinafter 2016 Frameworks Report].

[18] 547 U.S. 557 (2006).

[19] *See* Office of the White House, Report on the Legal and Policy Frameworks Guiding the United States' Use of Military Force and Related National Security Operations (2018) [hereinafter 2018 Frameworks Report].

[20] *See* Public Committee Against Torture, *supra* note 3. Under this framework, membership in a group, and the role an individual plays in that group, might be relevant to determine whether that individual is performing a "continuous combat function."

regime nonetheless provides only a relatively weak regulatory framework for transnational NIACs. To begin with, the law lacks specificity as it applies to these conflicts. The overwhelming bulk of legal rules articulated in treaties and in customary international law pertain to IACs. For example, of the several hundred articles of the four Geneva Conventions, only one—Common Article 3—applies to non-international conflicts with nonstate armed groups.[21] It sets an important floor, prohibiting atrocities, but does not provide much guidance to states or nonstate actors. AP II, which provides more detailed rules for such conflicts, has rectified this problem to some degree, but it is not nearly as widely ratified as the Geneva Conventions themselves. The United States has twice sought ratification of AP II, but the process remains incomplete.[22] A potent illustration of the paucity of clear rules governing NIACs can be found in the *U.S. Department of Defense Law of War Manual*. The *Manual* runs over one thousand pages; the chapter on NIACs is just forty-one pages long.[23] The vagueness and lack of specificity of the *jus in bello*'s NIAC rules has therefore led to much uncertainty for all actors in such conflicts, and it has provided a large opening for states to adopt competing interpretations. These challenges are evident if we review first, the targeting and use of lethal force against members of nonstate armed groups, and second, detention policies involving such persons.

1. Targeting

Additional Protocol I (AP I) provides the core *jus in bello* rules governing targeting decisions, laying out the principles of distinction, proportionality, precautions, unnecessary suffering, and necessity. These rules are widely accepted. Indeed, even states such as the United States that have not formally ratified AP I have accepted many of these rules as customary international law.[24] And to a significant degree these targeting rules are also accepted as

[21] *See, e.g.*, Civilian Persons Convention, *supra* note 1, art. 3.

[22] *See* Letter from Hillary Rodham Clinton, Secretary of State, and Robert Gates, Secretary of Defense, Recommending the Ratification of Additional Protocol II (Mar. 7, 2011), https://perma.cc/A5SC-67ZD; Message from the President of the United States Transmitting The Protocol II Additional to the Geneva Conventions of August 2, 1949 (Jan. 29, 1987), https://perma.cc/9J5S-3KLU.

[23] U.S. Dep't of Defense, Law of War Manual (2015) (including 2016 update), https://perma.cc/J6H3-PQ6T.

[24] *See* John B. Bellinger III & William J. Haynes II, *A US Government Response to the International Committee of the Red Cross Study Customary International Humanitarian Law*, 89 Int'l Rev. Red Cross 443 (2007); *see also* International Committee of the Red Cross, *Customary IHL Database*, https://ihl-databases.icrc.org/customary-ihl/eng/docs/home (last visited May 25, 2021).

customary international law that apply in NIACs.[25] However, when it comes to applying these rules to non-state actors—and in particular the principle of distinction as applied to such actors—the gaps and uncertainties become apparent.

The principle of distinction provides that parties to an armed conflict may not deliberately target civilians[26] or civilian objects.[27] If an individual is a combatant[28] or someone who is taking direct part in hostilities,[29] that individual may be the object of attack (provided other *jus in bello* principles are followed). However, nonstate actors are not easily classified. They do not typically qualify as combatants, for example, by wearing uniforms and meeting other requirements. Therefore, as noncombatants they may be targeted only for such time as they are taking direct part in hostilities.[30] Yet states and other entities disagree about the scope of this rule and its various elements.[31] In addition, separate from that question, the United States has maintained that mere membership in a particular armed group deemed hostile to the United States, such as specific terrorist organizations, renders one subject to attack.[32] Other states disagree with such a broad classification, asserting instead that the *only* relevant question in a NIAC is whether the individual is directly participating in hostilities.[33] Such disagreements, stemming from gaps in the law as it applies to nonstate actors, weakens the force of the *jus in bello* in this domain.

2. *Detention*

The gaps in the *jus in bello* are even greater for detention operations in NIACs. Common Article 3 sets a floor, barring torture and inhumane treatment, but provides little guidance on appropriate conditions for detainees. Detainees cannot, for example, benefit from prisoner-of-war status, a privilege reserved for captives who meet certain qualifications in international-armed

[25] *See id.*
[26] AP I, *supra* note 2, art. 51.2.
[27] *Id.*, art. 52.1.
[28] *Id.*, art. 43.
[29] *Id.*, art. 51.3.
[30] *Id.*
[31] *See, e.g.*, International Committee of the Red Cross, Interpretive Guidance on the Notion of Direct Participation in Hostilities Under International Humanitarian Law (2009); Stephen Pomper, *Toward a Limited Consensus on the Loss of Civilian Immunity in Non-International Armed Conflict: Making Progress Through Practice*, 88 Int'l L. Stud. 181 (2012).
[32] 2016 Frameworks Report, *supra* note 17, at 29.
[33] *See, e.g.*, Public Committee against Torture, *supra* note 3.

conflicts.[34] Articles 4–6 of AP II help close the gap, but significant major powers such as the United States have not joined.[35] There is also much debate about whether detainees have the right to have their detainee status reviewed, as well as the permissible amount of time a detainee may be held.[36] If the detaining power decides to criminally prosecute such detainees, the scope of their rights in such criminal proceedings is also unsettled.[37]

The US treatment of detainees at Guantánamo Naval Base over the past two decades highlights these ambiguities. As a matter of practice, the conditions of detention for these individuals have improved over the years.[38] But the United States has not ratified AP II, and these improvements do not reflect a sense of legal obligation. More controversially, many of these detainees have been held for years without charge or trial.[39] The United States maintains that the *jus in bello* permits such long-term detention.[40] Other states, NGOs, and tribunals argue, however, that the duration of detention is subject to more stringent limits.[41]

In addition, the United States has tried some of these detainees within a military commission system that has been controversial, especially in its earliest iterations, because it provided only minimal rights for the accused. The current version of the military commissions provides more substantial procedural rights, but they still do not match the rights US service members receive in trials under the Uniform Code of Military Justice.[42] Although it has increased protections for the accused as a matter of policy, the United States has argued that the *jus in bello* sets a fairly low floor for rights of nonstate

[34] *Id.*

[35] International Committee of the Red Cross, *Treaties, States Parties, and Commentaries*, https://ihl-databases.icrc.org/applic/ihl/ihl.nsf/Treaty.xsp?documentId=AA0C5BCBAB5C4A85C12563CD002D6D09&action=openDocument (last visited May 25, 2021).

[36] *See, e.g.*, David Cole, *Out of the Shadows: Preventive Detention, Suspected Terrorists, and War*, 97 Cal. L. Rev. 693 (2009); Robert M. Chesney, *Iraq and the Military Detention Debate: Firsthand Perspectives from the Other War, 2003–2010*, 51 Va. J. Int'l L. 549 (2011); Robert M. Chesney & Jack Goldsmith, *Terrorism and the Convergence of Criminal and Military Detention Models*, 60 Stan. L. Rev. 1079 (2008).

[37] *See, e.g.*, David Glazier, *Destined for an Epic Fail: The Problematic Guantanamo Military Commissions*, 75 Ohio State L.J. 904 (2014); Stephen I. Vladeck, *The Laws of War as a Constitutional Limit on Military Jurisdiction*, 4 J. Nat'l Sec. L. & Pol'y 295 (2010).

[38] *See, e.g.*, Laura A. Dickinson & James E. Baker, *The U.S. Military Commissions: Looking Forward, Report of the American Bar Association Standing Committee on Law and National Security*, May 25, 2018 [hereinafter ABA Report].

[39] *See id.*

[40] 2016 Frameworks Report, *supra* note 17, at 30.

[41] *See, e.g.*, 2015 IACHR Report, *supra* note 10; *see also* Laura A. Dickinson, *National Security Policy-making in the Shadow of International Law*, 2021 Utah L. Rev. 629 (2021).

[42] *See* ABA Report, *supra* note 38.

actors criminally charged in military proceedings.[43] Other states, NGOs, and tribunals disagree.[44]

C. The Expanded Scope of the *Jus in Bello* and Its Interaction with Other International Law Regimes

Paradoxically, as the scope of the *jus in bello* expands to address NIACs and nonstate armed groups, it could actually result in a *lower* standard of international law protection in these contexts. This is because some states couple an expansive view of the *jus in bello*'s scope with an argument that the *jus in bello* displaces other legal paradigms, such as IHRL. As a result, the relatively low floor set by the *jus in bello* for NIACs may be deemed to govern operations against members of nonstate armed groups, rather than the more protective IHRL regime.

The United States' approach is again instructive. Across multiple administrations, the United States has taken the position that the *jus in bello*, and not IHRL, applies globally to US counterterrorism operations, at least for certain terrorist organizations such as Al Qaeda.[45] Even outside geographic areas that are embroiled in armed conflict, the United States has maintained that, with respect to these hostile groups, a war is constantly taking place.[46] Accordingly, the *jus in bello* should govern. This interpretation of international law contrasts with the interpretation of many US allies, who maintain that the *jus in bello* does not apply globally to operations against terrorists such as Al Qaeda, instead adopting a more fact-specific analysis of whether an armed conflict is occurring in the particular geographic location where operations are contemplated.[47] If an armed conflict is not occurring, according to their analysis, the generally higher standards of IHRL would likely govern.[48]

These conflicting approaches regarding the applicable international legal paradigm have stark consequences for the treatment of nonstate actors in

[43] *Id.*
[44] *See* 2015 IACHR Report, *supra* note 10.
[45] *See, e.g.*, 2016 FRAMEWORKS REPORT, *supra* note 17; 2018 FRAMEWORKS REPORT, *supra* note 19.
[46] *See, e.g.*, 2016 FRAMEWORKS REPORT, *supra* note 17, at 18 (identifying military operations against Al Qaeda in the Arabian Peninsula (AQAP) as an ongoing armed conflict).
[47] *See, e.g.*, KENNETH WATKIN, FIGHTING AT THE LEGAL BOUNDARIES: CONTROLLING THE USE OF FORCE IN CONTEMPORARY CONFLICT (2016).
[48] *Id.*

extraterritorial counterterrorism operations outside traditional battlefields. One approach treats terrorists outside these traditional battlefields as criminals and deploys the law enforcement model for tracking, capturing, prosecuting, and—in certain very limited circumstances—killing them.[49] Within this model, the framework of IHRL would generally apply. In contrast, if terrorists are viewed as fighting a global war, then the battlefield itself is potentially global, and the largely less-restrictive *jus in bello* regime would apply. Or, if targeting terrorism suspects is seen as an act of national self-defense, then the law regarding the resort to force in national self-defense under the *jus ad bellum* might govern. Moreover, these legal regimes are not necessarily mutually exclusive. Not surprisingly, states and commentators have taken different positions regarding when, where, and under what circumstances IHRL, *jus in bello*, and self-defense regimes should apply, and how they overlap.[50]

The question of which legal regime (or combination) governs has consequences for decisions related to: (1) whether to capture or kill a terrorism suspect; (2) the rules applicable to targeted killings; (3) the level of acceptable civilian casualties; (4) how detention may be carried out; (5) the appropriate procedures and personnel to conduct operations; and (6) whether, and what type, of investigations are required in the face of allegations of misconduct.

For example, consider the US operation that killed Al Qaeda leader and US citizen Anwar Al-Awlaki in a 2011 drone strike in Yemen.[51] The operation sparked a heated debate in the United States and elsewhere about the possible legal basis for the strike.[52] At the time, there was a dispute within the international community whether the zone in which Al-Awlaki was killed was the site of an armed conflict.[53] Thus, in addition to significant questions about whether the US Constitution permitted such lethal action against a US citizen overseas, lawyers and policy makers disagreed about whether the action violated international law.[54] Central to that disagreement was a dispute

[49] *See id.* at 287–318.
[50] *See id.*
[51] *See* Mark Mazetti, Eric Schmitt, & Robert Worth, *Two Year Manhunt Led to Killing of Awlaki in Yemen*, N.Y. TIMES, Sept. 30, 2011.
[52] *See, e.g.*, Charlie Savage, *Secret US Memo Made Legal Case to Kill a Citizen*, N.Y. TIMES, Oct. 8, 2011.
[53] *See, e.g.*, Charlie Savage, *Court Releases Large Parts of Memo Approving Killing American in Yemen*, N.Y. TIMES, June 23, 2014.
[54] *See, e.g.*, Michael Ramsden, *Targeted Killings and International Human Rights Law: The Case of Anwar Al-Awlaki*, J. CONFLICT & SECURITY L. 385 (2011).

about which international legal paradigm, or paradigms, was applicable. Indeed, journalistic accounts suggest that even within the US government, lawyers and policy makers clashed over that question.[55]

Although the United States did not initially provide the legal basis for the Al-Awlaki strike,[56] the government has since clarified that it sees itself in a global war against Al Qaeda and ISIS and therefore views the battlefield as potentially worldwide for purposes of international law.[57] Moreover, the US position applies not only to targeted killings, such as the Al-Awlaki strike but also other extraterritorial counterterrorism operations, such as detention. And in both contexts, the US position differs fundamentally from that of many US allies, who have adopted a more confined view of the scope of the *jus in bello* and a broader vision for IHRL.

Thus, the *jus in bello* has survived the George W. Bush administration's early challenge to its applicability to nonstate actors involved in NIACs. Yet expansion of the *jus in bello* to cover transnational NIACs has resulted in ambiguities about precisely *how* the rules for targeting and detention apply. In addition, this expansion has ironically created space for arguments that would reduce the overall legal protections afforded by international law because states can claim that the *jus in bello* displaces the more protective IHRL regime. Accordingly, we see both the possibility that the *jus in bello* framework will be weakened over time in its application to these difficult contexts, and the possibility that international legal protections themselves may become diluted because the lower *jus in bello* standards will replace the more robust human rights requirements.

III. Privatization

Military and security privatization has also threatened to fray the fabric of the *jus in bello*. As I and others have described extensively elsewhere,[58] since

[55] *See* Savage, *supra* note 52; Savage, *supra* note 53.

[56] The United States did subsequently release a memo providing the legal reasoning that supported the strike. Memorandum for the Att'y Gen. Re: Applicability of the Federal Criminal Laws and the Constitution to Contemplated Lethal Operations Against Shaykh Anwar al-Aulaqi, Op. O.L.C. (July 6, 2010).

[57] 2016 Frameworks Report, *supra* note 17.

[58] *See generally* Deborah Avant, The Market for Force: The Consequences of Privatizing Security (2005); Dickinson, *supra* note 6; Sean McFate, The Modern Mercenary: Private Armies and What They Mean for World Order (2014); Peter W. Singer, Corporate Warriors: The Rise of the Privatized Military Industry (2008).

the end of the Cold War, states have turned increasingly to private companies to perform a broad range of military and security functions. At the high point of the conflicts in Iraq and Afghanistan, for example, the number of contractors soared to approximately 260,000, a ratio of contractors to troops that hovered for a number of years at approximately one to one.[59] More recently, Russian-backed private military and security contractors (PMSCs) formed an essential element of Russia's intrusion into Ukraine, particularly the ongoing conflict in the Donbas region in the east.[60] In addition, because of the rise of automated weaponry, contractors can now perform new functions with impacts on the battlefield, whether or not they themselves are located there. For example, a wide range of contractors participate in the operation of unmanned aerial vehicles, both for intelligence gathering and targeting purposes. Contractor functions reportedly include sifting through and analyzing intelligence before it is funneled to uniformed decision makers, including for targeting decisions.[61] Finally, the power of transnational corporations has grown independently of states, and, especially in the developing world, these corporations have themselves turned to other companies to provide security, especially in conflict zones.

All of this privatization potentially threatens the values that undergird the *jus in bello*. To be sure, this body of law applies to everyone in an armed conflict—public and private actors alike. Yet the mechanisms of accountability and oversight, such as the military chain of command, as well as criminal and civil penalties for violations, were not designed with privatized functions in mind.[62] Despite these strains, as in the case of organized armed groups, the *jus in bello* has proved relatively resilient.

[59] *See, e.g.*, COMMISSION ON WARTIME CONTRACTING, FINAL REPORT, TRANSFORMING WARTIME CONTRACTING: CONTROLLING COSTS, REDUCING RISK (2011) [hereinafter FINAL REPORT]. As the United States has brought troops home from the conflicts in the Middle East, the overall number of contractors in these regions has dropped as well, although a significant contractor presence remains. *See* U.S. DEP'T OF DEFENSE, CONTRACTOR SUPPORT OF U.S. OPERATIONS IN THE USCENTCOM AREA OF RESPONSIBILITY (July 2019), https://perma.cc/BGJ9-CH9U [hereinafter USCENTCOM].

[60] *See, e.g.*, Sergey Sukhankin, *War, Business and "Hybrid" Warfare: The Case of the Wagner Private Military Company (Part One)*, 15 EURASIA DAILY MONITOR (Apr. 19, 2018), https://perma.cc/2C6G-FFQG; *see also* Laura A. Dickinson, *The Future of Military and Security Privatization: Protecting the Values Underlying the Law of Armed Conflict*, *in* THE FUTURE OF THE LAW OF ARMED CONFLICT (Matt Waxman & Thomas W. Oakley eds., 2022).

[61] *See, e.g.*, Keric D. Clanahan, *Drone-Sourcing? United States Air Force Unmanned Aircraft Systems, Inherently Governmental Functions, and the Role of Contractors*, 22 FED. CIR. BAR. J. 6 (2012); A. Fielding-Smith et al., *Revealed: Private Firms at Heart of US Drone Warfare*, THE GUARDIAN, Feb. 12, 2015; A. Fielding-Smith & C. Black, *Pentagon's "Insatiable Demand" for Drone War Intelligence*, THE BUREAU OF INVESTIGATIVE JOURNALISM (July 30, 2015), https://perma.cc/F95V-6SZT.

[62] *See* DICKINSON, *supra* note 6.

A. The Threats Privatization Poses to the *Jus in Bello*

The *jus in bello* does not itself forbid military and security privatization. Indeed, this body of law assumes that some contractors will accompany armed forces. Efforts to ban contractors by defining them as illegal "mercenaries" have largely failed. As far back as the Hague Conventions of 1907, through several treaties on the status of mercenaries and the Additional Protocols to the Geneva Conventions, the international community has sought to draw boundaries around certain categories of "mercenary" behavior.[63] Postwar initiatives on the topic were caught in conflicting approaches, reflecting concerns about mercenarism in decolonizing Africa (prompting support for strongly worded bans in that context), and states' fears that overbroad bans could unduly restrain behavior that should be lawful in other contexts. As a result, both the International Convention Against the Recruitment, Use, Financing and Training of Mercenaries[64] and the Convention for the Elimination of Mercenarism in Africa[65] take a schizophrenic approach to the issue. Both treaties appear to penalize states for deploying mercenaries, but define mercenaries so narrowly, with intent requirements that are so difficult to prove, that the prohibitions are virtually meaningless. Furthermore, Additional Protocol I to the Geneva Conventions does not ban mercenarism.[66] Indeed, the US Representative to Protocol I's diplomatic conference noted how easy it would be for any party to a conflict to avoid the impact of the Protocol.[67] Thus, as I have written elsewhere, this tortured history has yielded little in the way of workable categories.[68]

Even though the *jus in bello* does not ban military and security contracting outright, the growing use of PMSCs for a broad range of functions threatens the *jus in bello*'s underlying values, in part because contractors are usually not inculcated in these values to the same extent as uniformed troops. In addition, the mechanisms of oversight and accountability for implementing the *jus in bello* were designed in a different era, when contractors were not performing such a broad range of functions.

[63] *See id.*

[64] International Convention Against the Recruitment, Use, Financing and Training of Mercenaries, Dec. 4, 1989, 2163 U.N.T.S. 75.

[65] Org. of African Unity [OAU], Convention for the Elimination of Mercenarism in Africa, July 3, 1977, OAU Doc. CM/817 (XXIX) Annex II Rev.1., 1490 U.N.T.S. 89.

[66] AP I, *supra* note 2, art. 47.

[67] *See* DICKINSON, *supra* note 6.

[68] *See id.*

The threat is greatest for contractors who are authorized to use force: for example, those working in security or interrogation. Although many of these contractors are risking their lives in conflict zones and are just trying to do their jobs, a number of high-profile incidents show how contractors in these domains sometimes flout the *jus in bello*'s fundamental principles. From the interrogation contractors at Abu Ghraib prison in Iraq who tortured detainees, to the security contractors who killed unarmed civilians in Baghdad's Nisour Square, contractors have committed serious abuses.[69] However, contractors whose roles include the use of force are not the only ones who pose problems. Contractors performing other roles, such as logistics, could undermine the values that undergird the *jus in bello* if they are armed for self-defense and then misuse their weapons during an armed conflict. Furthermore, a broader range of contractor misbehavior in conflict zones, such as human trafficking, forced labor practices, or actions that disrespect local culture, can undermine the military mission of governmental armed forces. Local populations do not usually distinguish between the actions of contractors and uniformed troops working for the same government; typically they blame military forces even when it is contractors who cause harm.

One might argue that there are bad actors within the ranks of uniformed troops as well, and a few abuses by contractors in war zones do not threaten to bring down the very foundations of the *jus in bello*. But the challenge is that the mechanisms of oversight and accountability that safeguard *jus in bello* values by protecting against governmental misconduct were not designed with today's broad range of contractors in mind. Contractors fall outside the chain of command, and so their actions are not subject to the same kinds of disciplinary measures as actions by uniformed personnel, or even civilian governmental personnel working with troops.[70] Indeed, any potential punishment of contractors in military courts runs up against not only the usual practical difficulties in providing sufficient proof of misconduct but also strong countervailing legal doctrines that limit the use of military courts

[69] *See* Final Report, *supra* note 59.

[70] The Military Extraterritorial Jurisdiction Act (MEJA) does provide civilian jurisdiction over extraterritorial crimes committed by contractors working for the Department of Defense or whose employment supports a Department of Defense mission. 18 U.S.C. §§ 3261, 3267. But loopholes in the statute leave some contractors for agencies other than the Department of Defense beyond its reach, and investigative challenges have plagued prosecutions under the statute. *See* Laura A. Dickinson, *Drone Contractors: An Oversight and Accountability Gap*, Just Security (July 21, 2015), https://perma.cc/AZP7-VWCK.

to try civilians. For example, in the United States, the use of military courts to try contractors presents significant constitutional concerns.[71] The transnational dimension of the problem is also a challenge, with contract firms often hiring employees from multiple nations. When abuses occur, victims and perpetrators often do not share the same nationality. The state where the harm takes place may not have the capacity to impose accountability, but courts from the perpetrator's home state, or the state of incorporation of the company, may be unwilling or unable to exercise extraterritorial jurisdiction.

Therefore, accountability and oversight, to the extent that it can be established, must come through a range of alternative mechanisms tailored to the current functions of military contractors. The next section discusses some of those alternative mechanisms.

B. Responses

Despite the tremendous pressure that outsourcing has put on the *jus in bello*, the last twenty years have produced a remarkable effort to respond to these pressures and to ensure that the humanitarian values embedded in the *jus in bello* remain protected. This effort has involved initiatives at both the international and domestic level to refine existing mechanisms of oversight and accountability—civil and criminal, military and civilian—and the development of new ones, including increased managerial oversight, reforms to the government contracting process, the development of public-private regulatory bodies and business management standards, improvement of the organizational culture within contract firms, and increased transparency regarding contracting practices. In addition, at the domestic level, some states have enacted regulations to cordon off some privatized functions—such as offensive combat and interrogation within armed conflict—as largely off limits to contractors. A good portion of my own writing has been devoted to this issue, and I am gratified to say that there have been enormous improvements.

At the international level, attempts to ban certain categories of contractors operating in conflict zones have largely failed. The various treaties seeking to ban "mercenaries" have not garnered significant support. A more recent initiative—the ongoing work of the UN Working Group on the use of mercenaries mandated by the UN Human Rights Council—has been similarly

[71] *See* Dickinson, *supra* note 6, at 50.

doomed, due partly to the decision to frame the Working Group's activities around the term "mercenaries."[72] Because "mercenary" carries so much stigma and baggage, the industry—including virtually all types of military and security firms—as well as many states refuse to engage meaningfully with the group.[73]

The more successful international approach has been to regulate, rather than prohibit, contractor activity in conflict zones. The so-called Montreux process, an initiative spearheaded by the ICRC, the Swiss government, and other national governments, has yielded significant results. This initiative, which also included sustained input from civil society groups and industry, produced a 2008 document entitled the Montreux Document on Pertinent International Legal Obligations and Good Practices for States Related to the Operations of Private Military and Security Companies During Armed Conflict.[74] Unlike the earlier treaties and the UN Working Group, the Montreux Document does not try to ban any specific category of contractors, although it does encourage states to limit the use of contractors who take a direct part in hostilities. Rather, the Montreux Document offers a framework for regulating the activities of contractors. It makes clear that military and security contractors must follow the *jus in bello* and that states that employ contractors are legally responsible for their behavior. The initiative also encompasses an ongoing, regular conference of states—the Montreux Document Forum[75]—that meets regularly and provides periodic reports on state compliance with these principles. The Forum includes major powers such as the United States and China, though not Russia.

[72] Human Rights Council Res. 42/9, U.N. Doc. A/HRC/RES42/9 (Sept. 26, 2019).

[73] *See* International Service for Human Rights, *Human Rights Council: Little Support for Proposed Convention Regulating Private Security Companies* (Sept. 23, 2010), https://perma.cc/K4N6-VAYB. A new draft treaty on mercenaries from the Working Group has received little interest and has languished within the Working Group for years. *See* Working Group on the Use of Mercenaries, Submission by the Working Group on the use of mercenaries as a means of impeding the exercise of the right of peoples to self-determination, ¶ 39, U.N. Doc. A/HRC/WG.10/2/CRP.1 (Aug. 6, 2012); International Service for Human Rights, *supra*. The Working Group has produced some useful reports that offer information about the use of contractors globally, but it has not been successful in providing a framework of legal oversight. *See* Gabor Rona, *A Tour de Horizon of Issues on the Agenda of the Mercenaries Working Group*, 22 Minn. J. Int'l L. 342–44 (2013).

[74] International Committee of the Red Cross, Montreux Document on Pertinent International Legal Obligations and Good Practices for States Related to the Operations of Private Military and Security Companies During Armed Conflict (2008).

[75] *Participating States and International Organizations*, Montreux Document Forum, https://www.montreuxdocument.org/about/participants.html (last visited May 25, 2021).

An offshoot of Montreux, the International Code of Conduct for Private Security Contractors (PSCs),[76] lays out in clear terms the responsibilities of security contractors, including with respect to the use of force. Although the *jus in bello* applies to all public and private actors operating in armed conflict, the PSC Code is significant because it specifically delineates what contractors must do to comply with the *jus in bello*, and it also lays out best practices that go beyond the *jus in bello*'s requirements.[77] Significantly, industry and civil society—not only states—helped draft the PSC Code. Furthermore, the PSC Code defines very specific substantive standards that PSCs themselves agree to observe directly by signing the PSC Code. In addition, the PSC Code has provided for the creation of an association, a mechanism of governance that includes not only governments but also civil society and the PSC industry, and brings these nonstate actors into the process of norm articulation and oversight.[78]

The Montreux process and PSC Code have been quite useful in articulating standards for certain categories of contractors and providing an implementation framework for states and the private sector. These initiatives have been especially effective for security contractors. The Montreux Document also provides some guidance for other types of contractors beyond PSCs, such as contractors providing military training and advice, and logistics, although there is no spinoff Code of Conduct for these contractors.

To be sure, while most democratic states can be expected to ban contractors from performing functions such as interrogation and offensive combat operations (and to use contractor firms that have signed on to the Montreux process), it is likely that powerful nondemocratic states such as Russia that do not robustly implement the *jus in bello* will expand their use of contractors in such roles. These contractors are even more likely to flout the *jus in bello* rules than if those states were acting directly, and the states may deny their connections to the contractors.[79] Moreover, in many cases, powerful states will be operating in partnership with weaker states in the developing world, and these states, in turn, will be less likely to adhere to the *jus in bello*. Finally, states may increasingly turn to contractors in the sphere of cyberspace and new military and intelligence technologies. The use of

[76] International Code of Conduct for Private Security Service Providers (2010), https://perma.cc/8V2P-DPAT.

[77] *See* Laura Dickinson, *Regulating the Private Security Industry: The Promise of Public/Private Governance*, 63 EMORY L.J. 417 (2013).

[78] *See id.*

[79] For a more detailed discussion of this problem, *see generally* Dickinson, *supra* note 60.

contractors in this domain could allow these states to exploit armed conflict thresholds to evade the strictures of the *jus in bello*.[80] In short, privatization might fuel what many have termed "hybrid war."[81]

Despite these strains, as in the case of nonstate armed groups, the *jus in bello* has proved relatively resilient. The ICRC and many states have come together to address the challenges of privatization in armed conflict. They have produced important soft law norms and best practices to help states protect the values of the *jus in bello* in an era of privatization. Even China, not a stalwart of the rules-based international order, has joined in this process.[82] Further, with respect to the conduct of security contractors, the international community—including the private sector—has developed codes of conduct and business management standards to improve compliance with *jus in bello* norms.[83] Although critical gaps remain, these efforts are significant and demonstrate the strength of *jus in bello* norms and institutions.

IV. Technological Change

Advances in military technologies are as old as military action itself. Yet recent technological shifts, and new shifts on the horizon, have the potential to disrupt modern warfare to an unprecedented degree and, as a consequence, the *jus in bello*. Such technologies include autonomous or semi-autonomous weapons systems, cyber operations, hypersonic weapons, bio-enhancement, and the like. In addition, big data increasingly will fuel many of these newer technologies, and the drive to acquire such data could undermine humanitarian principles. Finally, large-scale data storage may itself become an important target of military operations.

The commitment to respect fundamental principles of the *jus in bello*—military necessity and humanity—will in my view likely remain intact. But

[80] *See* Ido Kilovaty, *Cyber Conflict and the Thresholds of War* (Chapter 8 in this volume).

[81] *See, e.g.*, DICKINSON, *supra* note 6; Michael Kofman & Matthew Rojansky, *Kennan Cable No. 7: A Closer Look at Russia's "Hybrid War,"* WILSON CENTER (2015); Frank Hoffman, *On Not-So-New Warfare: Political Warfare vs. Hybrid Threats*, WAR ON THE ROCKS (July 28, 2014), https://perma.cc/6P6R-C5GT; Aurel Sari, *Legal Aspects of Hybrid Warfare*, LAWFARE (Oct. 2, 2015), https://perma.cc/K2E9-56SX.

[82] Government of Switzerland, Federal Department of Foreign Affairs, *Participating States of the Montreux Document* (2020), https://www.eda.admin.ch/eda/en/fdfa/foreign-policy/international-law/international-humanitarian-law/private-military-security-companies/participating-states.html.

[83] *See* Laura A. Dickinson, *Regulating the Privatized Security Industry: The Promise of Public/Private Governance*, 63 EMORY L.J. 417–54 (2013); *see also* DICKINSON, *supra* note 6.

the question will be whether new technologies are so disruptive that states and other actors will have difficulty balancing these somewhat conflicting aims. Will these new technologies enable more precise targeting that will better effectuate the principle of humanity and the corresponding principles of distinction, proportionality, and unnecessary suffering? Or will new technologies such as autonomous systems create such asymmetry in warfare that they will ultimately threaten the core of the humanity principle itself? Alternatively, will the proliferation of these technologies, some of which are relatively low cost, allow a broader range of states and nonstate actors to engage in armed conflict? Proliferation alone would not necessarily threaten the *jus in bello*, but if newly empowered actors are less likely to respect the rules-based international order, does the expansion of participants risk undermining *jus in bello* principles to an unprecedented degree?

These questions are difficult to answer, but there are reasons to be both pessimistic and optimistic. On the negative side of the ledger, the core *jus in bello* institutions have largely failed to provide effective fora where states could reach consensus around norms and best practices in this arena. For example, member states that are parties to the Convention on Certain Conventional Weapons[84] have not been able to agree on a regulatory framework for lethal autonomous weapons systems (LAWS).[85] Although experts have spoken forcefully on the need for new unified rules in this area, states have instead descended into a free-for-all of competing views. The heightened secrecy surrounding some of these technologies, such as cyber, has also hampered states from articulating their own views in a transparent way, which in turn has hindered the development of the law. Despite these failures, there are grounds for cautious optimism because there remains a strong underlying commitment to the fundamental goals of the *jus in bello*, even as various actors disagree about how to implement them. This section examines two areas of new technology—the potential use of LAWS and the increasing role of big data—to illustrate why the *jus in bello* is likely to be resilient even as these new technologies become more widespread.

[84] United Nations Convention on Prohibitions or Restrictions on the Use of Certain Conventional Weapons Which May be Deemed to be Excessively Injurious or to Have Indiscriminate Effects (and Protocols), October 10, 1980, 1342 U.N.T.S. 137 (as amended on Dec. 21, 2001).

[85] *See, e.g.*, Hayley Evans & Natalie Salmanowitz, *Lethal Autonomous Weapons Systems: Recent Developments*, Lawfare (Mar. 7, 2019), https://perma.cc/R4GQ-TZ9B; Rain Livoja, *Why It's So Hard to Reach an International Agreement on Killer Robots*, The Conversation (Sept. 11, 2018), https://perma.cc/33QF-D5B7; Chris Jenks, *Lethal Autonomous Weapons* (Chapter 7 in this volume).

A. Lethal Autonomous Weapons Systems

The development of weapons systems with autonomous capabilities is reshaping modern warfare. The US military has developed multiple weapons systems with at least some autonomous capabilities, including the US Navy's Phalanx system, which detects and neutralizes missiles that breach a warship's protective envelope, the US Army's comparable Counter Rocket, Artillery, and Mortar (C-RAM) System, for land-based defense, and the X-47B drone that can fly by itself during takeoff and landing. Other countries have produced and deployed such systems as well, from Israel's Harpies, which autonomously ferret out enemy radar and then dive-bomb to destroy them, to South Korea's robotic sentries that protect the border. As Chris Jenks's chapter in this volume discusses, these systems can either be fully or partially autonomous, depending on the degree of human intervention required to activate and control them.[86]

The use of such systems—and in particular the potential use of fully autonomous systems that can select targets among multiple options—has generated significant controversy among policymakers, activists, and legal scholars. While the creation of fully autonomous systems may be years, if not decades away, the prospect of full autonomy and the risks of even partial autonomy have raised concerns on multiple fronts. Human Rights Watch, with its provocatively titled campaign *Stop Killer Robots!*, has advocated a complete ban on autonomous systems.[87] The US Department of Defense has adopted a more moderate approach, instituting a temporary ban on lethal, fully autonomous systems, while at the same time providing policies to ensure meaningful human control over semi-autonomous systems.[88] Multiple governments and nongovernmental experts have engaged in ongoing discussions about whether existing *jus in bello* frameworks for approval of such systems and for targeting are sufficient to regulate them, or whether new rules are necessary.

[86] *See* Jenks, Chapter 7.

[87] *See* B. Docherty, *Losing Humanity: The Case Against Killer Robots*, at 2, HUM. RTS. WATCH (Nov. 19, 2012), https://perma.cc/N77J-EASX. For an argument for a more limited moratorium on only those weapons that are used to target human personnel, *see* Chris Jenks, *False Rubicons, Moral Panic, & Conceptual Cul-de-Sacs: Critiquing & Reframing the Call to Ban Lethal Autonomous Weapons*, 44 PEPP. L. REV. 1 (2016).

[88] U.S. DEP'T OF DEF., DIR. 3000.09, AUTONOMY IN WEAPON SYSTEMS (2012), https://perma.cc/NLG5-ETGS [hereinafter DOD Directive].

Critics worry that such systems will never operate in compliance with the fundamental principles of the *jus in bello*, including the principles of distinction, proportionality, and feasible precautions.[89] On the other hand, proponents argue that these weapons have the capacity not only to reduce military casualties but also to conduct more precise targeting that could reduce civilian casualties as well, because they would rely less on human judgment and might therefore provide an opportunity for more humane warfare, stripped of the irrationality, hot-blooded decision-making, and emotional toll of the battlefield.[90] Such weapons, according to these arguments, might paradoxically lead to better implementation of the distinction and proportionality principles.[91] Still others point to the ease with which these systems can proliferate among states and nonstate actors, creating new threats even as they provide increased military capabilities. For example, some have argued that the asymmetric harm such weapons can inflict flouts core principles of humanity that undergird the *jus in bello*, or that the promise of precision that such weapons offer may be overstated.[92]

1. *The Threats Autonomous Weaponry Poses for the* Jus in Bello

The scenario of the villain who designs and deploys autonomous weapons with the intent to wreak havoc on the world may be the dominant image of autonomous weaponry from pop culture, but it is not the focus of scholars and critics (and of course the *jus in bello*, however defined or applied, would presumably have no effect on such a global criminal). Rather, the core question for the *jus in bello* is whether, even if an autonomous system is designed with the intent to distinguish between military and civilian targets, such systems can ever actually do so effectively in practice. Markus Wagner, for example, has expressed skepticism that even highly sophisticated weapons systems could distinguish between an armed terrorist and a child playing with a toy gun. Applying the principle of distinction requires the kind of judgment that, he maintains, could never be programmed. Others fear that

89 *Id.*

90 *See, e.g.*, Matt Waxman & Kenneth Anderson, *Law and Ethics for Autonomous Weapon Systems: Why a Ban Won't Work and How the Laws of War Can*, The Hoover Institution (Apr. 13, 2013), https://perma.cc/C4UA-7DJN.

91 For an excellent overview of the debate about autonomous weapons and a moderate approach to the issue, *see* J. Vilmer, *Terminator Ethics: Should We Ban "Killer Robots"?*, Ethics & Int'l Affairs (Mar. 23, 2015), https://perma.cc/U6QD-TMDE.

92 *See, e.g.*, M. Wagner, *The Dehumanization of International Humanitarian Law: Legal, Political, and Ethical Implications of Autonomous Weapons Systems*, 47 Vand. J. Transnat'l L. 1371 (2014); Docherty, *supra* note 87.

even if autonomous weapons systems could be capable of implementing *jus in bello* principles, the use of such systems nonetheless poses multiple risks of harm because the systems could still malfunction. Paul Scharre at the Center for a New American Security has compiled a comprehensive analysis of such potential harms in a report, *Autonomous Weapons and Operational Risk*.[93] Scharre "assumes that lawful employment of autonomous weapons is feasible, at least for isolated situations." But for Scharre, the central risk in employing such systems "is that the system might not perform the tasks in a manner that the human operator intended."[94] In particular, he notes that the deployment of systems could result in large numbers of civilian casualties, friendly fire incidents, or unintended escalation in a crisis.

Scharre identifies four important risk factors to consider. First, there may be hazards inherent in a system, such as whether the system is capable of causing physical harm in an area that includes civilians, as well as the overall operational environment. For example, undersea usage or deployment in some other domain without civilians is obviously less risky than densely populated urban areas. Second, the time between system failure and corrective human action is key. Here, fully autonomous systems present the most risks because the human operator "lacks the ability to observe the autonomous system's behavior and undertake corrective action in sufficient time if the system fails to perform appropriately."[95] But even semi-autonomous weaponry may leave little time for a human operator to intervene. Third, there are the risks posed by adversaries, such as hacking.

Finally, the sheer complexity both of the system and its environment can increase the risk. Simpler systems will be easier to predict, while more complex systems are less transparent. Complex rule-based systems can pose significant problems due to malfunctions and bugs, system failures, lack of transparency to human operators, and unanticipated interactions with the environment (which increase as the systems grow more complex). Systems that are not rule-based but rather engage in so-called "machine learning" by evaluating and adapting to information from large data sets may pose the greatest challenge. Because such a machine's "internal cognitive processes are vastly different from a human's," this "significantly complicates a human's ability to predict how [the entity] might classify objects."[96] The risk

[93] Paul Scharre, Ctr. New Am. Sec. Autonomous Weapons And Operational Risk (Feb. 2016).
[94] *Id.* at 8.
[95] *Id.* at 10.
[96] *Id.* at 17.

of unintentional harms deriving from the interaction between humans and machines in complex organizational systems is therefore likely the most serious risk of harm that autonomous systems pose.

In light of their potential to cause unintentional harms, LAWS present a significant challenge for the *jus in bello*: the challenge of accountability.[97] In particular, these systems threaten the framework of individual criminal responsibility that many would argue undergirds the *jus in bello*. From the Nuremberg trials of Nazi war criminals, to proceedings before more recently established international courts and tribunals, to domestic civilian and military prosecutions, the *jus in bello* fundamentally requires that human beings be held individually responsible for war crimes. Although such prosecutions are rare, they constitute one of the core sanctions that seek to ensure compliance with this body of law. Autonomous weapons pose problems for this framework. As a number of scholars have pointed out, in the case of truly autonomous systems, there may be no human being with the requisite level of intent to trigger individual responsibility under existing doctrine.[98]

2. *Possible Responses*

The *jus in bello* could respond to such challenges. For example, international criminal law could be reformed to better address unintentional harms and to permit organizational accountability.[99] In addition, or in the alternative, greater emphasis on other forms of accountability, such as broader applications of tort liability and state responsibility might be useful supplements.[100]

I have argued previously that focusing narrowly on reforming international criminal law is at best a partial solution for adapting the *jus in bello* to meet these threats.[101] Indeed, given the potential for unintentional harms and human-machine interaction in complex organizational systems,

[97] *See* Wagner, *supra* note 92.

[98] *See id.*; J. Thurnher, *Examining Autonomous Weapon Systems from a Law of Armed Conflict Perspective*, *in* New Technologies and the Law of Armed Conflict 225 (H. Nasu & R. McLaughlin eds., 2014); M. Sassòli, *Autonomous Weapons and International Humanitarian Law: Advantages, Open Technical Questions and Legal Issues to be Clarified*, 90 U.S. Naval War C., Int'l L. Stud. 308 (2014).

[99] *See* Jens Ohlin, *The Combatant's Stance: Autonomous Weapons on the Battlefield*, 92 Int'l L. Stud. 1 (2016).

[100] *See* Rebecca Crootof, *War Torts: Accountability for Autonomous Weapons*, 164 Univ. Penn. L. Rev. 1347 (2016).

[101] Laura A. Dickinson, *The Impact of Emerging Technologies on the Law of Armed Conflict: The Overlooked Importance of Administrative Accountability*, *in* The Impact of Emerging Technologies on the Law of Armed Conflict (Ronald Alcala & Eric Talbot Jensen eds., 2019).

tinkering with criminal doctrines may not be the best approach. Instead, we may be better served in many situations by invoking what I call mechanisms of administrative accountability. And unlike, for example, the possibility of tort suits in international venues, administrative accountability mechanisms have the virtue of already existing, although they certainly can be improved.

By administrative accountability, I am referring to existing mechanisms, both military and civilian, that are often used for accidents and other types of problems. Their goal is not individual punishment, although they can involve financial and other penalties for individuals, such as loss of rank. They can be broader in their remedial scope, for example, leading to monetary payments to those who have been harmed. They can also be forward-looking, focusing on organizational reforms for the future. And because they are not taking away individuals' liberty, they can be more flexible in their procedures.[102]

Of course, administrative accountability is not a panacea. Certainly, because these mechanisms exist largely within the executive branch, guarantees of independence, impartiality, and transparency are critical, and reforms may be needed to better protect these values. But they do hold tremendous promise. In the end, I think some combination of international criminal law reform, expanded avenues of tort liability, and a more robust regime for administrative accountability could help bolster the *jus in bello* and allow it to respond to the threats posed by these new technologies.

B. Big Data

As with increasingly autonomous weapons systems, big data is emerging as a key component of military operations. Here we are talking about "the exponentially increasing amount of digital information being created by new information technologies such as mobile internet, cloud storage, social networking, and the 'internet of things'–and the advanced analytics used to process that data."[103] The ability of the warfighter to acquire, evaluate, and

[102] In the United States, examples include Commander's inquiries, fact-finding investigations pursuant to Army Regulation 15-6, Advisory Committee Task Forces, and Agency Inspector General inquiries. For further discussion of this approach, *see generally* Laura A. Dickinson, *Lethal Autonomous Weapons Systems: The Overlooked Importance of Administrative Accountability*, *in* The Impact of Emerging Technologies on the Law of Armed Conflict (Eric Jensen & Michael Schmitt eds., 2019).

[103] Paul B. Symon & Arzan Tarapore, *Defense Intelligence Analysis in the Age of Big Data*, 79 Joint Force Q. 5 (2015).

utilize such data will likely increase in importance in many combat contexts. Probability-based forecasts of enemy behavior, aggregation of weather and environmental conditions, anticipation and flagging of supply line vulnerabilities, and identification and tracking of targets can all significantly improve military capabilities. At the same time, targeting the adversary's data and data systems may provide important military advantages in armed conflict. And a multitude of actors, including humanitarian and human rights organizations, may also seek to utilize big data from a variety of sources to engage in functions such as aid delivery or the identification of atrocities. Furthermore, with big data's growing role, acquisition of, access to, analysis of, and dissemination of such data will be a crucial function that will likely require partnerships not only with allies but also the private sector.

Therefore, like autonomous weaponry, big data raises a variety of legal issues and challenges in armed conflicts, as well as for extraterritorial military actions that might fall below the armed conflict threshold. A significant scholarly and policy literature has touched on some of these issues in the context of evaluating artificial intelligence (AI) and its application to weapons systems, as AI often depends on the existence of big data and is a powerful tool to evaluate it.[104] In addition, debates about cyber operations above and below the armed conflict threshold have addressed international legal issues related to the targeting of data.[105]

Big data will likely present a number of tough challenges for the *jus in bello*. First, if data is targeted in an armed conflict, is it an "object" within the meaning of the *jus in bello*, and therefore subject to the *jus in bello*'s targeting rules related to objects? If so, then new policy guidelines in this area may be needed. Second, does the deliberate targeting of data without kinetic effects constitute an attack within the meaning of the *jus in bello*? Third, if the geographical location of data happens to be outside the zone of hostilities, should that be relevant to an analysis of whether there is a nexus to an armed conflict? And with regard to each of these issues, the interaction of the *jus in bello* with human rights law will pose complexities.

[104] *See, e.g.*, Anderson & Waxman, *supra* note 90; Ashley Deeks, *Predicting Enemies*, 104 VA. L. REV. 1529 (2018).

[105] *See, e.g.*, RÉPUBLIQUE FRANCAISE, MIN. DES ARMEÉS, DROIT INTERNATIONAL APPLIQUÉ AUX OPÉRATIONS DANS LE CYBERSPACE (2019) ["International Law Applicable to Operations in Cyberspace"]; Heather A. Harrison Dinniss, *The Nature of Objects: Targeting Networks and the Challenge of Defining Cyber Military Objectives*, 48 ISRAEL L. REV. 1 (2015); Michael N. Schmitt, *Wired Warfare 3.0: Protecting the Civilian Population During Cyber Operations*, 101 INT'L REV. RED CROSS 333 (2019); Kilovaty, Chapter 8.

A related set of issues arises not from targeting of data itself but rather from the use of big data in targeting decisions. For example, biases in data create potential operational risks and could lead to misidentification of targets.[106] To what extent does the *jus in bello*'s principle of distinction impose an obligation to weed out such biases? Does the principle of feasible precautions require testing of the algorithms that are used to distill big data in order to ensure there are no systemic problems that could lead to mistaken targeting of civilians? Is the use of big data to operate a particular weapon system itself a weapon that must undergo weapons review procedures? Are there any transparency or "explainability" rules that derive from the *jus in bello* or that should be adopted as a matter of policy?

Finally, governments and NGOs may increasingly turn to big data to help identify and respond to *jus in bello* violations because data can help determine whether atrocities are being committed. Accordingly, might the use of big data analysis trigger a state's obligation under the *jus in bello* to investigate such atrocities? In addition, if analysis of big data *could* reveal the existence of atrocities, might the *failure* to assess such data be a violation of the obligation to investigate?

In the end, big data, like the emergence of LAWS, seems likely to prompt a translation exercise for states and others in the international community. This process will involve considerable debate about how *jus in bello* principles and rules should apply to the contexts in which autonomous weaponry and big data are used or targeted. Gaps in the law as it governs these situations will lead to disagreements, and potentially to self-serving interpretations of existing doctrine. Yet there is no real sign that these new developments are prompting states or others to question the core values at the root of the *jus in bello* itself. Finally, as discussed previously, in some contexts this new technology might actually enable *greater* compliance with *jus in bello*'s core values.

V. Urbanization

Urbanization is another trend with potentially profound consequences for the *jus in bello*. Experts project the growth of cities in the near future to

[106] *See, e.g.*, Cong. Rsch Serv., R45178, Artificial Intelligence And National Security 30 (2019), https://perma.cc/9VV6-DFYJ.

increase exponentially, with the emergence of more and more megacities around the globe. Megacities pose significant challenges for the *jus in bello* because population density makes it very difficult for even well-intentioned combatants to uphold the principle of humanity in an armed conflict situation. Entities that use military force will struggle to apply the principles of distinction and proportionality in urban warfare, and the humanitarian costs of military operations will multiply. It is not surprising that the ICRC has made humanitarian protection in urban warfare one of its top initiatives in recent years.

In some respects, urbanization may pose a bigger threat to the *jus in bello* than the other forces described in this chapter. This conclusion may seem surprising, but urbanization exposes fissures in the *jus in bello* itself in a way that the forces discussed previously do not. The long-running transnational NIACs have in some ways obscured the problem, because counterinsurgency warfare, though posing its own challenges, tends to minimize civilian casualties. In contrast, an interstate armed conflict waged on modern urban terrain could cause staggering numbers of civilian casualties.

A. The Rise of Urban Warfare

"The future of the world's population is urban," the United Nations has emphasized.[107] The first two decades of the twenty-first century have produced a marked rise in urbanization. Projections for the future anticipate an exponential increase in urbanization in the years to come. And while we often associate megacities only with China, this is a worldwide trend. By 2018, the number of cities with at least one million inhabitants had grown to 548, and in 2030, a projected 706 additional cities will expand to that size.[108] In fact, policy makers predict that by 2030 two-thirds of the world's population will live in urban areas.[109] Furthermore, megacities, defined as cities with more than ten million inhabitants, are rapidly emerging around the globe. From Kolkata to Kinshasa, Beijing to Bogota, Manila to Mumbai, thirty-three megacities spread across multiple continents had emerged by 2018, with the

[107] Dep't Econ. & Soc. Aff., World Urbanization Prospects, U.N. Doc. ST/ESA/SER.A/420, at 1 (2018) [hereinafter World Urbanization].

[108] Dep't Econ. & Soc. Aff., The World's Cities in 2018: Data Booklet, U.N. Doc. ST/ESA/SER.A/417 (2018) [hereinafter Data Booklet].

[109] Peter Maurer, *War in Cities: What Is at Stake?*, 98 Int'l Rev. Red. Cross 639 (2016).

greatest future increase in such cities projected in South America, Africa, and Asia.[110] Unplanned development and rising inequality in dense urban areas often result in a lack of access to critical infrastructure that increases health risks and leaves the urban poor particularly vulnerable.[111]

As the world's cities have rapidly expanded, they have also become the site of complex counterterrorism operations and armed conflicts. The dense populations of Aleppo, Gaza, Mosul, and Donetz have all recently borne the brunt of intense fighting in NIACs involving terrorist groups.[112] The armed conflict in Yemen has also ravaged residents of the beleaguered country's cities.[113] Armed conflicts in such locations have taken a particular toll on the cities' poor, as the conflicts tend to disrupt already strained critical infrastructure, exacerbating the problems of poverty and disease, spurring mass displacement, and worsening humanitarian disasters.[114] In the conflicts in Iraq and Syria, urban warfare has led to 70 percent of the armed conflicts' civilian casualties.[115]

Yet the harms of NIACs in dense urban environments pale in comparison to the potential catastrophe if peer or near-peer states were to engage in international armed conflict. Perhaps no potential conflict presents the risk of catastrophic harm more starkly than the prospect of renewed fighting on the Korean Peninsula. Estimates project that even a conventional war on Korean territory could lead to an unprecedented death toll. The war on the peninsula in the 1950s resulted in more than two million civilian casualties, while 220,000 South Korean military personnel were killed. Casualties from any future war could be far higher, in part because of the risk to residents of the megacity Seoul, situated only about fifteen miles from the border with North Korea.[116] If Pyongyang's multiple rocket launcher systems were directed against Seoul, "their range would be sufficient to rain fire across the city and beyond . . . and [t]he world would see civilian casualty numbers equal to the entire Syrian conflict in a matter of days."[117] A war between India and Pakistan could be equally devastating.

110 Data Booklet, *supra* note 108.

111 World Urbanization, *supra* note 107, at 4.

112 Maurer, *supra* note 109.

113 *Id.*

114 *Id.*

115 Margarita Koanev, The Future of Urban Warfare in the Age of Megacities 43 (2019), https://perma.cc/L7SZ-JPGN.

116 *See* Patrick Cronin, If Deterrence Fails: Re-Thinking Conflict on the Korean Peninsula 13 (2014).

117 Todd Soth & Jeff Schogol, *War with North Korea: An Inside Look at How US Troops Would Respond Worldwide*, Military Times, May 21, 2017.

B. The Threats Urbanization Poses for the *Jus in Bello*

The heightened risk of civilian casualties in urban settings puts tremendous pressure on the *jus in bello*. In a dense urban environment, the principle of distinction becomes virtually impossible to apply because armed forces will struggle to distinguish between military targets and civilian ones.[118] For example, much civilian infrastructure is dual use: "separating military targets from the civilian population can be extremely difficult because the very infrastructure civilian populations rely upon—roads, bridges, power stations, food distribution centers, and clean water sources—can also be used by enemy forces for military purposes."[119] Similarly, even when armed forces can distinguish military targets, the high level of potential harm to civilians and civilian objects in any operation makes applying the principle of proportionality extremely challenging.

The development of more precise weapons and better intelligence gathering techniques, which has mitigated this problem to some degree, has still not been able to prevent extraordinarily high casualty counts in urban contexts. In the US-led battle to wrest Mosul from ISIS, for example, US and coalition officials used extraordinary efforts to protect civilians through the collection and analysis of highly precise intelligence, strict targeting procedures, and "meticulously calibrated angles of attack to ensure minimal collateral damage."[120] Yet even with such efforts, between nine thousand and eleven thousand civilians were killed in the nine-month battle.[121]

Because of this difficulty, the ICRC has called on states to halt the use of all explosive weapons in urban environments: "The unacceptable levels of civilian harm we continue to witness in urban conflicts—be they in Afghanistan, Iraq, Libya, Syria, Ukraine, or Yemen—has led the ICRC to call on States and all parties to armed conflict to avoid the use of explosive weapons with a wide impact area in populated areas, due to the significant likelihood of indiscriminate effects."[122] Others have resisted

[118] N. Durhim, *Protecting Civilians in Urban Areas: A Military Perspective on the Application of International Humanitarian Law*, 98 Int'l Rev. Red. Cross 177 (2016) ("[The] very nature of cities makes it complicated for armed forces to apply the principle of distinction.").

[119] Koanev, *supra* note 115, at 45.

[120] *Id.*

[121] S. George, *Mosul Is a Graveyard: Final IS Battle Kills 9,000 Civilians*, AP News, Dec. 20, 2017.

[122] Gilles Carbonnier, *We Witness Unacceptable Levels of Civilian Harm in Urban Conflicts* (Oct. 1, 2019), https://perma.cc/DZ4L-2KTY.

this call, observing that civilian casualties are "grim," but a lawful part of war.[123]

Because wealthy states may increasingly be able to deploy relatively precise weapons and other advanced techniques, such as heightened intelligence gathering, the question arises whether such states have a legal obligation to do so. Article 57 of Additional Protocol I provides that "in the conduct of military operations, constant care shall be taken to spare the civilian population, civilians, and civilian objects."[124] With respect to attacks, those who plan or authorize an attack must "take all feasible precautions in the choice of means and methods of attack with a view to avoiding, and in any event, minimizing, incidental loss of civilian life, injury to civilians and damage to civilian objects."[125] The ICRC, states, and commentators have debated whether the ability of a state to use an expensive but precise weapon makes it "feasible" and therefore obligatory for such states.[126] Some commentators have also argued that states with a greater capacity for intelligence gathering have an obligation to deploy that capacity to comply with the feasible precautions principle in urban warfare.[127]

Another dimension of the challenge results from the often deliberate actions by terrorist groups to take advantage of the urban environment to drive up potential citizen casualty counts and therefore dissuade their adversaries from attacking. For example, such groups may house their headquarters in or near civilian sites such as hospitals, and make extensive use of so-called "human shields." In using these tactics, terrorist groups violate the *jus in bello* themselves, while also making it even harder for adversary states to observe the principles of distinction, proportionality, and feasible precautions.[128] Indeed, some scholars have argued that "ever-increasing urbanization is creating significant pressure on the doctrine of precautions . . . [s]tretching the 'feasibility' standard beyond its capacity to adequately protect civilians."[129]

[123] Thomas Ayres, *The Use of Explosives in Cities: A Grim but Lawful Reality of War*, 87 Joint Force Q. 26 (2017).

[124] AP I, *supra* note 2, art. 57.

[125] *Id.*

[126] *See, e.g.*, ICRC, Expert Meeting: Explosive Weapons in Populated Areas: Humanitarian, Legal, Technical, and Military Aspects (2015).

[127] *See, e.g.*, Jonathan Horowitz, *Precautionary Measures in Urban Warfare: A Commander's Obligation to Obtain Information*, ICRC Humanitarian Law & Pol. (Jan. 10, 2019), https://perma.cc/JGV9-R2VW.

[128] *See, e.g.*, Eric Talbot Jensen, *Precautions against the Effects of Attacks in Urban Areas*, 98 Int'l Rev. Red Cross 147 (2016).

[129] *Id.* at 147.

Finally, there may be disagreements over how to quantify the harm to civilians and civilian objects when applying the principle of proportionality to attacks on infrastructure in urban environments. The interconnectedness of urban services, already fragile in many cities, increases the risk of harm to civilian infrastructure in urban warfare:

> For example, a high-impact explosive weapon hitting a single pipe can deprive 100,000 people of water and may also destroy the neighborhood's sewage system, which can cause thousands of people to become ill and exacerbate the already overwhelming burden on hospitals.[130]

It is clear that such consequences should be incorporated into the civilian harm component of the proportionality analysis, but the sheer magnitude of such harms means that one side of the equation will always be extremely high in urban environments. In addition, how should combatants measure the reverberating effects? Should *any* deaths that are foreseeable be included in the civilian harm calculation?[131] Or, should a distinction be drawn between direct and indirect, or remote, effects?

C. An Insurmountable Challenge?

Like the other challenges to the *jus in bello* discussed previously, urbanization presents a translation problem for states, NGOs, intergovernmental organizations, and commentators interpreting the law. This translation exercise, however, unlike the others, may produce such significant disagreement that it could stretch the legal framework to the breaking point. Not only are there gaps in the law in this domain—gaps that different parties may interpret to their own advantage—but in this case the very pressure that urbanization places on the law's balance between military necessity and humanity may be too much to bear.

The ICRC's call, discussed previously, to end the use of explosive devices in urban warfare is illustrative. The ICRC, motivated by humanitarian goals, understandably seeks to protect civilians from the inevitable harm caused by warfare in dense urban environments. Indeed, in such environments it may

130 Koanev, *supra* note 115, at 46.

131 Isabel Robinson & Ellen Nohle, *Proportionality and Precautions in Attack: The Reverberating Effects of Using Explosive Weapons in Populated Areas*, 98 Int'l Rev. Red Cross 107 (2016).

be fundamentally *impossible* to balance humanitarian protection with military necessity. But if that is the case, then it would appear almost impossible to conduct war in cities at all. On the other hand, it is unrealistic to expect that warfare will never occur in cities in the future. The problem is that any balance between military necessity and humanitarian protection may become impossible to maintain. And the very premise of the *jus in bello*—that these two goals can be balanced—may no longer hold.

We may not yet have reached the breaking point. And it may be that states' deployment of new, more precise, weapons and advanced intelligence gathering capabilities can preserve the possibility for parties to balance military necessity and humanitarian protection in conducting attacks in urban environments. But as the world becomes even more urban and the number of megacities proliferates, we may see the core balances of the *jus in bello* become obsolete.

VI. Conclusion

Chill winds are blowing in the international arena. From the rise of transnational terrorism, to the increased use of private contractors, to the growing deployment of new military technologies, to the growth of megacities, a variety of forces threatens to shake the very foundation of the rules-based international order. Yet the *jus in bello* has thus far proved remarkably resilient in the face of such forces. Most states have not abandoned their core commitment to balance the twin goals of this body of law: military necessity and humanitarian values. And states seem unlikely to do so in the near future, even as it may prove challenging for them to agree on principles to adapt the law to fit new circumstances.

7
Autonomous Weapons

Chris Jenks

I. Introduction

On November 27, 2020, Mohsen Fakhrizadeh, Iran's top nuclear scientist, was killed by an attack on his vehicle in the suburbs of Tehran.[1] Commodore Ali Fadavi, the deputy commander of Iran's Revolutionary Guards, claimed that the attack was carried out remotely and that "[n]o terrorists were present on the ground."[2] Fadavi explained that a machine gun was mounted on a pickup truck, that both the truck and machine gun were operated remotely via satellite, that the machine gun utilized facial recognition software to identify Fakhrizadeh, and that the truck self-destructed after the attack.[3] Iran's President Hassan Rouhani blamed Israel for the attack, but did not explain the basis for that conclusion or provide any supporting evidence.[4]

Details of the attack remain limited and somewhat conflicting; what really happened may never be publicly known.[5] Yet Commodore Fadavi's version of the story was certainly plausible. Portable, remotely operated weapons,[6] driverless vehicles,[7] and facial recognition programs[8] are

[1] Frank Gardner, *Mohsen Fakhrizadeh: Iran Scientist Killed by Remote-Controlled Weapon*, BBC, Nov. 30, 2020.

[2] Reuters Staff, *Iran Says Smart Satellite-Controlled Machine Gun Killed Top Nuclear Scientist*, REUTERS, Dec. 7, 2020.

[3] *Id.*

[4] Parisa Hafezi, *Iran's Leader Promises Retaliation for Nuclear Scientist's Killing*, REUTERS, Nov. 28, 2020.

[5] *See* Reuters Staff, *supra* note 2; *but see* David D. Kirkpatrick et al., *Killer Robot? Assassination of Iranian Scientist Feeds Conflict Accounts*, N.Y. TIMES, Dec. 2, 2020.

[6] *See* MARKETS AND MARKETS, *Remote Weapon Station Market* (Feb. 10, 2020), https://www.marketsandmarkets.com/Market-Reports/remote-weapon-station-market-172094776.html.

[7] *See* Evan Ackerman, *This Year, Autonomous Trucks Will Take to the Road With No One on Board*, IEEE SPECTRUM (Jan. 4, 2021), https://spectrum.ieee.org/transportation/self-driving/this-year-autonomous-trucks-will-take-to-the-road-with-no-one-on-board.

[8] *See* Electronic Freedom Foundation, *Face Recognition*, https://www.eff.org/pages/face-recognition (last visited Mar. 2, 2021).

Chris Jenks, *Autonomous Weapons* In: *Is the International Legal Order Unraveling?*. Edited by: David L. Sloss, Oxford University Press. © Oxford University Press 2022. DOI: 10.1093/oso/9780197652800.003.0008

available not only to governments[9] but increasingly through the commercial market.[10]

Regardless of what actually happened in Iran, the fact that such a remote attack is feasible underscores both the advances in weapons technology and their potential impact on the international legal order. There is no one technological descriptor for these advances. Some are the result of advances in robotics and new uses for data, including the role of big data in predictive analytics. Others are the result of one of more aspects of artificial intelligence (AI), including deep and machine learning, cognitive computing, and natural language processing. Given that there is neither a commonly accepted definition of AI[11] nor an "agreed-upon taxonomy that might be used as the basis for forming a common language,"[12] this chapter eschews the definitional quagmire that often bogs down discussions about emerging weapons technologies.

Instead, this chapter uses the term "autonomous" to refer to the "ability of a machine to execute a task or tasks, without human input, using interactions of computer programming with the environment."[13] An autonomous system is "a system—whether hardware of software—that, once activated, can perform some tasks or functions on its own."[14] The term "weapons" refers to "all arms, munitions, materiel, instruments, mechanisms, or devices that have an intended effect of injuring, damaging, destroying or disabling personnel or property," and the term "weapon system" refers to "the weapon itself and those components required for its operation."[15] Taken together, an autonomous weapon, for the purposes of this chapter, is one that can independently

[9] For example, just one Norwegian defense manufacturer has sold more than 20,000 remote weapon systems to more than twenty-three countries. *See* Kongsberg Defence & Aerospace, *Kongsberg Delivers Its 20,000th Remote Weapon Station (RWS)* (Oct. 23, 2020), https://www.kongsberg.com/newsandmedia/news-archive/20202/kongsberg-delivers-its-20000th-remote-weapon-station-rws/.

[10] *See* Rachel Smith, *A Beginners Guide to Building Your Own Face Recognition System to Creep Out Your Friends*, Towards Data Sci. (Sept. 30, 2019), https://towardsdatascience.com/a-beginners-guide-to-building-your-own-face-recognition-system-to-creep-out-your-friends-df3f4c471d55.

[11] Tim Simonite, *This Researcher Says AI Is Neither Artificial nor Intelligent*, Wired, Apr. 26, 2021 (interviewing Kat Crawford, author of Atlas of AI, in which Crawford argues that technology experts misunderstand artificial intelligence).

[12] John Dowdy, *AI and Autonomy: Trying to Piece It All Together*, LinkedIn (June 11, 2018), https://www.linkedin.com/pulse/ai-autonomy-trying-piece-all-together-john-dowdy/.

[13] Vincent Boulanin & Maaike Verbruggen, SIPRI, Mapping the Development of Autonomy in Weapon Systems (2017).

[14] *Id.*

[15] Int'l Comm. Red Cross, A Guide to the Legal Review of New Weapons, Means and Methods of Warfare: Measures to Implement Article 36 of Additional Protocol I of 1977, at 9 n.17 (2006).

select and attack targets.[16] These are weapons where the system performs the critical functions of acquiring, tracking, selecting, and attacking targets.[17]

The rationale for adopting a definition of autonomous weapons in general, and the one above in particular, is multifaceted. First, this chapter assesses the impact of autonomous weapons on the international legal order, so some definition of "autonomous" is required. Second, under this definition, autonomous weapons are not an abstraction or potential future development. Rather, as will be discussed later, autonomous weapons have been in use since the mid 1970s.[18] While that acknowledgment comes with the added benefit of providing a way out of an otherwise endless and circular discussion,[19] its primary utility is in yielding discrete, extant, systems upon which to make an assessment. Part of that assessment will project into the near future, but the definition allows for grounding the analysis in the reality of current systems.

The vast majority of extant autonomous weapons are large, expensive, defensive, and anti-materiel in nature.[20] However, anti-personnel and offensive autonomous weapons are now in limited use,[21] and more states and increasingly nonstate actors have access to some form of this technology.[22] What's happened over the last forty years is essentially what has always happened throughout history: technological advances have led to increased weapons capabilities. But "[u]ntil the present time, a decision to act depended on human cognition. With autonomous [weapons], this will not be the case."[23] Recent advances differ from prior technological developments in that a

[16] *See* INT'L COMM. RED CROSS, AUTONOMOUS WEAPON SYSTEMS: TECHNICAL, MILITARY, LEGAL AND HUMANITARIAN ASPECTS 57 (2014).

[17] *See id.*

[18] *See* BOULANIN & VERBRUGGEN, *supra* note 13, Appendix Table A.

[19] For example, during United Nations meetings on autonomous weapons in 2016, a representative of Human Rights Watch (HRW) insisted "there is a common understanding in the room. . . . [that w] e are talking about future weapons . . . [that] will be able to select and engage targets on their own." Stephen Goose, Statement, Convention on Certain Conventional Weapons (Apr. 12, 2016), http://www.unog.ch/80256EDD006B8954/(httpAssets)/252007F8C3EB3E1EC1257FAE002F4DE5/$file/HRW + intervention+Goose + 12+April + 2016.pdf.

Within minutes of HRW claiming that autonomous weapons referred to future weapons, a representative from the ICRC spoke and acknowledged that "[s]ome weapon systems in use today can select and attack targets without human intervention." Int'l Comm. Red Cross, Statement, Convention on Certain Conventional Weapons (Apr. 11, 2016), http://www.unog.ch/80256EDD006B8954/. (httpAssets)/9324B81015529E3DC1257F930057AF12/$file/2016_LAWS + MX_GeneralExchange_Statements_ICRC.pdf.

[20] *See* INT'L COMM. RED CROSS, *supra* note 16, at 65.

[21] *See* United Nations Security Council, Letter Dated 8 March 2021 from the Panel of Experts on Libya Established pursuant to resolution 1973 (2011) addressed to the President of the Security Council, S/2021/229 (Mar. 8, 2021) (describing the 2020 offensive use of an autonomous weapon, a Turkish made loitering munition, during a battle in Libya's ongoing civil war).

[22] *See* BOULANIN & VERBRUGGEN, *supra* note 13, at 44–45, 50–54.

[23] John R. Allen & Amir Husain, *On Hyperwar*, 143 NAVAL INST. PROC. 30 (2018).

portion of the new capabilities stem from computers and machines performing an increasing number of weapon systems functions that were previously either not possible or performed by humans.

As Russian President Vladimir Putin noted in 2017, technology advances "come[] with colossal opportunities, but also threats that are difficult to predict."[24] Bearing that difficulty in mind, this chapter explores the threats autonomous weapons may pose and the benefits they may provide to the international legal order, specifically the international law regulating the use of force.

To do so, this chapter distinguishes between two categories of autonomous weapons: "high-end" and "over-the-counter" systems. The current high-end systems operate in the air, in maritime environments, and on land. They include air defense systems, active protection systems, robotic sentry weapons, and loitering weapons, all with autonomous engagement modes. They also include decentralized, self-organizing, swarms of hundreds or even thousands of systems.

First World countries have harnessed increased computing power and staggering amounts of data to produce cutting-edge technology, which while not currently comprising a weapon, may foretell possible future weapons. This nonweapons technology includes unmanned aerial systems of all sizes that are capable of taking off from and landing on an aircraft carrier, operating at night, at high altitude, in subterranean and subsurface environments. Some of this technology is expensive and designed for repeated use. Other aspects are lower cost and considered disposable. These systems can operate from anywhere for hours to days to indefinitely, and they are capable of performing numerous tasks with little to no human intervention.

One byproduct of technology advancing to produce high-end systems is what this chapter refers to as "over-the-counter" systems. "[I]t's very easy to purchase small, off-the-shelf drones and weaponize them."[25] Third World countries and organized armed groups are able to assemble such systems with minimal infrastructure and support compared to manned aircraft.[26] Over-the-counter systems take several different forms, including developing

[24] James Vincent, *Putin Says the Nation that Leads in AI "Will Be the Ruler of the World,"* The Verge (Sept. 4, 2017), https://www.theverge.com/2017/9/4/16251226/russia-ai-putin-rule-the-world.

[25] Paul Scharre, *Between a Roomba and a Terminator: What Is Autonomy?*, War on Rocks (Feb. 18, 2015), http://warontherocks.com/2015/02/between-a-roomba-and-a-terminator-what-isa utonomy/.

[26] *See* David Hambling, *Houthis Step Up Long-Range Drone Attacks on Saudi Oil Facilities*, Forbes, Mar. 31, 2021.

new ways of incorporating old and new systems. For example, in its recent armed conflict with Armenia, Azerbaijan incorporated antiquated biplanes and cutting-edge Israeli loitering munitions.[27] Similarly, drug cartels in Mexico are strapping explosives and metal (to produce shrapnel) to aerial drones and crashing them into members of rival cartels.[28]

Over-the-counter systems also include primitive drone swarms. In 2019, the first known "coordinated massive swarm drone strike" took place in Saudi Arabia. The strike "disrupted 5.7 million barrels of crude oil production, representing half of the kingdom's output" and was "potentially executed by a non-state actor on a budget."[29]

In terms of forecasting future over-the-counter systems, this chapter suggests that actors will either manufacture devices with autonomous functions (like navigation), perhaps using 3D printers, or simply purchase them online. These systems—for example, aerial drones or driverless cars—could have explosives placed in or on them and then be used as lower-end autonomous weapons by simply colliding into their targets without sacrificing someone to fly or drive.

This chapter highlights the impact of both high-end and over-the-counter autonomous weapons on three different subsets of international law regulating the use of force: the *jus ad bellum*, which governs "the conditions under which States may resort to war or to the use of armed force in general"; the *jus in bello*, which is the international law "regulat[ing] the conduct of parties engaged in an armed conflict";[30] and laws regulating exports of weapons technologies.

This chapter suggests that autonomous weapons pose significant challenges for *jus ad bellum* and export control regimes, likely weakening them or lessening their effectiveness.

In terms of *jus ad bellum*, the challenges have been largely manageable up until now. But the impending ubiquitous nature of autonomous weapons will lessen the effectiveness of the UN Charter's restriction on the use of force,

[27] Paul Iddon, *The Last Azerbaijan-Armenia War Changed How Small Nations Fight Modern Battles*, Forbes, Mar. 25, 2021.

[28] Luis Chaparro, *"Like a Flying Ant": An Operative Describes How Mexico's Cartels Use Drones to Attack Enemies and Smuggle Drugs*, Bus. Insider (June 1, 2021), https://news.yahoo.com/flying-ant-operative-describes-mexicos-123100529.html

[29] India Block, *Massive Swarm Drone Strike on Saudi Oil Facility Demonstrates Destructive Potential of Autonomous Weapons*, Dezeen (Sept. 16, 2019), https://www.dezeen.com/2019/09/16/drone-strike-saudi-arabia-aramco-oil-supply/.

[30] Int'l Comm. Red Cross, *What Are Jus Ad Bellum and Jus In Bello?* (Jan. 22, 2015), https://www.icrc.org/en/document/what-are-jus-ad-bellum-and-jus-bello-0.

because the barriers to entry for an increasing number of state[31] and nonstate actors to acquire technology capable of employing armed force have never been lower. The proliferation of unmanned systems has led to their inevitable use by terrorist groups and nonstate actors, either as independent actors or as proxies of nation-states.[32]

With autonomous weapons, entities are able to use force remotely, without putting their members at risk. As a result, those entities may be increasingly willing to use force. Over-the-counter systems will empower both states and nonstate actors not only to initiate armed force of a type and degree not previously available, but to do so in a way that renders attribution difficult, while triggering the authority of the state against which force was used to use force itself in self-defense.

For export control of higher end systems, lines of computer code or programming are the key features that separate a weapon from an autonomous weapon; this fact poses significant inspection and verification challenges. At the same time, over-the-counter systems, whether produced through 3D printing or a converted civilian use product, are not easily subject to export control regimes.

The effect autonomous weapons have on *jus in bello* is likely to be mixed. Autonomous weapons will be more accurate and precise than humans, which could lead to less force being used and in a more discriminating manner. This would benefit both civilians and members of the armed forces. At the same time, autonomous weapons, at least for the time being and perhaps always, lack important human abilities—including empathy and assessing context—which could lead to unnecessary uses of force that may violate international humanitarian law (IHL). Swarming autonomous weapons present a number of challenges. With high-end systems, a malfunction could be replicated hundreds or a thousand times over, and over-the-counter swarm systems suggest the potential for a new era of indiscriminate attacks.

This chapter first outlines the challenges in defining autonomous weapons and then surveys developments in both high-end and over-the-counter systems. From there, the chapter transitions to assessing the impact of

[31] *See* David Hambling, *The "Magic Bullet" Drones Behind Azerbaijan's Victory over Armenia*, FORBES, Nov. 10, 2020.

[32] *See* Colin P. Clarke, *Approaching a "New Normal": What the Drone Attack in Venezuela Portends*, THE RAND BLOG (Aug. 13, 2018), https://www.rand.org/blog/2018/08/approaching-a-new-normal-what-the-drone-attack-in-venezuela.html.

autonomous weapons, first on *jus ad bellum*, then *jus in bello*, and finally on arms/export control regimes.

II. Definitional Challenges and Autonomy

As the Congressional Research Service politely noted in 2020, "[n]o single, universally accepted definition of [autonomous weapons] is used in international discussions."[33] Similarly, the chair of a 2014 United Nations meeting on autonomous weapons explained that "there is no ready-made, generally accepted definition of what is an autonomous system."[34] The result, according to the UN Institute for Disarmament Research, has been international discussions that

> lack[] focus, tacking between things (for example, drones, robots and systems), a characteristic (autonomy) and uses (defensive measures? targeting? kill decisions?), in an inconsistent and often confusing way. One of the reasons there are so many different terms being proposed as the object of discussion is that some actors are trying to capture a mix of variables of concern (such as lethality or degrees of human control), while others are talking about more general categories of objects.[35]

This should not be surprising given the wildly varied understandings of what is meant by autonomy in general, let alone as applied to weapons systems.[36] A significant part of the challenge is the result of misunderstanding machine autonomy. Autonomy is a technological descriptor and not more. "[A]utonomy isn't a discrete property of a work system, nor is it a particular kind of technology; it's an idealized characterization of observed or anticipated interactions between the machine, the work to be accomplished, and the situation."[37]

[33] Congressional Research Service, *International Discussions Concerning Lethal Autonomous Weapon Systems* https://fas.org/sgp/crs/weapons/IF11294.pdf (last visited June 7, 2021).

[34] Michael Biontino, Summary of Technical Issues at CCW Expert Meeting on Lethal Autonomous Weapons Systems (LAWS), German Permanent Missions Geneva (May 16, 2014) (on file with author).

[35] U.N. Inst. for Disarmament Research (UNIDIR), Framing Discussions on the Weaponization of Increasingly Autonomous Technologies 3 (2014).

[36] *See* Biontino, *supra* note 34.

[37] Jeffrey M. Bradshaw et al., *The Seven Deadly Myths of Autonomous Systems*, IEEE Intelligent Systems, May–June 2013, at 4, http://www.jeffreymbradshaw.net/publications/IS-28-03-HCC_1.pdf.

Autonomy does not operate in binary terms, meaning that a system isn't either autonomous or not. As the US Department of Defense (DoD) eventually learned, it is neither useful nor helpful to think of autonomy in levels.[38] Thinking of autonomy in levels is problematic because "autonomy is relative to the context of activity. Functions can't be automated effectively in isolation from an understanding of the task, the goals, and the context. . . . [L]evels of autonomy encourage reductive thinking. For example, they facilitate the perspective that activity is sequential when it's actually simultaneous."[39]

This is in part due to the dynamic nature of functions within a system.[40] Many functions can be executed "concurrently as well as sequentially . . . and can have a different allocation scheme to the human or computer at a given time."[41] As a result, attempting to plot autonomy as a linear and single axis progressively and discretely demarcated by whether humans are in, on, or out of a functional loop, both oversimplifies and misrepresents.[42] Use of in/on/out of the loop is, in the end, just another form of conceptualizing autonomy in levels, which, as discussed previously, is neither useful nor helpful.

There is not a single spectrum along which autonomy moves. Instead, autonomy is better thought of across several spectra: (1) the "nature of the human–machine command and control relationship"; (2) the "complexity of the machine"; and (3) the "type of decision being automated."[43]Within each spectrum, the amount or quality of functions a machine performs often changes as the system operates.[44]

Because of the multiple spectra, attempting to differentiate machine functions as either automatic, automated, or autonomous lacks practical utility.[45] Those terms may, at most, aid in understanding, at a descriptive or superficial level, only one of the three spectra through which we conceptualize autonomy—the complexity of the machine. The range of complexity of the machine includes automatic at the lower end, to automated in the middle, to autonomous at the higher end.[46] But again this is only one spectrum. Further lessening the already limited utility of this view of autonomy

[38] Dep't of Def., Def. Sci. Bd. Task Force Report: The Role of Autonomy in DoD Systems (2012).

[39] Bradshaw, *supra* note 37, at 4.

[40] *See id.*

[41] *Id.*

[42] *See* Scharre, *supra* note 25.

[43] *Id.*

[44] *See id.*

[45] *See id.*

[46] *See id.*

is that there are no clear boundaries between automatic, automated, or autonomous.

This chapter adopts the US DoD Defense Science Board's proposal to think of autonomy as "a capability of the larger system enabled by the integration of human and machine abilities."[47] This approach recognizes that the operation of all machines requires some degree of human involvement. And it means that "there exist no fully autonomous systems."[48] As one commentator observed, "the question of when we will get to 'full autonomy' is meaningless. [A] better framework would be to ask what tasks are done by a person and which by a machine."[49]

In terms of functions, this chapter focuses on acquiring, tracking, selecting, and attacking targets to differentiate autonomous weapons. Where the weapon is capable of performing those critical functions without further human intervention, this chapter considers the weapon autonomous. This understanding of an autonomous weapon is consistent with formulations by the International Committee of the Red Cross (ICRC) and the former UN Special Rapporteur on extrajudicial, summary, or arbitrary executions.[50]

This chapter acknowledges the challenge in delineating between semi-autonomous[51] systems—where a human launches or fires but then the system prioritizes targets—and systems that loiter, potentially for extended periods of time, and select targets. This chapter elects for overbreadth as opposed to underdetermination and considers loitering systems to be autonomous.[52] There are, of course, limits to that overbreadth and what this chapter is able consider. The chapter focuses on physical weapons, meaning that it does not consider weapons that operate only in cyberspace.

III. The Technology of Autonomous Weapons

At the high end, technological advances are facilitating new types of autonomous weapons, largely for First World powers and state militaries. At the other, over-the-counter end, modifying those systems and/or how they are

[47] Dep't of Def., *supra* note 38, at 23.
[48] *Id.*
[49] Scharre, *supra* note 25.
[50] *See* Int'l Comm. Red Cross, *supra* note 16; Christof Heyns, *Report of the Special Rapporteur on Extrajudicial, Summary or Arbitrary Executions*, U.N. Doc. A/HRC/23/47, at ¶ 38 (Apr. 9, 2013).
[51] *See* Dep't of Def. Directive 3000.09, Autonomy in Weapon Systems (2012).
[52] *See* Boulanin & Verbruggen, *supra* note 13, at 50.

used, making less sophisticated variants, and even online ordering of civilian items with autonomous capabilities and then using them as weapons, enables both state and nonstate actors to possess previously unattainable technological capabilities.

A. High-End Autonomous Weapons

Militaries of wealthy countries account for the high-end advances in autonomous weapons, because these advances require resources beyond the capacity of many states and nonstate actors. Resources include funding measured in the hundreds of millions or billions of dollars,[53] sophisticated computers capable of processing huge amounts of data, and the data itself.[54]

For example, in 2017, China released a security strategy that envisioned China as the "front-runner and global innovation center in AI" by 2020.[55] In 2018, Russia's Military Industrial Committee "set a target of making 30 percent of military equipment robotic by 2025." And the United States has stated as part of its national security strategy that the DoD will "invest broadly [as in billions of US dollars] in military application of autonomy, artificial intelligence, and machine learning, including rapid application of commercial breakthroughs, to gain competitive military advantages."[56] For the fiscal year 2021 defense budget, the DoD requested $1.7 billion for autonomy.[57]

This section first surveys technological developments by category over the last forty years. It then discusses one particular weapon system, "swarms." Finally, it highlights some nonweapon military technology that could factor into either future high-end or over-the-counter systems.

[53] *See* David Klein, *Fiscal 2020 Defense Budget Request Includes Billions for Unmanned Systems*, Unmanned Systems Mag. (June 24, 2019), https://www.auvsi.org/unmanned-systems-magazine-fiscal-2020-defense-budget-request-includes-billions-unmanned-systems.

[54] *See, e.g.*, Matthew Stewart, *The Future of Computation for Machine Learning and Data Science*, Toward Data Sci. (Oct. 24, 2019), https://towardsdatascience.com/the-future-of-computation-for-machine-learning-and-data-science-fad7062bc27d.

[55] Tom Simonite, *For Superpowers, Artificial Intelligence Fuels New Global Arms Race*, Wired (Aug. 8, 2018), https://www.wired.com/story/for-superpowers-artificial-intelligence-fuels-new-global-arms-race/.

[56] Dep't of Defense, Summary of the 2018 National Defense Strategy 7 (2018).

[57] *See* Office of the Under Secretary of Defense (Comptroller)/Chief Financial Officer, Defense Budget Overview: United States Department of Defense Fiscal Year 2021 Budget Request 1–9 (Feb. 2020).

1. *Autonomous Weapons Survey*

The Stockholm International Peace Research Institute (SIPRI) conducted a "one-year mapping study on the development of autonomy in military systems in general and weapon systems in particular."[58] Published in 2017, the study includes a series of tables that delineate different categories of autonomous weapons. The categories include: Air Defence Systems with Autonomous Engagement, Active Protection Systems With Autonomous Engagement, Robotic Sentry Weapons With Autonomous Engagement, and Loitering Weapons With Autonomous Engagement.

In the first category—Air Defence Systems with Autonomous Engagement—eighteen countries have developed systems used by well over a hundred countries.[59] Some of the systems are land-based, while others are naval systems, including the oldest system, Russia's AK-630, which was completed in 1976.[60] These weapon systems are designed as anti-materiel systems, meaning that they are designed to target incoming projectiles, aircraft, and ships. That said, there have already been incidents where such systems have killed humans.

In separate incidents during the 2003 invasion of Iraq, US Patriot air defense systems, operating in an autonomous mode, misidentified friendly aircraft as enemy, leading to the downing of a US F-18 and a British Tornado, killing the crews of both.[61]

Active Protection Systems With Autonomous Engagement are "weapon systems that are designed to protect armoured vehicles against incoming anti-tank missiles or rockets."[62] Some fifteen countries have developed and use these types of weapons.[63]

Robotic Sentry Weapons With Autonomous Engagement are gun turrets that can detect, track, and engage targets. They use smaller caliber ammunition and "are usually employed as anti-personnel weapons."[64] The SIPRI study identified only three such systems produced and used by two countries, Israel and the Republic of Korea.[65] Significantly, these systems depart from the historical practice of using autonomous weapons as anti-materiel weapons.

58 Boulanin & Verbruggen, *supra* note 13, at vii.
59 *See id.* at 36, Appendix Table A.
60 *See id.*
61 *See* Int'l Comm. Red Cross, *supra* note 16, at 72.
62 Boulanin & Verbruggen, *supra* note 13, at 41, Appendix Table B.
63 *See id.*
64 *Id.* at 44.
65 *See id.*, Appendix Table C.

Loitering Weapons With Autonomous Engagement are "a hybrid type of weapon system, which fits a niche between guided munitions and unmanned [drones]."[66] The loitering function refers to the system's ability to operate for an extended time period to identify and engage targets. These weapons may be used either offensively or defensively. A human launches or fires a loitering weapon. That fact removes it from some definitions of autonomous weapons. But as discussed previously, this chapter considers loitering weapons to be autonomous because loitering systems perform target selection—unlike semi-autonomous systems.

Loitering weapons are sometimes referred to as either "kamikaze" or "suicide" weapons, because they deliver an explosive charge by crashing into the target. Significantly, according to SIPRI, "loitering weapons are the only 'offensive type' of weapon system that is known to be capable of acquiring and engaging targets autonomously."[67] Israel is currently the only country to have produced and sold such weapons.[68]

2. *Swarms*

If a human is no match for a single autonomous weapon system, consider the impact of a swarm of hundreds or even thousands of autonomous weapons acting in concert. Swarming refers to "decentralized self-organizing behavior" in animals and insects.[69] In the military context, this is perhaps best illustrated by the US Air Force efforts with the Perdix small aerial drone. The Perdix system is 6½ inches long, with a wingspan of approximately one foot. It has foldable wings that allow the Perdix to be packed in a canister that is launched by an aircraft. The Perdix is powered by a propeller and able to fly at least seventy miles per hour for at least twenty minutes.[70]

As the DoD explained:

> Perdix are not preprogrammed, synchronized individuals. They share a distributed brain for decision-making and adapt to each other, and the environment,

[66] *Id.* at 50.

[67] *Id.* at vii.

[68] *See id.*, Appendix Table E. Israel produces two variants of the Harpy loitering munition and also the Harop system.

[69] John A. Sauter et al., *Performance of Digital Pheromones for Swarming Vehicle Control*, *in* PROCEEDINGS OF THE FOURTH INTERNATIONAL JOINT CONFERENCE ON AUTONOMOUS AGENTS AND MULTIAGENT SYSTEMS (2005); *see also* Manish Mahant et al., *A Profound Survey on Swarm Intelligence*, 2 INT'L J. ADVANCED COMPUTER RES. 31 (2012).

[70] *See* Strategic Capabilities Office, Perdix Fact Sheet, https://dod.defense.gov/Portals/1/Documents/pubs/Perdix%20Fact%20Sheet.pdf?ver=2017-01-09-101520-643 (last visited May 26, 2021).

> much like swarms in nature. Because every Perdix communicates and collaborates with every other Perdix, the swarm has no leader and can gracefully adapt to changes in drone numbers. This allows this team of small inexpensive drones to perform missions once done by large expensive ones.[71]

In 2016, the Air Force conducted a test involving more than one hundred Perdix systems.[72] The test "[s]howed off Perdix's collective decision-making, adaptive formation flying, and self-healing abilities. The drones collectively decide that a mission has been accomplished, fly on to the next mission, and carry out that one. The benefit of the swarm is that if one drone drops out—and a few appear[ed] to crash—the group can rearrange itself to maintain coverage."[73]

The Perdix was built using 3D printed parts and is not designed to be recoverable.[74] Thus, the Perdix may be employed without concerns about putting a human pilot in harm's way, or losing an expensive system. The Air Force continues to research swarming technology.[75]

Similarly, the US Navy has been testing swarming aerial systems[76] and also swarming autonomous patrol boats,[77] all of which are autonomous weapons or have a mode or setting by which the system selects and engages targets.

In addition to the United States, China,[78] France, India,[79] Iran, Israel, Russia,[80] Turkey, and the United Kingdom[81] are all developing comparable

[71] Amy McCullough, *The Looming Swarm*, AIR FORCE (Mar. 22, 2019), https://www.airforcemag.com/article/the-looming-swarm/.

[72] *See* Kyle Mizokami, *The Pentagon's Autonomous Swarming Drones Are the Most Unsettling Thing You'll See Today*, POPULAR MECHANICS (Jan. 9, 2017), https://www.popularmechanics.com/military/aviation/a24675/pentagon-autonomous-swarming-drones/.

[73] *Id.*

[74] *See* Perdix Fact Sheet, *supra* note 70.

[75] *See* McCullough, *supra* note 71.

[76] *See* John Keller, *Navy Developing Swarms of Cooperating Drones to Launch Overwhelming Attacks*, INTELLIGENT AEROSPACE (May 11, 2015), https://www.intelligent-aerospace.com/military/article/16538468/navy-developing-swarms-of-cooperating-drones-to-launch-overwhelming-attacks.

[77] *See* Jeremy Hsu, *U.S. Navy Tests Robot Boat Swarm to Overwhelm Enemies*, IEEE SPECTRUM (Oct. 5, 2014), http://spectrum.ieee.org/automaton/robotics/military-robots/us-navy-robot-boat-swarm.

[78] *See* Joseph Trevithick, *China Conducts Test of Massive Suicide Drone Swarm Launched from a Box on a Truck*, THE DRIVE (Oct. 14, 2020), https://www.thedrive.com/the-war-zone/37062/china-conducts-test-of-massive-suicide-drone-swarm-launched-from-a-box-on-a-truck.

[79] *See* David Hambling, *Indian Army Shows Off Drone Swarm of Mass Destruction*, FORBES (Jan. 1, 2021).

[80] *See* Sameer Joshi, *"Drone Swarms" Are Coming, and They Are the Future of Wars in the Air*, THE PRINT (Feb. 2, 2021), https://theprint.in/defence/drone-swarms-are-coming-and-they-are-the-future-of-wars-in-the-air/596842/.

[81] *See id.*

swarming systems. In 2019, then US Secretary of Defense Mark Esper claimed that Chinese weapons manufacturers were selling autonomous weaponized aerial drones[82] that are purportedly "capable of forming an intelligent swarm and launch[ing] coordinated attacks."[83] More recently, one author claimed that "the UK may have the world's first operational swarm drone unit by the middle of 2021 to perform tasks including suicide missions inside enemy lines and overwhelming adversary air defences," and that Russia is attempting to operationalize a high density swarm in coordinated saturation strike missions involving one hundred simultaneously launched drones, each with a small warhead.[84]

3. *Potentially Adaptable Military Technology*

Using the US military as an example, the Air Force, Navy, and Army are all experimenting with removing humans from vehicles, vessels, and aircraft, and increasing the quantity and difficulty of tasks that machines and computers perform. These are not currently autonomous weapons, because the weapons are not performing select and engage functions without human intervention. However, in some cases, the systems are capable of performing select and engage functions, meaning the technology exists but is not currently being used. In other cases, the technology could potentially be incorporated into either a future sophisticated autonomous weapon or over-the-counter weapon.

Adaptable Aerial Technology: The F-35 Joint Strike Fighter may be the last manned fighter aircraft that the United States develops. Instead, the Air Force is transitioning older, previously manned fighter aircraft into unmanned autonomous aircraft as part of the "Loyal Wingman" program.[85] In 2021, the Air Force plans to test a manned fighter against an autonomous drone as part of an effort that could "revolutionize air-to-air combat in ways that have so

[82] *See* Patrick Tucker, *SecDef: China Is Exporting Killer Robots to the Mideast*, Def. One (Nov. 5, 2019), https://www.defenseone.com/technology/2019/11/secdef-china-exporting-killer-robots-mideast/161100/.

[83] Liu Xuanzun, *Chinese Helicopter Drones Capable of Intelligent Swarm Attacks*, Global Times (May 9, 2019), https://www.globaltimes.cn/content/1149168.shtml.

[84] Joshi, *supra* note 80.

[85] *See* Tyler Rogoway et al., *F-15 Eagle Seen Loaded with Loyal Wingman Drone for Previously Unknown Tests*, The Drive (July 21, 2020), https://www.thedrive.com/the-war-zone/34982/highly-modified-air-launched-loyal-wingman-drone-tested-with-air-force-f-15-eagle.

far been limited to the realm of fiction."[86] It is not clear how much of a competition the test will be.

In August 2020, the Air Force conducted a virtual dogfight between an autonomous fighter (ALPHA) and a manned aircraft to "demonstrate the feasibility of developing effective, intelligent autonomous agents capable of defeating adversary aircraft in a dogfight."[87] The autonomous fighter easily won all five rounds. "[E]very 6.5 milliseconds ALPHA can take in the entirety of sensor data, organize the data and create a complete mapping of the scenario, analyze its current [course of action] and make changes, or create an entirely new" course of action.[88] In contrast, manned fighter aircraft are not able to perform anywhere close to their maximum capacity. Fighter aircraft could turn, climb, and descend much more aggressively without what some call the "weak link"—the human pilot.[89] So an autonomous unmanned aircraft could operate in ways that a manned aircraft simply cannot match. As a result, removing humans from the cockpit of fighter aircraft seems a relatively near-term possibility.

In 2019, the Air Force announced the unfortunately named "Skyborg" program. Through Skyborg, the Air Force is "developing a family of unmanned aerial vehicles (UAVs) designed to fly a limited number of sorties and cheap enough to use in threat environments where the risk of attrition is too high for manned aircraft. These 'attritable/reusable' UAVs will employ artificial intelligence-enabled autonomy to team with other aircraft to conduct multiple missions."[90] In March 2021, the Air Force successfully tested the Valkyrie drone, which carried and released the ALTIUS-600, a smaller drone.[91] The combination of the two suggests a significantly increased capability to use force without putting members of the military at risk. The

[86] Joseph Trevithick, *Manned Fighter to Face Autonomous Drone Next Year in Sci-Fi Movie-Like Showdown*, The Drive (June 4, 2020), https://www.thedrive.com/the-war-zone/33866/manned-fighter-to-face-an-autonomous-drone-next-year-in-a-sci-fi-movie-like-showdown.

[87] Patrick Tucker, *An AI Just Beat a Human F-16 Pilot In a Dogfight—Again*, Def. One (Aug. 20, 2020), https://www.defenseone.com/technology/2020/08/ai-just-beat-human-f-16-pilot-dogfight-again/167872/.

[88] Patrick Tucker, *The Air Force Doesn't Know How to Test Its Future Robotic Wingmen*, Def. One (Oct. 20, 2016), https://www.nextgov.com/cio-briefing/2016/10/air-force-doesnt-know-how-test-its-future-robotic-wingmen/132538/.

[89] *See* Timothy P. Schultz, The Problem with Pilots: How Physicians, Engineers, and Airpower Enthusiasts Redefined Flight (2018).

[90] Mark Gunzinger & Lukas Autenried, *The Promise of Skyborg*, Air Force Mag. (Nov. 1, 2020), https://www.airforcemag.com/article/the-promise-of-skyborg/.

[91] *See* Valerie Insinna, *Valkyrie Drone Launches Even Smaller Drone from Inside Payload Bay*, Def. News (Apr. 5, 2021), https://www.defensenews.com/air/2021/04/05/the-valkyrie-drone-launches-an-even-smaller-drone-from-inside-its-payload-bay/.

Valkyrie can fly some three thousand miles without a pilot on board. At any point, the Valkyrie could then launch a series of smaller drone swarms.

Adaptable Maritime Technology: The US Navy is developing unmanned autonomous surface and undersea vessels and vehicles that portend a future of constant maritime aerial presence.[92] One such system is the MQ-25A Stingray, an autonomous, aircraft carrier capable, aerial refueling system.[93] Another system is the MQ-4C Triton Broad Area Maritime Surveillance Vehicle, a high-altitude aerial surveillance system capable of operating for up to thirty hours without refueling.[94]

The Navy has made a policy choice not to have offensive autonomous weapons, or at least not yet. One of the undersea autonomous systems the Navy is developing is the Orca, a fifty-ton submersible currently envisioned as a sensor/detection platform.[95] One commentator has suggested that the Orca could be used as a "moor-pedo"—a hybrid of a mine moored to the bottom of the ocean and a homing torpedo.[96] Thus, the commentator claims that the Orca could become a "strategic underwater weapon" that could "reshape[s] naval conflict."[97]

Adaptable Ground Based Technology: The US Army has tested swarms of autonomous ground and aerial systems.[98] The tests, which "could eventually scale up to 250 drones and ground robots," demonstrated how the systems "analyzed two city blocks to find, surround, and secure a mock city building."[99] These systems are not autonomous weapons, but like the Navy systems discussed previously, that is the result of a policy choice, not technology limitations.

The Army is also developing a Next Generation Combat Vehicle program, which includes an "optionally manned fighting vehicle" and three versions

[92] *See* RONALD O'ROARKE, CONG. RSCH. SERV., R45757, NAVY LARGE UNMANNED SURFACE AND UNDERSEA VEHICLES: BACKGROUND AND ISSUES FOR CONGRESS (2020).

[93] *See* NAVAIR, *MQ-25 Stingray*, https://www.navair.navy.mil/product/MQ-25A-Stingray (last visited Dec. 7, 2020).

[94] *See* NAVAL TECHNOLOGY, *MQ-4C Triton Broad Area Maritime Surveillance UAS*, https://www.naval-technology.com/projects/mq-4c-triton-bams-uas-us/ (last visited Dec. 7, 2020).

[95] *See* H.I. Sutton, *The U.S. Navy's New Orca Drone Submarine Could Get Offensive Role*, FORBES (Dec. 17, 2019).

[96] Brian Dulla, *The Moor-pedo: A Strategic Underwater Weapon to Reshape Naval Conflict*, U.S. NAVAL INST. BLOG (Dec. 2, 2019), https://blog.usni.org/posts/2019/12/02/the-moor-pedo-a-strategic-underwater-weapon-to-re-shape-naval-conflict.

[97] *Id.*

[98] *See* Jay Peters, *Watch DARPA Test Out a Swarm of Drones*, THE VERGE (Aug. 9, 2019), https://www.theverge.com/2019/8/9/20799148/darpa-drones-robots-swarm-military-test.

[99] *Id.*

of robotic combat vehicles.[100] Technological improvements also underpin the Army's efforts at autonomous convoy operations, as well as "obstacle detection, collision avoidance, lane departure, tip-over warnings and vision enhancements for low-visibility conditions."[101] As will be discussed in the next section, driverless technology has the potential to be weaponized as vehicle-borne explosive devices, where an attacker need not sacrifice a human driver.

B. Over-the-Counter Systems

One byproduct of technology advancing to produce high-end systems is that less advanced autonomous weapons—over-the-counter systems—are now easier and cheaper to manufacture and acquire. In some cases, individuals can manufacture autonomous weapons by using a 3D printer and programs available online. In other cases, over-the-counter systems may be converted to or misused as lower-end autonomous weapons.

Unmanned systems are proliferating, primarily in the air, but also ground and maritime systems. Many of these systems are available for purchase online, with the price point continuing to drop.[102] Most of these systems require human involvement to guide, direct, or control certain functions or tasks. But the machines themselves are performing more and more tasks. Even when they do not, they are subject to relatively easy and inexpensive modifications allowing the machine to do so.[103]

1. Over-the-Counter Aerial Systems

There are currently over 1.7 million aerial drones registered in the United States.[104] By way of comparison, the United States has the largest number of

[100] Andrew Feickert, Cong. Rsch. Serv., R45519, The Army's Optionally Manned Fighting Vehicle Program: Background and Issues for Congress (2020).

[101] David Vergun, *Autonomous Vehicles to Exploit Capabilities of Machines, Soldiers*, U.S. Army (July 1, 2014), https://www.army.mil/article/129040/autonomous_vehicles_to_exploit_capabilities_of_machines_soldiers.

[102] A generic search for "drone" on Amazon.com, the world's largest online marketplace, yields 10,000 devices, several hundred of which are available for under $25.

[103] *See* Jeremy S. Cook, *Build an Autonomous Drone for Less than $200*, Hackster.io (2019), https://www.hackster.io/news/build-an-autonomous-drone-for-less-than-200-8716b22ecb64.

[104] Federal Aviation Administration, *UAS by the Numbers* (Dec. 15, 2020), https://www.faa.gov/uas/resources/by_the_numbers/.

helicopters in the world, some 9,348.[105] Globally, the small drone market in 2019 was valued at $7.7 billion. By 2027, the value is expected to reach $35 billion, although both amounts include military purchases.[106]

The Federal Aviation Administration (FAA) recently stated: "A few decades ago, drones were confined to science fiction or notions of the future. Today, unmanned Aircraft Systems, or drones, are rapidly becoming a part of our everyday lives. They are quickly increasing in numbers and complexity."[107] The FAA made that statement shortly before announcing rules that "make way for the further integration of drones into our airspace. . . . They get us closer to the day when we will more routinely see drone operations such as the delivery of packages."[108] The rule changes mean that drones may now be flown over people and at night, among other modifications.

An aerial drone delivery package will perform most, if not all, tasks related to flying, including collision avoidance and navigation. That's exciting when thought of in terms of Amazon or a food delivery service delivering orders more rapidly. But over-the-counter aerial systems could be (and already have been) misused and weaponized. Rather than carrying two kilos of food, the drone might carry two kilos of an explosive or flammable substance that is directed toward a military or civilian target, such as a head of state.[109] Enterprising bad actors could utilize this approach with a number of systems, creating in effect a low-cost swarm, which, while lacking most of the capabilities of high-end counterparts, could still be brutally effective.[110]

[105] *See* Statista, *Commercial Helicopters Fleet of the Leading Countries 2019*, https://www.statista.com/statistics/778282/commercial-helicopters-fleet-size-country/#:~:text=The%20United%20States%20has%20by,largest%20fleet%2C%20that%20of%20Canada.

[106] *See* Fortune Business Insights, *Small Drone Market Size* (Nov. 30, 2020), https://www.globenewswire.com/news-release/2020/11/30/2136618/0/en/Small-Drone-Market-to-Reach-USD-35-009-4-Million-by-2027-Backed-by-Increasing-Military-Expenditure-Worldwide-Says-Fortune-Business-Insights.html#:~:text=Filings%20Media%20Partners-,Small%20Drone%20Market%20to%20Reach%20USD%2035%2C009.4%20Million%20by%202027,Says%20Fortune%20Business%20Insights%E2%84%A2.

[107] Federal Aviation Administration, *supra* note 104.

[108] Federal Aviation Administration, *Press Release—U.S. Department of Transportation Issues Two Much Anticipated Drone Rules to Advance Safety and Innovation in the United States* (Dec. 28, 2020), https://www.faa.gov/news/press_releases/news_story.cfm?newsId=25541; *see also* NPR, *U.S. Announces New Rules for Drones and Their Operators* (Dec. 29, 2020) https://www.npr.org/2020/12/29/951010863/u-s-announces-new-rules-for-drones-and-their-operators.

[109] *See* Clarke, *supra* note 32.

[110] *See* Block, *supra* note 29.

2. *Over-the-Counter Maritime Systems*

Compared to aerial systems, there has been less development of maritime systems. At the same time, maritime systems have the potential to perform more functions than either aerial or ground based systems. This is due to there being less chance of an unintended collision or incident impacting civilians under or on the surface of the water. As a result, there are maritime systems that perform a greater range of tasks without human involvement.[111] Maritime uses include commercial shipping, environmental monitoring, mapping the seafloor and surface, and subsurface inspection of infrastructure.

It is not difficult to envision the results of continued advances in autonomy in over-the-counter maritime systems. In Yemen, for example, the Houthis have employed "drone boats"—unmanned boats filled with explosives—which are then directed toward Saudi shipping targets.[112] The boats are remote controlled and therefore not autonomous weapons—not yet, anyway.

3. *Over-the-Counter Ground Systems*

The development of unmanned ground vehicles tends to fall into one of two categories: driverless technology and tasks deemed too dangerous, dirty, or dumb (mindlessly repetitious) for humans to perform. For the dangerous, dirty, and dumb tasks, commercial applications include agriculture, disaster response, manufacturing, and mining. But concerns about weaponizing over-the-counter ground systems refer mostly to driverless technology.

Similar to weaponizing over-the-counter aerial systems by programming them to fly into targets, driverless vehicles may also be driven into targets. Consider the 2016 terror attack in Nice, France, in which a single person driving a nineteen-ton cargo truck into a pedestrian area killed eight-four people.[113] Now consider that in 2021 a US company is testing driverless tractor-trailer trucks and plans to operate them without a human driver by 2024.[114] As the technology improves and proliferates, the cost will drop, and it will become easier to acquire.

[111] *See* Brian Sprowl, *The Present and Future of Commercial Unmanned Maritime Systems*, AUVSI (Oct. 22, 2019), https://www.auvsi.org/unmanned-systems-magazine-present-and-future-commercial-unmanned-maritime-systems.

[112] *See* Christopher P. Cavas, *New Houthi Weapon Emerges: A Drone Boat*, Def. News (Feb. 19, 2017), https://www.defensenews.com/digital-show-dailies/idex/2017/02/19/new-houthi-weapon-emerges-a-drone-boat/.

[113] *See* Alissa J. Rubin, Adam Nossiter, & Christopher Mele, *Scores Die in Nice, France, as Truck Plows Into Bastille Day Crowd*, N.Y. Times, July 14, 2016.

[114] *See* Ackerman, *supra* note 7.

All the technology discussed previously—the sophisticated and the over-the-counter, the weapons, and the civilian applications susceptible to misuse—will impact the international legal order in differing ways. This chapter next considers the impact on *jus ad bellum*, the international law governing resorting to force, focusing on the UN Charter's qualified prohibition.

IV. *Jus ad Bellum*

Article 2(4) of the UN Charter requires that "[a]ll Members shall refrain in their international relations from the threat or use of force against the territorial integrity or political independence of any state, or in any other manner inconsistent with the Purposes of the United Nations."[115] The ICRC has referred to this prohibition against the use of force among states as a "core ingredient[]" of *jus ad bellum*."[116]

The effectiveness of the *jus ad bellum* depends critically on states' compliance with the basic prohibition on the use of force in Article 2(4). The harder and more costly it is for states to violate Article 2(4), and the greater the probability of attribution when they do, the more effective the ban. Autonomous weapons, both sophisticated and over-the-counter, threaten to undermine the prohibition on use of force for several reasons. Autonomous weapons enable state and nonstate actors to use force in ways previously unavailable and at less cost, both in terms of dollars spent to acquire the weapons and human life put at risk to employ them. At the same time, attribution for uses of force involving autonomous weapons is becoming increasingly difficult. The resulting plausible deniability renders such uses of force more likely.

The barriers to entry for an increasing number of state[117] and nonstate actors to acquire technology capable of employing armed force have never been lower. The lowered barriers reduce several different costs. Ultimately, reducing the cost of war might "lower the threshold for engaging in war."[118]

[115] UN Charter, art. 2(4).
[116] Int'l Comm. Red Cross, *supra* note 30.
[117] *See* Hambling, *supra* note 31.
[118] Marko Kovic, *The Strategic Paradox of Strategic Weapons*, ZIPAR Pol'y Brief (Feb. 2018), https://zipar.org/policy-brief/strategic-paradox-autonomous-weapons/#:~:text=The%20result%20is%20a%20strategic,by%20creating%20great%20security%20risks.

A. Lowering the Cost of Resort to Force

The increased development and use of autonomous weapons may result in what one commentator termed a "strategic paradox."[119] At the outset, it's important to note that the cost of armed conflict is measured in several ways—financially, politically, socially, and morally.[120] Autonomous weapons would alter the cost-benefit analysis associated with armed conflict, in some ways perhaps positively and in others negatively.

Arguably, lowering the threshold for employing force has already occurred even without autonomous weapons. Consider the use of remotely piloted weaponized drones. The United States has engaged in thousands of drone strikes in various states. What if weaponized drone technology did not exist, and the United States was considering those thousands of targets? For some, perhaps, use of missiles or artillery may have been an option. But for others, the targeting decision may have involved a manned aircraft or sending in special operations forces, placing them at risk. Obviously, it is impossible to know which of the strikes the United States would or would not have conducted. Some combination of decreased financial cost, and the technology being available to deliver lethal force remotely without putting members of the US armed forces at risk, factored into the US decision to conduct those drone strikes.

Even still, those drone strikes exposed the aerial systems to being shot down or crashing. Systems like the Reaper and Predator cost roughly $16 million each,[121] and each missile fired another $70,000.[122] When there is a crash, the US Air Force often will drop a two-thousand-pound bomb on the wreckage to prevent its salvage, incurring still more cost, and if a manned aircraft is used to drop the bomb, more risk.[123] Contrast that with the Perdix, made using a 3D printer and not designed to be recovered. Whereas the advent of aerial drones—like the Reaper and Predator, which are not

[119] *Id.*
[120] *See id.*
[121] *See* Kyle Rempfer, *Taliban Posts Photos of MQ-9 Reaper They Claim to Have Shot Down; US Says It Simply Crashed*, AIR FORCE TIMES (Nov. 9, 2018), https://www.airforcetimes.com/news/your-air-force/2018/11/09/taliban-posts-photos-of-mq-9-reaper-they-claim-to-have-shot-down-us-says-it-simply-crashed/.
[122] *See* Joseph Trevithick, *Here Is What Each of the Pentagon's Air-Launched Missiles and Bombs Actually Cost*, THE DRIVE (Feb. 18, 2020), https://www.thedrive.com/the-war-zone/32277/here-is-what-each-of-the-pentagons-air-launched-missiles-and-bombs-actually-cost; *see also* Deniz Cam & Christopher Helman, *The Quiet Billionaires Behind America's Predator Drone That Killed Iran's Soleimani*, FORBES, Jan. 7, 2020.
[123] *See* Rempfer, *supra* note 121.

autonomous weapons—began to erode the foundational *jus ad bellum* rule codified in Article 2(4), autonomous weapons, and swarming systems in particular, may accelerate that erosion.

On the positive side of the ledger, employing sophisticated autonomous weapons holds out the prospect of armed conflict without putting as much human life at risk, whether members of the armed forces or even more so civilians. This benefit would be even greater if one side's autonomous weapons were attacking the other side's autonomous weapons. Thus, a state may potentially engage in an armed conflict in a manner that poses less risk to human life. At the opposite end, over-the-counter autonomous weapons allow nonstate actors to avoid putting members of their group at risk. Instead of needing suicide bombers, organized armed groups can focus on the bombing, crashing autonomous air- or ground-based systems into targets.

Another factor that may influence (and increase) the use of autonomous weapons is the challenge they pose in terms of attribution. Autonomous weapons, in particular over-the-counter systems, lessen the likelihood that their use may be attributed to a particular state or nonstate actor. Whether this is viewed as removing a disincentive or adding an incentive, in either case more force is more likely to be used, furthering the erosion of the Article 2(4) norm.

B. Attribution and State Responsibility

A state is responsible for its internationally wrongful acts, "i.e. for conduct attributable to it under international law and which constitutes a breach of an international obligation of the State."[124] As a result, a state "may have to bear international responsibility for the comportment of its armed forces whenever they actively participate in an armed conflict."[125]

State responsibility may also be imputed based on the conduct of an organized armed group operating in another state. According to the International Court of Justice (ICJ), the test for imputing state responsibility is whether "effective control" of the organized armed group exists.[126] According to

[124] Frits Kalshoven, *State Responsibility for Warlike Acts of the Armed Forces: From Article 3 of the Hague Convention IV to Article 91 of Additional Protocol I of 1977 and Beyond*, 40 Int'l & Comp. L.Q. 827 (1991).

[125] *Id.*

[126] *See* Military and Paramilitary Activities in and Against Nicaragua (Nicar. v. U.S.), Judgment, 1986 I.C.J. 14 (June 27).

the International Criminal Tribunal for the former Yugoslavia, the test is whether "overall control" exists.[127] This chapter does not attempt to resolve that difference.[128] The point is that under international law there are direct and indirect ways by which a state is responsible, but they depend on being able to identify the actor using or employing force. Autonomous weapons make that identification more difficult, which ultimately results in lessening the effectiveness of the Article 2(4) prohibition.

The starting point for why autonomous weapons make attribution difficult is that they allow for the use of force with a far smaller "footprint" of personnel. Consider the backdrop of the 1986 ICJ case from which the effective control test originated. The United States was supporting over twenty thousand contras, insurgents fighting the Nicaraguan government in Nicaragua. Presumably, the United States believed that size force was necessary to effectuate regime change, despite that outcome not being realized. Now flash forward to the Wagner Group, a Russian private military company with about three thousand to five thousand trained Russian and Ukrainian fighters.[129] The Wagner group has operated in Ukraine, Syria, Sudan, the Central African Republic, and most recently Libya. In Libya, Wagner personnel supported the Libyan National Army (LNA), improving the precision of their artillery and mortar fires, "exact[ing] a heavy psychological toll with sniper fire and enable[ing] [the LNA] to seize territory for the first time."[130] According to the US ambassador to Libya, the Wagner group's involvement was a "game changer."[131]

The Wagner Group is a fraction of the size of the contras, but it arguably proves the value of a trained, well-equipped, and supported force. At the same time, while it is easier for Russia to mask the involvement of the Wagner Group than it was for the United States to hide its support of a small contra army, the Wagner group still consists of hundreds, if not thousands of people. In 2018, some six hundred Wagner contractors, "armed with tanks and

[127] *See* Prosecutor v. Tadić, Judgment (Appeals Chamber), Case No. IT-94-1-A (Int'l Crim. Trib. for the former Yugoslavia, July 15, 1999).

[128] *See* Antonio Cassese, *The Nicaragua and Tadić Tests Revisited in Light of the ICJ Judgment on Genocide in Bosnia*, 18 Eur. J. Int'l L. 649 (2007).

[129] Nathaniel Reynolds, *Putin's Not-So-Secret Mercenaries: Patronage, Geopolitics, and the Wagner Group*, Carnegie Endowment for Int'l Peace (July 8, 2019), https://carnegieendowment.org/2019/07/08/putin-s-not-so-secret-mercenaries-patronage-geopolitics-and-wagner-group-pub-79442.

[130] Paul Stronski, *Implausible Deniability: Russia's Private Military Companies*, Carnegie Endowment for Int'l Peace (June 2, 2020), https://carnegieendowment.org/2020/06/02/implausible-deniability-russia-s-private-military-companies-pub-81954.

[131] *Id.*

artillery, launched an assault on a position of the Syrian Democratic Forces [SDF], a largely Kurdish military force that had worked closely with the U.S.-led anti-Islamic State coalition in northeast Syria."[132] US advisers who were imbedded with the SDF called in airstrikes, artillery, and helicopters, killing an estimated three hundred members of the Wagner Group.[133] This led to both media attention and embarrassment for the Kremlin. Mercenary groups are illegal within Russia, but the Wagner group had served "as the tip of the spear of the Kremlin's proxy wars abroad," while providing a "degree of plausible deniability."[134] Deniability was impossible following the four-hour battle, with hundreds of dead Russian contractors.

Now consider the attack against the Iranian scientist discussed at the start of this chapter. There was no one driving the truck or manning the machine gun, at least not physically in Iran. As technology continues to advance, there will be less need for large numbers of personnel to physically "pull triggers" in the territory of another state. Instead, all that will be needed is a limited ground support team for the autonomous weapons. Consider the difficulty in surreptitiously utilizing and logistically supporting hundreds of members of the Wagner group (who were armed with tanks and artillery), compared to a small, covert team that infiltrates a state, sets up platforms to launch a series of drone swarms, and exfiltrates the state before the drone swarms launch.

Now consider the aftermath of the two attacks. With the Wagner Group, there were hundreds of dead contractors to deal with and presumably hundreds of wounded. With the covert swarm attack, the swarm is programmed to either impact a designated target or self-destruct, and similar to the truck used in the Iran attack, the launch platform could also be set to self-destruct. This is not to say that attribution for the swarm attack could not be determined. Self-destruct mechanisms don't always work, and even when they do, blast debris may still be analyzed. But compared to the Wagner Group attack, the drone swarm attack has a much better chance of avoiding attribution.

While over-the-counter systems lack the capabilities of their sophisticated counterparts, they have the "benefit" of posing far greater attribution challenges. Only a few countries in the world have or can afford to acquire the most sophisticated systems. If and when those systems are used, the

[132] *See* Neil Hauer, *The Rise and Fall of a Russian Mercenary Army*, Foreign Pol'y (Oct. 6, 2019), https://foreignpolicy.com/2019/10/06/rise-fall-russian-private-army-wagner-syrian-civil-war/.

[133] *See id.*

[134] Amy Mackinnon, *New Report Exposes Brutal Methods of Russia's Wagner Group*, Foreign Pol'y (June 11, 2020), https://foreignpolicy.com/2020/06/11/russia-wagner-group-methods-bouta-killing-report/.

pool of those potentially responsible would be small. As sophisticated systems proliferate, attribution will become harder. But over-the-counter systems, particularly civilian products with autonomous features that can be weaponized, currently pose attribution challenges, challenges which will likely only increase.

The Houthis in Yemen illustrate these attribution challenges. Iran has sold relatively sophisticated aerial drones to the Houthis. But the Houthis then began locally making (copying) those drones in Yemen. As a result, when the Saudis recover a drone used in an attack, it is not clear based on the drone whether the Iranians or the Houthis were responsible. In terms of over-the-counter systems, the Houthis have employed simple but effective "glorified model airplane[s] with an explosive on the front and a propeller on the back."[135] In one attack, purportedly conducted by the Houthis, a relatively primitive aerial drone outfitted with explosives to which ball bearings were added flew a preprogrammed route and crashed into or near the Yemini government's head of military intelligence, killing him and several others.[136] Identifying who employed such over-the-counter systems is challenging. In 2019, the United Nations formed a panel to examine aerial drones that the Saudi military recovered following attacks. The panel was unable to identify the drones specifically as they were "built from parts sourced internationally. The rear-mounted engines were either German [] [or] Chinese [] bought on the open market."[137]

While not sold as weapons, lower-end commercial drones can easily be used as weapons. As discussed in the introduction, ISIS, Hezbollah, and the Houthi rebels have all used primitive weaponized unmanned aerial vehicles. "Primitive" means using a literal over-the-counter system to drop small explosives or to fly the system into a target. As discussed previously, this was the method used to target and kill the head of Yemini military intelligence. Similarly, in 2018, two lower-end systems equipped with two pounds of plastic explosives were used as part of an assassination attempt against Venezuelan President Nicolas Maduro, ushering in "a foreboding new era—terrorism by unmanned aircraft."[138]

[135] Geoff Brumfiel, *In Yemen Conflict, Some See a New Age of Drone Warfare*, NAT'L PUB. RADIO (May 29, 2019), https://www.npr.org/2019/05/29/726760128/in-yemen-conflict-some-see-a-new-age-of-drone-warfare.

[136] *See id.*

[137] Hambling, *supra* note 31. Such systems also create export control challenges.

[138] Clarke, *supra* note 32.

Using over-the-counter systems is not limited to individual drones. As discussed in the introduction, a primitive drone swarm was used, purportedly by the Houthis, to attack Saudi oil refineries. And in Syria, thirteen bomb-laden drones attacked a Russian military base.[139] Even without explosives, imagine terrorists flying a number of aerial drones into the crowd at a stadium.[140] As one commentator noted, "[e]ven if a drone attack fails to result in large numbers of fatalities, the attempt could still achieve an attacker's goal of perpetuating the psychological dimension of terrorism."[141]

The attacks on the Saudi oil refineries and Russian military base highlight a functional challenge with attribution. For neither of those attacks is the identity of the state or nonstate actor clear. The attribution challenge is greatest with over-the-counter systems.[142] This challenge is not limited to those two incidents. In 2019, aerial drones swarmed US warships off the coast of California, and by 2020 the US Navy was still unable to identify the drones or who was responsible.[143] And beginning in late 2020, a series of unidentified drone swarms was seen in Colorado, Nebraska, and Kansas. Those drones remain unidentified, along with the responsible party.[144]

The attribution challenges exacerbate the pressure that autonomous weapons place on *jus ad bellum*, pressure that is likely to increase, particularly due to proliferating over-the-counter systems. As referenced previously, attribution challenges either lessen a disincentive not to use force or increase the incentive to do so. Given those attribution challenges, combined with the overall lowering of the financial and human cost of resorting to force, autonomous weapons are likely to further erode the Article 2(4) norm.

[139] *See* David Reid, *A Swarm of Armed Drones Attacked a Russian Military Base in Syria*, CNBC, Jan. 11, 2018; BART ELIAS, CONG. RES. SERV., PROTECTING AGAINST ROGUE DRONES (Sept. 3, 2020), https://fas.org/sgp/crs/homesec/IF11550.pdf.

[140] *See* Clarke, *supra* note 32.

[141] *Id.*

[142] *See* Sarah Kreps, *Why It's So Hard to Defend Against Drones*, WORLD POL. REV. (Oct. 4, 2019), https://www.worldpoliticsreview.com/articles/28240/why-it-s-so-hard-to-defend-against-drones.

[143] Tom Porter, *Mysterious Drones Swarmed US Warships, and the Navy Has No Idea Where They Came from More Than a Year Later*, BUS. INSIDER (Apr. 6, 2021), https://www.businessinsider.com/navy-still-no-id-drones-swarmed-california-2021-4.

[144] Amelia Tait, *Attack of the Drones: The Mystery of Disappearing Swarms in the US Midwest*, THE GUARDIAN, Apr. 18, 2021.

V. *Jus in Bello*

For *jus in bello*, critics question whether the use of autonomous weapons would comply with IHL, while proponents contend that their use might be not only desirable but required under the IHL obligation to take constant care to "spare the civilian population, civilians and civilian objects."[145] Similarly, some express concern regarding accountability following "costly mistakes"[146] involving autonomous weapons and suggest that the dictates of public conscience should be leveraged in support of regulation or a ban.[147] In contrast, others contend that existing IHL is adequate so long as states, when studying, developing, acquiring, or adopting a new autonomous weapon, assess its employment under IHL.[148]

A predicate challenge to the *jus in bello* discussion is the continued confusion as to what is meant by the term autonomous weapon. Since 2014, parties to the UN Convention on Certain Conventional Weapons (CCW)[149] have not been able to agree on how to define an autonomous weapon, or even describe its characteristics. Speaking as the chair of the 2014 CCW meetings on autonomous weapons, Ambassador Michael Biontino noted:

> During the whole debate on technical issues of lethal autonomous weapons systems, the notion of autonomy and its definition was at the center of interest. It became quite obvious that there is no ready-made, generally accepted definition of what is an "autonomous system" and as to where to draw the line between "autonomous" and "automatic" or "automated."[150]

There are currently 125 parties to the CCW, the purpose of which is "to ban or restrict the use of specific types of weapons that are considered to cause

[145] Protocol Additional to the Geneva Conventions of 12 August 1949, and Relating to the Protection of Victims of International Armed Conflicts, art. 57(1), June 8, 1977, 1125 U.N.T.S. 3 [hereinafter AP I].

[146] *See* Kelsey D. Atherton, *Autonomous War Machines Could Make Costly Mistakes on Future Battlefields*, Popular Science (May 17, 2021) (describing UNIDIR's report on the risks of autonomous weapons).

[147] *See* Int'l Comm. Red Cross, Peter Maurer speech announcing a new ICRC position on autonomous weapons (May 17, 2021), https://www.icrc.org/en/document/peter-maurer-role-autonomous-weapons-armed-conflict.

[148] AP I, *supra* note 145, art. 36.

[149] Convention on Prohibitions or Restrictions on the Use of Certain Conventional Weapons which may be deemed to be Excessively Injurious or to have Indiscriminate Effects, Oct. 10, 1980, 1342 U.N.T.S. 137 [hereinafter CCW].

[150] Biontino, *supra* note 34.

unnecessary or unjustifiable suffering to combatants or to affect civilians indiscriminately."[151] There are five Protocols to the CCW: (I) nondetectable fragments; (II) mines, booby traps, and other devices; (III) incendiary weapons; (IV) blinding laser weapons; and (V) explosive remnants of war. Some believe that autonomous weapons could and should be the subject of a sixth protocol, while others believe discussions on regulation or a ban are premature.[152]

Proponents of regulation may be reluctant to refine the discussion because if autonomous weapons are viewed as this chapter does—a weapon capable of performing the critical functions of acquiring, tracking, selecting, and attacking targets without further human intervention—then they already exist and have for some time. The fact that autonomous weapons exist does not mean they could not be subject to regulation, but it significantly alters the discussion. That scores of countries have spent billions of dollars acquiring autonomous weapons, which have been in use for decades and with little controversy, is a difficult foundation for regulatory discussions. This fact also may explain why a number of states parties to CCW are also reluctant to refine the discussion.

Arguably, the CCW discussions to date border on being outside the treaty's purpose to regulate *specific* types of weapons. So long as the discussion is framed in terms of a generalized technological descriptor like autonomy, it is difficult to envision the international discussions moving in any direction other than circular.

In addition to the terminology confusion, there is not even agreement on how to apply IHL. Critics of autonomous weapons claim that autonomous weapons "are unable to comply with IHL principles."[153] But IHL imposes obligations on states and parties to an armed conflict, and "it is for individual human beings . . . to ensure compliance with those obligations."[154] As the United States reiterated at a 2017 CCW meeting, "[i]t is not the case

[151] United Nations Office for Disarmament Affairs, The Convention on Certain Conventional Weapons, https://www.un.org/disarmament/the-convention-on-certain-conventional-weapons/ (last visited June 7, 2021).

[152] *See* Int'l Comm. Red Cross, *supra* note 16.

[153] Daniele Amoroso, *Jus In Bello and Jus Ad Bellum Arguments Against Autonomy in Weapons Systems: A Re-appraisal*, 43 QIL 5, 7 (Oct. 31, 2017), http://www.qil-qdi.org/jus-bello-jus-ad-bellum-arguments-autonomy-weapons-systems-re-appraisal/.

[154] Group of Governmental Experts of the High Contracting Parties to the Convention on Prohibition or Restrictions on the Use of Certain Conventional Weapons Which May Be Deemed to Be Excessively Injurious or to Have Indiscriminate Effects, Autonomy in Weapons Systems, Submitted by the United States of America, para. 10, CCW/GGE.1/2017/WP.6 (Nov. 10, 2017) (U.S. Working Paper).

that [IHL] requires that a weapon, even a semi-autonomous or autonomous weapon, make legal determinations."[155] Similarly, some contend that employing autonomous weapons would yield an accountability gap.[156] It is unclear why that would be the case. "As with all decisions to employ weapon systems, persons are responsible for their individual decision to use weapons with autonomous functions."[157]

A fair amount of the IHL confusion flows from conflating the legality of the weapon system itself with the law applicable to a weapon system's use. The legality of a weapon system refers to the IHL prohibition against employing "weapons, projectiles and material and methods of warfare of a nature to cause superfluous injury or unnecessary suffering."[158] But this prohibition "only addresses a weapon's systems effect on the targeted individual, not the manner of engagement (autonomous)." Admittedly, "an autonomous system could be used as a platform for a weapon that would violate the prohibition, such as a bomb containing fragments that are designed to be difficult to locate during [medical] treatment."[159] Under that scenario, the combination of the platform and the weapon would "render the autonomous weapon system unlawful per se." But as Schmitt stresses, that "*possibility* is not a valid basis for imposing an across the board pre-emptive ban."[160]

In terms of the law applicable to a weapon system's use, Schmitt explained the conflation with a quote from Seneca that "[a] sword is never a killer, it is a tool in the killer's hands."[161] For example, the US armed forces make extensive use of the M4 carbine as an individual weapon. The M4 is a lawful weapon, but it may be used in an unlawful manner: to shoot prisoners of war, for example. When that occurs, the problem is not the M4, the problem is with the service member who used the M4 in an illegal manner. The question is not whether the M4 itself is capable of distinction but whether it may be employed in a discriminate manner.

[155] Amoroso, *supra* note 153.

[156] *See* HUMAN RIGHTS WATCH, MIND THE GAP: THE LACK OF ACCOUNTABILITY FOR KILLER ROBOTS (Apr. 9, 2015).

[157] U.S. Working Paper, *supra* note 154.

[158] Michael N. Schmitt & Jeffery S. Thurnher, *"Out of the Loop": Autonomous Weapon Systems and the Law of Armed Conflict*, 4 HARV. NAT. SEC. J. 233 (2013).

[159] *Id.*

[160] *Id.*

[161] Michael N. Schmitt, *Autonomous Weapon Systems and International Humanitarian Law: A Reply to the Critics*, HARV. NAT. SEC. J. FEATURES (2013), https://harvardnsj.org/2013/02/autonomous-weapon-systems-and-international-humanitarian-law-a-reply-to-the-critics/.

Along those same lines, simply because there are circumstances where an autonomous weapon could be used in an indiscriminate manner does not mean the weapon is per se illegal.

> What has been missed in much of the dialogue so far is that even an autonomous weapon system that is completely incapable of distinguishing a civilian from a combatant or a military objective from a civilian object can be used lawfully in certain environments. Not all battlespaces contain civilians or civilian objects.[162]

As a result, this chapter envisions continued development of autonomous weapons inversely proportional to their use in battlespaces with civilians or civilian objects. What this means is that we should expect greater development of autonomous weapons that operate on the surface and subsurface of the water and at very high altitudes because there are fewer civilians or civilian objects there. We should expect slower or less development of ground-based autonomous weapons, given that domain tends to contain civilians and civilian objects. Most of the ground-based systems will likely be defensive and/or anti-materiel.

This chapter suggests that the effect of autonomous weapons on *jus in bello* is likely to be mixed. IHL seeks to minimize suffering in armed conflict. To the extent that autonomous weapons may be more accurate and precise than humans, that could result in more discriminate uses of forces and less collateral damage and suffering. This would benefit both civilians and members of the armed forces.

At the same time, as discussed previously in the *jus ad bellum* section, employing autonomous weapons may become increasingly viable and less costly than other systems, resulting in more uses of force, with the corresponding potential for collateral damage and suffering. Moreover, autonomous weapons, at least for the time being and perhaps always, lack important human abilities, including empathy and assessing context, which could lead to unnecessary uses of force that may violate IHL.

Swarming autonomous weapons present a number of challenges. With high-end systems, a malfunction could be replicated hundreds or a thousand times over, and over-the-counter swarm systems suggest the potential for a new era of indiscriminate attacks. The combined effect is likely to be a

162 Schmitt & Thurnher, *supra* note 158, at 246.

further weakening of IHL's ability to regulate armed conflict. The over-the-counter systems discussed in this chapter technically qualify as autonomous weapons, as this chapter defines that term. Misusing or weaponizing an aerial drone, driverless vehicle, or boat to collide at a GPS coordinate would in many cases would violate multiple IHL norms and rules.

VI. Export Control Challenges

One of the main objectives of arms control is to "make war less likely."[163] In a way, arms control represents an administrative implementation of the *jus ad bellum* limitations on using force. Effective arms control regimes reinforce those limitations, while an ineffective one suggests either greater potential for the use of force or at least the absence of a deterrent. The current arms control regimes do not lend themselves well to regulating sophisticated or over-the-counter autonomous weapons. Either the current regimes need to be modified, or new ones developed, if arms control is to account effectively for autonomous weapons.

The United States utilizes a series of domestic and international or multilateral export control regimes. On the domestic side, the Department of Commerce administers the Export Administration Act and the Export Administration Regulations, which control "dual use" products having both military and civilian applications. The Department of State administers regulations under the Arms Export Control Act and the International Traffic in Arms Regulations, which deals with defense articles and services. Lastly, the Treasury Department administers laws and regulations that impose economic sanctions on certain countries.

In terms of multilateral export control regimes, the United States is one of thirty countries that are members of

- The Wassenaar Arrangement on export controls for conventional arms and dual-use goods and technologies;
- The Nuclear Suppliers Group on controls of nuclear and nuclear related technology;
- The Australia Group on controls of chemical and biological technology that could be weaponized; and

[163] John D. Maurer, *The Purposes of Arms Control*, 2 Tex. Nat. Sec Rev. 9 (2018).

- The Missile Technology Control Regime on the control of aerial vehicles capable of delivering weapons of mass destruction.

These multilateral export control regimes, to varying degrees, regulate hardware, software, know-how, and data.[164] All of the regimes include software, but "software as an enabler of autonomous functions has not been addressed by any export control provision so far."[165] The International Panel on the Regulation of Autonomous Weapons (iPRAW) contends that data as a delineator for an autonomous weapon for export control purposes would be "difficult to define (and verify")).[166] iPRAW contends that of the four multilateral export control regimes, the Australia Group and the Wassenaar Arrangement are the "most promising."[167] That prediction is more of a relative than an absolute statement.

According to iPRAW, the potential of the Australia Group is its "catch-all clause." It bears emphasis that the Australia Group addresses only "chemicals and biological agents as well as related equipment, technologies, and knowledge to countries and non-state entities suspected of pursuing chemical or biological capabilities."[168] The overwhelming majority—possibly all the current and potential near term autonomous weapons—do not have anything to do with chemicals or biological agents/equipment, and thus would never implicate the Australia Group or its catch-all clause. If an autonomous weapon were to involve chemical or biological agents/equipment, the catch-all clause "requires member countries to be able to halt the transfer of any export, regardless of whether it appears on the group's control lists, if an importer might use it in a chemical or biological weapons program."[169]

In terms of the Wassenaar Arrangement, iPRAW suggested the potential utility of that regime's list of dual-use goods and technology. Under the Wassenaar Arrangement:

> Dual-use goods and technologies to be controlled are those which are major or key elements for the indigenous development, production, use or

[164] iPraw, *LAWS and Export Control Regimes: Fit for Purpose* (Apr. 2020), https://www.ipraw.org/wp-content/uploads/2020/04/iPRAW_WP_ExportControls.pdf.
[165] *Id.*
[166] *Id.*
[167] *Id.*
[168] Daryl Kimball, *The Australia Group at a Glance*, Arms Control Ass'n (Mar. 2021), https://www.armscontrol.org/factsheets/australiagroup#:~:text=The%20catch%2Dall%20provision%20requires,chemical%20or%20biological%20weapons%20program.
[169] *Id.*

enhancement of military capabilities. For selection purposes the dual-use items should also be evaluated against the following criteria:

- Foreign availability outside Participating States.
- The ability to control effectively the export of the goods.
- The ability to make a clear and objective specification of the item.
- Controlled by another regime. [An item which is controlled by another regime should not normally qualify to be controlled by the Wassenaar Arrangement].[170]

Similar to the Australia Group, it is unclear whether a significant number of types of autonomous weapons would meet all the criteria to fall within the ambit of the Wassenaar Arrangement. In terms of sophisticated autonomous weapons, making a clear and objective specification of the item is yet another reminder of the problematic nature of the word "autonomy." As previously discussed, autonomy is a generalized technology descriptor that seems almost the polar opposite of "clear and objective specification." In terms of over-the-counter autonomous weapons, or weaponized civilian applications, the ability to control export of the goods effectively is very much in question.

Potentially further exacerbating the difficulties in controlling the proliferation of autonomous weapons is the development of 3D printing and additive manufacturing. Additive manufacturing "has the potential to produce any physical object based on technical data . . . [that] can be easily transferred using email or other means of electronic communication that are hard for authorities to detect and prevent."[171] As SIPRI recently documented, files containing the information needed for a 3D printer to produce a complete and functioning firearm have been available online since 2013.[172] Adding to that challenge is the concern that additive manufacturing may facilitate producing weapons that avoid detection using metal detectors, X-ray scanners, and other screening devices.[173]

170 Wassenaar Arrangement, Criteria for the Selection of Dual-Use Goods and Technologies for the Sensitive List as amended in 2004, https://www.wassenaar.org/app/uploads/2016/01/08Criteria-for-the-Selection-of-Dual-Use-Goods-including-Sensitive-and-Very-Sensitive-Items.pdf.

171 Mark Bromley & Giovanna Maletta, SIPRI, The Challenge of Software and Technology Transfers to Non-Proliferation Efforts (2018).

172 *Id.*

173 *See* N.R. Jenzen Jones, *Small Arms and Additive Manufacturing: An Assessment of 3D-printed Firearms, Components, and Accessories*, *in* New Technologies, New Control Challenges Small Arms Survey (2015).

Ultimately, the patchwork nature of the current multilateral export control regimes does not suggest they will be of much utility in limiting exports of autonomous weapons. The fact that there is not an export control provision in existence that applies to software as an enabler of autonomous weapons only further lessens the chances of control.

Both high-end and over-the-counter autonomous weapons pose export control challenges. The start of the challenges is that what distinguishes an autonomous weapon is essentially lines of computer code. While it is unclear how many lines of code would be needed for an autonomous weapon, by way of comparison, estimates are that driverless cars will require one billion lines of code, "nearly 1,000 times more than the 145,000 [lines of code] NASA needed to land Apollo 11 on the moon."[174] Autonomous weapons presumably will require even more coding. How the presence or absence of certain computer code in a system could be verified is not clear.

As a result, none of the current export control regimes is a particularly good fit for autonomous weapons. Additionally, to the extent that there is an autonomous weapons arms race: "States have an interest in preserving any advantage they may have over other countries and maintaining some opacity over the maturity of their national capabilities."[175] As one expert noted, "[t]he absence of agreed international standards that could provide meaningful parameters of control-list items further complicates regime discussions."[176] As a result, there is not yet a way to distinguish items of concern from general purpose items. Moreover, "[e]ven after parameters are identified, the control list items need to be designed in a way that ensures both controllability—meaning that the volume of controlled transfers can be handled by the responsible authorities—and relevance—meaning that the technical thresholds will not become obsolete within a short period of time."[177]

In terms of high-end systems, the lack of an agreed definition of "autonomy," and the lack of an applicable existing control regime suggest that formal control mechanisms do not seem at all likely in the foreseeable future. Depending on how sophisticated the weapon is (and how many countries

[174] Tristan Shale-Hester, *Driverless Cars Will Require One Billion Lines of Code, Says JLR*, Auto Express (Apr. 16, 2019), https://www.autoexpress.co.uk/car-news/106617/driverless-cars-will-require-one-billion-lines-of-code-says-jlr.

[175] Kolja Brockmann, SIPRI, Challenges to Multilateral Export Controls: The Case for Inter-Regime Dialogue and Coordination (2019).

[176] *Id.*

[177] *Id.*

are capable of producing it), there is the possibility of informal controls. For over-the-counter systems, that Pandora's box seems long opened. These systems, particularly aerial drones, present a unique proliferation challenge given that they are not designed as weapons but may be easily converted to or used as weapons.

VII. Conclusion

While the assessment of autonomous weapons' effect on *jus in bello* is mixed, over-the-counter systems and the misuse or weaponizing of civilian applications may well tip the overall balance toward undermining that law's ability to regulate the conduct of hostiles.

Ultimately, autonomous weapons pose significant challenges for both *jus ad bellum* and export control regimes. The ongoing proliferation of both high-end and over-the-counter systems is already lowering the barriers to use of force. Reducing the financial and human cost of using force, and increasing the possibility of avoiding attribution, will combine to lessen the effectiveness of the UN Charter's regulation of the use of force.

Export control regimes have yet to grapple with regulating and verifying lines of computer code or the enormity of the dual-use challenge that autonomy poses. Unless and until current export control regimes are adapted, or a new regime developed, export controls for autonomous weapons are unlikely to reinforce the international legal order.

8

Cyber Conflict and the Thresholds of War

Ido Kilovaty

I. Introduction

The internet has revolutionized society globally in the last three decades, making remote communications and exchange of information instantaneous, inexpensive, reliable, and decentralized. Cyberspace, the concept on which the internet is based, allows global interconnectivity for digital devices, including desktop computers, smartphones, routers, smart thermostats, and personal digital assistants like Alexa and Google Home.

This societal dependence on cyberspace appeals to states that find this space easy to master, inexpensive, remote, and often anonymous.[1] It comes therefore as no surprise that in recent years states have utilized cyberspace to carry out operations against each other, with effects ranging from mere inconvenience in the form of a website defacement on one end,[2] to actual kinetic effects in the real world in the form of physical damage to infrastructure,[3] as well as injuries and deaths.[4]

States, however, are not the only actors conducting operations in cyberspace.[5] Cyberspace is characterized by its democratizing nature, which has enabled nonstate actors, such as hacking groups, political activists, rebel groups, and terrorist organizations, to take advantage of the societal dependence upon cyberspace and the ease with which cyber operations can be

[1] *See, e.g.*, Oona Hathaway et al., *The Law of Cyber Attack*, 100 CAL. L. REV. 817, 842 (2012) ("because highly industrialized states are generally more dependent upon computer networks and are more vulnerable to cyber-attacks, cyber-attacks may prove to be a powerful weapon of the weak").

[2] Catalin Cimpanu, *US, UK Formally Blame Russia for Mass-Defacement of Georgian Websites*, ZDNET (Feb. 20, 2020), https://www.zdnet.com/article/us-uk-formally-blame-russia-for-mass-defacement-of-georgian-websites/.

[3] Kim Zetter, *An Unprecedented Look at Stuxnet, The World's First Digital Weapon*, WIRED, Nov. 3, 2014.

[4] Melissa Eddy & Nicole Perlroth, *Cyber Attack Suspected in German Woman's Death*, N.Y. TIMES, Sept. 18, 2020.

[5] *See, e.g.*, Nicolò Bussolati, *The Rise of Non-State Actors in Cyberwarfare*, *in* CYBER WAR: LAW AND ETHICS FOR VIRTUAL CONFLICTS (Jens Ohlin, Kevin Govern, & Claire Finkelstein eds., 2015).

Ido Kilovaty, *Cyber Conflict and the Thresholds of War* In: *Is the International Legal Order Unraveling?*. Edited by: David L. Sloss, Oxford University Press. © Oxford University Press 2022. DOI: 10.1093/oso/9780197652800.003.0009

carried out. Indeed, in recent years, some of the most noteworthy cyber operations were arguably sponsored and carried out by nonstate actors.[6]

Both states and nonstate actors who are engaged in offensive cyber operations benefit from tools that afford anonymity online, such as botnets and IP address spoofing.[7] While anonymity online can be seen as a desirable feature for free speech, it can also be used to undermine attribution efforts, a central element in both the *jus ad bellum* and *jus in bello* regimes. This attribution challenge is further exacerbated by the secrecy and plausible deniability in this space, making it significantly harder to hold the perpetrators accountable.

On top of the attribution challenge, cyber operations enable a wide array of nonkinetic effects that, while not physical in nature, can nonetheless cause significant harms to democracy, privacy, public discourse, and integrity and availability of computer systems and networks. Although the harms themselves are not new, the scale, evasiveness, and damaging nature of nonkinetic cyber operations are unprecedented.

The introduction of cyber operations into the arsenals of both state and nonstate actors has been a profound challenge for international law and the rule of law. Some, including the UN Secretary General Antonio Guterres and former President Barack Obama, went so far as to characterize cyberspace as a "Wild West."[8] This chapter explores two regimes that are particularly challenged by the unique and novel nature of offensive cyber operations: *jus ad bellum* and *jus in bello*.

Although these two legal regimes are distinct in nature—the former focuses on the resort to force, while the latter regulates the conduct of hostilities—there are certain elements and assumptions that apply to both. For example, both regimes create thresholds that primarily take into account criteria like kinetic effects, physicality of force, and violence.

[6] *See Significant Cyber Incidents*, Ctr. for Strat. & Int'l Stud., https://www.csis.org/programs/technology-policy-program/significant-cyber-incidents (last visited June 1, 2021) (timeline records of significant cyber incidents since 2006).

[7] Sharngan Aravindakshan, *Cyberattack: A Look at Evidentiary Thresholds in International Law*, 59 Indian J. Int'l L. 285, 287 (2021).

[8] *See* U.N. Secretary-General, Remarks to the General Assembly on the Secretary-General's Priorities for 2020 (Jan. 22, 2020), https://www.un.org/sg/en/content/sg/speeches/2020-01-22/remarks-general-assembly-priorities-for-2020; White House, Office of the Press Secretary, Remarks by the President at the Cybersecurity and Consumer Protection Summit, Stanford University (Feb. 13, 2015), https://obamawhitehouse.archives.gov/the-press-office/2015/02/13/remarks-president-cybersecurity-and-consumer-protection-summit.

This chapter looks at a substantial challenge to the international legal order in the context of cyber conflict: namely, the nonkinetic nature of cyber operations, which is evaluated against our current understanding of the *jus ad bellum* and *jus in bello* frameworks.

Both the *jus ad bellum* and *jus in bello* have certain thresholds of severity and magnitude, above which the framework applies. Any act below these thresholds would not immediately trigger the relevant legal framework. The nonkinetic nature of most offensive cyber operations often leads states to conclude that the law of armed conflict is silent as to the legality of these operations, resulting in a space where accountability is scarce.

This chapter argues that the current international legal order is in danger of creating a lawless cyberspace, where states engage in offensive cyberspace behavior based on an assumption that any effects below the thresholds of war are permissible. To respond to the novelty of effects and unique characteristics of cyber operations, international law is in dire need of a revolution that fully encompasses the differences between kinetic operations and cyber operations. Without this revolution, cyberspace is at risk of becoming a lawless space, with no boundaries or norms of conduct to restrict harmful state-sponsored cyber operations.

This chapter proceeds as follows. Section II will lay out the different types of cyber operations, both kinetic and nonkinetic. Section III will then explore what this chapter refers to as "war's thresholds": namely, use of force, armed attack, and armed conflict. Section IV will assess the current gaps that arise from the existing thresholds and their application to nonkinetic cyber operations. Section V will look at a few challenges that may undermine the development of the law in a desirable direction.

II. Cyber Operations

This chapter defines cyber operations broadly to highlight the diversity of methods and possible outcomes that these operations may yield. The *Tallinn Manual on the International Law Applicable to Cyber Operations* has taken a similar approach, by defining cyber operations as "the employment of cyber capabilities to achieve objectives in or through cyberspace."[9]

[9] TALLINN MANUAL 2.0 ON THE INTERNATIONAL LAW APPLICABLE TO CYBER OPERATIONS 564 (Michael N. Schmitt & Liis Vihul eds., 2017).

Since cyber operations is a broad concept, it includes actions with kinetic effects that cause injuries or deaths to people. Cyber operations that are designed to cause a physical, destructive outcome are usually referred to as "cyber attacks."[10] One example of a cyber attack is the use of malware to infect industrial cyber physical systems, causing harm to the physical infrastructure at the targeted facility.

While cyber operations may be kinetic, therefore qualifying as "cyber attacks," the vast majority of cyber operations are of nonkinetic nature, resulting in effects that are not physically destructive, but arguably harmful, nonetheless.[11] As Josh Rovner observed: "[C]yber operations may provide a non-kinetic option for leaders who feel pressure to act in a crisis, but who are wary of using force."[12] Examples in this category are numerous: election interference, disinformation campaigns, nonphysical disruption, and more.

This section presents the different categories of cyber operations. This categorization is not an exhaustive list, though it reflects the nonkinetic nature of most cyber operations, which is particularly challenging for the *jus ad bellum* and *jus in bello*'s thresholds of war.

A. Kinetic Cyberwarfare

Although the vast majority of cyber operations result in nonkinetic effects, under certain circumstances, cyber operations may cause kinetic effects in the physical world, involving primarily "direct or indirect physical damage, injury or death" through the exploitation of vulnerabilities in computer systems and networks.[13] Cyber-physical systems, the internet of things, and other manifestations of the "physical internet" are all contributors to the link between cyberspace and physical space. In short, these systems involve "the tight conjoining of and coordination of computer systems and physical

[10] *Id.* at 415 ("A cyber attack is a cyber operation, whether offensive or defensive, that is reasonably expected to cause injury or death to persons or damage or destruction to objects.").

[11] *See* Harriet Moynihan, *The Application of International Law to State Cyberattacks: Sovereignty and Non-Intervention*, 3 CHATHAM HOUSE (Dec. 2019) ("in practice, the vast majority of cyber operations by states take place below the threshold of use of force, instead consisting of persistent, low-level intrusions that cause harm in the victim state but often without discernible physical effects").

[12] Josh Rovner, *Cyber War as an Intelligence Contest*, WAR ON THE ROCKS (Sept. 16, 2019), https://warontherocks.com/2019/09/cyber-war-as-an-intelligence-contest/.

[13] Scott Applegate, *The Dawn of Kinetic Cyber*, *in* 2013 5TH INTERNATIONAL CONFERENCE ON CYBER CONFLICT 163, 164 (K. Podins, J. Stinissen, & M. Maybaum eds., 2013).

processes,"[14] with applications in medical devices, critical infrastructure control (energy, water, communications), defense systems, and more.[15]

Cyber operations targeting cyber-physical systems are far from theoretical. The Olympic Games Operation provides an example of a cyber operation with significant physical effects. In that case, the computer worm Stuxnet infected the supervisory control and data acquisition (SCADA) system at the Iranian nuclear facility in Netanz, undermining the integrity of the system and causing the centrifuges to spin out of control. The Stuxnet worm caused irreversible physical destruction, destroying a thousand centrifuges.

Stuxnet, however, is not the only documented cyber operation that caused kinetic effects. Other examples include: a staged cyber operation by the Department of Homeland Security targeting a replica of a power plant's control system, resulting in physical destruction;[16] vulnerable medical devices that could cause physical injuries and death to patients;[17] smart vehicles that can be hijacked and controlled remotely;[18] and more.

Kinetic cyberwarfare, while disconcerting and dangerous, does not present too many novel legal challenges. Due to the resemblance of the effects in both traditional warfare and kinetic cyberwarfare, existing legal frameworks are still workable to a large extent. There are, however, some conundrums that the new nature of cyberwarfare presents, for example, with regard to attribution and the duty of due diligence. Nonetheless, kinetic cyberwarfare does not challenge international law to the extent that other types of cyber operations do.

B. Election Interference

Cyber operations may also be used to interfere in elections. The methods used in digital election interference are not unique to election interference; they may be used for online manipulation, doxing, spreading fake news and disinformation, and hacking of state election officials and voting machines.

[14] *Id.* at 164.

[15] *Id.*

[16] *Id.*

[17] U.S. Food & Drug Admin., FDA informs patients, providers and manufacturers about potential cybersecurity vulnerabilities for connected medical devices and health care networks that use certain communication software (Oct. 1, 2019), https://www.fda.gov/news-events/press-announcements/fda-informs-patients-providers-and-manufacturers-about-potential-cybersecurity-vulnerabilities.

[18] Andy Greenberg, *Hackers Remotely Kill a Jeep on the Highway—With Me in It*, WIRED, July 21, 2015.

However, digital election interference has given rise to a substantial body of work on international law applicable to these operations, as the relevant legal authorities—human rights law, nonintervention, sovereignty—may apply differently depending on whether a cyber operation targets the election infrastructure.

Election interference can take two forms: direct and indirect. Direct interference is the use of cyber operations to target voting machines and voting officials. Indeed, Russian interference in the 2016 US presidential election demonstrated the targeting of election officials, when the Main Directorate of the General Staff of the Armed Forces of the Russian Federation (GRU) sought to identify vulnerabilities in computers used by individuals and entities involved in the administration of the elections.[19] In addition, the GRU targeted private firms who manufacture and administer software and hardware related to the election.[20]

In addition, election interference may take a more indirect and subtle form. Indirect election interference does not target the election infrastructure or voting officials of the state, but focuses on the public discourse and disclosure of information (for example, through doxing[21]). Through an indirect election interference, the attackers are able to manipulate or distort public discourse and preferences by targeting social media platforms or by leaking sensitive and scandalous documents, as was the case during the 2016 Russian interference in the US election.

C. Online Manipulation and Disinformation

While certain forms of online manipulation can be acts of election interference, online manipulation is in a category of its own, as it is often unrelated to an election or only indirectly influences an election process. For example, there is now ample evidence to show that states are using social media platforms for information control. Manipulation and disinformation are used to suppress human rights, discredit political opponents, and drown out political dissent.[22]

[19] U.S. Dep. of Just., Special Counsel Robert S. Mueller, III, Report on the Investigation into Russian Interference in the 2016 Presidential Election, Volume I 50 (2019).

[20] *Id.*

[21] Ellen Nakashima & Shane Harris, *How the Russians Hacked the DNC and Passed Its Emails to WikiLeaks*, Wash. Post, July 13, 2018.

[22] Samantha Bradshaw & Philip Howard, The Global Disinformation Order: 2019 Global Inventory Of Organized Social Media Manipulation (2019).

There is not a precise or widely accepted definition of online manipulation. One approach, adopted by Susser, Roessler, and Nissenbaum, frames manipulation as a "kind of influence—an attempt to change the way someone would behave absent the manipulator's interventions."[23] Online manipulation, then, is an action taken online by the manipulator to steer users toward a decision that they otherwise would not make. Another definition, proposed by Shaun Spencer, considers manipulation as "an intentional attempt to influence a subject's behavior by exploiting a bias or vulnerability."[24] While this definition seems to be related to advertisement and marketing, it is not limited to that context.[25]

A Chatham House research paper authored by Kate Jones categorizes these influence operations under "disinformation."[26] According to Jones, disinformation means "false or manipulated information that is knowingly shared to cause harm."[27] This conception suggests that while manipulation influences the manipulee, disinformation causes actual harm. For the purposes of this chapter, the two are considered together because they both involve distortion of information to achieve a certain goal.

In recent years, states have increasingly become more involved in cyber operations that seek to manipulate internet users abroad. While Russia's efforts to shape public opinion and sow distrust on the eve of the 2016 US presidential election is a well-documented example of state-sponsored online election interference, a report by the Oxford Internet Institute identified as many as seventy countries involved in online manipulation operations in 2019 alone, up from forty-eight in 2018 and twenty-eight in 2017.[28]

Indeed, the introduction of social media platforms globally has made it easier for governments to engage in online manipulation extraterritorially. This is largely enabled by the business model of these platforms, which seek to grab user attention and increase the time that users spend on the platform.

[23] Daniel Susser, Beate Roessler, & Helen Nissenbaum, *Online Manipulation: Hidden Influences in a Digital World*, 4 Geo. L. Tech. Rev. 1, 13 (2019).

[24] Shaun Spencer, *The Problem of Online Manipulation*, 2020 U. Ill. L. Rev. 959, 990 (2020).

[25] *Id.*

[26] Kate Jones, *Online Disinformation and Political Discourse: Applying a Human Rights Framework*, Chatham House (Nov. 2019).

[27] *Id.* at 7.

[28] Bradshaw & Howard, *supra* note 22, at 2; *See also* David L. Sloss, Tyrants on Twitter: Protecting Democracies from Information Warfare (2022) (showing that since 2014, Russia has interfered in the elections of at least twenty-one European countries, including the EU parliamentary elections).

The side effect of this model, as Jones aptly observes, is that "social media uses techniques not just to inform but also to manipulate audience attention."[29]

Therefore, the interconnectedness and global nature of social media platforms enables cyber operations seeking to manipulate political discourse. Such operations may achieve their goals through the "creation of disinformation and divisive content; the use of specific methods to maximize the distribution of that material; and the use of personal data in order to maximize the influence of the material over individuals."[30]

D. Disruption

Cyber operations may cause disruption to the normal functioning of the target. Disruption may be temporary, either short-term or long-term, and differs from destruction because its effects are limited in time, whereas destruction is permanent and irreversible. Although there are numerous methods to cause disruption, the use of distributed denial-of-services (DDoS) techniques may be the most prominent example. In 2007, Estonia suffered a wave of DDoS attacks arising from a controversial removal of a Soviet-era memorial in Tallinn. There seems to be a consensus that Russia was behind the DDoS attack against Estonia, but its degree of involvement remains contested. The DDoS attacks paralyzed the Estonian economy, government, and emergency services for a period of time, but they did not cause any direct physical effects.

Disruption may seem not as threatening as destruction in the context of cyber operations, but it is still perceived as a national security threat, and certainly a matter of international concern. Ironically, this international concern is reflected in the official Russian position on the matter, which states: "The information weapon is particularly dangerous when used against military and civilian buildings and State systems and institutions, the disruption of the normal functioning of which constitutes a direct threat to national security."[31]

[29] Jones, *supra* note 26, at 9.
[30] *Id.* at 10.
[31] U.N. Secretary-General, *Developments in the Field of Information and Telecommunications in the Context of International Security*, 2, U.N. Doc. A/56/164/Add.1 (Oct. 3, 2009).

Indeed, in recent years, the cyber disruption of the electric grid has been a concern globally. In December 2015, the western and capital regions in Ukraine suffered an electrical power outage due to a cyber operation allegedly linked to Russia.[32] This was the first documented case of a cyber operation causing a blackout, but it will certainly not be the last. For example, in 2019 the *Washington Post* reported that a cyber operation had caused a disruption to electric grid operations in the western United States, overwhelming the grid with a DDoS attack.[33] In other instances, there were indications that foreign actors had been probing the US electric grid for vulnerabilities.[34] Experts believe that, if successful, a cyber operation against the electric grid could cause "power losses in large portions of the United States that could last days in most places and up to several weeks in others."[35] The impact of such an operation on the US economy is estimated to be between $250 billion and $1 trillion, according to a Cambridge University report.[36]

While disruption against the electric grid is of concern at present, it is merely one example of the wide array of disruptions achievable through cyberspace. Additional disruptions could target emergency services,[37] air-traffic control,[38] stock exchange trading,[39] water supply systems,[40] and more. In many scenarios, these disruptions could bring about the requisite kinetic effects to trigger Article 2(4). However, when the effects are limited to disruption alone, or kinetic effects that are too remote in time and causation, it may be difficult to apply kinetic-based war thresholds.[41]

[32] Ellen Nakashima, *Russian Hackers Suspected in Attack That Blacked Out Parts of Ukraine*, Wash. Post, Jan. 5, 2016.

[33] Joseph Marks, *The Cybersecurity 202: A Cyberattack Just Disrupted Grid Operations in the U.S. But It Could Have Been Far Worse*, Wash. Post, May 6, 2019.

[34] Robert Knake, *A Cyberattack on the U.S. Power Grid*, Council on For. Rel. (Apr. 3, 2017), https://www.cfr.org/report/cyberattack-us-power-grid.

[35] *Id.*

[36] Lloyd's & University of Cambridge Centre for Risk Studies, Business Blackout: The Insurance Implications of a Cyber Attack on the US Power Grid (2015).

[37] Yisroel Mirsky & Mordehcai Guri, *DDoS Attacks on 9-1-1 Emergency Services*, IEEE Transactions on Dependable & Secure Computing (Jan. 3, 2020).

[38] U.S. Gov't Accountability Off., GAO-15-221, FAA Needs to Address Weaknesses in Air Traffic Control Systems (2015).

[39] Hanna Ziday, *New Zealand Spy Agency Investigating "Severe" Cyberattack on Stock Exchange*, CNN, Aug. 28, 2020.

[40] Catalin Cimpanu, *Two More Cyber-Attacks Hit Israel's Water System*, ZDNet (July 20, 2020), https://www.zdnet.com/article/two-more-cyber-attacks-hit-israels-water-system/.

[41] Tallinn Manual 2.0, *supra* note 9, at 334 (proposing legal criteria for a use of force analysis in the cyber context, including immediacy of effects and directness. While there are no firm thresholds in this context, the sliding scale may be helpful to assess the legal consequences of a cyber operation).

III. War's Thresholds

The array of nonkinetic cyber operations reflects a growing trend of states resorting to these measures rather than the more physically destructive kinetic cyber operations. The question, therefore, is whether the existing *jus ad bellum* and *jus in bello* thresholds are appropriate for the devastating nature of today's nonkinetic cyber operations. This is not to say that every such operation should constitute a use of force or armed attack, potentially justifying self-defense, but rather that a recalibration of these thresholds in light of new cyber techniques is required.

Surely, many of these nonkinetic cyber operations would already be covered by existing peacetime principles, such as nonintervention, sovereignty, and self-determination. For example, if a cyber operation that interferes in an election is found to be coercive and targeted at the *domaine réservé*, it will necessarily violate the principle on nonintervention.[42] However, as some commentators have observed, the contours of these principles may be blurry and outdated given the realities of cyber operations, allowing the unique characteristics of cyber operations and cyberspace to evade the scope of these longstanding principles.[43]

There is a great deal to be said about nonintervention, sovereignty, and self-determination, and many of the threshold recalibration proposals may also apply to peacetime international law. However, this chapter's purpose is to explore how our current understating of the *jus ad bellum* and *jus in bello* is too narrow and outdated.

This chapter uses the overarching term "war's thresholds" to refer to three separate thresholds recognized by international law. While "war" is by and large not a legal term of art,[44] it is used in this chapter in the interest of

[42] Steven Barela, *Cross-Border Cyber Ops to Erode Legitimacy: An Act of Coercion*, JUST SECURITY (Jan. 12, 2017), https://www.justsecurity.org/36212/cross-border-cyber-ops-erode-legitimacy-act-coercion/.

[43] *See, e.g.*, Michael Schmitt, *Grey Zones in the International Law of Cyberspace*, 42 YALE J. INT'L L. ONLINE 1, 6 (2017) (arguing that there is a grey zone with regard to the applicability of the sovereignty principle to nonkinetic cyber operations); Jens Ohlin, *Did Russian Cyber Interference in the 2016 Election Violate International Law?*, 95 TEX. L. REV. 1579, 1596–97 (2017) (identifying three main problems with the use of self-determination in the cyber operation context: its use in the decolonization context, the difficulty of identifying a sovereign will ex ante, and past election interferences by the United States); Ido Kilovaty, *The Elephant in the Room: Coercion*, 113 AJIL UNBOUND 87 (2019) (arguing that the coercion element of nonintervention excludes nonkinetic cyber operations that qualify as "persuasion, criticism, public diplomacy, propaganda . . . retribution, [and] mere maliciousness").

[44] CHRISTINE GRAY, INTERNATIONAL LAW AND THE USE OF FORCE 6–7 (2004) (noting that the term "war" was replaced by "use of force").

simplicity and for the purpose of avoiding conflation between existing terms. The observations made with regard to these thresholds are often systemic and a result of the current structures of the *jus ad bellum* and *jus in bello*.

The three thresholds that are the focus of this chapter are: (1) use of force under Article 2(4) of the UN Charter; (2) armed attack under Article 51 of the UN Charter; and (3) armed conflict under international humanitarian law.

A. Use of Force

The prohibition on the use or threat of force contained in Article 2(4) of the UN Charter represents the first *jus ad bellum* threshold.[45] Article 2(4) reads: "All Members shall refrain in their international relations from the threat or use of force against the territorial integrity or political independence of any state, or in any other manner inconsistent with the Purposes of the United Nations."[46]

The key term in the prohibition on the use of force is "force," which the UN Charter does not define.[47] Scholars are divided on what actions constitute the use of "force."[48] For some, "force" suggests the use of weapons that produce kinetic effects, while for others, the notion of force encompasses other effects as well.

Nonetheless, the dominant view on the use of force prohibition and cyberwarfare is that cyber operations are in violation of Article 2(4) whenever they produce effects that are equivalent to the kinetic effects of traditional weapons.[49] This approach has been referred to as the "effects-based approach."[50] An iteration of this approach appears in the *Tallinn Manual 2.0*, where the Group of Experts posited that "consequences involving physical harm to individuals or property will in and of themselves qualify as use of force."[51] This approach was also articulated by the State Department's Legal Adviser, Harold Koh, who argued that "if the physical consequences of a cyber attack work the kind of physical damage that dropping a bomb or

45 *See* FRANCOIS DELERUE, CYBER OPERATIONS AND INTERNATIONAL LAW 276 (2020).

46 U.N. Charter, art. 2(4).

47 DELERUE, *supra* note 45, at 285.

48 JAMES CRAWFORD, BROWNLIE'S PRINCIPLES OF PUBLIC INTERNATIONAL LAW 747 (8th ed. 2012).

49 MARCO ROSCINI, CYBER OPERATIONS AND THE USE OF FORCE IN INTERNATIONAL LAW 54 (2014).

50 *See* Hathaway, *supra* note 1, at 845; *see also* Matthew Waxman, *Cyber Attacks and the Use of Force: Back to the Future of Article 2(4)*, 36 YALE J. INT'L. L. 421, 437 (2011).

51 TALLINN MANUAL 2.0, *supra* note 9, at 334 (Rule 69).

firing a missile would, that cyber attack should equally be considered a use of force."[52]

Herein lies the problem. While cyber operations that result in physical effects would undoubtedly be considered uses of force, those that cause only virtual effects, even if severe, would not qualify as prohibited uses of force under the effects-based approach. While some would argue that this is a feature of the *jus ad bellum* framework, there is a plausible argument that such exclusion is a bug and that the use of force framework needs to evolve alongside these devastating virtual effects resulting from cyber operations. In other words, some nonkinetic cyber operations should be considered weapons,[53] and in severe cases, as events crossing the thresholds of war.

While states like Australia, Germany, the United Kingdom, and the United States subscribe to the effects-based approach to the use of force prohibition, states like France have begun to acknowledge the problem of nonkinetic cyber operations. As evidenced by France's Declaration on International Law in Cyberspace, the qualification of a cyber operation as a use of force should include additional criteria that go beyond the kinetic and physical. The Declaration reads: "In the absence of physical damage, a cyberoperation may be deemed a use of force against the yardstick of several criteria." Some of these nonexhaustive criteria include "the circumstances prevailing at the time of the operation, such as the origin of the operation and the nature of the instigator (military or not), the extent of intrusion, the actual or intended effects of the operation or the nature of the intended target."[54] The French reading of Article 2(4) as applied to cyber operations is, however, not the majority view on this point.

B. Armed Attack

Jus ad bellum's upper threshold is that of an "armed attack." Article 51 of the UN Charter recognizes a self-defense exception to the use of force prohibition

[52] Harold Koh, *International Law in Cyberspace*, 54 HARV. INT'L. L.J. ONLINE 1, 4 (2012).

[53] *See* Yoram Dinstein, *Cyber War and International Law: Concluding Remarks at the 2012 Naval War College International Law Conference*, 89 INT'L L. STUD. 276, 280 (2013) ("cyber . . . must be looked upon as a new means of warfare--in other words, a weapon: no less and no more than other weapons").

[54] INTERNATIONAL LAW APPLIED TO OPERATIONS IN CYBERSPACE, MINISTÈRE DES ARMÉES (2019), https://www.defense.gouv.fr/content/download/567648/9770527/file/international+law+applied+to+operations+in+cyberspace.pdf.

if "an armed attack occurs."[55] While a small group of states, including the United States, consider the use of force and armed attack to be synonymous, the two thresholds are distinct. As the International Court of Justice (ICJ) iterated in the *Nicaragua* case, armed attacks are "the most grave forms of the use of force."[56] This view suggests that there is a certain threshold of intensity above which use of force would qualify as an armed attack.[57] However, even outside the cyber context, there is no consensus about how to draw the line that separates armed attacks from lesser uses of force.

C. Armed Conflict

Armed conflict is the third threshold of war, which is distinct from the two *jus ad bellum* thresholds. Armed conflict is the *jus in bello* threshold above which the body of international humanitarian law applies. While Common Articles II and III mention the threshold of armed conflict, the criteria for an armed conflict are not laid out.[58] Rather, the threshold was developed by international tribunals. Notably, the International Criminal Tribunal for the former Yugoslavia in the *Tadic* case defined an international armed conflict as "a resort to armed force between States."[59] For the non-international counterpart, the definition focuses on intensity and organization. As the *Tadic* court articulated, a non-international armed conflict exists when there is protracted armed violence between organized armed groups within a state.[60]

The threshold of armed conflict raises two distinct categories of questions in the context of cyberwarfare. First, can cyber operations in themselves cross the threshold of an "armed conflict"? In other words, can cyber operations

[55] U.N. Charter, *supra* note 46, art. 51.

[56] Military and Paramilitary Activities in and Against Nicaragua (Nicar. v. U.S.), Merits, 1986 I.C.J. Rep. 14, 101, ¶ 191 (June 27).

[57] *See* Rep. of the Indep. Int'l Fact-Finding Mission on the Conflict in Georgia, Vol. II, 242 (2009) ("the prohibition of the use of force covers all physical force which surpasses a minimum threshold of intensity").

[58] Geneva Convention for the Amelioration of the Condition of the Wounded and Sick in Armed Forces in the Field arts. 2–3, Aug. 12, 1949, 6 U.S.T. 3314, 75 U.N.T.S. 31; Geneva Convention for the Amelioration of the Condition of the Wounded, Sick and Shipwrecked Members of the Armed Forces at Sea arts. 2–3, Aug. 12, 1949, 6 U.S.T. 3316, 75 U.N.T.S. 85; Geneva Convention Relative to the Treatment of Prisoners of War arts. 2–3, Aug. 12, 1949, 6 U.S.T. 3316, 75 U.N.T.S. 135; Geneva Convention relative to the Protection of Civilian Persons in Time of War arts. 2–3, Aug. 12, 1949, 6 U.S.T. 3516, 75 U.N.T.S. 287.

[59] Prosecutor v. Dusko Tadic, Case No. IT-94-1-A, Decision on the Defence Motion for Interlocutory Appeal on Jurisdiction, ¶ 70 (Int'l Crim. Trib. for the Former Yugoslavia Oct. 2, 1995).

[60] *Id.*

alone satisfy the "resort to armed force" threshold in the International Armed Conflict context and the intensity requirement in the Non-International Armed Conflict context?

Second, assuming we are already in an armed conflict, how does international humanitarian law deal with kinetic and nonkinetic cyber operations used during an armed conflict?

1. Cyber Operations Triggering Armed Conflict

The key to answering the first question, that is, whether cyber operations can be the sole trigger of an international or a non-international armed conflict, is whether these cyber operations count as "armed."[61] While neither "armed" nor "conflict" is defined by international humanitarian law, the concept suggests the existence of hostilities.[62] Therefore, any resort to violence between two states would suffice for it to be considered an international armed conflict, while a degree of intensity and organization would still be required for a non-international armed conflict.

The connection between hostilities, violence, and nonkinetic cyber operations is unclear. However, under the current understanding of international humanitarian law, it appears that the use of nonkinetic cyber operations would not count as the initiation of an armed conflict, whether international or non-international.

The threshold of hostilities and violence giving rise to an armed conflict may seem reasonable at first blush, as in the pre-cyber era the use of military force usually led to serious humanitarian concerns. However, the nature of today's nonkinetic cyber operations is likely to create similar humanitarian concerns: widespread disruption of critical infrastructure, massive online disinformation campaigns, and election interference may all lead to significant harms to civilians, often of irreversible nature.

Whether kinetic or nonkinetic cyber operations could alone initiate an armed conflict would largely depend on our understanding of "hostilities" and "violence." Even assuming it were possible, international humanitarian law and the rules on the conduct of hostilities pose an additional challenge to the regulation of cyber operations during war.

[61] Tallinn Manual 2.0, *supra* note 9, at 383.
[62] *Id.*

2. Attack

International humanitarian law protects civilians from "attacks" that are either disproportionate, directed at civilian targets, or indiscriminate. Article 49(1) of Additional Protocol I of the Geneva Conventions defines "attacks" as "acts of violence against the adversary, whether in offense or in defense."[63] The existence of an "armed conflict" is a prerequisite for applying the principles of distinction and proportionality to "attacks." Thus, it is critical to understand when a cyber operation can be considered an "attack."

The term "attack" has received several definitions from countries and bodies around the world. For example, the International Committee of the Red Cross (ICRC) commentary to Additional Protocol I and the International Criminal Tribunal for the former Yugoslavia have found that the term "attack" means combat action.[64] Meanwhile, Heather Dinniss's commentary argues that "attacks" do not include the dissemination of propaganda, embargoes, or other nonphysical means of psychological or economic warfare since Article 49's definition of attacks as "acts of violence". denotes physical force.[65] This strict physical understanding of "attacks" as it relates to cyber operations will be considered in section IV of this chapter.

3. Distinction

The *jus in bello* seeks to protect civilians from "the calamities of war" by creating a distinction between civilians and combatants, military objectives, and civilian objects. The basic rule of distinction in Article 48 of Additional Protocol I provides: "Parties to the conflict shall at all times distinguish between the civilian population and combatants and between civilian objects and military objectives and accordingly shall direct their operations only against military objectives."[66] The Commentary to Additional Protocol I explains that "operations" in the context of Article 48 includes

[63] Protocol Additional to the Geneva Conventions of 12 August 1949, and Relating to the Protection of Victims of International Armed Conflicts art. 49(1), June 8, 1977, 1125 U.N.T.S. 3 [hereinafter Additional Protocol I].

[64] *See* Int'l Comm. of the Red Cross, Commentary on the Additional Protocols of 8 June 1977 to the Geneva Conventions of 12 August 1949 ¶ 1880 (Yves Sandoz et al. eds., 1987), https://www.loc.gov/rr/frd/Military_Law/pdf/Commentary_GC_ Protocols.pdf; Prosecutor v. Strugar, Case No. IT-01-42-T, Judgment (Int'l Crim. Trib. for the Former Yugoslavia, Jan. 31, 2005); Michael Bothe et al., New Rules for Victims of Armed Conflicts: Commentary on the Two 1977 Protocols Additional to the Geneva Conventions of 1949, at 289 (1982).

[65] Heather Dinniss, Cyber Warfare and the Laws of War 197 (2012).

[66] Additional Protocol I, *supra* note 63, art. 48.

"all movements and acts related to hostilities that are undertaken by armed forces."[67]

Distinction is a bedrock principle for the conduct of hostilities. Distinction obligates parties to direct their attacks to military targets and to spare civilians and civilian objects. This principle also reinforces both humanitarian and strategic considerations due to direct attacks being permissible only against military objectives. This is illustrated by Article 52(2) of Additional Protocol I, which states that "[a]ttacks shall be limited strictly to military objectives."[68] This means that "the civilian population as such, as well as individual civilians, shall not be the object of attack"[69] and that "civilian objects shall not be the object of attack."[70]

It would therefore be illegal to initiate a cyber operation directly targeting civilians, if the operation were considered an "attack." While the case of kinetic cyber operations as attacks is quite straightforward, it is debatable whether the term "attack" includes nonkinetic cyber operations. As noted by Heather Dinniss:

> it is common ground that computer network attacks which result in physical damage to civilian property, injury or death to civilians constitute attacks under international humanitarian law and are thus prohibited. However, the status of computer network attacks directed at civilian objects that do not result in such deleterious effects remains the subject of debate.[71]

Excluding nonkinetic cyber operations from the scope of "attack" would mean that civilians and civilian objects could legitimately become a direct target of such operations without it being considered a violation of the principle of distinction. This would be an undesirable outcome whereby states would be unaccountable for any disruption caused intentionally to civilians during an armed conflict.

4. *Proportionality*

The *jus in bello* adds another layer of protection for civilians and civilian objects, even if an attack is not directed at a civilian or civilian object, and

67 *See* ICRC Commentary on AP I, *supra* note 64, ¶ 1875.
68 Additional Protocol I, *supra* note 63, art. 52(2).
69 *Id.*, art. 51(2).
70 *Id.*, art. 52(1).
71 DINNISS, *supra* note 65, at 197.

even if the employed methods are capable of discriminating between protected and unprotected targets. The *jus in bello* assumes that even if these attacks do not target a civilian or civilian object and discriminate between protected and unprotected targets, incidental damage to civilians and civilian objects is still possible. Therefore, for additional protection, Article 51(5)(b) provides that "an attack which may be expected to cause incidental loss of civilian life, injury to civilians, damage to civilian objects, or a combination thereof, which would be excessive in relation to the concrete and direct military advantage anticipated" is indiscriminate and, therefore, illegal.[72] This principle is commonly referred to as "proportionality," and along with distinction represents a fundamental principle of modern international humanitarian law.[73]

Article 51(5)(b) notably uses the term "damage" as opposed to "destruction," which broadens the scope of its applicability. Damage means "harm . . . impairing the value or usefulness of something,"[74] and therefore an act or acts "disrupting the functioning of certain systems by interfering with their underlying computer systems can amount to damage insofar as it impairs their usefulness."[75]

Yet even after determining the principle of proportionality ought to apply to cyber operations, these operations still pose a great challenge to the principle of proportionality. Military advantage is often complicated to calculate, and might be either biased or arbitrary, but assessing collateral damage after a conventional military operation is relatively straightforward. The same cannot be said for cyber operations. After all, once a malicious tool is released, there may be little control over the eventual exposure,[76] and the subsequent physical, economic, and societal effects that such malicious tool is capable of causing.[77] Moreover, cyber operations blur the lines between collateral damage, nonkinetic harms, and inconveniences, making any proportionality

[72] Additional Protocol I, *supra* note 63, art. 51(5)(b).

[73] Roscini, *supra* note 49, at 219.

[74] Cordula Droege, *Get off My Cloud: Cyber Warfare, International Humanitarian Law, and the Protection of Civilians*, 94 Int'l Rev. The Red Cross 533, 559 (2012).

[75] *Id.*

[76] Dinniss, *supra* note 65, at 203 ("Viruses and worms are two methods of computer network attack which are particularly likely to fall into this category [of indiscriminate attacks] as their effects are often not limited by their creators.").

[77] Karine Bannelier-Christakis, *Is the Principle of Distinction Still Relevant in Cyberwarfare?*, *in* Res. Handbook on Int'l L. & Cyberspace 343, 349–50 (Nicholas Tsagourias & Russell Buchan eds., 2015) (comparing states with varying degrees of reliance upon cyberspace as a factor affecting the expected collateral damage).

analyses in the nonkinetic context highly challenging. Cyber operations can cause new types of harms, including, but not limited to, disruption harms, election interference, manipulation, disinformation, and more. However, the traditional rubric for damage assessment does not properly weight the new types of harm produced by these operations.

Another critical difficulty is determining the temporal scope of the collateral damage anticipated. Since the effects of cyber operations can often materialize after some time has elapsed, the exact proximity of the effects to the initial operation is highly ambiguous,[78] and this gap might be used by some actors to claim that certain harms are too distant to be linked to the initial operation.

IV. Cyber Operations and War's Thresholds

The thresholds of war—namely, use of force, armed attack, and armed conflict—create a challenge for the regulation of cyberwarfare. These three thresholds were created in the pre-cyber era, when devastating nonkinetic cyber operations did not exist and therefore could not have been considered.

First, this section contends that war's thresholds are outdated given the introduction of cyber operations. This is not to say that the thresholds are also outdated for the non-cyber world, but that cyber operations present such a level of devastation and undermining of essential state interests and human rights that the existing thresholds should be reconsidered.

Second, this section looks at alternatives to war's thresholds. After all, international law regulates activities below the threshold of war. The degree of propriety of these alternatives varies given the context, though they are not without problems. For certain cyber operations, like disruption, these alternatives may be more appropriate while for other cyber operations, like election interference, we may need to devise a different approach. Nonetheless, the main point of this chapter remains—a revolution is needed to address the current state of affairs in cyber operations.

[78] *Id.* at 350.

A. Are the Thresholds Outdated?

The observation that war's thresholds focus on physical aspects of conflict (armed force, kinetic effects), while at the same time, most cyber operations would not reach these thresholds despite potentially causing devastating nonphysical effects, suggests that perhaps these thresholds are outdated.

As Marc Shack observed, "[A]rticle 2(4) was written to keep powerful States from using the sharpest tool in their coercive toolbox—military might—to interfere with other, less powerful States."[79] Given that military might in this day and age includes military might in cyberspace, this threshold needs to be reconsidered. Shack further concludes that "the strict physicality of the immediate effect, while clearly important, can hardly be decisive. The broader effects of an attack should be considered too, physical or otherwise."[80]

Indeed, cyberspace capabilities are of the utmost importance to the most powerful militaries worldwide. Maintaining their power means that they also need to develop offensive and defensive capabilities in cyberspace. The *jus ad bellum* and *jus in bello* rarely touch on these novel capabilities. As Adm. Mike Gilday, US chief of naval operations, observed: "[W]e're not fighting a war where international norms exist. But make no mistake, we are in conflict day-in and day-out in the cyber realm."[81]

Therefore, the analysis should be indifferent toward the physicality of the use of force, armed attack, or armed conflict, but rather the equivalence of the result. For example, dropping a bomb on a server farm that stores sensitive government data should be considered the same as malware launched remotely against the same server farm to wipe out sensitive data permanently. I have previously made a similar argument in the context of economic cyber attacks.[82]

[79] Marc Schack, *Did the US Stay "Well Below the Threshold of War" with Its June Cyberattack on Iran*, EJIL: TALK! (Sept. 2, 2019), https://www.ejiltalk.org/did-the-us-stay-well-below-the-threshold-of-war-with-its-june-cyberattack-on-iran/.

[80] *Id.*

[81] Naomi VanDuser, *NCWDG Celebrates Opening of Cyber Foundry*, DEFENSE VISUAL INFORMATION DISTRIBUTION SERVICE (Feb. 18, 2020), https://www.dvidshub.net/news/363356/ncwdg-celebrates-opening-cyber-foundry#.Xkx8I44ONeo.twitter.

[82] Ido Kilovaty, *Rethinking the Prohibition on the Use of Force in the Light of Economic Cyber Warfare: Towards a Broader Scope of Article 2(4) of the UN Charter*, 4 J.L. CYBER WARFARE 210 (2015).

B. Recalibrating War's Thresholds

While not physical, the devastating nature of nonkinetic cyber operations should be regulated by both the *jus ad bellum* and *jus in bello* through a reimagination of war's thresholds. This recalibration of thresholds is not meant to exclude or modify the ways they already apply to kinetic cyber operations, but rather to adapt to the growing concern arising from nonkinetic cyber operations. This section explores some opportunities for recalibration.

1. *Rethinking Force*

A recalibration of war's thresholds requires rethinking the concepts of *force*, *armed attack*, and *violence*, all of which are used to distinguish events below and above key thresholds. In light of nonkinetic cyber operations, these thresholds need to be either interpreted to encompass the wide range of devastating harms that these operations could cause, or a new threshold would have to be introduced alongside the existing ones to ensure accountability for harmful nonkinetic consequences.

First, the concept of "force" would need to be reimagined. The current understanding of force emphasizes the existence of kinetic effects: deaths, injuries, and damage to physical property. This interpretation significantly constrains the ability of Article 2(4) to deter and limit the occurrence of nonkinetic cyber operations. To be clear, whether a cyber operation qualifies as a violation of the use of force prohibition would matter only for deterrence (of states that prefer not to violate the law) and international responsibility (for cases where such operations do take place). The redefinition of "force" would not necessarily open the floodgates for self-defense actions, which would be in the domain of "armed attack."

Rethinking the concept of "force," or when used conjunctively as "armed force," is also critical for the *jus in bello* context. International humanitarian law applies only in armed conflict situations, which involve a resort to force by states,[83] or protracted armed violence in cases of non-international armed conflicts.[84]

In the international armed conflict context, it is an open question whether *ad bellum* "force" and *in bello* "armed force" are synonymous, in which case reinterpreting force in light of cyber operations would contribute to both

[83] Prosecutor v. Dusko Tadic, Case No. IT-94-1-A, Decision on the Defence Motion for Interlocutory Appeal on Jurisdiction, ¶ 70 (Int'l Crim. Trib. for the Former Yugoslavia, Oct. 2, 1995).

[84] *Id.*

frameworks.[85] However, as the ICJ noted in the *Nicaragua* case, not every instance of the use of armed force in violation of Article 2(4) would create an armed conflict, thus triggering the application of international humanitarian law.[86] In cases where use of armed force does not result in an armed conflict, it is critical to set the criteria for cyber operations that both cross and do not cross the threshold of armed conflict.

2. *Rethinking Armed Attack*

Article 51 of the UN Charter requires an "armed attack" before self-defensive measures are legitimized. This is considered to be a high threshold that encompasses only the most grave uses of force. Our understanding of "armed attack" in the cyberspace context would have to include the most severe nonkinetic effects, such as massive critical infrastructure disruption causing massive interruption in essential services (such as power, water, sewage), and attacks against the economy resulting in significant financial losses and economic shutdown. This is less of an idea to justify more self-defense and more a proposal to equate kinetic effects with the most severe nonkinetic effects caused by cyber operations. While some would argue that some of these effects are already contained within the definition of "armed attack," it is not at all clear that they are.

As reflected in the *Tallinn Manual*, cyber operations that focus on intelligence gathering or limited interruption and inconvenience would not reach the threshold of armed attack. On the other end, a cyber operation that "seriously injures or kills a number of persons or that causes significant damage to, or destruction of, property would satisfy the scale and effects requirement."[87] While these two ends of the spectrum are uncontested, the precise threshold of armed attack is unclear.[88]

In addition, the threshold of armed attack does not currently address two important issues related to cyber operations. First, could victim states consider the effects of nonkinetic cyber operations cumulatively? That is, if each cyber operation taken alone is below the threshold, can their collective effects

[85] Jason Beckett, *New War, Old Law: Can the Geneva Paradigm Comprehend Computers*, 13 Leiden J. Int'l L. 33, 41 (2000).

[86] *See* Military and Paramilitary Activities in and Against Nicaragua (Nicar. v. U.S.), Merits, 1986 I.C.J. Rep. 14, 101, ¶ 191 (June 27); *see also* Roscini, *supra* note 49, at 128; *compare* Beckett, *supra* note 85, at 41 (arguing that use of force and resort to armed force are synonymous questions as "any use of force is regulated by IHL").

[87] Tallinn Manual 2.0, *supra* note 9, at 341.

[88] *Id.*

ever cross the threshold of armed attack? And, second, whether armed attack is solely concerned with the immediate physical consequences or if it also considers the "extent of the ensuing effects," which go beyond the immediate physical consequences and may include other effects that materialize over time.[89] In the nonkinetic context, it is desirable to focus on the latter rather than the former, as it takes into account severe consequences that naturally arise further on the chain of events.

3. *Rethinking Violence*

Finally, the third key concept that is overdue for rethinking is *violence*. Violence is important more broadly because it assumes that physical aggression between human beings, whether directly or indirectly, is condemnable and thus needs to be restrained by the laws regulating war. A narrow definition of "violence" is not necessarily tenable in the era of virtual violence, in which cyber operations may harm people and damage property in a more indirect, and sometimes less tangible manner.

Violence is relevant in the *in bello* context in cases of non-international armed conflicts. These conflicts arise out of "protracted" armed violence between governmental authorities and armed groups, or between armed groups.[90] The relationship between protracted armed violence and cyber operations is unclear, and whether cyber operations could in themselves satisfy this intensity requirement and trigger a non-international armed conflict is equally controversial.[91]

However, as Marco Roscini suggests, "with regard to disruptive cyber operations not resulting in physical consequences, it is likely that only multiple coordinated cyber operations seriously disrupting the functioning of several or all critical infrastructure of a heavily digitally reliant state for a prolonged time may potentially be considered by states to reach the intensity requirement needed for the application of the law of non-international armed conflict in the absence of associated kinetic hostilities."[92] While this

[89] *Id.* at 343 (discussing a disagreement over the characterization of a cyber operation "against a major international stock exchange that causes the market to crash." While some experts argued that such financial damage would not constitute an armed attack, other experts "emphasized the catastrophic effects" that such an operation would cause, thus reaching the threshold of an armed attack).

[90] Prosecutor v. Dusko Tadic, Case No. IT-94-1-A, Decision on the Defence Motion for Interlocutory Appeal on Jurisdiction, ¶ 70 (Int'l Crim. Trib. for the Former Yugoslavia, Oct. 2, 1995).

[91] *See* David Wallace & Christopher Jacobs, *Conflict Classification and Cyber Operations: Gaps, Ambiguities and Fault Lines*, 40 U. Pa. J. Int'l L. 643, 687 (2019) ("the traditional binary classification paradigm is being stressed both substantively and procedurally. The emergence of cyber operations will only exacerbate these stresses").

[92] Roscini, *supra* note 49, at 153.

view represents one extremity of the spectrum, it suggests that kinetic effects are not the sole factor for the intensity requirement. At the same time, the intensity requirement and the concept of protracted armed violence would need to be further clarified in light of nonkinetic cyber operations.

Violence is also a central tenet for the concept of "attacks" under international humanitarian law.[93] Attacks are defined as "acts of violence against the adversary, whether in offence or in defence."[94] As the commentary to Additional Protocol I to the Geneva Conventions suggests, "the term 'acts of violence' denotes physical force. Thus, the concept of 'attacks' does not include dissemination of propaganda, embargoes, or other non-physical means of psychological or economic warfare."[95] This understanding appears to be somewhat outdated in the context of cyber operations.

Whether a cyber operation counts as an "attack" is critical for the determination of whether the rules on conduct of hostilities apply. If nonkinetic cyber operations do not qualify as "attacks," then they are not constrained by distinction, proportionality, military necessity, and humanity. On the other hand, if they are, then distinction, proportionality, military necessity, and humanity would be at play. The harmful nature of nonkinetic cyber operations calls for an expansion of what is considered an "attack" in order to protect civilians from the effects of sophisticated cyberwarfare.[96] However, this proposition is likely to garner some pushback from states that would resist any restrictions on the conduct of cyber operations.[97]

4. *Nonkinetic Effects*

One way to recalibrate war's thresholds—use of force, armed attack, and armed conflict (violence)—is to involve severe nonkinetic effects within the ambit of these thresholds. These nonkinetic effects may take many different forms. They may, for example, involve the deletion or alteration of sensitive data stored on government computers. Or, alternatively, they may disrupt political processes or target critical infrastructure SCADA systems. Some of

[93] *See* Michael Schmitt, *"Attack" as a Term of Art in International Law: The Cyber Operations Context*, 4th International Conference on Cyber Conflict 283, 290 (2012).

[94] Additional Protocol I, *supra* note 63, art. 49.1.

[95] Bothe et al., *supra* note 64, at 289.

[96] Ido Kilovaty, *Virtual Violence—Disruptive Cyber Operations as "Attacks" under International Humanitarian Law*, 23 Mich. Tel. & Tech. L. Rev. 113, 116 (2016); *see also* Ido Kilovaty, *Violence in Cyberspace: Are Disruptive Cyber Operations Legal under International Humanitarian Law?*, Just Security (Mar. 3, 2017).

[97] Pete Pascucci & Kurt Sanger, *Why a Broad Definition of "Violence" in Cyber Conflict Is Unwise and Legally Unsound*, Just Security (Mar. 8, 2017).

these nonkinetic cyber operations are more harmful than others, which is to suggest that not all nonkinetic effects will necessarily reach the prerequisite thresholds of war.

Despite the challenges with this recalibration discussed in the next part, severe nonkinetic cyber operations will ultimately lead to an interpretation of war's thresholds that encompasses their harmful consequences. Whether this will be achieved through new customary international law, a new cyber-specific treaty, or a reinterpretation of existing treaties is yet to be determined.

This subsection argues that there are some serious nonkinetic consequences that need to be embedded within the current thresholds of war. Specifically, three kinds of cyber operations ought to be considered on par with kinetic effects. They are: *cyber operations against data*, *disruption of political processes*, and *disruption of critical infrastructure*. Specific legal issues with each category are discussed in turn.

5. *Cyber Operations against Data*

Cyber operations that target data, broadly speaking, present a difficult case for war's thresholds. The nonphysical nature of digital data makes cases of data deletion, alteration, or corruption difficult to analyze under Article 2(4).[98] Many such state-sponsored cyber operations have already taken place, including the North Korean operation against Sony[99] and the Iranian malware targeting Saudi Aramco.[100] In both cases, the deletion of sensitive data has been the goal and the actual result.

Some scholars, like Michael Schmitt, argue that such operations against data cannot be considered as uses of force or armed attacks, unless the data is "immediately convertible into tangible objects, like banking data."[101] On the other hand, the legality of cyber operations against data is still a matter of debate and could evolve accordingly.[102] However, this future development does not negate the challenges of the current legal limbo, where different

[98] Roscini, *supra* note 49, at 55.

[99] Kim Zetter, *Sony Got Hacked Hard: What We Know and Don't Know So Far*, Wired, Dec. 3, 2014.

[100] Humeyra Pamuk, *Exclusive: U.S. Probe of Saudi Oil Attack Shows It Came from North—Report*, Reuters, Dec. 19, 2019.

[101] Michael N. Schmitt, *Cyber Operations in International Law: The Use of Force, Collective Security, Self-Defense, and Armed Conflicts*, *in* Proceedings of a Workshop on Deterring Cyberattacks: Informing Strategies and Developing Options for U.S. Policy 164 (2010).

[102] Michael Schmitt, *The State of Humanitarian Law in Cyber Conflict*, Just Security (Jan. 6, 2015), https://www.justsecurity.org/18891/state-humanitarian-law-cyber-conflict/ ("It must be cautioned that international law evolves to reflect the values of the international community.").

authorities disagree on the legality of cross-border data destruction, alteration, and manipulation.[103]

Cyber operations against data raise some significant challenges in the *in bello* context as well. For example, do such operations qualify as "attacks" under international humanitarian law, thus regulated by the principles of distinction, proportionality, and humanity?

The view that cyber operations against data violate the laws of war, however, represents the minority view. The majority believe that cyber operations that alter or destroy civilian data without generating kinetic consequences, for instance, deaths, injuries, or physical destruction or damage, are not attacks under the current state of the laws of war.[104]

This fact demonstrates another gap in the thresholds of war as they apply to cyber operations of nonkinetic nature. The value of data is increasing, and if unconstrained, states may mount such attacks against sensitive data without facing consequences.

6. *Disruption of Critical Infrastructure*

In recent years, cyber operations aimed at disrupting critical infrastructure have gained traction, raising concerns as to the humanitarian nature of such disruption. Some examples include an attack against a dam in New York,[105] a steel mill in Germany,[106] Ukraine's electric grid,[107] the National Health Service in the United Kingdom,[108] and others.[109] In some circumstances,

[103] Ryan Goodman, *Cyber Operations and the U.S. Definition of "Armed Attack,"* Just Security (Mar. 8, 2018), https://www.justsecurity.org/53495/cyber-operations-u-s-definition-armed-attack/ ("This is an area where views are developing in one direction, but what happens in the limbo period between now and then, when some States and legal authorities hold one view and others hold different ones? That seems like a dangerous period for calibrating the use of force in cyber.").

[104] Schmitt, *supra* note 102.

[105] U.S. Dep't of Just., Manhattan U.S. Attorney Announces Charges Against Seven Iranians for Conducting Coordinated Campaign of Cyber Attacks Against U.S. Financial Sector on Behalf of Islamic Revolutionary Guard Corps-Sponsored Entities (Mar. 24, 2016), https://www.justice.gov/usao-sdny/pr/manhattan-us-attorney-announces-charges-against-seven-iranians-conducting-coordinated.

[106] Kim Zetter, *A Cyberattack Has Caused Confirmed Physical Damage for the Second Time Ever*, Wired, Jan. 8, 2015.

[107] Dragos, Inc., CRASHOVERRIDE: Analyzing the Malware that Attacks Power Grids (June 12, 2017), https://www.dragos.com/resource/crashoverride-analyzing-the-malware-that-attacks-power-grids/.

[108] Report by the Comptroller and Auditor General, Investigation: WannaCry Cyber-attack and the NHS (Apr. 25, 2018), https://www.nao.org.uk/wp-content/uploads/2017/10/Investigation-WannaCry-cyber-attack-and-the-NHS.pdf.

[109] *See, e.g.*, Sergio Caltagirone, *Industrial Cyber Attacks: A Humanitarian Crisis in the Making*, Humanitarian L. & Pol'y (Dec. 3, 2019), https://blogs.icrc.org/law-and-policy/2019/12/03/industrial-cyber-attacks-crisis/.

these attacks would result in physical consequences, for example, the destruction of hardware. However, in most scenarios, these attacks involve damage that is either digital or informational, not involving any physical destruction albeit clear disruptive effects.

The disruptive nature of such operations raises two questions. First, what level of disruption is bad enough that international law ought to consider it a use of force, or even an armed attack. Second, can the humanitarian effects of such disruption lead to it being classified as an armed conflict?

Rethinking *force*, *armed attack*, and *violence* may help in conceptualizing disruption in this context. Does disruption count as "force" or "violence"? What intensity of disruption would reach the level of an armed conflict?

V. Challenges Ahead

Accepting the outdated nature of war's thresholds in regard to cyber operations is only the first step. International law can adapt to new challenges through the crystallization of new customary international law, introduction of a new treaty, or new interpretations of existing treaties. This section argues that these three methods are unlikely in the context of cyber operations.

In addition, in recent years, private tech corporations have become increasingly involved in developing conceptual frameworks for cyber operations. One example includes Microsoft's president, Brad Smith, and his proposal for a Digital Geneva Convention.[110] Ever since then, new initiatives and institutions have begun to emerge to fill the gaps that states have not addressed.

A. The Role of Customary International Law

Recalibrating war's thresholds could in theory be achieved through the emergence of new customary international law. However, in practice, this may be a challenge given the unique nature of cyberspace. Primarily, cyberspace enables anonymity, and with sophisticated actors who use advanced

[110] Brad Smith, *The Need for a Digital Geneva Convention*, Microsoft (Feb. 14, 2017), https://blogs.microsoft.com/on-the-issues/2017/02/14/need-digital-geneva-convention/.

techniques and tools, this anonymity may undermine attribution altogether. Cyberspace is therefore plagued with secrecy, which poses difficulties for the creation of customary international law.[111]

In addition to this inherent anonymity, states are generally nontransparent when it comes to their cyber operations. As Gen. Michael Hayden has admitted, the cyber domain remains "hideously over-classified."[112] Brian Egan identified this difficulty in a speech given at Berkeley in which he highlighted the need for "increased transparency . . . to clarify how the international law on non-intervention applies to States' activities in cyberspace."[113]

In particular, the emergence of a new standard may be hindered by the transparency challenge identified by Efrony and Shany. The building blocks of a new norm of customary international law include information about the occurrence of a cyber intervention, the method used, direct and indirect consequences, and the response (or lack thereof) of the victim state. But in the cyber context, it is difficult to access such evidence due to the secrecy that states maintain by default in that space, whereby they are reluctant to present evidence publicly to avoid revealing their means, methods, and confidential intelligence. The optionality and parallel tracks strategies identified by Efrony and Shany are emblematic of this evidentiary challenge, as they make public attributions less likely with fewer states making them, which in turn makes the crystallization of customary international law more remote. The covert nature of cyber operations has become the norm since states believe that publicity or transparency "might expose their vulnerabilities, adversely affect their offensive or defensive capabilities, and weaken their power of deterrence."[114]

[111] *See* Michael Schmitt, *Taming the Lawless Void: Tracking the Evolution of International Law Rules for Cyberspace*, 3(3) Tex. Nat'l Sec. Rev. 32 (2020) ("Most state cyber operations are highly classified or otherwise shielded from observation by other states. Practice that is not visible does not contribute to the crystallization of a new customary law. Additionally, states have shown a general reluctance to engage in the verbal practice that might suffice to fill that void. For example, they have seldom condemned the cyber operations of other states as violations of international law.").

[112] Rudy Takala, *Former Spy Chief Complains about "Hideous Over-Classification"*, Wash. Examiner, Oct. 28, 2015.

[113] Brian Egan, Legal Adviser, U.S. Dep't of State, Address at University of California-Berkeley School of Law: International Law and Stability in Cyberspace (Nov. 10, 2016), https://2009-2017.state.gov/s/l/releases/remarks/264303.htm.

[114] Dan Efrony & Yuval Shany, *A Rule Book on the Shelf? Tallinn Manual 2.0 on Cyber Operations and Subsequent State Practice*, 112 Am. J. Int'l L. 583, 631 (2018).

B. New Treaties

Some of the required revisions to the *jus ad bellum* and *jus in bello* could be achieved through a new treaty. Indeed, Itamar Mann and I have argued that it may be possible for states to agree on a limited treaty addressing basic definitions and boundaries in cyberwarfare.[115] However, given recent global developments, especially the recent collapse of the UN Group of Governmental Experts process, reaching an agreement on these issues in written form may prove challenging.[116]

Michael Schmitt observed: "A new treaty governing cyberspace appears unlikely, at least on a global scale."[117] In a similar vein, during the Open-Ended Working Group session in February 2020, the Australian representative said: "A legally binding instrument in this space would take years to negotiate. It would likely end up with the lowest common denominator result and offer less protection than we currently have with the existing framework."[118]

At this point, it seems unlikely that states will come together any time soon to negotiate a multilateral treaty addressing cyber operations and cyberspace. There are, however, less formal and less binding multilateral processes that may have more promise as compared to a new treaty.

C. New Interpretations

A more promising way to achieve a consensus on how international law applies to cyber operations is through a reinterpretation of existing treaties and customary international law.

In recent years, the UN Group of Governmental Experts (UN GGE) process has shown some promise on achieving such consensus. However, the collapse of the UN GGE process in 2017 reflected major disagreements between the United States, Russia, China, Cuba, and other nations on issues

[115] Ido Kilovaty & Itamar Mann, *Towards a Cyber-Security Treaty*, JUST SECURITY (Aug. 3, 2016), https://www.justsecurity.org/32268/cyber-security-treaty/.

[116] *The Year in Review: The Death of the UN GGE Process?*, COUNCIL ON FOR. REL. (Dec. 21, 2017), https://www.cfr.org/blog/year-review-death-un-gge-process.

[117] Schmitt, *supra* note 111, at 35.

[118] UNITED NATIONS, UN WEB TV, "OPEN-ENDED WORKING GROUP ON DEVELOPMENTS IN THE FIELD OF INFORMATION AND TELECOMMUNICATIONS IN THE CONTEXT OF INTERNATIONAL SECURITY, SECOND SUBSTANTIVE SESSION," Feb. 10–14, 2020 (quoted in Schmitt, *supra* note 111, at 35).

such as how the right of self-defense applies in cyberspace, as well as the law of countermeasures in response to cyber operations.[119]

Another process, the UN Open-Ended Working Group, released its final report in March 2021, where it concluded that "States reaffirmed that international law, and in particular the Charter of the United Nations"[120] applies to cyber operations. However, the final report ended short of making any specific interpretations or normative recommendations. It observed that "States also concluded that further common understandings need to be developed on how international law applies to State use of ICTs."[121]

Both the UN GGE and Open-Ended Working Group demonstrate that reaching a common understanding of how to apply international law to cyber operations is difficult. States seem unlikely to reach any consensus, whether formal or informal, on how international law applies to cyber operations.

D. Norms Created by Private Tech Corporations

As traditional forms of international lawmaking have not proven to be promising in the context of cyberwarfare, private tech companies have taken it upon themselves to fill the gap.

In 2017, Brad Smith, president and chief legal officer of Microsoft, gave a speech at the United Nations in Geneva, in which he called for the creation of a Digital Geneva Convention to address current gaps with regard to cyber operations and international law.[122] According to Smith, there are considerable gaps with regard to the protection of civilians from harmful cyber operations. To demonstrate these gaps, Smith provided the recent example of the WannaCry ransomware attack,[123] which affected as many as two hundred thousand computers in one hundred fifty nations around the world.[124] This was not a military-to-military kind of cyberattack but

[119] *See Year in Review*, *supra* note 116.

[120] Open-ended Working Grp. on Dev. in the field of Info. & Telecomm. in the context of Int'l Sec., Final Substantive Report, U.N. Doc. A/AC.290/2021/CRP.2 (2021).

[121] *Id.*

[122] *Brad Smith Takes His Call for a Digital Geneva Convention to the United Nations*, Microsoft (Nov. 9, 2017), https://blogs.microsoft.com/on-the-issues/2017/11/09/brad-smith-takes-call-digital-geneva-convention-united-nations/.

[123] Nicole Perlroth & David E. Sanger, *Hackers Hit Dozens of Countries Exploiting Stolen N.S.A. Tool*, N.Y. Times, May 12, 2017.

[124] Elizabeth Piper, *Cyber Attack Hits 200,000 in at Least 150 Countries: Europol*, Reuters, May 14, 2017.

rather an indiscriminate ransomware worm that infected any computer it touched.[125] Most notably, as many as seventy thousand computers belonging to the United Kingdom's National Health Service hospital network were severely affected.[126]

Since Smith gave his speech at the United Nations, there have been some developments involving efforts by the private tech sector to provide an alternative to the dysfunctional international lawmaking landscape. One example is the Cybersecurity Tech Accord, a public commitment of sixty global tech companies to "protect and empower our users and customers, and thereby to improve the security, stability, and resilience of cyberspace."[127]

A more recent development is the establishment of the CyberPeace Institute in late 2019.[128] The CyberPeace Institute involves both for-profit and nonprofit entities within an organization that seeks to protect civilians from cyber attacks, assist in accountability, and advance soft law norms for responsible behavior in cyberspace.[129]

These developments may either supplement existing legal frameworks for cyber operations or motivate states to take over and be more transparent about their offensive and defensive activities in cyberspace in a manner that would support the creation of new customary international law or adoption of a new treaty or new interpretations of existing treaties. However, these private initiatives are not in any way formal international lawmaking as the idea is currently understood and therefore cannot serve as an adequate substitute for it.

VI. Conclusion

Cyber operations primarily cause nonkinetic effects, and the *jus ad bellum* and *jus in bello* are not fully adapted to this reality. International law, therefore, needs a revolution in how it conceptualizes the broader idea of

[125] White House, Office of the Press Secretary Press Briefing on the Attribution of the WannaCry Malware Attack to North Korea (Dec. 19, 2017), https://www.whitehouse.gov/briefings-statements/press-briefing-on-the-attribution-of-the-wannacry-malware-attack-to-north-korea-121917 ("In May of this year, a dangerous cyberattack known as WannaCry spread rapidly and indiscriminately across the world.").

[126] Sarah Neville, *NHS Systems to Be Strengthened after Cyber Attack*, FIN. TIMES, July 12, 2017.

[127] *See* Cybersecurity Tech Accord, https://cybertechaccord.org/accord/ (last visited June 1, 2021).

[128] *See* CyberPeace Institute, *Who We Are*, https://cyberpeaceinstitute.org/who-we-are (last visited June 1, 2021).

[129] *Id.*

cyberwar. A lawless cyberspace is a very real danger that may become a reality if existing outdated law is eroded and no other law takes its place. This chapter argues that nonkinetic cyber operations are harmful, and in some cases may be devastating to the point that the law of war needs to seek ways to deter and regulate them, in the same way that it deters the use of force or attacks against civilians during an armed conflict. This gap requires that we rethink broader concepts of *force*, *armed attack*, and *violence* to capture the novel nature of nonkinetic cyber operations capable of destroying, altering, and manipulating valuable data, and disrupting critical infrastructure. There are, however, numerous challenges and opportunities that may both hinder and support such development in the future, and it is important to be mindful of these challenges as states become both attackers and victims in this battlefield.

PART THREE

INTERNATIONAL ECONOMIC LAW AND INSTITUTIONS

9

The Experimental Evolution of Trade Law

Kathleen Claussen[1]

I. Introduction

International trade law, more than many other areas of international law, has been characterized by its institutional experimentation. Each trade-law period's institutional design has sought to respond to decisive moments—whether geopolitical, commercial, or otherwise. The present moment may be another such critical juncture as the "trade rule of law" that has dominated trade law and policy since the 1990s has come under challenge.

As detailed elsewhere in this volume,[2] free trade advocates heralded the success since the 1990s of the so-called establishment narrative.[3] Although not without controversy,[4] the commitment of states to a free trade system embodied in a dense web of rules with a dispute settlement system at the World Trade Organization (WTO) was the first of its kind.[5] In the early 2000s, commentators from the Global North viewed this system as working to the benefit of both rich and poor states.[6] The future of this robust institutional structure for the maintenance of global economic stability now hangs in doubt, however. An increasingly complex institutional design governs

[1] The author thanks James Gathi, Sergio Puig, Wayne Sandholtz, Richard Steinberg, and the other contributors to the volume for their helpful comments on earlier drafts. Thanks in particular to David Sloss for the invitation to contribute to the volume and for his detailed feedback on this chapter.

[2] *See* Richard H. Steinberg, *The Rise and Decline of a Liberal International Order* (Chapter 1 in this volume).

[3] Nicolas Lamp, *How Should We Think about the Winners and Losers from Globalization? Three Narratives and Their Implications for the Redesign of International Economic Agreements*, 30 Eur. J. Int'l L. 1359 (2019).

[4] *Id.*; *see also* Simon Lester, *Three (Or More) Narratives about Globalization's Winners and Losers*, Int'l Econ. L. & Pol'y Blog (Dec. 12, 2018), https://ielp.worldtradelaw.net/2018/12/three-or-more-narratives-about-globalization.html.

[5] *See generally* Kathleen Claussen, *The Other Trade War*, 103 Minn. L Rev. Headnotes 1 (2018).

[6] *See, e.g.*, Jennifer Hillman, *An Emerging International Rule of Law?—The WTO Dispute Settlement System's Role in its Evolution*, 42 Ottawa L. Rev. 269 (2011); Pascal Lamy, *The Place of the WTO and Its Law in the International Legal Order*, 17 Eur. J. Int'l L. 969 (2007).

Kathleen Claussen, *The Experimental Evolution of Trade Law* In: *Is the International Legal Order Unraveling?*. Edited by: David L. Sloss, Oxford University Press. © Oxford University Press 2022.
DOI: 10.1093/oso/9780197652800.003.0010

what we think of as trade, and not all of that design continues to receive support from the most important players.

What was once considered a successful trade rule of law characterized by the legalization and judicialization of trade rules has been overshadowed by the use of unilateral exercises of power, in spite of that framework. The United States and China have engaged for more than two years in what some have called a "trade war," with collateral damage and direct effect on other advanced and developing economies.[7] Various manifestations of that trade war appear to some to be incompatible with a rule of law approach.[8] And yet, none of the players in the war has fully abandoned the 1990s' trade rule of law. Rather, the present moment is one that challenges the old design and seeks to drive an alternative with some new rules and different structures.[9] As we do not yet know what that future may hold, it is difficult to evaluate the prospects of experiments yet to come. In fact, our terms of assessment may be miscalibrated, conditioned by the establishment view for the last three decades.

This chapter works through this complicated moment by unpacking the once-dominant trade law narrative, grievances that have arisen under it, and prospects for the future. This survey reinforces the chapter's central claims: that trade law and its institutions continue to evolve and that experimentation in trade law has not reached its end. Economic law and policy—part national and part international in our globalized world—is in a constant state of flux, with immensely complicated drivers of change, seen and unseen. I present three broad areas where trade law remains unsettled: in the relationship between domestic and international tools; in the place and space for wealth redistribution; and in the shape of an institutional framework that can itself be flexible and responsive as new issues arise.

Section II of this chapter examines the establishment view of the trade rule of law and how it has come under challenge. What some see as a "fraying" of an ideal structure for managing trade law and policy, I identify as another

[7] Chad P. Bown & Melina Kolb, *Trump's Trade War Timeline: An Up-to-Date Guide*, PETERSON INST. FOR INT'L ECON. (Feb. 8, 2021), https://www.piie.com/blogs/trade-investment-policy-watch/trump-trade-war-china-date-guide.

[8] *See, e.g.*, *Factbox: Winners and Losers in Trump's Trade War with China*, REUTERS, June 19, 2019.

[9] Hearing to consider the nomination of Katherine C. Tai, of the District of Columbia, to be United States Trade Representative, with the rank of Ambassador Extraordinary and Plenipotentiary Before the S. Fin. Comm., 117th Cong. (2021) (statement of Katherine Tai, Ambassador-designate), https://www.finance.senate.gov/hearings/hearing-to-consider-the-nomination-of-katherine-c-tai-of-the-district-of-columbia-to-be-united-states-trade-representative-with-the-rank-of-ambassador-extraordinary-and-plenipotentiary (commenting on the need for new rules).

turn in trade law's experimentation. Section III analyzes four institutional challenges that arise from this turn, although there are others. It considers the work of the WTO dispute settlement system, the WTO's other institutional features, the invocation of national security as a justification to depart from the establishment approach, and trade agreements. Section IV looks to the future, imagining the possibilities for institutional change and a new conception of the trade rule of law going forward.

II. The Trade Rule of Law and Its Present Challenges

I begin this story with what has been seen as the "establishment view" since the 1990s: the view that all countries gain from free trade in the aggregate, despite that there are winners and losers.[10] For more than two decades now, the entrenchment of a rule of law system in trade governance has facilitated market liberalization and orderly resolution of economic and regulatory conflicts.[11] A liberal and multilateral narrative undergirded by a theory of comparative advantage and justified by the idea that such a system would "raise all boats" led to the expansion, additional codification, and judicialization of rules constraining state authority in international trade.[12] While the General Agreement on Tariffs and Trade (GATT) had been in place for half a century, those rules had not previously been subject to a robust enforcement and compliance regime.[13]

The centerpiece of the establishment view is the WTO and its dispute settlement system: a commitment by members to abide by the rules and to allow panels to adjudicate disputes between or among them. Commentators praised the system for allowing states to prioritize cooperative solutions over unilateral action.[14] Since its inception in 1995, WTO members have brought more than five hundred disputes to the WTO dispute settlement mechanism.[15] Many considered the trade law system a model for successful global governance. According to James Bacchus, "the GATT-based trading system

[10] Lamp, *supra* note 3.

[11] *See, e.g.*, Andrea Durkin, *Rule of Law Is the Bedrock of Trade Agreements*, HINRICH FOUND. (Jan. 24, 2020), https://www.hinrichfoundation.com/research/tradevistas/sustainable/rule-of-law-trade/.

[12] *See, e.g.*, Harlan G. Cohen, *What Is International Trade Law For?*, 113 AM. J. INT'L L. 326 (2019).

[13] *See* Kathleen Claussen, *Old Wine in New Bottles? The Trade Rule of Law*, 44 YALE J. INT'L L. ONLINE 61, 61–62 (2019) (introducing the "trade rule of law" idea).

[14] *See* Hillman, *supra* note 6.

[15] World Trade Organization, *Chronological List of Disputes Cases*, https://www.wto.org/english/tratop_e/dispu_e/dispu_status_e.htm (last visited June 3, 2021).

has been establishing the international rule of law in international trade, rule by rule, and case by case."[16]

Like other rule of law concepts, the trade rule of law has been prized at both the international and domestic levels because it involves a system of rules that restrict the arbitrary exercise of government power, preserve formal equality among states, and provide an effective dispute resolution mechanism. The trade rule of law prioritizes principles of procedural fairness, transparency, understandability, consistency, effective enforcement, and congruence in administration. Central to the trade institutions created during the 1990s are stability and predictability.

Support for these dominant principles has not been uniform, however. Initially, pushback from civil society threatened the sustainability of the WTO institutions, as exemplified by the "Battle of Seattle" protests at the 1999 WTO ministerial. Alternative voices have demanded greater attention to growing economic inequality within the developed world, the promotion of labor law and human rights protections in regional trade agreements, and the prioritization of environmental concerns, among other impacts.[17] These voices have grown louder as the purview of trade law has expanded.[18] Opponents of such wide-ranging expansion of trade law's scope have argued that economic growth should not be prioritized over distributional concerns without a broader conversation about impact and principles.[19] And while these questions about winners and losers have strengthened, the global economy has changed, with the growth of complex global value chains and the increased importance of digital trade. Capital has also become more mobile. More players entered the rule-making conversation, most notably China.

As a consequence of these trends, the consensus around the liberal and judicialized trade rule of law has begun to unravel. That fraying in turn has created a challenge to the normative foundation underlying the trade rule of law institutions. Governments and scholars have begun to reconsider precisely what values should guide a twenty-first-century trade rule of law,

[16] James Bacchus, *Groping Toward Grotius: The WTO and the International Rule of Law*, 44 HARV. INT'L L.J. 533, 539 (2003); *see also id.* at 542 (describing the compulsory jurisdiction and enforcement power of the WTO dispute settlement system).

[17] Lamp, supra note 3 (comparing the critical narrative and the "Trump narrative"); James T. Gathii & Sergio Puig, *The West and the Unraveling of the Economic World Order: Thoughts from a Global South Perspective* (Chapter 2 in this volume).

[18] *See* Kathleen Claussen, *Our Trade Law System*, 73 VAND. L. REV. 151 (2020).

[19] *See* Lamp, *supra* note 3.

raising questions about what trade law is for and who participates in the construction and interpretation of trade law.[20]

In recent years, norms about the appropriate trade rules have been upended. Other priorities have grown in popularity: those that emphasize protectionism, sometimes on the basis of national security and with populist overtones. The 2016 election of Donald Trump in the United States precipitated much greater emphasis on these alternatives as viable policy tools for the United States, beyond their more limited use during the early 2000s by the George W. Bush administration. In 2017, the United States withdrew from the Trans-Pacific Partnership Agreement and adopted a more strident tone, criticizing the WTO's faults.[21] Leadership within the Trump administration emphasized the importance of bringing home to the United States the decision-making authority regarding trade rules.[22] That position—that bureaucrats in Geneva ought not to decide trade disputes—was not new, but for the first time since 1995 it was the view of those leading the US government. Invocations of "fair trade" rather than "free trade," and an emphasis on American jobs have dominated the conversation in the United States since 2016, and contributed to the popularity of the Trump administration's rhetoric on questions of international trade. These changing narratives, themselves with competing and overlapping drivers, are now at the center of debates about the future of trade law institutions and the future of a trade rule of law.

Economic demonization rhetoric in the United States has also fueled advocacy for alternative approaches. As concerns about terrorism receded, attention refocused attention on China and its rise. Early in its tenure, the Trump administration began an investigation into China's trade practices related to intellectual property.[23] Unwilling to rely upon the WTO to control China's trade policies as the Obama administration had largely sought to do, the Trump administration turned to tariffs to provide leverage for a bilateral deal that would effectuate the changes it believed necessary to make sure that China was "playing by the

[20] Cohen, *supra* note 12; Gregory Shaffer, *Retooling Trade Agreements for Social Inclusion*, 2019 U. Ill. L. Rev. 1 (2019); Frank Garcia & Tim Meyer, *Restoring Trade's Social Contract*, 116 Mich. L. Rev. Online 78 (2017).

[21] *See infra* section III.

[22] *See, e.g.*, Chad Bown & Soumaya Keynes, *Trade Policy Under Trump: Interview with Stephen Vaughn*, Trade Talks Podcast (Nov. 25, 2019), https://www.tradetalkspodcast.com/podcast/93-us-trade-policy-before-trump-with-ambassador-michael-froman/.

[23] Office of the U.S. Trade Representative, Initiation of Section 301 Investigation, 82 Fed. Reg. 40213 (Aug. 24, 2017).

rules."[24] This new narrative embraced the existing rules, at least rhetorically, but rejected the institutions through which those rules were agreed to be enforced. No longer did the United States find the WTO a sufficient or desirable institution for resolving trade differences.

Many traditional US allies criticized the Trump administration's approach on China, which also had collateral effects on those allies. Some allies retaliated after the United States imposed supplemental tariffs on steel and aluminum.[25] Several countries invoked WTO rules, claimed that the United States was violating those rules, and then initiated dispute settlement proceedings at the WTO. Some also imposed retaliatory tariffs on products from the United States, prompting the United States to launch WTO proceedings against those members for those actions. To a neutral and casual observer, it may have appeared that the rules had lost their efficacy if they were unable to contain this type of tit-for-tat battle of retaliatory tariffs. By 2018, the system appeared on the verge of unraveling entirely.

Thus far in this retelling, the tale of an unraveling consensus is a story about one superpower that took issue with another with considerable fallout for US allies. It was a power struggle in the fraying of the establishment consensus, but that consensus suffered from other flaws that have further contributed to the fraying. There were signs of strain within the system before Donald Trump became president, calling into question the idea of a trade rule of law in at least four respects: first, with respect to its liberal foundations; second, as to its principal actors; third, as to its intended or actual effects; and fourth, with respect to its misaligned incentives.

For several years, commentators have pushed back against the establishment view. As Harlan Cohen has written, the "raise all boats" or "grow the pie" idea has moved to the periphery, with other stories filling the gap.[26] Those stories largely reflect problems in wealth distribution, as Tim Meyer has noted, and the disconnect between the free trade agenda and other

[24] *See, e.g.*, Peter Morici, *The West Has Got to Make China Play by the Rules*, MARKETWATCH (July 1, 2020), https://www.marketwatch.com/story/the-west-has-got-to-make-china-play-by-the-rules-11593550533. *But see* Simon Lester, *Why Did Donald Trump's Trade War on China Fail?*, CATO INST. COMMENTARY (Jan. 25, 2021), https://www.cato.org/commentary/why-did-donald-trumps-trade-war-china-fail.

[25] *See* Kathleen Claussen, *Trade War Battles: The International Front*, LAWFARE (July 27, 2018), https://www.lawfareblog.com/trade-war-battles-international-front#:~:text=Trade%20War%20Battles%3A%20The%20International%20Front.%20A%20surprise,initial%20outlook%20for%20Juncker%E2%80%99s%20visit%20was%20not%20good (listing several dispute settlement requests brought by US trading partners at the WTO).

[26] *See* Cohen, *supra* note 12; Steinberg, Chapter 1 (distinguishing between liberalism and hyperliberalism).

agendas that are now considered part of trade.[27] Nowhere does the establishment trade rule of law expressly accommodate the values of distribution or development, although those values may have seemed implied or the natural extension of such a system. Other institutions at either the domestic or international level were tasked with the problems of development and distribution, creating various misalignments in the public view and in the law.[28] Greg Shaffer refers to this framework as a "two-step": achieve growth at the international level and then leave it to domestic political systems to manage the redistribution.[29] Moreover, as trade expanded and trade agreements since the 1990s put increased emphasis on labor, environment, and sustainable development, the distributional causes and effects became still more shrouded. The establishment prioritization of growing the pie was just one of several competing interests, as the scope of trade law expanded to encompass additional regulatory areas, such as environmental regulation and intellectual property.

As trade law's reach has expanded, the major themes of the establishment trade rule of law have declined in importance in favor of the accommodation of these new narratives and their guiding principles. Some of those principles prioritize domestic industry, while some are more populist in nature, to name just two among many.[30] What distinguishes them are their different visions for the purpose and elements of a trade rule of law system.

Central to this multidimensional conversation is the establishment narrative's inflexibility and inability to address these other voices. Although trade law and institutions have evolved over time, a crisis of responsiveness to these growing concerns inhibited the establishment from successfully incorporating or addressing them. The result has been a clash of ideas over how to handle the establishment's redistributive failures; how to handle increased reliance on a dispute settlement mechanism that was unanticipated and unintended; how to handle changes in the global economy, such as the growth of China; and how to handle changes in technology, among others. The rigidity of establishment policies and an inability to recognize the discontent has created an appearance that these policies cannot accommodate other issues to the satisfaction of the biggest players. The failure to conclude new

[27] *See* Timothy Meyer, *Misaligned Lawmaking*, 73 Vand. L. Rev. 151 (2020).
[28] *Id.*
[29] Shaffer, *supra* note 20, at 3 (laying out the two-step).
[30] Nicolas Lamp and Anthea Roberts helpfully lay out the distinctions among these rationales in their forthcoming book (manuscript on file with author). For example, they equate protectionism with economic motivations and populism with sovereigntist dimensions.

rules, such as through the Doha Development Agenda, is just one example. As Cohen suggests, continued multilateralism may become more difficult, not only by dispersing power more broadly and thereby decreasing the value of issue linkages but also by raising the value and costs of cooperation in ways that encourage both exit (to avoid costs) and free-riding (to retain value).[31] The difficulty of maintaining a multilateral trade rule of law is exacerbated by the vast differences in the political and economic structures of the most important actors. These challenges and divergent views play out in the "establishment" institutions to which the next section turns.

III. Institutional Challenges

Although, as noted previously, the challenges facing the preexisting trade rule of law are manifestations of deeper challenges to principles, the institutions supporting the establishment view have been the main locus of contestation. The multilateral rules and institutions of international trade were intended to reduce the likelihood of trade wars by ensuring the values of the trade rule of law, such as predictability, transparency, cooperation, and dispute settlement. However, as support for those ideals among governments has shifted, the institutions and the rules unsurprisingly have come under fire.[32] This section lays out the institutional difficulties the trade law system faces at the start of 2021 as a result of dissatisfaction with the establishment trade rule of law.

A. The WTO Appellate Body

At the center of the pushback on WTO reform is a debate over its dispute settlement function and the way in which dispute settlement has occurred. Once termed the "crown jewel" of the WTO, the dispute settlement mechanism seems to have lost its shine, at least to some. Elsewhere, I have referred to this as "the other trade war" to distinguish it from the tariff battle in light of the legal and conversational battles through which this debate has played out.[33] The principal focus of the debate is the appropriate role of the WTO Appellate Body (AB).

[31] Harlan Cohen, *Multilateralism's Life Cycle*, 112 AM. J. INT'L L. 47 (2018).
[32] *See* Andrew T. Guzman, *Global Governance and the WTO*, 45 HARV. INT'L L.J. 303 (2004).
[33] Claussen, *supra* note 5, at 2. I draw from that essay in this section.

The system that predated the WTO under the GATT was widely considered to suffer from a number of weaknesses, especially in the area of dispute settlement.[34] The establishment of the WTO in 1995 heralded a new chapter with the creation of an appellate review mechanism to correct serious legal errors or fundamental flaws in panel reports.[35] The European Union and the United States were the primary advocates of such a mechanism, although neither intended to create "a strong international court."[36] Rather, the AB was "an inspired afterthought" in the negotiations.[37] The AB is a standing body of seven persons, three of whom serve on any one dispute.[38] Those seven persons are appointed by consensus of all WTO members; thus, a single member can block an appointment of one of the adjudicators by refusing to join the consensus.[39] AB members serve four-year terms with the possibility of being reappointed once, again by consensus.[40]

In the first two decades of the WTO, the AB rose in prominence and solidified its control over the regime governing international trade.[41] Many WTO members and commentators have expressed strong support for the AB's work.[42] Yet, despite praise and its increased use, certain WTO members, especially the United States, have voiced concerns about the AB regarding both the substance of its decision-making and the procedures it has applied. The United States commented as early as February 2001 that the AB had "arrogated to [itself] the right to censure particular Members for any reason" and that, in another case, "the Appellate Body's findings . . . verged on an interpretation of a WTO agreement, even though such interpretations could be made only by Members. . . . This was a new obligation, not found in the WTO

[34] *See What's Needed for the GATT After the Uruguay Round?*, 86 ASIL Proc. 69, 69–71 (1992). *See also* Gregory Shaffer, Manfred Elsig, & Sergio Puig, *The Extensive (But Fragile) Authority of the WTO Appellate Body*, 79 L. & Contemp. Prob. 237–73 (2016) (explaining the evolution of the AB and its distinction compared to the prior system).

[35] The GATT Uruguay Round: A Negotiating History, 1986–1992, at 2767–68 (Terrance P. Stewart ed., 1993).

[36] Peter Van den Bossche, *From Afterthought to Centerpiece: The WTO Appellate Body and Its Rise to Prominence in the World Trading System*, *in* The WTO at Ten: The Contribution of the Dispute Settlement System 286, 294 (G. Sacerdoti et al. eds., 2006).

[37] Van den Bossche, *supra* note 36, at 293.

[38] Understanding on Rules and Procedures Governing the Settlement of Disputes, art. 17.1, Apr. 15, 1994, Marrakesh Agreement Establishing the World Trade Organization, Annex 2, 1869 U.N.T.S. 401.

[39] *Id.*, arts. 2.4, 17.2.

[40] *Id.*, art. 17.2.

[41] *See, e.g.*, Robert Howse, *The World Trade Organization 20 Years On: Global Governance by Judiciary*, 27 Eur. J. Int'l L. 9 (2016); Andrew Lang, *The Judicial Sensibility of the WTO Appellate Body*, 27 Eur. J. Int'l L. 1095 (2016).

[42] *See* Richard H. Steinberg, *Judicial Lawmaking at the WTO: Discursive, Constitutional, and Political Constraints*, 98 Am. J. Int'l L. 247 (2004).

Agreements."[43] Similar comments have also been made over the years by Mexico, Pakistan, Malaysia, Chile, and Argentina, among others.[44] Members also have expressed concern that the AB has commented on issues not raised in the dispute, not essential to the dispute's resolution, or not within the dispute's terms of reference.[45]

In August 2018, the United States announced that it would block all appointments and reappointments to the AB until its concerns about "persistent overreaching" by the AB were addressed.[46] Eventually, this refusal to appoint new members led to a stoppage of work by the start of 2020.[47] Some WTO members have created an alternative mechanism to substitute for the lack of a functioning AB, but the success of that alternative mechanism remains to be seen.[48]

Reconciling competing views about the AB now appears essential to resolving the current WTO impasse. Debate over the successes and failures of the WTO's hybrid court/arbitration model has prompted fundamental questions, just as the long-standing concerns about the WTO AB's judicialization are legal and teleological.

B. WTO beyond the AB

The AB "crisis" is not the only WTO-related concern raised by governments and critics. There are other institutional aspects of the WTO's functioning that have precipitated conversations about its importance and significance. Above all, after twenty-five years, the rules embodied in the WTO agreements would benefit from review and update.[49] They are inadequate to cover new trends and developments, particularly in technology. They are not suitable to

[43] Dispute Settlement Body, *Minutes of the Meeting Held in The Centre William Rappard on 19 January 2001*, WTO Doc. WT/DSB/M/97, ¶ 5 (Feb. 27, 2001); Dispute Settlement Body: *Minutes of the Meeting Held in The Centre William Rappard on 16 May 2001*, WTO Doc. WT/DSB/M/105, ¶ 42 (June 19, 2001).

[44] *See* Claussen, *supra* note 5.

[45] Bryce Baschuk, *U.S. Blocks Korean Judge from WTO Appellate Body*, Bloomberg, May 24, 2016.

[46] Dispute Settlement Body, *Minutes of DSB Meeting*, WTO Doc. WT/DSB/M/417, ¶ 12.2. (Aug. 27, 2018).

[47] *See, e.g.*, Robert McDougall, *The Crisis in WTO Dispute Settlement: Fixing Birth Defects to Restore Balance*, 52 J. World Trade 867 (2018); Shaffer, Elsig, & Puig, *supra* note 34.

[48] World Trade Organization, *Statement on a Mechanism for Developing, Documenting and Sharing Practices and Procedures in the Conduct of WTO Disputes—Multi-Party Interim Appeal Arbitration Arrangement Pursuant to Article 25 of the DSU*, WTO Doc. JOB/DSB/1/Add.12. (Apr. 30, 2020).

[49] *See, e.g.*, Roberto Azevedo, *The World Trade Organization Needs an Update*, Int'l Ctr. for Def. & Sec. (Nov. 22, 2019), https://icds.ee/en/the-world-trade-organization-needs-an-update/.

address nonmarket economies, such as China's. Several looming grievances raised by WTO members about the current system relate to China's behavior within the system since it joined in 2001.[50] China's state-directed economic system is difficult to discipline under existing rules and their interpretations by the AB. Some of the issues today deemed insufficiently covered by the rules include: the question of whether government subsidies are appropriate and under what circumstances; state-owned enterprises and how they ought to be treated under the WTO agreements; and digital trade and intellectual property issues not adequately covered by the existing rules, including forced technology transfers.[51] These questions—as they relate to China and more generally—dominate many of the conversations about potential WTO reforms, but so far little agreement has been reached, let alone the consensus required under WTO rules.

Also related to China, but extending beyond its narrow focus, are the issues of transparency and notifications. The WTO establishes a peer monitoring and enforcement system, in which WTO members provide information about their trade policies and practices for review by other members. Unfortunately, a handful of WTO members regularly neglect to provide such information in a timely or comprehensive manner. To date, little recourse has been available for other members negatively affected by such obfuscation. The United States and other members have called for new sanctions on members that fail to meet their transparency obligations.[52]

WTO members have also raised concern in recent years over the flexibility that the WTO rules afford developing countries and the categorization of certain members as developing countries. There is no shared standard as to which members may be considered "developing."[53] Rather, members self-declare. Upon so doing, those members have access to greater latitude and policy space in their domestic rule-making. This self-designation system has led to accusations of abuse and controversy over whether the existing

[50] *See, e.g.*, Off. U.S. Trade Representative, 2020 Report to Congress on China's WTO Compliance (Jan. 2021), https://ustr.gov/sites/default/files/files/reports/2020/2020USTRReportCongressChinaWTOCompliance.pdf.

[51] *Id.*

[52] U.S. Mission to the WTO, Statement delivered by Amb. Dennis C. Shea in the WTO Council for Trade in Goods, *Procedures to Enhance Transparency and Strengthen Notification Requirements Under WTO Agreements* (Apr. 11, 2019), https://geneva.usmission.gov/2019/04/12/procedures-to-enhance-transparency-and-strengthen-notification-requirements-under-wto-agreements/.

[53] U.S. Mission to the WTO, Statement delivered by Amb. Dennis C. Shea in the WTO General Council Meeting, *Procedures to Strengthen the Negotiating Function of the WTO* (Dec. 9, 2019), https://geneva.usmission.gov/2019/12/09/ambassador-shea-procedures-to-strengthen-the-negotiating-function-of-the-wto/.

system is appropriate. Some members have advocated the development of benchmarks to be imposed that would restrict such self-designation where certain thresholds in economic strength are met.[54]

C. National Security

Between 2015 and 2020, more states have also invoked and relied upon national security arguments as a justification for the implementation of policies contrary to the spirit, if not the letter, of the international instruments underpinning the trade rule of law. Many of these references to national security have to do with concerns about technology as a means of collecting personal information, or information about commercial secrets and innovations, or information about the government. For example, the United States has raised concerns about the national security threat posed by Chinese technology firms like Huawei, although China says those concerns are unfounded.[55] Other references to national security appear to mask concerns about job loss and globalization moving industrial manufacturing to cheaper labor markets.[56] Still others involve physical threats to borders and claims to interference with state sovereignty.[57] The security-driven conversation in trade has created significant tension between what appear to be two competing paradigms, each demanding full policy space.[58] The first prioritizes liberalization while the second prioritizes protectionist policy with a security justification.

The rhetoric on national security has led to institutional challenges at the domestic and international levels. At the domestic level, governments have used national security rhetoric to justify policy choices that conflict with the liberal understanding of the trade rule of law. In the United States, for example, the executive branch has used security-based delegations from the legislature to raise tariffs, impose export controls, and prevent foreign direct

[54] *Id.*

[55] *See, e.g.*, Arjun Kharpal, *China's Huawei and ZTE Officially Designated "National Security Threats" by the FCC*, CNBC, June 30, 2020.

[56] *Economic Security as National Security: A Discussion with Dr. Peter Navarro*, Ctr. for Strategic & Int'l Stud. (Nov. 13, 2018), https://www.csis.org/analysis/economic-security-national-security-discussion-dr-peter-navarro.

[57] Panel Report, *Russia—Measures Concerning Traffic in Transit*, WTO Doc. WT/DS512/R (adopted Apr. 5, 2019).

[58] *See, e.g.*, Harlan Grant Cohen, *Nations and Markets*, 23 J. Int'l Econ. L. 793 (2020); Kathleen Claussen, *Trade's Security Exceptionalism*, 72 Stan. L Rev. 1029 (2020).

investment, among other activities.[59] The United States has justified using these tools, as detailed further in section IV, referring to exceptions recognized in the WTO agreements. The GATT contains a national security exception permitting states to depart from their commitments when their security interests so require.[60] Until recently, that exception was almost never invoked at the WTO. Rarely used and even more rarely litigated, the national security exception has recently become a topic of increased tension among member states; at least three members have relied upon it in disputes to justify or excuse actions that would otherwise violate WTO rules.[61]

Apart from criticisms of the legitimacy of these actors relying on the national security exception, there is also widespread recognition that the GATT national security exception, drafted in the 1940s, does not clearly accommodate twenty-first-century threats, such as cybersecurity threats. The characterization of these debates and possible futures falls beyond the scope of this chapter. Suffice it to say that the national security debates inside and outside the WTO have threatened to upend its previously heralded stability, just as the other institutional challenges highlighted previously have done. Exceptionalizing security within trade or vice versa is not sustainable.[62] If anything, the national security invocations are perhaps the most potentially damaging to the stability of the system, should they be relied upon widely, especially after the pandemic and global recession of 2020.[63]

D. Trade Agreements and Their Alternatives

The shifting winds in the support for the WTO cannot be viewed in a vacuum. Alongside the WTO's changing tides, free trade agreements (FTAs) have continued to multiply, as have other forms of trade agreements. FTAs, also commonly referred to as regional trade agreements, given that they often have been regional in scope, have increased in number and reach since

[59] *See generally* Claussen, *supra* note 58.

[60] *See* General Agreement on Tariffs and Trade, art. XXI, Oct. 30, 1947, 55 U.N.T.S. 187, 266.

[61] *See, e.g.*, Panel Report, *Saudi Arabia—Measures concerning the Protection of Intellectual Property Rights*, WTO Doc. WT/DS567/R (under appeal as of July 28, 2020); *Russia—Traffic in Transit*, *supra* note 57.

[62] *See generally* Claussen, *supra* note 58; Cohen, *supra* note 58.

[63] Julian Arato, Kathleen Claussen, & J. Benton Heath, *The Perils of Pandemic Exceptionalism*, 114 Am. J. Int'l L. 624 (2020) (warning about the dangers of overreliance on exceptions, including national security and public health exceptions in trade law).

the 1990s.[64] FTAs provide reciprocal benefits between two or more partners. As of September 2020, according to the WTO, 306 FTAs were in force.[65] As late as 1995, that number was only a few dozen.[66]

Views on FTAs are mixed. On the one hand, FTAs promote liberalization; on the other, FTAs can diminish the importance of globalism. Undoubtedly, however, FTAs have grown in popularity and continue to be institutional tools of choice for many economies in their trade policies. FTAs have pushed forward with disciplines that go far beyond the WTO Agreements. Through them, the scope of trade law has expanded and become more integrated and less siloed; as a result, the trade instruments are more like omnibus instruments than ever before. By 2020, trade law encompassed not only traditional border measures such as tariffs but also other legal mechanisms that would not have fallen under the trade umbrella in prior decades. FTAs from around the world, but especially among G20 countries, regularly include enforceable principles related to environment, labor, digital trade, and many more topics that would never succeed as a matter of global, multilateral negotiation. By pushing forward these new topics, FTAs set standards and contribute to norms and expectations as to what trade regulation ought to include and what can be demanded of trading partners.[67]

Other forms of trade agreements deal with commercial issues, but do not seek to reduce tariff barriers to zero. These often shorter agreements, some of which may be inconsistent with WTO rules, typically cover single sectors on a bilateral basis. Since the 1990s, the increase in bilateral trade agreements of this type has signaled an alternative approach to conducting trade business.[68] Within the globalized economy, states are regulating their foreign commerce through these alternative means, with agreements such as these covering issues as diverse as tariffs, intellectual property, digital trade, distilled spirits, national security, automobiles, rules of origin, and regulatory barriers in agriculture.[69]

64 *See, e.g.*, Claudia Hofmann, Alberto Osnago, & Michele Ruta, *The Content of Preferential Trade Agreements*, 34 World Trade Rev. 1 (2017); Henrik Horn, Petros C. Mavroidis, & André Sapir, *Beyond the WTO? An Anatomy of EU and US Preferential Trade Agreements*, 33 World Econ. 1565 (2010).

65 World Trade Organization, *Regional Trade Agreements*, https://www.wto.org/english/tratop_e/region_e/region_e.htm (last visited June 3, 2021).

66 *Id.*

67 *See* Dani Rodrik, *What Do Trade Agreements Really Do?*, 32 J. Econ. Persp. 73, 82–88 (2018).

68 *See* Kathleen Claussen, *Trade Executive Agreements* (work in progress, on file with author).

69 *Id.*

IV. Reform or Reconciliation?

With the WTO's future under consideration and the politics on trade changing, certain governments, most notably the United States, have turned their attention to alternative—and critics would say illegal under the present rule structure—tools for achieving trade policy aims. This section surveys those alternatives and analyzes their place in a forward-looking regime. The future is uncertain, but for trade there is at least a reasonably clear menu of possible futures with different push and pull factors.[70] Finally, this section concludes with comments on new directions informed by these challenges and their responses.[71] My goal is not to promote specific outcomes or policy tools, especially given the immense uncertainty of the present moment, but rather to survey possible future directions. Given trade law's history of experimentation, I expect that experimentation to continue as the underlying political priorities continue to evolve.

A. Old Tools with New Uses

The use of unilateral tools, particularly by the Trump administration, has reinvigorated debates about the appropriate use of those tools. For example, in March 2018 the United States first imposed tariffs on steel and aluminum from around the world, citing the threat those imports caused to US national security. US trading partners and commentators quickly rejected the administration's position as a thinly veiled pretext for protectionist intervention on behalf of US manufacturing, exacerbated by inconsistent messaging from various parts of the executive.[72] The widespread rejoinder that the United States was acting unlawfully according to both domestic and international law led to litigation at the WTO, with governments around the world imposing retaliatory tariffs on products from the United States.

[70] *Cf.* Tom Ginsburg, *The Future of Liberal Democracy in the International Legal Order* (Chapter 3 in this volume).

[71] *See generally* OISIN SUTTLE, DISTRIBUTIVE JUSTICE AND WORLD TRADE 37–48 (2018) (describing theories).

[72] *See* Damian Paletta, *Top Trump Trade Officials Still at Odds After Profane Shouting Match in Beijing*, WASH. POST, May 16, 2018; Logan Pauley, *Consistent Inconsistency Crippling Trump's China Trade Ambitions*, THE HILL, May 31, 2018, https://thehill.com/opinion/finance/390085-consistent-inconsistency-crippling-trumps-china-trade-ambitions. *See also* Anthony Esposito & David Ljunggren, *Global Auto Powers Plotting Response to Trump Auto Tariff Threats*, REUTERS, July 28, 2018.

In fact, under domestic law, many of the Trump administration's actions were lawful. The administration invoked narrow exceptions to the ordinary domestic liberalization rules. The Trump administration's use of Section 301 of the Trade Act of 1974 to impose tariffs on China suffered also from challenges to its lawfulness. Critics contended that the United States advanced disingenuous and conflicting aims: the tariffs sought to prompt China to open its market to US investors, while the administration sought to maintain production in the United States.[73]

The tools and policy choices that have prompted reconsideration of our trade rule of law are not new. Nevertheless, certain elements make this moment noteworthy. First, the present use of tariffs has emerged against the background of an experimental multilateral system. Second, to the extent that China is the focus of concern and action, China is specially situated. Its state-centric economy presents unique challenges that the prior period's rules and governance mechanisms are not well designed to accommodate. But what makes this moment perhaps most notable is the express acknowledgment by the United States of its intent to reform trade law institutions and its exercise of the leverage to do so. Notwithstanding that the United States has deployed its powerful influence to use tariffs or precipitate reform on dozens of prior occasions, the use of unilateral tools together with its injurious position at the WTO beginning in 2017 is different. Accordingly, this moment—at the start of 2021—is a remarkably unique juncture. It has given rise to organizational questions that governments have yet to address: questions of institutional adequacy, how to manage harm caused by those institutions, and how to handle outliers.

B. Future Institutions

There is little evidence to suggest that trade law's experimentation will abate. Trade law rules and institutions maintain a central role in determining state economic choices and global value chains. Many commentators viewed the US presidential election in November 2020 as a harbinger of times to come. And yet, both Donald Trump and Joe Biden rejected the establishment view, at least to some extent. Thus, the 2020 presidential contest in the United

[73] *See* Off. U.S. Trade Representative, *USTR Updates Section 301 Investigation* (Nov. 20, 2018), https://ustr.gov/about-us/policy-offices/press-office/press-releases/2018/november/ustr-updates-section-301.

States was just one piece of a broader puzzle in navigating the future of trade law and policy. What are the possible futures for the trade rule of law as we have come to know it? That is, what rules-based frame can accommodate today's competing discourses, if any? One can imagine at least four possible futures—which I will call reinvigoration, replacement, retention, or return.

One future may involve the reinvigoration of the WTO system, with continued legalization at the global level. There is widespread agreement that WTO reform is both necessary and beneficial.[74] Still, the United States has rejected all serious proposals for reform, even proposals that are responsive to at least some of its concerns. The United States has continued to call for reforms, while simultaneously criticizing its trading partners' proposed reforms.[75] In December 2018, the United States took the floor at the WTO General Council to make the point that the proposals advanced to modify the existing rules are insufficient because they would require changes to the system.[76] Rather, the United States wishes to see the AB abide by the rules as written. The United States also called for further "discussion" about why the AB "depart[ed]" from the rules in the first place.[77] In August 2020, US Trade Representative Robert Lighthizer set out a short vision for the possible reinvigoration of the WTO, but as of this writing, none of those ideas has gained traction.[78] So far, many WTO members continue to participate actively in the WTO and in the creation of new agreements, even while dispute settlement takes on a role of lesser importance and there is little indication of an appetite for reform.[79] Depending on the course taken by the Biden administration, there could be more or less reinvigoration. If the former, this option would strengthen the establishment trade rule of law to the greatest extent, supporting multilateral institutions over others.

[74] Philip Blenkinsop, *EU Trade Chief Urges U.S. to Join Talks on WTO Reform*, REUTERS, Nov. 27, 2018.

[75] Dennis Shea, U.S. Trade Representative, Remarks at the Center for Strategic and International Studies (Oct. 12, 2018) (transcript available at https://www.c-span.org/video/?452885-1/deputy-us-trade-representative-world-trade-organization).

[76] Brett Fortnam, *Shea: Appellate Body Reform Proposals Fail to Address U.S. Concerns*, INSIDE U.S. TRADE, Dec. 13, 2018, https://insidetrade.com/daily-news/shea-appellate-body-reform-proposals-fail-address-us-concerns.

[77] *Id.*

[78] Robert Lighthizer, *How to Set World Trade Straight*, WALL ST. J., Aug. 28, 2020.

[79] In the President's 2018 Trade Policy Agenda, the administration laid out its view on the importance of strengthening the multilateral system generally. *See* OFF. U.S. TRADE REPRESENTATIVE, THE PRESIDENT'S TRADE POLICY AGENDA 28 (2018), https://ustr.gov/sites/default/files/files/Press/Reports/2018/AR/2018%20Annual%20Report%20I.pdf. But it has repeatedly rejected enhancing or advancing dispute settlement.

A second possibility would involve replacement of the WTO by a set of regional trading blocs or plurilateral arrangements defined less by region and more by ideology.[80] Since 2017, the United States has prioritized bilateral arrangements, and most states that are members of regional trading blocs remain committed to those regional arrangements. Not all such regional arrangements take on forms like the North American Free Trade Agreement or the European Union. China's influence through its Belt and Road Initiative may have even more far-reaching effects. Likewise, the recent conclusion and entry into force of the African Continental Free Trade Area has complemented long-standing subregional arrangements that have facilitated trade among the countries on the continent.[81] Although attempts to connect the Americas, or to connect countries across the Pacific through the Trans-Pacific Partnership, have not achieved the most fulsome reach, they have laid the groundwork for other regional and plurilateral agreements. These agreements may be the main loci of future rule-making, given the inability of WTO members to negotiate agreement on new rules. Likewise, a few smaller agreements at the WTO with limited membership have reached completion and implementation, despite other ongoing controversies.[82] Finally, there may be an increased role under this scenario for power blocs like the G20 and G7, or intergovernmental organizations like the Organisation for Economic Cooperation and Development, even if they do not maintain lawmaking functions. Rather, they may serve a significant leadership role for normative development in the absence of a strong multilateral system. In this way, trade may move closer to finance and some other areas of international economic law.[83] This option envisions the institutional focus at the regional or plurilateral level. It situates the trade rule of law in smaller complementary or competitive architectures. Although likely a second-best to the establishment narrative, this option preserves many of the same normative commitments in at least some parts of the world.

Third, retention of some of the existing multilateral and regional institutions, but without further development of new rules or resolution of

[80] Tom Ginsburg and Richard Steinberg prioritize variations on this option in other terms (Ginsburg's duopoly and Steinberg's spatial and economic fracturing). *See* Ginsburg, *supra* note 70; Steinberg, Chapter 1.

[81] *See* James Gathii, *Introduction to the Symposium on Africa and the Future of International Trade Regimes*, 111 AJIL Unbound 369 (2017).

[82] *See, e.g.*, Agreement on Trade in Civil Aircraft, April 12, 1979, 1186 U.N.T.S. 2 (entered into force Jan. 1, 1980).

[83] *See, e.g.*, Wolfgang Alschner, *Shifting Design Paradigms: Why Tomorrow's International Economic Law May Look More Like the Tax Regime than the WTO*, 114 Am. J. Int'l L. 270 (2020).

the dispute settlement issues highlighted previously, could lead to more of the recent same. If states are unwilling to find compromise in reform efforts, we may see some degree of the status quo, with states selecting among alternative courses of action for disputes. Under this scenario, ongoing trade disputes managed through domestic tools—such as the "trade war" between the United States and China—would become frequent and anticipated features of the institutional landscape. To be sure, the "trade war" vocabulary suffers from several flaws.[84] It exacerbates the perceived dichotomy between unilateral and multilateral action when, in fact, domestic and international tools could be complementary or cooperative. The retention model results in clash rather than collaboration. States maintain their own different interpretations of multilateral rules, which sustains competitiveness among them rather than cooperation. This model tests the bounds of institutional capacity and challenges the authority of existing institutions, thereby weakening the establishment trade rule of law deliberately and collaterally.

Fourth, we could see a return to the pre-WTO era, when international rules were selectively enforced and, consequently, mattered less. Under this fourth scenario, unilateral tools would dominate trade policies. Domestic trade rules would govern the trade rule of law, with states invoking domestic authorities to take trade action or purposively act contrary to international rules. This fourth option is most likely if the United States remains outside the system, rather than a constructive player within it. But it is not only the United States that may reject the alternatives. Other members have experimented with unilateral trade measures or undertaken trade wars, either on their own or as manifestations of other types of disputes.[85] The final outcomes in these disputes may trigger a broader dissatisfaction with the multilateral system and a turn away from binding dispute settlement through that system. Further, given present tensions, the stalled negotiating function of the WTO, with few legislative outcomes or new rules at the multilateral level since its inception, does not bode well for the future of multilateralism.

Of these four options—reinvigoration, replacement, retention, or return—each seems reasonably plausible. There may still be a fifth option that draws from each of these. A reconciliation model may draw on features of each of

[84] Claussen, *supra* note 13, at 63.
[85] *See, e.g.*, Lindsay Maizland, *The Japan-Korea Trade Dispute: What to Know*, Council on Foreign Relations, Aug. 5, 2019, https://www.cfr.org/in-brief/japan-south-korea-trade-dispute-what-know; Panel Report, *Saudi Arabia—Measures Concerning the Protection of Intellectual Property Rights*, WTO Doc. WT/DS567/R (under appeal as of July 28, 2020); Panel Report, *Russia—Measures Concerning Traffic in Transit*, WTO Doc. WT/DS512/R (adopted Apr. 5, 2019).

the preceding models so that no one approach dominates the future of trade law. Since trade law is among the legal regimes that are "too complex to be reduced to a simple choice between unilateralism and multilateralism,"[86] rather than adopt a "lateral" vernacular that emphasizes seemingly competing interests, commentators and participants in the trade law regime ought to adopt language that recognizes the past use, present demonstration, and greater future potential for trade law. According to this reconciliation approach, a better tactic may be to adjust our collective understanding of an appropriate balance of international and domestic trade policy devices. The dominant binary representation inhibits dialogue on constructive rethinking. It should not be surprising to encounter both domestic tools (tariffs, among others) and international tools (such as bringing new dispute settlement proceedings at the WTO[87] or concluding new international instruments[88]) at work in this environment. What is required is a shift in perspective that recasts unilateral tools and multilateral rules as complementary parts of a resilient and adaptive trade law system. A reconciliation model sees international and domestic mechanisms as mutually reinforcing, where international rules cover some but not all the space, leaving some policy choices to domestic or unilateral action.

Retaining the robust use of domestic tools while some states rely on multilateral or plurilateral agreements could constitute a hybrid trade rule of law—one dominated not by the absence of rules but rather a blend of global, regional, and domestic rules. The rules at these three levels are flexible enough to accommodate this hybrid model in which states rely on them even if they act at those rules' margins. This is a different concept of the trade rule of law from the present dominant model. It may be seen by the establishment as weaker, but it actually preserves some of the establishment model's normative foundations through its deferential features.

Central to a reconciliation model is a better accounting of distributive goals. Several scholars have argued persuasively for shifting to a system in which trade law and trade institutions no longer occupy the driver's seat in

[86] José E. Alvarez, *Contemporary International Law: An "Empire of Law" or the "Law of Empire"?*, 24 Am. U. Int'l L. Rev. 811, 815 (2009).

[87] *See, e.g.*, *United States Files WTO Complaint on China's Protection of Intellectual Property Rights*, World Trade Org. (Mar. 26, 2018), https://www.wto.org/english/news_e/news18_e/ds542rfc_26mar18_e.htm.

[88] *See, e.g.*, United States–Mexico–Canada Agreement, Can.-Mex.-U.S., Nov. 30, 2018, Off. U.S. Trade Representative, https://ustr.gov/trade-agreements/free-trade-agreements/united-states-mexico-canada-agreement/agreement-between; *see also* David Shepardson, *Trump Administration Says to Open Trade Talks with EU, UK, Japan*, Reuters, Oct. 16, 2018.

our international and domestic economic policies, and instead move to the passenger seat, allowing for other domestic redistributive policies to take the lead.[89] The global pandemic laid bare how trade and economic policy is dominant in our global institutions, instead of issues related to global health.[90] The result is an overreliance on exceptional authorities to exempt action in favor of public welfare, rather than designing rules to accommodate public welfare goals other than free trade.[91] The fact is that much of our present framework is well entrenched and difficult to undo. Despite the backlash and controversies that dominate the rhetoric and attention of commentators, the basic infrastructure of our system remains.

Evolution and experimentation within our present framework have permitted members to adopt their own pathways and have simultaneously created a rift in their understandings of how the system works, what it is for, what it is capable of, and where it should go. The future path depends on domestic politics, is constrained by the WTO consensus requirement, and is overshadowed by other matters that the current system was not designed to address.

Our trade institutions are resilient and can be adaptive. But the degree and nature of upheaval and reorganization to be expected over the coming decade remains unclear. As additional conversations about a revised trade rule of law framework are underway, they will need to consider rule competition and, perhaps most importantly, the matter of administration and compliance with any shared rules. There is ample space for additional innovation. Trade's legalization is unlikely to fade to nothing.[92] Moreover, the values associated with the trade rule of law that guide our trade law interactions through the institutions described in section III need not be discarded. What remains to be seen is how the international and the domestic can be more cooperative and functional.

[89] *See, e.g.*, Cohen, *supra* note 12.

[90] Jen Patja Howell, *The Lawfare Podcast: Global Trade and Investment in the Coronavirus Era*, May 15, 2020, https://www.lawfareblog.com/lawfare-podcast-global-trade-and-investment-coronavirus-era.

[91] *See* Arato, Claussen, & Heath, *supra* note 63.

[92] *See, e.g.*, Timothy Meyer, *Saving the Political Consensus in Favor of Free Trade*, 70 Vand. L. Rev. 985, 1014–20 (2017); Shaffer, *supra* note 20.

V. Conclusion

Trade law is both vulnerable and resilient: constantly in motion, but also adaptable in light of shifts in view. The present moment of change is disappointing to many who saw the establishment of a trade rule of law in the 1990s as the end of those regularized shifts in the sand. The stability of the system appears now to have been fleeting, and yet there are elements that will have a lasting impact. Moreover, that institutional framework's inflexibility is partly responsible for the current challenges. As described here, existing institutions are unlikely to fade entirely, but they may be reworked to accommodate the pressures that have come to light in recent years. The future is likely to hold a new idea of the trade rule of law. Its legalization and possibly its judicialization may be reshaped. Some may think the trade rule of law label inapplicable to the new arrangement that emerges from this moment, but some of its central features are likely to remain. Above all, trade law's experimentation will continue.

10

Strength in Obscurity

The Resilience of International Investment Law

Jeremy Rabkin

I. Introduction

Many fields of international law are now under great strain. Amidst hand-wringing over the general trends, it is easy to overlook the norms and procedures protecting foreign investment. They do not get much attention. But they have largely maintained their place in the past decade. And their place, judged by the volume of legal disputes pursued, is not small. Disputes about the rights of foreign investors are regularly referred to international arbitration. In the first two decades of the current century, such disputes generated many times more legal rulings than all disputes submitted to the permanent tribunals associated with the United Nations or other global organizations.[1]

International tribunals generally focus on disputes between states. But some three thousand investment treaties now allow individual investors (usually private business firms) to pursue compensation claims against foreign states. The procedure has come to be known as investor-state dispute settlement (ISDS). The spread and development of this practice has rightly been called "one of the most remarkable phenomena in international law" in our time.[2]

[1] The World Bank's International Centre for the Settlement of Investment Disputes (the largest but not the only forum for such cases) recorded decisions in 707 disputes between January 2000 and June 2020. The United Nations' International Court of Justice (sometimes called the "World Court") ruled on thirty cases in that period; the International Criminal Court completed only twenty-two cases, the International Tribunal for the Law of the Sea only twenty-five, the Appellate Body of the World Trade Organization less than two hundreds.

[2] K.J. Vandevelde, *A Brief History of International Investment Agreements*, 12 U.C. Davis J. Int'l L. & Pol. 157 (2005).

Jeremy Rabkin, *Strength in Obscurity* In: *Is the International Legal Order Unraveling?*. Edited by: David L. Sloss, Oxford University Press. © Oxford University Press 2022. DOI: 10.1093/oso/9780197652800.003.0011

It is remarkable, first, because it has reached this scale in such a short time. ISDS scarcely existed, as a regular practice, before 1990. It is also remarkable because the norms involved had been urged by Western states for more than two centuries but seemed to be losing their force through most of the twentieth century. In this area, new procedures have revived, and in some ways expanded old, struggling norms.

II. Earlier History: The Compensation Doctrine under Increasing Challenge

A. Before World War II

Since the formative period of international law in the seventeenth century, states have tried to protect the personal safety of their nationals when traveling abroad and also secure protection for the property held by their nationals in foreign lands. In the seventeenth and eighteenth centuries, European states concluded treaties (often bilateral, sometimes multilateral), promising to respect the property of foreign merchants from the signatory states. By the nineteenth century, major states insisted the obligation to respect foreign owned property was an obligation under customary international law, regardless of whether particular treaties applied. Britain successfully pursued such claims against Portugal and Sicily in the early nineteenth century.[3]

There was continuing difficulty, however, getting all states to embrace this norm (or embrace a common understanding of its implications). Outside Europe, powerful states regularly resorted to force to make host states pay compensation on property claims of their nationals. The most active was Britain, with the world's largest navy and the willingness to deploy its guns against coastal targets in recalcitrant states. Britain deployed military force against Latin American nations on at least twenty-six occasions between 1820 and 1914 to "enforce claims of British subjects" and "protect [their] property."[4]

Often, the threat of force was enough to secure an agreement to submit the claims involved to a panel of arbitrators chosen by the disputing states.

[3] Charles Lipson, Standing Guard: Protecting Foreign Capital in the 19th and 20th Centuries 11, 12 (1985).
[4] *Id.*, at 54.

With its own growing strength in the Western Hemisphere, the United States entered into approximately forty such arbitrations with Latin American countries between 1829 and 1910.[5]

Not surprisingly, a doctrine associated with foreign force came to be seen as an affront to the independence of states on the receiving end. Latin American republics typically offered generalized guarantees of property rights in their national constitutions and civil codes. In practice, these paper guarantees did not secure owners against government default on contract claims or outright seizures under flimsy pretexts with limited legal process. The Argentine jurist, Carlos Calvo, tried to refute claims for foreign intervention with the argument that foreign states could not demand more protection for their nationals (when the latter were in a foreign country) than the host state provided to its own citizens.[6] Mexico and other states in the region sometimes required foreign investors to agree to waive claims to diplomatic protection by their home states in what came to be known as a "Calvo clause."[7]

Western states, supported by legal analysts, insisted they retained a residual right to protect their own nationals from abuse, a sovereign right that private citizens could not disavow.[8] British and German warships bombarded Venezuela to force (among other things) compensation for their nationals (1902–03). President Theodore Roosevelt then offered his "Corollary to the Monroe Doctrine" (1904): if foreign states had legitimate claims in the Western Hemisphere, the United States would try to enforce them rather than allow outside powers to take military action in the Americas.

The Second Hague Peace Conference (1907), the first major international conference to include Latin American states, tried to address their protests over such interventions. But the convention negotiated there prohibited resort to force only for claims based on nonpayment of government loans, and then only so long as the debtor state agreed to have such claims submitted to international arbitration.[9] An American scholar exulted that the agreement was "emphatically a peace-measure," which "will banish foreign

[5] Lionel Summers, *Arbitration and Latin America*, 3 Cal. W. Int'l L.J. 1, 7 (1972).

[6] *See* Carlos Calvo, Derecho Internacional de Europa y America (1863).

[7] On the ensuing history, *see* Daniel Shea, The Calvo Clause (1955).

[8] The US–Mexico Claims Commission reviewed contending claims in *North American Dredging (USA) v. United Mexican States*, 4 Rev. Int'l Arb. Awards 26 (1926) (repudiating the idea that an American company could sign away the right of the US government to exert diplomatic protection on its behalf, though upholding contractual obligation to exhaust local remedies).

[9] Hague Convention II Respecting the Limitations of the Employment of Force for the Recovery of Contract Debts, Oct. 18, 1907, 36 Stat. 2241.

fleets from [Latin] American waters."[10] The Argentine diplomat Luis Drago, who had originally advocated the ban on force for such claims, worried that the Hague convention was actually "legalizing war as a process for the collection of debts in the last resort."[11] Ten Latin American states ratified only with reservations, insisting that in their view resort to force would be wrong whether arbitration could be arranged or not.

In 1910, the first president of the American Society of International Law, Elihu Root, offered a learned rejoinder, insisting that it was no excuse for host states to abuse foreigners simply because they often treated their own citizens that way ("national treatment"). The treatment of foreigners must at least satisfy the "minimum standard of treatment"—"the protection which . . . conforms to the established standard of civilization."[12] The argument may have carried a bit more authority coming from Root, who had recently served as Secretary of War in Theodore Roosevelt's cabinet.

The doctrine proved harder to maintain after the exhausting struggles of the First World War and the upheavals that followed. Bolsheviks in Russia confiscated foreign property as systematically as property belonging to Russians. Revolutionaries in Mexico seized land belonging to foreigners (as well as wealthy Mexicans). The new League of Nations tried to promulgate compensation standards for takings of foreign-owned property. Even in a period when the Soviet Union remained outside the League, the membership of the League (which did include most states in Latin America) could not reach agreement on a formulation of the standard.

In the 1930s, President Franklin Roosevelt proclaimed a "Good Neighbor Policy," eschewing resort to force against Latin nations. That did not end debate on protections for foreign investors, since their claims could still be pressed by home states through diplomatic protests and demands for arbitration. A New Deal legal scholar warned that the logic of excluding outside challenge to abuse of foreign investors could equally justify "a universal

[10] James Brown Scott, *Work of the Second Hague Peace Conference*, 2 AM. J. INT'L L. 1, 15 (1908). Others were more skeptical: "Instead of prohibiting the employment of force under all circumstances for the collection of public debts, as the Drago Doctrine demanded, the use of force is merely postponed till arbitration has been tried." Edward Elliott, "*Development of International Law by the Second Hague Conference*," 8 COLUM. L. REV. 96, 103 (1908).

[11] Paul Reinsch, *Failures and Successes at the Second Hague Conference*, 2 AM POL. SCI. REV. 204, 207 (1908).

[12] Elihu Root, *The Basis of Protection for Citizens Residing Abroad*, 4 AM. J. INT'L L. 517, 521 (1910). He acknowledged that the United States had fallen short of this "general standard" by failing to punish lynch mobs after they attacked Chinese, Mexican, and Italian nationals in the last decades of the nineteenth century.

destruction of the rules sheltering aliens from injury."[13] A prominent New York lawyer offered a more colorful version of the challenge: if Soviet Russia followed up confiscation of property with "the nationalization of women," would other states allow that local law to be made "applicable to aliens"?[14] Amidst the threat of impending war in Europe, Secretary of State Cordell Hull protested Mexican nationalization of petroleum drilling sites owned by US companies. He insisted that Mexico must provide "adequate, effective and prompt payment for the properties seized"—a demand that came to be known as the "Hull Rule."[15]

The return of world war did not quell the debate. For some commentators, it merely raised the stakes. At the beginning of 1941, when Nazi Germany and Soviet Russia were still de facto allies and dividing most of continental Europe between them, the *American Journal of International Law* devoted space to an article on "Expropriation of Foreign Property." It concluded with the warning that since "the totalitarian states, in their internal structure, have come to replace the system of private property by one of state-regulation," the "outcome of the world struggle will also decide the fate of . . . international law concerning the expropriation of private property."[16]

Even after Mexico joined the United States in declaring war against Germany, Mexican officials thought it timely to denounce diplomatic protests on behalf of fellow nationals in another country as an "instrument of oppression," reflecting the "totalitarian doctrines" against which free nations were then fighting. The *American Journal of International Law* soon published a riposte from an American lawyer, warning that Mexico's position—rejecting the right of foreign governments even to make peaceful protests against disregard of property claims of their own citizens—"marks the final and logical phase of a determined campaign against one of the most fundamental pillars of international law."[17]

[13] A.H. Feller, *Some Observations on the Calvo Clause*, 27 Am. J. Int'l L. 461, 468 (1933). Feller held several senior positions in the Roosevelt administration during the 1930s and became legal counsel to the UN secretariat in 1945.

[14] Frederic R. Coudert, *The Mexican Situation and Protection of American Property Abroad*, 24 Am. Bar Ass'n J. 813, 822 (1938). ("The Totalitarian State is necessarily inimical to the growth and development of international law because it avowedly seeks its ends outside of law and through preponderant force.")

[15] US Secretary of State to Mexican Ambassador, Aug. 22, 1938, reprinted in 3 G. Hackworth, Digest of International Law 658–59 (1942).

[16] John H. Herz, *Expropriation of Foreign Property*, 35 Am. J. Int'l L. 242, 262 (1941).

[17] Alwyn V. Freeman, *Recent Aspects of the Calvo Doctrine and the Challenge to International Law*, 40 Am. J. Int'l L. 121, 122 (1946) (with citations to the Mexican claims at the Inter-American Bar Association conference in the summer of 1944). Freeman took the trouble to note: "Yet in Nazi

B. Eclipse of the Doctrine of Compensation during the Cold War

For some decades after the Second World War, there seemed to be less and less agreement on compensation obligations owed to foreign investors. On the one hand, a triumphant Soviet Union was left to reorganize Eastern Europe in its own image. New communist governments followed the Bolshevik example by expropriating private property, including that owned by foreigners, without any compensation to owners. Meanwhile, Western states began to relinquish control of former colonies in Asia and Africa. The apparent success of socialism in Soviet Russia encouraged many new states to adopt state-directed development schemes. Accordingly, many newly independent states soon insisted on repudiating not only foreign political control but foreign ownership of major assets, such as mining and oil-drilling operations. They often acknowledged some obligation to compensate owners but almost always in accord with their own standards of adequacy rather than what firms claimed as the minimum international standard.

Two other factors worked to undermine the compensation doctrine. First, by its terms, the UN Charter prohibits the use of force, except in self-defense. The exception for self-defense did not obviously include defense of private property in a foreign state, merely because the property happened to belong to a complaining state's own nationals. States with sizable military capacity did not always adhere to strict interpretations of the Charter's restrictions, of course. But they were not as confident about resorting to force even against the sorts of countries that could not readily retaliate (and had therefore been the target of gunboat diplomacy to enforce compensation claims in earlier times).

A second inhibiting factor was that, as the Cold War intensified, Western states came to see themselves in competition with the Soviet Union for influence and support among states describing themselves as "non-aligned" (or "Third World"). Third World states constituted the majority of the UN General Assembly by the 1960s. Communist governments cheered the efforts of Third World states to supplant foreign control of major economic sectors in their territories. For Western states to intervene on behalf of their

Germany the only real protection afforded to foreign individuals who otherwise would have suffered as did natives was through this same maligned institution of diplomatic protection!" *Id.* at 146.

own investors was to add new burdens to the geo-strategic aims of Western diplomacy.

So postwar Western interventions on behalf of Western property claims were either disguised or entangled with larger claims. That was true of the CIA-backed coup against the leftist Iranian premier Mohammed Mossadegh in 1953 (at least in part to thwart nationalization of Western oil companies there). It was true of British and French intervention in Egypt in 1956, ostensibly to protect international traffic through the Suez Canal from war between Egypt and Israel (but also to challenge Egypt's seizure of the canal from European owners). Similarly, after Castro's regime in Cuba began to nationalize American-owned companies, the United States helped organize a landing by a Cuban exile force at the Bay of Pigs in 1961 (in hopes it could be depicted as a domestic rebellion against tyranny rather than a US intervention to enforce compensation claims by US companies).

With Western states focused on Cold War diplomacy, however, even such efforts (loudly denounced by communist and Third World leaders) were mostly half-hearted and ineffectual. Western hesitation encouraged bolder measures by developing nations. The tide of expropriations accelerated, reaching (by the count of a UN study) 875 expropriations in 62 countries between 1960 and 1974.[18]

UN resolutions on the relevant obligations of states followed a similar trajectory. In 1962, the General Assembly adopted a resolution affirming "Permanent Sovereignty Over Natural Resources." It acknowledged that "reasons of public utility, security or the national interest" could justify "nationalization, expropriation or requisitioning" of private property, even property belonging to foreigners, but insisted that "the owner shall be paid appropriate compensation . . . in accordance with international law."[19] By 1974, the UN General Assembly felt it could proclaim a "Charter of Economic Rights and Duties of States," which affirmed the "right" of every state "to nationalize, expropriate or transfer ownership of foreign property" merely "taking into account . . . all circumstances that the [expropriating] state considers pertinent" and emphasizing "the question of compensation . . . shall be settled under the domestic law of the nationalizing state" (without mention of international standards).[20] The United States and a

[18] Jeswald Salacuse & Nicholas Sullivan, *Do BITs Really Work?*, 46 Harv. Int'l L.J. 67, 75 (2005).
[19] G.A. Res. 1803, ¶ 4 (Dec. 14, 1962).
[20] G.A. Res. 3281 (XXIX), art. 2(c) (Dec. 12, 1974).

number of other Western countries that had supported the 1962 resolution decided to abstain from supporting the 1974 resolution.

Meanwhile, a 1970 UN General Assembly resolution purporting to define "principles of international law" insisted that "every state has the inalienable right to choose its political, economic, social and cultural systems without interference in any form by other states."[21] The same resolution not only denounced interference by armed force but "the use of economic, political or any other type of measures to coerce another state," implying that capital exporting states could not join together to impose sanctions on states engaged in expropriation. In fact, there was dwindling interest in such measures, even among Western states. A political science study in the mid-1980s concluded that efforts to coerce compensation through organized sanctions had proven so ineffective, even among Western states, "few have shown much enthusiasm for resurrecting the old standards."[22]

III. Post-Cold War: Revived and Extended Compensation Law through New Procedures

The end of the Cold War saw a dramatic reversal in global trends, restoring and actually extending the historic compensation doctrine. But the reversal achieved such success because it built on a new legal architecture already being developed, almost without notice, in the last decades of the Cold War. The trend built on the small and quiet practice of negotiating individual treaties that came to be known as bilateral investment treaties (BITs). They affirmed obligations of host states to provide "fair and equitable treatment" for foreign investment and to compensate for loss of property.

The first BIT was concluded between West Germany and Pakistan in 1959. Germany had seen almost all its foreign investments confiscated during World War II. (Confiscation was one of the main contributions to the Allied cause by many countries in Latin America, for example.) Given fear and suspicion left by its wartime conduct, West Germany was also particularly concerned to affirm its postwar commitment to peaceful diplomacy. Over the next decade, however, France, Switzerland, Netherlands, Italy, and other Western European states negotiated their own BITs. The treaties adopted

21 G.A. Res. 2625, Declaration of Principles of International Law on Friendly Relations and Cooperation Among States (Oct. 24, 1970).

22 Lipson, *supra* note 3, at 267, 275.

similar phrasing, typically providing that disputes would be referred to the International Court of Justice (ICJ) or to a mutually agreed arbitration forum.

Starting in the mid-1960s, an important innovation was included: provisions allowing private investors to pursue such claims. These private claims would have to be directed to an alternate forum, since the ICJ is authorized to hear only disputes between states. The United States offered to embrace the practice in a model BIT developed by the Carter administration in the late 1970s.

An initiative of the World Bank helped the new approach gain momentum. In 1965, the Bank proposed that its members should embrace a formal treaty to facilitate this type of arbitration: the International Convention on the Settlement of Investment Disputes Between States and Nationals of Other States (ICSID Convention). The treaty did not, in itself, commit signatory states to accept arbitration of investment disputes, but offered a framework for doing so. In 1966, the World Bank established its own International Centre for Settlement of Investment Disputes (ICSID), which provided services to facilitate arbitration. Without specifying the law to be applied, these arrangements could help states and investors pursue arbitration of claims regarding compliance with BIT guarantees.

ICSID was not the only way to implement BIT guarantees. In 1966, the United Nations established the UN Commission on International Trade Law (UNCITRAL). It soon proposed its own approach to arbitration, which states (and investors) might choose to adopt in resolving disputes about BIT terms. Commercial arbitration services also opened their doors to investor-state disputes, notably the Stockholm Chamber of Commerce, whose services had been accepted by US and Soviet governments for some state-to-state trade disputes starting in the 1970s. In 1978, the World Bank's ICSID established an "Additional Facility," which offered arbitration services for states that were not parties to the ICSID Convention, but might still want to pursue arbitration of claims under ICSID auspices. The proliferation of potential fora ran along with the growth in willingness of states to commit to BITs. By the end of the 1980s, there were already some four hundred BITs.[23]

Then in 1990, suddenly and unexpectedly, the Soviet empire collapsed. Former Eastern European satellites sought to establish Western-style market economies and invited investment from Western companies. In Africa, Asia, and Latin America, countries that had been locked in stagnation as they tried

[23] Vandevelde, *supra* note 2, at 172.

to shield themselves from foreign interference noticed the growth achieved by Asian "Tigers" in the 1980s (Hong Kong, South Korea, Taiwan, Singapore, Malaysia), with factories financed by foreign investors. In response to these new circumstances, dozens of new countries sought to negotiate investment treaties. By 2005, there were more than two thousand BITs, a five-fold increase from 1990. In the same fifteen years, foreign direct investment (FDI) soared from $239 billion per year to $3.1 trillion per year: more than a twelve-fold increase.[24] Arbitrations followed a similar surge. In the five years preceding 2005, ICSID facilitated arbitration for 118 disputes; in the first five years of the previous decade (1990–94), it had assisted only six arbitrations.[25]

Latin American states had uniformly rejected the World Bank's ICSID convention when it was launched in the 1960s. They began to reconsider this stance by the 1980s, and almost all had joined by the end of the 1990s. Amidst a profusion of new BITs, Mexico agreed to investment protections in a new regional trade agreement—the North American Free Trade Agreement (NAFTA). Law journals carried articles speculating about the "death of the Calvo clause."[26]

The stick of military intervention had shriveled to almost nothing but the carrot of access to foreign capital drew much of the world to embrace investor-state arbitration agreements. Even China signed many such agreements, initially to coax foreign investors to China.[27] Doctrines of just compensation seemed to be achieving, after all, an established place in the international law of the twenty-first century. It was a "remarkable" turn, indeed.

Meanwhile, the scope of protections had begun to expand. During the Cold War, disputes usually focused on the amount of compensation for outright expropriation ("nationalization"). By the 1990s, host states rarely attempted outright seizures of foreign property, but might still try to force

24 There was a considerable drop in FDI at the end of the following decade, plunging to $1.3 trillion in 2018, and expected to drop still further under the influence of the COVID pandemic. But the trend does not seem to have stimulated a comparable plunge in BIT repudiations or refusals to arbitrate. It may reinforce competition to reassure investors.

25 ICSID, 2020 Caseload Statistics, https://icsid.worldbank.org/resources/publications/icsid-caseload-statistics (last visited May 27, 2021).

26 Denise Manning-Cabrol, *The Imminent Death of the Calvo Clause and Rebirth of the Calvo Principle*, 26 Law & Pol'y in Int'l Bus. 1169 (1995); Wenhua Shan, *Is Calvo Dead?*, 55 Am. J. Comp. L. 123 (2007) (warning that nationalist assertions might return in more difficult economic circumstances).

27 M. Sornarajah, International Law on Foreign Investment 207 (4th ed. 2017) (noting that China began negotiating BITs in the 1980s "to signal . . . its willingness to give guarantees of protection" but limited arbitration to disputes about the amount of compensation. China's later treaties, aimed at protecting Chinese investment abroad, are "very similar to those which Western industrialized states sign.").

foreign investors to sell off their properties or abandon their contract claims. So BITs included language prohibiting not only direct confiscation but expropriation "indirectly through measures tantamount to expropriation or nationalization."[28]

In 1981, the US and Iran agreed to a settlement of differences arising from a fourteen-month confrontation, provoked by the seizure of American diplomats in Tehran and escalating through seizures of property and assets on both sides. The United States and the new Islamic Republic agreed to submit competing claims to a special Iran-US Claims Tribunal at The Hague (with three judges appointed by the United States, three by Iran, three by mutual agreement). In ensuing decades, the Tribunal reviewed some four thousand claims, upholding many claims based on extortionate conduct by the Iranian regime toward American firms. Its rulings were then frequently cited by other arbitration panels to award compensation for "creeping expropriations"—a series of increasingly severe restrictions forcing firms to cease operations—and also for a "multiplicity of inappropriate regulatory acts, omissions, and other deleterious [government] conduct" undermining "the indispensable normative and legal framework without which private industry . . . cannot survive."[29] One scholar, emphasizing the influence of the Iran-US Claims Tribunal's rulings, called it "the most significant arbitral body in history."[30]

Challenges to abusive regulatory measures (as opposed to direct confiscation) soon appeared in NAFTA disputes, as American companies protested regulatory policies in both Canada and Mexico (and in a few cases, where Canadian-owned firms protested regulatory policies in various US states). Somewhat similar challenges were pursued (under BITs) against Australia and several countries in Europe. It shocked advocates for environmental regulation and other types of social regulation that obscure arbitration proceedings could challenge regulatory measures in Western democracies.

These concerns merged with a general current of anxiety or resistance to "globalization" that spread through Western (as well as non-Western) states starting in the late 1990s. The passions ignited by this movement were made painfully evident by a riot in Seattle, Washington—the so-called Battle in

[28] U.S.-Russia BIT, art. III(i), discussed in Michael Reisman & Robert D. Sloane, *Indirect Expropriation and Its Valuation in the BIT Generation*, 75 Brit. Yrbk. Int'l L. 115, 118 (2004) (asserting that the provision has come to be "mirrored in substance in virtually all BITs").

[29] *Id.*, at 118–19.

[30] David D. Caron, *The Nature of the Iran–United States Claims Tribunal and the Evolving Structure of International Dispute Resolution*, 84 Am. J. Int'l L. 104 (1990).

Seattle—as protests against a conference of the World Trade Organization in November 1999 spiraled out of control. The mood of protest did affect the practice of investor-state arbitration. But ISDS proved somewhat better situated to weather the storm.

IV. ISDS in Larger Context

To understand the durability of ISDS, it helps to compare it with two other innovations in international law since World War II. These are, first, international treaties to protect human rights and, second, international agreements to promote trade between nations. These projects are parallel to investor protection treaties in that all seek to strengthen legal safeguards for private activity. They might well have been pursued together. In some regional organizations, they have been. But as worldwide undertakings, they emerged in quite different political settings and have developed along quite different trajectories, with notably different results.

A. International Protection for Human Rights

International protection for human rights, in the sense of protection for individuals against their own governments, was largely unknown before the Second World War. The drafters of the UN Charter, eager to build support for the new organization, declined to invest the organization with wide-ranging powers in the field of human rights. The Charter gives the Economic and Social Council a weak power to "make recommendations for the purpose of promoting respect for, and observance of, human rights" (Article 62). By contrast, the Security Council was given much more robust powers to "determine" and "decide" and "take action by land, sea and air forces"—but only in relation to "action" for "international peace and security" (Articles 39, 41, 42).

The same consensual strategy guided the drafting of the Universal Declaration of Human Rights, endorsed by the General Assembly in 1948. As a "declaration," it would not be legally binding. And in the effort to secure "universal" agreement, it steered away from controversial questions. In 1789, new governments in the United States (US Bill of Rights, Amendment V) and in France (Declaration of the Rights of Man and the Citizen, Article

XVII—on "the inviolable and sacred right to property") included express guarantees against confiscation of property (except for public use and then only with "just" compensation).[31] The United Nations' Universal Declaration offers only the weak admonition that "no one shall be *arbitrarily* deprived of his property" (Article 17, emphasis added), leaving open the scope for *systematic* confiscation. Communist and socialist governments found it easy to accept that very vague guarantee, especially given other provisions which defined "human rights" to include government guarantees of employment, education, housing, medical care, and an "adequate standard of living" (Article 25).

Subsequent conventions imposed new obligations on states, but offered no further protection for private property. The Covenants on Civil and Political Rights and on Economic and Social Rights (1966) are legally binding treaties, as are separate human rights conventions against race discrimination (1965), sex discrimination (1979), torture (1985), mistreatment of children (1989), and mistreatment of people with disabilities (2006). All these conventions—even the Covenant on Economic Rights—disregard protections for private property rights, as if "human rights" were entirely disconnected from economic activity in the private sector.

Whatever their views, almost all governments found it safe to embrace most of these conventions. Thus, the Soviet Union embraced the Covenant on Civil and Political Rights, while Saudi Arabia embraced the Convention on the Elimination of All Forms of Discrimination Against Women. By mixing rights guarantees with long-term social policy aims, human rights conventions seem to encourage the notion that all rights may be contextual and adaptable. At any rate, they contain very weak enforcement mechanisms, so they impose few obvious costs for states that sign and then violate their terms. One study found that human rights compliance actually tended to decrease among nations that ratified more human rights conventions.[32] Every state may interpret convention provisions in its own way, giving itself the benefit of what it takes to be implied exceptions. Monitoring committees established under several of the conventions may "comment" on state practices

[31] States in Western Europe that joined the Council of Europe also agreed to enshrine protection for private property in the European Convention for the Protection of Human Rights (originally drafted in 1950), but only in a separate 1952 Protocol. "Property" rights were not part of the original "human rights" consensus, even among countries in Western Europe, most of which had important parties calling themselves "socialist" or "social democratic," or (as France and Italy did) "communist" (i.e., pro-Soviet) parties.

[32] Oona Hathaway, *Do Human Rights Treaties Make a Difference?*, 111 Yale L.J. 1935 (2002).

and "recommend" reforms, but no convention requires states to heed the monitors (which include members from some of the world's most brutal and repressive regimes—such as Russia, China, Cuba, Saudi Arabia, Pakistan).

BITs have pursued a very different approach. They are, of course, focused on the property claims that human rights treaties neglect. That is, to start with, a reason they are worth seeking, even with states that have already pledged to respect all the various human rights conventions. They are not affirmations of general governing ideals but commitments to compensate injuries to a particular set of claimants (foreign investors from the other nation in the bilateral treaty).

Where the human rights conventions receive their international affirmation or fulfillment (such as it is) in speeches and reports at UN conferences, BITs with ISDS provisions culminate in legal proceedings before international arbitrators who are empowered to make binding decisions. A victim of human rights abuses can hope that filing complaints with a UN monitor will generate moral pressure for his government to change its ways. The complaining investor in ISDS has a reasonable expectation of receiving direct payments in compensation for proven loss. Compensation awards may run to tens or even hundreds of millions of dollars, and there are legal mechanisms to enforce payment, though they are not always entirely reliable.[33]

In sum, compared with international human rights treaties, BITs have been much narrower in coverage but much more effectual where they do apply. A human rights treaty purports to be a pledge of good conduct given to all other signatory states. But a promise to all states does not necessarily engage any other state in particular. It is a promise that does not seek anything from others, since it expresses what each signatory state commits to do for, or avoid doing to, its own citizens.

[33] The 1959 New York Convention (officially, "Convention on Recognition and Enforcement of Foreign Arbitral Awards") commits signatories to enforce arbitration awards, regardless of where they occur or what they cover. Typically, they are awards in commercial disputes between private parties but disputes between governments and private firms are not excluded. There are now 165 states that are parties to this Convention, though not all have exactly the same domestic legal rules about which assets are subject to seizure to satisfy an award and of course, given the distribution of foreign assets, states vary in their capacity to seize sufficient assets to satisfy a large award. Still, despite opportunities to resist payment, there is often steady pressure to do so. So, for example, after years of legal wrangling in various national courts, Argentina in 2013 agreed to pay over $500 million to settle five separate arbitration awards against it. It continued to resist payment on other awards but did not repudiate the treaties committing it to arbitrate such disputes. For recent analysis of Argentina's maneuvering constraints, *see* Yoram Z. Haftel & Hila Levi, *Argentina's Curious Response to the Global Investment Regime*, 23 J. Int'l Rel. & Dev. 744 (2020).

By contrast, BITs are motivated by concern to draw in foreign investors—and by the reasonable concern that investors will withdraw or remain aloof if not reassured by legal guarantees. The motivations and incentives are more compelling because more focused. It has been said that "human rights [conventions] are best observed in the places that need them least."[34] ISDS agreements are designed to provide reassurance for investors in places where reassurance is most necessary.

B. International Trade Agreements

Efforts to liberalize trade restrictions started at almost the same time as the international human rights program. This was also something new in international affairs. Before World War II, trade agreements had rested primarily on bilateral treaties rather than multilateral treaties. These early treaties tended to have early expiration dates (most often three or five years), emphasizing their dependence on subsequent diplomacy. Renegotiation prospects were the main goad to compliance.

The era of multilateral trade agreements began in 1947 with the signing of the General Agreement on Tariffs and Trade (GATT). It followed the traditional pattern of emphasizing diplomatic bargaining on concessions to favored trade partners. Little attempt was made at proclaiming universal principles or securing comprehensive agreement. Only twenty-seven states signed up for the limited, tariff-cutting program of the GATT—largely nations of Western Europe and the British Commonwealth, along with the United States—at a time when the United Nations had fifty-seven members.

Trade liberalization was then pursued step by step, discarding projects that proved too controversial. Almost fifty nations sent delegates to a 1948 conference in Havana, which drafted a "charter" for an International Trade Organization (ITO). Along with a mandate to monitor implementation of tariff reductions, the ITO Charter did include protections for foreign investors (from member states) against unfair treatment by host states.[35]

[34] Stephen Hopgood, *Human Rights on the Road to Nowhere*, *in* HUMAN RIGHTS FUTURES 290 (Stephen Hopgood, Jack Snyder, & Leslie Vinjamuri eds. 2017) (citing past research by social scientists).

[35] BORZU SABAHI, NOAH RUBINS, & DON WALLACE, INVESTOR-STATE ARBITRATIONS 50 (2nd ed. 2019) (stating that "governments of developing countries were hostile to certain provisions of the [proposed ITO] charter, especially those related to the protection of foreign investments"), 632–33 (describing ITO investment provisions).

Partly for this reason, the ITO was rejected by states in Latin America and provoked skeptical reactions from Senate Republicans in the United States. It never went into effect.

Subsequent rounds of tariff reduction continued under GATT for nearly half a century thereafter, without delving into protections for investors. Successive GATT agreements sought deeper tariff reductions on a wider range of products and then sought to curtail subsidies for domestic producers (as an impediment to free competition with foreign producers). By the early 1990s, as more and more states sought to participate, a new agreement established a permanent World Trade Organization (WTO) to oversee international trade agreements.

Still, there was no provision for investor protections. The WTO included more formalized procedures for arbitration of disputes about compliance. But dispute settlement under GATT reflected its reliance on ongoing diplomatic bargaining. The WTO adopted the GATT practice whereby complaints could be pursued only by member states, initially in direct negotiation, and only after that by submission of the interstate dispute to arbitration. There was no mechanism for private firms to pursue complaints (except by urging their governments do so on their behalf).

In the early 1990s, negotiators working on the design of the new WTO had agreed to postpone investor protections to separate negotiation. Later in that decade, trade ministers convened by the Organisation for Economic Co-operation and Development (OECD) spent several years negotiating a Multilateral Agreement on Investment (MAI). It came under intense criticism and had to be abandoned when major Western countries, starting with France, backed away. Even in the United States there was resistance.[36]

After establishment of the WTO in 1995, getting agreement on additional trade liberalization was difficult. A new trade liberalization round, named for the initial launch conference in Doha, foundered on disagreements between developing countries and more affluent states. There have been no new agreements (within WTO) on further trade liberalization in more than a quarter century since the founding agreements negotiated in the early 1990s.

[36] The Organisation for Economic Co-operation and Development (OECD) grew out of the distribution of Marshall Plan funding to Western European states in the late 1940s (under the Organisation for European Cooperation and Development). OECD has retained the original emphasis on encouraging market-oriented policies but has only a reporting and data-collection role. On the spread of critical concerns about the MAI in the late 1990s, *see* Juergen Kurtz, *NGOs, the Internet and International Economic Policy Making: The Failure of the OECD Multilateral Agreement on Investment*, 3 MELB. J. INT'L L. 213 (2002).

Before the advent of the WTO, successive GATT rounds had generated an average of two new agreements per decade over the course of forty years.

The obvious alternative seemed to be regional trade agreements among like-minded states, but they have encountered resistance, as well. The 1993 North Atlantic Free Trade Agreement (NAFTA) had been negotiated in parallel with the agreements that launched the WTO. NAFTA did include provisions for investor protection. After 2010, Western states focused on a Transatlantic Trade and Investment Partnership (TTIP), linking EU states with NAFTA nations, while a similar Trans-Pacific Partnership (TPP) sought to link East Asian states (and Australia and New Zealand) with North and South American nations. These agreements would have followed NAFTA in offering broad protections for foreign investment as well as further reductions in tariffs and other trade barriers.

But again there was political resistance. Hillary Clinton, who had encouraged and promoted both measures as secretary of state, felt compelled to oppose TPP as the Democratic candidate for president in 2016. Donald Trump took the same position and announced US withdrawal from TPP negotiations on his first day in the White House. The TTIP negotiations lingered in comatose condition. President Trump also announced a determination to renegotiate NAFTA.

In 2018, the eleven other parties to the original TPP agreed on a somewhat revised version, rebranded as the Comprehensive and Progressive Agreement for Trans-Pacific Partnership (CPTPP), which included the originally envisioned investor protection measures. Countries like Australia, where the government had previously expressed qualms about ISDS, bowed to the urging of Malaysia, which strongly supported investor protections. The 2019 United States–Mexico–Canada Agreement (USMCA), negotiated to replace NAFTA, sharply reduced NAFTA's investor protection provisions. Robert Lighthizer, Trump administration trade negotiator, seemed to echo Latin American rhetoric from a century earlier, when he insisted (as advocates for the Calvo Doctrine had) that outside protections for investors raised a "question of sovereignty." "Why should a foreign national be able to come in and . . . have more rights than Americans have in the American court system?"[37]

[37] "U.S. Trade Policy Agenda," Hearing Before House Committee on Ways and Means, Mar. 21, 2018 (statement of Robert Lighthizer, responding to initial questioning from Chairman Brady). Commentators on international investment law have noted the implications of such insistence that foreign investors receive no more protection than US nationals. It would be "ironic" if the United

Yet for all its loud protests against "trade agreements," the Trump administration did not repudiate a single one of the many freestanding BITs to which the United States had become party. It even expressed willingness to consider joining CPTPP (the Pacific trade pact), if some changes were made, but it did not focus on ISDS provisions as a stumbling block to US participation. In its first months, the Biden administration embraced USMCA as an "improvement" over NAFTA. Though in general eager to highlight its repudiation of Trump policies, the Biden administration did not express any great interest in negotiating new trade agreements. Both political parties in Washington had major constituencies expressing wariness about free trade. But not so much about investor protection agreements.

Much of the difference may reflect the greater political salience of trade agreements. Foreign producers may compete with domestic producers. Trade liberalization may then threaten jobs and wages of those dependent on the domestic producers. Foreign investment is usually expected to generate new jobs by expanding economic activity in the host nation. Meanwhile, compared with a bilateral treaty, a multilateral trade agreement is, almost by definition, likely to affect many more domestic interests (by opening the way for competing imports from more countries).

It is possible to negotiate an agreement to reduce trade barriers on a bilateral basis and a fair number of such treaties have been put into effect. But the main effort in trade liberalization has focused on multilateral agreements. Trade negotiators have sought, since the beginning of GATT, to bring multiple parties together to achieve deeper or wider concessions overall, through a process of log-rolling. Different states have different domestic industries they hope to protect (at least somewhat) and different export markets where they seek greater access. A range of participants allows for more productive negotiations. The game is for state A to offer concessions of particular interest to state B, so that B will entice C to join, in order to persuade D to make the concessions most attractive to A. The result is that trade agreements are usually quite long and detailed, as they try to codify all the various side bargains that persuaded all parties to accept the final deal.

Investor protection agreements are different. Though a bilateral treaty only affects two states, they tend to follow standard templates, with brief general provisions that are easier to negotiate. States have thus subscribed to many

States, "long the leading opponent of the Calvo Doctrine," came to be "considered its proponent." SABAH, RUBINS, & WALLACE, *supra* note 35, at 630.

more BITs than trade agreements. While the WTO reports 306 "regional trade agreements" (mostly bilateral), the UN Conference on Trade and Development (UNCTAD) reports 2,341 BITs now in force (with another 319 trade agreements that include investor protections). ICSID reports that the solid majority—some 60 percent of its cases—arise from bilateral agreements rather from investor protection provisions in wider trade agreements. The United States is signatory to nineteen bilateral trade agreements but forty-seven BITs (though seven of the latter have not been ratified).

Investor protection agreements have provoked criticism in Western countries, especially from advocates of social regulation fearful that international arbitration will relieve foreign-owned firms from compliance with environmental or worker safety standards. There have also been complaints from developing countries that arbitrators tend to side with Western investors and disregard the special needs of poor countries.[38] But most countries still do want foreign investment. Even beyond the contrasts noted here, there are reasons why efforts to reassure foreign investors have proven more durable than efforts to lower trade barriers.

V. Elements of Resilience

In 2013, a collection of essays on international arbitration surveyed a range of different complaints. One of the contributors reported a prevalent perception that "arbitration has fallen into an autumn of decline and decay, shedding leaves of efficiency and coherence to reveal barren branches of rules without responsibility."[39] In the five years that followed, ICSID arbitration cases increased by over 38 percent compared with the previous five-year period, and overall cases (including non-ICSID arbitration) by 65 percent.[40]

[38] *See* Gus Van Harten, *Arbitrator Behaviour in Asymmetrical Adjudication*, 50 OSGOODE HALL L.J. 211 (2012) (finding favorable outcomes of arbitration more likely for US investors and less so for investors from France and the United Kingdom, and not at all for German investors, but the samples for European cases are in single digits). *But see* Susan Franck & Lindsey Wylie, *Predicting Outcomes in Investment Treaty Arbitration*, 65 DUKE L.J. 459 (2016) (disputing such findings, based on a larger sample). *See also* "Public Statement on the International Investment Regime," Osgoode Hall Law School, York University, Aug. 31, 2010 (statement signed by some eighty scholars from North America, Europe, and Asia, criticizing arbitration under BITs as a "threat to democratic choice" and urging governments to "withdraw from investment treaties" and "refuse to pay arbitration awards against them").

[39] William Park, *Procedural Tension in International Arbitration*, *in* INTERNATIONAL ARBITRATION 3 (John Norton Moore ed., 2013). Park cites critics directly assessing ISDS experience.

[40] There were a total of 179 ICSID cases between 2009 and 2013, and a total of 247 ICSID cases from 2014 to 2018, an increase of 37.99%. ICSID, 2020 Case Statistics, available at https://icsid.

True, the overall number of BITs in force declined in the second decade of the new century. Three populist governments in South America (Venezuela, Bolivia, and Ecuador) denounced existing agreements, as a sign of their determination to resist foreign interference with their redistributionist policies. New members of the European Union agreed to renounce BITs they had negotiated in the 1990s with older members of the European Union. India, after several unfavorable rulings from arbitrators, renounced all its existing BITs.

But more telling is that few other countries followed these examples. Neither willingness to commit to BITs nor readiness to go forward with arbitration seems to have been affected by a substantial decline in overall foreign direct investment in 2017–19. According to UNCTAD, changes in national laws involving foreign investment in this period continued to be overwhelmingly on the side of "liberalization"—that is, designed to attract more foreign investment, as they remained open to investor protection.[41] Even the nationalist Modi government in India tried to win agreement to new BITs rather than renouncing all participation in ISDS.

There seem to be enduring attractions to the arbitration arrangements that have developed in the field of investment protection. One might think of them as the "three Ds": de-politicize, de-localize, and de-center.

The advantage most touted by advocates, such as the World Bank's ICSID, is to *depoliticize* disputes by recasting what were traditionally seen as confrontations between states into self-contained investor-state disputes. As the Egyptian-born Secretary-General of ICSID, Ibrahim Shihata, put it in the Centre's 1984 report: ICSID "provide[s] developing countries with a response which, compared to the Calvo Doctrine, is . . . more adequate in the depoliticization of disputes . . . without inviting the abuses of diplomatic protection."[42]

worldbank.org/sites/default/files/publications/The%20ICSID%20Caseload%20Statistics%20%282021-1%20Edition%29%20ENG.pdf. If we include non-ICSID cases, there were a total of 233 cases between 2009 and 2013, and a total of 384 cases from 2014 to 2018, an increase of 65%. UNCTAD, World Investment Report 2020.

41 UNCTAD, World Investment Report 2019, at 15 (reporting on more than one hundred changes in fifty-five countries finding some two-thirds as "liberalizing"), with an uptick in "liberalizing" changes reported in 2020. Overall, FDI contracted by over 20% between 2017 and 2018 and recovered only slightly in 2019—and was projected to drop more sharply in 2020 in response to the Covid pandemic.

42 ICSID, Annual Report (1984) at 4 (cited, with many similar statements, in Sergio Puig, *Emergence & Dynamism in International Organizations: ICSID, Investor-State Arbitration & International Investment Law*, 44 Geo. J. Int'l L. 531, 547 (2013)).

By framing disputes as between the host state and the investor, the process removes the investor's home state from the wrangling. The investor who invokes ICSID agrees, by its terms, to forgo "diplomatic protection" (protests on its behalf by its home state). That is useful in several ways. It allows the host state to respond to legal challenges to its policies without losing face (with its own people) by seeming to knuckle under to a bullying foreign government. Disputes often feature home states that would not have sent out a naval force even in the old days. They involve many states that do not have conjurable associations with the CIA, the British Empire, or some other former colonial power in the affected territory.[43] The system puts all home states (along with all foreign investors) on the same level.

On the other hand, ISDS removes investment disputes from the geostrategic calculations of the home state. It is not necessary for the home state's foreign ministry, or even its trade ministry, to agonize over whether (or how) to confront the host state over the particular dispute. It can all be left to arbitrators to sort out. ISDS, then, has some of the attractions of a domestic legal proceeding, where government officials find it convenient to say: "We need to wait for the legal process to play out." It removes the dispute from the desk of the relevant government officials (at least in the home state of the investor). That is a large part of what it means to "de-politicize"—it removes the issue from the responsibility of political officials. They may welcome the chance to keep their attention focused elsewhere.

At the same time, the dispute is largely *delocalized* from the legal system of either the host country or the home country. In the mid-1980s, ICSID revised its arbitration rules to clarify that parties could seek provisional measures from domestic courts only with the explicit consent of both the foreign investor and the affected state. This amendment was part of a "strategic effort to cement ICSID's status as a self-contained system and disassociate its proceedings from the scrutiny of national courts."[44] To remove the dispute from the courts of the host country is, of course, often the main aim of the complaining investor. The investor seeks a more neutral forum, more open to the concerns of foreign claimants. At the least, investors want to avoid a court

[43] Among the top twenty sources of foreign direct investment in 2017–2018 were: Japan, Germany, Netherlands, Canada, Spain, South Korea, Singapore, Switzerland, Italy, Sweden, Taiwan, Thailand, United Arab Emirates, and Ireland. UNCTAD, World Investment Report 2019, at 4. The United States was not among the top twenty capital exporters, though it was the number one capital importer. *Id.* at 3.

[44] Puig, *supra* note 42, at 553–54 (noting that ICSID attorneys at the time advocated for the "self-contained" character of its arbitrations in academic commentary).

that may be predisposed to favor the government that appoints and pays the salaries of the judges (and may dangle prospects for career advancement).

There is a certain compensating advantage for the host state. The issue is not whether any particular national law or policy is valid but whether the foreign investor is entitled to compensation. No ISDS arbitration can reach into the legal system of the host state and declare the disputed law or policy invalid within that national system. The same law or policy might be applied to nationals of the host state without fear that they will challenge it (since their own citizens have no access to international arbitration). The same law or policy might be applied even to other foreign investors: other investors might view it as not particularly harmful or be satisfied by some different offsetting or compensating offer from the host state. In fact, most ISDS claims have not turned on the validity of a general law, but the administrative determinations applying it to the local operations of the complaining foreign investor.[45] The defendant state could see individualized arbitration as an exercise in "pragmatism," where the state, "acting in a semi-private role" (as partner to the arbitration agreement), settled on a particular form of "dispute resolution in relationship-specific foreign investment protection."[46]

Here again, the contrast between ISDS and trade disputes is particularly relevant.[47] At the WTO (as in most regional trade agreements), the complaining state usually wants the actual policy changed. Only states can pursue disputes before WTO arbitration panels. They do not typically turn on the complaint of one affected company, because states don't often gear up a trade dispute on the complaint of just one company. When they do get started, WTO disputes are often joined by multiple complaining states or at least draw in amicus filings by other states (and by nonstate organizations that want certain issues presented to the panel). The aim remains getting the state complained against to remove the objectionable policy, with the threat that the complaining state (or states) may impose offsetting retaliatory tariffs if it does not. WTO panels cannot order compensation payments to be paid to companies that claim they have been victimized by the policy in the past.

[45] Jeremy Caddel & Nathan Jensen, *Columbia FDI Perspective No. 120: Which Host Country Government Actors Are Most Involved in Disputes with Foreign Investors?*, VALE COLUMBIA CENTER ON SUSTAINABLE INT'L INVESTMENT (Apr. 28, 2014) (reporting that some 90% of ISDS rulings focused on complaints against administrative determinations rather than general laws).

[46] Puig, *supra* note 42, at 558.

[47] On political trade-offs between trade regimes and investor protection schemes, *see* Sergio Puig, *Merging International Trade and Investment Law*, 33 BERK. J. INT'L L. 1 (2015).

The aim of WTO arbitration is to determine whether a disputed state policy should be changed in the future.

ISDS, by contrast, focuses on providing a remedy for the past financial losses of the complaining investor. The investor remains in control of its claim and may accept a compromise at any time. Pressure to change underlying state policies is at best indirect. Some states have agreed to arbitration so long as the outcome remains confidential—a way of limiting its wider impact.

Finally, the scheme is *decentered*. There is no one central authority in charge of investor protection laws. That is a way of lowering the stakes but also of accommodating change. There has never been a single overarching treaty that sets out the law of investor protection. There is not full agreement on which arbitration results should be regarded as settled precedents or what weight any recognized precedent should be given.

Some commentators have claimed that the accumulated precedents of many arbitration awards are developing an increasingly settled international economic law.[48] Others dispute the claim, characterizing the accumulating precedents as "soft law" or a very specialized "common law," distinct from general obligations under customary international law.[49] A more skeptical commentator argues that the practice seems to combine elements of private commercial arbitration with public international law in a scheme that is "undertheorized" and "a conceptual mess."[50] Arriving at the best characterization is less urgent than it may seem. The Statute of the International Court of Justice (Article 59) stipulates that its decisions are binding only on the parties, so technically they are not precedents establishing a binding law. Nonetheless, the ICJ itself cites its past rulings as if they had significant precedential weight, so advocates before the court do so, and commentators and governments do so as well. That does not prevent governments from disregarding ICJ rulings (regarding other states) when they find them implausible or disagreeable.

[48] Stephen M. Schwebel, *The Influence of Bilateral Investment Treaties on Customary International Law*, 98 ASIL Proc. 27 (2004); Andreas Lowenfeld, *Investment Agreements and International Law*, 42 Colum. J. Trans'l L. 123 (2003); Reisman & Sloane, *supra* note 28.

[49] Andrew Guzman & Timothy Meyer, *International Common Law: The Soft Law of International Tribunals*, 9 Chi. J. Int'l L. 515 (2009); Frederic G. Sourgens, *Law's Laboratory: Developing International Law on Investment Protection as Common Law*, 34 Nw. J. Int'l L. & Bus. 181 (2014).

[50] Althea Roberts, *Clash of Paradigms: Actors and Analogies Shaping the Investment Treaty System*, 107 Am. J. Int'l L. 45, 47 (2013).

ISDS agreements can be renegotiated to emphasize state concerns. The United States twice made changes in its model BIT (under President G.W. Bush and again under Obama) to emphasize reserved powers over domestic regulation. New standards might raise complications, if all past precedents actually had the status of settled international law. But no one disputes that states may change some elements of their agreements. On the other hand, few informed observers doubt that arbitration panels may still consider precedents from earlier rulings, especially if they find some way to square them with new (but generally vague) terms in updated agreements. A recent survey finds states do not, in fact, rush to renegotiate BITs even after unfavorable decisions that seem to expand investor protections more than participating states might have expected.[51]

The rejection of regional or multilateral treaties with ISDS provisions does not displace or exclude reliance on BITs. Even in the absence of BITs, firms may sign contracts with states that provide for arbitration of ensuing contract disputes. At the margin, there may be enforcement challenges. India persuaded a US federal district court that an arbitration ruling ordering it to reinstate off-shore drilling rights for a foreign oil company could not be enforced by the court because ordering specific performance against a sovereign state (as opposed to damage payments) would violate US public policy.[52] Such precedents do not bind courts in other countries and cannot be settled by a single international authority.

Charles Brower, an arbitrator of many investor-state claims (including as judge for the Iran-US Claims Tribunal) offers this sensible reminder: "There is not a single, monolithic international investment law regime." Instead, there are some three thousand separate treaties that states can adjust in regard to substance and "agree to arbitrate under any of various institutions and rules" or "specify" particular adjustments or exceptions in the procedure. Brower sees the existence of "competing regimes" as offering "the benefit of experimentation that can lead to best practices over time."[53]

Brower's hopes for "best practices" may be optimistic. But it remains true that the range of alternatives can accommodate demands from particular states or influential critics without threatening the overall structure. So, for

[51] Cree Jones & Weijia Rao, *Sticky BITs*, 61 Harv. J. Int'l L. 357 (2020).
[52] Hardy Expl. & Prod. v. Gov't of India, 314 F. Supp. 3d 95 (D.D.C. 2018).
[53] Charles Brower & Sadie Blanchard, *What's in a Meme? The Truth About Investor-State Arbitration*, 52 Col. J. Transnat'l L. 689, 776 (2014) (citing Thomas Waelde, *Improving the Mechanisms for Treaty Negotiation and Investment Disputes: Competition and Choice as the Path to Quality and Legitimacy*, Y.B. Int'l Investment L. & Pol'y 2008–09, 505 (2009)).

example, in the summer of 2020, after consultation with legal experts and governments, UNCITRAL and ICSID introduced a joint proposal on rules to guard against conflicts of interest among arbitrators of ISDS disputes. The proposal would not prevent states from choosing other arbitrators in other fora, but will likely establish a professional standard.[54] Judges of the ICJ announced (on their own initiative) that they would not participate in ISDS arbitration as personal sideline activities, because their ICJ priorities might distract them from impartial attention to the immediate investor dispute.

VI. Expectations and Lessons

The future of investment protection law will depend, of course, on larger trends in the world. ISDS would have no place in an apocalyptic future where cross-border trade and investment had dwindled to insignificance. ISDS could be equally irrelevant if all nations agreed to live under a world government where borders no longer matter.

Short of these extreme possibilities, the future might bring a formalization and centralization of the current arrangements, where a single, generally accepted world investment court handles cases based on an authoritative case law previously built up by that court. That global court might draw its authority from a more detailed global treaty, setting out fundamental principles and fundamental exceptions in the law of investor protection.

Or we might see a reversion to a world in which states refuse to let themselves be summoned to arbitration by private investors: a restoration of sovereign immunity across the board. But this second alternative future is no more likely than the first. There are substantial reasons to doubt that the world will go very far toward either alternative, so long as it remains a world of sovereign states with extensive cross-border trade and investment.

The institutional path of the European Union might seem to strengthen the case for centralization. The European Court of Justice (ECJ) already exercises appellate authority over national courts in questions involving EU norms and regulation and has jealously guarded this authority. In 2018, the ECJ ruled that EU member states could not maintain BITs among

[54] Chiara Giorgetti, *ICSID and UNCITRAL Publish the Anticipated Draft of the Code of Conduct for Adjudicators in Investor-State Dispute Settlement*, Kluwer Arb. Blog, available at http://arbitrationblog.kluwerarbitration.com/2020/05/02/icsid-and-uncitral-publish-the-anticipated-draft-of-the-code-of-conduct-for-adjudicators-in-investor-state-dispute-settlement/.

themselves, since this would allow for inter-state dispute resolution among EU states outside the Court's supervision.[55] The EU states which had signed such agreements (principally former communist states in the years before they joined the European Union) agreed to repudiate them. The ruling was also expected to prevent resort to arbitration under the 1991 Energy Charter Treaty for intra-EU disputes.[56] When the European Union negotiated a trade agreement with Canada, the agreement provided for investor protection, but with disputes to be submitted to a permanent court rather than ad hoc arbitration panels.[57] In negotiations over Britain's departure from the European Union, European negotiators tried hard (though ultimately unsuccessfully) to secure Britain's commitment to leave some trade-related and investment disputes with the European Union to be settled by the ECJ.

The attraction of a permanent court is that it may be more predictable, given a stable membership. It may also be more attentive to states, since its membership would be determined exclusively by states (as opposed to ISDS panels, where investors have a say in which arbitrators will decide their case). The European Union—a sort of quasi-state—may be particularly drawn to this approach, since it seems to enhance the authority of the European Union itself (acting as trade negotiator for its member states) and of supranational authority in general (displacing the nationalist or sovereigntist tendencies of states, including EU member states). One can imagine the European Union trying to promote such arrangements in trade deals with other nations or regions across the world, perhaps then inducing different regional courts to accept a common global appeals court.

But whether other states would wish to go along is very doubtful. Compared to arbitration under ISDS agreements, where private claimants have a say in the selection of arbitrators, a centralized system might seem to offer more control for states. But the control over selection would more likely reflect the views of some states more than others: at best, the views of a majority, more likely the views of the most influential or most alert states. Smaller states might be wary. Larger states might also be wary, for fear of

[55] Case C-284/16, Slovak Republic v. Achmea BV, EU:c:2018:158 (Mar. 6, 2018).

[56] April Lacson, *What Happens Now? The Future of Intra-E.U. Investor-State Dispute Settlement Under the Energy Charter Treaty*, 51 Int'l L. & Pol. 1327 (2019). In July 2020, the European Union initiated negotiations to "modernize" the Energy Charter Treaty (with thirty members, including Russia and former Soviet states, along with all EU members).

[57] Canada-European Union Comprehensive Economic and Trade Agreement (CETA), Can.-E.U., Oct. 30, 2016, http://ec.europa.eu/trade/policy/in-focus/ceta/ceta-chapter-by-chapter/. The arrangement was endorsed by the ECJ in its advisory opinion issued on April 30, 2019.

being outvoted or outmaneuvered, or deprived of influence they might exert in alternate fora. In December 2020, China and the European Union announced agreement on a preliminary treaty on investment protection. Unlike the EU-Canada treaty, the EU treaty with China provided for submission of disputes to a panel of arbitrators chosen for the occasion, rather than a permanent, standing court.[58] The United States has shown the same wariness as China. In negotiations over NAFTA, the United States vetoed a Canadian proposal for a central court (and it did not reappear in negotiations for the USMCA).

The pattern is evident among other states in other settings. Quite apart from trade or investment disputes, states often submit disputes to ad hoc arbitration. Many of these disputes could be submitted to the International Court of Justice or the International Tribunal for the Law of the Sea (ITLOS). So, for example, ITLOS has compulsory jurisdiction (meaning signatories of the Law of the Sea treaty must accept it) for disputes arising from seizures of individual ships. Apart from such very specialized cases, ITLOS heard only six cases on all other sea-related issues (such as maritime boundaries and regulatory authority at sea) between 2000 and 2001. In the same period, the ICJ decided nine cases involving maritime disputes. Arbitrators affiliated with the Permanent Court of Arbitration (hosting ad hoc arbitrations) heard twenty-nine such cases in the same period.[59]

Most states may prefer this approach because they want to select judges (arbitrators) for the purpose at hand. They may also wish to lower the stakes by choosing a forum whose decision will have less weight as a precedent. States may be willing to submit to arbitration, but not to let a permanent body develop extensive case law, which may leave them with new obligations or new restrictions.

There remains the alternative possibility that states will withdraw consent to any form of international dispute settlement and demand that foreign

[58] EU-China Comprehensive Agreement on Investment, Jan. 22, 2021, https://trade.ec.europa.eu/doclib/press/index.cfm?id=2237. The dispute resolution provisions here envision state-to-state arbitration but do not exclude investor claims. The European Parliament voted to defer approval in May 2021, in the midst of a dispute between China and the European Union over EU sanctions against Chinese officials for abuses of Uyghurs and Chinese countersanctions. But most observers predicted the agreement would ultimately be approved.

[59] *See* ITLOS, List of Cases, https://www.itlos.org/en/main/cases/list-of-cases/ (last visited June 17, 2021); International Court of Justice, Contentious Cases, https://www.icj-cij.org/en/contentious-cases (last visited June 17, 2021); Permanent Court of Arbitration, Cases, https://pca-cpa.org/cases/ (last visited June 17, 2021). For analysis of why states prefer to rely on arbitrators selected for the particular dispute, *see* Eric Posner & John C. Yoo, *Judicial Independence in International Tribunals*, 93 Cal. L. Rev. 1 (2005).

investors simply pursue their claims in domestic courts. It is in their own courts, presumably, that governments have the most control over the selection of judicial decision makers and the most likelihood of a sympathetic hearing. But to start with, this approach risks raising doubts and concerns with foreign investors, so they might withdraw their investments or decline to expand them. That is a particular problem for states that depend on outside capital, because their own legal systems may seem unreliable to outsiders.

There remains another obvious difficulty. Refusing to submit investor disputes to outside arbitration does not mean the host state will be left to itself. In addition to the reaction of other investors, there may be reactions from their home states, particularly those that feel their nationals have been abused. Today, the response is very unlikely to be a military intervention. But it may still involve unpleasant consequences.

The historic attraction of BITs was not merely to reassure investors, but to assure their home states that they need no longer stand on guard or on call to protect investors. Without ISDS, a state that provokes protest from a foreign investor may escape arbitration with the investor but still be tumbled into diplomatic confrontation. The home state of the investor may decide that the offending state is an unsuitable partner in other fields, costing it valued opportunities. Or the home state might, after a few such episodes, still demand that a state-to-state arbitration resolve accumulated grievances, as was the common resort in the early twentieth century.

ISDS is less fraught for defending states. Only a third of ISDS arbitrations have resulted in awards of financial compensation for complaining investors.[60] A state that is ordered to make compensation may still attempt to resist payment (or prompt, full payment) without generating a diplomatic imbroglio. The investor may resort to courts in other countries to try to enforce its compensation claims, but the defending state may invoke various legal defenses to resist such claims. Argentina petitioned a US court to vacate an arbitral award in favor of a British firm (under an Anglo-Argentine investment treaty). On appeal to the US Supreme Court, the Court ruled in favor of

[60] According to UNCTAD's Investment Policy Hub, arbitrators issued favorable rulings for investors on 30% of decided cases, while 37% of cases upheld the challenged state (counting cases decided by the end of 2019). Other cases were settled by agreement of the parties or withdrawn by unilateral action of the investor, presumably on indications of a likely unfavorable result (https://investmentpolicy.unctad.org/investment-dispute-settlement). ICSID reports that 31% of its cases (as of June 30, 2020) granted awards in whole or part to the investor, while 34% found for the state, either for lack of jurisdiction or on the merits. The ICSID Caseload—Statistics, Jan. 28, 2021, at https://icsid.worldbank.org/resources/publications/icsid-caseload-statistics (covering 768 cases under ICSID Convention or Additional Facility Rules since 1972).

the British investor, but not without a vigorous dissent by two justices, raising possible issues for the future.[61]

A state can make full payment on an award but affirm that it does not accept the reasoning behind the judgment or all its implications. A state can insist that BITs be renegotiated without rejecting the general approach. States can seek adjustments to their commitments without wholesale withdrawal from the network of BIT commitments. Even threats to renegotiate formal commitments may exert some pressure on arbitrators, who may find it easier to accommodate the emerging mood than would a permanent court, more concerned about its own institutional reputation and perhaps more tied to its own prior decisions.

It is true, of course, that too many concessions will start to hollow out the procedure, leaving it a kind of formality with little real weight as a constraint on state conduct or as a reassuring safeguard for foreign investors. Before things go that far, however, there are likely to be pressures for arbitrators to give more weight to underlying economic realities.

A world recovering from dislocations wrought by a pandemic and other uncertainties has seen a considerable decline in flows of foreign direct investment.[62] But that will probably make states more eager to retain or replace foreign investments in a more competitive environment. Cheap foreign imports, from China and other low-cost producers, have generated protest by affected local industries and their employees (or former employees). Foreign investment tends to be much less controversial.

There is also a structural obstacle to mobilizing opposition to investor protection agreements. The decentralized or dispersed nature of the system—a network of many small strands rather than a single grand structure—makes it less vulnerable to political pressure. Advocates can mobilize opposition to a grand bargain like the TPP or the MAI because it threatens harm (or can be depicted as doing so) for a great many varied interests. That is harder for any particular BIT. Thus, even as the United States has withdrawn from major global or regional trade treaties with investor protection provisions, the

[61] BG Group v. Republic of Argentina, 572 U.S. 25 (2014). The arbitrators held that Argentina had denied "fair and equitable treatment" to BG, which owned MetroGas in Argentina. The dissent by Chief Justice Roberts, joined by Justice Kennedy, protested that Argentina's consent to an investment treaty with the United Kingdom (home of BG) did not imply consent to arbitration with a private firm in the particular circumstances of this dispute.

[62] The OECD reports a 50 percent drop in "global flows of foreign direct investment" (that is, new investment) for the first half of 2020 (compared with the same period in 2019), bringing the total back to the level reached in 2013. OECD, FDI in Figures (Oct. 2020).

United States has continued to negotiate and commit itself to individual BITs with particular countries. These focused agreements do not rouse nearly the same amount of opposition since so much less is at stake in any one particular investment agreement with a particular partner.

In a similar way, the dispersed character of these agreements means that disputes under a particular bilateral treaty do not threaten the whole scheme. Countries can repudiate some agreements without withdrawing from the entire network of BIT commitments. India, after repudiating most of its BITs in 2016, soon announced a new model BIT (ostensibly offering more protection for domestic regulation and more precision in defining eligible "investors") and then concluded a major new agreement with Brazil, while also pursuing new agreements with other states.[63]

There have been notable gaps in the reach of the BIT network. Proposed treaties between the United States and China and the United States and India have stalled in negotiation, as each side has found new reasons for delay. But the ultimate effects of such setbacks are somewhat offset by the potential for multinational corporations to restructure their investments so they can qualify for protection under a BIT that covers subsidiaries in a different home state.[64] Individual investors have sometimes, in the absence of a BIT, insisted (and gained) contract language assuring resort to international arbitration for disputes about improper state interference.

The larger political context is also more favorable. We do not now live in a world where Western capital-exporting states face a large bloc of states inspired by socialist expropriation doctrines. Today, even advanced economies welcome, and have come to depend on, foreign investment. Even developing countries see home-based businesses conduct some of their operations in foreign countries. Over a thousand BITs (more than a third of the total) are between non-Western states on both sides. China has become one of the largest investors in foreign-based enterprises; it is a party to numerous BITs designed to safeguard those investments.

[63] *See* Prabhash Ranjan & Pushkar Anand, *The 2016 Model Indian Bilateral Investment Treaty: A Critical Deconstruction*, 38 N.W. J. Int'l L. & Bus. 1 (2017) (warning that provisions do not strike an acceptable "balance between investment protection and host state's right to regulate" because they are too protective of state regulation). Still, unlike populist regimes in South America, India did not repudiate ISDS in principle. It remains to be seen whether India will be satisfied with what foreign firms are prepared to invest there without BIT protection, or whether it will change its announced bargaining position (its "model") to secure more new BITs.

[64] Brower & Blanchard, *supra* note 53, at 763 (citing UK BIT describing covered firms as "UK nationals" if "constituted under the law in UK," without reference to ultimate ownership).

In the 1970s, disputes about protections for foreign investors under international law stirred debate at the United Nations, enlisting the superpowers of that era on opposite sides. In today's world, China and the United States—which disagree on so much else—are in general agreement that international law assures protection for foreign investors against abusive treatment by host states. Under ISDS arrangements, each dispute can stand on its own as a local disagreement to be "settled" rather than an affirmation or challenge to a global doctrine.

For all these reasons, ISDS is more likely to remain an enduring element in the landscape of contemporary international law. As it is dispersed, adaptive, incremental—and also iterative and somewhat reciprocal (similar issues arise again and again but not always with interests arranged on the same sides)—it has some of the features of the common law. It works as markets do, directing attention to trade-offs and shared interests across particular transactions.

ISDS will likely prove more enduring than efforts to mobilize the world community for centrally directed projects or fully standardized programs. There was international law, even international arbitration, long before there was a United Nations or a set of permanent international courts. International law seems to work best when smoothing interactions between national legal systems rather than subordinating them to a global agenda.

11
Anti-Bribery Law

*Paul B. Stephan**

I. Introduction

International anti-bribery law came into its own during the twenty-first century. Its impact on business behavior has been enormous. Over the last twenty years, regulators have imposed sanctions, and the regulated have invested in compliance, at unprecedented levels. Firms around the world bear these costs. One is hard-pressed to identify any other area of law that has seen such a manifest expansion of its transnational impact.

Were one looking for evidence of the persistence of international cooperation and the ongoing relevance of international law in today's world, this story would seem to fit. At first blush, the growth of transborder anti-bribery law enforcement represents a clear win for international liberalism. This regulatory regime does not aspire to suppress international business transactions, but rather to use transparency and accountability to protect multinational enterprises from a significant vulnerability. Anti-bribery law rests on a belief that markets and contract and property rights must be protected from covert behavior that, left unchecked, would subvert their benign social functions. The extension and deepening of this regime thus looks like successful international cooperation to strengthen global capitalism and the international rule of law.

Several factors complicate the picture, however. First, anti-bribery law is not, strictly speaking, anticorruption law. The groundbreaking US statute, as well as those that follow in its path, criminalizes corrupt payments, not corruption generally.[1] The existing regime focuses on the supply-side of

* I am grateful to comments by David Sloss and Richard Steinberg as well as suggestions by other participants in this project at our February 2020 meeting in Santa Clara. Responsibility for errors and misjudgments remains mine alone.

[1] Foreign Corrupt Practices Act of 1977, Pub. L. No. 95-213, Tit. I, Dec. 19, 1977, 91 Stat. 1495 (codified as amended at 15 U.S.C. §§ 78dd-1, 78dd-2, 78dd-3).

Paul B. Stephan, *Anti-Bribery Law* In: *Is the International Legal Order Unraveling?*. Edited by: David L. Sloss, Oxford University Press. © Oxford University Press 2022. DOI: 10.1093/oso/9780197652800.003.0012

corruption—payments of bribes by multinational firms—and not the demand-side: that is, solicitation and procurement of corrupt benefits by public officials. We have no good way of measuring the impact of regulating the former on the scale of the latter. We do not know whether the anti-bribery regime improves the quality of public services by suppressing bribe-taking or simply shifts the market for bribes to payers who can avoid the contemporary transnational regime, presumably local actors who do not have a substantial presence in countries that regulate bribe payments.

Second, the regime depends on international law, but not the global institutions and cosmopolitan commitments that current world politics have placed under siege. Rather, formal international cooperation, manifested in the OECD Convention on Combating Bribery of Foreign Public Officials in International Business Transactions (OECD Convention)[2] and, to a much lesser extent, the UN Convention Against Corruption,[3] mostly bolster competition among national regulators by reducing traditional sovereignty-based barriers to extraterritorial regulation. International anti-bribery law relies on negative comity, where states strive mostly to stay out of the way of other states' regulatory efforts. A handful of states vigorously prosecute bribery of foreign government officials, and the rest acquiesce.

The first section of this chapter describes the rise of transborder anti-bribery law in this century against the background of its twentieth-century origins. It focuses on the role of a hegemon, namely, the United States, and the impact of its conduct on other rich-world states. During the last century, other states passively resisted US initiatives. Then, at the dawn of the new century, some undertook their own anti-bribery programs in response to US regulation. At the international level, this response took the form of treaties accepting national regulation but not parceling out primary regulatory jurisdiction among states. Cooperation among prosecutors grew, but almost

[2] OECD Convention on Combating Bribery of Foreign Public Officials in International Business Transactions, Dec. 17, 1997, S. Treaty Doc. No. 105-43, 2802 U.N.T.S. 225 (entered into force Feb. 15, 1999) [hereinafter OECD Convention].

[3] United Nations Convention Against Corruption, Oct. 31, 2003, S. Treaty Doc. No. 109-6, 2349 U.N.T.S. 41 (entered into force Dec. 14, 2005). This instrument followed quickly on the heels of the OECD Convention. Today it has 187 parties. Its substantive obligations largely follow those in the OECD Convention, but reporting and peer review measures are largely absent. It has provided employment for a certain number of experts and bureaucrats, but its accomplishments otherwise are hard to detect. *See* Kevin E. Davis, Between Impunity and Imperialism: The Regulation of Transnational Bribery 49 (2019) ("So far the UN mechanism has been less successful."). It seems to exemplify that class of multilateral treaties that states join to forestall international pressure, rather than to carry out a program. *See* Oona A. Hathaway, *Do Human Rights Treaties Make a Difference?*, 111 Yale L.J. 1935 (2002) (describing class). Accordingly, this chapter does not discuss it further.

entirely through informal mechanisms. What resulted is a remarkably robust regulatory regime with almost all of the action occurring at the national level.

The next two sections ask why this kind of international cooperation unfolded as it did. The first focuses on striking parallels between the development of transborder anti-bribery enforcement and the rise of transborder anti-cartel law a generation earlier. Thirty years before anti-bribery law became a thing, the United States took the initiative in attacking international cartels when the rest of the world ignored them. The object was not to dismantle global capitalism, but rather to save it from a deformation that frustrated economic growth and human flourishing. Other countries in the West resisted the US move, in some instances robustly. By the 1980s, however, rich countries came to embrace this form of regulation, not by institutionalizing it at the international level, but rather through coordinated withdrawal of sovereignty-based resistance. International cooperation exists, but through informal fora and other contacts among prosecutors, rather than by the creation of international legal obligations and international institutions to administer them. As with the later anti-bribery project, anti-cartel policy thrived through the scaling back of international-law-based claims about the limits of prescriptive jurisdiction, not through creation of new international institutions.

Section IV then explores the political economy of transborder anti-bribery law. It considers why states regulate behavior that, as a first-order matter, harms foreigners while enriching domestic firms (unlike anti-cartel policy, which focuses on injury to domestic consumers). It rebuts arguments that altruism and a cosmopolitan sense of justice motivate states. Rather, this regulation, like the earlier anti-cartel actions, can best be explained as an effort to save the system of global markets, international business and investment, and transnational private ordering from itself. States have come to embrace these efforts, but have not sought to enforce them through international law. This approach instead puts the onus on powerful states acting as norm entrepreneurs to promote the rule of domestic law internationally.

On balance, the development of anti-bribery law during this century suggests a process of evolutionary adaptation, not revolutionary change and disruption. This chapter considers, however, whether the forces that have undone the liberal internationalist aspirations of the 1990s pose a threat to the contemporary transborder anti-bribery regime. Recent events in China, Brazil, and the United States provide some evidence that anticorruption campaigns can be diverted to dark ends, namely, providing politicians a pretext to crush opponents, thereby reinforcing state power as a means of private enrichment. These episodes raise the prospect of weaponizing anti-bribery law as a means of escalating international conflicts. National initiatives with systemic international benefits, which the anti-cartel law and anti-bribery regimes illustrate, are not immune from the broad economic, social, and political forces that have emerged in this century. That trans-border anti-bribery efforts have prospered during this period of unrest may indicate something about the resilience of global capitalism, but is not proof of the durability of the liberal international order that existed at the end of the twentieth century.

II. The Rise of Anti-Bribery Law

As recently as fifty years ago, most rich countries regarded the bribery of foreign officials as a normal cost of doing business. They even allowed a tax deduction for these payments. In the 1970s, however, the United States moved in a different direction. Until the end of the century, no other country followed. During the final years of the Clinton administration, that changed.

The United States began prosecuting the bribery of foreign officials due to a mix of historic accident, path dependency, and the pressure of bilateral superpower competition. During its investigation of the involvement of US corporations in the 1972 presidential campaigns, the Securities and Exchange Commission (SEC) uncovered facilities (undocumented accounts funded by false invoices) used by many large companies to make illegal payments. The SEC's chief of enforcement, Stanley Sporkin, continued the investigation after President Richard Nixon resigned. Sporkin learned that companies had created these facilities originally to deliver bribes to foreign leaders as a means of procuring contracts from their governments. After assembling this evidence, the SEC claimed that these mechanisms and the bribes they facilitated constituted per se fraud on investors and asserted jurisdiction to suppress the practice.[4] Congress in 1977 enacted the Foreign Corrupt Practices

[4] Securities Act Release No. 5466, 39 Fed. Reg. 10,237 (1974); *see generally* Sec. & Exch. Comm'n, 94th Cong., Report of the Securities and Exchange Commission on Questionable and Illegal Corporate Payments and Practices to the Senate Committee on Banking, Housing and Urban Affairs (Comm. Print 1976); Note, *Disclosure of Payments to Foreign Government Officials under the Securities Acts*, 89 Harv. L. Rev. 1848 (1976).

Act (FCPA), which both ratified the SEC position and added federal criminal penalties to the enforcement mix.[5]

Three aspects of the new criminal statute were significant. First, it focused on paying, rather than taking, bribes. Second, it covered bribes paid to public actors (including political party officials and legislators) but not to persons in private firms. Third, it applied not only to US persons (active personality jurisdiction), but to any bribe payer associated with a company that qualified as an "issuer" under US securities law. This meant that any firm that tapped into US capital markets, as well as people associated with such firms, faced potential criminal liability as well as SEC regulation. As we shall see, this jurisdictional feature, a product of the statute's peculiar origins in Sporkin's investigation, proved significant when the United States later sought to build a transnational anti-bribery regime.

Why the United States adopted the FCPA, when the rest of the rich world continued to treat bribery of foreign governments as a normal business practice, remains a puzzle. Outside of North America and Northern Europe, many political leaders saw reaping rewards from the facilitation of government contracts as a perquisite of public office. International development agencies, including the World Bank, accepted this attitude as natural and made no serious effort to change it. The United States had already moved a step away from the rich-world consensus in 1969 by denying the tax deductibility of such bribes, but it otherwise had done little to suppress the practice.[6]

The geopolitical context suggests one possible reason why the United States launched its anti-bribery campaign. The mid-1970s witnessed serious, sometimes tortured self-appraisal by the United States of its position in the world. The Vietnam tragedy and the Watergate debacle spurred reforms and investigations, including enactment of the War Powers Act of 1973, the Impoundment Control Act and the Trade Act in 1974, and the 1975 Rockefeller Commission and Church Committee inquiries into the Central Intelligence Agency. These responses to executive overreach and misbegotten foreign policy played out against a background of apparent Soviet geopolitical gains through victories in proxy wars in Southeast Asia and

[5] For a fuller narrative, *see* Pierre-Hugues Verdier & Paul B. Stephan, *International Human Rights and Multinational Corporations: An FCPA Approach*, 101 B.U. L. Rev. 1359, 1393–96 (2021).

[6] Tax Reform Act of 1969, Pub. L. No. 91-172, § 902(b), Dec. 30, 1969, 83 Stat. 487, 710 (codified at 26 U.S.C. § 162(c)).

Africa.[7] In this environment, Sporkin's revelations, involving bribes paid to leaders of key Cold War allies such as Japan and Saudi Arabia, demanded a response. Otherwise, the United States would have left unrebutted its adversaries' charge that global capitalism, of which the United States was the perceived leader, exercised its hegemony through corrupting local élites to the detriment of the people they supposedly served. That the world seemed to be moving the adversaries' way made the need for a response even more urgent.

The challenge for the United States was to balance several competing interests: demonstrating commitment to the people in the developing world who did not want to have their leaders suborned by First World firms; not alienating too much the corrupt leadership of Cold War allies; and not imposing excessive costs on US firms competing for business in parts of the world where corruption was commonplace. From the time of enactment of the FCPA until the end of the Cold War, the United States struck a balance that minimized the interests of the developing world while not ignoring them altogether. It imposed significant fines on companies in the cases exposed by Sporkin, but did not use criminal sanctions; afterward it occasionally prosecuted flagrant acts of corruption, especially when the bribes harmed US firms that lost business by not playing along; and it generally tolerated devices available especially to large and experienced firms to outsource bribery, such as by working through distributors and similar independent contractors.

For the next twenty years, this compromise remained fairly stable. Business interests tried to use the Omnibus Trade and Competitiveness Act of 1988, the most important reform of US international business law since the 1974 Trade Act, to undermine the FCPA, but the amendments enacted instead codified existing government positions.[8] The US Chamber of Commerce and other business groups grumbled about US firms losing out to rich-world competitors, especially German and Japanese firms, but to little avail. At the same time, neither the Justice Department nor the SEC sought to test the limits of their prosecutorial powers.[9]

During the 1990s, things began to change. First and foremost, the Soviet Union came to an ignoble end, highlighting a general trend away from economic autarky and seemingly bringing in a new age of political and economic

[7] *See* Paul B. Stephan, *Courts, the Constitution, and Customary International Law: The Intellectual Origins of the Restatement (Third) of the Foreign Relations Law of the United States*, 44 Va. J. Int'l L. 33, 53–58 (2003) (describing crisis of political élites in the United States during this period).

[8] Pub. L. No. 100-418, § 5003(a), (c), 102 Stat. 1107, 1415, 1419 (1988).

[9] *See* Rachel Brewster, *Enforcing the FCPA: International Resonance and Domestic Strategy*, 103 Va. L. Rev. 1611, 1646–47 (2017) (summarizing data on FCPA prosecutions and fines).

liberalism as well as international cosmopolitanism and institutionalism. Apartheid fell in South Africa, while left and right authoritarians gave way to apparently liberal democrats elsewhere in the developing world. The international rule of law seemed to have come into its own. The United Nations gave its blessings to a US-organized armed conflict with Iraq; the Council of Europe, NATO, and the European Union absorbed much of the former Warsaw Pact and even parts of the former Soviet Union; and the General Agreement on Tariffs and Trade became the ward of a new World Trade Organization.[10] The Cold War had ended, and the US-led West seemed to triumph.[11]

If the US anti-bribery regime emerged as a response to the dictates of the Cold War, one might have expected some scaling back once that struggle ended. But the opposite happened. In 1995, the administration sponsored James Wolfensohn as the new president of the World Bank, with the understanding that he would end that institution's business-as-usual approach to corruption.[12] More significantly, the Clinton administration turned to the Organisation for Economic Co-operation and Development (OECD) as a platform to push rich and semi-rich countries to join the struggle against transborder bribery.[13] The United States saw the rooting out of official corruption as fundamental to its program for remaking the world in what it believed to be the American image, an international society based on market capitalism, the rule of law, respect for human rights, and effective representative democracy.

The transformation of the world economy after 1989–91 surely raised the salience of anti-bribery law. Many large states—China, India, and Russia in particular—had opened themselves to foreign trade and investment without

[10] Paul B. Stephan, *The New International Law—Legitimacy, Accountability, Authority, and Freedom in the New Global Order*, 70 U. Colo. L. Rev. 1555 (1999).

[11] I questioned that assessment at the time. *See, e.g.*, Paul B. Stephan, *The Fall—Understanding the Collapse of Soviet Communism*, 29 Suffolk U. L. Rev. 17 (1995).

[12] *See* James D. Wolfensohn, *Fighting Corruption Is Central to Development*, *in* Voice for the World's Poor: Selected Speeches and Writings of World Bank President James D. Wolfensohn, 1995–2005, at 175, Report No. 34362 (2005); Hassane Cissé, *Crossing Borders in International Development: Some Perspectives on Human Rights, Governance, and Anti-Corruption*, 55 Va. J. Int'l L. 1, 2–6 (2014). Most international financial institutions, following the lead of the World Bank, developed anti-bribery rules for private actors participating in projects that they back. Evidence of actual enforcement, however, is scant.

[13] *See* Davis, *supra* note 3, at 43; Daniel K. Tarullo, *The Limits of Institutional Design: Implementing the OECD Anti-Bribery Convention*, 44 Va. J. Int'l L. 665, 668–80 (2004). As Tarullo notes, the United States also negotiated a Convention Against Corruption with the Organization of American States during this period, and the Council of Europe produced a Criminal Law Convention on Corruption. *Id.* at 666, nn. 3, 4 (citing treaties). I am unaware of any evidence of these two treaties doing any work independent of the OECD Convention.

necessarily ridding themselves of the pervasive corruption that had accompanied their closed economies. Meanwhile, international finance grew massively during this period, with the US dollar further entrenched as the world's principal currency. As a result, global capitalism faced many more opportunities for business in regions where public corruption was endemic at a time when international business had become more dependent on dollar-based finance. Because the United States had tied its anti-bribery regime to access to US capital markets, these factors provided a unique opportunity for regulatory leverage.[14]

The immediate fruit of the Clinton administration's effort was the OECD Anti-Bribery Convention. As of 2020, all thirty-seven OECD members have joined the Convention and enacted domestic implementing legislation, as have Argentina, Brazil, Bulgaria, Costa Rica, the Russian Federation, and South Africa.[15] Typical of OECD treaties, the Convention functions as an action plan, more than as a source of mutual and reciprocal obligations under international law. Parties agree to enact domestic legislation that criminalizes the bribery of foreign public officials, and to hold firms accountable for such conduct.[16] The Convention does not, however, give concrete guidance as to the specifics of the offenses and other accountability mechanisms. Rather, it creates a monitoring and reporting function based on peer review to enable the hectoring of underperforming states.[17]

The Convention's parties also agree to coordinate their actions in cases where more than one state asserts jurisdiction over an offense.[18] Significantly, the Convention does not provide a formula for resolving conflicts of jurisdiction and in particular does not oblige a party to defer to any other state where such conflicts exist. Instead, it effectively limits, even if it does not

[14] For discussion of some of the international legal responses to these changes in the global economy, *see* Jeremy Rabkin, *Strength in Obscurity: The Resilience of International Investment Law* (Chapter 10 in this volume).

[15] Costa Rica at present is a candidate for accession to the OECD. Brazil, China, and South Africa enjoy a special relationship with the OECD as "key partners." India and Indonesia also are key partners but have not joined the Convention. Argentina and Russia do not have any formal special relationship with the OECD but do participate in particular projects and committees.

[16] OECD Convention, *supra* note 2, arts. 1, 2. Because many of the OECD countries do not recognize criminal liability for legal, as opposed to natural, persons, the second provision was necessary to create a level playing field between common-law and civil-law countries.

[17] *Id.*, art. 12. The parties have implemented this process through a quarterly meeting of national chief prosecutors for bribery offenses at OECD headquarters, as well as through regularly scheduled audits of enforcement programs by peer enforcers (not OECD staff or experts).

[18] *Id.*, art. 4.

conclusively reject, the right of one state to block another's prosecution based on impermissible interference with matters within its sole competence.

All parties to the Convention currently are in full compliance, in the sense that they have satisfied its one clear positive obligation to enact specified legislation. Enforcement of the adopted laws, however, has been largely absent. It took years for any country other than the United States to bring a prosecution, and only a handful of states vigorously enforce their laws today. One important economic power, Japan, has yet to bring a single case. Were one to assess the Convention solely by the criterion of whether it moved the parties to prosecute bribery by firms within their jurisdictions, one would have to count it a damp squib at best.[19] But this is not the right way to look at what the Convention did.

What happened in the wake of adoption of the OECD Convention was a significant upsurge in US prosecutions under the FCPA. Rachel Brewster, drawing on a database she created to identify trends, reports that both SEC and Department of Justice enforcement actions started to grow by 2001, and by 2007 hit levels that were roughly an order of magnitude higher than those before 1998.[20] Practices that US prosecutors had tolerated, such as outsourcing bribery through third parties, came under fire.[21] The penalties assessed since the signing of the Convention grew at an even greater rate and indicate a significant shift toward actions against foreign-headquartered enterprises.[22]

This increase in US actions against foreign firms induced a new interest in anti-bribery enforcement on the part of other Convention parties. Germany, the United Kingdom, and Switzerland became relatively active enforcers of anti-bribery law after the United States brought high-profile actions against firms based in their countries. More recently, France seemingly has moved in this direction on the heels of the US prosecution of one of its national champions.[23] The inference seems irresistible: the Convention cleared a path

[19] Rachel Brewster & Christine Dryden, *Building Multilateral Anticorruption Enforcement: Analogies between International Trade & Anti-Bribery Law*, 57 Va. J. Int'l L. 211, 238–41 (2018) (reporting data on enforcement actions by Convention parties).

[20] Brewster, *supra* note 9, at 1648–49.

[21] Practitioners saw the turning point as the SEC enforcement action against InVision Technologies. In the Matter of GE InVision, Inc. (formerly known as InVision Technologies, Inc.), Respondent Admin. Proc. File No. 3-11827, Securities and Exchange Comm'n, Feb. 14, 2005 (basing liability on receipt of e-mails reporting on bribes paid by independent distributor).

[22] Brewster, *supra* note 9, at 1651–55. A comprehensive and searchable database for FCPA enforcement actions, created by the Sullivan & Cromwell law firm, is available at Foreign Corrupt Practices Act Clearinghouse, http://fcpa.stanford.edu.

[23] Brewster & Dryden, *supra* note 19, at 242–47, 255–57.

for increased US extraterritorial enforcement against foreign bribe payers, enabling the United States also to go after its own firms more vigorously. Only after their firms became the subject of significant US actions did other Convention parties begin to police their own, in some prominent cases by entering into collaborative prosecutorial arrangements with US authorities.[24]

This new regime has had significant consequences for multinational firms. The ongoing appetite for access to US capital markets has induced a wide range of corporations from around the world to expose themselves and the people who work for or with them to US enforcement jurisdiction. The OECD Convention has freed the United States to exercise that jurisdiction without fear of retaliation from other states. Today, large multinational corporations devote significant resources to both prevention and investigation of corrupt payments to foreign officials, whether made directly out of corporate resources or through independent middlemen.[25]

Some observers worry that an enforcement regime led by a single country invites competition from states that will shelter firms from US anti-bribery rules. A common argument is that as China's role in the global economy grows, more firms will move away from US capital markets and the accompanying anti-bribery regulation to take advantage of lower compliance costs and, perhaps, greater opportunities to pursue business opportunities based on bribery.[26] To date, however, this does not seem to have happened. To be sure, capital allocations by multinational firms take place in a very noisy environment, even more so under conditions of the COVID-19 pandemic. We cannot say with complete confidence whether businesses with a choice have stayed away from the United States because of its rules. We do continue to

[24] *Id.*; *see also* Brewster, *supra* note 9, at 1671 ("The OECD Anti-Bribery Convention allowed U.S. authorities to achieve a competition-neutral strategy by making use of the FCPA's (long dormant) expansive jurisdiction."); Stephen J. Choi & Kevin E. Davis, *Foreign Affairs and Enforcement of the Foreign Corrupt Practices Act*, 11 J. Empirical Leg. Stud. 409 (2014) (demonstrating a positive correlation between level of US sanctions and robustness of defendant's home-state anti-bribery regime).

[25] *See* Mike Koehler, *Foreign Corrupt Practices Act Ripples*, 3 Am. U. Bus. L. Rev. 391, 395–402 (2014); Veronica Root Martinez, *The Outsized Influence of the FCPA?*, 2019 U. Ill. L. Rev. 1205, 1209–10.

[26] *See, e.g.*, Andrew Brady Spalding, *The Irony of International Business Law: U.S. Progressivism and China's New Laisser-Faire*, 59 UCLA L. Rev. 354, 395 (2011) (asserting existence of Chinese competitive advantage); Andrew Brady Spalding, *Unwitting Sanctions: Understanding Anti-Bribery Legislation as Economic Sanctions Against Emerging Markets*, 62 Fla. L. Rev. 351, 397–98 (2010) (describing "black knight" scenario of increasing foreign direct investment by states that encourage bribery).

see, however, Chinese multinational firms coming to the United States for capital, notwithstanding the regulatory burden that accompanies that step.[27]

Finally, one might note that the contemporary international anti-bribery regime emerged through state agencies (prosecutors and diplomats) without competitive pressure from private actors. Unlike many other regulatory schemes in the United States, US anti-bribery law does not enable private actors to compete with public law enforcers to expose wrongdoing and bring lawbreakers to justice. The FCPA does not provide for private lawsuits. An effort to use civil Racketeer Influenced and Corrupt Organizations Act (RICO) suits as an indirect means of FCPA enforcement was underused and became untenable in light of later Supreme Court jurisprudence.[28]

In sum, once the United States doubled down on its regulatory program during the 1990s, the OECD Convention and the dependence of many international firms on US capital markets provided the tools for creating the contemporary international anti-bribery regime. The question remains, however, why the United States made this choice. Notwithstanding the ideology of the post-Soviet moment and the increased risk of multinational corporations engaging in bribery of foreign officials once formerly autarkic, but still corrupt, states opened up their economies, it is not self-evident why the United States chose to make a significant investment of political good will and regulatory resources in this enterprise. Its partners were reluctant and other potential cooperative projects existed, especially once the terrorist threat reemerged in the late 1990s.

The next two sections of this chapter offer responses to this question. The United States had a precedent for the kind of regime that emerged for bribery. The anti-cartel consensus that had taken shape by the end of the 1980s showed the way. That consensus arose out of conflict between the United States and its allies that was resolved only after most of the major economic powers in the West came to see the benefits to consumers from the suppression of cartels generally as more important than the local rents

[27] For 2011–20, nearly a third of all corrupt practices addressed by US enforcers of the FCPA (50 out of 157) involved Chinese officials. Foreign Corrupt Practices Act Clearinghouse, *supra* note 22.

[28] *See* Environmental Tectonics v. W.S. Kirkpatrick Co., 847 F.2d 1052 (3d Cir. 1988) (upholding RICO civil suit based on facts arising out of FCPA prosecution), *aff'd on other grounds*, W.S. Kirkpatrick Co., Inc. v. Environmental Tectonics Corp., Int'l, 493 U.S. 400 (1990) (act of state doctrine does not apply to claim). *But see* RJR Nabisco, Inc. v. European Community, 136 S. Ct. 2090 (2016) (limiting civil suits under RICO to violations producing a domestic injury to persons or property). Injuries resulting from bribery of foreign officials occur in places where foreign officials exercise authority, which would not be the United States. Accordingly, the kinds of civil RICO suits that the Third Circuit endorsed in *Environmental Tectonics* seem to be out of bounds after *RJR Nabisco*.

derived from state-sponsored or protected export cartels. Something similar then happened with respect to bribery. Rich-world exporters came to see advantages from the suppression of bribery as long as a reasonably effective system existed to regulate their most significant competitors elsewhere in the rich world. Led by the United States, rich-world governments satisfied that demand.

III. The Competition Law Precedent

International competition law has a long and complicated history. This section focuses on the parts of that history that became relevant to the international anti-bribery project. It thus concentrates on one aspect of competition law, namely, suppression of international cartels.

International cartels (consortiums of firms that agree not to compete with each other so as to support high prices) emerged as a significant form of organization of the world economy during the interwar period. They became a target of US enforcers as World War II drew to an end, in part because some cartels involved domestic producers collaborating with enemy-alien firms.[29] For the next forty years, most other rich countries—Australia and Canada, as well as the large European powers—pushed back. They claimed that international law did not permit the United States to regulate business activity carried out on another state's territory, even if that activity had a significant commercial effect on the US economy.

Effective cartels induce producers not to compete with each other by forgoing exports to other members' markets. Suppression of international cartels thus necessarily requires punishing agreements among foreign producers not to do something on the territory of the targeted country. In a world that allocated regulatory jurisdiction mostly on the basis of territoriality and nationality, going after foreign firms for what they did on foreign territory seemed beyond the pale. The United States rationalized its approach by arguing that international law permitted the suppression of overseas activity that had an intended and significant harmful effect on economic activity within the regulating state's territory. The rest of the rich world argued

[29] *See* United States v. Aluminum Co. of America, 148 F.2d 416, 442–45 (2d Cir. 1945) (upholding liability of cartel participant as to overseas activity); James Rahl, *International Cartels and their Regulation*, *in* Competition in International Business 240 (Oscar Schacter & Robert Hellawell eds., 1981).

that this position had no basis in international law. As part of their resistance, states criminalized compliance with US investigations into cartel activity and authorized firms subject to damages awards for violation of US antitrust law to "claw back" damages paid through civil suits against their judgment creditors.[30]

This conflict reflected a particular political economy. Having as it did the world's richest domestic market, the United States objected to collusion among producers to restrict quantity and thus to raise prices in that market. Its consumers bore the largest share of injury, measured by the difference between prices paid and the prices that would have occurred in the absence of collusion. Other countries regarded losses to their consumers as less significant than the chance that their national champions could obtain monopoly superprofits through cartel participation. Both the United States and the other market-oriented economic powers understood cartels to function as a means of redistributing wealth from consumers to producers; their position on cartels turned on the net of their own consumers' losses and producers' gains.[31]

As late as the early 1980s, conflicts between US extraterritorial enforcement of its anti-cartel law and other countries defending their national champions broke out. The Laker Airways dispute, involving barriers to entry into the trans-Atlantic air passenger market erected by an incumbent cartel comprising national airlines, spawned parallel suits in the United States and the United Kingdom, as well as remarkable procedural innovations, in particular the anti–anti-suit injunction. The United States asserted a right to suppress conduct that had the direct effect of raising the cost of international airfares for US travelers; the British courts defended the right of the United Kingdom to decide for itself how British airlines would go about their business.[32]

[30] *See, e.g.*, Rio Tinto Zinc Corp. v. Westinghouse Electric Corp., [1978] A.C. 547 (H.L.) (rejecting US discovery with respect to uranium cartel); Gulf Oil Corp. v. Gulf Canada Ltd., [1980] 1 S.C.R. 39 (Can. Sup. Ct.) (same); Joseph E. Neuhaus, *Power to Reverse Foreign Judgments: The British Clawback Statute under International Law*, 81 Colum. L. Rev. 1097 (1981).

[31] This account, like political-economy stories generally, ignores noneconomic explanations of the conflict, such as cultural differences and differences in the degree of integration between political and economic élites.

[32] *Compare* Midland Bank v. Laker Airways Ltd., [1986] 1 Q.B. 689 (Ct. App.) (enjoining US suits against British participants in cartel), *with* Laker Airways Ltd. v. Sabena, 731 F.2d 909 (D.C. Cir. 1984) (enjoining non-British cartel participants from seeking anti-suit injunction against potential plaintiff in British courts). *Midland Bank* was a traditional anti-suit injunction; the *Sabena* case enjoined the defendants from following in Midland Bank's steps, and hence blocked a suit to obtain an anti-suit injunction.

Even as European states were defending their right to protect home-state cartel participants, cracks in rich-world opposition to US regulation emerged. Canada, the Federal Republic of Germany, and Australia entered into executive agreements with the US government in an effort to manage jurisdictional conflicts. The agreements adopted a notify-and-consult model accompanied by a promise of confidentiality as to investigative information exchanged. They contained no substantive rules, but rather formalized a process that could limit conflicts.[33]

Meanwhile, European anti-cartel law began to move in the direction of consumer protection. The 1957 Treaty Establishing the European Economic Community had endowed the European Commission with the authority to impose competition law, including the suppression of cartels, regardless of national law. No cases arose for over a decade, and then those that did involved only producers within the Community. If one were to view the European Economic Community (EEC) as a single state for competition law purposes, then the Commission's practice did not undermine the strict territoriality asserted by national regulators.

In the 1980s, however, the Commission went after the wood pulp cartel. This group included Canadian, Finnish, Swedish, and US firms, none of which produced wood pulp within the Community. In 1988, the European Court of Justice upheld the Commission's assertion of jurisdiction.[34] It did not expressly endorse the "effects" theory of regulatory (prescriptive) jurisdiction espoused by the United States, but most readers found its approach irreconcilable with any other conception of regulatory authority.[35] From a political economy perspective, it appeared that the EEC had come to recognize the net benefits of cartel suppression. Once one saw the EEC as an integrated single market, the lost consumer surplus from international cartel participation outweighed local producers' monopoly superprofits. EEC-based public intervention followed.

[33] Joint Statement Concerning Cooperation in Anti-Trust Matters, Nov. 3, 1969, United States–Canada, 8 I.L.M. 1305 (1969); Agreement Between the Government of the United States of America and the Government of the Federal Republic of Germany Relating to Mutual Cooperation Regarding Restrictive Business Practices, June 23, 1976, 15 I.L.M. 1282 (1976); Agreement between the Government of the United States of America and the Government of Australia Relating to Cooperation on Antitrust Matters, June 29, 1982, 21 I.L.M. 702 (1982).

[34] Joined Cases 89, 104, 114, 116, 117, and 125 to 129/85, A. Ahlström Osakeyhtiö v. Commission, 1988 E.C.R. 5193. Finland and Sweden joined the European Union, the successor to the European Economic Community, years later.

[35] *See* Restatement (Fourth) of the Foreign Relations Law of the United States § 409 reporters' note 2 (Am. Law Inst. 2018) (describing resistance to and then acceptance of effects principle with respect to prescriptive jurisdiction of economic regulation).

Shortly thereafter, the Community and the United States entered into an executive agreement to promote competition-law cooperation.[36] This pact committed the parties to notify each other of investigations that might affect important interests of the other side and to consult over concerns about these effects. It neither committed the parties to conform their competition policies nor definitively allocated prescriptive jurisdiction. It did implicitly endorse, however, the concept that overlapping assertions of jurisdiction were a natural part of competition law enforcement and were to be accommodated whenever possible. When the substance of competition policy converged, as with cartels, it bolstered cooperative enforcement.

During the 1990s, the entente memorialized in the executive agreement facilitated several cooperative prosecutions of international cartels.[37] The OECD's competition committee became a venue for coordinating activity among developed-world enforcers.[38] Throughout the present century the US government has continued to target cartels in tandem with foreign prosecutors.[39] The Trump administration, whatever its reservations about international cooperation in general, continued to participate in the Competition Committee as well as advertising its accomplishments in pursing international cartels.[40]

[36] Agreement Between the Government of the United States of America and the Commission of the European Communities Regarding the Application of Their Competition Laws, arts. II, V, VI, Sep. 23, 1991, 30 I.L.M. 1487 (1991). The European Court of Justice later ruled that the Commission had exceeded its powers by proceeding without full involvement of the Council. Case C-327/91, French Republic v. Commission, 1994 E.C.R. I-3641. The Commission and Council then jointly ratified the agreement, essentially unchanged, on behalf of the European Communities. Decision of the Council and the Commission of 10 April 1995 Concerning the Conclusion of the Agreement Between the European Communities and the Government of the United States of America Regarding the Application of Their Competition Laws, 1995 O. J. (L95) 45. The new agreement was signed on June 4, 1998. There is no evidence that the four-year gap in an agreement being in force had any effect on prosecutorial behavior.

[37] Antitrust Div., U.S. Dept. of Justice, Final Report of Advisory Committee on International Antitrust Policy 163–200 (2000) (describing anti-cartel cooperation), https://www.justice.gov/atr/final-report.

[38] *See, e.g.*, OECD, Cartels and anti-competitive agreements, https://www.oecd.org/competition/cartels/. The Clinton administration promoted an international Competition Network as an informal means of including enforcers from the developing world into the mix. It presently includes almost exclusively Western Hemisphere governments, and not many of them. https://www.internationalcompetitionnetwork.org/members/.

[39] To facilitate this cooperation, US prosecutors successfully sought limits on the ability of private plaintiffs to compete with their actions in US courts. Brief for the United States as Amicus Curiae Supporting Petitioners, F. Hoffman-La Roche Ltd. v. Empagran, S.A., 542 U.S. 155 (2004) (No. 03-724) (defending limitation on private claims to those based on domestic injury).

[40] Antitrust Division Spring Update 2019, Cartels Beware: The Antitrust Division Prepares for Trial and Continues Criminal Investigations in Key Markets, Mar. 26, 2019, https://www.justice.gov/atr/division-operations/division-update-spring-2019/cartels-beware.

To summarize, the international experience with cartel suppression evolved from sharp conflict with a hegemon, in its initial stage, to the development of significant international cooperation that did not depend on international institutions or substantive international legal obligations, in its final stage. During the transition period, the United States and its adversaries drew back from what amounted to a game of chicken and began exploring opportunities for sharing prosecutorial resources as well as staying out of each other's way. When the Clinton administration began pushing for collective action in the anti-bribery field, the cooperative international anti-cartel regime had been in place for roughly a decade following twenty years of prior development.

IV. Anti-Bribery Regimes and National Interest

Collective action to suppress international cartels reflects a fairly simple economic calculus. The issue is who suffers and who benefits from particular interventions. Most states with large-scale economies suffer greater losses to their consumers than they gain from producer monopoly superprofits.[41] Dividing the surplus created by the suppression of cartels thus presents a fairly easy-to-solve bargaining problem. Each state can act as a proxy for its producer and consumer groups without too much difficulty.[42]

In the case of anti-bribery actions, the political economy is murkier. Identifying the winners and losers from corrupt transactions and the mechanisms that keep the winners in power is challenging. One might view corruption as simply a tax on outsiders seeking access to a nation's economy, with the revenues going to designated public officials rather than to the public fisc. Indeed, one could conceive of bribe collecting as a form of tax-farming, with public servants "paying" into general revenues by accepting

[41] The statement in text applies to cartels for commodities that generate few positive externalities, such as technological innovation and other forms of knowledge. The presence of significant positive externalities from production may alter the calculus for states that host producers. *See* Paul B. Stephan, *Global Governance, Antitrust, and the Limits of International Cooperation*, 38 CORNELL INT'L L.J. 173 (2005).

[42] The statement in text brackets the well-documented tendency of producer groups to prevail over consumers in straightforward political contests. VILFREDO PARETO, MANUAL OF POLITICAL ECONOMY 379 (Ann S. Schwier & Alfred N. Page eds., Ann S. Schwier trans., 1971) (1927); Anne O. Krueger, *Government, Trade, and Economic Integration*, 82 AMER. ECON. REV. 109, 110–11 (1992) (providing various examples of small, well-organized interest groups extracting protective measures from the legislature). This evidence does not refute the point that, if a sufficiently large disparity exists between the values of consumer and producer interests, the former will prevail.

lower formal compensation in return for the privilege of collecting bribes. The political economy then becomes fairly straightforward: Are bribe-collectors paying the sovereign enough for the privilege of collecting bribes? If this were all that is going on, the politics focus simply on the pricing of the privilege.[43]

It is more common, however, to think of corruption as a rent collected by public servants to the harm of the general welfare, with the deadweight loss increasing as the cost of ousting incumbents rises.[44] For this reason, corruption is often associated with autocracy, just as clean government is associated with transparency and political accountability.[45] Anticorruption regimes, unlike anti-bribery rules, thus require tackling fundamental issues of political structure. This presents significant challenges to outsiders, in particular states with jurisdiction over potential bribe-paying firms. One might stipulate that, ceteris paribus, people would be better off if their states were not corrupt autocracies. Designing mechanisms to replace such regimes in ways that do not generate new rents for those who displace the former incumbents, however, has proven exceedingly difficult.[46]

Reconceiving the project as anti-bribery, rather than anticorruption, simplifies the issues. One only has to identify the conditions under which foreign firms would find a ban on paying bribes acceptable. One may assume that firms would prefer to avoid the direct costs of bribery (the payment) as well as the indirect costs—mainly monitoring the compliance of bribed persons with the terms of the bribe contract and screening bribe solicitations for quality and credibility. If so, potential bribe payers would support suppression of bribery whenever bribery-related costs were greater than the cost of losing business opportunities to competitors who do not have to comply with a ban on bribes. Expanding the scope and effectiveness of the ban thus

[43] *See* Gary S. Becker, *A Theory of Competition Among Pressure Groups for Political Influence*, 98 Q.J. Econ. 371 (1983) (describing conditions under which competition among rent-seekers disperses private rents).

[44] *See generally* Susan Rose-Ackerman, *The Law and Economics of Bribery and Extortion*, 6 Ann. Rev. L. & Soc. Sci. 217, 219 (2010) ("The social costs of bribery include the inefficiencies introduced by payoffs, the unfair distribution of a public benefit, and the erosion of legal entitlements to act free of threats to person or property.").

[45] There is, of course, a view that the statement in text has it exactly backward, that successful oppression and injustice benefit from opaque means of subjugation disguised by seeming transparency. *See, e.g.*, David Kennedy, *The International Anti-Corruption Campaign*, 14 Conn. J. Int'l L. 455 (1999). One need not embrace critical theory to doubt whether there exists a clear and broadly appealing conception of the optimal balance between administrative discretion and constraints on self-dealing by public officials.

[46] *See, e.g.*, Ivan Krastev & Stephen Holmes, The Light that Failed (2019) (discussing failures of the post-autocratic project in Europe).

lowers the costs to potential bribe payers of their compliance with the ban by reducing opportunity costs.

Scholars have elaborated on the factors that would induce potential bribe payers to welcome otherwise costly restrictions on bribery (potential sanctions plus monitoring and bonding mechanisms designed to suppress bribe payments by persons for whom a firm is accountable).[47] First, firms might believe that the creation of "black accounts" creates incentives for employees and agents to embezzle from the firm, and potential losses from such behavior may outweigh the benefits from additional business gained. Second, firms might appreciate that they are not very good at assessing the quality of bribe demands, namely, the likelihood that a public official will deliver the proffered service, and might regard a general ban as a desirable bonding mechanism.[48] Third, even more would welcome dispensing with the costs of paying bribes, both direct and indirect, as long as a substantial portion of their competitors were similarly constrained.[49]

The first two of these explanations would apply to some firms even in the absence of even-handed enforcement, but the last depends on solving a collective action problem. Even-handed anti-bribery enforcement against the rich world's multinational firms requires either a sharing of prosecutorial responsibilities among a salient coalition of states or leadership by a hegemon that could overcome resistance by other states. The former presents rich opportunities for defection. It is not irrelevant that few examples of sustained successful prosecutorial collaboration exist in international economic law generally.[50] The anti-cartel program of the 1970s and 1980s demonstrated how the latter approach could work.

[47] *See* Michael C. Jensen & William H. Meckling, *Theory of the Firm: Managerial Behavior, Agency Costs and Ownership Structure*, 3 J. Fin. Econ. 305, 323–26 (1976) (defining monitoring mechanisms as those used to observe agent behavior, and bonding mechanisms as constraints imposed on agents to limit disloyalty). Jensen and Meckling define agency costs (the costs associated with entering into an agent-principal relationship) as the sum of monitoring and bonding costs plus the residual costs in an agent-principal relationship that monitoring and bonding mechanisms do not abate. *Id.* at 308.

[48] A bonding mechanism forbids an agent from undertaking activity that might benefit the principal in some instances because the overall risk of principal harm is too great. *Id.* at 326; *see* Paul B. Stephan, *Regulatory Competition and Anticorruption Law*, 53 Va. J. Int'l L. 53, 62–63 (2012) (describing bribery as an agency cost to firms).

[49] Brewster, *supra* note 9, at 1667–72 (US government obtained international-competition neutrality so as to overcome business resistance); Sean J. Griffith & Thomas H. Lee, *Toward an Interest Group Theory of Foreign Anti-Corruption Laws*, 2019 U. Ill. L. Rev. 1227, 1252–57 (depicting development of coalition among capital-exporting states to suppress bribery based on lobbying by business groups). The stories told by Brewster and Griffith-Lee are more complementary than rivalrous: both turn on the willingness of businesses to embrace anti-bribery enforcement if, but only if, enforcers did not discriminate among competitors seeking government contracts.

[50] International trade law might be seen as a counterexample. *See* Brewster & Dryden, *supra* note 18. The trade regime, however, seeks to limit government action (tariff collection and comparable

There remains the question of why a multilateral treaty emerged as part of the response to this collective action problem, when nothing similar came out of the disputes over anti-cartel cooperation. Rachel Brewster has proposed the most convincing explanation. She explains: "International acceptance of foreign anti-corruption norms, predominantly the entry into force of the OECD Anti-Bribery Convention, allowed American prosecutors to successfully target foreign and domestic corporations."[51] The Convention, in other words, established negative comity sufficient to clear the way for US extraterritorial enforcement, even without formally doing so. Simply by affirming that they regarded bribery of foreign officials as worthy of regulation, the treaty parties implicitly surrendered any objection to US regulation to that end, even if that regulation reached their nationals.

To summarize, international anti-bribery law reflects a search for a solution to a collective action problem. Most multilateral firms would prefer not to bribe foreign government officials for a variety of reasons, but only if their principal competitors also would not bribe. Requiring national prosecutors to share the burden of enforcing the anti-bribery norm would risk defection. But, as the experience with anti-cartel law demonstrated, the United States could solve the problem through leveraging its jurisdiction over many multinational firms. Other states either could join in, if only to forestall more stringent action by the United States, or instead allow the United States to take charge.[52] The OECD Convention supports this form of international cooperation, even if it did not mandate it.

V. Anti-Bribery and the Rise of National Populism

The preceding sections demonstrate that anti-bribery law has prospered even during a period when nationalist populism around the world has

rule enforcement) rather than mandate it. Protecting shared-enforcement regimes from interested shirking presents distinct challenges.

[51] Brewster, *supra* note 9, at 1655.

[52] During this century the United States has done something similar with respect to regulation of financial institutions. It has leveraged its role as a global financial center to require international banks to comply with its rules regarding money laundering and sanctions against rogue states as well as its anti-bribery rules. Rather than favoring its own banks, the United States appears to have used its capacity as a hegemon to generate public goods for the benefit of the international financial system. *See* Pierre-Hugues Verdier, Global Banks on Trial: U.S. Prosecutions and the Remaking of International Finance (2020).

undermined global institutions and law-based international cooperation. They also indicate that the form of international cooperation necessary for anti-bribery law to flourish—mostly negative comity pursuant to which states seek not to obstruct the actions of other states—may explain this paradox. Where a hegemon has the capacity to organize a solution to a collective action problem—here, even-handed enforcement of an anti-bribery norm across rich-world multinational corporations—the defection of other states poses less of a threat to the regime as a whole. Not dependent on cooperation with other states, the hegemon can proceed as long as the regime produces substantial benefits for it.

This insight, however, should not be taken as a claim that the anti-bribery regime is immune from the forces that have disrupted international cooperation in other areas. To be sure, anti-bribery law is not at the moment in the crosshairs of national populist movements around the globe. Unlike the body of international law governing international flows of goods, people, and capital, it is not accused of having brought about the economic and moral ruin of salient groups within otherwise prospering nations.[53] Yet it still remains vulnerable.

As discussed earlier in this chapter, one reason why the international regime suppressing transnational bribery has succeeded is that the regime has limited ambition. It has not attempted to impose a uniform international standard on the probity of public servants, and indeed does not address bribe solicitation as such. Yet as nationalist populists use anticorruption rhetoric as one of the channels for disrupting domestic politics, spillover to international transactions becomes a real risk. The even-handedness on which the anti-bribery regime depends may dissipate, bringing the regime down as its foundation crumbles.

The threat to even-handedness is the risk that, in a world where international cooperation faces greater challenges, states, in particular a hegemon in a multipolar system, will wield anti-bribery law as a weapon to pursue other foreign policy objectives. We already have seen nationalist populists exploit anticorruption law to advance their rise to power. One might worry that anti-bribery law will follow.

Consider China's President Xi Jinping, whose ascent has produced an even more authoritarian and antiliberal regime than the one he inherited. As part of his ascent, Xi used domestic anticorruption law to liquidate his principal

[53] *See* Paul B. Stephan, *Sovereignty and the World Economy*, 17 U. St. Thomas L.J. 649 (2021).

adversaries, first and foremost, Bo Xilai. Similarly, Brazil's nationalist populist President Jair Bolsonaro came to power in large part due to *Operação Lava Jato*, a transborder anti-bribery investigation that exposed corruption in the leadership of the Workers' Party that previously led the country. In both cases, anti-bribery authorities were at least influenced, if not commandeered, by political elements that used charges of corruption to advance transformative and illiberal politics.

The United States, where nationalist populism has produced especially consequential results, saw an escalation in the rhetoric of international corruption. The heart of the first impeachment charges against President Trump was the claim that he solicited a bribe from Ukrainian President Zelensky, namely, adverse action against his assumed opponent in the 2020 presidential election, as the price of releasing aid already due Ukraine as a matter of law. More generally, Trump's opponents depicted him as in the pocket of Russian kleptocrats. Trump and his supporters made symmetrical charges, namely, that the prior Ukrainian administration (as well as the Chinese government) rendered favors to candidate Joe Biden to grease cooperation with the United States. As in China and Brazil, charges of receiving international bribes became weaponized, with the alleged payers potentially drawn into the conflict.

These are instances where the domestic politics focused on bribe-taking, but we have seen a few instances where a charge of bribe-paying has become politicized. Representative is the Bitkov affair. Guatemala's independent anti-bribery commission went after Russian refugees for alleged corrupt payments to local officials. Some charged that the commission acted at the behest of Russia. The Guatemalan government, allegedly under US pressure, shut down the commission. Whether the commission's prosecution was justified, incompetent, or suborned is impossible to determine, at least from this distance, but the intrusion of international politics seems clear. Such interference undermines the premise of the regime, namely, disinterested suppression of all bribes to foreign officials.

Worse may be in store. It is not crazy to anticipate, for example, that anti-bribery law might become one of the tools that US policy makers will use in their battles with China. Already we have seen a US indictment of a significant Chinese businessperson—Meng Wanzhou, the chief financial officer of Huawei, as well as the founder's daughter—for financial fraud connected to sanctions evasion. More recently, the United States has charged her with involvement in a criminal conspiracy to steal US trade secrets. Whatever the merits of the government's case, the effect on international relations has been great. One can easily imagine this prosecution, premised on alleged false accounting to hide illegal payments, unfolding instead as an anti-bribery case. More generally, one can envision the United States and China descending into a practice of tit-for-tat anti-bribery prosecutions, each targeting the other's national champions. China's immediate response to the first indictment—arresting and detaining Canadian businesspeople while Canada considers the US request to extradite Meng—points to how things might play out.

To be sure, such confrontations are not inevitable. The global economy is enormous, and its trashing would come with large costs. Perhaps China and the United States face too much interdependence to take the kinds of steps that a weaponized anti-bribery campaign would represent. Perhaps, if the two superpowers need to relearn how to cooperate and build trust, strengthening anti-bribery enforcement might be a place to start. Perhaps China will come to see bribery as a costly and ineffective means of advancing economic projects such as the Belt and Road Initiative and seek to join the United States in suppressing transborder bribery.[54] The feel-good story—China and the United States using anti-bribery law as the basis for a broader range of cooperation—can no more be ruled out than the pessimistic tit-for-tat alternative.[55]

The point is a cautionary one. The turn toward robust global anti-bribery policy over the course of the twenty-first century reflects the importance of the global economy. It represents an important instance of international cooperation to protect and preserve that economy. But it does not confer immunity from the prevalent deep hostility to the international order. Indeed, current anti-bribery policy and the institutions that enforce it remain vulnerable to capture by domestic political forces intent on disrupting that order.

[54] On possible futures of the China–United States relationship, *see* Tom Ginsburg, *The Future of Liberal Democracy in the International Legal Order* (Chapter 3 in this volume).

[55] *But see* Griffith & Lee, *supra* note 49, at 1257, 1263–66 (envisioning competition between US anti-bribery coalition and China-led, bribery-tolerant coalition). Indications that the United States is considering repurposing its anti-bribery regime to use as an instrument for geopolitical competition comes from the Biden administration's June 3, 2021, memorandum on corruption and national security, which in turn draws on its March 2021 interim national security guidance. The former's reference to a need to counteract "strategic corruption" by foreign adversaries, and the latter's reference to "weaponized corruption," implies a new function for US anti-bribery law that would go beyond protecting the integrity of transnational markets. Presidential Action, Memorandum on Establishing the Fight Against Corruption as a Core United States National Security Interest § 2(f) (June 3, 2021); Interim National Security Strategic Guidance 7 (Mar. 2021) ("Anti-democratic forces use misinformation, disinformation, and weaponized corruption to exploit perceived weaknesses and sow division within and among free nations, erode existing international rules, and promote alternative models of authoritarian governance.").

One might look at the anti-bribery turn as an example of how international cooperation can serve important human ends and still recognize that it may contain the seeds of its own destruction.

VI. Conclusion

The contemporary world provides many reasons to think that the international liberal moment has come and gone. The course of the international anti-bribery regime over the present century, however, gives ground for guarded optimism. During a period when international institutions and the international law that they generate and rely on have come under attack from a wide range of interests and critics, legal regulation of transborder bribery has been remarkably consequential and resilient. This chapter explains why these two trends are not necessarily inconsistent.

The international bribery regime, unlike international projects such as the World Trade Organization, does not entail the pooling of resources at the international level to pursue collective benefits. Rather, the international anti-bribery regime consists of building widespread consent to a jurisdictional rule that allows states to tie bribery regulation to capital-market access, rather than to traditional rules such as corporate nationality. As long as the state associated with the largest capital market, the United States, commits to anti-bribery regulation that does not discriminate between US and foreign nationals, many other states have been willing either to accede to US jurisdiction or to compete with the United States by developing their own anti-bribery enforcement.[56]

The domestic political forces that have undermined other international legal projects do not seem to have impeded the significant growth and effect of the anti-bribery regime. This may change: national populists who portray legacy political structures as oppressive may yet link domestic corruption to foreign bribery and weaponize anti-bribery law as a political instrument. Yet one may also imagine the benefits of suppressing bribery as substantial enough to induce otherwise adversarial politicians and states to cooperate in the project. Much remains to be revealed.

[56] On the possibility of beneficial regulatory competition over anti-bribery policy, *see* Stephan, *supra* note 48, at 64–67.

PART FOUR

HUMAN RIGHTS AND RELATED ISSUES

12

Authoritarianism, International Human Rights, and Legal Change

Wayne Sandholtz

I. Introduction

The international legal order in human rights, constructed over the decades following World War II, faces a period of flux. According to critics, the global human rights system is collapsing under the weight of its own illusions, insularity, detachment from the everyday problems of real people, and overall failure to improve lives.[1] The skeptics have pointed to challenges that are largely internal to the human rights movement and the international legal regime it has labored to build and apply. But a more serious threat to the future of the human rights international legal order is external to it: the resurgence of authoritarian regimes and practices in a growing number of countries around the world.

The problem is not just that established authoritarians have hardened their grip on power, but that hitherto democratizing countries, and even some established democracies, have experienced a rise in authoritarian modes of politics and governance. Increasing authoritarianism is not just a matter of more frequent, direct violations of basic civil, political, and personal integrity rights.[2] Resurgent authoritarianism will strain the international human rights legal regime in at least two ways. First, authoritarian states are likely to weaken international human rights institutions by blocking criticism of autocratic regimes and practices, declining to participate in human rights review processes, and withdrawing—in either a practical or a formal sense—from

[1] Moyn, Hopgood, and Posner are among the most visible critics: SAMUEL MOYN, THE LAST UTOPIA: HUMAN RIGHTS IN HISTORY (2010); STEPHEN HOPGOOD, THE ENDTIMES OF HUMAN RIGHTS (2013); ERIC A. POSNER, THE TWILIGHT OF HUMAN RIGHTS LAW (2014).

[2] In this chapter, I use the terms "authoritarian" and "autocratic" interchangeably, though distinctions between the two may be useful in other contexts.

Wayne Sandholtz, *Authoritarianism, International Human Rights, and Legal Change* In: *Is the International Legal Order Unraveling?*. Edited by: David L. Sloss, Oxford University Press. © Oxford University Press 2022.
DOI: 10.1093/oso/9780197652800.003.0013

international human rights institutions (like the human rights treaty bodies and the regional human rights courts).

This chapter, however, emphasizes a second plane on which resurgent authoritarianism threatens to undermine international human rights law (IHRL): the domestic dimension. It focuses on the domestic level because domestic institutions are the front line in vindicating international human rights. IHRL has practical effects mainly at the domestic level, to the extent that it empowers people to mobilize political pressure or to vindicate rights in local courts.[3] IHRL improves human rights practices when it is incorporated into domestic law and when domestic actors—journalists, activists, advocates, civil society organizations (CSOs), elected officials, and judges—leverage international human rights norms to pressure governments by exposing and condemning violations, to hold perpetrators accountable, and to gain justice for victims. Authoritarian regimes undermine or dismantle these domestic mechanisms, eroding the capacity of domestic actors to deploy international human rights norms in their local contexts. As a result, even though IHRL may be left in place on paper, the domestic mechanisms through which it can have real effects are under threat from resurgent authoritarianism.

The perspective shaping this analysis, in other words, is that the international human rights legal order integrates both international (including regional) and domestic levels.[4] I suggest that authoritarian regimes will likely not seek to dismantle or withdraw from the system of formal international law. The complex of human rights treaties and institutions will remain largely intact, though partially hollowed out by resistance and by ritualized, nonsubstantive participation by authoritarian regimes. The greater danger is to the domestic mechanisms that can make IHRL effective. In many parts of the world, the dismantling of domestic tools for claiming, vindicating, and expanding rights will undercut the international human rights legal order from below.

[3] SALLY ENGLE MERRY, HUMAN RIGHTS AND GENDER VIOLENCE: TRANSLATING INTERNATIONAL LAW INTO LOCAL JUSTICE (2006); BETH A. SIMMONS, MOBILIZING FOR HUMAN RIGHTS: INTERNATIONAL LAW IN DOMESTIC POLITICS (2009); David Sloss & Wayne Sandholtz, *Universal Human Rights and Constitutional Change*, 27 WM. & MARY BILL RTS. J. (2019).

[4] IHRL is thus a transnational legal order as conceptualized by Halliday and Shaffer. It consists of legal norms and practices that develop and settle in a recursive process involving multiple kinds of actors across multiple levels, including the local, national, regional, and international. *See* Terence C. Halliday & Gregory Shaffer, *Transnational Legal Orders*, *in* TRANSNATIONAL LEGAL ORDERS (Terence C. Halliday & Gregory Shaffer eds., 2015).

The next section presents a picture of the surge in authoritarianism, focusing on three key authoritarian practices that undermine domestic mechanisms of human rights accountability. These core authoritarian strategies include abolishing judicial independence; limiting, or eliminating, freedom of expression, including freedom of the press; and restricting CSOs. The subsequent section assesses the likely consequences of resurgent authoritarianism for: (1) the formal regime of IHRL (treaties and related institutions); and (2) domestic tools for holding governments accountable for rights violations. The final section speculates about possible alternative futures for IHRL.

II. Twenty-First-Century Authoritarianism

Authoritarianism is clearly resurgent in the twenty-first century, across world regions and across regime types. Entrenched authoritarians have intensified their repression (Azerbaijan, Burundi, Cambodia, Egypt, Iran). Countries that had appeared to be consolidating democracies (Brazil, Hungary, Poland) or transitioning toward democracy (Philippines, Turkey) are now seen as "backsliders." And regimes in established democracies like India, Israel, and the United States have embraced some authoritarian rhetoric and policies.

Authoritarianism in the twenty-first century differs from earlier versions in both its typical means of gaining power and its core strategies for maintaining power. In previous eras, autocrats generally seized power through revolutions or coups d'etat. In the 1970s and 1980s, about 60 percent of autocrats came into power through a coup d'etat, whereas only 10 percent did so by perverting democratic institutions. By contrast, in the decade 2000–10, authoritarians were as likely to gain power through democratic erosion as through coups.[5] Huq and Ginsburg draw a similar distinction, between "authoritarian reversion" and "constitutional retrogression." The former denotes "rapid, wholesale collapse into authoritarianism,"[6] for example, via a coup. In the latter, retrogression, authoritarian leaders or parties gain power through democratic elections, then gradually and incrementally erode essential democratic institutions. In time, a formerly democratic system devolves into

[5] Erica Frantz & Andrea Kendall-Taylor, *The Evolution of Autocracy: Why Authoritarianism Is Becoming More Formidable*, 59 Survival 57, 60–61 (2017).

[6] Aziz Z. Huq & Tom Ginsburg, *How to Lose a Constitutional Democracy*, 65 UCLA L. Rev. 78, 92 (2018).

a hybrid regime (with both democratic and authoritarian elements) or an authoritarian one.[7] Huq and Ginsburg note a decline in coups d'etat in recent years and an increase in constitutional retrogression.[8] Or, as Frantz and Kendall-Taylor put it:

> Contemporary autocrats are coming to power through a process of "authoritarianisation", or the gradual erosion of democratic norms and practices. Democratic leaders, elected at the ballot box through reasonably free and fair elections, are slowly undermining institutional constraints on their power . . . in ways that make it difficult to pinpoint the moment at which the break with democratic politics occurs.[9]

Data compiled by the Varieties of Democracy project (V-Dem) support these assessments. Analyzing V-Dem data, Lührmann and Lindberg point out that "[d]emocratic erosion became the modal tactic during the third wave of autocratization," whose beginning they date to 1994. "Here, incumbents legally access power and then gradually, but substantially, undermine democratic norms without abolishing key democratic institutions. Such processes account for 70%" of democratic reversals in the third wave.[10]

The twenty-first-century version of authoritarianism also tends to differ from its predecessors in its primary tools and strategies for staying in power. One difference is that today's authoritarians generally (not always) rely less on brutal physical repression. Autocrats in the 1960s and 1970s routinely resorted to political detention, torture, disappearances, and extrajudicial killing to suppress dissent and eliminate opponents.[11] Today's authoritarians often operate within democratic frameworks and exploit formally legal processes to subvert them. Scheppele labels practitioners of the current approach "autocratic legalists." These are autocrats "who hijack constitutions . . . to benefit from the superficial appearance of both democracy and legality within

[7] *Id.* at 94–98.

[8] *Id.* at 93–96. Numerous insightful scholars have addressed democratic recession or democratic erosion. *See, e.g.*, Larry Diamond, *Facing Up to the Democratic Recession*, 26 J. DEMOCRACY 141 (2015).

[9] Frantz & Kendall-Taylor, *supra* note 5, at 60.

[10] Anna Lührmann & Staffan I. Lindberg, *A Third Wave of Autocratization Is Here: What Is New About It?*, 26 DEMOCRATIZATION 1095, 1105 (2019).

[11] Of course, many of today's authoritarians do employ the same kinds of physical violence: extrajudicial killings in the Philippines, large-scale detentions of journalists in Turkey, mass arrests of Uighurs in China and their transfer to concentration camps, and more. The point here is that many of today's autocrats do not rely on violent repression but instead hollow out democratic institutions using ostensibly legal means.

their states. They use their democratic mandates to launch legal reforms that remove the checks on executive power, limit the challenges to their rule, and undermine the crucial accountability institutions of a democratic state."[12] Moreover, technologies—the internet, social media platforms, and artificial intelligence—have enabled modern autocrats to regulate the flow of ideas and information more efficiently. Not only can authoritarian governments censor communication they object to, they can monitor email and social media to track and block regime critics and political opposition. Autocrats "are harnessing a new arsenal of digital tools to counteract what has become the most significant threat to the typical authoritarian regime today: the physical, human force of mass antigovernment protests."[13] Digital tools are less expensive than massive human surveillance and internal spying; once citizens understand the reach of comprehensive state monitoring, "they alter their behavior without the regime having to resort to physical repression."[14]

The resurgence of authoritarian practices in recent decades has been so dramatic that it is apparent in a variety of broad indicators. For example, Freedom House provides one of the longest-running, highly visible assessments of the state of freedom and democracy around the globe. For several years, Freedom House has been calling attention to the erosion of democracy and the rise of authoritarianism. Its 2018 annual report, titled *Democracy in Crisis*, declared that democratic values were "under assault and in retreat globally" and that "[p]olitical rights and civil liberties around the world deteriorated to their lowest point in more than a decade in 2017."[15] The 2020 document reported that "2019 was the 14th consecutive year of decline in global freedom," that "64 countries experienced deterioration in their political rights and civil liberties while . . . just 37 experienced improvements," and that "the negative pattern affected all regime types."[16] In fact, twenty-five of forty-one "established democracies" (those with at least twenty consecutive years of democracy prior to 2006) experienced declines over the past fourteen years.[17] The V-Dem 2020 report concurs, finding that "[d]emocracy declined in 26 countries during 2019, up from 18 in 2017," and that over the previous ten years, "more nations have become characterized by

[12] Kim Lane Scheppele, *Autocratic Legalism*, 85 U. Chi. L. Rev. 545, 547 (2018).
[13] Andrea Kendall-Taylor et al., *The Digital Dictators: How Technology Strengthens Autocracy*, Foreign Aff., Mar.–Apr. 2020, at 104.
[14] *Id.*
[15] Freedom House, Freedom in the World 2018: Democracy in Crisis (2018).
[16] Freedom House, Freedom in the World 2020: A Leaderless Struggle for Democracy (2020).
[17] *Id.* at 10.

autocratization than by democratization." Indeed, "[f]or the first time since 2001, democracies are no longer in the majority."[18] And the declines have occurred not just in countries that were already autocracies, but in democracies: "[O]ver the last decade, the rise in electoral autocracies is mainly the result of democracies gradually breaking down. Seven of these became electoral autocracies over the last year from 2018 to 2019."[19]

III. Authoritarianism and International Human Rights Law

Rising authoritarianism is likely to weaken IHRL, not by dissolving or modifying the body of international human rights treaty law but by undermining the mechanisms that give it effect. Put differently, the next decade or two may not see any significant change in formal international human rights law and institutions. Rather, if authoritarian modes of politics and governance continue to spread and become entrenched, the practices of IHRL—and therefore its effectiveness—will be diminished. The argument here takes as given that international law is more than a set of legal rules. My approach has affinities with Brunnée and Toope's interactional theory of international legality. In their account, the legitimacy of international law, and thus the sense of obligation held by actors, is based on: (1) the law's congruence with wider social norms; (2) its consistency with the criteria of legality;[20] and (3) supportive "practices of legality."[21] These three factors interact to create legitimate international law and engender in its subjects the "fidelity" that leads to compliance.[22] IHRL will therefore be weakened, even if the formal law remains unchanged, to the extent that authoritarian regimes undermine "practices of legality." This section assesses the likely effects of rising authoritarianism on practices of human rights legality at the international level; the next section examines the threat to human rights practices of legality at the (crucial) domestic level.

[18] Varieties of Democracy Inst., Autocratization Surges—Resistance Grows: Democracy Report 2020 (2020).

[19] *Id.* at 13.

[20] The criteria of legality are based on Fuller's eight principles of legality. *See* Lon L. Fuller, The Morality of Law (1964).

[21] Jutta Brunnée & Stephen J. Toope, Legitimacy and Legality in International Law: An Interactional Account 55, 101, 119 (2010).

[22] *Id.*

The international human rights legal order consists of the network of human rights treaties, both global and regional, plus their associated institutions. Many international human rights norms are considered to have attained customary international law status, including, in the view of some scholars, those listed in the Universal Declaration of Human Rights. International and domestic courts have also recognized a growing number of international human rights norms as customary international law.[23] After a brief description of formal IHRL, the discussion turns to practices in the associated institutions, which include the human rights treaty bodies, the regional human rights courts, and the Human Rights Council (HRC), its Universal Periodic Review (UPR) process, and the array of UN special rapporteurs who report to the HRC on specific human rights topics.

IHRL is embodied in a network of treaties. The global human rights regime has expanded dramatically since the 1948 Genocide Convention, in terms of the number of treaties, the range of rights covered, and the number of states parties. Figure 12.1 depicts that expansion for ten core human rights treaties.[24]

As shown in Table 12.1, some of these treaties have achieved nearly universal ratification (CRC, CEDAW), whereas some of the more recent ones have been ratified by barely a quarter of states (CED, CRMW). In addition to the global treaties, regional human rights treaties cover more than half of states in the world: the African Charter on Human and Peoples' Rights (54 states parties), the European Convention on Human Rights (47 states parties), and the American Convention on Human Rights (23 states parties).

Rising authoritarianism is unlikely to lead to widespread abandonment of existing human rights treaties.[25] But it also seems unlikely that new

[23] Malcolm N. Shaw, International Law 259–61 (2003); Dinah L. Shelton, Advanced Introduction to International Human Rights Law 77 (2014).

[24] The ten treaties include (in chronological order) the Genocide Convention, the Convention on the Elimination of All Forms of Racial Discrimination (CERD), the International Covenant on Civil and Political Rights (ICCPR), the International Covenant on Economic, Social, and Cultural Rights (ICESCR), the Convention on the Elimination of All Forms of Discrimination against Women (CEDAW), the Convention against Torture (CAT), the Convention on the Rights of the Child (CRC), the Convention on the Rights of Migrant Workers (CRMW), the Convention on the Rights of Persons with Disabilities (CRPD), and the Convention on Enforced Disappearances (CED).

[25] A few states have withdrawn from human rights–related international institutions. Burundi and the Philippines have exited the Rome Statute. Trinidad and Tobago (1998) and Venezuela (2012) denounced the American Convention on Human Rights. Jamaica (1997) and Trinidad and Tobago (2002) withdrew from the First Optional Protocol to the International Covenant on Civil and Political Rights, which allows the Human Rights Committee to receive individual communications. Guyana (1999) also withdrew from the First Optional Protocol but immediately re-acceded with a reservation. *See* United Nations Treaty Collection, Status of Treaties, Optional Protocol to the International Covenant on Civil and Political Rights, https://treaties.un.org/Pages/ViewDetails.aspx?src=TREATY&mtdsg_no=IV-5&chapter=4&clang=_en#2 (last visited Jan. 12, 2021);

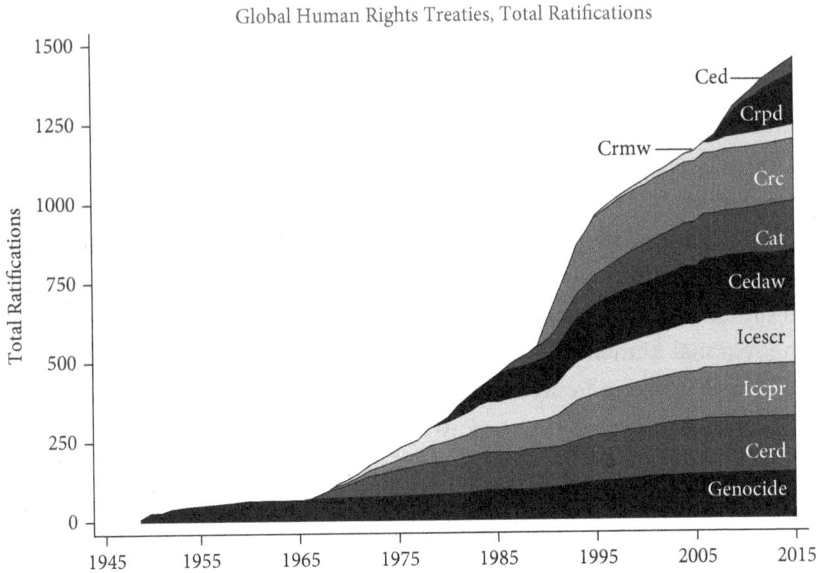

Figure 12.1 Global Human Rights Treaties, Total Ratifications

Table 12.1 States Parties to Human Rights Treaties, 2021

CRC	196
CEDAW	189
CERD	182
CRPD	182
ICCPR	173
ICESCR	171
CAT	171
GENOCIDE	152
CED	63
CRMW	56

Note: Total UN membership in early 2021 was 193 states. Some entities that are not UN member states are registered as parties to some of the treaties. For example, both the Holy See and the State of Palestine are listed as parties to the Convention on the Rights of the Child (CRC).

Source: Office of the High Commissioner for Human Rights, *Status of Ratification* (2021), https://indicators.ohchr.org/.

see also Laurence R. Helfer, *Overlegalizing Human Rights: International Relations Theory and the Commonwealth Caribbean Backlash against Human Rights Regimes*, 102 COLUM. L. REV. 1832 (2002). These few instances are the exceptions that prove the rule.

human rights treaties will be adopted in the near future, given apparently declining global interest in multilateralism, which itself may be due in part to rising authoritarianism. Treaty withdrawal would have symbolic importance, signaling an open rejection of human rights principles and norms. Autocratic governments would see little to gain from formally renouncing human rights treaties and would expect some reputational cost. No leader, regardless of how abusive of rights domestically, wants to be seen as opposing or rejecting human rights. Thus the "wholesale rejection of rights is rare."[26] Authoritarians often deploy the rhetoric of democracy and human rights, even as their actions erode rights in practice. Or, governments routinely justify rights violations by invoking other basic norms, "like counterterrorism, sovereignty and non-interference," or "traditional values."[27] Autocrats can erode the international human rights legal order without having to take the step of formal renunciation.

Rather than seeking to dismantle formal international law, authoritarians can gradually hollow out the institutions designed to monitor state human rights practices and promote compliance with human rights treaties. These include the UN HRC, ten human rights treaty bodies,[28] three regional human rights courts,[29] and subregional courts with human rights jurisdiction.[30] We know from existing research that authoritarian regimes generally "have little reason . . . to bear the costs of membership [in IOs] . . . or have their actions scrutinized and publicized by the organization."[31] Authoritarian states resist intrusive international organizations (IOs) and continually emphasize norms of sovereignty and noninterference in domestic affairs. The reluctance to allow scrutiny by IOs is surely even stronger in the human rights domain, given that rights-repressive measures are a key autocratic tool for holding onto power. The point is not that authoritarian governments will attempt a frontal assault on international organizations; direct efforts to dissolve or prune back the authority of IOs would provoke resistance from other states

[26] Stephen Hopgood et al., *Conclusion: Human Rights Futures*, *in* HUMAN RIGHTS FUTURES 316 (Stephen Hopgood et al. eds., 2017).

[27] *Id.*

[28] For general information about the human rights treaties bodies, *see* Office of the High Comm'r for Human Rights, Monitoring the Core International Human Rights Treaties (2020), https://www.ohchr.org/EN/HRBodies/Pages/Overview.aspx (last visited Nov. 4, 2020).

[29] The European Court of Human Rights (ECtHR), the Inter-American Court of Human Rights (IACtHR), and the African Court on Human and Peoples' Rights (ACtHPR).

[30] These include the Economic Community of West African States (ECOWAS) Community Court of Justice and the East African Community (EAC) Court of Justice.

[31] Edward D. Mansfield & Jon C. Pevehouse, *Democratization and the Varieties of International Organizations*, 52 J. CONFLICT RESOL. 269, 276 (2008).

and would be politically costly. Rather, authoritarians can weaken international human rights institutions in less obtrusive ways.

Authoritarian regimes can weaken human rights IOs from within. They can participate in minimalist, pro forma ways or scale back their level of activity. But authoritarian governments can, and do, take more active steps. China and Russia, for example, have regularly "used [their] veto in the Security Council to shield other authoritarian countries from international demands to protect human rights and to block interventions that would force governments to end abuses."[32] Autocracies also inhibit human rights initiatives in the General Assembly. Boockmann and Dreher report a clear difference in the voting behavior of democracies and autocracies with respect to human rights resolutions in the General Assembly. Across different measures of democracy, the more autocratic a country is, the more likely it is to vote against a human rights resolution.[33] Ginsburg notes that authoritarian states engage in a "concerted effort to neutralize multilateral forums as vehicles for democracy promotion" and human rights,[34] pointing to their successful effort to gain seats on the HRC, the UN intergovernmental body charged with the "promotion and protection of all human rights around the globe."[35] In fact, for the 2020 Council session, nearly half of the membership (21 out of 47 countries) consisted of autocracies. (See Table 12.2.) The success of authoritarian governments in gaining election to the HRC comes despite the nominal requirement that members of the Council have a strong record of respecting human rights. The number of autocracies in the Council undermines its credibility as a mechanism for encouraging states to improve their rights performance. In fact, authoritarian states in the Council amount to an informal group "that oppose[s] a more activist human rights agenda."[36] China, the largest and most influential autocracy, took a more activist approach after its election to the HRC in 2013. China proposed its first resolutions in the Council in 2017 and 2018. "Both resolutions emphasized national sovereignty, called for quiet dialogue and cooperation rather than investigations and international calls to action, and pushed the Chinese

32 Jessica Chen Weiss, *A World Safe for Autocracy? China's Rise and the Future of Global Politics*, Foreign Aff., July–Aug. 2019, at 92, 95.

33 Bernhard Boockmann & Axel Dreher, *Do Human Rights Offenders Oppose Human Rights Resolutions in the United Nations?*, 146 Pub. Choice 443, 455–58 (2011).

34 Tom Ginsburg, *Authoritarian International Law?*, 114 Am. J. Int'l L. 221, 255 (2020).

35 Human Rights Council, *United Nations Human Rights Council*, https://www.ohchr.org/EN/HRBodies/HRC/Pages/Home.aspx (last visited Nov. 4, 2020).

36 Ted Piccone, China's Long Game on Human Rights at the United Nations, at 3 (2018).

Table 12.2 Autocracies in the Human Rights Council, 2020

Country	V-Dem Regime Type	Term Expired
Afghanistan	Electoral autocracy	2020
Angola	Electoral autocracy	2020
Armenia	Electoral autocracy	2022
Bahrain	Closed autocracy	2021
Bangladesh	Electoral autocracy	2021
Burkina Faso	Electoral autocracy	2021
Cameroon	Electoral autocracy	2021
Democratic Republic of the Congo	Electoral autocracy	2020
Eritrea	Closed autocracy	2021
Fiji	Electoral autocracy	2021
Libya	Closed autocracy	2022
Mauritania	Electoral autocracy	2022
Nigeria	Electoral autocracy	2020
Pakistan	Electoral autocracy	2020
Philippines	Electoral autocracy	2021
Qatar	Closed autocracy	2020
Somalia	Closed autocracy	2021
Sudan	Closed autocracy	2022
Togo	Electoral autocracy	2021
Ukraine	Electoral autocracy	2020
Venezuela (Bolivarian Republic of)	Electoral autocracy	2022

Note: V-Dem classifications. Total Council membership = 47.

model of state-led development as the path to improving their vision of collective human rights and social stability."[37] As the number of autocracies in the world increases, those with seats on the Council may well be emboldened to further dilute its capacity to pursue its mission.

The HRC also conducts the most comprehensive, global human rights reporting mechanism, the UPR. The UPR takes place in five-year cycles; each UN member state is reviewed in each cycle. The review considers the report submitted by the state under review, plus additional documents submitted by human rights organizations, other UN treaty bodies and agencies, and domestic stakeholders. Each review produces a report that contains questions,

[37] *Id.* at 4.

comments, and recommendations.[38] Not surprisingly, the nature and quality of state participation varies widely. In a 2009 report to the HRC, early in the first review cycle, the nongovernmental organization (NGO) UN Watch rated the degree to which countries participated "constructively" in the process, based on their submissions related to countries with poor human rights records. Negative points were given to interventions that praised or covered up for the country being reviewed, while positive scores were awarded for challenges to the rights-violating country. Among the sixteen states that were rated as "destructive" to the UPR process, all but two were autocracies under the V-Dem classification.[39] In addition, the content of recommendations varies between democracies and nondemocracies, regardless of the actor under scrutiny. Democracies tend to recommend changes to domestic law and governance. Nondemocratic states target their recommendations to joining or ratifying international human rights treaties, rather than encouraging domestic change.[40]

The strategy of participating in international human rights institutions in ways that weaken them manifests itself in other ways. Authoritarian states can go through the motions of submitting the periodic reports required in most human rights treaty bodies, but without accepting external criticisms or committing to substantive reforms. For example, Creamer and Simmons find that autocracies are as likely as democracies to file the reports required by the Committee against Torture. But "[d]emocracies generally submit reports that identify implementation and compliance shortcomings and that respond to concerns of the treaty-monitoring body—autocracies, much less so."[41] A similar dynamic likely holds in the other human rights treaty bodies.

Finally, autocracies will likely increase their "pushback" against regional human rights courts. As Ginsburg has argued, rising authoritarianism generally implies "less use of formal third-party adjudication, and more emphasis on state-to-state negotiation and diplomacy as preferred mechanisms for resolving disputes, since third-party dispute resolution has the potential to

[38] Office of the High Commissioner for Human Rights, *Universal Periodic Review*, https://www.ohchr.org/EN/HRBodies/UPR/Pages/UPRMain.aspx (last visited May 22, 2021).

[39] UN Watch, Mutual Praise Society: Country Scorecard and Evaluation of the Universal Periodic Review System of the U.N. Human Rights Council (2009), https://unwatch.org/mutual-praise-society/ (last visited Nov. 10, 2020).

[40] Mi Hwa Hong, *Legal Commitments to United Nations Human Rights Treaties and Higher Monitoring Standards in the Universal Periodic Review*, 17 J. Hum. Rts. 660, 661 (2018).

[41] Cosette D. Creamer & Beth A. Simmons, *Do Self-Reporting Regimes Matter? Evidence from the Convention Against Torture*, 63 Int'l Stud. Q. 1051, 1053 (2019).

deliver surprise losses."[42] Of course, some degree of state resistance to international human rights courts and noncompliance with their judgments is "normal" state behavior.[43] But authoritarian states have been the ones to withdraw from the jurisdiction of human rights–related courts in recent years, including Burundi and the Philippines from the International Criminal Court and Venezuela from the Inter-American Court of Human Rights.

In sum, authoritarians seek to undermine international human rights institutions from within, appearing superficially to participate but doing so in ways that weaken the institutions and diminish their credibility. Authoritarian states file reports and respond to complaints and "observations" in ways that deploy human rights rhetoric but deflect blame, criticize their critics, and block conclusions that point out abuses. In that sense, authoritarians replicate in international human rights institutions the same approach they have used in their domestic political institutions: preserve the forms of democracy and rights but empty them of substantive capacity. The larger the number of authoritarians in the world, the greater their ability to support each others' efforts to subvert international human rights institutions from within.

IV. Authoritarians and Domestic Rights Accountability

Research in international law and international relations has long recognized that human rights treaties do not directly, of themselves, improve respect for rights.[44] In fact, it is by now well established that IHRL has practical effects mainly at the domestic level, to the extent that it is incorporated into

[42] Ginsburg, *supra* note 34, at 225.

[43] *See* the recent work on "backlash" against international courts, including Daniel Abebe & Tom Ginsburg, *The Dejudicialization of International Politics?*, 63 INT'L STUD. Q. 521 (2019); Karen J. Alter et al., *Backlash against International Courts in West, East, and Southern Africa: Causes and Consequences*, 27 EUR. J. INT'L L. 293 (2016); Mikael Rask Madsen et al., *Backlash against International Courts: Explaining the Forms and Patterns of Resistance to International Courts*, 14 INT'L J.L. IN CONTEXT 197 (2018); Wayne Sandholtz et al., *Backlash and International Human Rights Courts*, *in* CONTRACTING HUMAN RIGHTS: CRISIS, ACCOUNTABILITY, AND OPPORTUNITY (Alison Brysk & Michael Stohl eds., 2018).

[44] Wade M. Cole, *Human Rights as Myth and Ceremony? Reevaluating the Effectiveness of Human Rights Treaties, 1981–2007*, 117 AM. J. SOC. 1131 (2012); Emilie M. Hafner-Burton & K. Tsutsui, *Human Rights in a Globalizing World: The Paradox of Empty Promises*, 110 AM. J. SOC. 1373 (2005); Emilie M. Hafner-Burton & Kiyoteru Tsutsui, *Justice Lost! The Failure of International Human Rights Law to Matter Where Needed Most*, 44 J. PEACE RES. 407 (2007); Oona A. Hathaway, *Do Human Rights Treaties Make a Difference?*, 111 YALE L.J. 1935 (2002).

domestic law and empowers people to mobilize political pressure or to litigate for rights.[45] IHRL improves human rights practices when domestic actors—journalists, activists, victims, advocates, CSOs, elected officials, and judges—leverage international human rights norms to expose and condemn violations; pressure governments to hold perpetrators accountable; litigate claims to gain justice for victims; and change domestic laws and how they are enforced. As argued previously, domestic actors, institutions, and practices are integral parts of the international human rights legal order. Indeed, domestic arenas are the front line in vindicating international human rights. This perspective is compatible with Koh's transnational legal process model, in which international law has effects on state behavior to the extent that it is internalized in domestic actors, institutions, policies, and laws.[46]

States bear primary duties under IHRL to respect and to ensure respect for rights. Domestic actors can invoke international human rights treaty commitments to hold governments accountable for violations through a combination of electoral and administrative mechanisms and litigation. Rising authoritarianism undermines IHRL from below by vitiating the primary mechanisms through which IHRL affects rights in practice where they matter most: at the domestic level.

A. Core Authoritarian Strategies

Although twenty-first-century authoritarianism differs in some respects from earlier versions, as noted previously, for the concept of "authoritarianism" to be analytically useful, it needs to have a stable core. Political scientists have identified the essence of authoritarianism as a "mode of governing which is intolerant of public opposition and dissent." Authoritarian governance occurs when "rulers see public opposition as a major threat to the extent or continuation of their power, and believe that they can work to undermine it with relative impunity."[47] One advantage of this definition is that it allows the analyst not just to assess autocracies but also to evaluate

[45] *See* Merry, *supra* note 3; Simmons, *supra* note 3.

[46] Harold Hongju Koh, *Why Do Nations Obey International Law?*, 106 Yale L.J. 2599 (1997); Harold Hongju Koh, *The 1998 Frankel Lecture: Bringing International Law Home*, 35 Hous. L. Rev. 623 (1998).

[47] David Beetham, *Authoritarianism and Democracy: Beyond Regime Types*, 13 Comp. Democratization 2, 12 (2015).

authoritarian conduct *within democracies*. This is an important advantage at present given significant authoritarian shifts in countries that are formally and hitherto functionally democratic. Authoritarian practices—in whatever type of regime they are found—aim to eliminate, or in Glasius's terms, "sabotage," accountability.[48] Accountability is "a relationship between an actor and a forum, in which the actor has an obligation to explain and to justify his or her conduct, the forum can pose questions and pass judgement, and the actor may face consequences."[49] Authoritarian practices remove constraints on the exercise of government power by reducing or eliminating potential sources of criticism, opposition, and accountability.

Research has been strikingly convergent on three key institutions that authoritarians target in order to consolidate unaccountable power: judicial independence, which entails the institutional authority to review government acts for their consistency with basic rights; freedom of expression, especially freedom of the press; and freedom to assemble and organize, not just to contest elections but to influence government and hold it accountable through CSOs. Beetham, for example, declares that authoritarians can institutionalize the suppression of opposition by restricting freedom of expression (including the press) and freedom of association (civil society), and by subordinating the courts to the executive.[50] Glasius offers restraints placed on journalists and NGOs as examples of sabotaging accountability.[51] Müller notes that authoritarians (focusing on populist authoritarians) remake the state to enlarge and entrench their power by exerting control over the courts, intimidating or silencing the press that reports critically, and condemning or suppressing NGOs and other civil society groups that criticize the regime.[52] Mudde and Rovira Kaltwasser similarly point out that "[a]mong the most targeted institutions are the judiciary and the media."[53] In today's world, authoritarian governments target not just the traditional print and

[48] Marlies Glasius, *What Authoritarianism Is . . . and Is Not: A Practice Perspective*, 94 INT'L AFF. 515, 521 (2018).

[49] Mark Bovens, *Analysing and Assessing Accountability: A Conceptual Framework*, 13 EUR. L.J. 447, 450 (2007).

[50] Beetham, *supra* note 47, at 13.

[51] Glasius, *supra* note 48, at 528.

[52] Jan-Werner Müller, *The Rise and Rise of Populism?*, *in* THE AGE OF PERPLEXITY: RETHINKING THE WORLD WE KNEW (2018), https://www.bbvaopenmind.com/wp-content/uploads/2018/03/BBVA-OpenMind-Jan-Werner-Muller-The-Rise-and-Rise-of-Populism-1.pdf.

[53] CAS MUDDE & CRISTÓBAL ROVIRA KALTWASSER, POPULISM: A VERY SHORT INTRODUCTION 81 (2017). Mudde and Rovira Kaltwasser address populism, but their arguments clearly apply also to populist authoritarianism.

broadcast media but also exploit social media for purposes of surveillance and control.[54]

Recent work highlights the tactics of elected authoritarians, who make use of electoral success and existing legal processes to undermine democracy and rights. Scheppele identifies the core tactics of "autocratic legalists," highlighting as common elements the assertion of political control over the judiciary, the modification of electoral rules to guarantee legislative majorities or supermajorities, and reduction or elimination of independent media.[55] Huq and Ginsburg's analysis of the "constitutional retrogression" path of authoritarianism points to the elimination of institutional checks, especially through independent courts; control of information and communication, including restrictions on journalists; and curtailing the activities of lawyers, NGOs, and private foundations (civil society in my terminology).[56] And Kaufman and Haggard note that "elected authoritarians" use their power "in a step-by-step fashion to weaken institutions of horizontal accountability." It is an incremental process that "typically begin[s] by using executive and legislative authority to undermine the independence of the judiciary, law enforcement agencies, and the press."[57] In short, researchers from a variety of disciplines and perspectives have identified a core set of targets for authoritarians intent on dismantling the institutions of accountability: independent courts, a free press, and active CSOs.

Core authoritarian practices thus undermine essential means of holding governments accountable. The right to free expression is essential if rights violations are to be exposed, publicized, and condemned. Civil society is crucial for mobilizing pro-rights actors in both political and judicial realms. CSOs pressure government officials, marshal support for candidates, organize direct political action, and engage in "naming and shaming." In the judicial realm, CSOs are crucial in locating victims, providing them legal

[54] Rebecca MacKinnon, *Liberation Technology: China's "Networked Authoritarianism,"* 22 J. Democracy 32 (2011).

[55] Scheppele, *supra* note 12, at 549. *See also* Nancy Bermeo, *On Democratic Backsliding*, 27 J. Democracy 5, 10–11 (2016) ("[E]lected executives weaken checks on executive power one by one, undertaking a series of institutional changes that hamper the power of opposition forces to challenge executive preferences. The disassembling of institutions that might challenge the executive is done through legal channels, often using newly elected constitutional assemblies or referenda.").

[56] Huq & Ginsburg, *supra* note 6, at 130–35.

[57] Robert R. Kaufman & Stephan Haggard, *Democratic Decline in the United States: What Can We Learn from Middle-Income Backsliding?*, 17 Persp. on Pol. 417, 418 (2019).

Table 12.3 Authoritarian Strategies, V-Dem Indicators

Authoritarian Strategy	Indicator
Undermine judicial independence	Government attacks on the judiciary (v2jupoatck)
	Court packing (v2jupack)
Curtail freedom of expression	Freedom of discussion (average of v2cldiscm (men) and v2cldiscw (women))
	Government media censorship (v2mecenefm)
Constrain civil society	CSO entry and exit (v2cseeorgs)
	CSO repression (v2csreprss)

Note: V-Dem variable names in parentheses.

assistance, and representing them in judicial proceedings. Independent courts are essential for ensuring that the laws that protect rights are applied, even against state officials.

B. Authoritarian Strategies in Domestic Arenas

Have regimes that moved toward authoritarianism over the past decade implemented the three core strategies? Based on V-Dem data for all three, the answer is a clear "yes." I chose two V-Dem indicators for each of the three core authoritarian strategies, listed in Table 12.3.[58] The indicators regarding judicial independence and civil society are self-explanatory; the measures for freedom of expression may require additional explanation. The first, "freedom of discussion," captures the scope for people to express ideas and opinions in society at large. It thus includes, in principle, all modes of communication. The second, "government censorship," measures the degree to which government employs direct or indirect means of censoring print or broadcast media. Note that "indirect means" include a variety of methods for governments to control media.[59] I identify states moving toward

[58] Michael Coppedge et al., V-Dem Country-Year Dataset v12, https://www.v-dem.net/vdemds.html; Michael Coppedge et al., V-Dem Codebook v12, https://www.v-dem.net/static/website/img/refs/codebookv12.pdf [hereinafter V-Dem Codebook].

[59] V-Dem Codebook, *supra* note 58, at 187 ("Indirect forms of censorship might include politically motivated awarding of broadcast frequencies, withdrawal of financial support, influence over printing facilities and distribution networks, selected distribution of advertising, onerous registration requirements, prohibitive tariffs, and bribery.").

authoritarianism in two alternative ways. The first follows the classification of the Regimes of the World (RoW) project, which identifies countries' regime type as either (in order of increasing authoritarianism) "liberal democracy," "electoral democracy," "electoral autocracy," or "closed autocracy."[60] Movement toward authoritarianism consists of any shift in a country's classification to a more authoritarian category during the period 2009–19.[61] The second method of identifying authoritarian shifts is to take a decline in V-Dem's Liberal Democracy Index (LDI) as a sign of movement toward authoritarianism.[62]

I determine the change in a country's score on each of the six indicators of authoritarian strategies over the period 2009–19, then count the number of indicators for which each country experienced a decline. (Higher scores for each variable indicate greater democracy, lower scores represent greater autocracy). The data show clearly that states moving toward authoritarianism deploy the core authoritarian strategies to a striking degree. Table 12.4 reports the average number of authoritarian strategies that increased among states that underwent an authoritarian shift, compared to states that did not. The difference between the two groups of states is large and significant. In addition, many of the countries that have moved in an authoritarian direction have seen an increase in all or nearly all of the six authoritarian strategy indicators. Of the twenty-nine countries that dropped in the RoW classification (to a more authoritarian category), five countries show greater authoritarianism in all six indicators, and nine countries show it in five.[63] Moreover, this is a conservative approach to measuring that difference because a large number of states that declined on the LDI did not drop to a lower RoW category. Among the ninety-eight states with a decrease in the LDI, eighteen states show greater authoritarianism in all six indicators, and twenty-seven states (including the United States) show it in five.[64] In short, states that experienced a rise in authoritarianism, under either measure, experienced a dramatic increase in authoritarian strategies for reducing domestic accountability.

60 Lührmann & Lindberg, *supra* note 10; V-Dem Institute, *supra* note 18, at 11.

61 A change from "liberal democracy" to "electoral democracy" thus counts as a shift toward authoritarianism.

62 The Liberal Democracy Index (v2x_libdem) is an aggregate measure including electoral democracy plus basic civil liberties and the rule of law. *See* V-Dem Codebook, *supra* note 58, at 43.

63 For more country details, *see* Table 12.A1 in the appendix.

64 For more country details, *see* Table 12.A2 in the appendix.

Table 12.4 Average Number Out of Six Indicators Showing an Authoritarian Shift, 2009–19

	Countries that:			
	Dropped to a more authoritarian category (N)	**Did not drop to a more authoritarian category (N)**	**Difference**	**Significant difference?**
Average number of six authoritarian strategy indicators	4.28 (29)	3.21 (146)	1.07	yes (p = 0.0010)
	Declined on the Liberal Democracy Index (N)	**Did not decline on the Liberal Democracy Index (N)**	**Difference**	**Significant difference?**
Average number of six authoritarian strategy indicators	4.31 (98)	2.21 (77)	2.1	yes (p = 0.0000)

Note: The number of countries in each group is indicated in parentheses.

A brief review of some national experiences can add substantive content to the general trends shown in the data. President Recep Tayyip Erdogan of Turkey has assiduously pursued the three core authoritarian strategies. He has closed down more than one hundred independent news organizations and led the world each year from 2016 through 2018 in arrests of journalists (only to take second place to Xi's China in 2019).[65] He packed the courts with loyalists. Erdogan's April 2017 referendum massively expanded his powers and opened the way for him to extend his time in office potentially until 2029.[66] Erdogan has taken advantage of the coronavirus pandemic to further stifle dissent and press freedom.[67]

[65] Elana Beiser, Comm. to Protect Journalists, China, Turkey, Saudi Arabia, Egypt Are World's Worst Jailers of Journalists (2019).

[66] Patrick Kingsley, *Erdogan Claims Vast Powers in Turkey after Narrow Victory in Referendum*, N.Y. Times, Apr. 16, 2017.

[67] Marc Pierini, Carnegie Endowment for Int'l Peace, Emerging From the Pandemic, Turkey Rolls Out a More Assertive Foreign Policy (2020).

Viktor Orban may be the most accomplished implementer of authoritarian strategies. After his party, Fidesz, won a two-thirds supermajority in parliament, Orban deployed that unstoppable advantage to rewrite the constitution and restructure Hungary's institutions. The 2011 constitution was passed by parliament in nine days without public comment and without a national referendum. "The main victim of the new constitution was the judiciary, especially the Constitutional Court, whose justices would be selected not as they had been before, through an all-party parliamentary committee, but directly by parliament. With Fidesz holding a supermajority in parliament, Orban could pack the court with sympathetic judges," which he did.[68] A new law placed all government-supported radio and television broadcasters under a new corporate structure headed by Fidesz supporters and placed the new organization under a state media authority run by Fidesz loyalists. "As a result, the public networks are more tightly supervised today than they were in the final period of the communist regime."[69] Newspapers were also brought under a new entity controlled by Fidesz; the new organization was exempted from laws designed to regulate media concentration. With a handful of exceptions, "every single media outlet in the country is now controlled by people close to the regime."[70]

Since taking power in 2015 elections, the Law and Justice Party (PiS) in Poland has steadily implemented the core authoritarian strategies. Its first target was the Constitutional Tribunal. The PiS government refused to seat five judges legally appointed by the Sejm (parliament), declined to publish Tribunal judgments that contradicted its policies, and ultimately appointed a majority of the judges. The government then moved to take control of the Supreme Court, exert control over the ordinary courts, and subordinate the National Council of the Judiciary.[71] The PiS regime moved against press freedom and civil society as well; it "enacted changes to media laws that promote government messaging; has sought to regulate NGOs; and, in March 2017, passed legislation limiting rights to assembly."[72]

[68] Paul Lendvai, *The Transformer: Orban's Evolution and Hungary's Demise*, Foreign Aff., Sept.–Oct. 2019, at 44, 51.

[69] *Id.*

[70] *Id.*

[71] Christian Davies, Freedom House, Hostile Takeover: How Law and Justice Captured Poland's Courts (2018); Anna Sledzinska-Simon, *The Polish Revolution: 2015–2017*, Int'l J. of Const. L. Blog (July 25, 2017), http://www.iconnectblog.com/2017/07/the-polish-revolution-2015-2017/ (last visited Nov. 12, 2020).

[72] Frantz & Kendall-Taylor, *supra* note 5, at 62.

Rodrigo Duterte has implemented similar authoritarian strategies since winning election in the Philippines in 2016. His government has "cracked down on the independent press, jailed a senator who investigated his death-squad past, and engineered the ouster of an independent minded chief justice of the Supreme Court."[73] Duterte has publicly threatened journalists, some of whom have reported negatively on his campaign of extrajudicial killings of supposed drug dealers (more than seven thousand have been killed). "Just because you're a journalist," he said, "you are not exempted from assassination, if you're a son of a bitch."[74]

In late 2020, Amnesty International reported on intensified repression in Tanzania ahead of the election that returned the authoritarian president John Magufuli to office for a second term. The measures taken by Magufuli's government followed the authoritarian playbook analyzed previously. Since taking power, the government weakened the judiciary "through executive appointments without independent parliamentary vetting."[75] It clamped down on the media through a law empowering it "to suspend and close media outlets for reporting on allegations of corruption and human rights violations."[76] A similar law granted the government "sweeping powers to police the internet."[77] Amnesty International concluded that "Magufuli's government has built up a formidable arsenal of laws to stifle all forms of dissent and effectively clamp down on the rights to freedom of expression and peaceful assembly ahead of elections on 28 October."[78] The government's actions "significantly eroded the rule of law and undermined respect for human rights."[79] Leading up to the October 2020 election, major media outlets had been banned and opposition candidates had been harassed, arrested, and physically attacked.[80] Magufuli won re-election in a tainted election.

Such examples could easily be multiplied, including Egypt under Abdel Fattah al-Sisi, Nicolás Maduro in Venezuela, and many more.

[73] Sheila S. Coronel, *The Vigilante President: How Duterte's Brutal Populism Conquered the Philippines*, Foreign Aff., Sept.–Oct. 2019, at 36, 42.
[74] Domenico Montanaro, *6 Strongmen Trump Has Praised—And the Conflicts It Presents*, Nat'l Pub. Radio, May 2, 2017.
[75] Tom Odula, *Tanzania Intensifies Repression ahead of Polls, Says Report*, Associated Press, Oct. 12, 2020.
[76] *Id.*
[77] *Id.*
[78] Amnesty International, *Tanzania: Laws Weaponized to Undermine Political and Civil Freedoms ahead of Elections*, Oct. 12, 2020.
[79] Odula, *supra* note 75.
[80] *Id.*

The consolidated autocratic regimes of Vladimir Putin in Russia and Xi Jinping in China have fully accomplished the three core authoritarian goals of establishing political control over the judiciary, eliminating independent news media, and repressing the ability of civil society to organize and engage in policy advocacy. Both have clamped down effectively on human rights and pro-democracy NGOs by restricting foreign funding or prohibiting it altogether.[81] That strategy has spread broadly among authoritarian governments.[82] Moreover, China has actively exported "surveillance and censorship technologies," making it "cheaper for other authoritarian and would-be authoritarian regimes to monitor their citizens,"[83] thus boosting the ability of governments to regulate expression and control civil society. For instance, "Chinese companies have . . . exported surveillance tools, including facial recognition, to more than 60 foreign governments, subsidizing the purchases to participants in its Belt and Road initiative."[84]

C. National Human Rights Institutions

Finally, authoritarian efforts to suppress key components of domestic rights accountability are directly relevant to a mechanism specifically designed to bridge IHRL and domestic accountability: national human rights institutions (NHRIs).[85] The concept of the NHRI dates to 1946, when the UN Economic and Social Council, as it prepared the Universal Declaration of Human Rights, suggested that states consider creating national human rights committees. NHRIs were not formally part of the human rights treaty system, and they received "intermittent attention over the next forty years."[86] The 1991 Paris Workshop produced the Paris Principles (the Principles), a set of standards for effective NHRIs. The Principles were included in the Declaration of the 1993 World Conference on Human Rights in Vienna, and the UN General Assembly endorsed the Principles in 1993, urging all

[81] Thomas Carothers, *The Backlash Against Democracy Promotion*, Foreign Aff., Mar.–Apr. 2006, at 55; Tom Ginsburg & Aziz Z. Huq, How to Save a Constitutional Democracy 50 (2018).

[82] Darin Christensen & Jeremy Weinstein, *Defunding Dissent: Restrictions on Aid to NGOs*, 24 J. Democracy 77, 80 (2013).

[83] Chen Weiss, *supra* note 32, at 97.

[84] Suzanne Nossel, *How to Stop the Export of Authoritarianism*, Foreign Pol'y, Oct. 5, 2020.

[85] *See* Katerina Linos & Tom Pegram, *Architects of Their Own Making: National Human Rights Institutions and the United Nations*, 38 Hum. Rts. Q. 1109 (2016).

[86] Thomas Pegram, *Diffusion across Political Systems: The Global Spread of National Human Rights Institutions*, 32 Hum. Rts. Q. 729, 739 (2010).

countries to establish NHRIs in accordance with those standards.[87] The Principles emphasize the independence and substantive authority of NHRIs and specify an active role vis-à-vis IHRL:

> 3(b) To promote and ensure the harmonization of national legislation, regulations and practices with the international human rights instruments to which the State is a party, and their effective implementation;
>
> (c) To encourage ratification of the above-mentioned instruments or accession to those instruments, and to ensure their implementation;
>
> (d) To contribute to the reports which States are required to submit to United Nations bodies and committees, and to regional institutions, pursuant to their treaty obligations and, where necessary, to express an opinion on the subject, with due respect for their independence;
>
> (e) To cooperate with the United Nations and any other organization in the United Nations system, the regional institutions and the national institutions of other countries that are competent in the areas of the protection and promotion of human rights.[88]

Monitoring of adherence to the soft-law Paris Principles is in the hands of the network of NHRIs themselves, organized in the Global Alliance of National Human Rights Institutions (GANHRI) (formerly the International Coordinating Committee of NHRIs).[89] The number of NHRIs grew from about 20 in 1990 to around 130 as of 2015.[90]

Though the NHRIs are not formally part of the human rights treaty system or the United Nations, they are increasingly integrated into IHRL mechanisms. An obligation to create an NHRI was included in the Optional Protocol to the Convention against Torture. NHRIs that receive the highest rating from GANHRI can submit documents in the HRC, including in the Universal Periodic Review process. The Office of the High Commissioner for Human Rights now includes an NHRI Unit.[91] Some NHRIs in Latin America can receive individual complaints, investigate and collect evidence, and recommend remedial actions, thus serving as a direct link between domestic

[87] United Nations General Assembly, Principles Relating to the Status of National Institutions (The Paris Principles), G.A. Res. 48/134 (Dec. 20, 1993).

[88] *Id.*

[89] Global Alliance of National Human Rights Institutions, *Global Alliance of National Human Rights Institutions*, https://ganhri.org/ (last visited Nov. 11, 2020).

[90] Linos & Pegram, *supra* note 85, at 1110.

[91] Pegram, *supra* note 86, at 740.

government institutions and civil society. Some NHRIs are also active in the Inter-American Human Rights System, representing victims at the Inter-American Commission and the Inter-American Court and monitoring state compliance with judgments of the latter.[92]

In short, NHRIs are domestic institutions with a direct role in advancing domestic compliance with international human rights treaties. That said, not all NHRIs are created equal. Autocracies are less likely to create NHRIs, and when they do, they tend to grant them more limited powers. Pegram finds that whereas the "ombudsman" model is favored by countries rated as "free" by Freedom House, the "commission" model is preferred by regimes classified as "not free." This difference is suggestive because the commission model is generally "an advisory body (with no investigatory powers) while all human rights ombudsmen have investigatory powers."[93] Furthermore, given the authoritarian drive to suppress domestic accountability mechanisms, we should expect that as authoritarian regimes become more consolidated, they will take steps to limit the independence and effectiveness of NHRIs. They can accomplish this by gaining greater control over the appointment and removal of NHRI officials, restricting NHRI budgets and staffing, trimming their authority to receive complaints or initiate legal proceedings, and ignoring or rejecting NHRI actions. Such an erosion would further weaken domestic avenues for giving effect to IHRL.

Authoritarian resurgence over the past decade has weakened the domestic accountability mechanisms that are essential for giving effect to international human rights legal norms. We have long known that ratifying a treaty does not automatically move states to improve respect for their citizens' rights. Rather, IHRL can be a tool for actors who press their own governments to live up to their international human rights commitments. International institutions associated with IHRL often exercise their main influence by empowering domestic actors. The regional courts, for example, order states to compensate victims of rights violations, and states generally comply. But the Inter-American Court also regularly orders "structural" remedies that require further state action and follow-up by nonstate actors. The HRC and the human rights treaty bodies lack the authority to issue legally binding judgments, so their most potent effect almost certainly comes through

[92] Thomas Pegram & Nataly Herrera Rodríguez, *Bridging the Gap: National Human Rights Institutions and the Inter-American Human Rights System*, *in* The Inter-American Human Rights System: Impact Beyond Compliance 170–79 (Par Engstrom & Maxine Molyneux eds., 2019).

[93] Pegram, *supra* note 86, at 755, 757.

empowering domestic actors. Their conclusions and judgments are levers that domestic actors can wield to advocate for domestic reforms. Former judge Diego García-Sayán of the IACtHR recognized this reality with respect to domestic courts: "The mechanisms of the Inter-American system are establishing guidelines and standards on very diverse issues. Nevertheless, the states are supposed to be the actors performing the leading role. Within the state, the judges are supposed to be the first guarantee of human rights."[94]

The same logic holds for all of the domestic accountability mechanisms. Advocates, litigators, activists, the news media, and the broader public can expose abuses, denounce violators, demand accountability, and bring political and legal pressure on governments to fulfill their human rights treaty commitments, but only if the channels for engaging in those activities remain open. Naturally, authoritarian governments consistently target these mechanisms of accountability. The data demonstrate just how successful authoritarians have been in recent years in curtailing, and in many cases eliminating, the essential domestic mechanisms of human rights accountability. In that sense, certain rights—the right to fair judicial process, the right to free expression and a free press, and the right to organize and mobilize outside of state control—are crucial to peoples' ability to deploy IHRL in their local contexts.

V. Alternative Futures

Alternative future paths for IHRL are possible. The first, the *end-times scenario*, sees the skeptical view of human rights playing out at the global level.[95] In this scenario, the system of IHRL collapses under the weight of disenchantment with oversold promises, the detachment of the human rights project from the everyday concerns of most of the world's people (especially regarding economic insecurity), and the smug insularity of the human rights complex. Human rights treaties might not be denounced, but they will steadily slip into irrelevance and desuetude as actors direct their energies elsewhere. This scenario seems unlikely because a set of liberal democracies can sustain the core of IHRL, even if the number of nonparticipating or

[94] Diego García-Sayán, *The Inter-American Court and Constitutionalism in Latin America*, 89 Tex. L. Rev. 1835, 1836 (2011).

[95] Hopgood, *supra* note 1; Moyn, *supra* note 1; Posner, *supra* note 1.

resistant states rises.[96] Indeed, for all of its existence, the international human rights regime has been developed and supported by a coalition of liberal states in the face of indifference or resistance from a substantial share of the world's countries.

A second possible future, the *two-worlds scenario*, foresees the development of two parallel but intersecting international communities. In one, consisting of durable democracies, states participate actively in human rights institutions, call out rights abusing governments, and assist states that show movement toward democracy and human rights. They continue to support and comply with regional human rights systems. In the second cluster of states, consolidated autocracies implement a version of international law that emphasizes sovereignty, noninterference, and the territorial integrity of existing states (to continue the suppression of internal minorities like the Uighurs and the Kurds). Autocracies water down or oppose human rights reports and resolutions in international fora and shield each other from criticism within international human rights institutions. As Professor Ginsburg has suggested, they invest in regional or subregional organizations like the Shanghai Cooperation Organization (SCO).[97] SCO treaties on countering terrorism and extremism commit states to criminalize and to prosecute not just relevant acts but also "ideology and practice."[98] The treaties also commit states to cooperate in detaining and extraditing terrorists and extremists. The SCO also targets separatism, demonstrating "that states may go quite far in punishing freedom of expression if it is designated as 'secessionist,' which in turn hampers the ability of an oppressed group to raise awareness of their conditions to the international plane."[99] The "new norms help ensure that member countries will not provide safe havens for dissidents from other countries," with the result that "SCO members now share information on each other's opposition groups, using extradition and denials of asylum to facilitate politically motivated prosecution and repression."[100] Hybrid states, showing some characteristics of both autocracy and democracy, may bounce opportunistically between the two communities.

[96] *See* Tom Ginsburg, *The Future of Liberal Democracy in the International Legal Order* (Chapter 3 in this volume).

[97] Ginsburg, *supra* note 34. The original members of the SCO were China, Kazakhstan, Kyrgyzstan, Russia, Tajikistan, and Uzbekistan; India and Pakistan joined in 2017.

[98] Ginsburg, *supra* note 34, at 251–52.

[99] *Id.* at 252.

[100] *Id.*

In the third scenario, *resilience of rights*, the current authoritarian wave turns out to be temporary. Authoritarian regimes find it hard to deliver prosperity and economic security and discover that the Chinese model of authoritarian state capitalism is not exportable. The Chinese model itself suffers from long-term demographic shifts (an aging population being carried by smaller, younger generations). Populations begin to chafe under authoritarian regimes that provide neither jobs nor rights, and popular movements begin to push autocrats out. A fourth wave of democracy begins, and IHRL and institutions provide a point of reference for the reformers, as well as a source of domestic legitimation. Existing and transitional democracies reinvigorate international human rights institutions, perhaps with an enhanced emphasis on environmental and economic rights.

Recent events suggest that the current wave of authoritarianism may not be unstoppable. Authoritarian regimes are also vulnerable.[101] They are vulnerable both because governing is difficult and because people continue to value democracy and rights. If autocrats fail to deliver economic improvements, they lose their principal claim to legitimacy. And even if autocrats do raise standards of living (and China so far appears to be an outlier on that score), their populations may value economic well-being *and* rights, as the struggle to reclaim democracy and rights in diverse countries indicates. In a variety of national settings, people have turned against the authoritarians and have sometimes succeeded in ousting them. As Carothers puts it, "all this attention on the decline of democracy has obscured a story that is just as important: many authoritarians, dictators, and other nondemocratic leaders are also in trouble. Just like their peers in free countries, many citizens in nondemocracies are deeply frustrated with their political systems and have in the last several years been acting on that unhappiness by challenging those in power."[102]

In a striking number of cases, autocrats have confronted major public resistance and in some notable instances have been toppled. Malaysia's prodemocracy movement has mobilized major demonstrations since 2007. The target of many of the protests, Prime Minister Najib Razak, was voted out in 2018. The monarchy installed a new unelected government in February 2020,

[101] *See* Minxin Pei, *China's Coming Upheaval: Competition, the Coronavirus, and the Weakness of Xi Jinping*, Foreign Aff., May–June 2020, at 82.
[102] Thomas Carothers, *Dictators in Trouble: Democracy Isn't the Only System under Stress*, Foreign Aff., Feb. 6, 2020.

but COVID-19 restrictions have limited protests since then.[103] The most recent large-scale protests in Thailand began when the military government banned the main opposition party in February 2020; those protests were continuing as of November 2020.[104] Mass protests against the authoritarian rule of Nicolas Maduro have been a consistent feature of life in Venezuela, particularly since 2014. Protests continued in the lead-up to December 2020 legislative elections, even though opposition leaders who remained in the country continued to be arrested and prosecuted.[105] In Nigeria, large crowds have protested against excessive police violence and impunity in a number of cities. Though the government has stated its intention to dissolve the police unit in question, protests are ongoing.[106]

Even successful authoritarians have come in for concerted opposition. Protests against Hungary's Viktor Orban began anew in October 2019 following his election to a third term. And opposition parties gained a significant number of seats in municipal elections in November 2019, including winning the mayor's office in Budapest.[107] In Turkey, Erdogan's ruling party suffered a narrow defeat in Istanbul's municipal elections in March 2019, leading Erdogan to declare a rerun of the vote on June 23 in Istanbul and municipalities. Protests ensued against the action, which was perceived as election manipulation. The original winner prevailed in the revote, with a larger vote total and a larger share.[108]

Popular opposition and protest have toppled some autocrats. In 2015, antigovernment protests broke out in Ethiopia, to which the government responded with a national state of emergency. Uprisings continued until the prime minister, Hailemariam Desalegn, resigned in February 2018.[109] In Sudan, mass protests against the autocratic Omar al-Bashir started in

[103] Richard Paddock, *Tens of Thousands of Protesters Call for Najib Razak, Malaysian Leader, to Resign*, N.Y. Times, Nov. 19, 2016; Richard Paddock, *Democracy Fades in Malaysia as Old Order Returns to Power*, N.Y. Times, May 22, 2020.

[104] Jonathan Head, *Thai Protests: Tens of Thousands Gather again in Mass Defiance of Government*, BBC News, Oct. 15, 2020; Richard Paddock & Muktita Suhartono, *Thailand's Leader Offers End to Crackdown on Pro-Democracy Protesters*, N.Y. Times, Nov. 2, 2020.

[105] *What Lies Behind the Protests in Venezuela?*, BBC News, Mar. 27, 2014; Mariana Martínez & Anatoly Kurmanaev, *Venezuela's Opposition Splits over Taking Part in Coming Elections*, N.Y. Times, Sept. 16, 2020.

[106] Tarila Marclint Ebiede, *The Massive Protests in Nigeria, Explained*, Wash. Post, Oct. 26, 2020.

[107] Nick Thorpe, *Budapest Election: Hungary's Orban in Shock Defeat*, BBC News, Oct. 14, 2019; Helene Bienvenu & Marc Santora, *Thousands of Hungarians Protest Against Newly Elected Leader*, N.Y. Times, Apr. 14, 2018.

[108] Mark Lowen, *Turkey's Erdogan Defends Istanbul Election Re-run Amid Protests*, BBC News, May 7, 2019; Mark Lowen, *Erdogan's Party Suffers Blow after Istanbul Re-run Poll Defeat*, BBC News, June 24, 2019.

[109] *Ethiopian Prime Minister Resigns after Mass Protests*, The Guardian, Feb. 15, 2018.

December 2018 and the military removed al-Bashir from power in April 2019. Following the coup, protests resumed against the ruling military government until a mixed civil-military ruling coalition was established in September 2019, promising elections.[110] When the autocratic president of Algeria, Abdelaziz Bouteflika, announced his candidacy for a fifth term in February 2019, he triggered massive peaceful demonstrations. Bouteflika stepped down in April 2019, and protests continued, demanding a democratic transition. When the military's preferred candidate won the election in December 2019, the protests resumed.[111]

The anti-authoritarian popular movements have not succeeded everywhere, and where they have driven autocrats from power, the aftermath has not been a rapid transition to democracy. But the point is that repression can reach its limits and that publics are often willing to defy the autocrats. Governing is difficult, even for authoritarians, and the currently resurgent authoritarianism is not a one-way trend. So a *two-worlds scenario* may be likely in the near term, but the *resilience of rights scenario* is also still an open possibility.

VI. Conclusion

Resurgent authoritarianism will not lead to substantive changes in formal IHRL. Autocrats stand to gain little from denouncing human rights treaties or from proposing new international instruments that would explicitly shield authoritarian regimes from external scrutiny. On the contrary, autocrats may expect some public relations payoff from remaining within the international human rights treaty system and related institutions. But authoritarian regimes will continue to weaken international human rights institutions from within by submitting pro forma reports, rejecting negative findings, and blocking criticism of fellow autocrats, all the while "talking the talk" of international human rights. In other words, IHRL is not likely to change at the level of formal law but rather in the institutional arrangements for applying it. Professor Ginsburg refers to this as a "concerted effort to

[110] *Sudan Coup: Why Omar al-Bashir Was Overthrown*, BBC News, Apr. 15, 2019.

[111] Adam Nossiter, *Hopes Fade for New Political Course in Algeria a Year After Popular Uprising*, N.Y. Times, Oct. 6, 2020; Adam Nossiter, *Military's Preferred Candidate Named Winner in Algeria Election*, N.Y. Times, Dec. 13, 2019.

neutralize multilateral forums as vehicles" for promoting democracy and human rights.[112]

Perhaps more importantly, rising authoritarianism means the erosion or destruction of domestic mechanisms for holding governments to their international human rights obligations. A substantial body of research shows that human rights treaties improve the fulfillment of rights when they empower domestic actors in domestic judicial, administrative, and political arenas. Activists, advocates, CSOs, legislators, and judges can invoke international human rights norms to enhance the legitimacy of their demands and increase the pressure on governments to improve respect for rights.[113] But when the mechanisms for exposing and publicizing violations, petitioning for redress, and demanding policy and legal change are eliminated, international human rights treaties can do little to empower domestic actors. Autocrats block those avenues. In order to maintain their grip on power, authoritarian regimes suppress mechanisms of accountability. They consistently target three in particular: independent courts, freedom of expression and of the press, and freedom of civil society to organize and participate in public life. Thus, resurgent authoritarianism neutralizes the crucial domestic means for applying and implementing IHRL. In Koh's terms, authoritarianism disrupts the dynamic of internalization that generates state compliance.[114]

But what comes after the current authoritarian wave? In my view, the first scenario—*end times*—is unlikely. The second—*two worlds*—is quite possible. And the third—*resilience of rights*—should not be dismissed out of hand.

[112] Ginsburg, *supra* note 34, at 255.

[113] Geoff Dancy & Kathryn Sikkink, *Ratification and Human Rights Prosecutions: Toward a Transnational Theory of Treaty Compliance*, 44 N.Y.U. J. INT'L L. & POL. 751 (2012); MARGARET E. KECK & KATHRYN SIKKINK, ACTIVISTS BEYOND BORDERS: ADVOCACY NETWORKS IN INTERNATIONAL POLITICS (1998); Ellen L. Lutz & Kathryn Sikkink, *International Human Rights Law and Practice in Latin America*, 54 INT'L ORG. 633 (2000); THOMAS RISSE-KAPPEN et al., THE POWER OF HUMAN RIGHTS: INTERNATIONAL NORMS AND DOMESTIC CHANGE (1999); SIMMONS, *supra* note 3; MERRY, *supra* note 3.

[114] Koh, *Why Do Nations Obey?*, *supra* note 46; Koh, *Bringing International Law Home*, *supra* note 46.

Appendix

Table 12.A1 Change in Indicators of Core Authoritarian Strategies, 2009–19

Countries that dropped at least one category in the Regimes of the World classification							
		Individual Indicators					
	Number of indicators showing increased authoritarianism	Attacks on the judiciary	Court packing	Suppression of free discussion	Media censorship	Restrictions on CSO entry	CSO repression
Czech Republic	6	↑	↑	↑	↑	↑	↑
Greece	6	↑	↑	↑	↑	↑	↑
Hungary	6	↑	↑	↑	↑	↑	↑
Poland	6	↑	↑	↑	↑	↑	↑
Turkey	6	↑	↑	↑	↑	↑	↑
Yemen	6	↑	↑	↑	↑	↑	↑
Albania	5	↑	↓	↑	↑	↑	↑
Bangladesh	5	↑	↑	↓	↑	↑	↑
Benin	5	↓	↑	↑	↑	↑	↑
Serbia	5	↑	↓	↑	↑	↑	↑
Tanzania	5	↑	↓	↑	↑	↑	↑
Ukraine	5	↑	↓	↑	↑	↑	↑
Bolivia	4	↓	↓	↑	↑	↑	↑
Iceland	4	↓	↑	↑	↓	↑	↑
Lithuania	4	↓	↓	↑	↑	↑	↑

(continued)

Table 12.A1 Continued

Countries that dropped at least one category in the Regimes of the World classification							
		Individual Indicators					
	Number of indicators showing increased authoritarianism	Attacks on the judiciary	Court packing	Suppression of free discussion	Media censorship	Restrictions on CSO entry	CSO repression
Maldives	4	↓	↓	↑	↑	↑	↑
Namibia	4	↑	↓	↑	↓	↑	↑
Slovakia	4	↑	↓	↑	↓	↑	↑
South Africa	4	↓	↓	↑	↑	↑	↑
Syria	4	↑	↓	↑	↓	↑	↑
Togo	4	↓	↓	↑	↑	↑	↑
Zambia	4	↓	↑	↓	↑	↑	↑
Burkina Faso	3	↓	↓	↑	↓	↑	↑
Comoros	3	↓	↓	↑	↓	↑	↑
Mali	3	↓	↓	↓	↑	↑	↑
Mauritius	3	↓	↓	↓	↑	↑	↑
Thailand	3	↓	↓	↑	↓	↑	↑
Malawi	2	↓	↓	↓	↓	↑	↑
Sudan	1	↑	↓	↓	↓	↓	↓
Total countries with increase in specific authoritarian practice:		15	10	23	20	28	28

Note: A "↑" indicates an increase in the authoritarian practice (a decrease in the underlying V-Dem indicator). A "↓" indicates a decrease in the authoritarian practice (an increase in the underlying V-Dem indicator).

Table 12.A2 Change in Indicators of Core Authoritarian Strategies, 2009–19

25 countries showing the greatest decline in the Liberal Democracy Index, 2009–19								
			Individual Indicators					
	Decline in Liberal Democracy Index	Number of indicators showing increased authoritarianism	Attacks on the judiciary	Court packing	Suppression of free discussion	Media censorship	Restrictions on CSO entry	CSO repression
Hungary	−0.358	6	↑	↑	↑	↑	↑	↑
Turkey	−0.357	6	↑	↑	↑	↑	↑	↑
Poland	−0.328	6	↑	↑	↑	↑	↑	↑
Serbia	−0.271	5	↑	↓	↑	↑	↑	↑
Brazil	−0.251	6	↑	↑	↑	↑	↑	↑
India	−0.186	6	↑	↑	↑	↑	↑	↑
Mali	−0.173	3	↓	↓	↓	↑	↑	↑
Thailand	−0.164	3	↓	↓	↑	↓	↑	↑
Nicaragua	−0.161	4	↓	↓	↑	↑	↑	↑
Zambia	−0.147	4	↓	↑	↓	↑	↑	↑
Bulgaria	−0.144	3	↓	↓	↑	↑	↓	↑
United States of America	−0.139	5	↑	↑	↑	↑	↑	↓
Comoros	−0.138	3	↓	↓	↑	↓	↑	↑
Burundi	−0.137	6	↑	↑	↑	↑	↑	↑
Romania	−0.136	5	↑	↓	↑	↑	↑	↑
Czech Republic	−0.131	6	↑	↑	↑	↑	↑	↑

(*continued*)

Table 12.A2 Continued

25 countries showing the greatest decline in the Liberal Democracy Index, 2009–19								
			Individual Indicators					
	Decline in Liberal Democracy Index	Number of indicators showing increased authoritarianism	Attacks on the judiciary	Court packing	Suppression of free discussion	Media censorship	Restrictions on CSO entry	CSO repression
Bangladesh	−0.126	5	↑	↑	↓	↑	↑	↑
Bolivia	−0.126	4	↓	↓	↑	↑	↑	↑
Croatia	−0.125	5	↓	↑	↑	↑	↑	↑
Ukraine	−0.116	5	↑	↓	↑	↑	↑	↑
Suriname	−0.113	5	↑	↑	↑	↓	↑	↑
Liberia	−0.111	4	↓	↓	↑	↑	↑	↑
Benin	−0.108	5	↓	↑	↑	↑	↑	↑
Burkina Faso	−0.101	3	↓	↓	↑	↓	↑	↑
Tanzania	−0.094	5	↑	↓	↑	↑	↑	↑
Total countries with increase in specific authoritarian practice			14	13	22	21	24	24

Note: A "↑" indicates an increase in the authoritarian practice (a decrease in the underlying V-Dem indicator). A "↓" indicates a decrease in the authoritarian practice (an increase in the underlying V-Dem indicator).

13

The International Criminal Law of the Future

Leila N. Sadat

I. Introduction

International criminal law (ICL) is one of international law's newer disciplines. It experienced three periods of intense growth during the past hundred years: during the interwar period of the twentieth century after the (failed) trial of the Kaiser; during and immediately following World War II as a result of the Nuremberg and Tokyo trials; and following the end of the Cold War with the establishment of ad hoc international criminal tribunals, the International Criminal Court (ICC), and significant action at the national and international level addressing transnational crimes, including terrorism.

The ICL project is very much linked to a central theme of this volume: the evolution of a rules-based international order. Indeed, particularly as regards the "core crimes" of aggression, crimes against humanity, genocide, and war crimes,[1] the decision to move from a purely political understanding of whether state actors ordering or committing such crimes were justified to a legal understanding of the same, has been, as I have written elsewhere, a journey from politics to law.[2] Although the concept of a rule-of-law-based system is admittedly challenging to define, one might conveniently adopt the principles elaborated by the World Justice Project: accountability, just

[1] *See, e.g.*, European Union Agency for Criminal Justice Cooperation, *Core International Crimes*, https://www.eurojust.europa.eu/crime-types-and-casework/crime-types/core-international-crimes#:~:text=The%20crime%20of%20genocide%2C%20crimes,well%2Dbeing%20of%20our%20world (last visited Jan. 16, 2020). Although Eurojust does not include the crime of aggression, in the view of this author it is a mistake to omit it. It was included in the Charters of the Nuremberg and Tokyo Tribunals and shares many characteristics with other core crimes.

[2] Leila Nadya Sadat, *International Criminal Justice: The Journey from Politics to Law*, *in* THE FOUNDERS: FOUR PIONEERING INDIVIDUALS WHO LAUNCHED THE FIRST MODERN-ERA INTERNATIONAL CRIMINAL TRIBUNALS 19–31 (David M. Crane, Leila N. Sadat, & Michael P. Scharf eds., 2018).

Leila N. Sadat, *The International Criminal Law of the Future* In: *Is the International Legal Order Unraveling?*. Edited by: David L. Sloss, Oxford University Press.
DOI: 10.1093/oso/9780197652800.003.0014

laws, open government, and accessible justice.[3] In other words, like international criminal justice itself, a rules-based international order requires that governments, as well as private actors, be held responsible for their actions under the law, a fundamental shift from the days when the sovereign could do no wrong. That this attempted transformation of ICL developed during a mere one hundred years is extraordinary, but cannot yet be taken for granted. This is particularly true as regards the law and mechanisms developed to address the core crimes, which were originally conceived as crimes committed by the state, to which there was therefore great resistance on sovereignty grounds, resistance that persists today.

As this chapter highlights, ICL uses a "crime control" approach for transnational crimes, but a "justice" or due process approach—perhaps with elements of restorative justice as well—for core crimes.[4] This results in a paradox: "Lesser" crimes such as terrorism are codified in treaties with robust interstate cooperation provisions, and even enforced by the UN Security Council or military action. Sanctions are harsh, "justice" is swift, and extrajudicial killing of suspected terrorists may be involved. State enforcement of drug crimes can involve cross-border kidnapping and harsh sentences, and states may employ their domestic criminal jurisdiction exorbitantly in cases involving corruption or organized crime. On the other hand, the "most serious crimes of concern to the international community as a whole"—genocide, crimes against humanity, and war crimes—are codified in treaties with weak enforcement provisions.[5] Core crimes are typically prosecuted in national and international jurisdictions, including the ICC, containing robust human rights protections for the accused, and are subject to significant jurisdictional, procedural, and enforcement constraints.

This chapter traces the contours of ICL's expansion over the past century; briefly surveys the relationship between that expansion, justice, and crime

[3] World Justice Project, *What Is the Rule of Law?*, https://worldjusticeproject.org/about-us/overview/what-rule-law (last visited Jan. 16, 2021).

[4] Neil Boister, *Transnational Criminal Law*, 14 Eur. J. Int'l L. 953 (2003). The crime control model is a theory of criminal justice, which emphasizes reducing crime through increased police and prosecutorial powers. A "due process" or "justice" model focuses upon individual liberties and rights and limiting government power. Herbert Packer, *Two Models of the Criminal Process*, 113 U. Pa. L. Rev. 1 (1964). A restorative justice model was added by Kent Roach, *Four Models of the Criminal Process*, 89 J. Crim. L. & Criminol. 671 (1999).

[5] The proposed new treaty on crimes against humanity would remedy this gap. *Proposed International Convention on the Prevention and Punishment of Crimes Against Humanity*, *in* Forging a Convention for Crimes Against Humanity 359 (Leila Nadya Sadat ed., 2013); Int'l Law Comm'n, Rep. on the Work of its Seventy-First Session, U.N. Doc. A/74/10, at 10-140 (2019) [hereinafter Int'l Law Comm'n Report].

control; and concludes with some tentative thoughts about ICL's likely future. The chapter cannot possibly cover all of ICL: the field is too vast. Nor can it address related questions of transitional justice after mass atrocities, meaning modalities other than the criminal law that are used to restore peace to troubled communities. Its aim is therefore more modest: to survey the existing landscape, discern current trends, and draw tentative conclusions about likely future developments. The five broad trends evinced by this short study point in opposite directions. Some echo the concerns raised in this volume about increasing illiberalism in global affairs as states advance nationalist justifications for the commission of atrocities or other crimes, or punish nonstate actors in increasingly harsh and extralegal ways for the commission of transnational crimes. Others, however, support the continued evolution of the rules-based international legal order. Which trends will predominate in the long term is unclear, but the election of Joe Biden as the forty-sixth president of the United States, given his commitment to the rule of law and multilateralism, suggests that the short-term trajectory is probably positive.

II. The Development of International Criminal Law in the Twentieth and Twenty-First Centuries

The term "international criminal law," like the term "rule of law," is subject to interpretation. This chapter defines ICL in classic fashion as the convergence of two disciplines: the penal aspects of international law and the transnational aspects of national criminal law.[6] Some suggest that "ICL" refers only to "core crimes," meaning genocide, crimes against humanity, war crimes, and aggression.[7] Yet even this list of offenses punishable as a matter of universal jurisdiction should arguably include piracy, slavery, and torture.[8] Moreover, after the September 11, 2001, attacks, terrorism, which was initially conceived as a transnational crime, took on many penal characteristics of the

[6] M. Cherif Bassiouni, *An Appraisal of the Growth and Development of International Criminal Law*, 45 REV. INT'L DE DROIT PENAL 405 (1974).

[7] *See, e.g.*, Mikkel Jarle Christensen, *Crafting and Promoting International Crimes: A Controversy Among Professionals of Core-Crimes and Anti-Corruption*, 30 LEIDEN J. INT'L L. 501 (2017); Christine Schwöbel-Patel, *The Core Crimes of International Criminal Law*, *in* THE OXFORD HANDBOOK OF INTERNATIONAL CRIMINAL LAW (Kevin Jon Heller et al. eds., 2020) [hereinafter THE OXFORD HANDBOOK]; Regina Menachery Paulose, *Beyond the Core: Incorporating Transnational Crimes into the Rome Statute*, 21 CARDOZO J. INT'L & COMP. L. 77 (2012).

[8] THE PRINCETON PRINCIPLES ON UNIVERSAL JURISDICTION, Principle 2(1), https://lapa.princeton.edu/hosteddocs/unive_jur.pdf.

core crimes, particularly as the regime governing terrorism became a blend of international criminal law and international humanitarian law (IHL). For this reason, the better view is that ICL includes the legal regime governing the core crimes as well as transnational criminal law (TCL). Thus, principles of jurisdiction, punishment, interstate cooperation, *aut dedere aut judicare*, and the like apply to the entire field, although differentially depending upon the nature and penal characteristics of the particular offense.[9] Today there are more than 320 international and regional criminal law treaties that cover crimes from interfering with submarine cables to genocide.[10]

The work of the international criminal tribunals in the 1990s brought new focus and interest to the subject of ICL, *stricto senso*, meaning the adjudication of international crimes by international courts and tribunals. TCL focuses upon matters such as extradition, control of transnational corruption, organized crime, drug trafficking, and terrorism, although particularly as regards terrorism, we now see an interplay between the rules of IHL and ICL. TCL is all about crime control: deterrence, capture, restraint, and punishment. ICL, with respect to the core crimes, has been more about justice. Although it has a deterrent element and involves arrest and punishment, because of the nature of mass atrocities, bringing peace and justice to afflicted communities has to be part of the equation, even as the criminal process is used with respect to specific perpetrators.[11] The potential convergence of these two branches of ICL offers the possibility of strengthening the crime control dimension of ICL applicable to core crimes and may enhance the justice dimension of TCL, particularly with respect to terrorism, where illiberal trends have caused the regime governing transnational terrorism to diverge from human rights norms.[12]

[9] M. Cherif Bassiouni, Introduction to International Criminal Law (2nd ed. 2012).

[10] In 2013, my co-authors and I counted 318 such treaties, but that did not include the new International Convention for the Protection of All Persons from Enforced Disappearance, which entered into force on December 23, 2010, or the 2014 Protocol to the Montreal Convention on Offenses and Certain other Acts Committed on Board Aircraft. *See* Jordan J. Paust et al., International Criminal Law: Cases & Materials 17–18 (2013).

[11] Neil Boister, An Introduction to Transnational Criminal Law 278 (1st ed. 2012).

[12] *See also* Frédéric Mégret, *The Unity of International Criminal Law*, *in* The Oxford Handbook, *supra* note 7, at 811. The title of this chapter pays homage to the late Judge Hans Peter-Kaul of Germany, who delivered a memorable address on *The International Criminal Court of the Future* on the occasion of the 6th Humanitarian Law Dialogs in Chautauqua, New York. Judge Hans Peter-Kaul, *The ICC of the Future* (Aug. 28, 2012), https://www.icc-cpi.int/NR/rdonlyres/8572B9B0-B827-466C-B67A-3C9C06A5E46E/284994/30082012_ChautauquaSpeech_THEICCOFTHEFUTURE_provis.pdf.

A. The Founding Period: 1919–46

Modern international criminal justice is generally traced to the adoption of the 1919 Treaty of Versailles following the First World War. The warring states inflicted horrific violence upon combatants and civilians alike, including the use of poison gas, ethnic cleansing, and genocide.[13] The use of modern weaponry rendered the conflict more devastating than earlier wars and caused many to believe that what had happened was not simply immoral or the continuation of "politics by other means,"[14] but a cataclysmic event, at least some aspects of which were *unlawful*, indeed, *criminal*.

The Commission on the Responsibility of the Authors of the War and on the Enforcement of Penalties proposed the creation of an international "high tribunal" for the trial of "all enemy persons alleged to have been guilty of offences against the laws and customs of war and the laws of humanity."[15] The US members of the Commission dissented, opining that although the actions of the Central Powers may have been immoral, they were not illegal.[16] The compromise was to try the German Kaiser for the "supreme offence against international morality and the sanctity of treaties." The Netherlands refused to extradite the Kaiser for trial, however, and only a handful of individuals were handed over to a German court in Leipzig, most of whom were acquitted. The effort was a fiasco.[17]

The idea of an international criminal jurisdiction, however, captured the imagination and led to multiple proposals for the establishment of a permanent international criminal court, particularly in Europe.[18] (US scholars and some of their British colleagues were decidedly less enthusiastic.[19]) The first treaty codification that followed proposed the establishment of an international criminal court for terrorism offenses. Unfortunately, the treaty never

[13] *See, e.g.*, David Matas, *Prosecuting Crimes Against Humanity: The Lessons of World War I*, 13 FORDHAM INT'L L.J. 86 (1989).

[14] Evan Luard, *von Clausewitz—The Political Purposes of War*, *in* BASIC TEXTS IN INTERNATIONAL RELATIONS: THE EVOLUTION OF IDEAS ABOUT INTERNATIONAL SOCIETY 243, 244 (2016).

[15] Commission on the Responsibility of the Authors of the War and on Enforcement of Penalties, *Report Presented to the Preliminary Peace Conference*, 14 AM. J. INT'L L. 95, 123 (1920).

[16] *Id.* at 128.

[17] WILLIAM A. SCHABAS, THE TRIAL OF THE KAISER (2019); M. Cherif Bassiouni, *The Status of Aggression in International Law: From Versailles to Kampala—And What the Future Might Bring*, *in* SEEKING ACCOUNTABILITY FOR THE UNLAWFUL USE OF FORCE 7, 16–18 (Leila Nadya Sadat ed., 2018).

[18] Leila Nadya Sadat, *The Nuremberg Paradox*, 58 AM. J. COMP. L. 151, 166–69 (2010).

[19] J.L. Brierly, *Do We Need an International Criminal Court?*, 8 BRIT. Y.B. INT'L. L. 81–88 (1927).

entered into force; India was the only state to ratify it.[20] However, increasing numbers of treaty instruments related to other transnational offenses were proposed and negotiated after the war, especially new conventions codifying the laws and customs of war.

When war and wartime atrocities came again to Europe in the 1930s and 1940s, the Allied powers (France, the Soviet Union, the United States, and the United Kingdom) announced their determination to punish the perpetrators, issuing declarations to this effect in 1942[21] and 1943.[22] These laid a foundation for the establishment of the International Military Tribunal at Nuremberg (IMT) and the International Military Tribunal for the Far East (IMFTE) in Tokyo.

As to the IMT, the Allies bickered about whether to hold a trial at all (Churchill advocated summary executions), and, once the decision was made to hold one, who should be charged and what procedural rules should apply.[23] Allegations of "victor's justice" plagued the tribunal, as the Allies—who had firebombed Dresden during the war and dropped two atomic bombs as the IMT Charter was being negotiated and signed—did not include charges relating to aerial bombardment. The Soviet Union also insisted on accusing the Germans of the Katyn Forest massacre, which Soviet forces had carried out. The judgment in the parallel proceedings held by the IMFTE was issued over a stinging dissent by the Indian judge, who objected to the exclusion of Allied crimes and the lack of judges from the vanquished nations on the bench, criticisms compounded by the doubtful procedural fairness of the trial itself.[24]

Yet even with these deficiencies, the Nuremberg trial in particular left an important legacy. The idea that human beings could assert rights under international law against their governments was innovative, as was the notion that leaders could be held legally responsible for their violation. The decision to hold a trial, and the accomplishment of the task to a high level

[20] *See* Convention for the Prevention and Punishment of Terrorism, League of Nations (Nov. 16, 1937), https://www.wdl.org/en/item/11579/; *see also* Ben Saul, *Attempts to Define Terrorism in International Law*, 52 NETH. INT'L L. REV. 57, 63 (2005).

[21] The *St. James Declaration*, Resolution by Allied Governments Condemning German Terror and Demanding Retribution (Jan. 13, 1942), *in* British and Foreign Papers, 1940–1942, at 1072 (Her Majesty's Stationary Office).

[22] The *Moscow Declaration*, Declaration of German Atrocities, Nov. 1, 1943, 3 Bevans 816, 834, DEPT. STATE BULLETIN (Nov. 6, 1943), at 310–11.

[23] TELFORD TAYLOR, THE ANATOMY OF THE NUREMBERG TRIALS: A PERSONAL MEMOIR (1992).

[24] Neil Boister & Robert Cryer, *The Tokyo International Military Tribunal: A Reappraisal*, 17, 323–27 (2008).

of professionalism, represented a real achievement. It may have been an American "show"[25] in terms of the material support and size of the various participating prosecutorial teams, but it built upon decades of European thought and legal analysis.[26] As recent scholarship has illuminated, the Soviet contribution was also critically important to building the aggressive war charges that the United States came to see as the most important element of the trial.[27] The judgment was well crafted, and the brilliant opening statement of Robert H. Jackson, Chief Prosecutor for the United States, is still quoted today. Nonetheless, whether Nuremberg would be a "one-off" historic event or would have enduring salience remained an open question.

B. 1946 to the Present Day

The Nuremberg Principles are deeply embedded in the UN Charter, which was negotiated and adopted contemporaneously. This is evidenced by the Charter's prohibition on the use of force against the territorial integrity and political independence of member states[28] and in the Charter's human rights provisions.[29] Indeed, modern human rights law—like modern international criminal law—rests upon the Nuremberg foundation. The corollary of the notion that individuals have duties under international law, expounded by the judgment of the IMT, is that they may also acquire rights thereunder.

The Nuremberg Principles were codified by the International Law Commission and presented to the General Assembly after the war.[30] At least some of the "law" associated with Nuremberg found its way into new global treaties on apartheid, genocide, the laws of war, and torture.[31] Although

[25] ELIZABETH BORGWARDT, A NEW DEAL FOR THE WORLD: AMERICA'S VISION FOR HUMAN RIGHTS 233 (2005).

[26] Sadat, *supra* note 18.

[27] FRANCINE HIRSCH, SOVIET JUDGMENT AT NUREMBERG (2020).

[28] U.N. Charter, art. 2, ¶ 4.

[29] *Id.*, arts. 55 & 56. *See also* MARY ANN GLENDON, A WORLD MADE NEW: ELEANOR ROOSEVELT AND THE UNIVERSAL DECLARATION OF HUMAN RIGHTS (2001).

[30] Int'l Law Comm'n, Rep. on the Work of its First Session, U.N. Doc. A/925 (1949).

[31] International Convention on the Suppression and Punishment of the Crime of Apartheid, Nov. 30, 1973, 1015 U.N.T.S. 243; Convention on the Prevention and Punishment of the Crime of Genocide, Dec. 9, 1948, 78 U.N.T.S. 277; Geneva Convention (I) for the Amelioration of the Condition of the Wounded and Sick in Armed Forces in the Field, Aug. 12, 1949, 75 U.N.T.S. 31; Geneva Convention (II) for the Amelioration of the Condition of Wounded, Sick and Shipwrecked Members of Armed Forces at Sea, Aug. 12, 1949, 75 U.N.T.S. 85; Geneva Convention (III) Relative to the Treatment of Prisoners of War, Aug. 12, 1949, 75 U.N.T.S. 135; Geneva Convention (IV) Relative to the Protection of Civilian Persons in Time of War, Aug. 12, 1949, 75 U.N.T.S. 287; Convention

aggression and crimes against humanity were never made the subject of similar specialized conventions, that effort is currently underway for crimes against humanity.[32] Understood broadly, the "Nuremberg Principles" eschew collective responsibility in favor of individual criminal responsibility; provide that no human being (even a head of state or other government official) is above the law with respect to the most serious crimes of concern to humanity as a whole; and that reliance upon internal law is no defense to crimes for which an individual may have responsibility under international law.[33]

At the international level, therefore, the Nuremberg Principles became a critical legal underpinning of the new world order. But Cold War politics impeded their implementation. The permanent members of the Security Council were often divided, meaning that the International Law Commission had difficulty advancing its work on a draft code of crimes and a statute for an international criminal court.[34] The Nuremberg Principles were also often honored in the breach as powerful states pursued their national interests. The United States invaded Vietnam; the Soviet Union invaded Afghanistan.[35] Indeed, as Samuel Moyn recently noted, although the Nuremberg judgment itself labeled war the "supreme international crime,"[36] a shift subsequently occurred in which *atrocities* during war became the focus of international law, rather than war itself.[37]

In the 1990s, the Security Council, finally freed from Cold War politics, established two new international criminal tribunals. The first addressed crimes committed during the war in the former Yugoslavia (the International

Against Torture and Other Cruel, Inhumane or Degrading Treatment or Punishment, Dec. 10, 1984, 1465 U.N.T.S. 85.

[32] Proposed International Convention on the Prevention and Punishment of Crimes Against Humanity, *supra* note 5. Leila Nadya Sadat, *Little Progress in the Sixth Committee on Crimes Against Humanity*, Case Wes. Res. J. Int'l L. (forthcoming 2022).

[33] Leila Nadya Sadat, *Shattering the Nuremberg Consensus: U.S. Rendition Policy and International Law*, 3 Yale J. Int'l Aff. 65, 66 (2008).

[34] Leila Nadya Sadat, *The Proposed Permanent International Criminal Court: An Appraisal*, 29 Cornell Int'l L.J. 665, 667 (1996) (formerly Wexler).

[35] *See* Taylor, *supra* note 23, at 636; Jean Allain, *The Continued Evolution of International Adjudication*, *in* Looking Ahead: International Law in the 21st Century 50, 55 (Can. Council of Int'l Law ed., 2012); Benjamin B. Ferencz, *The Nuremberg Principles and the Gulf War*, 66 St. John's L. Rev. 711, 719–20 (1992); Claude Lombois, Droit Pénal International 162 (1979).

[36] Trial of the Major War Criminals Before the International Military Tribunal 186 (1947), https://www.loc.gov/rr/frd/Military_Law/pdf/NT_Vol-I.pdf.

[37] Samuel Moyn, *From Aggression to Atrocity: Rethinking the History of International Criminal Law*, *in* The Oxford Handbook, *supra* note 7, at 341. *See also* Dianne Otto, *Women, Peace and Security: A Critical Analysis of the Security Council's Vision* (Jan. 9, 2017), https://blogs.lse.ac.uk/wps/2017/01/09/women-peace-and-security-a-critical-analysis-of-the-security-councils-vision/.

Criminal Tribunal for the former Yugoslavia (ICTY)); the second addressed crimes committed during the Rwandan genocide (the International Criminal Tribunal for Rwanda (ICTR)). The politics surrounding the creation and operation of these tribunals has been exhaustively documented by others;[38] suffice it to say, they faced tremendous political and logistical challenges, particularly in their early years. The Yugoslavia and Rwanda Tribunals had similar, but not identical, jurisdictions to the IMT, although neither tribunal included crimes against peace in its statute, limiting their jurisdictions to genocide, war crimes, and crimes against humanity.[39] The ICTY was the first court to be established in the middle of an armed conflict. It was tasked to investigate for the commission of atrocity crimes, a "novel experiment of dual-track justice and warfare"[40] that would become the model for the ICC.[41]

Although sometimes criticized as either too expensive or remote from the regions or peoples they served, the establishment of the ad hoc international criminal tribunals inspired states and nongovernmental organizations to establish a permanent international criminal court. This idea was reintroduced into the General Assembly's agenda in 1989 by a coalition of sixteen Caribbean and Latin American nations, led by Trinidad and Tobago, which proposed the establishment of a court to try offenses related to drug trafficking and other transnational crimes.[42] As negotiations progressed, however, the "treaty crimes" that had been at the core of Trinidad's proposal were ultimately jettisoned. In the ICC Statute, adopted on July 17, 1998, the Court's jurisdiction paralleled that of the Nuremberg and Tokyo Tribunals: crimes against humanity, genocide, war crimes, and aggression (subject to a separate jurisdictional regime).[43]

[38] *See, e.g.*, DAVID SCHEFFER, ALL THE MISSING SOULS: A PERSONAL HISTORY OF THE WAR CRIMES TRIBUNALS (2010).

[39] Statute of the International Criminal Tribunal for the Former Yugoslavia, S.C. Res. 827, Annex, U.N. Doc. S/RES/827 (May 25, 1993); Statute of the International Criminal Tribunal for Rwanda, S.C. Res. 955, Annex, U.N. Doc. S/RES/955 (Nov. 6, 1994).

[40] SCHEFFER, *supra* note 38, at 19.

[41] The establishment of the Rwanda and Yugoslavia Tribunals was followed by the creation of other international criminal courts and tribunals including the Special Panels for East Timor in 2000; the Special Court for Sierra Leone in 2002 (SCSL); the Extraordinary Chambers in the Courts of Cambodia in 2003 (ECCC); and the Special Tribunal for Lebanon in 2007. *See* Sadat, *supra* note 2.

[42] G.A. Res. 44/39, International criminal responsibility of individuals and entities engaged in illicit trafficking in narcotic drugs across national frontiers and other transnational criminal activities: establishment of an international criminal court with jurisdiction over such crimes (Dec. 4, 1989).

[43] Leila Nadya Sadat & S. Richard Carden, *The New International Criminal Court: An Uneasy Revolution*, 88 GEO. L.J. 381 (2000); Sadat, *supra* note 2.

The ICC Statute was adopted after years of difficult discussions and five long, hot weeks of grueling negotiations in Rome. It is longer and more complicated than the statutes of earlier tribunals, and the jurisdictional regime and procedure of the Court much more complex. In particular, the ICC, unlike the ICTY, the ICTR, and the Nuremberg Tribunal itself, is based upon the principle of "complementarity," meaning that the Court is intended as a Court of last, not first, resort that will hear only cases in which states are unable or unwilling to proceed.[44] Thus, under the Court's complicated admissibility rules, any state—even a state not party to the Statute—can divest the Court of jurisdiction by opening an investigation into a case in which jurisdiction is sought by the Court. Although the ICC has had its share of criticism since its creation in 1998, its establishment marked an important milestone in the construction of a rules-based international order.

The field of transnational crime also experienced exponential growth after World War II. Beginning in 1955, the UN Congress on Crime Prevention and Criminal Justice convened five-year congresses involving policy makers, practitioners, academics, intergovernmental organizations, and civil society. The UN Office on Drugs and Crime website features some of the many treaties negotiated to address, inter alia, maritime piracy, terrorism, corruption, drug trafficking, and organized crime.[45] In 1996, during the Annual Meeting of the American Society of International Law, one participant observed that, along with world interdependence and ease of communication, transport, trade, and migration, criminal elements "fully participat[e] in . . . global processes" and that transnational organized crime is "an almost natural component of the global international processes of change."[46]

There are now nineteen universal legal instruments against terrorism, as well as numerous UN Security Council Resolutions; a UN Convention against Corruption with 187 parties;[47] three major drug control treaties;[48]

[44] Rome Statute for the International Criminal Court, Preamble, art. 17, July 17, 1998, 2187 U.N.T.S. 3.

[45] United Nations Office on Drugs and Crime, *Treaties*, https://www.unodc.org/unodc/en/treaties/index.html?ref=menuside (last visited Jan. 7, 2021).

[46] Ugljesa Zvekic, *International Cooperation and Transnational Organized Crime*, 90 ASIL. Proc. 533, 533 (1996).

[47] United Nations Convention Against Corruption, Oct. 30, 2003, 2349 U.N.T.S. 41.

[48] Protocol Amending the Single Convention on Narcotic Drugs, 1961, Mar. 25, 1972, 976 U.N.T.S. 3; Convention on Psychotropic Substances, Feb. 21, 1971, 1019 U.N.T.S. 175; United Nations Convention Against Illicit Traffic in Narcotic Drugs and Psychotropic Substances, Dec. 19, 1988, 1582 U.N.T.S. 95.

and the UN Convention against Transnational Organized Crime[49] with 190 parties, having been ratified by virtually every country in the world. Many cases are tried annually under these conventions in national systems. The treaties contain many provisions like those undergirding prosecutions of core crimes, including provisions on extraterritorial jurisdiction, the obligation to extradite or prosecute,[50] and modes of liability.

There is a certain degree of cross-fertilization between treaties embodying core crimes and those involving transnational crimes. For example, Article 25(3)(d) of the Rome Statute incorporates a mode of liability drawn from the 1997 Convention on Terrorist Bombing.[51] Likewise, the Proposed Convention for the Prevention and Punishment of Crimes against Humanity,[52] as well as the International Law Commission's draft articles predicated thereon,[53] rely heavily on the UN Convention against Transnational Organized Crime and the UN Corruption Convention for provisions on interstate cooperation and mutual legal assistance.[54]

Domestic criminal law is about using state power to regulate, prohibit, and deter undesirable behavior (crime control). Likewise, ICL is often used by national and international jurisdictions for the same reason. For example, the United States has been attempting to use transnational prosecutions to address abuses committed by the Maduro regime in Venezuela. It recently indicted President Maduro himself,[55] and the US Department of Justice has been vigorously pursuing, in the United States and abroad, more than thirty indictments of individuals connected to the Maduro regime as part of an effort to exert "maximum pressure" on it.[56] At the same time, the humanitarian crisis in Venezuela is now also the subject of an ICC referral.[57] Although there

[49] United Nations Convention against Transnational Organized Crime, Jan. 8, 1997, 2225 U.N.T.S. 209.

[50] *See* Zdzislaw Galicki (Special Rapporteur), *Fourth report on the obligation to extradite or prosecute*, U.N. Doc. A/CN.4/648 (May 31, 2011).

[51] International Convention for the Suppression of Terrorist Bombings, Dec. 15, 1997, 2149 U.N.T.S. 256.

[52] Proposed International Convention on the Prevention and Punishment of Crimes Against Humanity, *supra* note 5.

[53] Int'l Law Comm'n Report, *supra* note 5.

[54] United Nations Convention against Transnational Organized Crime, Nov. 15, 2000, 2225 U.N.T.S. 209; United Nations Convention Against Corruption, Oct. 30, 2003, 2349 U.N.T.S. 41.

[55] Read the Justice Department's narcotrafficking indictment against Venezuela's Nicolás Maduro, Wash. Post, updated Mar. 26, 2020.

[56] Steptoe, FCPA/Anti-Corruption Developments: 2018 Year in Review 48–49 (2019), https://www.steptoe.com/images/content/1/8/v4/189874/2018-FCPA-Year-in-Review-Final-Feb-28-2019.pdf. *See also* Gibson Dunn, 2019 Year-End FCPA Update (2020), https://www.gibsondunn.com/2019-year-end-fcpa-update/.

[57] Venezuela responded by filing a case against the United States. *See* Statement of the Prosecutor of the International Criminal Court, Mrs Fatou Bensouda, on the referral by Venezuela regarding

is nothing per se problematic about international and national systems using ICL synergistically, in the case of Venezuela, the US effort may represent an abuse of TCL to extend its jurisdictions beyond its borders to punish individuals otherwise out of reach. A more felicitous example of international and national cooperation is the use of universal jurisdiction in national systems to try individuals accused of war crimes in Syria, using evidence developed either by nonstate actors or collected and processed by the International, Impartial, and Independent Mechanism charged by the General Assembly to assist in the investigation and prosecution of persons responsible for the most serious crimes under international law committed in Syria since March 2011.[58]

The rise in international terrorism beginning in the 1970s, and the September 11, 2001, attacks in particular, had a profound effect on ICL. Occurring just three years after the Rome Statute had been negotiated, the attacks provoked an injured and angry United States to move terrorism from the category of transnational to international crime, not via the establishment of a new treaty but through the Security Council. Resolution 1373, adopted immediately following the attacks, contained provisions requiring states to prevent and suppress the financing of terrorist acts, and prosecute or extradite suspected terrorists.[59] Two years prior, in 1999, Security Council Resolution 1267 had designated Osama bin Laden and his associates as terrorists and established a sanctions regime to cover individuals and entities associated with them and/or the Taliban, wherever located.[60] This extraordinary use of the Council's Chapter VII authority to designate individuals for sanctions in order to combat transnational crime is in contrast with the relatively cumbersome regime of the ICC Statute for the investigation, prosecution, trial, and sentencing of individuals accused of war crimes, crimes against humanity, and genocide.

the situation in its own territory (Feb. 17, 2020), https://www.icc-cpi.int/Pages/item.aspx?name=200217-otp-statement-venezuela.

[58] G.A. Res. 71/248, International, Impartial and Independent Mechanism to Assist in the Investigation and Prosecution of Persons Responsible for the Most Serious Crimes under International Law Committed in the Syrian Arab Republic Since March 2011 (Dec. 21, 2016). In 2021, Germany convicted a former Syrian secret police officer of aiding and abetting crimes against humanity. *See* Ben Hubbard, *German Court Convicts Former Syrian Official of Crimes Against Humanity*, N.Y. Times, Feb. 24, 2021, and in 2022 convicted a Syrian colonel for crimes against humanity. Jenny Hill, *German Court Finds Syrian Colonel Guilty of Crimes Against Humanity*, BBC News, Jan. 13, 2022, https://www.bbc.com/news/world-europe-59949924.

[59] S.C. Res. 1373, U.N. Doc. S/RES/1373 (Sept. 28, 2001).

[60] S.C. Res. 1267, U.N. Doc. S/RES/1267 (Oct. 15, 1999).

The United States responded to the attacks of 9/11 by coupling the crime control model with a military response involving the invasion of Afghanistan,[61] the subsequent invasion of Iraq,[62] the use of drones to kill purported terrorists in countries where suspected terrorists were thought to be operating,[63] and the use of the Guantánamo Bay prison camp and military commissions for detention and trial. After the attacks on the US embassies in Kenya and Tanzania, then Secretary of State Madeline Albright suggested that international terrorism would be the "war of the future."[64] That proved prophetic in 2001, with the George W. Bush administration's decision to use a military, as opposed to a civilian, conception of terrorism.

The resulting confusion not only disrupted "some crucial legal categories of international law"[65] but nearly twenty years later, has established neither peace[66] nor justice.[67] Osama bin Laden was tracked down and killed by the Obama administration in 2011, and the Al Qaeda network was severely crippled by US and coalition strikes.[68] However, Afghanistan and neighboring Pakistan remain deeply unstable. A study in 2015 estimated that more than 149,000 people died in Afghanistan and Pakistan since the 2001 invasion.[69] Particularly after the withdrawal of US forces in summer 2021, Afghanistan experienced a Taliban takeover and an increased risk of human rights violation and mass atrocities.[70] In 2001, many argued that the United States and

[61] Council on Foreign Rel., *The U.S. War in Afghanistan: 1999–2021*, https://www.cfr.org/timeline/us-war-afghanistan (last visited Feb. 28, 2022).

[62] *See* Sean D. Murphy, *Assessing the Legality of Invading Iraq*, 92 Geo. L. J. 173 (2004).

[63] Milena Sterio, *The United States' Use of Drones in the War on Terror: The (Il)legality of Targeted Killings under International Law*, 45 Case W. Res. J. Int'l L. 197 (2012).

[64] Leila Nadya Sadat, *Terrorism and the Rule of Law*, 3 Wash. U. Glob. Stud. L. Rev. 135, 139 (2004).

[65] Antonio Cassese, *Terrorism Is Also Disrupting Some Crucial Legal Categories of International Law*, 12 Eur. J. Int'l. L. 993 (2001).

[66] Council on Foreign Relations, *Global Conflict Tracker: War in Afghanistan*, https://www.cfr.org/global-conflict-tracker/conflict/war-afghanistan#:~:text=Throughout%202019%20and%20into%202020,Security%20Forces%20(ANDSF)%20bases%20and (last visited Jan. 20, 2021).

[67] David Glazier, *Destined for an Epic Fail: The Problematic Guantánamo Military Commissions*, 75 Ohio St. L.J. 903 (2014).

[68] Bruce Riedel, *Al-Qaida today, 18 years after 9/11*, Brookings Inst. (Sept. 10, 2019), https://www.brookings.edu/blog/order-from-chaos/2019/09/10/al-qaida-today-18-years-after-9-11/.

[69] Adam Taylor, *149,000 People Have Died in War in Afghanistan and Pakistan since 2001, Report Says*, Wash. Post, June 3, 2015. The United States lost more than seven thousand soldiers in Afghanistan and Iraq as a result of the invasion of those countries after 9/11, with tens of thousands more wounded. U.S. Dep't Defense, Casualty Status, https://www.defense.gov/casualty.pdf (last visited March 1, 2021). These figures are somewhat lower than those reported by other sources.

[70] In 2021, Afghanistan ranked second highest among 162 countries for the risk of mass killings, according to the US Holocaust Museum's Early Warning Project. Pakistan was first on the list. *See* Early Warning Project, *High Risk Countries*, https://earlywarningproject.ushmm.org/high-risk-countries (last visited May 23, 2021). It was thus unsurprising that the US withdrawal in summer 2021 led to a Taliban takeover and increased human rights violations. Michael D. Shear & Jim Tankersley, *Biden*

its allies should convene an international tribunal to assess criminal responsibility for the attacks, rather than rely solely on military force.[71] Their views were rejected. Although President Barack Obama moderated many Bush-era policies, most were never entirely repudiated, particularly the use of the Al Qaeda sanctions committee and the targeting and killing of terrorists (as opposed to capturing and prosecuting them). President Donald Trump subsequently executed a state official, Iranian General Qassim Soleimani, arguing that he was a terrorist.[72]

III. How Has ICL Fared during the Past Thirty Years?

The preceding survey suggests that ICL has become an integral part of the global legal order, important for the maintenance of international peace and security and transnational crime control. It is thus unsurprising that the past thirty years have seen exponential growth in the law and institutions established to combat transnational and international crime. But how successful has this effort been? With respect to the core crimes, although the ad hoc tribunals suffered some of the same difficulties experienced at Nuremberg, they ultimately became credible and successful international institutions, trying scores of defendants and creating important precedents that have added depth to our understanding of international criminal justice and the substantive law of war crimes, crimes against humanity and genocide, as well as international criminal procedure.[73] Because they were established by the Security Council and applied to specific situations, they were consistent with the political objectives of the great powers and were generally supported by

Defends Afghan Pullout and Declares an End to Nation-Building, N.Y. Times, Aug. 31, 2021, https://www.nytimes.com/2021/08/31/us/politics/biden-defends-afghanistan-withdrawal.html.

[71] *See, e.g.*, Anne-Marie Slaughter, *Al Qaeda Should Be Tried Before the World*, N.Y. Times, Nov. 18, 2001.

[72] Dareh Gregorian & Jane C. Timm, *Trump on Soleimani Strike: "His Reign of Terror Is Over,"* NBC News, Jan. 3, 2020.

[73] The ICTY indicted 161 persons, 90 of whom were sentenced. Two cases are currently in retrial before the MICT. International Criminal Tribunal for the Former Yugoslavia, *Infographic: ICTY Facts and Figures*, https://www.icty.org/en/content/infographic-icty-facts-figures (last visited March 1, 2021). The ICTR indicted ninety-three individuals and convicted sixty-two. Proceedings have concluded for eighty-six persons; two are fugitives who remain at large, and one former fugitive was recently rendered to the Tribunal: U.N. International Residual Mechanism for Criminal Tribunals, *The ICTR In Brief*, https://unictr.irmct.org/en/tribunal (last visited Mar. 1, 2021).

them, particularly the United States.[74] Although doubts have surfaced about whether victims have been well served by international justice as a whole, and some victims have clearly found the proceedings difficult to bear,[75] recent empirical studies suggest that individual victims of mass atrocities have a preference for retributive justice.[76] This is evident in national systems as well—even decades after crimes have been committed, victims typically want their day in court,[77] in addition to solace for their pain.

Unlike the ad hoc tribunals, the ICC, which has 123 states parties as of this writing, has not yet hit its stride. The Court has opened investigations into sixteen situations involving fifteen countries, and five additional situations are in the "Preliminary Examination" phase as of March 1, 2022. Two of the Court's active situations—in Libya and Darfur, Sudan—were referred by the Security Council, but have presented difficulties in terms of investigation and trial. Several other situations were referred by the territorial states themselves: this is true of the situations in Uganda, the Democratic Republic of the Congo, Mali, the Central African Republic, and one of the two situations in Venezuela (Venezuela II). Some referrals were made *proprio motu* by the Prosecutor, either with the consent of the territorial state (as in Côte d'Ivoire and Georgia), or against the will of the territorial state, as in the case of Burundi and the Philippines, which subsequently withdrew from the ICC Statute.[78]

The Court, like the ad hoc tribunals before it, has had a rocky start. The first trial (the *Lubanga* case) took too long and was criticized for narrow charges and evidentiary problems. The Court has had difficulty procuring much-needed financial resources and problems arresting its accused, thirteen of

[74] *See* Harry M. Rhea, *The United States and International Military Tribunals: An Historical Analysis*, 16 ILSA J. Int'l & Comp. L. 19 (2009). Russia, however, later soured on the ICTY. *See* Maja Zivanovic, *Russian Minister Says Hague Tribunal "Should Be Closed,"* Balkan Insight (Oct. 16, 2017), https://balkaninsight.com/2017/10/16/russian-minister-says-hague-tribunal-should-be-closed/.

[75] *See* Sarah Louise Steele, *Victim-Witnesses in the International Criminal Court: Justice for Trauma, or the Trauma of Justice?*, 12 Australian Int'l L.J. 99 (2005); Kimi King & James Meernik, *The Burden of Bearing Witness: The Impact of Testifying at War Crimes Tribunals*, 63 J. Conflict Res. 348 (2019).

[76] Geoff Dancy, Yvonne Dutton, & Eamon Aloyo, *Retributive or Reparative Justice? Explaining Post-Conflict Preferences in Kenya*, J. Peace Res. (forthcoming, 2022). *See generally* Refik Hodzic, *Living the Legacy of Mass Atrocities*, 8 J. Int'l Crim. Just. 113 (2010).

[77] Consider the crimes against humanity cases brought in France fifty years after World War II by victims of Vichy collaborators. After fifty years, victims were still hopeful that the French courts could deliver justice. Leila Sadat, *The Interpretation of the Nuremberg Principles by the French Court of Cassation: From Touvier to Barbie and Back Again*, 32 Colum. J. Transnat'l L. 289 (1994) (formerly Wexler).

[78] Int'l Crim. Court, *Situations under investigation* (Mar. 1, 2022), https://www.icc-cpi.int/pages/situation.aspx.

whom are still at large as of this writing.[79] It has struggled with the pretrial process, and some of its recent judgments were so controversial that observers spoke of a "judicial meltdown." States have occasionally tampered with witnesses and/or evidence, or simply refused to cooperate.[80] The Court has endured bruising attacks by the United States, including legislation threatening countries with the loss of financial and military assistance if they failed to sign an ICC immunity agreement with the United States,[81] and subsequently imposing sanctions upon the Prosecutor and one of her deputies.[82]

Critics allege that the Court is both too strong and too weak;[83] that it has targeted Africa because it is a tool of the West,[84] or alternatively, that it has brought politically motivated prosecutions against Western states; that the Prosecutor has targeted defendants who are too high-ranking,[85] or has, conversely, brought only cases against low-level accused.[86] As Darryl Robinson has observed, it seems that no matter what it does, "the ICC cannot win."[87] The Court occupies—to paraphrase the late Judge Patricia Wald—"a small center in a whirling international vortex" in which almost everything it does "has political implications."[88] Thus, a certain degree of criticism is inevitable and, given the many setbacks the Court has had recently, warranted.

The Syrian and North Korean situations remain jurisdictionally outside the reach of the ICC because Russia and China are willing to veto resolutions that could refer those cases to the Court. Likewise, the United States remains outside the reach of the Court with respect to most of its military operations

[79] *See, e.g.*, Human Rights Watch, Unfinished Business: Closing Gaps in the Selection of ICC Cases (2011); Somini Sengupta, *Omar al-Bashir Case Shows International Criminal Court's Limitations*, N.Y. Times, June 15, 2015.

[80] Open Soc'y Justice Initiative, *Briefing Paper: Witness Interference in Cases Before the International Criminal Court* (Nov. 2016), https://www.opensocietyfoundations.org/sites/default/files/factsheet-icc-witness-interference-20161116.pdf; Prosecutor v. Uhuru Muigai Kenyatta, ICC-01/09-02/11-1037, Second Decision on Prosecution's Application for a Finding of Non-Compliance under Article 87(7) of the Statute (Sept. 19, 2016).

[81] American Servicemember's Protection Act of 2002 (codified at 22 U.S.C. §§ 7421–33).

[82] Exec. Order No. 13,928, 85 Fed. Reg. 36139 (June 11, 2020).

[83] *See* Jack Goldsmith, *The Self-Defeating International Criminal Court*, 70 U. Chi. L. Rev. 89 (2003).

[84] Adam Taylor, *Why So Many African Leaders Hate the International Criminal Court*, Wash. Post, June 15, 2015.

[85] *See, e.g.*, Simon Tisdall, *Bashir Slips out of Court's Grasp*, The Guardian, June 11, 2009 (recounting criticisms from African and Western officials alike).

[86] *See, e.g.*, William A. Schabas, *The Banality of International Justice*, 11 J. Int'l. Crim. Just. 545, 550 (2013) (arguing that the ICC has found excuses to not go after harder cases, focusing instead on prosecuting "global pariahs").

[87] Darryl Robinson, *Inescapable Dyads: Why the International Criminal Court Cannot Win*, 28 Leiden J. Int'l. L. 323, 324 (2015).

[88] Patricia A. Wald, *Running the Trial of the Century: The Nuremberg Legacy*, 27 Cardozo L. Rev. 1559, 1581–82 (2006).

because it is not a party to the Statute and is often (but not always) conducting its operations on the territory of non–states parties. This raises not only the specter, but the reality, of double standards, and gives individuals accused by the ICC the same argument that the Nuremberg and Tokyo defendants raised: that the "justice" dispensed by the Court is victor's justice only, not the kind of even-handed application of the law that would be expected from a Court exercising universal jurisdiction over international crimes. Finally, in the past two years, the Court has faced an avalanche of criticism that seems different in both degree and kind from before,[89] resulting in the Assembly of States Parties commissioning an Independent Expert Review that issued a 348-page report containing 384 recommendations in September 2020.[90] The ICC has received support from States, including the United States, relating to its recent intervention in Ukraine, providing an opportunity for the Court to perhaps reset the relationship with global stakeholders and demonstrate its utility in the face of mass atrocities.

TCL has had its share of criticism, as well. Examples such as the US pursuit of the Maduro regime or even the designation by the United States of regimes as "state sponsors of terror," or efforts to designate the Chinese Communist Party a "transnational criminal organization,"[91] have led to the observation that TCL, like ICL, may be used in a manner that is illiberal, Eurocentric, and even illegitimate.[92] The addition of the Al Qaeda Sanctions Committee to the repertoire of tools available to fight transnational terrorists, which provides the Security Council with sweeping powers to sanction individuals suspected of terrorist crimes across the globe, demonstrates the enormous power of this particular tool. Some have argued that the ICC represents an overly harsh criminal law approach to atrocity crimes, rather than an approach grounded in more restorative justice approaches.[93] However, with its narrow jurisdiction, extensive jurisdictional limitations and human rights centered procedural protections, the ICC is a much more human rights–friendly regime

[89] Leila Nadya Sadat, *Reforming the International Criminal Court: "Lean in" or "Leave,"* 62 Wash. U. J. L. & Pol'y 51 (2020).

[90] Independent Expert Review of the International Criminal Court and the Rome Statute System Final Report (Sept. 30, 2020), https://asp.icc-cpi.int/iccdocs/asp_docs/ASP19/IER-Final-Report-ENG.pdf.

[91] Hollie McKay, *NGOs, Activists Press Barr to Declare Chinese Communist Party a "Transnational Criminal Organization,"* Fox News, July 27, 2020.

[92] Kristin Ebner, *Transnational Criminal Law: A Tool to Further Western Interests?*, 10 King's Student L. Rev. 19 (2020).

[93] Payam Akhavan et al., *What Justice for the Yazidi Genocide?: Voices from Below*, 42 Hum. Rts. Q. 1 (2020).

than some of the regimes governing TCL, which involve extraordinary exercises of jurisdiction by states to situations well beyond their borders, and even, following 9/11, the use of military commissions and other exceptional jurisdictions to try alleged terrorists as so-called "unlawful enemy combatants."

IV. Discernible Trends and Tentative Conclusions

Given the current landscape, what will the ICL of the future look like? Based upon this brief *tour d'horizon*, five broad themes emerge.

First, there is a certain degree of convergence and deepening of the regimes applicable to international and transnational crimes occurring on several levels. As noted earlier, the treaties addressing transnational crimes like corruption[94] and narcotics trafficking have jurisdictional regimes and enforcement provisions that are robust and respond to (primarily) Western concerns about those crimes. Conversely, the treaties addressing international crimes such as genocide or torture have strong normative dimensions—even *jus cogens* status—but have weak interstate enforcement provisions. There is evidence that these very separate regimes are beginning to converge, as the following examples suggest.

During the initial drafting process for a new model treaty on crimes against humanity, a consensus emerged from consultations with more than 250 experts worldwide that strengthening enforcement provisions for ICL conventions regarding core crimes was critically necessary to the effectiveness of these treaties. Thus, the *Proposed International Convention on the Prevention and Punishment of Crimes against Humanity* drew its extradition, mutual legal assistance, and interstate enforcement provisions from treaties such as the UN Convention on Transnational Organized Crime.[95] The International Law Commission followed suit with its own Draft Articles on crimes against humanity, adopted in 2019.[96] ILC Draft Article 14 on mutual legal assistance, for example, has nine paragraphs drawn largely from the 2000 UN Convention against Transnational Organized Crime. In the

[94] *See* Paul B. Stephan, *Antibribery Law* (Chapter 11 in this volume).

[95] *Proposed International Convention for the Prevention and Punishment of Crimes Against Humanity*, *supra* note 5.

[96] International Law Commission, Report of the International Law Commission, Seventy-first Session, Geneva 29 April–7 June and 8 July–9 August 2019 U.N. Supplement No. 10 (A/74/10) (May 15, 2019), *available at* https://legal.un.org/ilc/reports/2019/english/a_74_10_advance.pdf.

Commission's words, "the more detailed provisions were best suited for draft articles on crimes against humanity. Such provisions provide extensive guidance to States, which is especially useful when there exists no mutual legal assistance treaty between the requesting and requested States."[97] Likewise, the new proposal for a Mutual Legal Assistance Treaty for core crimes (floated by Belgium, the Netherlands, Slovenia, Argentina, and Senegal), which has been joined by seventy-six states, is another example of this convergence.[98] There is also an effort to include some transnational crimes such as terrorism and "grand corruption" into the Rome Statute,[99] to bring them into harmony with other threats to international peace and security.

As regards core crimes, this convergence is salutary in many respects, because it will finally acknowledge the "crime control" dimension of prosecuting core crimes and more effectively enable national jurisdictions to cooperate to prevent and punish them. With respect to terrorism, the picture is more complex. As noted earlier, following the September 11, 2001, attacks in the United States, terrorism seemed to be elevated from transnational to core or international crime, *stricto senso*. Although it is the object of nineteen separate suppression conventions regarding its various manifestations, Security Council Resolution 1373 appeared to treat it as an international crime entitled to the normative features normally associated with *jus cogens* violations, including the right of states to exercise universal jurisdiction over terrorist offenders, not on the basis of a treaty, but under customary international law.[100] Moreover, the Council appeared to be creating "binding rules of international law—rather than mere commands relating to a particular situation—and, moreover, even creat[ing] a mechanism for monitoring compliance with them."[101]

Returning to the rule of law definition noted earlier, the lack of transparency in the Security Council sanction process and the increased militarization of the ICL terrorism regime sparked by the September 11 attacks have

[97] *Id.* at 134, ¶ 5.

[98] Draft Convention on International Cooperation in the Investigation and Prosecution of the Crime of Genocide, Crimes against Humanity and War Crimes (Mar. 20, 2020), https://www.gov.si/assets/ministrstva/MZZ/projekti/MLA-pobuda/MLA-Initiative-Draft-Convention-English.pdf.

[99] Ben Bloom, *Criminalizing Kleptocracy? The ICC as a Viable Tool in the Fight Against Grand Corruption*, 29 AM. U. INT'L L. REV. 627 (2014); Aviv Cohen, *Prosecuting Terrorists at the International Criminal Court: Reevaluating an Unused Legal Tool to Combat Terrorism*, 20 MICH. ST. U. COLL. L. INT'L L. REV. 219 (2012).

[100] S.C. Res. 1373 (Sept. 28, 2001). *See also* Paul Szasz, *The Security Council Starts Legislating*, 96 AM. J. INT'L. L. 901 (2002).

[101] *Id.* at 902.

created an illiberal approach to addressing international terrorist threats, inconsistent with human rights norms and inconsistent with trials of equally serious crimes at the international level, such as genocide, crimes against humanity, and war crimes. Since the sanctions are applied by the Security Council, the five permanent members have a much greater role in their enforcement than all other states. After extensive litigation in Europe, the Security Council created an ombudsperson to allow individuals placed on the list by the Sanctions Committee to obtain their removal. Yet serious concerns remain with the due process deficiencies in the 1267 Sanctions Regime, even though individuals are now able to petition to be removed from the list. The sanctions themselves are extraordinarily harsh and include the freezing of assets, travel bans, and embargos, actions that if carried out by a national jurisdiction would surely require a judicial process.[102] This double standard is harmful to human rights norms and arguably to global peace and security, as states may see "terrorists" as individuals undeserving of trials and impose summary execution or harsh preventive detention regimes instead.[103] This has the potential to increase rather than decrease global violence and instability. For this reason, it would be useful to bring terrorism and some of the other transnational crimes back into an international judicial framework for at least some cases so that unilateral activity—and particularly military activity—by states is decreased.

This has begun in a modest way. The Special Tribunal for Lebanon (STL), created by Security Council Resolution 1757 to address the assassination of the former Lebanese Prime Minister Rafiq Hariri,[104] included terrorism in its Statute. Additionally, some terrorism-related offenses were included in Article 4(d) of the ICTR Statute,[105] Article 3(d) of the Statute of the Special Court for Sierra Leone,[106] and Article 8 of the Statute for the Extraordinary

102 Jack I. Garvey, *Targeted Sanctions: Resolving the International Due Process Dilemma*, 50 Tex. Int'l L. Rev. 551 (2015). As another writer notes, because individuals are not notified, they have been listed until *after* it occurs, it is reminiscent of Alice in Wonderland: "sentence first . . . then a trial." Daniel Arshack & Marouschka Gunzburg, *Due Process for Those Maligned in United Nations Reports*, 42 Litigation 17, 19 (2015).

103 Agnes Callamard, *Report of the Special Rapporteur of the Human Rights Council on Extrajudicial, Summary or Arbitrary Executions*, U.N. Doc. A/73/314 (Aug. 6, 2018), *available at* https://reliefweb.int/sites/reliefweb.int/files/resources/A_73_42960.pdf.

104 S.C. Res. 1757 (May 30, 2007).

105 Statute of the International Criminal Tribunal for Rwanda, S.C. Res. 955 (Nov. 8, 1994), amended by S.C. Res. 1165 (Apr. 30, 1998).

106 Agreement between the United Nations and the Government of Sierra Leone on the establishment of a Special Court for Sierra Leone, Jan. 16, 2002, 2178 U.N.T.S. 137.

Chambers in the Courts of Cambodia.[107] Although objections are often made on the grounds that no uniform definition of terrorism exists, that was once true as well of crimes against humanity, which was nonetheless included in the statutes of all the international courts and tribunals (except the STL). Moreover, the UN General Assembly and the STL have made substantial progress in defining terrorism.[108] Finally, although terrorism was excluded from the ICC Statute in 1998, Annex I, Resolution E of the Final Act "*Recommends* that a Review Conference pursuant to article 123 of the Statute of the International Criminal Court consider the crimes of terrorism and drug crimes with a view to arriving at an acceptable definition and their inclusion in the list of crimes within the jurisdiction of the Court."[109] Proposals to do so have been made, but in recent years the struggles of the Court to gain a secure foothold have pushed that possibility to the side.[110]

Second, given the ongoing need for transnational cooperation regarding crime control, the field will continue to expand and grow, including the continued proliferation of international, regional, and mixed tribunals adjudicating cases of international and transnational crimes. National jurisdictions will remain critically important as well.

At the international level, while the ICC has been the subject of extensive criticism, reports of its death have been greatly exaggerated. The Court is busier than ever because many global situations cry out for its intervention. Even the decade-long struggle of Sudan's President Omar Al-Bashir to evade justice has ultimately resulted in the Appeals Chamber's decision confirming that heads of state have no immunity from prosecution before the Court,[111] and Sudan has stated it is likely to surrender Al-Bashir to the Court.[112] This

[107] Agreement between the United Nations and the Royal Government of Cambodia concerning the prosecution under Cambodian law of crimes committed during the period of Democratic Kampuchea, June 6, 2003, https://www.eccc.gov.kh/sites/default/files/legal-documents/Agreement_between_UN_and_RGC.pdf.

[108] G.A. Res. 73/211, Measures to eliminate international terrorism (Jan. 14, 2019). The STL Appeals Chamber issued a landmark ruling on the definition of terrorism, finding that a definition existed in customary international law that could be applied by an international tribunal. Interlocutory Decision on the Applicable Law: Terrorism, Conspiracy, Homicide, Perpetration, Cumulative Charging, Case No. STL-11-01/I (Feb. 16, 2011), https://www.stl-tsl.org/x/file/TheRegistry/Library/CaseFiles/chambers/20110216_STL-11-01_R176bis_F0010_AC_Interlocutory_Decision_Filed_EN.pdf.

[109] Final Act of the United Nations Diplomatic Conference of Plenipotentiaries on the Establishment of an International Criminal Court, U.N. Doc. A/CONF.183/10* (July 17, 1998).

[110] Press Release, General Assembly, *Facing Political Attacks, Limited Budget, International Criminal Court Needs Strong Backing to Ensure Justice for Atrocity Crimes*, President Tells General Assembly, U.N. Press Release, GA/12084 (Oct. 29, 2018).

[111] Situation in Darfur, Sudan, Prosecutor v. Omar Hassan Ahmad Al-Bashir, *Judgment in the Jordan Referral re Al-Bashir Appeal*, Case No. ICC-02/05-01/09 OA2 (May 6, 2019).

[112] *Omar al-Bashir: Sudan Agrees Ex-President Must Face ICC*, BBC, Feb. 11, 2020.

is not due to lofty feelings about the Court and the need for global justice, but because the Court is, like any criminal justice system, a practical tool for those in power or charged with keeping the peace. The ICC Prosecutor's decision to open an investigation into Russia's invasion of Ukraine was supported by forty-three states,[113] and accompanied by pledges of much-needed financial support.

The good news is that recent scholarship has demonstrated empirically that prosecutions by the ICC help prevent violence.[114] As Stuart Ford notes in his excellent summary of research findings, without empirical studies, suggestions that the Court can or cannot succeed have largely been based upon either anecdotes or theory.[115] Each approach is valuable but does not answer the hard question whether the Court can be effective in the real world. Recent empirical studies published thus far suggest that it can and has been; anecdotal evidence supports this conclusion.[116] Despite assertions that criminal indictments might interfere with peace, there is little evidence that any ICC indictment has done so. This argument was advanced in the Uganda situation and turned out to be wrong. It was also made in the Sudan referral, and while the indictments issued by Luis Moreno Ocampo, the former ICC Prosecutor, did set back humanitarian assistance temporarily, as Al-Bashir reacted to them,[117] they in no way impeded his ultimate fall from grace. Some scholars have argued that individuals such as Syria's Bashir Al-Assad might have stepped down but for the threat of criminal sanctions.[118] That argument is tenuous at best. Given the Russian Federation's protection of

113 Ukraine, Jurisdiction in the general situation, https://www.icc-cpi.int/ukraine.

114 *See* Stuart Ford, *The Biden Administration Should Engage with the ICC—The Evidence Shows that It Saves Lives*, JUST SECURITY (Jan. 28, 2021) (providing excellent summary of recent empirical studies).

115 Stuart Ford, *Can the International Criminal Court Succeed? An Analysis of the Empirical Evidence of Violence Prevention*, 43 LOY. L.A. INT'L & COMP. L. REV. 101 (2020).

116 On empirical evidence, *see, e.g.*, Benjamin J. Appel, *In the Shadow of the International Criminal Court: Does the ICC Deter Human Rights Violations*, 62 J. CONFLICT RES. 3, 4 (2018); Courtney Hillebrecht, *The Deterrent Effects of the International Criminal Court: Evidence from Libya*, 42 EMPIRICAL & THEORETICAL RES. IN INT'L REL. 616 (2016); James Meernik, *The International Criminal Court and the Deterrence of Atrocities*, 17 CIVIL WARS 318 (2015); Hyeran Jo & Beth A. Simmons, *Can the International Criminal Court Deter Atrocity*, 70 INT'L ORG. 443 (2016). On anecdotal evidence, *see* TIM ALLEN, TRIAL JUSTICE: THE INTERNATIONAL CRIMINAL COURT AND THE LORD'S RESISTANCE ARMY (2006); Leila Nadya Sadat, *Exile, Amnesty, and International Law*, 81 NOTRE DAME L. REV. 955 (2006).

117 *Genocide Continues as Sudan's Indicted Leader Games World—ICC Prosecutor*, UN NEWS, Dec. 9, 2010.

118 Daniel Krcmaric, *Should I Stay or Should I Go? Leaders, Exile, and the Dilemmas of International Justice*, 62 AM. J. POL. SCI. 486 (2018). *See also* DANIEL KRCMARIC, THE JUSTICE DILEMMA (2020).

Syria's dictator, there is little possibility of an ICC referral. Instead, impunity seems to have given Assad a license to kill.

Although Security Council dysfunction has prevented the Council from intervening to refer the Syrian or Myanmar situations to the ICC, independent mechanisms have been established to collect and evaluate evidence regarding those situations and prepare cases for trial. Some cases have already proceeded against Syrian defendants based on universal jurisdiction exercised by national courts in Europe.[119] The ICC has also extended its own jurisdiction over certain crimes committed on the territory of Myanmar that affected the territory of Bangladesh—relying on the *Lotus* case and other precedents.[120] Thus, we can expect a future expansion of international criminal jurisdiction over core crimes.

There has been a call for regional and specialty courts with international criminal jurisdiction. One of the interesting developments emerging from the African Union's political struggle with the ICC was the drafting of the Malabo Protocol. Although not yet in force, the Protocol proposes to amend the Statute of the African Court of Justice and Human Rights to vest the Court with international criminal jurisdiction.[121] While much of the focus regarding the Malabo Protocol has been on its controversial Article 46A*bis*—which immunizes heads of state, heads of government, and senior state officials—the depth and breadth of the protocol, which would give the Court jurisdiction over fourteen transnational and international crimes, is an interesting example both of convergence and expansion.[122] It also responds to general dissatisfaction with the current dysfunction in the Security Council and the imbalance of power in modern international relations.

Third, as ICL regimes and institutions grow stronger, they will engender more resistance, particularly the ICC. As Jean Monnet, one of the architects of the European Union, wrote many years ago, "resistance is always proportional to the degree of change one seeks to bring about."[123] The establishment

119 Human Rights Watch, "These are the Crimes we are Fleeing": Justice for Syria in Swedish and German Courts (Oct. 3, 2017), https://www.hrw.org/report/2017/10/04/these-are-crimes-we-are-fleeing/justice-syria-swedish-and-german-courts.

120 Decision on the Prosecution's Request for a Ruling on Jurisdiction under Article 19(3) of the Statute, ICC-RoC46(3)-01/18-37 (Sept. 6, 2018), https://www.icc-cpi.int/CourtRecords/CR2018_04203.PDF.

121 Protocol on Amendments to the Protocol on the Statute of the African Court of Justice and Human Rights, adopted by the Twenty-Third Ordinary Session of the Assembly of the African Union (June 27, 2014), https://au.int/sites/default/files/treaties/36398-treaty-0045_-_protocol_on_amendments_to_the_protocol_on_the_statute_of_the_african_court_of_justice_and_human_rights_e.pdf.

122 *Id.*

123 Jean Monnet, Memoires (1988).

of the ad hoc international criminal tribunals generated resistance from a limited number of states, mostly those directly affected by their work. The ICC has generated fierce resistance, particularly from China, Russia, and the United States, and pushback from the African Union, particularly as regards the Al-Bashir and Kenyatta cases. The United States has been particularly vocal about wanting the ICC, in the words of former National Security Adviser John Bolton, to "wither and collapse,"[124] leading some to wonder whether the Court will eventually fail under the weight of such intense political opposition.

Yet the establishment of courts and tribunals serve a useful purpose. The ICC and the system of global justice are useful in maintaining the stability of international *ordre public*, and therefore, as a general matter, are in the enlightened self-interest of states to support. They clearly can serve as a deterrent to future crimes; they motivate states to take care that crimes are not committed or are investigated swiftly if they are; and particularly in areas of the world where militias and other nonstate actors are the primary perpetrators, provide hapless governments and their populations a respite from criminal activity on their territory. The opposition of the great powers is to be expected, although the United Kingdom has stood firmly behind the Court,[125] as has France.[126] The open question is whether the opposition of other countries can, in the long term, be overcome, or whether it will eventually scuttle the Court entirely. The United States took forty years to ratify the Genocide Convention, but eventually did so. The Soviet Union ratified in 1954, and China ratified in 1983 (but was recently accused of genocide against the Uighurs).[127] Were the United States to join with the other 123 states parties, the Court would be greatly strengthened. If it does not and continues along a path of either indifference or hostility, the Court will

124 Don Kraus, *The Court of Last Resort*, Inst. for Pol'y Stud. (May 30, 2010), https://ips-dc.org/the_court_of_last_resort/.

125 Statement by Amb. Jonathan Allen, U.K. Chargé d'Affaires to the United Nations, *Promoting International Criminal Justice and the Rule of Law*, Nov. 2, 2020, https://www.gov.uk/government/speeches/promoting-international-criminal-justice-and-the-rule-of-law.

126 Statement by Jean-Yves Le Drian, Minister for Europe and Foreign Affairs, *International Criminal Court—Announcement of Individual Sanctions by the United States*, France Diplomacy, Sept. 3, 2020, https://www.diplomatie.gouv.fr/en/french-foreign-policy/international-justice/news/article/international-criminal-court-announcement-of-individual-sanctions-by-the-united.

127 United Nations Treaty Collection, Convention on the Prevention and Punishment of the Crime of Genocide, https://treaties.un.org/Pages/ViewDetails.aspx?src=IND&mtdsg_no=IV-1&chapter=4&clang=_en#5; Josh Rogin, *The Trump State Department's Final Act: Calling out China for Genocide*, Wash. Post, Jan. 19, 2021.

undoubtedly suffer. The ability of the Court to act swiftly in the Ukraine situation may be critically important.

Fourth, expanded and illiberal use of ICL by governments that are rejecting international institution-building and are, at the same time, using modalities of ICL as instruments of state power is likely, as are the continued use of exorbitant exercises of jurisdiction and even militarization of ICL as regards certain crimes, particularly terrorism.

In the absence of strong global governance, self-help will remain the rule of the day. This chapter has described how terrorism was slowly transformed from a transnational to an international crime over the past decades, and the September 11 attacks appear to have completed that process. This suggests that international tribunals could serve a useful purpose with respect to the investigation and punishment of suspected international terrorists, but states guard their sovereignty jealously and may prefer to apply their national laws to extraterritorial terrorist activity.[128] Military force has been used to attack nonstate "terrorist" actors, such as Al Qaeda and ISIS, and more recently, terrorism charges were used to justify Iranian General Qassim Soleimani's assassination by the United States. Other TCL regimes do not exhibit this kind of militarization—regimes protecting wildlife, money laundering, drug trafficking, and human trafficking, for example—because states do not believe their national security is threatened. But the use of the "terrorist" label as a trump card that allows for the imposition of specialized sanctions regimes by the Security Council, military commissions, or even the use of force or extrajudicial executions against alleged offenders, has potentially devastating human rights effects.

Fifth, debate will continue regarding the crime of aggression and aggressive war.

Finally, in thinking about the ICL of the future, there is the crime of aggression to consider. At Nuremberg, it was deemed "the supreme international crime." It was nonetheless difficult to codify. It was included in the Rome Statute as a crime within the jurisdiction of the Court in the 1998 text,[129] but jurisdiction over it was not activated until 2017 based upon a text negotiated and adopted at the 2010 Kampala Review Conference.[130] Even

[128] *See, e.g.*, International Convention against the Taking of Hostages, art. 5(1)(d), Dec. 17, 1979, 1316 U.N.T.S. 205 (conferring jurisdiction on the state of the victim's nationality regardless of the locus of the crime).

[129] Rome Statute of the International Criminal Court, *supra* note 44.

[130] Int'l Crim. Court, *Assembly Activates Court's Jurisdiction over Crime of Aggression* (Dec. 15, 2017), https://www.icc-cpi.int/Pages/item.aspx?name=pr1350.

then, the crime of aggression was subjected to a special jurisdictional regime, and a series of understandings that made it clear that states were not willing to place it on the same footing as other core crimes.[131] As of this writing, forty-three states have ratified the Kampala amendments,[132] leaving many states, even within the ICC family, outside the aggression amendments. In one of his last writings, Cherif Bassiouni, often called the "father" of international criminal law, argued that the compulsory amendments adopted at Kampala had placed the crime of aggression on "life support," but that more was needed. Surely this is correct. ICL instruments are adopted to protect different values. Although the offense of crimes against humanity law protects civilians, it offers no protection to soldiers or combatants. Aggression, on the other hand, criminalizes wrongful war making, and therefore directly protects combatants whose lives are otherwise forfeited under the laws of war—laws that may protect them from unnecessary suffering, but cannot save them from death.[133] In the nuclear age, prohibiting war is more vital than ever, and unlawful war making should receive the highest level of moral and legal condemnation.

V. Conclusion

The international criminal law of the future is likely to be increasingly robust, with continued codification of transnational crimes, overuse and abuse of terrorism as a category of offenses, and continued adjudication before international courts and tribunals, including the ICC. It is telling that in situations in which an ICC referral proved impossible, the General Assembly developed workarounds, creating new mechanisms, such as the International, Impartial, and Independent Mechanism for Syria, to amass evidence of crimes, either for future trials at the international level or in national systems. While there is still much talk of the peace versus justice debate, and states are attempting to confine the ICC by asserting immunities or objecting to

[131] Alex Whiting, *Crime of Aggression Activated at the ICC: Does It Matter?*, JUST SECURITY (Dec. 19, 2017). *See generally* CRIME OF AGGRESSION LIBRARY, THE CRIME OF AGGRESSION: A COMMENTARY (Claus Kreß & Stefan Barriga eds., 2016).

[132] United Nations Treaty Collection, Amendments on the crime of aggression to the Rome statute of the international criminal court, https://treaties.un.org/Pages/ViewDetails.aspx?src=TREATY&mtdsg_no=XVIII-10-b&chapter=18&clang=_en (last visited Mar. 1, 2022).

[133] Leila Nadya Sadat, *14th Annual Grotius Lecture Response*, 28 AM. U. INT'L. L. REV. 373, 377 (2012).

jurisdiction in particular cases, thus far, the regime of ICL codified at Rome and embedded in the ICC Statute remains intact. The simmering hostility of the United States, however, remains of concern, although the Biden administration has indicated that it is ready to assist the Court in very concrete ways.[134] If the United States continues this more constructive approach, and Karim Khan, the new Chief Prosecutor, and the six newly elected judges prove able and implement many of the reforms suggested in the Independent Expert Review, it is likely that the Court will manage and even thrive. If it suffers more serious missteps, along the lines of some of the self-inflicted wounds identified by the Independent Expert Report, however, the Court will face difficulties in the years to come.

It is difficult to have a system of global governance without a system of global criminal justice. The two go hand in hand. The question is what kind of system it will be. Efforts by the United States and other countries to extend their national jurisdictions extraterritorially to serve as the investigators and police of the world are likely to succeed only sporadically and are likely to increase interstate tensions. This has certainly been true in the case of Venezuela, where the long arm of the law has raised hackles not only in Venezuela but in countries like Spain, where the United States has sought the extradition of Venezuelan nationals to stand trial in the United States for financial crimes committed in Venezuela. For that reason, it may be useful to create mechanisms enabling some transnational crimes to become the subject of international adjudication so that their enforcement becomes more effective and multilateral. Indeed, an effort is now ongoing to establish a new global corruption court. Regional courts may also offer new possible venues, such as the African Court proposed by the Malabo Protocol. While it is difficult to make long-term predictions, at its best, a global system of criminal justice would have the ICC as its centerpiece, with many satellite courts at the international level and national jurisdictions filling in where regional and international courts are not engaged, are overwhelmed, or cannot exercise jurisdiction. Although the ICC will not directly exercise its jurisdiction in many cases, given its status as a court of last resort, its activities will be central to the system as a whole. Ideally, such a system will be human rights friendly, incorporating protections for the accused found in international human rights law, and state actors engaging in national prosecutions

[134] Statement on behalf of the United States of America, 20th Session of the Assembly of States Parties to the Rome Statute, Dec. 7, 2021, https://asp.icc-cpi.int/iccdocs/asp_docs/ASP20/ASP20.GD.USA.07.12.pdf.

will be encouraged to use best practices in their national systems. It will also respond to modern calls for a more restorative approach to criminal justice. The real danger is not that ICL will disappear. Rather, the risk is that attacks on its international and multilateral manifestations, such as the ICC, will cause it to become increasingly illiberal and unilateral, increasing friction between states and endangering international peace and security.

14

Migration and International Legal Disorder

Jaya Ramji-Nogales

I. Introduction

This volume engages with the questions of whether the international legal order is unraveling, and if so, whether that demise will be swift or gradual. These queries assume the existence of an international rules-based order: an order that hardly exists in the field of international migration law.[1] Most human movement across borders is barely governed by formal international law.[2] The crisis-based response framework constructed by international refugee law treats migration as exceptional rather than ordinary. In so doing, it fails to engage proactively with or respond to the needs of either migrants or destination states. Rather than recognizing migration as an expected component of greater globalization, and crafting laws and institutions to facilitate and regulate migration, this state of international legal disorder means that many migrants have no choice but to move outside of legal channels.[3] Populist politicians have capitalized on irregular migration flows to stoke nativist fears in many destination states, a development that threatens to undermine the international legal order.

The international rule of law is famously challenging to define and is perhaps most accurately described as a story that democratic states in the Global

[1] T. Alexander Aleinikoff, *International Legal Norms on Migration: Substance Without Architecture*, *in* International Migration Law: Developing Paradigms and Key Challenges 467 (Ryszard Cholewinski et al. eds., 2007); Jaya Ramji-Nogales, *Migration Emergencies*, 68 Hastings L.J. 609 (2017).

[2] Chantal Thomas, *Transnational Migration, Globalization, and Governance: Theorizing a Crisis*, *in* The Oxford Handbook of the Theory of International Law 16 (Anne Orford & Florian Hoffmann eds., 2016) [hereinafter Oxford Handbook].

[3] For a thorough discussion of the role of international law in constituting disorder, *see* James Thuo Gathii, *The Agenda of Third World Approaches to International Law*, *in* International Legal Theory: Foundations and Frontiers (Jeffrey Dunoff & Mark Pollack eds., 2019).

Jaya Ramji-Nogales, *Migration and International Legal Disorder* In: *Is the International Legal Order Unraveling?*. Edited by: David L. Sloss, Oxford University Press. © Oxford University Press 2022.
DOI: 10.1093/oso/9780197652800.003.0015

North tell about themselves to justify a framework of global legal structures that benefit their interests.[4] This is a story of greater global prosperity and security protected by a set of international laws and institutions that enable ever freer trade between democratic nations, protect the rights of all by virtue of their humanity, and minimize interstate armed conflicts. The diminution of sovereignty in favor of international cooperation is an important feature of this project. From "below," in the Global South, scholars have critiqued this order as an extension of the imperial project, a racialized civilizational hierarchy that justifies economic domination, military intervention, and the entrenchment of global power inequalities.[5] At the same time, feminist scholars have highlighted the absence of women from the institutions and lawmaking efforts that construct the international order, which has consequently reproduced existing gender hierarchies.[6]

The study of global migration law provides a trenchant vantage point from which to contrast the features of the international legal order with the story that is told about that order.[7] Indeed, if one were to argue that the international legal order contains the seeds of its own demise, its approach to global migration might be precisely one of those seeds. As international institutions and legal frameworks enabled greater trade and investment across borders, they failed to open those same borders to the movement of people in any meaningful way.[8] The 1951 UN Convention Relating to the Status of Refugees and its principle of non-refoulement—expanded through a variety of international and regional treaties and implemented by the UN High Commissioner for Refugees—has been a relatively effective component of the post–World War II international human rights landscape.[9] However,

[4] Daniel Joyce, *Liberal Internationalism*, *in* Oxford Handbook, *supra* note 2, at 4 (describing the international order as "a form of moral messaging and justification for conflict or economic domination.").

[5] *See, e.g.*, Antony Anghie, Imperialism, Sovereignty and the Making of International Law (2004); Balakrishnan Rajagopal, International Law From Below: Development, Social Movements and Third World Resistance (2003); John Reynolds, Empire, Emergency and International Law (2017).

[6] *See, e.g.*, Hilary Charlesworth & Christine Chinkin, The Boundaries of International Law: A Feminist Analysis (2000); Anne Orford, Reading Humanitarian Intervention (2003); Diane Otto, *Subalternity and International Law: The Problems of Global Community and the Incommensurability of Difference*, 5 Soc. & Legal Stud. 337 (1996).

[7] Jaya Ramji-Nogales & Peter Spiro, *Introduction to Symposium on Framing Global Migration Law*, 111 AJIL Unbound 1 (2017).

[8] Thomas, *supra* note 2; Jennifer Gordon, *People Are Not Bananas: How Immigration Differs from Trade*, 104 Nw. U. L. Rev. 1109 (2010).

[9] Convention relating to the Status of Refugees, art. 33, July 28, 1951, 189 U.N.T.S. 150. *See also* Convention Against Torture and Other Cruel, Inhuman or Degrading Treatment or Punishment, art. 3, Dec. 10, 1984, 1465 U.N.T.S. 85; American Convention on Human Rights, Nov. 22, 1969, 1144 U.N.T.S. 123; Cartagena Declaration on Refugees, Nov. 22, 1984, OAS Doc. OEA/Ser.L/V/

a closer look reveals that this regime's early success was due to its utility as an instrument to shame the Eastern bloc during the Cold War: a political balancing act that may no longer be sustainable.[10] Even when the refugee law framework aligned with the political interests of destination states, it offered protection to a minuscule proportion of those who desired to migrate. This was not an international legal order but a law of crisis, enabling exceptional migration in a few select emergency situations.[11]

Beyond non-refoulement, the international law of migration is almost entirely deferential to sovereign interests. It yields to domestic authority both in its failure to oblige states to admit refugees and through the narrow scope of the refugee definition, which limits substantially the number of migrants entitled to international legal protection once they have entered a state's territory. International migration law has aptly been described as the "last bastion of sovereignty," a regime that enables powerful migrant-receiving states to set their own terms for admitting migrants into their territory.[12] States in the Global North that admit tiny numbers of refugees can congratulate themselves on their humanitarianism, while keeping out far larger numbers of migrants and perpetuating global economic conditions that provoke at least some of this human movement across borders.[13] Moreover, when regulation

II.66/doc.10, rev. 1 (1984–85) [hereinafter Cartagena Declaration]; Convention for the Protection of Human Rights and Fundamental Freedoms, Nov. 4, 1950, 213 U.N.T.S. 221 [hereinafter ECHR]; African Charter on Human and Peoples' Rights, June 26, 1981, 1520 U.N.T.S. 217 [hereinafter Banjul Charter]; Convention Governing Specific Aspects of Refugee Problems in Africa, June 20, 1974, 1001 U.N.T.S. 45 [hereinafter OAU Convention].

[10] Rebecca Hamlin & Philip E. Wolgin, *Symbolic Politics and Policy Feedback: The United Nations Protocol Relating to the Status of Refugees and American Refugee Policy in the Cold War*, 46 INT'L MIGRATION REV. 586 (2012); GIL LOESCHER & JOHN A. SCANLAN, CALCULATED KINDNESS: REFUGEES AND AMERICA'S HALF-OPEN DOOR 1945–PRESENT (1998).

[11] Hilary Charlesworth, *International Law: A Discipline of Crisis*, 65 MOD. L. REV. 377 (2002); Dianne Otto, *Decoding Crisis in International Law: A Queer Feminist Perspective*, *in* INTERNATIONAL LAW AND ITS DISCONTENTS: CONFRONTING CRISIS 115, 135 (Barbara Stark ed., 2015).

[12] Catherine Dauvergne, *Sovereignty, Migration and the Rule of Law in Global Times*, 67 MOD. L. REV. 588, 588 (2004).

[13] Graziella Bertocchi & Fabio Canova, *Did Colonization Matter for Growth? An Empirical Exploration into the Historical Causes of Africa's Underdevelopment*, 46 EUR. ECON. REV. 1851, 1868, 1870 (2002) (empirical study finding "evidence that colonization did exert a direct effect on the growth pattern of African countries and that it also affected physical and human capital accumulation and the sociopolitical factors typically thought to explain growth" and that "colonies kept paying the consequences of their history even after political independence was achieved"); Obed Galor & Andrew Mountford, *Trading Population for Productivity: Theory and Evidence*, 75 REV. OF ECON. STUD. 1143, 1173 (2008) (empirical study finding that international trade has "widened the gap between the technological level as well as the skill abundance of industrial and non-industrial economies, enhancing the initial patterns of comparative advantage and generating sustained differences in income per capita across countries . . ." and suggesting that developed countries' sustained economic growth is associated with a lack of sustained economic growth in less developed countries); Daron Acemoglu, Simon Johnson, & James A. Robinson, *Reversal of Fortune: Geography and Institutions in*

of migration is left to domestic law, the terms are often set in a way that, at best, fails to account sufficiently for the motivations of migrants, and at worst, imposes nativist cruelties.[14] While the harms of such an approach are felt most acutely by the migrants themselves, a legal system that does not adequately respond to the motivations of actors it aims to regulate is likely to fail, as the subjects of that law have little incentive to comply with it.[15] It would be in the best interests of both states *and* migrants for international law to play a more effective role in regulating migration.

The contemporary political situation presents both an opportunity to move toward an effective international legal order on migration and a risk of eliminating even the narrow legal framework that currently governs migration. Populist nationalist politicians present a serious threat to the baseline refugee protections that form the existing international legal regime. In recent years, Australia, Europe, and the United States have implemented increasingly restrictive immigration policies despite the economic need for migrant labor.[16] In the asylum realm, destination states have externalized their borders, engaging in maritime interdiction and enlisting transit states to prevent asylum seekers from reaching their territory and lodging claims for protection. They have implemented a variety of restrictions on the substantive law of asylum, narrowing the legal grounds on which asylum can be granted, and limited access to asylum procedures, minimizing the number of eligible applicants who can seek protection.[17] In response to the COVID-19 pandemic, many states initiated a breathtaking display of sovereign authority, closing their borders to asylum seekers in violation of both

the Making of the Modern World Income Distribution, 117(4) Q. J. of Econ. 1231, 1235 (2002) (empirical study finding that European colonialism led to the creation of extractive institutions in certain countries in the Global South while developing institutions of private property in settler colonial nations that form part of the Global North, which made it harder for the former and easier for the latter to industrialize).

[14] Christian Breunig & Adam Luedtke, *What Motivates the Gatekeepers? Explaining Governing Party Preferences on Immigration*, 21 Governance: An Int'l J. of Pol., Admin., & Institutions 123 (2008).

[15] *See, e.g.*, Tom R. Tyler, *Multiculturalism and the Willingness of Citizens to Defer to Law and Legal Authorities*, 24 L. & Soc. Inquiry 983 (2000).

[16] Charles Kenny, *The Real Immigration Crisis: The Problem Is Not Too Many, but Too Few*, Foreign Aff., Nov. 11, 2019.

[17] David FitzGerald, Refuge Beyond Reach: How Rich Democracies Repel Asylum Seekers (2019); Andrew I. Schoenholtz, Jaya Ramji-Nogales, & Philip G. Schrag, The End of Asylum (2021); Violeta Moreno-Lax, Accessing Asylum In Europe: Extraterritorial Border Controls and Refugee Rights under EU Law (2017).

international refugee law[18] and public health recommendations.[19] Public fears easily sway against migrants. For that reason, an attempt to revise international legal protections for migrants could easily backfire.

Even so, the rise of nationalist populism and authoritarianism, as well as the political instability of the current moment, could also open up political space for a more pluralist international order around migration. The extreme cruelty of nationalist politicians may ironically lead to increased political engagement and support for migrants.[20] Concern about the rising power of authoritarian regimes such as China could present an incentive for migrant destination states to conclude agreements with source states as part of an attempt to shore up soft power. Migrants, diaspora members, and their friends and families at home might push the governments of those source states to request more robust international legal protections for migrants. Powerful destination states may have incentives to conclude regional agreements, in part to keep authoritarian states from building power near their borders.

If it is possible to work within this constrained political space, the goal should be to craft international legal agreements that more effectively balance the interests of migrants and destination states. Given the contemporary political obstacles, a globally ratified multilateral treaty is unlikely to garner signatories in the near future. Regional and plurilateral agreements offer a more realistic starting point, and may set the stage for a broader international agreement down the road. These agreements could begin to craft a new international legal order around migration that accounts for the motivations

[18] Jaya Ramji-Nogales & Iris Goldner Lang, *Freedom Of Movement, Migration & Borders*, 19 J. Hum. Rts. 593 (2020); Migration in the Time of Covid-19: Comparative Law and Policy Responses (Jaya Ramji-Nogales & Iris Goldner Lang eds., 2021) (ebook); E. Tendayi Achiume, Thomas Gammeltoft-Hansen, & Thomas Spijkerboer eds., *Symposium on Covid-19, Global Mobility and International Law*, 114 AJIL Unbound 312 (2020).

[19] Letter to HHS Secretary Azar and CDC Director Redfield Signed by Leaders of Public Health Schools, Medical Schools, Hospitals, and Other U.S. Institutions (May 18, 2020), https://www.publichealth.columbia.edu/public-health-now/news/public-health-experts-urge-us-officials-withdraw-order-enabling-mass-expulsion-asylum-seekers; Columbia Mailman School of Public Health et al., *Public Health Recommendations for Processing Families, Children and Adults Seeking Asylum or Other Protection at the Border* (Dec. 19, 2020), https://www.publichealth.columbia.edu/sites/default/files/public_health_recommendations_for_processing_families_children_and_adults_seeking_asylum_or_other_protection_at_the_border_dec2020_0.pdf.

[20] Joel Rose, *Americans Back Trump on Immigration—But Only to Stop COVID-19, Poll Finds*, Nat'l Pub. Radio (Aug. 5, 2020), https://www.npr.org/2020/08/05/898915843/americans-back-trump-on-immigration-but-only-to-stop-covid-19-poll-finds; Mohamed Younis, *Americans Want More, Not Less, Immigration for First Time*, Gallup (July 1, 2020), https://news.gallup.com/poll/313106/americans-not-less-immigration-first-time.aspx .

of migrants and regulates their transit, entry, reception, and integration.[21] Destination states depend on migrant labor and will do so increasingly for the foreseeable future; this interest could be leveraged in favor of an effective coordination regime. The ultimate legal framework would coordinate both labor migration and protection functions. Using risk prediction software to anticipate refugee flows and proactively planning coordinated responses, an effective international legal order on migration could distribute responsibility for refugee protection between states proximate to refugee flows that host the vast majority of at-risk populations, and other states, including but not limited to wealthier states in the Global North that host far fewer refugees. It would also provide safe and regular pathways, matching migrants seeking employment with destination states that need their labor, as well as enabling family reunification. While such an order would necessarily include regional and plurilateral (and perhaps eventually global) agreements focused on migration, it is also imperative to integrate migration issues into other fields of international law, including development, environmental law, labor law, and trade law.

It is important to recognize that migration is already happening. The point of such a regime would not be to increase the numbers of migrants but to ensure safer movement within lawful channels. In fact, a successful international legal order could decrease migration levels if those not selected for labor migration programs forego dangerous irregular journeys in favor of reapplying for future openings. Many refugees fleeing violence and instability prefer to seek protection closer to their home state so that they can return when the situation stabilizes;[22] those migrants might not make onward journeys if the situation in neighboring states presented them tenable opportunities for a dignified existence. Successful development, peacemaking, and anticorruption efforts could forestall migration entirely in some cases, because individuals are more likely to choose to remain at home if they see a viable future for themselves in their countries of origin.

Given the political obstacles, these changes will of course not happen overnight. The first steps might happen on a regional level, enabling states and international organizations to build programs that offer safe and regular

[21] Ramji-Nogales & Spiro, *supra* note 7 ("The field of global migration law explores transnational movement of people defined broadly. It covers a broad temporal scope, from causal factors and motivations for migration to exit, transit, entry, reception, and integration.").

[22] UNHCR, Global Trends: Forced Displacement in 2019, at 22, *available at* https://www.unhcr.org/5ee200e37.pdf.

opportunities to seek employment and protection. Destination states have strong political and economic incentives to regularize migration in their regions. Migrants can play an important role in powering the economies of their home states, adding private funds on top of international development efforts.[23] Yet the question that remains is whether these efforts can succeed, given that the appetite for inexpensive labor in destination states may create a preference for legally precarious migrants who can be paid less than a fair market wage.

II. International Migration in 2020

As we enter the third decade of the twenty-first century, absolute numbers of migrants have reached their highest levels ever, although the ratio of migrants to the world population has not changed substantially in the past forty years, remaining in the range of 2 to 4 percent.[24] In 2015, the most recent year for which data are available, migrants contributed $6.7 trillion to the global economy, which is about 9.4 percent of global GDP.[25] These figures provide an important reminder that migration is an ongoing phenomenon that is relatively small in size but that yields relatively large economic benefits.

The drivers of international migration are numerous and complex.[26] For those who move irregularly, the long-standing challenge of global inequality

[23] International Organization for Migration, *Global Migration Indicators 2018*, at 18, https://publications.iom.int/system/files/pdf/global_migration_indicators_2018.pdf (in 2018, migrants sent home $466 billion in remittances, which was more than three times official development assistance).

[24] *Id.* at 20 (in 2018, there were 258 million international migrants, comprising 3.4% of the world population; in 2000, there were 123 million international migrants, comprising 2.8% of the world population; and in 1980, there were 102 million international migrants, comprising 2.3% of the world population).

[25] *Id.* at 19.

[26] Though often depicted as the simplistic dualism "war or poverty," reasons for migration are complex, and generally do not include poverty. A recent survey found that 70% of respondents (who were migrants) cited economic reasons (both underemployment and unemployment) and 24% cited violence and insecurity. Lack of rights (18.5%), personal/family reasons (18.9%), and/or poor governance (16.6%) were the next most common responses. (The totals add up to more than 100% because survey takers could check more than one reason.) Mixed Migration Centre, *Drivers Revisited: Why People Migrate*, Mixed Migration Review 2018, at 78 (C. Horwood, R. Forin, & B. Frouws eds., 2018). *See also* Hein de Haas et al., *International Migration: Trends, Determinants, and Policy Effects*, 45 Population & Dev. Rev. 885, 893 (2019) ("The popular idea that south-north migration is essentially driven by poverty in origin countries ignores evidence that most migration neither occurs from the poorest countries nor is undertaken by the poorest segments of the population."); Heaven Crawley et al., Destination Europe? Understanding the Dynamics and Drivers of Mediterranean Migration in 2015, at 38 (2016) (77% of respondents left due to "conflict, persecution, violence, death threats and human rights abuse").

and the stubborn problem of corruption often lie at the root of the decision to migrate. From these sources flower a variety of incentives to move, including underemployment and unemployment. Violence and insecurity are also important factors in modern migration decisions. Climate change will also increasingly provoke movement, both because of sudden habitability challenges and because of slow onset shifts that negatively impact agricultural yields and profitability.[27] Migrants undertake dangerous journeys to seek political stability and to reunite with family, and because jobs are available to them in destination states regardless of their lawful status.

The international order itself has played a role in encouraging migration, particularly by low-wage workers. Both Jennifer Gordon and Chantal Thomas have traced the ways in which international economic regimes have led to increased migration as imports, inflows of foreign capital, and privatization eliminated employment opportunities in countries of origin.[28] Thomas traces the CAFTA-DR and its opening of Central American markets to US agricultural imports as well as the increased focus on export commodities.[29] These policies led to displacement from agricultural lands and increased economic volatility.[30] Though she is careful to qualify the causal nature of the relationship, Thomas notes the role of these policies in creating push-and-pull factors for migration.[31] Similarly, Gordon explains that in the wake of NAFTA, foreign capital moved quickly into Mexico, replacing small farms with corporate agriculture.[32] Many farmers and farm workers lost their livelihoods as a result, and some migrated to the United States in search of gainful employment.[33]

In some cases, then, the international legal order that has lowered barriers to trade and investment has provoked international migration. Yet because the barriers to migration have not been concomitantly lowered, many of those who suffer the consequences of international economic policies are not able to migrate lawfully. Irregular migration does not serve the interests of migrants themselves, who suffer violence and exploitation both on dangerous journeys north and in the destination states. It also does not serve

[27] Jaya Ramji-Nogales, *Slow-Onset Climate Justice and Human Mobility*, 93 Temple L. Rev. 671 (2021).

[28] Thomas, *supra* note 2, at 5; Gordon, *supra* note 8.

[29] Thomas, *supra* note 2, at 5, 7.

[30] *Id.* at 8–9.

[31] *Id.*

[32] Gordon, *supra* note 8, at 1115.

[33] *Id.*

the interests of low-wage workers in destination states, who must compete with migrants willing to sacrifice their living conditions in order to send remittances to family members still residing in their home states, and who are unlikely to complain about poor working conditions because they risk deportation.[34] Irregular migration also does not serve the interests of destination states, who lose control over decisions about who enters their countries, and with it important information about those individuals. Destination states may also forfeit tax revenues from migrants who are working without authorization. But this disposable labor force does serve the economic bottom line of certain corporations, who are able to pack meat and pick tomatoes much more cheaply than they would otherwise.[35]

III. Migration and International Legal Disorder

The story that many in the Global North tell about the international rules-based order has been subject to critique from the perspective of the Global South and the vantage of feminist legal theory. These critical scholars have highlighted the biases of the international order, tracing colonial continuities and ongoing economic domination.[36] The statist focus of international law and its emphasis on state sovereignty have played important roles in excluding the perspectives of non-Europeans and non-elite individuals.

The hierarchical and exclusionary nature of international law has been widely critiqued.[37] In 1985, Mohammed Bedjaoui famously offered a critique of four aspects of international law: the Eurocentric geographic bias, the religious-ethical focus on Christianity, the mercantilist economic motivations, and the imperialist political aims.[38] On the latter point, John Reynolds notes that "colonial power dynamics and legal concepts were and

[34] *See, e.g.*, Jennifer J. Lee, *Redefining the Legality of Undocumented Work*, 106 CAL. L. REV. 1617 (2018).

[35] Patrik Jonsson, *Trafficking: In Florida's Tomato Fields, a Fight for Ethical Farm Labor Grows*, CHRISTIAN SCI. MONITOR (Nov. 16, 2015), https://www.csmonitor.com/World/2015/1116/Trafficking-In-Florida-s-tomato-fields-a-fight-for-ethical-farm-labor-grows; Eric Schlosser, *Why It's Immigrants Who Pack Your Meat: What Trump Has Called an "Invasion" Was Actually a Corporate Recruitment Drive*, THE ATLANTIC (Aug. 16, 2019), https://www.theatlantic.com/ideas/archive/2019/08/trumps-invasion-was-a-corporate-recruitment-drive/596230/.

[36] *See, e.g.*, Gathii, *supra* note 3; REYNOLDS, *supra* note 5, at 25–26 (describing two generations of TWAIL scholars).

[37] Gathii, *supra* note 3, at 4.

[38] Mohammed Bedjaoui, *Poverty of the International Order*, *in* INTERNATIONAL LAW: A CONTEMPORARY PERSPECTIVE 152–54 (R. Falk, F. Kratochwil, & S.H. Mendlovitz eds., 1985).

remain integral to formation and development of . . . international legal norms."[39] He explains the ways in which international law instantiates and perpetuates racialized hierarchies and structural material inequalities, in particular through colonialist ideas around cultural superiority and "overt imperial violence."[40] In a similar vein, Dianne Otto describes the ways in which the "international legal order . . . legitimated colonialism and imperialism and . . . western domination of the world economy . . . ," but did so with a new legal and moral façade.[41] She has critiqued the international legal order as incommensurable with multiplicity, requiring assimilation rather than enabling transformation or even inclusion on real terms.[42]

Critical scholars have also highlighted the undemocratic nature of international lawmaking processes.[43] This concern pertains both to the power politics that underlie the international legal order, as well as the exclusion of individuals and nonstate actors from the process of determining principles and norms of international law.[44] International law's fictions of consent and formal equality obscure power disparities between states, masking a legal order based on European imperialism rather than genuine agreement to its terms.[45] The statist focus of international lawmaking also "silences individuals and other non-elite groups in the international arena."[46] From a feminist perspective, the lack of representation in law and lawmaking bodies creates and sustains a regime of deeply biased norms.[47]

The concepts of state sovereignty and territorial integrity play important roles in perpetuating the colonial origins of international law.[48] Antony Anghie explains the role that international law plays in creating the dichotomy between the "civilized" and universal and the "uncivilized" and particular, and then creating techniques to "normalize" the former.[49] In particular, he notes, these imperialist methods continue to be exercised through the sovereignty doctrine, which is used to exclude non-Europeans

39 Reynolds, *supra* note 5, at 28.
40 *Id.* at 24, 28.
41 Otto, *supra* note 6, at 343–45.
42 *Id.* at 338–39.
43 *Id.* at 337.
44 *Id.* at 337–38 (noting that "democratic pretensions always already capitulate to the *de facto* balance of global power").
45 *Id.* at 339, 342.
46 Charlesworth & Chinkin, *supra* note 6, at 69, 124.
47 *Id.* at 62, 98, 189–90.
48 Anghie, *supra* note 5, at 3; Otto, *supra* note 6, at 340. *See also* Vasuki Nesiah, *The Ground Beneath Her Feet: "Third World" Feminisms*, 4 J. Int'l Women's Stud. 30, 35 (2003).
49 Anghie, *supra* note 5, at 4.

from structures of power. In Anghie's words, "the colony, the primitive, is always and everywhere within sovereignty doctrine, if only because it must be excluded and managed."[50] Moreover, though the concept of sovereignty is structured by the colonial encounter, it is highly effective at obscuring these colonialist origins.[51] Hilary Charlesworth and Christine Chinkin also note that the international legal system's "mantle of rationality and objectivity is a chimera"[52] that disguises deep bias and inequality.

Migration, of course, implicates the full power of sovereignty and racialized fears around territorial integrity and often results from the structural global economic inequality that is the legacy of colonialism and is perpetuated by the international legal order.[53] While many aspects of the critiques of international law's hierarchies, exclusions, and democratic gaps play out in similar ways, in the migration arena the perceived interests of the Global North are perpetuated by the combination of international legal rules that protect state sovereignty along with the absence of international legal rules that constrain the sovereign power of states to exclude migrants. Without an effective international legal framework to coordinate the interests and needs of migrants and of destination states, those states are able to utilize the mantle of sovereignty to exclude migrants from lawful opportunities to enter their territories. Migrants enter nonetheless, but the sovereignty-based legal framework renders those who move outside of legal channels vulnerable to exploitation and abuse in transit to and after arrival in the destination state.

A. The Limited Protections of Non-Refoulement

Given the relationship between migration, sovereignty, and territorial control, it is perhaps unsurprising that the international legal framework on migration has been characterized by disorder rather than order. While there are some binding international legal norms relating to migration, they are narrow in scope, meaning that most human movement is insufficiently governed by international law. Or, to state the point differently, international law grants sovereign states a virtually unrestricted power to exclude

50 *Id.* at 314.
51 *Id.* at 312.
52 Charlesworth & Chinkin, *supra* note 6, at 95.
53 *See* sources cited in note 13.

migrants, and sovereign states exercise that power in a manner that creates disorder.

The principle of non-refoulement, which is constituted by international refugee law as well as international human rights law, has been relatively effective at changing state behavior. The international legal norm against returning refugees to countries where they fear persecution was first set out by the 1951 Convention Relating to the Status of Refugees and its 1967 Protocol.[54] With 148 states as members of one or both,[55] these agreements prohibit the return of a noncitizen to a country where he or she fears persecution on the basis of race, religion, nationality, political opinion, or membership in a particular social group. The 1984 Convention Against Torture, which has 173 states parties,[56] broadened the scope of the non-refoulement principle by prohibiting return of a noncitizen to a state where there are "substantial grounds for believing" that he or she would be in danger of torture, defined as intentional infliction of severe pain or suffering. This version of non-refoulement is in some ways narrower, as it requires that the torture be perpetrated with the consent or acquiescence of a state actor. The International Covenant on Civil and Political Rights contains a prohibition on return to torture that has been interpreted to mirror the provisions of the Convention Against Torture,[57] as does the European Convention on Human Rights.[58]

While the implementation of these treaties has been far from perfect, perhaps in part because none of them speak to the process through which refugees should be protected, the principle of non-refoulement has been

[54] Refugee Convention, *supra* note 9; United Nations Protocol Relating to the Status of Refugees, Jan. 31, 1967, 606 U.N.T.S. 267.

[55] *Status of the Convention Relating to the Status of Refugees*, U.N. Treaty Collection, https://treaties.un.org/Pages/ViewDetailsII.aspx?src=TREATY&mtdsg_no=V-2&chapter=5&Temp=mtdsg2&clang=_en; *Status of the Protocol relating to the Status of Refugees*, U.N. Treaty Collection, https://treaties.un.org/Pages/ViewDetails.aspx?src=TREATY&mtdsg_no=V-5&chapter=5&clang=_en; *see* U.N. High Comm'r for Refugees, States Parties to the 1951 Convention Relating to the Status of Refugees and the 1967 Protocol, http://www.unhcr.org/en-us/protection/basic/3b73b0d63/states-parties-1951-convention-its-1967-protocol.html (noting that 148 states are parties to one or both of these treaties) (last visited Mar. 10, 2021).

[56] United Nations Office of the High Commissioner for Human Rights, *Status of Ratification Interactive Dashboard*, https://indicators.ohchr.org/ (last visited Mar. 10, 2021).

[57] International Covenant on Civil and Political Rights, art. 7, Dec. 16, 1966, 999 U.N.T.S. 171 (entered into force Mar. 23, 1976); UN Human Rights Committee, *General Comment No. 20: Prohibition of torture or other cruel, inhuman or degrading treatment or punishment (article 7)* (1992), adopted at the Forty-fourth Session of the Human Rights Committee, A/44/40, Mar. 10, 1992.

[58] ECHR, *supra* note 9, art. 3; Soering v. United Kingdom, 161 Eur. Ct. H.R. (ser. A) 35 (1989); Chahal v. United Kingdom, 1996-V Eur. Ct. H.R. 1831.

widely accepted as a norm of international law.[59] Migrant receiving states in the Global North have created processes to determine whether noncitizens fit within the scope of protection of the non-refoulement principle, and in many cases allow those who do to remain lawfully in their territory. Though the principle of non-refoulement has often been politicized and its scope contested, states have internalized the principle in ways that influence state behavior to meet the protection needs of migrants who fit within its narrow scope. From 2010 to 2019, five million asylum seekers, meaning those who lodged claims within or at the borders of destination states, were granted protection.[60] In addition, outside of the asylum process, over fifteen million people were newly recognized as refugees, awarded protection as part of a group determination process and in some cases received only temporary status.[61] (Eighty-five percent of the world's refugees are hosted in the Global South, and over three-quarters live in protracted situations, in which over 25,000 refugees from the same state have resided in a host state for over five years;[62] 2.6 million refugees are housed in refugee camps, often in treacherous conditions.[63]) In 2020, states and private donors provided the UN High Commissioner for Refugees, the executive body governing the implementation of the Refugee Convention, with nearly $4.5 billion in funds—less than 50 percent of its budget, but still a testament to the power of the organization.[64]

Yet beneath these successes lurk at least two serious flaws. First, the principle of non-refoulement is a law of crisis.[65] Those seeking protection from persecution or torture are by definition in crisis, and international law jumps in to respond. This crisis approach obscures the larger structural inequalities that have set the stage for the migrants' flight, enabling destination states in the Global North to congratulate themselves for their humanitarianism while overlooking the ways in which they benefit from and contribute to the causes of the crisis. As a result, the solution provided by the non-refoulement

[59] There is still some contestation over whether it is a *jus cogens* norm. The prohibition on return to torture is generally considered a *jus cogens* norm; whether the prohibition on return to persecution is also a *jus cogens* norm is a matter of scholarly debate. *See* Guy S. Goodwin-Gill & Jane McAdam, The Refugee in International Law 348–51 (2007).

[60] UNHCR, *supra* note 22, at 4.

[61] *Id.*

[62] *Id.* at 2, 24.

[63] *Refugee Camps*, https://www.unrefugees.org/refugee-facts/camps/ (last visited Mar. 9, 2021).

[64] UNHCR, *Consequences of Underfunding in 2020*, https://www.unhcr.org/underfunding-2020/#:~:text=UNHCR's%20budget%20was%20%249.131%20billion,a%20funding%20gap%20of%2051%25 (last visited Mar. 9, 2021).

[65] Charlesworth, *supra* note 11; Otto, *supra* note 11.

principle is individualized rather than systemic. Instead of treating migration as a normal, even quotidian, feature of a globalized world, and anticipating and coordinating state responses to migration for a range of reasons, the non-refoulement framework characterizes migration as exceptional, meaning that only the exceptional migrant receives the protection of international law.

The second problem is that the principle of non-refoulement is far too narrow to address the numerous and complex reasons that humans choose to migrate. It is underinclusive both in terms of who is protected and with respect to the protections it provides. The narrow scope of the non-refoulement principle fails to protect many people facing serious harms, such as individuals fleeing generalized civil strife who are not individually targeted for harm but whose lives nonetheless may be at serious risk. Even for those who fit within the refugee definition, the principle provides only for nonreturn, prohibiting expulsion but failing to require admission. As a result, many refugees end up in precarious situations in host countries whose resources are insufficient to provide them with basic protections. Standing alone, the principle of non-refoulement fails to govern migration that takes place outside the crisis framework and even a substantial portion of crisis migration. The narrow scope of non-refoulement of course would not be problematic if it was part of a larger framework of international law relating to migration. When it comes to migration and migrants, however, other subfields of international law offer only legal disorder in the form of excessive deference to sovereignty.

B. Migration's Absences in International Law

Several subfields of international law have obvious links to migration yet fail to coordinate the needs and interests of migrants and states adequately or to alter state behavior effectively. None comes close to creating a framework of law that could be considered a form of governance, suggesting a failure to view migration as a regular feature of a globalized world. Migrants are silenced, even made invisible, in the subfields of international law where you would expect them to surface. International human rights law, international labor law, the law of the sea, and international trade law each provide some protections to some migrants, but generally exclude those fleeing violence or poverty or seeking employment. Most protections are provided to those lawfully present in destination states, meaning that those who need protection the most are least able to access it. Moreover, the framework fails generally to provide opportunities for safe and lawful transit and entry. Transnational criminal law, which has been at least partially successful in coordinating state behavior, criminalizes the process of migration, painting migrants, their facilitators, and criminal organizations with the same brush.[66]

Multilateral human rights treaties provide migrants with a set of rights similar to those accorded to citizens. The effectiveness of these rights assumes that humans are autonomous beings who can make demands against the sovereign and that the sovereign is required to obey and enforce human rights law. This conception of the universal subject as autonomous obscures the experience of undocumented migrants. Many of these rights are limited to noncitizens who are lawfully present in the destination country.[67] The set of general protections provided by human rights law cannot be accessed easily, and often not at all, by those who are unable to demand enforcement of their rights because they fear deportation.[68] Moreover, human rights law is designed to protect people who are content to remain in their home countries. It fails even to mention basic rights that are crucial to migrants fleeing generalized violence or poverty or seeking employment, such as the right to safe transit between countries, the right to enter a third country, or the right to remain in a third country.[69] Human rights law fails to create an effective framework to coordinate state behavior around transnational migration.

Given that many migrants cross borders to seek employment, international labor law seems a promising site for more robust regulation of migration. Moreover, international labor is a highly regulated field. The International Labor Organization counts nearly two hundred conventions, eight of which are considered fundamental, with ratifications by 155 to 198 states.[70] It has, however, created only three treaties relating to labor migration, and these

[66] *See* Leila Nadya Sadat, *The International Criminal Law of the Future* (Chapter 13 in this volume).

[67] For example, the ICCPR provides only migrants lawfully present in a state with freedom of movement and residence within a territory, as well as fair process in immigration proceedings. *See* International Covenant on Civil and Political Rights, arts. 12–13, Dec. 16, 1966, 999 U.N.T.S. 171.

[68] *See generally* Jaya Ramji-Nogales, *Constructing Human Rights: State Power and Migrant Silence*, *in* Beyond Borders: The Human Rights of Non-Citizens at Home and Abroad (Molly Land & Kathryn Libal eds., 2021); Jaya Ramji-Nogales, *Undocumented Migrants and the Failures of Universal Individualism*, 47 Vand. J. Trans'l L. 699 (2014); Gregor Noll, *Why Human Rights Fail to Protect Undocumented Migrants*, 12 Eur. J. Migration & L. 241 (2010).

[69] Ramji-Nogales, *Undocumented Migrants*, *supra* note 68.

[70] International Labor Organization, *Ratification By Convention*, https://www.ilo.org/dyn/normlex/en/f?p=1000:12001:16548995909848::::P12001_INSTRUMENT_SORT:1 (last visited Mar. 10, 2021).

agreements are ratified largely by migrant-sending states in the Global South rather than destination states in the Global North.[71] Similarly, the International Convention on the Rights of All Migrant Workers and Their Families has largely been ignored by destination states in the Global North.[72] Political opposition to establishing standards for labor migration in these receiving states has effectively quashed such efforts.[73] There is, as a result, no multilateral mechanism designed to enable states to negotiate and coordinate labor migration.[74] In contrast to investment and trade treaties, Jennifer Gordon notes that treaties related to labor migration tend to be far less comprehensive, and contain weaker protections with limited enforcement. Those treaties do not supersede domestic law and are usually negotiated in secret.[75] With the notable exceptions of the free movement regimes of the European Union and MERCOSUR, existing agreements tend to benefit high-wage workers.[76] In the end, despite a broad range of treaties and a capable treaty executive, international labor law fails to set out a comprehensive framework to regulate labor migration or to alter the behavior of destination states.

International trade law is constituted by a broad range of comprehensive treaties and has a powerful and well-funded international adjudicatory body, but it fails to address trade-related migration.[77] The World Trade Organization's General Agreement on Trade in Services is extremely narrow

[71] To be clear, most migration occurs within the Global South, but migrants who seek employment in the Global North need labor protections. Fifty states ratified the Migration for Employment Convention. Only nine are major migrant-receiving countries in the Global North: Belgium, France, Germany, Italy, the Netherlands, New Zealand, Portugal, Spain, and the United Kingdom. Convention (No. 97) concerning migration for employment (revised 1949), Int'l Labour Org., July 1, 1949, 120 U.N.T.S. 71. Twenty-five states ratified the Migrant Workers Convention. Only four are major migrant-receiving countries in the Global North: Italy, Norway, Portugal, and Sweden. Convention (No. 143) concerning migrations in abusive conditions and the promotion of equality of opportunity and treatment of migrant workers, Int'l Labour Org., June 24, 1975, 1120 U.N.T.S. 323. Thirty-one states ratified the Domestic Workers Convention. Only eight are major migrant-receiving countries in the Global North: Belgium, Finland, Germany, Ireland, Italy, Portugal, Sweden, and Switzerland. Convention (No. 189) concerning decent work for domestic workers, Int'l Labour Org., June 16, 2011, 2955 U.N.T.S. 407.

[72] International Convention on the Protection of the Rights of All Migrant Workers and Members of Their Families, July 1, 2003, 2220 U.N.T.S. 3.

[73] Virginia A. Leary, *Labor Migration*, *in* Migration and International Legal Norms 229 (T. Alexander Aleinikoff & Vincent Chetail eds., 2003).

[74] Gordon, *supra* note 8, at 1115.

[75] *Id.* at 1128–29.

[76] *Id.* at 1115. For a discussion of the MERCOSUR regime, *see* Diego Acosta, The National versus the Foreigner in South America (2018).

[77] Gordon, *supra* note 8, at 1121 ("The limited global map of rules and institutions regulating the migration of workers across borders presents a stark contrast to the many international agreements governing trade and investment."); Chantal Thomas, *Convergences and Divergences in International Legal Norms on Migrant Labor*, 32 Comp. Lab. L. & Pol'y J. 405, 434 (2011) (trade law does not address irregular migration).

in scope.[78] It does not govern labor migrants seeking employment and does not "affect measures regarding citizenship, residence or employment on a permanent basis."[79] The agreement largely defers to the preferences of member states, which use it to enable entry of high-wage workers.[80] Rather than constructing a legal framework that could enable a broader range of human movement in concert with the movement of goods and capital, international trade law has minimal effect on state behavior related to migration.[81]

Although many migrants rely on maritime transit routes, the law of the sea is also largely deferential to sovereign preferences.[82] The UN Convention on the Law of the Sea regulates the authority of different states to exercise jurisdiction over different parts of the oceans.[83] In terms of the content of the law of the sea, when it comes to migration and the treatment of migrants, domestic standards generally prevail.[84] Although several treaties set out substantive legal obligations to rescue people in distress at sea,[85] the law of the sea does not obligate any state to admit migrants rescued at sea, except on a temporary basis.[86] Even the applicability of the non-refoulement principle

[78] Marrakesh Agreement Establishing the World Trade Organization, Annex 1B, Apr. 15, 1994, 1867 U.N.T.S. 3 (entered into force Jan. 1, 1995) ("General Agreement on Trade in Services"), Annex on movement of natural persons supplying services under the Agreement. Michele Klein Solomon, *GATS Mode 4 and the Mobility of Labour*, *in* INTERNATIONAL MIGRATION LAW: DEVELOPING PARADIGMS AND KEY CHALLENGES 107 (Ryszard Cholewinski et al. eds., 2007) (explaining that GATS Mode 4 covers only citizens of one WTO member state temporarily providing a service in the territory of another member state).

[79] *Movement of Natural Persons*, World Trade Org., https://www.wto.org/english/tratop_e/serv_e/mouvement_persons_e/mouvement_persons_e.htm.

[80] *Id.*

[81] Gordon, *supra* note 8, at 1115; Sophie Nonnenmacher, *International Trade Law and Labour Mobility*, *in* FOUNDATIONS OF INTERNATIONAL MIGRATION LAW 312, 312–14 (Brian Opeskin et al. eds., 2012); Thomas Straubhaar, *Why Do We Need a General Agreement on Movements of People (GAMP)?*, *in* MANAGING MIGRATION: TIME FOR A NEW INTERNATIONAL REGIME? 110, 129–33 (Bimal Ghosh ed., 2000).

[82] For a superb explanation of the law of the sea and its relationship to migrant smuggling, *see* ANNE T. GALLAGHER & FIONA DAVID, THE INTERNATIONAL LAW OF MIGRANT SMUGGLING 227–49 (2014).

[83] United Nations Convention on the Law of the Sea, arts. 2, 3, 19(2)(g), 25, 33, 86, 89, 92, Dec. 10, 1982, 1833 U.N.T.S. 397. The UNCLOS has been ratified by 166 states and the European Union. The "right of innocent passage" enables foreign vessels to pass through territorial seas, but passage is not "innocent" if the vessel loads or unloads any person contrary to the immigration laws and regulations of the coastal state. *Id.*, art. 19(2)(g). *See also* Natalie Klein, *Assessing Australia's Push Back the Boats Policy Under International Law: Legality and Accountability for Maritime Interceptions of Irregular Migrants*, 15 MELB. J. INT'L L. 414, 420–21 (2014).

[84] GALLAGHER & DAVID, *supra* note 82, at 237.

[85] Four different treaties direct states to require ships flying their flags to assist people in distress at sea to the extent they are able to do so without endangering their own ship. UNCLOS, *supra* note 83, art. 98; International Convention for the Safety of Life at Sea, Annex ch. V, reg. 33, Nov. 1, 1974, 1184 U.N.T.S. 278 (2007 revision); Convention on the High Seas, art. 12(a), Sept. 30, 1962, 450 U.N.T.S. 11; International Convention on Salvage, art. 10, Apr. 28, 1989, 1953 U.N.T.S. 165.

[86] *See* Violeta Moreno-Lax & Efthymios Papastavridis, *Introduction: Tracing the Bases of an Integrated Paradigm for Maritime Security and Human Rights at Sea*, *in* "BOAT REFUGEES" AND

has been questioned when it comes to the high seas.[87] Adding into the mix transnational criminal law, which authorizes states to prevent unauthorized migrants from accessing their territory by sea,[88] the line between rescue and interdiction has become obscured. Again, although the law of the sea could play a role in regulating migration and protecting migrants at sea, it provides at best limited and sporadic gestures in that direction.

Beyond the principle of non-refoulement, transnational criminal law is the only subfield of international law that has successfully shifted norms related to migration. The human trafficking and migrant smuggling protocols of the UN Convention Against Transnational Organized Crime have been widely ratified and incorporated into domestic laws that criminalize human trafficking, migrant smuggling, and related activities.[89] This turn to criminalization of irregular migration is cause for concern, because it deflects attention from global structures of inequality that provoke migration. In a remarkable continuity with colonialism, transnational criminal law not only places the blame on those who move and those who assist them for the untenable situations in which they find themselves but also seeks to depict them as bad actors. Although international law should address transnational criminal organizations that exploit migrants, the migrants themselves should not

MIGRANTS AT SEA: A COMPREHENSIVE APPROACH 5 (Violeta Moreno-Lax & Efthymios Papastavridis eds., 2017) ("[A]lthough the UN Convention on the Law of the Sea and related instruments impose a series of obligations both on flag and coastal states with regard to persons in distress at sea, they fail to clearly allocate responsibility for those rescued or to pre-determine a precise port of disembarkation—whether the geographically closest to the shipwreck; the next port of call; one within the SAR Region of the coastal State concerned; or the 'safest' port in human rights and refugee law terms.").

[87] Sale v. Haitian Centers Council, 509 U.S. 155 (1993). The Guidelines on the Treatment of Persons Rescued at Sea, in contrast, reference the U.N. Refugee Convention. International Maritime Organization, Res. MSC. 167(8), UN Doc. MSC 78/26/Add.2, Annex 34, at 11 (May 20, 2004). *See also* Khlaifia v. Italy, App. No. 16483/12 (Eur. Ct. H.R. Dec. 15, 2016) (holding that Italy's expulsion of Tunisian nationals intercepted by the Italian Coast Guard and detained in Lampedusa was not a violation of Protocol 4, Article 4, which prohibits collective expulsion of non-citizens); CPCF v. Minister for Immigration and Border Protection [2015] HCA 1 (Austl.) (holding that the detention of 157 Sri Lankan Tamil asylum seekers at sea did not violate Australian law, with little analysis of its obligations under international refugee law).

[88] Protocol Against the Smuggling of Migrants by Land, Sea and Air, supplementing the United Nations Convention Against Transnational Organized Crime, art. 8, Jan. 28, 2004, 2241 U.N.T.S. 507; GALLAGHER & DAVID, *supra* note 82.

[89] United Nations Convention Against Transnational Organized Crime & the Protocols Thereto, Dec. 15, 2000, 2225 U.N.T.S. 209 (including the Protocol to Prevent, Suppress and Punish Trafficking in Persons, Especially Women and Children, Nov. 15, 2000, 2237 U.N.T.S. 319); Protocol Against Smuggling of Migrants, *supra* note 88; ANNE T. GALLAGHER, THE INTERNATIONAL LAW OF HUMAN TRAFFICKING 500 (2010); GALLAGHER & DAVID, *supra* note 82.

be lumped in the same category as the powerful cartels that exploit them.[90] Moreover, the smuggling and trafficking industries have arisen in response to many migrants' inability to move lawfully from their state of origin to their preferred destination state. The solution is to enable safe transit, not to punish those who seek to escape violence and poverty and find stable employment.

The international law of migration is a law of crisis and disorder. It belies the story of an international legal order that moves the international community toward greater prosperity, security, and freedom. It tells instead a story from the Global South, critical of the racial hierarchies and economic inequalities that underlie a system built around the exclusion of individuals from international lawmaking and the primacy of state sovereignty for the Global North, perpetuated by the fictions of consent and equality.

IV. An Effective International Legal Order on Migration

Although the colonial continuities of the international law of migration demonstrate amply the shortcomings of the international legal order, the emancipatory potential of international law remains.[91] Indeed, it is only by identifying and dismantling those imperialist features that international law can begin to live up to its promise. An effective international legal order on migration would combat racialized hierarchies by foregrounding the voices of individuals who are the subjects of the law.[92] The perspective of the Global North can no longer be taken as a baseline, and the alleged neutrality of that viewpoint must be replaced with an approach that incorporates a multiplicity of perspectives. It will be an ongoing challenge to incorporate non-elite interests given that international law is written by lawyers, but the recognition and prioritization of that goal would represent an important step forward toward meaningful inclusion.

Before taking that step, of course, the contemporary political space around migration must be navigated. Although the principle of non-refoulement is narrow and outdated, an effort to rework the foundations of international refugee law risks eliminating even the underinclusive protections that currently

[90] Gabriella Sanchez & Luigi Achilli, Critical Insights on Irregular Migration Facilitation: Global Perspectives (2019); Gabriella E. Sanchez, Human Smuggling and Border Crossings (2014).

[91] James Thuo Gathii, *The Promise of International Law: A Third World View*, 114 ASIL Proc. 165 (2020).

[92] Ramji-Nogales, *Constructing Human Rights*, *supra* note 68.

exist. Faced with a particularly virulent strain of nativism in global politics, this may seem an inopportune moment to reform the system. On the other hand, the cruel excesses of xenophobic politics have given rise to political awareness and activism that could improve migration law, and contemporary political instability has opened up antiracist spaces and movements that might be capable of moving international law on migration toward an inclusive new order.

Nativist politics have a long history in Europe and the United States. Only in recent years has the idea of demeaning entire groups of people on the basis of their race, religion, or ethnicity come to be viewed as unacceptable in democratic countries.[93] Voters who have not fully embraced that shift are most commonly associated with right-wing political beliefs, but may also favor left-wing economic policies.[94] While recent growth in nativism has been greater in right-wing political parties, parties on the left have collaborated on issues such as immigration control and securitization.[95] The increase in contemporary support for nativist politics can be ascribed to a number of complex factors, including a lack of trust in political leaders and a belief on the part of some voters that the system has left them behind.[96] The rise of these parties can also be attributed to a failure of leadership on the part of mainstream political parties, which have chosen to collaborate with, rather than reject, nativist politicians.[97] In other words, right-wing populism is not an exogenous phenomenon existing outside of conventional politics, but instead thrives on the "radicalization of mainstream values."[98]

While this may not appear to be a promising starting point for progressive reform of international migration law, recent polling data in the United States shows increased support for immigration.[99] It is possible that the cruel policies of the Trump administration, including family separations at the border, have mobilized voters to counteract his xenophobic politics. It remains to be

[93] *Rachel Kleinfeld & John Dickas, Resisting the Call of Nativism: What U.S. Political Parties Can Learn From Other Democracies* 4, 6–7 (Carnegie Endowment for International Peace, Working Paper, 2020).

[94] *Id.* at 5–6.

[95] Cas Mudde, *Three Decades of Populist Radical Right Parties in Europe. So What?*, 52 Eur. J. Pol. Res. 1, 13, 15 (2013).

[96] Andrew Geddes & Peter Scholten, The Politics of Migration and Immigration in Europe 238 (2016).

[97] *Id.* at 241; Kleinfeld & Dickas, *supra* note 93, at 2.

[98] Mudde, *supra* note 95, at 16 ("the populist radical right is not a normal pathology of European democracy, unrelated to its basic values, but rather a pathological normalcy, which strives for the radicalisation of mainstream values.").

[99] Rose, *supra* note 20; Younis, *supra* note 20.

seen whether the shift will be lasting and whether a similar shift will occur in Europe. In any case, a move toward a more pluralist international order in the migration space—an order that takes into account the perspectives of migrants and their countries of origin—will require substantial courage on the part of political leaders. The political instability of the current moment offers the possibility of a new, global antiracist politics that could take root and exert its power to support a more inclusive and pluralist approach to international migration law.

The political impetus for this reform would be most effective coming from a transnational social movement comprised of migrants themselves and diaspora and allies in destination states, as well as those impacted by migration in sending states. Such a political movement would prioritize the perspectives of migrants and their relatives and allies from the Global South in its demand for a restructuring of the international legal framework around migration. Migrants and diaspora members should work in solidarity with allies in destination states, as well as families and friends and returned migrants in countries of origin, to demand that these states work to craft a more effective legal regime governing migration. Social movements and civil society might advocate for the changes that migrants seek both inside international institutions and in the streets. These efforts will be most successful if they can benefit from transnational coordination, while at the same time ensuring that non-elite voices are incorporated. Those voices could then be amplified by a range of allies in both receiving and sending states.

An effective international legal regime governing migration would ensure that migrants are able to travel safely and lawfully from their home states to seek protection from harm and/or to obtain employment in destination states. In the long run, this would involve expanding the grounds for protection beyond the narrow non-refoulement principle to address contemporary harms comprehensively. It would also enable safe transit and entry for those whose protection claims are granted. At the same time, an effective international law of migration would prioritize autonomy, enabling refugees who prefer to seek protection in countries close to their home states to do so in a safe and dignified manner. It would also ensure safe and regular migration routes for migrants seeking to fill labor needs in destination states, requiring states to offer legal status that enables migrant workers to enforce their rights. This regime would play a role in developing capacity in countries of origin such that individuals who prefer to remain at home are able to secure employment that fulfills their human potential.

The asylum system is currently one of the few paths for many migrants to access employment opportunities; this is an unsustainable situation caused by path dependency in the structure of international law.[100] Given aging populations and declining birth rates, it is in the economic best interest of countries in the Global North to welcome labor migrants.[101] Given the dearth of visas, many current labor migrants are undocumented, which leaves them vulnerable to exploitation. An effective international legal regime, in short, would ensure the autonomy and safety of migrants through all parts of their journey and would push states to recognize the full range of reasons that humans cross international borders, while at the same time fulfilling labor market needs in destination states.[102] These aspirational goals are not likely to be realized in a multilateral international legal instrument in the near future, but through an iterative process, states in the Global North might be encouraged to take steps in this direction. Regional approaches also offer a promising starting point for a rules-based international order on migration.

In order to work toward an international regime that establishes binding legal obligations around migration, major migrant destination states in the Global North could establish a plurilateral agreement to admit migrants seeking protection and employment. Following the Paris Agreement of the UN Framework Convention on Climate Change, each state could determine its own obligation to admit a certain number of migrants in these two categories (seeking protection and employment) each year. These migrants would then be able to travel safely by airplane to the destination state, eliminating dangerous journeys and crowded border crossings, and creating revenue for airline companies and destination states. This approach should minimize irregular migration, enabling destination states to create more comprehensive records of the migrants within their territories. If sufficient resources are allocated toward this effort, labor markets in destination states should benefit from the entry of migrant workers, as should local workers whose wages will be less easily undercut by labor migrants in lawful status. If this iterative agreement proved successful over time, states might be willing to commit to an agreement that creates a binding obligation to admit a certain number of migrants per year, based on global protection needs and domestic labor needs.

[100] Ramji-Nogales, *supra* note 1.
[101] Kenny, *supra* note 16.
[102] Ramji-Nogales & Spiro, *supra* note 7.

The reforms might most effectively be located as an initial matter at a regional level, and in fact are already taking place through regional agreements and bodies in Africa and Latin America. The regional approach is important for at least three reasons. First, it is a space that is more likely to be able to incorporate the perspectives of migrants themselves into the legal conversation. Second, a focus on regional reforms would help shift the locus of knowledge production from the Global North to the Global South. While regional agreements and bodies in the former tend to perform a containment function that benefits destination states, the latter has provided a space for progressive reform of international migration law in ways that reflect the perspectives of migrants themselves. Of course, some regions include states from both the Global North and the Global South; in those cases, the political incentives of the former in containment must be balanced, possibly through the political power of migrants from the latter who reside in the former. Third, a regional approach recognizes that more migrants move within the Global South than from the Global South to the Global North.[103] While some migrants from the Global South travel beyond their regions to seek employment or protection, a regional approach offers promise to those who remain closer to home. Even this approach, in some cases, would benefit from funding from the Global North.

Though these regions are vast and diverse, a brief snapshot of migrant flows within Africa, the Americas, and Asia provides context for this analysis.[104] In terms of regional migration in Africa, in 2019, over twenty-one million Africans resided in another African country.[105] Cross-border migration within Africa has grown substantially since 2000 and emigration, particularly to Europe, has more than doubled since 1990. In 2019, over ten million African migrants lived in Europe, while 4.6 million lived in Asia and just over three million resided in North America. South Africa has long been the largest destination state in Africa, with around four million international migrants, followed by Cote d'Ivoire, Uganda, Ethiopia, and Sudan.[106]

[103] World Bank, *South-South Migration versus South-North Migration*, *in* MIGRATION AND REMITTANCES FACTBOOK (2016).

[104] These statistics are drawn from the International Organization for Migration's World Migration Report, which uses the six world regions defined by the UN Department of Economic and Social Affairs (Africa, Asia, Latin America and the Caribbean, Northern America, and Oceania). INTERNATIONAL ORGANIZATION FOR MIGRATION, WORLD MIGRATION REPORT 2020, Ch. 3, Appx. A, at 313 (2019).

[105] *Id.* at 54.

[106] *Id.* at 57.

In 2019, Egypt saw the largest number of emigrants; South Sudan, Somalia, Sudan, and Algeria were also in the top five migrant-sending states.

In the Americas, over twenty-six million migrants from Latin America and the Caribbean were residing in North America in 2019.[107] Mexico was by far the largest migrant-sending country in the region and is the second-largest country of origin in the world, after India. Most Mexican migrants reside in the United States, as do many Central Americans. Behind Mexico, Colombia, Venezuela, and Brazil were the next largest countries of origin in Latin America.[108] After the United States, Argentina was the largest destination state, followed by Venezuela, Colombia, and Mexico.[109]

Finally, in the Asian region, sixty-six million Asians lived in other countries within Asia in 2019; migration within the region has grown substantially since 1990, when the figure was thirty-five million.[110] Most other Asian migrants resided in North America and Europe. While India and China send the largest absolute numbers of migrants to live abroad, those numbers are small as a percentage of their populations.[111] Bangladesh, Syria, and Pakistan are also in the top five sending states. The top five destination states in Asia in 2019 were Saudi Arabia, the United Arab Emirates, Turkey, India, and Kazakhstan.[112]

Regional agreements offer great potential for safe movement as well as the risk of being captured as a containment strategy. A regional arrangement could process migrants seeking both protection and employment within their home countries, enabling them to travel lawfully to the destination state. Given the grave physical dangers of many migrant journeys, the promise of safe transit is tantalizing. The Biden administration has begun talks with the UN High Commissioner for Refugees about a program to enable Central American asylum seekers to have their claims adjudicated in their own countries.[113] President Biden has also said he will restore a previous program that aimed to enable certain Central American minors to apply for asylum within their home countries; that program was not successful because the processing centers were inaccessible to the children seeking

[107] *Id.* at 95.
[108] *Id.* at 97.
[109] *Id.* at 98.
[110] *Id.* at 68.
[111] *Id.* at 70.
[112] *Id.* at 71.
[113] Oliver Griffin, *U.N. in Talks with U.S. on Central American Refugees Applying for Asylum from Home*, Reuters, Feb. 9, 2021.

protection.[114] A new version of the program will require substantial planning and investment to function effectively and will need to avoid the pitfalls of current resettlement programs that accept a small fraction of refugees needing protection.

Regional bodies in the Global South have already begun to reform international migration law in a way that more faithfully represents the interests of migrants. The principle of non-refoulement, for example, has been expanded by regional human rights instruments in the Global South, which offer protection and rights to a larger group of noncitizens. The 1969 OAU Convention Governing Specific Aspects of Refugee Problems in Africa, for example, extends the non-refoulement principle beyond those individually targeted to include those fleeing destabilizing situations such as "external aggression, occupation, foreign domination or events seriously disturbing public order."[115] Explicitly referencing the OAU's broadened refugee definition, the 1984 Cartagena Declaration on Refugees, a nonbinding instrument adopted by ten members of the Organization of American States, similarly extends the non-refoulement principle to those fleeing "generalized violence, foreign aggression, internal conflicts, massive violations of human rights or other circumstances which have seriously disturbed public order."[116] These updates to the scope of non-refoulement protection more accurately reflect the forces that might prompt migrants to flee their home countries in search of protection and represent a strong starting point for the expansion of refugee protection.

Beyond the principle of non-refoulement, regional human rights law in Africa and Latin America has begun to extend rights to undocumented migrants, pushing to reform state practices. The African Charter on Human and Peoples' Rights provides for freedom of movement and residence to "every individual" within the state, explicitly including migrants who do not

[114] FAYE HIPSMAN & DORIS MEISSNER, MIGRATION POLICY INSTITUTE, IN-COUNTRY PROCESSING IN CENTRAL AMERICA: A PIECE OF THE PUZZLE (Aug. 2015), https://www.migrationpolicy.org/research/country-processing-central-america-piece-puzzle.

[115] OAU Convention, *supra* note 9, art. I(2). The OAU Convention has been ratified by forty-six members of the African Union (which has a total of fifty-five members). Morocco is the only migrant destination state that has opted out; the other countries that are not members are Djibouti, Eritrea, Madagascar, Mauritius, Namibia, Sahrawi Arab Democratic Republic, Somalia, and Sao Tome and Principe. *List of Countries Which Have Signed, Ratified/Acceded to the OAU Convention Governing the Specific Aspects of Refugee Problems in Africa*, https://au.int/en/treaties/oau-convention-governing-specific-aspects-refugee-problems-africa (last visited Mar. 9, 2021).

[116] Cartagena Declaration, *supra* note 9, Conclusion 3. The Cartagena Declaration was signed by Belize, Colombia, Costa Rica, El Salvador, Guatemala, Honduras, Mexico, Nicaragua, Panama, and Venezuela.

have lawful migration status.[117] This provision prohibits the detention of asylum seekers and restricts limitations on the movement of asylum seekers and migrant workers.[118] The Inter-American Principles on the Human Rights of All Migrants, adopted by the Inter-American Commission on Human Rights in 2019, represent perhaps the most progressive interpretation to date of human rights law with respect to undocumented migrants.[119] These nonbinding principles condemn refusal of entry at the border as well as indirect return or chain refoulement at territorial borders, entry points, and within transit zones. They offer what may be the first recognition under international law of migrants' right to determine their state of destination. The principles accord due process rights to all migrants, regardless of migration status, in immigration proceedings. Finally, they mandate that states consider measures to regularize the undocumented, examining how long they have lived in the host state, their family relations, their ties to the community, and the best interests of their children.

Outside of human rights law, regional law has created in two instances free movement and residence rights for nationals of member states. Under Article 45 of the Treaty on the Functioning of the European Union, citizens of EU member states are entitled to work and reside in other EU member states and to enjoy equal treatment with nationals in access to employment, conditions of work, and remuneration.[120] In South America, the 2002 MERCOSUR Residence Agreement provides nationals of nine countries in South America with the right to reside and work in all other member states.[121] The agreement that sets out this free movement regime is justified by the need to resolve the undocumented status of migrants within the region, in contrast to the European Union's economic focus on establishing an internal market.[122] The proposal was also justified by state needs and interests, highlighting the challenges of controlling large borders, the need to be able to identify

[117] African Commission on Human and Peoples' Rights, General Comment No. 5 on the African Charter on Human and Peoples' Rights: The Right to Freedom of Movement and Residence (Art. 12(1)), ¶ 8 (discussing Banjul Charter, *supra* note 9, art. 12(1)), https://www.achpr.org/legalinstruments/detail?id=74.

[118] *Id.*, ¶¶ 48, 51.

[119] Inter-American Commission on Human Rights, Inter-American Principles on the Human Rights of All Migrants, Refugees, Stateless Persons and Victims of Human Trafficking, Res. 04/19 (Dec. 7, 2019).

[120] Consolidated Version of the Treaty on the Functioning of the European Union, art. 45, 2012 O.J. (C326).

[121] Acosta, *supra* note 76. Member states to the agreement are Argentina, Bolivia, Brazil, Chile, Colombia, Ecuador, Paraguay, Peru, and Uruguay.

[122] *Id.* at 180–81.

migrants present within the country, and the importance to both national workers and migrant workers of status regularization in terms of fair wages and protection from exploitation.[123]

In the face of economic and environmental challenges, a human mobility approach that offers individuals a real choice between migrating and remaining in their home countries must also incorporate development, adaptation, and mitigation as part of the international legal framework around migration. States in the Global North can and should do more to encourage the creation of employment, education, and training opportunities in migrant-sending states. Regional approaches offer some promise in this regard, but risk being coopted as containment strategies.[124] On the environmental law front, the Platform on Disaster Displacement, guided by a Steering Group of eighteen states from the Global North and the Global South,[125] works with three international policy frameworks to address climate migration: the Global Compacts on Migration and Refugees, the Sendai Framework for Disaster Risk Reduction, and the UN Framework Convention on Climate Change.[126] The Sendai Framework focuses on risk anticipation, investment in risk reduction, and strengthening risk governance.[127] This is an important starting point, but the focus should be broadened to include slow onset climate change and expanded beyond the human rights obligations of the home state in response to climate change disasters to include the duties of migrant-receiving states in furthering adaptation and mitigation efforts.[128]

Finally, in terms of the substance of the law, a more effective approach to international migration law would begin by conceptualizing migrants as whole human beings who may have both protection and employment needs. To ensure protection, international institutions should be able to anticipate flows of migrants fleeing conflict, climate change, or other events that

[123] *Id.* at 180.

[124] Ramji-Nogales, *supra* note 1, at 639–42.

[125] Platform on Disaster Displacement, https://disasterdisplacement.org/ (last visited Mar. 10, 2021). Current members of the steering group are: Australia, Bangladesh, Brazil, Canada, Costa Rica, European Union, Fiji (Chair), France (Vice-Chair), Germany, Kenya, Madagascar, Maldives, Mexico, Morocco, Norway, Philippines, Senegal, and Switzerland.

[126] Platform on Disaster Displacement Strategy 2019–2022, at 3, https://disasterdisplacement.org/wp-content/uploads/2019/06/26062019-PDD-Strategy-2019-2022-FINAL_to_post_on_website.pdf (last visited Mar. 10, 2021).

[127] United Nations Office for Disaster Risk Reduction, Sendai Framework for Disaster Risk Reduction 2015–2030, ¶¶ 20, 30(l) (2015).

[128] Bruce Burson et al., *The Duty to Move People Out of Harm's Way in the Context of Climate Change and Disasters*, 37 Refugee Surv. Q. 379, 383 (2018); Ramji-Nogales, *supra* note 27.

seriously disturb public order. These organizations could then play a role in proactive planning, offering both financial and logistical support for neighboring states likely to host the largest numbers of migrants and providing solutions for those who cannot stay safely near home. Historically, states in the Global North have provided insufficient support for states in the Global South that host the vast majority of refugees.[129] This is a thorny collective action problem that will require substantial political effort to shift behavior. In order to provoke this shift, the relevant legal obligations must be grounded in either serious plurilateral legal commitments or binding international or regional law.

Global migration is, of course, a symptom of deep structural inequality. The question remains whether any reform of the international legal order can contribute to the eventual resolution of that inequality, without which international law will serve the interests of powerful nations rather than unleashing its emancipatory potential. In particular, given ongoing economic domination, it may be exceedingly unrealistic to expect that migrants and their allies will be able to leverage social movements to make their voices heard in international migration law. Yet the current moment may present an opportunity to reframe state interests to demonstrate that both migrants and destination states can benefit from a more effective international legal order around migration.

[129] Currently, 85% of refugees are hosted in the Global South. UNHCR, *Figures at a Glance*, https://www.unhcr.org/en-us/figures-at-a-glance.html (last visited May 28, 2021).

Index

For the benefit of digital users, indexed terms that span two pages (e.g., 52–53) may, on occasion, appear on only one of those pages.

Note: Tables and figures are indicated by *t* and *f* following the page number

Abu Ghraib prison in Iraq, 197
accountability for multinational enterprises, 338
ad hoc tribunals, 411
adaptable aerial technology, 229–31
adaptable ground technology, 231–32
adaptable maritime technology, 231
Additional Protocols to Geneva Conventions, 9, 184, 186, 189–90, 196, 212–13
Afghanistan, 38, 55–56, 187, 409–10
Africa, 66, 69, 99, 447–48
African Charter on Human and Peoples' Rights, 369, 449–50
African Continental Free Trade Area, 302
African Court of Justice and Human Rights, 419
African Court on Human and Peoples' Rights, 15
African Union, 84–85, 99, 152–53
An Agenda for Democratization (Boutros-Ghali), 83–84
aggression, the crime of, 399–400, 421–22
Al-Awlaki, Anwar, 193–94
al-Bashir, Omar, 390–91, 417–18
Al Qaeda, 55–56, 192, 193–94, 409–10
Al Qaeda Sanctions Committee, 413–14
al-Sisi, Abdel Fattah, 383–84
Alliance of Small Island States, 127
Álvarez, José, 71–73
American Branch of the International Law Association (ABILA), 1
American Journal of International Law, 308
American Society of International Law, 406
Amnesty International, 383
Anghie, Anthony, 434–35
anonymity online, 252
anti-bribery law
  competition law, 349–53
  criminalization of transnational bribery, 10–11
  introduction to, 3–4, 338–41
  national populism and, 356–60
  OECD Anti-Bribery Convention, 345–48
  regimes and national interest in, 353–56
  rise of, 341–49
  rising Chinese power and, 19–20
  robust enforcement of, 15–16
  summary of, 360
  transborder anti-bribery law, 340
  before WWII, 7–8
anti-cartel law, 340–41, 350, 351, 356
anti-materiel weapons systems, 226
anti-migrant animus, 20
anticipatory self-defense, 151, 163, 170*f*, 180
anticorruption law, 338–39, 357–58. *See also* anti-bribery law
antigovernment protests, 366–67, 390–91
antiliberal regimes, 357–58. *See also* illiberal democracy
Arend, Anthony, 154–55
armed attacks, 262–76
armed conflict, 18, 133–38, 263–68
arms control treaties, 24–25
Arms Export Control Act, 246
artificial intelligence (AI), 208
Asia, 66, 69, 448
Asian Infrastructure Investment Bank, 70

Association of Southeast Asian Nations (ASEAN), 84–85
asylum
applications to EU, 129–30
denials of, 388
migration law and, 428–29, 436–37, 446, 448–50
austerity programs of neoliberal economics, 78–79
Australia Group, 246, 247
authoritarian international law, 20, 62–63, 93, 96, 104
authoritarian international organizations, 87
authoritarianism and human rights
in China, 89, 91–98, 357–58, 372–73, 389, 429
core strategies, 376–79
in domestic arenas, 379–84
domestic rights accountability, 375–87
international human rights law and, 364–65, 368–76, 370*f*, 370*t*
liberal democracy, erosion of, 89, 91–98, 365–66, 367–68, 386, 392
national human rights institutions, 384–87
possible futures, 387–91
shifts in, 381*t*, 393*t*, 395*t*
summary of, 391–92
in twenty-first century, 365–68
autocratic governments, 31, 369–71
autocratic legalists, 366–67, 378
autonomous, defined, 217–18
autonomous weapons. *See also* drones/drone warfare
adaptable aerial technology, 229–31
adaptable ground technology, 231–32
adaptable maritime technology, 231
definitional challenges, 222–24
export control challenges, 246–50
high-end autonomous weapons, 225–32
introduction to, 18, 24–26, 216–22
jus ad bellum, 220–21, 235–41, 250
jus in bello and, 221, 242–46, 250
lowering the threshold for use-of-force, 236–37
over-the-counter aerial systems, 232–33
over-the-counter ground systems, 234–35
over-the-counter maritime systems, 234
over-the-counter systems, 219–20, 221–22, 232–35
potentially adaptable technology, 229–32
research survey on, 226–27
state responsibility and, 237–41
swarms of, 227–29, 245–46
technology of, 224–35
Autonomous Weapons and Operational Risk report, 204–5
autonomy, defined, 222

Bandung Conference (1955), 78, 81, 91
Barber, William, 69–70
Bassiouni, Cherif, 421–22
"Battle of Seattle" protests, 288
Bedjaoui, Mohammed, 67–68, 433–34
Beijing effect, 93
Belt and Road Initiative (BRI), 50–51, 94–95, 96, 302, 359
Bharatiya Janata Party, 86–87
Biden, Joe, 16–17, 51, 58–59, 300–1, 358, 448–49
big data and *jus in bello*, 207–9
bilateral investment treaties (BITs)
China and, 91
EU and, 329
gaps in, 334
historic attraction of, 331
international investment law, 10–11, 12–13, 314–18, 323
introduction to, 7–8
renegotiation of, 332, 333–34
Bill and Melinda Gates Foundation, 23
bin Laden, Osama, 408, 409–10
bipolarity and liberal international order, 52–54
blockchain-based schemes, 102–3
Bo Xilai, 357–58
Bolivia, 99
Bolsonaro, Jair, 357–58
bomb-laden drones, 240–41
borders and migration inequality, 128–33
Bosselmann, Klaus, 114–16, 117n.46
Botswana, 169–70
Bouteflika, Abdelaziz, 390–91
Boutros-Ghali, Boutros, 83–84
Brazil, 357–58

Bretton Woods Institutions, 70, 71–72, 73–74
Brexit, 38–39, 56–57
bribery. *See* anti-bribery law
Bribery Convention (OECD), 12
Brussels effect, 93
Bush, George W., 151, 194, 289, 409

Calvo Doctrine, 324
Canada, 315
Capital and Ideology (Picketty), 74–75
capital-exporting states, 7–8, 12–13
capital-importing states, 7–8
Capital in the Twenty-First Century (Picketty), 74–75
capitalism, 71, 75–76, 340–41
Caribbean, 448
Cartagena Declaration on Refugees, 449
Castro, Fidel, 310
Center for a New American Security, 204–5
Central Intelligence Agency (CIA), 342–43
Chad, 169–70
Charter for the Economic Rights and Duties of States, 69
Charter Liberalism, 90
Chemical Weapons Convention, 23
China
  admission into WTO, 13–14
  authoritarianism of, 89, 91–98, 372–73, 389, 429
  autonomous weapons and, 225
  Belt and Road Initiative, 50–51, 94–95, 96, 302, 359
  BITs and, 334
  climate change and, 5
  Cold War with, 28–29
  cyber law in, 97
  cyber troops, 28
  democratic decline in, 89
  digital authoritarianism and, 33
  duopoly with US, 89, 101–4
  economic rise of, 289–90
  EU treaty with, 330
  human rights in, 97
  liberalism and, 72, 89–103
  reunification with Taiwan, 92, 94–95
  rise of power, 19–20, 28–30, 47–48, 58–59
  socialist market economy of, 38–39, 50–51
  sovereignty-based international order and, 4
  urbanization of, 210–11
  US climate change cooperation, 27
  US trade relations and, 286, 289–90, 299–300, 302–3, 358–59
  US trade war with, 16–17, 21–34
Church Committee inquiry, 342–43
civil society, 288, 445
civil society organizations (CSOs), 364, 377–79
civilian casualties, 193, 212–13
classical liberalism, 42
climate change and international legal order
  attempts to slow or reverse, 113–23
  borders and migration, 128–33
  case studies on, 123–38
  climate system forecast, 109–12
  conflict over, 133–38
  extreme climate events, 129, 134–35
  fragmentation in practice, 115–19
  global commitments to, 60
  global instability and, 114–15
  implications for, 112–13
  introduction to, 106–8
  migration law and, 451
  North-South divide and, 123–28
  shared origins of, 119–23
  summary of, 138–39
  as threat to, 5, 20–21, 26–27
Clinton, Hillary, 321
coercive diplomacy, 42–43
Cohen, Harlan, 290–92
Cold War
  bipolarity, 37–38
  with China, 28–29
  compensation doctrine in international law, 312–14
  corrupt leadership of allies, 343
  hyper-liberalism and, 2
  military power during, 46
  non-refoulement principle, 426–27
  Nuremberg Principles, 404–5
  overview of, 5–6, 8–11, 28
  rise of populism, 72–73
  with Soviet Union, 46
  US liberalism during, 49–50
collective self-defense, 179

colonialism
  dispossession, 62–63
  domination of people and place, 121
  economic world order and, 62–68
  inequalities during, 62–68
  international law and climate change, 120–21
  international legal order and, 113, 119
  migration law and, 433–34
  postcolonial hierarchies, 121–23
colonization and climate change, 127
COMINTERN, 87
Commission on the Responsibility of the Authors of the War and on the Enforcement of Penalties, 401
compensation doctrine in international law
  Cold War era, 312–14
  overview of, 308–18
  post-Cold War era, 314–18
  pre-World War II, 308–11
competition law, 349–53
Comprehensive and Progressive Agreement for Trans-Pacific Partnership (CPTPP), 30, 321–22
Congress of Vienna, 87
Constitutive Act of the African Union, 152–53
Convention on Combating Bribery of Foreign Public Officials in International Business Transactions (OECD Convention), 339. *See also* anti-bribery law
Convention on the Elimination of All Forms of Discrimination Against Women (CEDAW), 10, 316–17.
cooperative transatlantic governance, 38
core authoritarian strategies, 376–79
core crimes, 398, 399–400, 414–15
Correlates of War data, 155–56
corruption. *See* anti-bribery law; anticorruption law
Costa Rica, 160
Council of Europe, 87–88
Counter Rocket, Artillery, and Mortar (C-RAM) System, 203
counterterrorism, 72, 192–93, 369–71
COVID-19 pandemic, 75, 86–87, 102–3, 347–48, 389–90, 428–29
Craig, Robin, 114
crimes against humanity, 13, 399–400
Cuba, 159–60, 310
Cultural Revolution (China), 92–93
customary international law
  cyber conflicts/operations and, 274, 276–77, 278, 280
  economic world order and, 65–66
  international criminal law and, 415
  international investment law and, 308, 326
  international legal order and, 369
  jus in bello, 184, 188–90
  rules-based international order, 10
  use of force and, 144–45, 151
cyber attacks, 254, 261–62
cyber conflicts/operations
  armed attacks, 262–76
  armed conflict, 263–68
  critical infrastructure disruptions, 275–76
  customary international law, 276–77
  cyber attacks, 254, 261–62
  against data, 274–75
  disinformation campaigns, 256–58
  disruption goals, 258–59
  distinction in hostilities, 265–66
  election interference, 255–56
  future challenges, 276–80
  jus ad bellum, 252–53, 260–68
  jus in bello, 252–53, 260–68
  kinetic cyber operations, 254–55, 264
  new interpretations, 278–79
  new treaties, 278
  nonkinetic cyber operations, 254–55, 260, 264, 273–74
  online manipulation, 256–58
  overview of, 253–59
  private tech companies and, 279–80
  proportionality and, 266–68
  summary of, 280–81
  thresholds of war, 268–76
  as use-of-force, 149n.19
  use of force and, 261–62
cyber law, 97
cyber weapons, 18, 24–26
CyberPeace Institute, 280
Cybersecurity Tech Accord, 280

Declaration on International Law in Cyberspace (France), 262
decolonization, 66
democracy. *See also* liberal democracy
 architecture of, 83–85
 community of democracies, 98–99
 decline of, 71–72
 global decline of, 17, 20
 political hyperliberalism, 41
 in recession, 57
 recommended policies *vs.* autocratic dominance, 373–74
 self-determination with, 78–79
 spread of, 15
 US foreign policy toward, 49, 50
 US military spread of, 22–23
democracy charters, 84–85, 87
Democracy in Crisis (Freedom House), 367–68
democratic deficit, 78–79
Democratic Party, 16–17
democratic revival, 89, 98–101
democratization, 50, 55, 367–68
Deng Xiaoping, 91, 92
depoliticizing disputes, 324
detention/detainees, 190–92, 193
deterrence, 42–43, 46–47, 270, 277, 400
digital authoritarianism, 33
Digital Geneva Convention, 276, 279–80
Dinniss, Heather, 266
direct election interference, 256
disinformation campaigns, 256–58
dispersion of power, 19, 39, 56
dispute settlement system, 58, 287–88
Dispute Settlement Understanding, 13–14
distinction in hostilities, 265–66
distributed denial-of-services (DDoS), 258
Doha Development Agenda, 291–92
Doha Round of Development, 70–71
domestic criminal law, 407–8
domestic rights accountability, 375–87
Dominican Republic-Central America FTA (CAFTA-DR), 432
Doudou Thiam, 66–67
Drago Doctrine, 65–66
drones/drone warfare. *See also* autonomous weapons
 bomb-laden drones, 240–41
 cost concerns, 236–37
 drone swarms, 220
 over-the-counter aerial systems, 232–33
 Perdix small aerial drone, 227–28
 unauthorized sale of, 240
 unmanned drones, 227, 240
 Valkyrie drone, 230–31
drought-induced water shortages, 122–23
dualism, 115–16, 121, 431n.26
duopoly, 89, 101–4
Duterte, Rodrigo, 383

Economic Community of West African States (ECOWAS), 84–85, 95
economic demonization rhetoric, 289–90
economic hyperliberalism, 40–41, 54–56, 57–58
economic independence, 66
economic inequality, 20, 71, 126, 288, 435
economic power, 22–23, 39–40, 42–44, 59, 346, 348–49, 350
economic rationality, 115–16
economic rights, 2
economic world order
 colonialism and, 62–68
 fair and differential treatment, 79–81
 international economic law, 64–67, 76–81
 liberalism and, 71–76
 post-World War II, 63–71, 77
 preservation of, 71–81
 self-determination with democracy, 78–79
 summary of, 81
 thwarting of reforms, 69–71
Economist Intelligence Unit, 86
Ecuador, 99
Egypt, 383–84
elected authoritarians, 378
election interference, 255–56
electoral autocracy, 86–87
Elephant graph, 88
end-times scenario, 387–88, 392
Energy Charter Treaty, 329
Enlightenment, 115–16, 118–19
Environmental Protection Agency, 116–17
Erdogan, Recep Tayyip, 381, 390
Esper, Mark, 228–29

Estonia, 258
Ethiopia, 390–91
European Convention on Human Rights, 369, 436
European cosmology, 115–16
European Court of Human Rights, 3
European Court of Justice (ECJ), 329
European Economic Community (EEC), 351
European imperialism, 434
European Union (EU)
  anti-cartel law, 351
  bilateral investment treaties, 323, 329
  Brexit and, 38–39, 56–57
  free movement regimes of, 439–40, 450–51
  Hungary and, 100
  institutional path of, 329–30
  rule of law in, 87–88
  treaty with China, 330
Executive branch managerialism, 78–79
Export Administration Act, 246
Export Administration Regulations, 246
export control challenges, 246–50
expropriation of property, 8n.26
external legitimacy, 77–78
Extraordinary Chambers in the Courts of Cambodia, 13, 416–17
extraterritorial jurisdiction, 406–7
extreme climate events, 129, 134–35
extreme poverty, 109–10
extremism, 97, 388

fair and differential treatment, 79–81
Fakhrizadeh, Mohsen, 216
Farer, Tom, 154–55
Federal Aviation Administration (FAA), 233
Federal Republic of Yugoslavia, 158–59
feminist legal theory, 433
Fidesz party, 382
Financial Times, 63–64
Five Eyes, 98–99
five interlocking injustices, 69–70
flawed democracy, 86–87
Foal Eagle exercises, 55–56, 59
food security concerns, 135–36
Foreign Corrupt Practices Act (FCPA), 10–11, 341–43, 348
foreign direct investment (FDI), 296–97, 313, 319n.31, 323, 329n.50
France, 234, 262
Franck, Thomas, 146–47
free market liberalism, 2, 101
free movement of people, 1–2
free movement regimes of EU, 439–40, 450–51
free speech, 252
free trade agreements (FTAs), 30, 297–98
Freedom House, 34, 85, 86–87, 367–68, 386
freedom of association, 377–78
freedom of expression, 377–78

G7 countries, 31–32
García-Sayán, Diego, 386–87
General Agreement on Tariffs and Trade (GATT)
  bipolarity and, 52–53
  economic power and, 43–44, 43*f*
  introduction to, 9–10, 13–14, 39–40, 43*f*
  migration law and, 440–41
  signing of, 318–20
  trade rule of law and, 287, 293, 296–97
  unipolarity and, 54
  US share of GATT/WTO GDP, 39–40, 43*f*
Geneva Conventions, 6–7, 9, 11, 184, 188–89, 273
genocide, 13, 119–20, 399–400, 414
Genocide Convention, 11, 369, 420–21
Gilded Age, 74–75
Glennon, Michael, 146, 154–55
Global Alliance of National Human Rights Institutions (GANHRI), 385
Global Compacts on Migration and Refugees, 131, 451
global economic order. *See* economic world order
global financial crisis, 17–18, 88
Global North
  capitalism in, 71, 75–76
  colonialism and, 69–71
  economic inequality and, 40–41
  economic world order and, 62
  foreign aid and investment from, 64
  international economic law, 64–65

knowledge production shifts, 447
migration law and, 425–26, 427–28, 429–30, 435–38, 443, 446, 451–52
North-South inequality, 2, 123–33
post-World War II international economic order, 2
trade law and, 285–86
Global South
Chinese exports to, 33
colonialism and, 67–68, 69–71
democratic deficit of, 78–79
economic inequality and, 40–41
economic world order and, 62
humans as part of ecosystems, 118–19
international economic law, 64–65
knowledge production shifts, 447
migration law and, 425–26, 443, 445, 449, 451–52
North-South inequality, 2, 123–33
overconsumption of resources, 119
post-World War II international economic order, 2
views on expropriation, 8n.26
Global War on Terror, 92
globalization, 29–30, 88, 296, 425
Gonzalez, Carmen, 107, 121
government censorship, 379–80
grave breaches, 11
Grear, Anna, 116
Great Recession, 56, 70–71
Group of Government Experts (GGE), 24–25
Guantánamo Bay prison camp, 191, 409
The Guardian, 64
Guatemala, 358
guided munitions, 227
gunboat diplomacy, 65–66
Guterres, Antonio, 252

Hague Conventions (1907), 149–50, 196
Hague Peace Conference, 6–7
Hakimi, Monica, 160–61
hard power, 42–43, 49, 50
Hariri, Rafiq, 416–17
Hayden, Michael, 277
hegemonic stability theory, 39
Henderson, Christian, 146–47
Hendrix, Cullen, 136–38
high-end autonomous weapons, 225–32
Honduras, 99
horizontal rules, 3, 4
Houthi movement, 240
human climate niche, 110–11
human rights, 10, 97, 99, 109–10, 318–21, 439. *See also* authoritarianism and human rights
Human Rights Council (HRC), 15, 369, 372–74, 373*t*
human rights law, 11–12, 115, 439. *See also* international human rights law
human rights norms, 15, 17
Human Rights Watch, 203
humanitarian intervention, 152–54, 169–77, 174*f*
humanitarian liberalism, 2, 22–23
Humphreys, Stephen, 112–13
Hungary, 87–88, 100, 390. *See also* Orban, Viktor
Hurricane Laura, 111
hurricane-related flooding, 125–26
Hussein, Saddam, 187
hyperliberalism, 2. *See also* economic hyperliberalism

illegal immigrants, 88–89
illiberal democracy, 86–88
imperial international law, 65–66
imperialism, 434
Impoundment Control Act, 342–43
Indigenous communities, 79, 118–20
indirect election interference, 256
industrial espionage, 93
Industrial Revolution, 125
information and communications technology (ICT), 33
Inter-American Commission on Human Rights, 385–86
Inter-American Court of Human Rights (IACtHR), 385–87
Inter-American human rights system, 385–86
Inter-American Principles on the Human Rights of All Migrants, 449–50
Intergovernmental Panel on Climate Change (IPPC), 106
international armed conflicts (IACs), 185–86, 189

International Bank for Reconstruction and Development (IBRD), 52–53
international cartels, 349–50
International Centre for Settlement of Investment Disputes (ICSID), 12–13, 312–14, 322, 323, 324–25, 328
International Code of Conduct for Private Security Contractors, 200
International Committee of the Red Cross (ICRC), 9, 184, 187–88, 209–10, 212–13, 214–15, 224, 235, 265
International Convention Against the Recruitment, Use, Financing and Training of Mercenaries, 196
International Convention on the Rights of All Migrant Workers and Their Families, 439–40
International Convention on the Settlement of Investment Disputes Between States and Nationals of Other States (ICSID Convention), 312–14, 323
International Court of Justice (ICJ), 68, 127, 149, 237–38, 262–63, 312
International Covenant on Civil and Political Rights (ICCPR), 10, 83–84, 316–17, 436
International Covenant on Economic, Social, and Cultural Rights (ICESCR), 10, 316–17
International Criminal Court (ICC), 3, 13, 14–15, 55, 99, 375, 397, 406, 410–24
international criminal law (ICL)
  crime control approach, 398
  development of, 399–410
  founding of, 401–3
  future trends, 414–22
  ICC and, 397, 406, 410–24
  impact of, 410–14
  introduction to, 397–99
  Nuremberg Principles, 403–10
  summary of, 422–24
  transnational criminal law, 23, 399–400, 410–11, 413–14
International Criminal Tribunal for Rwanda (ICTR), 13, 14–15, 55, 404–6
International Criminal Tribunal for the former Yugoslavia (ICTY), 13, 14–15, 55, 237–38, 263, 404–6
international economic law, 64–67, 76–81, 101. *See also* international investment law
international economic order. *See* economic world order
international environmental agreements, 27
international environmental law (IEL), 107, 139
international human rights law (IHRL)
  authoritarianism and, 364–65, 368–76
  Human Rights Council and, 15, 369, 372–74, 373*t*
  Inter-American Commission on Human Rights, 385–86
  Inter-American Court of Human Rights, 385–87
  Inter-American human rights system, 385–86
  Inter-American Principles on the Human Rights of All Migrants, 449–50
  International Covenant on Civil and Political Rights, 10, 83–84, 316–17, 436
  International Covenant on Economic, Social, and Cultural Rights, 10, 316–17
  jus in bello, 185–86, 187
  Office of the High Commissioner for Human Rights, 385–86
  Optional Protocol to the Convention against Torture, 385–86
  rules- based order and, 3
  UN Commission on Human Rights, 10, 15, 84n.6
  UN Convention Against Torture, 10, 436
  UN Convention on the Elimination of All Forms of Racial Discrimination, 10
  UN Convention on the Rights of the Child, 10
  UN Human Rights Council, 198–99
  Universal Declaration of Human Rights, 2, 10, 83–84, 316, 369, 384–85
  Universal Periodic Review, 369, 373–74, 385–86
international humanitarian law (IHL). *See also jus in bello*
  armed attacks and, 265, 273

autonomous weapons and, 221, 242, 243–44
cyber operations and, 264
pre-World War II, 6–7
international investment law
doctrine of compensation, 308–18
expectations and lessons in, 331–37
ICSID Convention, 312–14, 323
international protection for human rights, 318–21
introduction to, 3, 307–8
investor-state dispute settlement, 12–13, 307–8, 318–37
resilience in, 325–31
trade agreements, 321–25
International Labor Organization (ILO), 7–8, 138–39, 439–40
International Law Association, 130–31
International Law Commission, 68, 130–31
international legal disorder, 425, 433–43
international legal order (ILO), 6–8, 7*t*, 20–21, 106–8, 112–13, 443–52
International Maritime Organization (IMO), 27, 118
International Military Tribunal at Nuremberg (IMT), 11, 402–3
International Military Tribunal for the Far East (IMFTE) in Tokyo, 402
International Monetary Fund (IMF), 38–39, 44, 44*f*, 45*f*, 52–53, 63–64, 69–70, 73–74, 77
International Panel on the Regulation of Autonomous Weapons (iPRAW), 247
international refugee law, 132–33, 425, 428–29, 436, 443–44. *See also* migration law
international security cooperation, 47–48
international trade agreements, 321–25. *See also* trade agreements
international trade law. *See* General Agreement on Tariffs and Trade; trade law; trade rule of law; World Trade Organization
International Trade Organization (ITO), 319
International Traffic in Arms Regulations, 246
International Tribunal for the Law of the Sea (ITLOS)., 330
investor-state arbitration, 3–4, 315
investor-state dispute settlement (ISDS), 12–13, 307–8, 318–37
Iran, 216, 240
Iran-US Claims Tribunal, 314–15
Iraq, 14, 167, 187, 197, 226
irregular migration, 425, 432–33, 442–43, 446
Islam, Raqul, 123–24
Islamic Republic, 314–15
Islamophobia, 72
Israel, 158–59, 171, 175–76, 175n.79, 219–20

Jackson, Robert H., 402–3
Japan, 23, 86
job losses, 40–41
judicial enforcement, 3–4
jus ad bellum. *See also* UN Charter and use of force
armed attacks, 262–63
autonomous weapons, 220–21, 235–41, 250
cyber conflict, 252–53, 260–68
as horizontal rules, 3
Iraq's invation of Kuwait and, 14
Kellogg-Briand Pact and, 8
national self-defense under, 192–93
post-Cold War era, 11–12, 16–17
privatization and, 194–201
rising Chinese power and, 19–20
use of force laws, 220
jus in bello. *See also* international humanitarian law
Additional Protocols to Geneva Conventions, 9, 184, 186, 189–90, 196, 212–13
application of, 188–92
armed attacks, 262–76
autonomous weapons and, 221, 242–46, 250
autonomous weapons threat to, 18
big data and, 207–9
in Cold War era, 9
cyber conflict, 252–53, 260–68
enforcement of, 3–4
international law regimes and, 192–94
introduction to, 184–85
lethal autonomous weapons systems, 202, 203–7

jus in bello (*cont.*)
non-international armed conflicts, 185–94
nonstate armed groups, 185–94
post-Cold War era, 11–12, 14–16
post-9/11 era, 186–88
rising Chinese power and, 19–20
summary of, 215
technological change, 201–9
urban warfare and, 209–15
urbanization threat to, 212–14
violence and, 272

Kampala Review Conference, 421–22
Kellogg-Briand Pact, 8
kinetic cyber operations, 254–55, 264
Koh, Harold, 261–62
Kuwait, Iraq's invasion of, 14
Kyoto Protocol, 70–71

laissez-faire capitalism, 38
Latin America, 10, 55, 64–66, 448
Law and Justice Party (PiS), 382
Law of the Sea Convention, 118
League of Nations, 121–22
Lebanon, 171, 175–76
legal instruments against terrorism, 406–7
legal taxonomies, 118
lethal autonomous weapons systems (LAWS), 202, 203–7, 209
LGBT individuals, 97
liberal democracy, 15, 31–32, 73–74
liberal democracy, erosion of
architecture of democracy, 83–85
authoritarian power through, 89, 91–98, 365–66, 367–68, 386, 392
causes of, 88–89
democratic revival and, 89, 98–101
duopoly and, 89, 101–4
impact on human rights, 34
in international legal order, 82–83
possibilities for global order, 103–5
trends in, 85–88, 86*t*
Liberal Democracy Index (LDI), 379–80
liberal international order
bipolarity and, 52–54, 53*f*
dimensions of, 41–42
economic power and, 43–44
introduction to, 1–3, 37–41
military power and, 45–48
multipolarity and, 56–59
periodization and, 52–59
power shifts and, 42–51, 43*f*
soft power and, 49–51
summary of, 59–61
unipolarity and, 54–56
liberalism
antiliberal regimes, 357–58
bipolarity and liberal international order, 52–54
Charter Liberalism, 90
China and, 72, 89–103
classical liberalism, 42
during Cold War, 49–50
economic hyperliberalism, 40–41, 54–56, 57–58
economic world order and, 71–76
free market liberalism, 2, 101
humanitarian liberalism, 2, 22–23
hyperliberalism, 2
political hyperliberalism, 41
Libyan National Army (LNA), 238
Lighthizer, Robert, 301
limitless commodification processes, 114–15
loitering weapons, 227
"Loyal Wingman" program, 229–30

Maduro, Nicolás, 240, 383–84, 389–90, 407–8
Magufuli, John, 383
Malabo Protocol, 419
Malaysia, 389–90
malware attacks, 254
Mao Zedong, 92–93
Marshall Fund, 73–74
Marshall Plan, 31, 33
mass atrocities, 145–46, 398–99, 400, 409–11
materialism, 115–16
Meng Wanzhou, 358–59
mercenaries, 99, 196, 198–99, 238–39
MERCOSUR, 439–40, 450–51
Mexico, 129–30, 448
migration law. *See also* international refugee law

current policy impact, 132–33
failures in, 438–43
international legal disorder, 425, 433–43
international legal order on, 443–52
introduction to, 425–31
irregular migration, 425, 432–33, 442–43, 446
non-refoulement principle, 426–27, 435–38, 443–44, 445, 449–50
post-Cold War era, 11–12
as sovereignty-based international order, 11–12
in twenty-first century, 431–33
Milanovic, Branko, 88
militarized interstate disputes (MIDs), 155–63, 156*f*, 158*f*
military power, 22–23, 42–43, 45–51, 59, 98
Military Tribunal at Nuremberg, 11
Missile Technology Control Regime (MTCR), 23, 25, 247
Modi, Narendra, 86–87
modus vivendi, 60–61
Monnet, Jean, 419–20
monoculture agriculture, 126
Montreux Document on Pertinent International Legal Obligations and Good Practices for States Related to the Operations of Private Military and Security Companies During Armed Conflict, 199
moral worth, 75
Morrison, Scott, 92
Multilateral Agreement on Investment (MAI), 320
multilateral export control agreements, 25, 26
multilateral human rights, 10, 439
multilateral trading system, 9–10, 56–57, 322
multilateralism, 37, 43, 91, 96–97, 291–92, 303–4, 369–71, 398–99, 429–30
Mutua, Makau, 73
mutual legal assistance treaties, 414–15

national human rights institutions (NHRIs), 384–87
national security state, 72
natural resources competition, 136
neocolonialism, 64–65, 119
Nepal, 23
net zero carbon emissions, 26
New International Economic Order, 62, 67, 69
new weapons technologies, 18, 24–26
Next Generation Combat Vehicle program, 231–32
Nicaragua, 160, 238
Nigeria, 389–90
9/11. *See* September 11, 2001 attacks
Nixon, Richard, 341–42
Nkurumah, Kwame, 64–65
nomadic societies, 120–21
non-international armed conflicts (NIACs)
detention operations, 190–92
jus in bello, 185–94
targeting decisions and, 189–90
urban warfare and, 211
non-refoulement principle, 426–27, 435–38, 443–44, 445, 449–50
nongovernmental organizations (NGOs), 27, 185, 187–88, 373–74
nonjudicial enforcement, 3–4
nonkinetic cyber operations, 254–55, 260, 264, 273–74
nonstate actors, 23, 25–26
nonstate armed groups, 185–94
North American Free Trade Agreement (NAFTA), 57–58, 302, 313–14, 315, 321, 330, 432
North Atlantic Treaty Organization (NATO), 55–56, 100
North-South inequality, 2, 123–33
Nuclear Non-Proliferation Treaty, 23
Nuclear Suppliers Group (NSG), 25, 246
Nuremberg Principles, 403–10

OAU Convention Governing Specific Aspects of Refugee Problems in Africa, 449
Obama, Barack, 252, 289–90, 409–10
Office of the High Commissioner for Human Rights, 385–86
official development assistance (ODA), 32
Olympic Games Operation, 255

online manipulation, 256–58
Operation Enduring Freedom, 55–56
Operation Iraqi Freedom, 17–18
Opium Wars, 91
Optional Protocol to the Convention against Torture, 385–86
Orban, Viktor, 86–87, 100, 382, 390. *See also* Hungary
Organisation for Economic Co-operation and Development (OECD), 12, 320, 344, 345–48, 352, 356
Organization of African Unity (OAU), 15
Organization of American States (OAS), 84–85, 99
Otto, Dianne, 433–34
over-the-counter aerial systems, 232–33
over-the-counter ground systems, 234–35
over-the-counter maritime systems, 234
over-the-counter weapon systems, 219–20, 221–22, 232–35
overconsumption of resources, 119

pacta sunt servanda, 60
Pakistan, 175n.79, 409–10
Paris Agreement, 127, 139, 446. *See also* climate change and international legal order
Paris Principles, 384–85
People's Liberation Army (PLA), 47–48
Perdix small aerial drone, 227–28
Permanent Court of Arbitration, 330
philanthropic foundations, 31
Picketty, Thomas, 74–75
Platform on Disaster Displacement, 451
plurilateral trade agreements, 304
Poland, 87–88, 382
political agency of poor, 75
political hyperliberalism, 41
political independence, 66, 144–45, 235, 261, 403
political modernization theory, 41
populism, 72–73, 356–60, 425, 428–29
postcolonialism, 62–63, 121–23
postwar liberal international order, 42–51
potentially adaptable technology, 229–32
poverty, 75, 109–10
prisoner-of-war status, 190–91
private military and security contractors (PMSCs), 194–95, 196
private tech companies, 279–80
privatization and *jus ad bellum*, 194–201
proportionality and cyber conflicts, 266–68
Proposed Convention for the Prevention and Punishment of Crimes against Humanity, 407
proto authoritarians, 87–88
Protocol on the Status of Refugees, 11
Putin, Vladimir, 38–39, 46–47, 219, 383–84

Race and the Undeserving Poor (Shilliam), 75
Rachman, Gideon, 63–64
racism, 20, 62, 72, 119–20
Racketeer Influenced and Corrupt Organizations Act (RICO), 348
radicalization of mainstream values, 444
Razak, Najib, 389–90
refugee, narrowness of definition, 11
refugee law. *See* international refugee law; migration law
Regimes of the World (RoW) project, 379–80
Regional Comprehensive Economic Partnership, 102
regional security cooperation, 47–48
regional trade agreements, 30, 288, 297–98, 313–14, 321, 322, 326
Reisman, Michael, 146–47
Republic of Palau, 127
resilience of rights scenario, 389, 392
Resilient Supply Chain Initiative (RSCI), 29–30
restorative justice, 398, 413–14
right-wing political parties, 444
rights-repressive measures, 371–72
robotic sentry weapons, 226
Rockefeller Commission inquiry, 342–43
Rome Statute for the International Criminal Court, 13, 407, 408
Roscini, Marco, 272–73
Rouhani, Hassan, 216
rule of law, 87–88, 112–13, 138–39. *See also* trade rule of law

rules-based international order
brief history of, 5–18
climate change as threat to, 5, 20–21, 26–27
in Cold War era, 2, 5–6, 8–11
dispersion of power, 22–23
end of US hegemony, 15–18
global decline of democracy, 17, 20, 30–34
international legal order before WWII, 6–8, 7*t*
introduction to, 1–5
new weapons technologies, 18, 24–26
post-Cold War era, 11–15
response to threats, 21–34
rising Chinese power and, 19–20, 28–30
sovereignty-based international order *vs.*, 2–4, 3n.4, 5–6
threats to, 18–21, 21*t*
Russia, 28, 38–39, 46–47, 89, 256, 257, 372–73
Russia-China Declaration on the Promotion of International Law, 93–94

Saudi Arabia, 316–17
Scharre, Paul, 204–5
secret ballots, 83–84
Securities and Exchange Commission (SEC), 341–42, 343
self-defense
anticipatory self-defense, 151, 163, 170*f*, 180
collective self-defense, 179
cyber operations and, 260
under *jus ad bellum*, 192–93
rights in UN Charter, 147–50, 151, 309
self-determination, 68, 78–79
Sendai Framework for Disaster Risk Reduction, 451
separatism, 97, 388
September 11, 2001 attacks, 50–51, 72, 186–87, 399–400, 408–10
Shanghai Cooperation Organization (SCO), 87, 97, 388
Shihata, Ibrahim, 324
Shilliam, Robbie, 75
Simpson, Gerry, 90
Sino-Japanese War (1895), 91
Slaughter, Anne-Marie, 71–72
Smith, Brad, 276, 279–80
social media, 28, 256, 257–58, 366–67, 377–78
social movements, 445, 452
socialist market economy, 38–39, 50–51
socioeconomic development and climate change, 136–37
soft power, 42–43, 49–51, 52, 100, 429
Soleimani, Qassim, 72, 409–10
South Africa, 169–70
South Korea, 55–56, 59, 86, 211
sovereignty-based international order, 2–4, 3n.4, 5–6, 7–8, 11–12
sovereignty doctrine, 434–35
Soviet Union, 24, 50, 316–17, 343–44
Special Court for Sierra Leone, 13, 416–17
Special Tribunal for Lebanon (STL), 13, 416–17
Sporkin, Stanley, 341–42
Stern, Nicholas, 124–25
Stockholm Chamber of Commerce, 313
Stockholm International Peace Research Institute (SIPRI), 226–27, 248
Stop Killer Robots! campaign, 203
supervisory control and data acquisition (SCADA) system, 255, 273–74
Supreme Iraqi Criminal Tribunal, 13
swarms of autonomous weapons, 227–29, 245–46
Syria, 158–59, 167
Syrian Democratic Forces (SDF), 238–39
systemic racism, 63–64

Taiwan, 92, 94–95
Taliban, 409–10
Tallinn Manual on the International Law Applicable to Cyber Operations, 253, 261–62
targeted killings, 72, 193, 194
targeting decisions in NIACs, 189–90
technological change and *jus in bello*, 201–9
terrorists/terrorism, 23, 193, 251–52, 421. *See also* September 11, 2001 attacks
Thailand, 389–90
Third World Approaches to International Law (TWAIL), 121
3D printing, 248

thresholds of war
armed attacks and, 271–72
in cyber operations, 268–76
nonkinetic effects, 273–74
as outdated, 269
recalibration of, 270–76
use of force and, 270–71
violence and, 272–73
torture crimes, 414
Trade Act, 342–43
trade agreements. *See also* North American Free Trade Agreement
free trade agreements, 30, 297–98
international trade agreements, 321–25
plurilateral trade agreements, 304
regional trade agreements, 30, 288, 297–98, 313–14, 321, 322, 326
trade rule of law and, 297–98
trade law, 11–12, 17–18, 19–20, 115, 285–86
trade rule of law
future institutions, 300–5
institutional challenges, 292–98
introduction to, 16–17, 285–87
national security and, 296–97
policy aims, 299–305
present challenges, 287–92
summary of, 306
trade agreements and, 297–98
unilateral tools in, 299–300
WTO and, 285–87, 290, 292–96
Trans-Pacific Partnership (TPP), 289, 321
Transatlantic Trade and Investment Partnership (TTIP), 16–17, 57–58, 321
transborder anti-bribery law, 340
transborder bribery, 10–11, 359
transnational criminal law (TCL), 23, 399–400, 410–11, 413–14
transparency for multinational enterprises, 338
Treaty of Versailles, 401
Treaty of Westphalia, 90
Treaty on the Functioning of the European Union, 450–51
Trump, Donald
"America First" approach, 51
authoritarian populism of, 82–83, 98–99
bribery charge against, 358
execution of Qassim Soleimani, 409–10
NAFTA and, 321
trade rule of law and, 289, 299, 300–1
trade war with China, 16–17
unilateral tools and, 299
on US commitment to NATO, 58–59
Tsai Ing-Wen, 92
Turkey, 390
two-worlds scenario, 388, 392

Uexkull, Nina von, 134–35
Ukraine, 259, 358
UN Charter
adoption of, 8–9
armed attacks and, 271–72
illiberalism and, 86–87
international protection for human rights, 318–21
liberalism and, 72–73
number of sovereign states signing, 19
Nuremberg Principles, 403–10
UN Charter and use of force
abroad *vs.* nonstate actors, 151–52
accepted grounds for, 148–50
anticipatory self-defense, 151, 163, 170*f*, 180
Article 51 and, 147–48, 157–61, 158*f*, 262–63
black letter law of, 144–45, 147, 150, 167, 174–75, 181–82
ceasefire violation justifications, 149–50, 168–69, 168*f*
challenges to, 145–47
collective self-defense, 179
communications data, 165–69, 166*f*, 167*f*, 168*f*, 170*f*, 172*f*, 174*f*
contested claims patterns, 169–77
contested forms of, 150–54
cyber operations and, 261
dictionary-based methods of analysis, 161–63, 164*t*, 165*t*
extralegal arguments, 154
extralegal justifications, 177–81, 178*f*
general prohibition on, 144–45
humanitarian intervention, 152–54, 169–77, 174*f*
introduction to, 143–44
justifications for, 157–81
legal justifications, 148
mentions of reprisals, 175–77, 176*f*

militarized interstate disputes, 155–63, 156*f*, 158*f*
patterns in, 154–57
reprisals, 152
response to armed attack, 149
self-defense rights, 147–50, 151, 309
summary of, 181–82
UN Commission on Human Rights, 10, 15, 84n.6
UN Commission on International Trade Law (UNCITRAL), 313
UN Conference on Trade and Development (UNCTAD), 322
UN Congress on Crime Prevention and Criminal Justice, 406
UN Convention Against Corruption, 339, 406–7
UN Convention Against Torture, 10, 436
UN Convention against Transnational Organized Crime, 406–7
UN Convention on Certain Conventional Weapons (CCW), 242–44
UN Convention on Terrorist Bombings, 407
UN Convention on the Elimination of All Forms of Racial Discrimination (CERD), 10
UN Convention on the Law of the Sea (UNCLOS), 58, 93–94, 441–42
UN Convention on the Rights of the Child (CRC), 10
UN Convention on Transnational Organized Crime, 414–15, 442–43
UN Convention Relating to the Status of Refugees, 11, 426–27, 436
UN Corruption Convention, 407
UN Economic and Social Council, 384–85
UN Framework Convention on Climate Change, 446, 451
UN General Assembly, 10, 310–11, 316, 372–73, 384–85, 416–17
UN Group of Governmental Experts (UN GGE), 261–62, 278–79
UN High Commissioner for Refugees, 426–27, 448–49
UN Human Rights Council, 198–99
UN Institute for Disarmament Research, 222
UN Office on Drugs and Crime, 406
UN Official Documents System (ODS), 157–58
UN Open-Ended Working Group, 279
UN Security Council
authoritarian regimes and, 372–73
colonial inequalities, 63–64
international criminal law, 398, 415–17
international legal order, 408
Iraq's invasion of Kuwait, 14
legal instruments against terrorism, 406–7
Operation Iraqi Freedom, 17–18
rising Chinese power and, 19–20
rules-based international order and, 3, 8–9, 13
UN Charter Article 51 and, 147–48
underrepresentation of Global South in, 78
UN Special Rapporteur on Extreme Poverty and Human Rights, 109–10, 124–25
UN Working Group on the use of mercenaries, 198–99
undocumented migrants, 439
Uniform Code of Military Justice, 191–92
unilateralism, 303–4
United Kingdom (UK), 111–12, 152–53
United Nations (UN), 22–23, 83–85, 96–97
United States-Mexico-Canada Agreement (USMCA), 57–58, 321. *See also* North American Free Trade Agreement
United States (US)
anti-cartel law, 350–51, 356
autonomous weapons and, 225
BITs and, 334
China climate change cooperation, 27
Chinese trade relations and, 286, 289–90, 299–300, 302–3, 358–59
climate change and, 5
democratic revival and, 89, 98–101
duopoly with China, 89, 101–4
economic demonization rhetoric, 289–90
economic hyperliberalism, 40–41, 54–56
economic power of, 39–41
end of US hegemony, 15–18
export control challenges, 246–50
as flawed democracy, 86

United States (US) (*cont.*)
foreign policy toward democracy, 49, 50
foreign policy toward racialization, 72
invasion of Iraq, 226
Iran-US Claims Tribunal, 314–15
liberal democracy and, 89–103
military spread of democracy, 22–23
post-World War II hegemony of, 82
Soviet Union relations with, 24
trade war with China, 16–17, 21–34
Universal Declaration of Human Rights, 2, 10, 83–84, 316, 369, 384–85
Universal Periodic Review (UPR), 369, 373–74, 385–86
unlawful enemy combatants, 413–14
unmanned aerial vehicles (UAVs), 230–31
unmanned drones, 227, 240
urban warfare and *jus in bello*, 209–15
urbanization threat to *jus in Bello*, 212–14
U.S. Department of Defense Law of War Manual, 189
US Chamber of Commerce, 343
US Department of Defense (DoD), 203, 223, 224
US Department of Homeland Security, 255
US Department of Justice, 343
US National Climate Assessments, 109
US Supreme Court, 331–32
US Treasury Department, 246
use of force, 149n.19, 220, 236–37, 261–62. *See also* UN Charter and use of force

Vagts, Detlev, 92
Valkyrie drone, 230–31
Varieties of Democracy project (V-Dem), 366, 367–68, 379–80, 379*t*
Venezuela, 407–8. *See also* Maduro, Nicolás
vertical rules, 3, 4
violence and thresholds of war, 272–73

Wagner Group, 238–39
WannaCry ransomware attack, 279–80
war crimes, 13, 399–400, 401–3, 410–11
War Powers Act, 342–43
warming-induced benefits, 125
Warsaw Pact, 37–38, 87
Washington Consensus, 22–23, 50, 55, 71–72, 122–23
Wassenaar Arrangement, 246, 247–48
weapons of mass destruction (WMD), 24, 145–46, 151, 154–55, 171
weighted voting, 69–70, 77
Westphalian sovereignty, 90
White, Kyle Powys, 123–24
white privilege, 63–64
white racial superiority, 65–66
World Bank
bipolarity and, 52–53
colonial inequalities and, 63–64
ICSID Convention and, 312–14
neoliberal economic regime of, 73–74
weighted voting, 69–70, 77
World Conference on Human Rights, 384–85
world economic order. *See* economic world order
World Justice Project, 397–98
World Trade Organization (WTO)
Appellate Body of, 292–94
China in, 91, 96–97
climate regime and, 116–17
colonial inequalities and, 63–64
dispute settlement system, 58, 287–88
Doha Round of Development, 70–71
dysfunctional nature of, 38–39
economic power and, 43–44, 43*f*
establishment of, 320
future importance of, 22–23
General Council, 301
global trade relations of, 102
rules-based international order and, 3, 13–14, 16–17, 22–23
trade liberalizing rules, 40–41
trade rule of law and, 285–87, 290, 292–96
unipolarity and, 54
World War II, 1–2, 6–8, 7*t*

xenophobia, 72, 443–45
Xi Jinping, 89–90, 96, 357–58

Yameen, Abdulla, 95
Yoo, John, 154–56

Zelaya, Manuel, 99